THE
STORY OF
MAPS

The city of Constantinople looking south towards the Sea of Marmora. This manuscript map, from a Turkish sea atlas, *The Shapes of the Islands of the Mediterranean*, was made in 1526 at Gallipoli.

THE
STORY OF
MAPS

Lloyd A. Brown

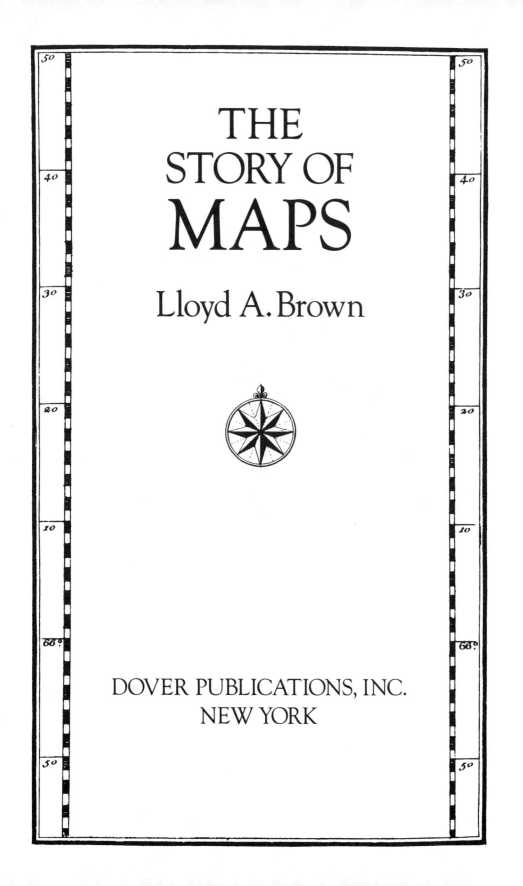

DOVER PUBLICATIONS, INC.
NEW YORK

Published in Canada by General Publishing Company,
Ltd., 30 Lesmill Road, Don Mills, Toronto, Ontario.
Published in the United Kingdom by Constable and
Company, Ltd.

This Dover edition, first published in 1979, is an
unabridged and unaltered republication of the work
originally published in 1949 by Little, Brown and Company. Two navigational charts from Waghenaer's *Spieghel der Zeevaerdt* which were used as decorative end-
papers in the original edition have been captioned and
reproduced here following the Table of Contents. The
frontispiece, originally in color, is reproduced here in
black and white. The Dover edition is published by special
arrangement with Little, Brown and Company, 34 Beacon St., Boston, Mass. 02106.

International Standard Book Number: 0-486-23873-3
Library of Congress Catalog Card Number: 79-52395

Manufactured in the United States of America
Dover Publications, Inc.
180 Varick Street
New York, N.Y. 10014

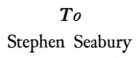

To
Stephen Seabury

Preface

Any survey history is, of necessity, a co-operative venture, involving the resources of many libraries and the specialized knowledge of numerous individuals, both living and dead. During the past four years I have been granted privileges and extended courtesies in libraries and archives such as would warm the heart of any research worker, and by virtue of these amenities I succeeded in digging out a great deal of material which proved vital to my story. Therefore, it is a pleasure to acknowledge my indebtedness to the American Geographical Society, the American Neptune, Inc., American Philosophical Society, Bibliothèque Nationale, Clarendon Press (Oxford), Columbia University, Enoch Pratt Free Library, Fogg Museum of Art, Free Library of Philadelphia, Goucher College, Harvard University, International Map Company, John Carter Brown Library, John W. Garrett Library, Johns Hopkins University, Library of Congress, National Maritime Museum (Greenwich), New York Public Library, Princeton University, Semitic Museum (Harvard University), United States Geological Survey, United States Hydrographic Office, United States Naval Observatory, University of Michigan, Walters Art Gallery, Welch Medical Library, William L. Clements Library, and Yale University.

Historians of bygone days whose writings I have used must go unthanked, but I have endeavored to pay them tribute by scrupulously citing each one, either in my Notes or in the Bibliography. My contacts with the living, both historians and other persons in possession of special talents or information of different kinds, are another matter. My conversations and correspondence with them have been my chief source of pleasure during the writing of this book, and I am happy to acknowledge publicly my indebtedness to Randolph G. Adams, Burton W. Adkinson, Don C. Allen, Elizabeth Baer, S. Whitimore Boggs, Commander C. R. Brent, Robert Brown, Arthur Cavanagh, John Coolidge, Florence E. Dragoo, Bertha Frick, Frederick R. Goff, E. P. Goldschmidt, Douglas H. Gordon, Jean Gottman, Gertrude Hess, Philip Hofer, E. H. Hugo, Ella Hymans, William A. Jackson, Frederick Keator, Clara Egli LeGear, David C. Mearns, Dorothy Miner, Martinus Nijhoff, Robert H. Pfeiffer, Peter J. Prevas, Constance Anne Price, Frank Robbins, Jacob H. Skop, Colton Storm, R. Catesby Taliaferro, Walter Whitehill, Alvina M. Woodford, and Lawrence C. Wroth.

In addition to the above individuals, I wish to express my sincere thanks to the staff of the Peabody Institute Library for their patience, co-operation and loyalty, and to the Library Committee of the Board of Trustees, whose blessing and support made possible this book.

LLOYD ARNOLD BROWN

Contents

Navigational chart showing the English Channel and the coast of England from Plymouth to Weymouth in 1583. From the first volume of Lucas Janssz Waghenaer's sea atlas *Spieghel der Zeevaerdt* (1584).

ſmen daer voorbij zeÿlt; twe mÿlen van v. zÿn.

Gedaente van S. Andries Landt, twe
mÿlen van v. wesende.

PARS.

Weÿmouth

Dorcester

S: Andreas Landt.

Borthlÿn.

Byrtport.

Tſlott

Porth-
landt.

Tias van Poortlandt.

SEPTENTRIO. N.

Noordt ten ooſten.

Noordt noordt ooſt.

Noordt ooſt ten noorden.

Noordt ooſt.

Noordt ooſt ten ooſten.

Ooſt noordt ooſt.

van

Ooſt ten noorden.

ORIENS. O.

Ooſt ten zuijden.

Zuijdt zuijdt ooſt.

Zuijdt ooſt t'ooſten.

Zuijdt ooſt.

Zuijdt ooſt ten zuijden.

Zuijdt zuijdt ooſt.

landt.

Beſchrÿuinghe der Zee-
cuſten van Engelandt,
tuſſchen Pleÿmouth en
Porthlandt, met zÿne
principale hauenen,
elcx in heure gedaente.

Navigational chart showing the Baltic Sea, the northern coast of Poland (then part of Pomerania) and the Danish island Bornholm, c. 1583. From the second volume of Lucas Janssz Waghenaer's sea atlas *Spieghel der Zeevaerdt* (1585). (For the proper orientation hold the chart with the north direction at the top.)

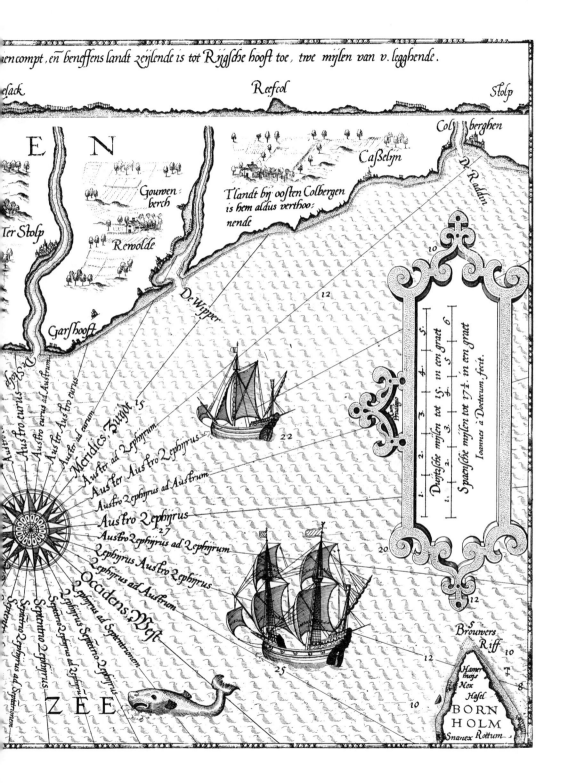

esack   Reefcol   Stolp

E N

Colsberghen

De Radilin

Casselijn

Gouven berch

Tlandt bij oosten Colbergen is hem aldus verthoo: nende

Ter Stolp

Rewolde

De Wipper

Garshooft

10

Paulus

Duijtsche mijlen tot 15. in een graet
Spaensche mijlen tot 17½. in een graet

Ioanes à Doeteum. fecit.

6
5
4
3
2
1

5
4
3
2
1

Meridies, Zuijdt 25

Auster ad Zephyrum

Auster Austro Zephyrus

Austro Zephyrus ad Austrum

Austro Zephyrus
27

Austro Zephyrus ad Zephyrum

Zephyrus Austro Zephyrus

Zephyrus ad Austrum

Occidens, West

Zephyrus ad Septentrionem

Zephyrus Septentrio Zephyrus

Septentrio Zephyrus

Septentrio Zephyrus ad Zephyrum

Septentrio Zephyrus ad Septentrium

Austrozephyrus

Auster Austro zephyrus

Auster Austro ad eurus

Auster ad eurus

Auster ad eurum

22

20

12

12

25

10

10

Brouvers Riff

Hamer huijs
Nex
Hasel

BORN HOLM

Snanex Rottum

ZEE

Illustrations

THE
STORY OF
MAPS

Introduction

THIS is the story of maps: the men who made them and the methods they employed, what can be found on them and the devious ways by which the information required for their compilation was obtained. There is no other such chronicle in print, though in the past seventy-five years or so it has been many times reasserted that the world is becoming increasingly aware of and interested in maps. Unfortunately this statement has often represented the wishful thinking of a small group of scholars and collectors who, from generation to generation, have supported the study of maps both old and new. But in the past five years the assertion has actually begun to mean something.

When hostilities began in Europe in 1939, every map collection of any consequence in the United States and abroad was quickly dusted off, and even some of the smaller, little-known collections in private hands were ferreted out. It was discovered that the world had been mapped, to be sure, but how? Obsolete maps and charts of remote, forgotten islands, lagoons, plateaus and jungle trails suddenly became prized possessions, guarded with unremitting vigilance. The world had been mapped, yes. Nevertheless, there was something radically wrong. The old familiar paths were there (though the scale was often too small to have any great military value), but the theater of war did not always follow the old familiar pattern, and it shortly developed that the world, all of it, had not been mapped after all. History tells us why.

The recent world war has brought about this new interest in world cartography because, regardless of our political views regarding isolationism, the vast, unfamiliar world with which we have lately had to deal has relentlessly closed in around us. Our interest in it is no longer the casual interest of neutral observers; it is the interest of persons who have come to realize that the map of the world is our map and that it is time to learn a little more about it.

There are several reasons why this story has not been written before; they are ancient reasons which apply generally to any such historical survey. Robert Hooke (1635–1703), the English physicist and "experimental philosopher," stated the case neatly and concisely in a Preface written for a friend.[1]

There are but few who, though they know much, can yet be persuaded they know any thing worth Communicating, and because the things are common and well known to them, are apt to think them so to the rest of Mankind; This Prejudice has done much mischief in this particular as well as in many other, and must be first remov'd. There are others that are conscious enough of their own Knowledge, and yet either for want of

Ability to write well, or of use to Compose, or of time to Study and Digest, or out of Modesty and fear to be in Print, or because they think they know not enough to make a Volume, or for not being prompted to, or earnestly solicited for it, neglect to do it; others delay to do it so long till they have forgotten what they intended. Such as these Importunity would prevail upon to disclose their knowledge, if fitting Persons were found to Discourse and ask them Questions, and to Compile the Answers into a History.

There are several other reasons not mentioned by Robert Hooke. Firsthand biographical material for a history of cartography, especially in the pre-Christian era, is rare; consequently, whole chapters, covering centuries of human thought, must remain rather impersonal, if not nebulous. It is necessary to depend on second- or third-hand accounts of men and their accomplishments, and often these are merely fragments which have been many times recopied and retranslated. Sometimes the record is no better than the hearsay of contemporaries. For example, there are instances where Strabo wrote that Poseidonius said that Aristotle was said to have written . . . This disorderly array of data is not at all satisfying to the soul of a true scholar, for by the time he has finished weighing the pros and cons and comparing variant codices he has, more than likely, bogged down somewhere in the vicinity of the Middle Ages and has reached the age of retirement, feeling that he has earned a long rest. Or, after appraising the available data, he prefers not to write at all rather than depend on such fragile evidence to support him.

As it stands today, the literature on the history of map making consists of countless "papers," monographs and longer studies concerned with a personality or a period of history. Such studies have been written by persons who have had the time and energy to exhaust a minute point or a single chapter, but who have lacked either the time or the inclination to make a survey covering a period of more than five thousand years and involving the personalities and accomplishments of innumerable individuals from every conceivable walk of life.

Therefore, in order to compile a one-volume survey history, it is necessary to confine the story to a straight and more or less narrow path, to keep close to the line of progress and merely suggest the bypaths, such as the numerous factors which retarded scientific conquest of the unknown. It is also necessary and safe to assume an advanced state of cultural development on the part of mankind when the evidence is not as clear as we would like to have it. Enough allusions, hints and incidental remarks have come down through the ages to suggest that all has not been revealed by the record; in fact, it would be folly to assume otherwise. For instance, in the fourth book of his *Geography*, Strabo wrote that in earlier times the Massiliotes had a good supply of ships, "as well as of arms and instruments that are useful for the purposes of navigation and for sieges." Now, we can assume, as some historians have, that these aids to navigation did not amount to much, that actually they were crude affairs because the culture of the period was thus and so. Or we can leave the question open and wonder, rightfully, just how far the Phoenicians had actually gone in the development of the compass, the astrolabe and other aids to navigation. I prefer to leave the question open. Again, Strabo relates that Saleucus, the Chaldean astronomer, spoke of an irregularity of the tides in certain places during different phases of the moon. Saleucus is therefore given credit for having solved the riddle or discovered the law which governs the diurnal inequality of the tide in the Indian Ocean. Strabo merely mentions this in passing to illustrate another point he wishes to make. What else did Saleucus know about the universe? Have we any right to assume that this was his only contribution to science? On the contrary, a few hundred similar casual references to the lesser lights of history make one very cautious when mentioning dates of discovery and invention.

Priority claims are important to the party or parties of the first part, even in the realm of research which yields no profit of a pecuniary variety; but in treating historically the accomplishments of men who lived two thousand or three thousand years ago, the question of priority is strictly academic, especially when the invention or discovery concerns knowledge which might possibly have been more common than is supposed. Astronomy, for instance, was probably a part of every man's knowledge, even in very ancient civilization, a heritage passed down either by word of mouth or in the writings of the priests. Therefore the known facts regarding the heavens were no more worthy of special note than the rising of the sun or the fact that the desert was full of sand.

Priority claims for certain individuals constitute the theses of hundreds of learned works, and they have inspired many a critical debate which has added materially to our knowledge of the past. However, in the case of historical cartography, they have often tended to obscure the picture as a whole. A perfect example of just such an intellectual impasse was reached some years ago in connection with Aristarchus. It seems that Archimedes, a younger contemporary of Aristarchus, reported that the latter wrote a book of hypotheses (now lost), one of which was that the sun and the fixed stars remain unmoved and that the earth revolves around the sun in the circumference of a circle. He thus anticipated the Copernican hypothesis by several hundred years. Astronomers, including Sir Thomas Heath, accepted this claim on behalf of Aristarchus with philosophic calm, and there the matter rested until G. V. Schiaperelli, another first-rate scholar, published two papers and then a third.[2] From his studies he concluded that Heraclides of Pontus either invented or copied from an earlier writer the system of the universe associated with the name of Tycho Brahe and that he also originated the Copernican hypothesis as well. Now this was a very important claim, and Heath did not take it lightly. In a book of 424 pages he reviewed the whole history of Greek astronomy up to the time of Aristarchus, concluding his study with a new translation of the astronomer's writings accompanied by critical notes on all known texts.[3] Both writers produced studies worthy of the highest praise, but they limited themselves to a point or two in a big story. Writers on the history of cartography have often limited their studies in the same way and for the same reasons, which partially accounts for the fact that there is no current survey history of map making.

If biographical data and primary textual sources are scanty, the maps and charts themselves are yet more difficult to find. Even the most important ones, the subject of textual wrangling among the Greek philosophers themselves, have disappeared entirely. Maps, charts and globes are expendable; and there is an abundance of evidence to prove that countless numbers of them were destroyed through sheer carelessness and indifference. But there are other reasons why original map sources are scarce, and why there are wide gaps in the chronological sequence of map development.[4]

Ancient maps were designed primarily for travelers, soldiers and mariners. Traveling in ancient times was a hazardous business. Conveyances were crude when available and the condition of the roads, up to the development of civil engineering in Rome, negated the small comfort to be had from a crude wagon or iron-shod chariot. Highwaymen were as common as hostels were rare; consequently many "traveler's pictures," road maps and itineraries rotted by the wayside with their owners' bodies. Fire, flood and shipwreck accounted for many more.

The very material used in the making of maps, charts and globes contributed to their destruction. No medium or material has yet been discovered which can be used for map making and nothing else. For example, both Charles the Great (Charlemagne), Roman emperor and king of the Franks, and King Roger of Sicily, ordered maps made on solid silver plates. Servants and conquering soldiers might not be interested in such productions from the standpoint of geography, but solid silver — ! Copper and brass were just as tempting. The brass globes of Archimedes and others made in his day were natural bait for a thief looking for bright metal. Or, as one writer has suggested, a hollow metal globe, cut in two, would make two fine camp kettles for an invading army. Lead could be made into bullets; parchment and vellum would make good cartridges, also a strong spine for a bookbinding. If a map were old and obsolete and parchment was scarce, the old ink and rubrication could be scraped off and the skin used over again.[5] This practice, accounting for the loss of many codices as well as valuable maps and charts, at one time became so pernicious because of the scarcity of writing material that in 691 A.D. a synodical decree was handed down forbidding the mutilation or destruction of any of the Scriptures or writings of the Church Fathers by such means.

A part of the map known as the Peutinger Table, a rare example of Roman cartography, was found in use as a flyleaf of a book in the city library of Treves, generally considered the oldest German city. Another rare fragment of a Roman map of Spain, cut in stone, was found built into the wall of the Abbey of Saint John, near Dijon in France. Stones bearing inscriptions make just as good building material as those without scratches on them. A fishmonger near the British Museum once discovered that parchment or limp vellum, though defaced by ancient ink and paint, was better than oiled paper for wrapping fish. Before the authorities caught up with him, numerous rare manuscripts had found their way into London kitchens, and from thence to the trash bin.

Large maps have always been inconvenient to store flat and open, so they were often folded, many of them into books. This practice accounted for the loss of many important cartographic documents. Continued folding and unfolding produced wear and tear, and if a map were stout enough to withstand this sort of treatment, a guillotine wielded by a careless or indifferent bookbinder often completed the dissection if not the total destruction of the document.

At the beginning of the Christian era, and for the next twelve hundred years or so, only the brave and the pagan indulged in geographic speculation. It was impious if not downright sinful to probe the mysteries of the universe, and the explanations set forth by the Church in regard to the heavens and the earth, as well as the maps produced under the supervision of the clergy, were sufficiently vague and awe-inspiring to satisfy all but the most skeptical observers of natural phenomena. So while both ecclesiastical and pagan manuscripts were collected openly, maps were made furtively, studied secretly, and in many cases destroyed promptly.

Heretics and barbarians, meaning whoever happened to be the enemy at the time, were not the only ones to destroy maps. It seems to be an assumption of long standing that the latest map is the best one, regardless of the area involved or the compiler; but this is frequently not so. An original map may be the product of a careful survey while a later, more resplendent *copy* may be a hasty, inaccurate job produced to sell in quantity at a large profit. Unfortunately the out-of-date map is usually discarded or destroyed when a new one comes along, even though military campaigns have been won with the aid of "obsolete," long-forgotten maps and charts, a statement which holds good as of this date.

With the exception of commercial publications designed to entertain as well as edify, maps and charts have always been surrounded by an aura of mystery and secrecy which has had much to do with their destruction, and retarded at the same time the dissemination of geographic knowledge. They were dangerous things to have around. The earliest extant records show that the informative nature of a map has always been fully appreciated. If your neighbor coveted your ox or your ass, your hidden granary or your secret supply of salt, your treasure chest or your harem, it was not sensible to leave a papyrus roll lying around showing the exact location of your possessions. Let the thief "case" the place himself before raiding it. Thus, there are no examples extant of the cadastral surveys made by the "geometers" of early Egypt. Chances are they were destroyed by members of the families who ordered the surveys made.

Since the beginning of time, maps have been associated with military intelligence as well as local adventure and intrigue. Because they were potential sources of information to the enemy, maps of an empire or even a city were closely guarded. The location of roads and navigable streams by which an army might threaten the security of a city, the location of military objectives such as arsenals, barracks, water mains, dockyards and public buildings, was not information to be divulged any more than necessary to a hostile world. For this reason the Roman Emperor Augustus, who ordered the compilation of a detailed survey of his empire, had all maps and related data locked up in the innermost vaults of the palace, and allowed only partial copies to be distributed, and then only on the advice of his imperial councilors, to generals going off to the wars or to the schools of the provinces for educational purposes. Domitian is said to have punished severely one of his councilors for indiscreetly divulging information contained on such maps, and later history tells of many persons who suffered death for similar treasonable offenses. The situation today remains essentially unchanged. The legends concerning the secrecy attached to navigational charts and ships' logbooks which stud the maritime history of every nation are timeless. In emergencies, all such confidential and informative documents take precedence over cargo, the ship itself and the safety of the crew. One story tells of a loyal Carthaginian sea captain whose ship was pursued and intercepted by a Roman squadron. Rather than let his log and charts, keys to the secret of a lucrative Carthaginian trade, fall into Roman hands, he ran his ship on the rocks and drowned his crew. When he finally reached home he was given a hero's welcome. This is by no means an isolated example.

The old Spanish custom of weighting charts, not to mention log and code books, with lead so that they could be quickly jettisoned is still as popular as it is effective should the enemy try to board. This sort of practice, combined with the general reluctance of statesmen and sovereigns to duplicate and distribute important maps and charts, has contributed to their scarcity and has left the historian to guess what maps were made and what was on them. Often it is necessary to accept second- or third-hand evidence that a map was actually made; its contents must therefore be conjectural or hearsay.

From the beginning of Spanish exploration of the New World, in fact from the first voyage of Columbus, all maps and charts of the New World were deposited for safekeeping in the archives of Seville, and only a limited number of copies were made for the use of the most trustworthy Spanish sea captains. None of the original maps or charts made by the great explorers was allowed to be engraved and printed, so that today, for one reason or another, the primary documents relating to Columbus, Cortes, Magellan and countless others, are lost, probably forever. What maps and charts we do have of the great maritime explorations and discoveries have been compiled from miscellaneous notes and drawings that escaped the vigilance of the Spaniards and Portuguese. For example, an Englishman, Robert Thorne by name, acquired a place for himself in history by spiriting out of Seville a map and report on the West Indies, which he probably copied from confidential sources in the royal archives. He sent the documents to a fellow countryman, Dr. Edward Lee (or Ley), ambassador of Henry VIII to the court of the Emperor Charles, with a warning. "Also this Carde [chart] and that which I write . . ." he said, "is not to be shewed or communicated. . . . For though there is nothing in it prejudiciall to the Emperour, yet it may be a cause of paine to the maker: as well for that none may make these Cardes, but certaine appointed and allowed for masters, as for that peradventure it would not sound well to them, that a stranger should know or discover their secretes:

and would appear worst of all, if they understand that I write touching the short way to the spicerie by our Seas." [6]

Representatives of foreign powers were not the only offenders when it came to the illegal appropriation of maps and charts that were not meant for public distribution, for a chart showing a new trade route or the details of a newly discovered harbor was always a negotiable document. The "Casa de la Contratación de las Indias" was a noble attempt on the part of its founders, in the reign of Ferdinand of Spain, to pool all information relating to the seven seas, so that the best maps and charts would be available to the Spanish mariners responsible for the establishment of new sea routes to the New World and the Orient. But human frailty often prevailed and money talked. Information was withheld from the pool and sold on the side; Portuguese gold assayed as heavily as Spanish. [7]

Whole editions of books and maps were bought up and destroyed by the Spanish authorities because they told too much or pictured the wrong things, and there was always a prison cell or a little machine waiting for the author and publisher of confidential maps and charts. In the sixteenth century genuine Spanish charts of any part of the Americas were real maritime prizes, rated as highly by the French and English as the gold bullion which might be in the ships' strong rooms. One such priceless haul was made by the English adventurer and freebooter Woodes Rogers. [8] While cruising in behalf of some merchants of Bristol along the coast of Peru and Chile he captured some charts which were so "hot" that they were immediately engraved in London and published by John Senex. Other nations, especially those that made any pretense of carrying on a maritime trade, have been guilty at one time or another of this same thirst for knowledge, and piracy is the term which most adequately describes the technique employed in acquiring it.

∽   ∽   ∽

The history of science as a whole is the record of a select group of men and women who have dared to be wrong, and no group of scientists has been more severely criticized for its errors than cartographers, the men who have mapped the world. Hundreds of weighty tomes have been written to prove how very wrong were such men as Ptolemy, Delisle and Mitchell. For every page of text, for every map and chart compiled by the pioneers in cartography, a thousand pages of adverse criticism have been written about them by men who were themselves incapable of being wrong because they would never think of exposing themselves to criticism, let alone failure.

Yes, the early cartographers, without exception, were wrong, gloriously wrong in the same way Columbus was wrong when he thought he had made a landfall on the coast of Asia; the way Harrison was wrong when he built his first timekeeper; the way Edison was wrong when he used a bamboo filament in his incandescent lamp instead of tungsten. The remarkable achievements of early scientists, not to mention their personalities, have become lost in a maze of critical commentaries and ponderous verbiage. And yet the men who mapped the world were colorful figures from all walks of life. Some were astute and learned scientists: astronomers, mathematicians, physicists and naturalists, men of high ideals and ability. Others were military men, local burghers, river pilots, religious zealots, merchant seamen and resourceful rascals. For the most part they led interesting and exciting lives; some were starkly tragic. A few perpetrated swindles, falsifying data and withholding information at the cost of lives, fortunes and even empires. Some suffered ostracism for their radical views regarding the universe, others died in their defense.

The world has been mapped, after a fashion, and this story tells how the job was done, stressing methods and apparatus rather than the end product, the hundreds of thousands of maps and charts produced, representing centuries of trial and error. Each early map and chart is a story in itself, often incorporating a little folklore and philosophy, some art both good and bad, and a smattering of scientific fact. Most of them contain enough errors to delight the critical scholar; consequently a great many individual maps have been written up in minute detail, adding valuable fragments to the picture as a whole. But how was the framework built? How did "they," meaning the early map makers, do such accurate work centuries before they were supposed to have the necessary knowledge and equipment?

The mapping of the world, with every coastal outline, every river, lake and mountain, town and city in its proper place with regard to distance and direction, depends upon a simple geometric proposition, namely, that the intersection of two lines is a point. In other words, to "locate" a spot on the earth, to "fix" it cartographically, it is only necessary to know two things: its latitude and longitude, two lines which intersect at the desired spot, and lo and behold, it is done. But right here simplicity breaks down and complications begin to set in.

The better to appreciate some of these complications, let us assume a globe representing the earth's surface divided into a geometrical network of parallels of latitude and meridians of longitude spaced at intervals of one degree of arc. Let us also assume that each point marking the intersection of a parallel and meridian has been accurately "fixed" by astronomical observation. We thus have a network of 64,080 points on our globe, not counting the two poles. Actually it would not be possible to locate that many points on the earth itself because nearly three quarters of them would be over water. Yet even after we have reduced the number by three quarters, we still have 16,020 points located on dry land, the very minimum required for an accurate framework of the earth drawn to scale. Study the globe and consider the difficulties of transporting men and apparatus to many of those points, assuming that someone was willing to stand the cost of an expedition. Then you will not be surprised to learn that as late as 1740 Johann Gabriel Doppelmayr, a German astronomer and mathematician, estimated that not more than 116 places on the face of the earth had been correctly located, places whose distance north or south of the equator (latitude) and east or west of a prime meridian (longitude) had been accurately determined by astronomical observation. Seventy-seven years later, in 1817, Franz August von

Etzel, another geographer, estimated that the number of places correctly located had been increased to 6000, two thirds of which were on the continent of Europe. This is far short of the number of places required for the most elementary framework of a world map. Again in 1885, Captain George M. Wheeler of the U. S. Corps of Engineers had the following report to make on the state of the world in maps: "In the summing up it can but be noticed, notwithstanding the admirable persistent efforts of European Governments, how little comparatively of the land surface of the globe is made known to us in plentiful topographical detail, by rigid mathematical and instrumental processes." These pessimistic reports do not mean that map making had made no real progress after two thousand years or more, and they do not mean that there were no reliable maps or charts before the middle of the eighteenth century. Actually, cartography had made great strides; thousands of maps, charts and globes had been made before 1800, and some very good ones at that. They only mean that map making on a world scale, with distance and direction carefully determined, presented some interesting problems which took centuries of labor to solve, and it is this kind of mapping that Doppelmayr, von Etzel and Wheeler were talking about.

Referring again to the hypothetical globe, dotted with 16,020 correctly located points which are nothing more than corner posts for a map grid, the next step is to run the lines connecting them, north and south, east and west. These lines will average roughly 58 miles to a side. Each line must be geometrically true, of course, or the areas cannot be closed. Running a line 58 miles long involves, among other things, over-the-horizon surveying (geodesy), taking into consideration the curvature of the earth and numerous other complicating factors. Then having successfully enclosed each section measuring a degree on a side, we are left with 16,020 parcels of land, averaging 3390 square miles, approximately the size of Delaware and Rhode Island combined, which are entirely blank. There is considerable terrain in any 3390 square miles!

There is only one way to compile an accurate map of the earth and parts thereof, and that is to go into the field and survey it; likewise, there is only one way to establish a series of base lines of reference from which such surveys can be made, and that is to send out expeditions to the far corners of the earth equipped with astronomical apparatus and surveying instruments. This represents a tremendous undertaking requiring time, centuries of it, and money. It also requires an incentive. The nations that have been most interested in the establishment of colonies and a world trade have contributed more than others to the establishment of a science of cartography; those nations which have resisted exploitation and the intrusion of outsiders, regardless of their mission, have hindered the cause. The net result today is a map of the world which is spotty, both literally and figuratively. Much remains to be done. Writing in 1932, Kenneth Mason, an English geographer, said, "I have hinted that the world is discovered, but I doubt whether a hundredth part of the land surface of the globe is surveyed in sufficient detail for modern requirements. If the pioneer's day is nearly over, the specialist-explorer's dawn is only breaking."

CHAPTER I

The Earth Takes Shape

CARTOGRAPHY was not born full-fledged as a science or even an art; it evolved slowly and painfully from obscure origins. The first and most important stage of its development took place during the last hundred years of the pre-Christian era in Alexandria, the Roman capital of Egypt.[1] Situated only twelve miles from the Canobic mouth of the Nile, the city at that time had become a clearinghouse of information, where the news of the world was sifted and weighed. Also weighed in Alexandria were the spices, ores and precious baubles brought in from Upper Egypt and the heart of Africa, the fabulous produce of India and Arabia, destined for resale or ultimate consumption in "the greatest emporium in the inhabited world."

Twenty-five years before the birth of Christ there was no better place to live than Alexandria. It was a cosmopolitan city, a melting pot of humanity from the far corners of the earth, a rendezvous of cutthroats and kings. Culturally it had gone far in the three hundred years since its founding. Richly endowed with the wonders of nature, it had added considerably to its inheritance in the way of architectural masterpieces, art treasures and books, until it rivaled in beauty and importance the Eternal City itself. Alexandria had become the virtual center of the Hellenic world, a show place for travelers and a haven for scholars, a place where a man could think.

Among the European travelers who crossed *Mare Nostrum* in 25 B.C. to visit the city of Alexandria was a young man named Strabo, a native of Amasia in Pontus, and an important figure in this chronicle.[2] Strabo was a curious visitor, and was better qualified than most to appreciate what he was about to see. Born in 63 B.C., he had received an elaborate education, thanks to a family of considerable wealth. While in Rome he had studied under Tyrranion, whom Cicero considered an able philosopher and a geographer of distinction. Strabo had become a confirmed Stoic, a faithful disciple of Zeno of Citium, founder of the sect, for whom physics, ethics and logic constituted the "expedient arts" necessary for the exercise of philosophy in the acquirement of knowledge. Wisdom and knowledge were synonymous. Strabo had no time for Aristotle and his Peripatetic School.

After completing his formal education, Strabo traveled, an itinerant scholar in search of intellectual diversion and stimulation. He journeyed as far west as the coast of Tyrrhenia (Etruria) opposite Sardinia; towards the south he had sailed from the Euxine Pontus as far as the frontiers of Ethiopia. For a time he took in the sights in and around Rome, and from there went to Corinth. He knew Pontus well; he had visited Mylasa, Alabando, Tralles, Magnesia, Smyrna and Beirut. He considered all this something of an accomplishment: "You could not find another person among the writers on Geography who has travelled over much more of the distances just mentioned than I." As a fitting climax to his travels, Strabo went to Alexandria, probably by way of Pelusium, where he could explore the Nile with his friend Aelius Gallus, prefect of Egypt, and examine the wealth of material in the royal libraries. Whether he planned at the time to write an eighteen-volume treatise on geography no one knows, but he went to Alexandria for a visit and stayed five years. What kind of a city did he find there?

When Alexander the Great, conquering hero and "liberator," entered Egypt in the autumn of 332 B.C. to free the people from the Persian yoke, his first concern was to choose a site on which to build a city which would be appropriate for the future capital of the country he was about to liberate. He selected the narrow strip of land between the Mediterranean Sea and Lake Mareotis (Sebaca, Birk Mariout or Mariut), and close to the western extremity of the delta. Memphis had been ruled out as a site because it was too far inland and too Egyptian, while the ancient and notorious market city of Naucratis was too disreputable and unsavory. Furthermore, Greece was interested in diverting the wealth of Egypt into her own warehouses, which meant that a good harbor was paramount. Alexander's site may not have looked promising to some, but it had the necessary harbor, and at that time it was the only place along the coast of the delta which was not in danger of being buried by the silt brought down by the Nile.

On his first and only visit to the site, Alexander found nothing but a tiny settlement (Rhacotis) squatting near the shore, the remains of a small military garrison established many years before. The ancient kings of Egypt had fortified it against the fools and knaves who sailed the seas; in particular the Greek adventurers and pirates from Cyrene and Crete who were forever marauding along the coast. In addition to the garrison, small bands of armed herdsmen tended their flocks up and down the shore, roving patrols capable of dealing with small parties that might attempt to land without invitation. Opposite the settlement of Rhacotis about a mile off shore was the island of Pharos, connected with the mainland by a mole or breakwater which served both as a thoroughfare and an aqueduct.

Three hundred years brought vast changes to Egypt and its capital city.[3] Under the shrewd and for the most part intelligent reign of a succession of Ptolemies and Cleopatras, the maritime commerce of the Phoenicians on the Red Sea, formerly an exclusive monopoly, was diverted from the Isthmus of Suez direct to Alexandria by way of a canal running from the capital to Arsinoë near the site of the present city of Suez. Egypt now possessed an elaborate system of canals capable of floating vessels of tremendous burden, and all canals led to Alexandria, the toll city of the commercial world. Each year, under the impetus of royal command and dreams of fabulous profits, merchants sent their ships farther and farther away from their home ports, seeking new markets and a wider variety of trade goods for barter in the capital city. High taxes were levied in Egypt, but the people who paid them suffered more or less silently because they knew that for every extravagance indulged in by the royal household there would be a new temple erected in honor of one of their beloved gods or goddesses; it had happened many times before, each one surpassing the last, with the result that Alexandria had become a city of great beauty.

Approaching Alexandria from the sea, the first of its many wonders was visible on the horizon more than twenty miles out: [4] the white marble beacon tower on the eastern tip of Pharos, guiding the navigator to the city. The island itself, which Strabo described as oblong, lay parallel to the mainland, a natural break-water and a forbidding barrier against sudden attack. The mole (Heptastadium) linking the island to the mainland had been enlarged, and the T-shaped promon-tory thus formed gave the city two excellent harbors. The western, Eunostus ("Harbor of the Happy Return"), was used chiefly by merchant shipping, and was connected with Lake Mareotis by a canal, which in turn received shipping from the Nile by means of other canals.

The entrance to the eastern or Great Harbor was narrow, guarded on the seaward side by low rocks, some partly submerged, "which at all hours roughen the waves that strike them from the open seas." [5] The light on Pharos was no welcoming gleam, for the two harbors as well as the land approaches to the city were strongly guarded. All approaching vessels were met by ships of the Royal Navy and escorted through the narrow channel. Crews and passengers were carefully scrutinized, and no person could enter or leave the city without a pass-port. Augustus Caesar was in power.

Once inside the harbor the sight which greeted Strabo and his fellow passengers was awe-inspiring. Along the shore a solid phalanx of mansions and palaces of the royal house of Egypt rose up from the water's edge, each with its private harbor and boat wells for the royal barges. The water was so deep that the very largest vessels could tie up at the steps. The grounds of the royal residences were elaborately landscaped with magnificent groves of trees and formal gardens. The outbuildings and lodges were painted a variety of colors, and gaily colored awnings and pavilions dotted the broad expanse of cut stone. Farther along the shore towards the city was the Admiralty Port, partly hidden by the crescent-shaped island of Antirrhodos. Just beyond it was a man-made peninsula projecting far out into the harbor, built by Mark Antony during his extended visit as the house guest of the reigning monarch, Cleopatra VI. At the tip of the peninsula Antony had built a sumptuous lodge, the better to view the harbor, which he named Timonium, presumably after Timon of Athens who likewise had mis-givings concerning his social and political contacts with his fellow men.

Not all the inhabitants of Alexandria were privileged to enjoy the sea breezes which cooled the royal residences along the waterfront, but the climate of the city as a whole has been called salubrious by all writers before and after Strabo. As Strabo himself pointed out, other cities situated near lakes and smaller bodies of water sweltered in the summer heat; the air was heavy with moisture, and from the marshy shallows "filth-laden" air rose to assail the nostrils, the source of pestilential disease, especially malaria. But at Alexandria, when the Nile was full and Lake Mareotis flooded, stagnant water was sluiced out to sea through the canal, so that no marshy matter was left to corrupt the rising vapors. At the same time the Etesian wind blowing all summer from the northwest brought clean air from across a vast expanse of water, "so that the Alexandrians pass their time most pleasantly in summer." [6] The mean temperature of the delta is 81° F. in summer and 57° in winter.

The general plan of the city was fixed upon at the time of its founding, based on the drawings of the Greek architect Hippodamus. Strabo saw it in its prime. Its streets were wide and at right angles to one another, the main thoroughfares measuring a full plethron (101.2 feet) across, and even the narrowest were practicable for chariot driving. Some of the streets were flanked by wide colonnades built for the shelter of pedestrians and for sheer adornment. Fully one fourth of the buildings in the city were royal palaces, "for just as each of the kings, from love of splendour, was wont to add some adornment to the public monuments, so also he would invest himself at his own expense [that is, out of the tax money] with a residence, in addition to those already built." [7]

The building and beautifying of temples was even more important to the Ptolemies and Cleopatras than the construction of sumptuous palaces. No gods ever received such magnificent tributes to their sanctity as the deities of Lower Egypt. Nothing was spared that might add to the beauty of their temples and shrines; and the cost, based on the 18 talents spent on the construction of the lighthouse on Pharos, was hardly worth mentioning.

For those inhabitants who were interested in the more pagan forms of worship there was the city of Canobus, only 120 stadia from the eastern gate of Alexandria. A good road connected the two cities but it was more fashionable to take one of the many boats that operated day and night by way of the canal of Schedia, carrying people "who played the flute and danced without restraint" to the houseboats and resorts "adapted to relaxation and merry-making of this kind." [8]

Two structures in the city of Alexandria merit special attention. The first was the Paneium, dedicated to the god Pan, which Strabo describes as a "height," made by the hand of man on the top of a hill at the western end of the city. It resembled a fir cone, and was ascended by a spiral road, "and from the summit one can see the whole of the city lying below it on all sides." [9] This is all Strabo has to say about it, but in spite of the fact that the "height" was dedicated to a god, it probably doubled as an astronomical observatory and possibly a fire tower; but this is nothing but conjecture. The second structure, and the one which most interested Strabo, was the Museum which housed the royal Library.

The exact nature of the Museum is one of the most tantalizing of the unsolved riddles of ancient Egypt, because of what it may have contained. The little that is known about it has only whetted the curiosity and, unfortunately, the imagination of investigators who have tried to find out more. Strabo said the Museum was connected with the royal palaces, which would place it in the Bruchium quarter not far from the waterfront. It had a public walk, and Vitruvius the architect said, "spacious Exedras . . . with seats, where philosophers, rhetoricians and all others who take delight in studies can engage in disputation." Attached to the building or near it was the common mess hall for "the men who share the Museum. This group of men not only hold property in common, but also have a priest in charge of the Museum, who formerly was appointed by the kings, but is now appointed by Caesar." [10] These are the principal allusions to the Museum made by contemporaries who worked there. However, several interesting legends have come down through the ages, a few of them fairly well founded, as legends go.[11]

One legend has it that Ptolemy Soter, the probable founder of the Museum, had in mind a university of Alexandria, patterned after the celebrated schools at Athens that had fostered the development of Greek art and science, because at the time he visited Greece (308–307 B.C.) he tried to induce Stilpo of Megara, the Cynic philosopher, to come to Egypt. He also attempted, unsuccessfully, to lure Theophrastus, Aristotle's successor, and Menander the dramatist, away from their native soil. He had better luck with Demetrius the Phalerean, who had recently been forcibly ejected from Athens by his namesake and was looking for a safe place to stay.

It seems highly probable that like hundreds of monarchs before and after the Ptolemaic dynasty, Soter had a healthy respect for learning but did not know exactly what to do with it or the people who possessed it. So he did what a monarch in good standing usually did — he bought, or tried to buy, the commodity on the open market. This solution, which centuries later made possible the founding of the Académie Royale des Sciences, the Royal Society and similar learned bodies in such monarchies as could afford them, proved mutually beneficial to the parties concerned and elevated learning-for-its-own-sake from a starvation basis to one verging on frowsy respectability. It should be noted in passing that from the beginning the head of the Museum at Alexandria was a priest and a Greek. The priesthood, at that time, not only dictated the will of the gods, as it had for more than three thousand years, but the priests' sacred office gave them the supervisory task of seeing that philosophy and science stayed within the bounds of theological propriety. As a group, they represented the elite among the learned.

The activities of the Museum revolved around the Library instituted by Ptolemy Soter. Under the direction of Philadelphus, his successor, a strenuous campaign of collecting was carried on; scouts were sent out to all parts of Greece and the known parts of Asia to gather up everything they could lay hands on in the way of a manuscript — cost no object. It was at this time that the Library began to acquire a reputation as a great repository. Many important private collections were doubtless added to the Library, but the record tells of only one such acquisition, and about that there is some doubt. According to Athenaeus, the library of Aristotle, the first private library in history, was sold to Philadelphus by Neleus, who inherited it from Theophrastus, and it finally ended up in the Library at Alexandria.

Ptolemy Euergetes, who succeeded Philadelphus, was even more zealous in his collecting. He used the simple expedient of having everyone searched before they were allowed to enter the city of Alexandria. Any books found on their persons or in their luggage were confiscated and immediately copied. The original was placed in the royal Library and the copy was presented to the owner without thanks. Euergetes was an omnivorous collector totally lacking in philosophic bias; he took anything, whether it was Hebrew, Egyptian or Greek. If the manuscript was in a foreign language he had it translated and put both the original and the translation in the Library. By the time he had relinquished the throne and Eratosthenes, his Librarian, had died, the collection in the Museum had grown to 490,000 volumes; there were also 42,800 volumes in the library of the Serapaeum. Such was the city of Alexandria as Strabo found it.

Strabo occupies a peculiar position in history and in this narrative. It is doubtful whether he made a single original contribution to human knowledge or whether he ever compiled a map. If he had done so or if he only thought he had, he would have said so. His ego was sublime! Yet his *Geography* is the principal key to the history of ancient cartography, simply because the manuscript survived and was published, while the writings and maps of his contemporaries as well as those of the "ancients" before him were lost or destroyed. Nearly all that is known about Greek cartography prior to the work of Claudius Ptolemy (fl. 150 A.D.) can be traced back to the writings of Strabo of Amasia and no further. It is fortunate, therefore, that Strabo was a historian with broad interests and a flair for description as well as a geographer interested in origins and customs that a more scientific writer might have considered extraneous.

Some of Strabo's fame, then, came to him by default, but for the most part it was well earned. Presumably he spent most of five years in the Library at Alexandria, poring over the writings of the ancient philosophers and scientists, gathering material for his *Geography*. There within the walls of a single building he found the knowledge of the ages, the elements from which the science of cartography evolved, arranged under such topical headings as *The Sphere, On Nature, On the Fixed Stars, On Inventions, On Eratosthenes, Against Eratosthenes, Iliad* and *Odyssey*. He was selective in his reading, and though he digressed in his writing, he strove to record only the facts concerning the larger issues of his subject, "except as some petty thing may stir the interest of the studious or the practical man." At times he was repetitious, and frequently used more illustrations than necessary to drive home an important point. However, this was part of a plan to promote in his readers the virtue of not marveling at anything, a fundamental precept of Stoicism. His intention was to heap wonder upon wonder until his readers were so surfeited with wonderful things that they would, like all good Stoics, become inured to them. This policy proved fortunate for posterity.

In describing the various elements of geography and cartography, Strabo allowed himself to become mildly enthusiastic about some things and fairly warm about others, but at no time did he permit himself to marvel at anything in the usual sense, least of all the writings and accomplishments of his fellow men. These he censured unstintingly, often without good cause. Concerning his sources, he said, "If I shall, on occasion, be compelled to contradict the very men whom in all other respects I follow most closely, I beg to be pardoned; for it is not my purpose to contradict every individual geographer, but rather to leave the most of them out of consideration — men whose arguments it is unseemly even to follow — and to pass upon the opinion of those men whom we recognize to have been correct in most cases. Indeed, to engage in philosophical discussion with everybody is unseemly, but it is honourable to do so with Eratosthenes, Hipparchus, Poseidonius, Polybius, and others of their type." [12]

In his discussion of the several elements which go to make up cartography Strabo, like some of his successors, was not certain as to what kind of information should be embraced by "the science of geography," but he was emphatic concerning "the special branch of geography" [13] which treats with the broader issues such as the nature of the universe, the movement of the heavenly bodies including the earth; the general character of the earth, its shape and size, the inhabited parts versus the uninhabited parts. All those who undertake to know and describe such things, he said, "must look to the vault of heaven"; they must devote special attention to astronomy and geometry; in fact this special study of the universe, he thought, properly represents a union of meteorology, astronomy and geometry, "since it unites terrestrial and celestial phenomena as being very closely related, and in no sense separated from each other, 'as heaven is high above the earth.' " He put it even more emphatically when he said, "It is impossible for any man, whether layman or scholar, to attain to the requisite knowledge of geography without the determination of the heavenly bodies and of the eclipses which have been observed. . . ." [14] Such phenomena, he said, are important distinguishing features in treating countries widely separated. In these statements Strabo put his finger on the crux of the problem of map making, and it should be kept in mind that the first steps in acquiring knowledge about the earth came by indirection, through the study of the heavens. Astronomy has been called the "handmaiden" of cartography, but the term is a misnomer implying a subservient place in the scheme; actually cartography has been the dependent. Progress in the science of cartography has never moved ahead of developments in astronomy, and our world map of today has been made possible largely because of the high degree of accuracy achieved by astronomical observers.

Strabo found that mankind had been looking to the vault of heaven, as he recommended, for thousands of years before his time, but not primarily for information about the earth. The sky was man's almanac, telling him when to sow and when to reap, when to hunt and fish, when to worship and when to sleep. As early as 4241 B.C., to be exact, the passage of a calendar year of 365 days was noted and set down in the record of important events. [15] This interval of time, this completed cycle, was determined by two successive observations of Sirius, the Dog Star, made just before sunrise when Sirius is first visible on the horizon, a phenomenon which does not repeat itself at any place oftener than once a year. And it is highly probable that a systematic study of the skies for theological purposes was begun in the earliest period of Babylonian and Assyrian history — that is, in the nomadic or "Euphratean" period, some 3000 years before Christ.

Astrology came into vogue, apparently, as some of the more ancient forms of worship, involving blood sacrifice, fell into disfavor.[16] For instance, there was the ancient method of soul-searching which consisted of going directly to the source in order to determine the wishes and temper of the gods. It was believed that if the deity for whom a sacrifice was being made was in a receptive mood he would identify himself with the soul of the animal, which resided in the liver, and forthwith deity and liver would be in complete harmony and accord. Hence it was only necessary to conduct a post-mortem on the sacrificial animal, accompanied by rigid protocol, of course, and make a careful examination of the liver. This happy state of affairs made it possible for tribal priests and exponents of local gods to predict marvelous things. But the system had its disadvantages. Even to the trained eye, a liver had its limitations, and the priesthood was often left with knotty interpretations to make without much help from the liver. However, it was probably not the lack of resourcefulness on the part of the priesthood but the vast amount of unexplained phenomena visible in the sky which led to the abandonment of hepatology and the evolution of a polytheism founded on the celestial bodies.

For centuries, wandering tribes in Babylonia and Assyria, guarding their flocks at night, watched with awe and fear as the sun sank below the horizon and the stars came up against the black dome of the heavens. They watched them slowly move across the sky, up to the zenith and then slowly down, disappearing finally below the horizon on the other side. This was not all. Some of the larger stars seemed to move independently, cutting diagonally across the path of the moving heavens. Frequently a star would dash from its place and come streaking down the sky, leaving behind it a trail of fire that threatened to destroy or engulf the earth. More terrifying than any of this was the great circle of cold light that moved periodically across the heavens, far bigger than any of the stars and with a path all its own. It came and went in cycles. The first night it would appear as a mere crescent sliver of light with a faint outline completing the disc; the next night the crescent would be larger and the darkened disc smaller until finally, no less than twelve times a year, it arose a fiery red ball, shrinking in size and turning golden as it approached the zenith. This phenomenon was an obvious sign from one of the gods; the priests called it Nannar or Sin, "the illuminer," and in some regions it was En-zu, lord of wisdom. But regardless of what god was responsible for such a glorious display of power, it was clear that the heavens should be studied and if possible interpreted.

The worship of the heavenly bodies imposed a serious burden of responsibility on the priestly exponents of the cult in the valleys of the Tigris and Euphrates. Once the celestial bodies had become the rulers and guardians of the universe, it was up to the priests to study the periodicity of their movements and their relationship to one another, for if the heavens could be correctly interpreted, disaster might be averted and the anger of the gods appeased. It followed that if the priests could forecast far in advance just what might be expected of the sun, moon and stars, their standing in the community would be greatly enhanced. So it happened that a religious cult took over the responsibility of amassing data concerning the laws of the universe and the nature of the earth.

Written records concerning the heavenly bodies were faithfully kept by the guardians of the temple. Astrological data were handed down from generation to generation without interruption for well over two thousand years so that, at the time of Alexander the Great, it had become enormous in volume and amazing in quality. The system became elaborate, varying in complexity with the industry and ingenuity of the priests who kept the records; and it was changed from time to time. Some gods and their celestial counterparts lost caste regionally; some were obliged to share their glory and their temples with other deities. For example, Shamash the sun-god was the offspring of Nannar the moon-god, and consequently subservient to him. But Shamash was also justice, who brought evil and injustice to light. He also released sufferers from the clutches of demons. Subservient to Shamash was Ninib, sun-god of morning and of springtime; Nergal was the sun-god of noon and the summer solstice.

As soon as there were enough data to work on, five of the planets were incorporated into the system. Jupiter became associated with Marduk, who, among his many duties, was patron deity of the ancient city of Babylon. Venus was associated with Ishtar, the principal goddess who presided over all living things. An exacting deity, she could on occasion cause the fields to wither and living things to die. In her better moods, however, she held the power to fertilize and make life bountiful. Saturn became identified with Ninib who was at times the god of healing, and at other times the god of war and of the chase, who went abroad with lethal weapons. Mercury became Nebo or Nabu, "the proclaimer," god of wisdom, responsible for the introduction of the art of writing. His priests were personally responsible for the correct interpretation of all celestial phenomena. Mars became associated with Nergal, the "raging king" and "the burner," who was also associated with the custody of the nether regions and the rule of the dead. Those celestial bodies which were not incorporated in the astrotheological system became part of an elaborate folklore out of which came the constellations. This arrangement of star groups was presented to the Greeks by two of their more prominent astronomers, Aratus and Eudoxus, substantially as it originated in Babylonia, perhaps as early as 2800 B.C.[17]

The peculiarities of the moon were noted in detail. Its exact position in the heavens, the position of the horns, the halo visible when the moon is new, and the ring or "stall" around the full moon, all these were studied with care by the astrologers of Babylonia and Assyria. Eclipses, both solar and lunar, were the most spectacular manifestations of godly activity and received special attention. Likewise the angular path of the sun, its daily rate of change, the limits of its height in the sky at different times of the year, were noted, and eventually all such information led to a theory regarding the ecliptic. But the perfection of the theory and the ultimate division of the ecliptic into twelve equal parts of 30° each (the zodiac) probably came after the fall of the Babylonian Empire in 539 B.C.

The transition of Babylonian stargazing from a theological pursuit into a disinterested, scientific study was a natural step which probably took place so quietly and gradually that it was hardly noticed. As observations grew more complicated and observers became more preoccupied with their findings, a slow emergence of astronomy was inevitable. Whether the disintegration of Babylonian polytheism was a cause or an effect of this evolution is a debatable question. Another question of interest is why the records of the astrologers escaped when many of the graven images associated with their pagan form of worship were destroyed. However, once liberated from the inhibiting influence of the religious cult responsible for their being, both astronomy and mathematics made better progress; the new findings of one stimulated greater activity in the other. Working in close co-operation, they began to achieve real stature as sciences. And most essential to the further development of both was the enormous star literature compiled and handed down by the Babylonian priesthood.

The amazing quality of the Babylonian star data can best be appreciated by examining a few of their calculations. One of their oldest records concerned the "Saros," a cycle of 18 years and 11 days, or 223 lunations, at the end of which time the moon very nearly returns to her original position in the sky with respect to the sun and to her nodes and perigee. More remarkable, perhaps, was the observation that there is a definite periodicity in the behavior of certain planets. It was noted, for instance, that Venus returns in almost 8 years to a given point in the sky, and Mercury does the same, but only once in 46 years; Saturn takes 59 years, while Mars and Jupiter take 79 and 83 years respectively. These latter figures, representing a life span or more, prove that the methods and apparatus used to obtain them were handed down from generation to generation; and the positive confirmation that these phenomena represented cycles and not merely coincidence, means that accurate, uninterrupted observations had been made over a long period of time. It also explains how it was possible, in ancient times, to predict lunar eclipses with great accuracy. Not all data were accurate, and at times the error was great, as in the calculation of the perigee of the sun's orbit. These calculations seem never to have been closer than 10° to the true value. On the other hand, the length of the sidereal year was only 4½ᵐ too long! [18]

Eventually the stream of human knowledge began to flow from East to West, and in 640 B.C. a Babylonian savant named Berossus founded a school on the island of Cos (Stanko or Stanchio) at the mouth of the Gulf of Halicarnassus. At the same time Greek scholars began to explore on their own account the learning of Egypt as well as Babylonia.[19] A general exchange of information began between Europe and Asia; but as far as astronomy was concerned, it stood and moved alone, far ahead of other fields of learning, and for centuries no attempt was made to apply its findings to the basic problems of geography and cartography.

The sixth century B.C. saw great intellectual activity among the Greeks. Prose writing was introduced and pronounced a huge success. The Ionic school of philosophy made the first imperfect attempts at a scientific approach to learning under the guiding hand of Thales of Miletus, its founder, and the earliest recorded essays on philosophical speculation appeared. One of the foremost subjects of dispute among the philosophers was the universe, its nature, its size and significance, the part played by our earth in the scheme of things. Many concluded, as Strabo did, that the science of geography was, "quite as much as any other science, a concern of the philosopher." [20] And in all matters concerning the earth and its place in the universe, Strabo, like the Greek philosophers before him, turned to their earliest and most authoritative source of information, the one whose writings embodied most closely the accepted Greek conceptions and the most popular answers. This authority was none other than Homer, the epic poet, whose dates are unknown, whose background is a perfect blank, whose writings have caused as many heated arguments as those of William Shakespeare.

Whether the *Odyssey* and the *Iliad* are compilations of folklore brought together by one or more writers, or whether they represent, as Strabo felt, profound geographical knowledge on the part of one man, will probably remain forever a mystery.[21] What is important about these poetic masterpieces is that they reflect geographical conceptions which were current in Greece for about five hundred years, and which influenced in no small degree the trained minds of later generations that should have known better.

Homer wrote of brave men, of their military conquests and their travels. His fanciful ideas and poetic allegory, according to Strabo, by no means reflected the profundity of the poet's knowledge of the inhabited world, all parts of it. On the contrary, like the playwright of Elizabeth's time who wrote historical drama to entertain the people of London, Homer made the story good while he was about it. Both gentlemen, it seems, exerted an influence on future thought far beyond their original intent.

In reviewing the literature of early geography and the early conceptions of the earth, all books lead to Homer, whom Strabo called the founder of the science of geography, "for Homer has surpassed all other men, both of ancient and modern times, not only in the excellence of his poetry, but also, I might say, in his acquaintance with all that pertains to public life. . . . And this acquaintance made him busy himself . . . about the geography both of the individual countries and of the inhabited world at large, both land and sea; for otherwise he would not have gone to the uttermost bounds of the inhabited world, encompassing the whole of it in his description." [22] Strabo studied him carefully.

The earth, according to Homer and his disciples, was a plane disc surrounded by a constantly moving ocean river "Oceanus." [23] Resting on the rim of the earth's disc was the high vault of heaven, an inverted hemisphere. In need of additional support, the skies were propped by a series of tall pillars, not visible, whose structural safety was in the care of Atlas. Later his broad shoulders became the principal supporting members. Hyperion, the Titan sun-god, rose daily "from the deep stream of gently-flowing Oceanus," and every night sank again beneath the waves, "drawing black night over earth, the grain-giver." There were those who, venturing far out to sea, had heard the hissing roar as the fiery ball of the sun plunged beneath the water. But no one knew exactly where Hyperion came from or where he went or how he got dried out at night.

The stars did the same thing, traversing the heavens, "after having bathed in Oceanus." That is, all except the Bear. "She alone hath no part in the baths of Oceanus." Strabo, who was acquainted with two Bears, was confident that Homer knew of the lesser one as well, but admitted that the Little Bear might not have been marked out as a constellation in Homer's time. Strabo further defended this statement of Homer's by emending it and adding his own version of what the poet meant to say. He felt that Homer was explaining that the entire arctic circle and not just the Bear marks the boundary beyond which stars neither rise nor set, and that by Oceanus Homer meant the horizon beneath which the stars set and from above which they rise. Strabo himself maintained that the arctic circle touches the most northerly part of the inhabited world. Homer wrote of other star groups such as "the late-setting Boötes," and the Pleiades, the Hyades and the mighty Orion. He also mentioned Sirius.

There were four winds in Homer's world. Boreas, the north wind, blew from Thrace, a wind that rolled up mighty waves. Notus, the south wind, was a stormy petrel bringing sudden squalls, hence dangerous to navigators. Zephyrus, the west wind, was often represented as a stormy wind, but not by Homer, who knew the west, where the climate was temperate and the people prosperous. In the west was the Elysian Field itself and the ends of the earth, "where is Rhadamanthus of the fair hair, where life is easiest. No snow is there, nor yet great storm; but always Oceanus sendeth forth the breezes of the clear-blowing Zephyrus." In that same general direction were the Islands of the Blest (the Canary Islands, perhaps), lying westward of most western Maurusia (Morocco, approximately). Eurus, the east wind, was seldom mentioned.

Oceanus, according to Homer, ebbed and flowed, a gentle swell going nowhere in particular. No distinction was made between the inner and outer sea, the Ocean and the Mediterranean; it was all one and the same to Homer. Strabo agreed with Homer that the limits of the inhabited world were washed by the sea because, he reasoned, our senses tell us so; for no matter in which direction man has traveled sea has been found. Strabo thought it very unlikely that the great Western Sea was divided into two parts as some believed, separated by an isthmus; in fact he argued that those who had tried to sail around the circumfluent ocean turned back only "because of their destitution and loneliness," [24] and not because they encountered a land barrier such as a continent in their path. Moreover, the ebb and flow of the tide in every inhabited region proved that there was one and only one ocean, an opinion not shared by all writers. Strabo was a little uncertain, but felt it best to accept the theory of one continuous ocean because he and the rest of the Stoics believed that the greater the mass of water surrounding the earth, the better the heavenly bodies would be held together by the vapors arising therefrom!

From Homer's time to the introduction of prose writing in Greece there were no professed writers on history and geography, although allusions to geographical matters in the poetry of Hesiod indicate that there was a certain amount of activity in his day.[25] Atlas, from his "local habitation" in the Far West, now supported the heavens, "with his head and unwearied hands, under the pressure of stern necessity, standing at the furthest limits of the earth, in front of the clear-voiced Hesperides." They, in turn, stood guard over the golden apples and the trees that bore the precious fruit, "beyond the waters of Oceanus."

Strabo next turned to the Greek philosophers who began to exert considerable influence on geographical thought about 600 B.C. Much of the activity in the realm of philosophy was centered around the Ionic school founded by Thales at a time when Miletus (Palatia) was the most important city in Greece.[26] Situated on the southern shore of the Latmic Gulf near the mouth of the Maeander River, Miletus was an ideal outlet for the trade of Southern Phrygia. Its four harbors carried on a brisk trade with ancient Egypt by way of Naucratis and with the Black Sea cities of the North. Beginning with Thales, Miletus spawned many a noteworthy scholar and scientist including Anaximander, Anaximenes and Hecataeus. Even their severest critics admitted that these men made important contributions to learning. Eratosthenes went so far as to say that the first worthy successors to Homer in geographical circles were Anaximander, the first Greek to publish a map, and Hecataeus, who wrote an important two-volume treatise on geography entitled *Travels round the Earth*.[27]

Among the Miletan philosophers there was much talk about the probable size and shape of the earth and its place in the universe before any attempt was made to draw a picture of it. On the whole it was fairly elevated conversation, and even though some of the most brilliant ideas expounded at the time seem fantastic today, they were no more so than the present concept of an earth spinning on its axis at the rate of more than a thousand miles an hour and tearing through space at the rate of 18½ miles per second in an elliptical orbit around a stationary sun — facts which we accept on faith without a trace of emotion.

Anaximander of Miletus [28] was an able astronomer and geographer, one of the pioneers in exact science among the Greeks. He taught, if he did not discover, the obliquity of the ecliptic. He is said to have introduced the gnomon and sundial into Greece. Yet his philosophy did not gibe with his science. In spite of his mentor Thales, who taught that the earth was disc-shaped and supported by water on which it floated like a log or ship, Anaximander postulated a kind of primal chaos out of which had sprung a central mass, the earth, cylindrical in shape and poised in space. Surrounding the earth at a great distance were numerous balls of fire previously thrown off by the earth and left spinning in the cosmos like fiery wheels or air bubbles. The habitable part of his world was disc-shaped (presumably the top of the cylinder), and considerably larger than Homer's world. It extended westward to the Cassiterides or Tin Islands (Scilly Islands), beyond the Pillars of Hercules, and eastward to the Caspian Sea, which he thought was a continuation of the eastern part of Oceanus. The Aegean Sea occupied the center of his world.

Anaximenes,[29] who studied under Anaximander at Miletus, rejected the views of his teacher regarding the earth, visualizing instead of a cylinder a rectangle, buoyed up and cushioned in the heavens by compressed air. Everything, in fact, was air in varying degrees of density, and bodies such as earth, sun and stars were nothing more than finely adjusted condensations of air, either hot or cold. He believed that the heavenly bodies were transported around the fixed earth at a great distance, and supported, like the earth, by atmospheric pressure. Regarding the sun's disappearance at night, Anaximenes advanced a novel explanation, and one that persisted for many years in certain circles: the light of the sun was intercepted at night by a high range of mountains — imperfectly located geographically in the vicinity of the extreme north.

Hecataeus, the youngest of the Miletans,[30] defended the disc-shaped world and the circumfluent ocean, although he is said to have had at his disposal sailing directions covering the territory from the Indus River to the Red Sea; he knew of the campaign of Darius in Scythia (513 B.C.) and from the merchants and travelers who put in at Miletus he must have heard that there was more than compressed air beyond the horizon. Certainly no mariner of the time would have helped perpetuate the idea of a sluggish, "gently-flowing Oceanus," but his own travels seem to have taught him little in regard to the earth.

The first tentative approach to the truth about the shape of the earth came from Pythagoras the Ionian, who founded a school of philosophy at Crotona about 523 B.C.[31] A great name in the history of science, Pythagoras is credited with several important scientific hypotheses which turned out to be correct. Perhaps his most important theory was that the earth, instead of being flat or disc-shaped, was spherical. How he arrived at such a fantastic conclusion, the keystone of cartography, is a mystery. Various suggestions have been advanced as to his method of reasoning; a favorite one, attributed to him by his followers and exponents, was that the earth is spherical simply because "the sphere is the most beautiful of solid figures." Other writers favor the idea that he reached this portentous conclusion by observation of the heavens and the correct interpretation of what he saw there. At any rate, the Pythagoreans, who elaborated the ideas propounded by the master, built around their spherical earth a new cosmic system, departing in many respects from all previous concepts including those of Pythagoras himself. They stuck to his spherical earth but abandoned the geocentric hypothesis, removing the earth from the center of the universe and reducing it to the status of a planet like Jupiter and the sun. Then they proceeded to fabricate a system wherein the celestial bodies including the sun revolve around a "central fire" of mysterious origin. The logic back of this move goes something like this: "The worthiest place is appropriate to the worthiest occupant, and fire is worthier than earth. . . ." Therefore, the central body in the universe must be a central fire, but not the sun. Still another celestial body was introduced which the Pythagoreans called *antichthon*, a sort of counter-earth, on the opposite side of the rotating universe and therefore invisible from the earth. Some authorities held that in this scheme of the universe the earth remained fixed in space, while certain of the Pythagoreans believed that it revolved around the central fire in an oblique circle, the same as the sun and the moon, in which case the earth supposedly made one revolution around the central fire in a day and a night, or every twenty-four hours.

The complex theories regarding the universe advanced by Eudoxus and Callippus, two learned astronomers, involving a system of concentric spheres and abstruse mathematical formulae, added little but confusion to the evolving

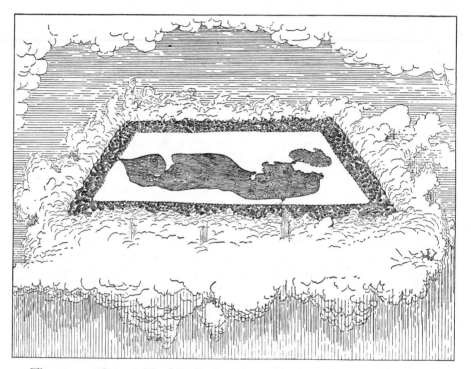

The rectangular world of Anaximenes (*c.* 500 B.C.) was watery yet supported in space by compressed air. The Mediterranean washed its nearer shores while beyond the horizon flowed the great circumfluent Ocean Sea.

picture of the world.[32] They were beautiful theories, but Aristotle, in reviewing the opinions of earlier astronomers, felt constrained to modify them considerably and in some instances to substitute his own ideas on the subject. The universe, said he, is finite and it is spherical. The stars are spherical. Why? Because nature does nothing without a purpose; therefore nature gave the stars a form least like that of animate things, which possess organs of locomotion, a shape least favorable for any independent movement. The earth, also, is spherical, he said, in spite of the contention made by some that the line of the horizon which cuts the rising and setting sun is straight and not curved. This apparent straight line, he reasoned, was an optical illusion created by the tremendous expanse of the horizon and the comparatively small sphere of the sun observed at sunrise and sunset, a combination which was confusing if not misleading to the observer. His other reasons for subscribing to the theory of a spherical earth were clearer and based on observations which any person could make with the naked eye. During a partial eclipse of the moon, for example, the line of demarcation is always curved, regardless of the amount of the eclipse; on the other hand, the line of demarcation across the face of the moon at her various phases may be straight or curved in either direction. Therefore the eclipse, which is caused by the interposition of the earth, proves that the earth is a sphere. His second point was to prove valuable in the progress of cartography. Certain stars, he pointed out, which are above the horizon in Egypt and Cyprus are not visible farther north; moreover, certain stars that set in those places, remain always above the horizon in regions farther north. These things being so, and because there is such a perceptible change in the horizon between places so near together, it follows that the earth must be spherical, and not such a big sphere at that.

Aristotle [33] did not agree with Thales that the earth floats on water, asserting that it was a theory contrary to experience. We see water resting or floating on the earth, but we never see earth floating anywhere. He also rejected the theory advanced by Anaximenes, Anaxagoras and Democritus that the earth, like a flat lid or wagon wheel, rides in space supported by compressed air. Aristotle tried to prove that the earth has no motion whatever, and in criticizing his colleagues who opposed the idea he distinguished between those who favored a motion of translation and those who believed that the earth rotates on an axis through its poles. Nothing was said about the possibility of two different motions, a revolution of the earth within the celestial sphere and an axial rotation.

The radical hypotheses advanced by Aristarchus of Samos (*c.* 310–230 B.C.), "the mathematician," completed the early philosophic framework of astronomy in its relation to cartography.[34] A pupil of Strato the astronomer, who succeeded Theophrastus as head of the Peripatetic School in 288 B.C., Aristarchus left to posterity many mechanical appliances as well as theoretical data of the first importance. A versatile scientist, Aristarchus of Samos wrote a work *On the sizes and distances of the sun and moon,* a treatise in many respects ahead of the times. He perfected an improved sundial, the base of which was a concave hemisphere instead of a plane, with a vertical pointer or style fixed at the center so that direction and the height of the sun could be calculated at a glance. He wrote on optics, light and color. "And," wrote Heath, "there is not the slightest doubt that Aristarchus was the first to put forward the heliocentric hypothesis. Ancient testimony is unanimous on the point, and the first witness is Archimedes, who was a younger contemporary of Aristarchus, so that there was no possibility of a mistake." [35] Moreover, it is generally unknown or overlooked that Copernicus himself admitted that the theory should be attributed to Aristarchus.

Writing on the universe and the earth's place within it, Archimedes said, "But Aristarchus brought out a book consisting of certain hypotheses, wherein it appears, as a consequence of the assumption made, that the universe is many times greater than the 'universe' just mentioned. His hypotheses are that the fixed stars and the sun remain unmoved, that the earth revolves about the sun in the circumference of a circle, the sun lying in the middle of the orbit. . . ." [36] A second witness in behalf of Aristarchus and his remarkable contribution to science was Plutarch: "Only do not, my good fellow, enter an action against me for impiety in the style of Cleanthes, who thought it was the duty of Greeks to indict Aristarchus of Samos on the charge of impiety for putting in motion the Hearth of the Universe, this being the effect of his attempt to save the phenomena by supposing the heaven to remain at rest and the earth to revolve in an oblique circle, while it rotates, at the same time, about its own axis." [37] Indicted he was, by his contemporaries, and few persons at the time could afford to give credence to such a wild hypothesis, and even after Copernicus rephrased it 1800 years later, it was not convincing to more than a few radical thinkers.

No sooner had the hypotheses of Pythagoras been generally accepted, and the earth had taken the shape of a sphere, than estimates were made as to its size. Of the early guesses, Plato's, set forth in his *Phaedo*, was the largest, at least by implication. "I believe," he said, through his medium Socrates, "that the earth is very large and that we who dwell between the Pillars of Hercules and the river Phasis live in a small part of it about the sea, like ants or frogs about a pond, and that many other people live in many other such regions. . . ." [38] Aristotle was more conservative and more specific. He said that observations of the stars prove that the earth is spherical and that its size is not great. He also said that the mathematicians of his day estimated the earth's circumference at 400,000 stadia.[39] (Note: for the convenience of the reader all linear measure originally expressed in stadia will be given in miles — 10 stadia = 1 mile.) [40] Archimedes, in his *Sand-reckoner*, said that this figure had since been reduced by common consent to about 30,000 miles.[41] By then, the measurement of the earth's circumference had become a popular subject among the learned, but for a great many years nothing was said about methods.

The earliest reliable account of how the earth was first measured relates to Eratosthenes of Cyrene, born in 276 B.C.[42] A versatile man of learning with a thorough background in science and philosophy, Eratosthenes spent considerable time in Athens, and while there he was sought out by Ptolemy Euergetes, the reigning monarch of Egypt, who was looking for a man to succeed Callimachus as head of the Alexandrian Library. Some historians say he was also looking for a scholar to tutor his son Philopator (Ptolemy IV). However, if Eratosthenes actually undertook this additional responsibility, the tutoring seems to have had little effect on the royal heir, for he later inaugurated his reign by murdering his mother and otherwise contributing generously towards the decline of the dynasty.

Eratosthenes wrote on many subjects, both scientific and philosophical, but his most outstanding contribution to the science of cartography was a sound method of measuring the size of the earth, a classic of its kind and the first of many to go on the record. The original account, like most of his writings, is lost, but thanks to Cleomedes the astronomer (*c.* 50 B.C.) the method and the result have survived.[43]

Eratosthenes based his measurement on certain known or alleged facts: (1) that the linear distance between Alexandria and Syenê (Assuan) was 500 miles; (2) that Alexandria and Syenê were situated on a north-south line, or as Cleomedes put it, "under the same meridian circle"; (3) that Syenê was located at the extremity of the Summer Tropic zone (on the Tropic of Cancer), a fact supposedly confirmed by Pliny, Arrian and others, because in Syenê, at the summer solstice, the sun was directly overhead at midday; at that time the gnomon cast no shadow and the sun's rays were reflected from the very bottom of the deepest wells. Now, by observation it was noted that on the day of the summer solstice the midday sun at Alexandria was not overhead, but instead it cast a shadow at an angle equal to one fiftieth part of a circle. This being so, the angular distance between Alexandria and Syenê was equivalent to one fiftieth of the distance around the earth. Therefore, if the linear distance between the two cities was 500 miles, the linear distance around the earth would be 50 times 500 or 25,000 miles. It was all so simple it should have been thought of before. The accuracy of this value depends, of course, on the value of the "stadium" as a unit of linear measure at the time, and it looks as though the point will never be settled to the satisfaction of all; but if the several different values are averaged, the measurement of the earth by Eratosthenes would come within 200 or 300 miles of the true value, *if the earth were a perfect sphere.* This popular and natural assumption, which persisted until 1671 A.D.,[44] was the one theoretical error in the method employed by Eratosthenes and one which can hardly be held against him. In all other respects his method was essentially the same as that used by modern astronomers to measure the earth.

As for the other errors in his measurement, they were caused by faulty information contributed by tradition and popular belief. For example, Syenê is not on the Tropic of Cancer but in latitude 24° 5′ 30″, approximately 37 miles north of it. And again, the distance between Syenê and Alexandria was probably not more than 453 miles. Syenê does not lie on the meridian of Alexandria, but 3° 3′ east of it. The difference in latitude between Syenê and Alexandria which Eratosthenes took as one fiftieth part of a great circle or 7° 12′ of arc, is actually 7° 5′, which produces another error in the final result. It seems highly probable that Eratosthenes was aware of the likelihood of error in his result, because he apparently revised his final result upward, making it 25,200, a number readily divisible into 360 parts, or into the number of degrees in a great circle, each degree of arc being equal to 70 miles. If he had stuck to his original figure of 25,000 geographical miles (250,000 stadia) he would have come remarkably close to the truth, for the circumference of the earth at the equator is very close to 25,000 *English* miles — 24,899 according to Herschel's measurement. A very nice result for a beginner who had no telescope or, presumably, precision instruments of any kind.

The second recorded attempt to measure the earth was made by Poseidonius

of Apameia.[45] His result was not good, but he deserves a place in this history because of the confusion he caused among the early historians and because his
estimate, reported by Strabo, was accepted and perpetuated for centuries, instead
of the value determined by Eratosthenes.

Poseidonius (*c.* 130–51 B.C.) was one of the most learned of the Stoic philosophers. Surnamed "the Rhodian," he conducted a school on the island of
Rhodes which attracted scholars from all parts of the world. Though not an
astronomer, "in the strict sense of the word," as one historian put it, he nevertheless incorporated in his philosophy not only astronomy but geography, mathematics and meteorology; he also wrote a history in 52 books. In a few instances
he outdid the astronomers, as in his measurement of the distance of the sun from
the earth, which came closer to the truth than the figure arrived at by Hipparchus.
His measurement of the earth was based on the same general principles used by
Eratosthenes, but instead of calculating the difference in the altitude of the sun
at two different places on the day of the summer solstice, Poseidonius used a star.
The story was reported in detail by Cleomedes as follows:

In parts of Greece the bright star Canopus was invisible, but at Rhodes, where
Poseidonius was working, it rose just high enough to graze the horizon and then
set again immediately. At Alexandria, still further south, the meridian height of
Canopus was equal to "a fourth part of a 'sign,'" that is, one forty-eighth part
of the zodiac circle. This was just another way of saying that the difference in
the angular height of Canopus at Alexandria and at Rhodes was 7° 30′. The linear
distance between the two places was generally agreed to be 500 miles; therefore,
the circumference of the earth would be 48 times 500 or 24,000 miles.

Here again, the method employed by Poseidonius was sound enough, but his
result was off because his data were inaccurate. In the first place, the angular
distance between Rhodes and Alexandria (that is, the difference in latitude) instead of being 7° 30′ is 5° 15′, or less than one sixtieth part of a great circle.
Heath points out that the error in taking the meridian height of the star probably occurred at Rhodes, where the effects of refraction at the horizon would
vitiate the observation considerably; in other words, an accurate observation of a
star just grazing the horizon would be extremely difficult, if not impossible. The
second error, the distance of 500 miles between Alexandria and Rhodes, resulted
from a traditional estimate made by mariners, men who have never been famous
for their understatements. It was the maximum estimate. Some authorities reckoned
the distance at 400 miles and Eratosthenes, according to Strabo, said the distance
was only 375 miles. However the estimate made by Poseidonius and reported
by Cleomedes was 24,000 miles for the circumference of the earth, and there it
would have remained had it not been for Strabo. But in discussing the more recent
measurements of the earth, Strabo mentioned "the one which makes the earth
smallest in circumference . . . that of Poseidonius, who estimates its circumference at about one hundred and eighty thousand stadia [18,000 miles]. . . ."[46]

Why should there have been such a vast discrepancy between the figure reported by Cleomedes and that recorded by Strabo? Heath supplies an ingenious

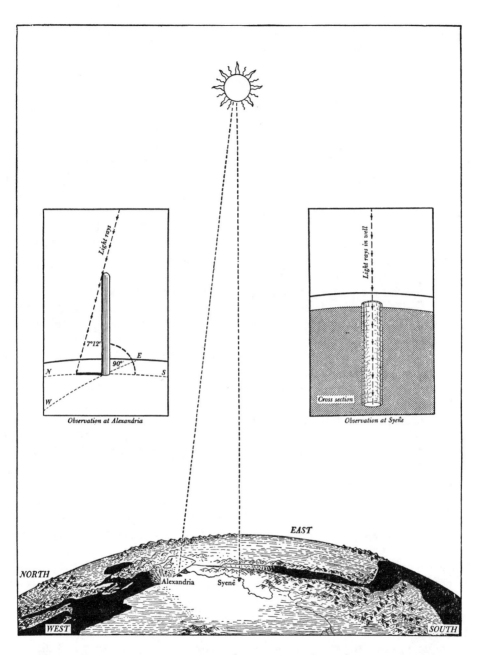

The earliest known measurement of the earth's circumference was made by Eratosthenes about 240 B.C. His calculations were based on (1) the angular height of the sun and (2) the linear distance between Alexandria and Syenê.

answer which makes both authorities correct up to a point. Strabo, he reasons, was favorably inclined towards the writings of Eratosthenes and suspicious of popular opinion on any subject, scientific or otherwise. So when he came to report on Poseidonius, he rejected the popular figure of 500 miles as the distance between Alexandria and Rhodes and used the figure set down by Eratosthenes, which was 375 miles. At the same time, both reporters on Poseidonius (Cleomedes and Strabo) seem to have agreed that the arc between the two cities was equal to one forty-eighth part of a great circle meridian. Now 48 times 500 miles is 24,000 miles and 48 times 375 miles is 18,000 miles.[47] If we accept this line of reasoning we must assume that either Strabo or Cleomedes or both had a secondhand account of Poseidonius to work with, a description of his method without figures, and took the liberty of filling in the details. However, the smaller value was recorded by Strabo, the historian's historian, with the result that 18,000 miles was generally accepted as the circumference of the earth, and 50 miles the value of a degree of arc, two standards which were destined to change the course of history and torment geographers for many years to come.

In discussing the progress of cartography, Strabo referred to the map drawing of "the ancients," but, in keeping with his avowed policy of ignoring all but the most authoritative of the "modern" writers, he said almost nothing to indicate just how ancient the "ancients" were. He mentioned none of them by name and was vague as to the development of cartography up to Homer's time, yet map making is perhaps the oldest variety of primitive art, because from the very beginning it was art with a purpose. It is as old as man's first tracings on the walls of caves and in the sands. Moreover, the ability to depict with sticks and stones or with a piece of chalk a portion of the earth's surface, however small, is so universal and timeless that it might even be considered instinctive. This fact has been noted by countless explorers who have had dealings with primitive people. When all other methods of communication fail, the universal language of the simple map and chart comes to the rescue.

The earliest maps were based on personal experience and familiarity with a local situation. They showed the path through the forest to the neighboring tribe; places where game, water and salt could be found; the distance and direction of enemy tribes. Nomadic life complicated the picture somewhat; wandering tribes needed to know how to cross the desert without dying of thirst and how to get home after grazing their flocks for many miles during the summer season. Making war, an ancient method of acquiring land, meant knowing your neighbor's territory and not forgetting it. Commerce with other tribes and nations meant knowing still more about distance and direction; the farther away the markets the more accurate the routes to and from them had to be. Distance and direction became increasingly important as civilization expanded, and like the records of the early astrologers, geographical accounts and pictures, the way to get from place to place, were set down — after a fashion — on stone, papyrus and parchment. Few of them survived.

The maps and globes of Strabo's "ancients" fall into two general groups: representations of the whole world and maps of local areas. Which came first is a question, because on the earliest maps a representation of the home town might just as well be considered a map of the world, for that is exactly what it was to the person who made it — his world — a flat surface whose center could be marked with an X at the point of observation and whose limits were the circular horizon as it appeared from where he was standing. The circular horizon and the circular world expanded in direct proportion to man's mobility, and he probably speculated on how far he would have to travel before the horizon, the jumping-off place, could be reached. On a national scale, there were various geographical centers of the world. Greece was the center of the world to the Hellenes, and Delphi was the center of Greece. Every country went through this stage of development and at one time there were as many centers of the world as there were nations. The disc-shaped world, or what remained of the concept after Homer's time, expanded finally until it included the Mediterranean basin, the Black Sea, Egypt, Babylonia and Assyria, but maps of this world are nonexistent. All that can be proved from the literature is that such maps existed throughout the pre-Christian era.

The earliest positive evidence of map making stems from Babylonia, where a cadastral (real estate) survey for the purpose of taxing property was functioning in the age of Sargon of Akkad (*c.* 2300 B.C.), and there are clay tablets in the British Museum dating back to 2300 or 2100 B.C., which contain surveying notes.[48] One of these depicts in a rough way a part of lower Babylonia encircled by a "salt water river," or *Oceanus*. A papyrus in the Turin Museum depicts the triumphal return of Seti I (1366–1333 B.C.) from Syria, and shows the road from Pelusium to Heroöpolis embellished with quaint details. Apollonius of Rhodes, who became Librarian at Alexandria in 196 B.C., reported in his *Argonautica* that the inhabitants of Colchis, a colony dating from the time of Rameses II (about 1250 B.C.), preserved as heirlooms certain graven wooden tablets on which land, sea, roads and towns were accurately set down. There are several other examples of early maps and plans made a thousand years or more before Anaximander, whom the Greeks revered as the inventor of cartography.

Traces of world maps have been found in the earliest literature relating to geography, regardless of the then current conception of the earth's size and shape. Hecataeus, who wrote so glibly about his world travels, was responsible for a bronze tablet upon which was engraved "the whole circuit of the earth, the sea and the rivers." Herodotus reported that about 500 B.C. this map was shown to Cleomenes, king of Sparta, by Aristagoras, tyrant of Miletus, who was trying to organize a revolt against the Persians and wanted some Spartan assistance. The map was probably an adaptation of an earlier one made by Anaximander.

In Aristophanes's comedy *The Clouds* (423 B.C.), a map of the world was brought onto the stage, whereupon a disciple of the Sophists pointed out certain familiar places such as Athens to the audience. The dialogue ran as follows: [49]

STREPSIODES. This then (*pointing to a geometrical instrument*); how is it useful?

DISCIPLE. To measure up land.

STREPSIODES. Do you mean the allotment-land?

DISCIPLE. No! the whole world . . . Here you have the circuit of all the earth. D'ye see? Here is Athens.

Democritus of Abdera (*c.* 450–360 B.C.), cofounder with Leucippus of the atomic theory, made a map of the inhabited part of the world. Dicaearcus of Messana, a pupil of Aristotle (326–296 B.C.), wrote a description of the earth illustrated with maps. Also part of this work, in all probability, was his treatise on the method of measuring the height of mountains.

Enough specimens of early globes were written about to indicate that they came into rather common use shortly after the earth was generally considered to be a sphere. The Museum of Naples has a globe two meters in diameter which is doubtless a product of the fourth century B.C. The globe is supported on the shoulders of a human figure representing Atlas. It may have been built by or for Eudoxus (d. 386 B.C.), the celebrated astronomer and philosopher. Aratus of Soli (b. 315 B.C.) refers in his poetical *Prognostics* to a globe in his possession. Archimedes had a celestial globe of glass with a small terrestrial globe suspended inside it. Hero of Alexandria, the geometer, had a similar one. Hipparchus, the astronomer-librarian, had a globe which he used in the Alexandrian library. About 140 B.C. Crates of Mallus constructed a globe on which he set forth the Stoic conception of the world.

Among the tales in the *Variae Historiae* brought together by Aelian in the third century A.D. was one which illustrates the progress of cartography up to the time of Strabo.[50] "When Socrates saw Alcibiades puffed up by his wealth, boasting of its abundance and still more about his lands, he led him to a certain place in the city where there was deposited a plate having on it the circuit of the earth, and bade him look for Attica thereon. When Alcibiades had found it, Socrates bade him point out his own lands. And on his replying, 'But they are nowhere drawn.' 'These then,' said he, 'make you boast, though they are not even a part of the earth.'" In 25 A.D. few men could step up to a map and say, "This is my land and this my country." Only a few could give a name to the countries bordering Our Sea, and the limits of the inhabited world were largely a mystery.

CHAPTER II

The Habitable World

I F THE EARTH were really a sphere and anywhere near as large as Eratosthenes said it was, then the philosophers and astronomers, the geographers and geometers were faced with several interesting questions. How much of the earth was habitable and how much of it actually inhabited? Certainly not all of it. There were rumors of far-off countries beyond the Pillars of Hercules, below the Island of the Fugitive Egyptians and in the remote regions of the Far East. If these countries really existed, how far were they from the civilized world and how could the geometers partition that part of the world which was habitable from that which would not support life? In short, how could the spherical earth be divided and classified in an orderly manner when there were so few landmarks to go by?

Dicaearcus of Messana made a start by drawing a straight east-west line across the map of the habitable world as he knew it.[1] This "diaphragm," or "partition" as it was called, extended from the Pillars of Hercules through the Mediterranean, along the Taurus and Imaus (Himalaya) mountains to the Eastern Ocean. As a straight east-west partition, the line was not a huge success. The precise location of its western terminal was in doubt as much as three hundred years later, at least in geographical circles, and Strabo discussed at length the possibility of establishing the location of the Pillars at some future date. Going east from the Pillars, the line disintegrated rapidly, veering first to the north and then to the south as Dicaearcus selected the points through which it ought to pass. Beyond the Mediterranean to the east the line passed through mountains that were known by rumor only and entered an ocean whose existence was only assumed. The partitioning of the sphere, then, was not going to be so easy, and in their search for a point or line of departure, a way of keeping a line headed in the proper direction, geographers again turned to the heavens, specifically to the sun. The sun gave to cartography its first three standard lines of partition: the equator, the Tropic of Cancer and the Tropic of Capricorn, lines that gave some meaning to the term "parallel."

The basic facts concerning the sun's behavior came from the common man, the shepherd and the farmer, the fisherman and the camel driver of primitive civilization. Like all living things, he needed the sun to warm him, but he also needed its heat to support him, to make grass grow, and grain. He recognized the sun as the giver and supporter of life, and was vitally interested in its habits long before the priestly cult took over the custody of the calendar and the responsibility of predicting eclipses. He studied it before he worshiped it. Certain

things about the sun were apparent to any observant person, besides the fact
that every morning it rose in one part of the heavens and at night disappeared on
the opposite side. It did not always rise and set in the same place. At certain times
of the year it rose late and set early; at other times it rose early and set late. The
arc it described across the heavens varied from day to day and from month to
month. This was important because each appreciable change in the height of the
sun brought a change in season. Not only the length of the day and night but
the hotness of the day and the coldness of the night were affected. These changes
corresponded with the growing cycle of plant life and the fertility of animals.
The day the sun reached the lowest point in the heavens, when the night was
longest and the hours of sunshine were too few to warm a body, there was rejoicing, even in the discomfort of the day or hour, because tomorrow there would
be just a little more warmth and the night would not be quite so long, though
it might be just as cold. The winter solstice (December 21) was celebrated long
before the birth of the Christ child. Why? Because the sun was coming back.[2]
By the time it had reached the halfway mark three months later, when day and
night were of equal length (the equinox), there was further cause to celebrate;
life was abundant and fertility everywhere apparent. Not only the earth but life
itself was being replenished. At the other extreme, the longest day of the year,
when the sun had reached its full height in the heavens, there was also a period
of great rejoicing; for many it was harvest time, for others it was merely a time
to keep indoors during the middle of the day. Shamash was now in all sincerity
"the burner." For everyone, the summer solstice (June 21) was the climax of all
good things which the sun-god had to bestow on mortal man. Soon the autumnal
equinox would come again and the earth would begin to die.

    It did not require the services of a priest to prophesy these things, any more
than it took an astrologer to point out the fact that the polestar remained in a
fixed position, year in and year out, while millions of stars revolved around it,
from the right hand to the left. Such things were common knowledge, even
though the untutored man might be a day or two off in his reckoning of these
fundamental solar changes. However, the orientation of ancient monuments such
as those at Stonehenge indicate that ancient man did his best with what he had
to keep track of the important periods of seasonal change. He learned to place
his markers so that the sun's annual climb from south to north along the eastern
horizon could be plotted, in a crude sort of way, to warn him when it was time
to celebrate and when to mourn. The priestly cult of Egypt and Chaldea improved upon his technique, pinning down the days of important seasonal change,
and Greek philosophers, with the aid of the gnomon and sundial, went a step
further. They brought down to earth and applied to their maps the equinox and
the solstices.

    The origin of the gnomon was humble indeed. In its most primitive form it was
a shepherd's staff, a tent stake stuck in the ground, or any other kind of rod, tree
or vertical shaft, which, by casting a shadow in the sunlight indicated the sun's
position. The slant of the shadow told the herdsman and the moneylender how

the day was progressing, while the length of the shadow indicated the passage of the seasons. The former was more obvious to the observer than the latter, but it was the ratio between the height of the gnomon and the length of the shadow it cast which was first applied to cartography and which established the first three parallels of latitude on the map. The day of the equinox, when the hours of daylight and darkness were equal, occurred twice a year. To the earth's inhabitants it

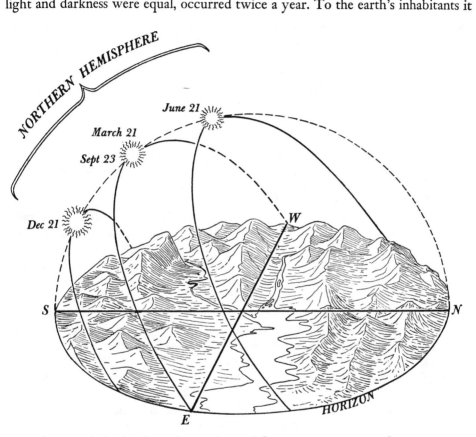

The sun's behavior from day to day and from year to year was known to primitive man. Astronomers marked the days of the equinoxes and the solstices.

was the midpoint between the northern and southern limit of the sun's annual pilgrimage up and down the heavens. On the days of the equinox it rose in the east and set due west, and, said the astronomers, on those days the gnomon cast no shadow on the equinoctial line because the sun was directly overhead. The equinoctial line was an "equatorial" line as well, an imaginary great circle at right angles to the axis of the earth dividing the sphere into northern and southern hemispheres. This fact was recognized by astronomers, but for a long time it had no bearing on map making in general or the map of the habitable world, because the region of the equinoctial or equatorial line was thought to be uninhabitable and therefore of no concern to geographers. But gradually, as time went on, this first, most familiar astronomical base line was taken over by geographers and cartographers. It had several things to recommend it. First of all, it was a neat, geometrical partition of a sphere, perpendicular to the earth's axis, which appealed to the mathematical brethren. Second, it could be utilized as a convenient base line of reference from which data concerning the habitable parts of the earth could be calculated theoretically without departing from the realm of civilization. Third, it furnished mankind with a standard day. The equinox was the *mean* day, with reference to the number of hours of daylight. The sand glass and water clock (clepsydra) were graduated on the basis of the equinoctial day, from sunrise to sunset, into hours, half hours and quarter hours, and it was the day on which sundials were oriented. There were doubtless several ways of determining the day of the equinox, besides relying on the calendar or on the calculations of astronomers, which were not in wide circulation. Several practical methods have been suggested, any one of which would have been feasible with no other instruments than a gnomon or sundial.[3]

The second and third parallels laid down on the spherical earth were closely related to the equatorial or equinoctial line, and were literally parallel to it. Strabo and his ancients called them, logically, the Summer Tropic and the Winter Tropic, because they marked the two extremes of the sun's annual course and corresponded to the summer and winter seasons of Strabo's habitable world. To Strabo, the Summer Tropic represented the maximum height of the sun, the longest day of the year in the northern hemisphere, the summer solstice, when most of the habitable world was hot. Later it was named the Tropic of Cancer, because on the day of the solstice the Crab (Cancer), the fourth sign of the Zodiac, made its first appearance.[4] And anyone living in Syenê knew that at the time of the summer solstice the sun was directly overhead and that the index (style) of the sundial and the gnomon cast no shadow. This fact was agreed to by most astronomers and confirmed by Pliny and Arrian, for in Syenê "is also the well that marks the summer tropic, for the reason that this region lies under the tropic circle and causes the gnomons to cast no shadow at midday; for if from our region, I mean that of Greece, we proceed towards the south, it is at Syenê that the sun first gets over our heads and . . . it also casts its rays into wells as far as the water, even if they are very deep; for we ourselves stand perpendicular to the earth and wells are dug perpendicular to the surface."[5] At all other times in Syenê the shadow of the gnomon fell "towards the darkness" and the polestar; never towards the equinoctial, which meant that Syenê was the northern limit of the sun's climb. And at various places between Syenê and the equator, the shadow cast by the gnomon sometimes fell one way and sometimes the other, depending on the season, and at all such places there were two actual and several apparent days when the sun was directly overhead and the gnomon cast no shadow.

The corresponding parallel in the southern hemisphere, the Winter Tropic, was known by reputation only. Observations of the sun at the time of the winter

The earliest known map (*left*), found at Nuzi near Kirkuk, dates from the dynasty of Sargon of Akkad, about 2400–2200 B.C. The Babylonian tablet at right is a ground plan dating from the sixth or seventh century B.C.

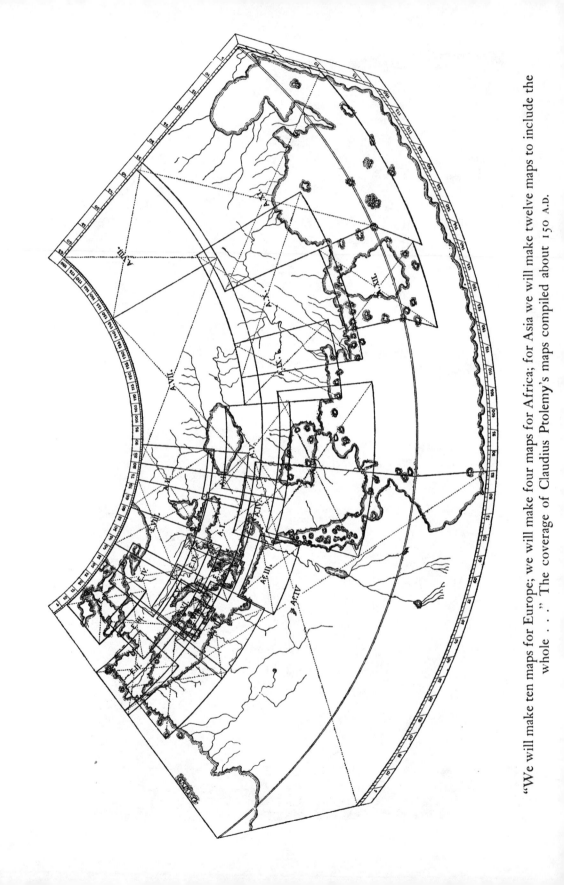

"We will make ten maps for Europe; we will make four maps for Africa; for Asia we will make twelve maps to include the whole . . ." The coverage of Claudius Ptolemy's maps compiled about 150 A.D.

solstice were made from a distance: no one in Greece had been to the region to see it pass directly overhead or to note that the gnomon cast no shadow on the ground. It was observed, however, that on the day of the winter solstice the He-Goat (Capricorn), the tenth sign of the Zodiac, first made its appearance on the horizon.[6] So it was that in subsequent discussions of the tropics in connection with the location of places and the determination of latitudes it was the *Summer* Tropic, lying within the habitable world, which was studied. The length of the longest day of the year in hours became a standard index of latitude, but nothing was said about the shortest day. Just where these three parallels should be placed with respect to places on the earth and from thence onto a map, was a highly debatable point. Also a problem was how to establish intermediate lines (parallels) that were too far apart to measure by surveying. Another question was, how far apart were the tropics and what was the distance between each tropic and the equator?

Astronomers were able to contribute the answers to these questions because they were the core of their studies of the ecliptic, an imaginary great circle in the heavens so named because it was the path along which solar and lunar eclipses took place. The ecliptic is defined in several ways, all of which describe one or more results of the fact that the axis of the earth is tilted or inclined instead of being in line with the axis of the celestial sphere. Likewise, the terrestrial equator projected, instead of coinciding with the celestial equator, makes an oblique circle against the celestial sphere; hence the plane of the ecliptic is inclined to the plane of the celestial equator. The ecliptic is defined as the apparent path of the sun extended to the celestial sphere, the path of the sun among the stars.[7] To ancient astronomers, it was obvious that the plane of the ecliptic did not coincide with the plane of the terrestrial equator. It was apparent, therefore, that the axis of the earth could not coincide with the axis of the celestial sphere. The most sensible demonstration of the obliquity of the ecliptic was the annual course of the sun, and it was recognized that the angle involved was equivalent to the arc between the sun at the equinox and the sun at either the Tropic of Cancer (summer solstice) or the Tropic of Capricorn (winter solstice). Among Greek astronomers a traditional value for the obliquity of the ecliptic was 24°. Nothing is said about how this angle was determined. Greek mathematicians arrived at the same figure by geometrical means. They said the obliquity of the ecliptic was equal to the angle subtended at the center of a circle by the side of a regular fifteen-angled figure inscribed in the circle, or 24°.[8] Theon of Alexandria gave Eratosthenes credit for a closer approximation, when the latter found that the angular distance between the two tropic circles was 11/83rds of a meridian circle, or 47° 42′ 40″. Therefore the obliquity of the ecliptic, the angular distance between the equator and either tropic, would be one half of that value, or 23° 51′ 20″. At the time, the actual value would have been 23° 45′ 4″. Today it is about 23° 26′ 46″.[9]

The astronomical location of the tropics did not solve the problem of establishing parallels of latitude, by any means; but it pointed the way. It gave cartographers their first three east-west partitions, literally parallel with one another, and established the limits of the two tropic (torrid) zones or "climata." It also furnished data which contributed to the theoretical location of the two arctic (frigid) zones, likewise of astronomical origin but later adopted by cartographers and set down on the map.

Early Greek astronomers used the term "arctic circle" not in connection with the frigid zones of the earth near the poles, but with reference to a celestial circle. Our Arctic Circle, on the map and on the earth itself, is fixed for convenience sake at 66° 30', while in Greek astronomy the arctic circle varied according to the position of the observer and his horizon. At the equator, for example, the arctic circle was nonexistent, because all of the stars comprising the Great Bear were below his horizon, and would remain so at any point in the southern hemisphere. Further north, however, at a station such as Alexandria or Massilia, the arctic circle would be described on the celestial sphere so as to include all such stars, including the polestar, as remained always above the horizon; in other words, the "circle" would be tangent to the horizon of the observer. Thus the arctic circle would increase in radius as the observer moved north, and the radius, with the polestar as a center, would likewise be an indication of the latitude of the observer. In other words, going north from the equator, the angular height of the polestar increased in the same proportion as the radius of the arctic circle, so that at the Pole the angle of the polestar would be 90° and the circumference of the arctic circle would be equal to the circle tangent to the horizon at 24°.[10]

Pytheas seems to have brought the arctic circle down to earth in his first references to Thule. In referring to its latitude he said it was the most northern inhabited region and that at Thule the arctic circle corresponds with the Summer Tropic (Tropic of Cancer), which is to say that the height of the polestar at Thule is the same as the angular height of the Summer Tropic above the equator, that is, about 24°, approximately the location of the Arctic Circle from the North Pole. In other words, if Pytheas, like Eratosthenes and Strabo, placed the Summer Tropic at 24° north of the equator, the latitude of Thule would be 66°, the complement of the Summer Tropic.[11]

There are numerous references to the "arctic circle" used in this sense by early Greek writers, and of course by Strabo. Speaking of the latitude of various places in the habitable world, Strabo says, "The Cinnamon-producing people are the first to whom the Little Bear is wholly inside the arctic circle and always visible; for the bright star at the tip of the tail, the most southerly in the constellation, is situated on the very circumference of the arctic circle, so that it touches the horizon." [12] He might have stated it in much simpler terms by saying that the height of the polestar (the latitude) at the cinnamon-producing country (Somaliland) is so many degrees and minutes of arc, or is equal to the length of the Little Bear. There were, then, two arctic circles, one of them loosely fixed with respect to the earth and varying in size according to the position of the observer; and a second one, fixed mathematically as it is today on modern maps. Both, apparently, were in common use when Strabo investigated the subject.

In addition to the three primary zones or "climata" established by the sun and accepted by astronomers and geographers, there were others. In fact the climata were the subject of endless controversies among Strabo's worthies. How many were there and how could they be defined, literally and figuratively? And what connection was there between the various climata and habitability? Thales and Pythagoras had divided the sphere of the universe into climata or zones, five of them: the arctic, which is always visible; the summer tropical; the equatorial; the winter tropical; the antarctic, which is never visible.[13] These celestial circles were later transposed to the earth and from thence to the map of the world. The conservative element were content to divide the earth into five zones: the "torrid" zone, which included the band between the two tropic circles, two "temperate" zones, lying between the tropic circles and arctic circles (fixed), and two "frigid" zones, extending from the fixed arctic circles to each pole. The hair-splitters insisted on differentiating between the northern and southern tropics, separated by the equator. A few may have had suspicions that the northern tropic zone would support life as far south as the equator; but no man was fool-hardy enough to suggest that the torrid region south of the equator was habitable. Some, including Poseidonius, divided the earth into seven zones, subdividing the area bounded by the tropics near the equator into two narrow zones, roughly five degrees on either side, where the sun was said to be directly overhead, or nearly so, about a half month each year. These super-torrid zones were described as thoroughly parched, in the literal sense of the word. They are sandy, wrote Strabo, "and produce nothing but silphium [the terebinth shrub] and some pungent fruits that are withered by the heat; for those regions have in their neighborhood no mountains against which the clouds may break and produce rain, nor indeed are they coursed by rivers; and for this reason they produce creatures with woolly hair, crumpled horns, protruding lips, and flat noses (for their extremities are contorted by the heat); and the 'fish-eaters' also live in these zones." [14] Just how fish-eaters could subsist in a region which lacked rivers and was parched and shriveled, was not explained by Poseidonius or by Strabo.

Regardless of the number of zones established for the spherical earth, certain facts were known about the world beyond the Mediterranean. Obviously some of it was too hot for human habitation while other parts were too cold to endure. Firsthand experience with the midday sun of Upper Egypt was enough to convince anyone that there must be a limit further south beyond which man could not survive. It was also logical to assume that in the desolate northern parts of Europe and Asia, where the sun never shone more than a few hours each day, there must be a point where man, not to mention vegetation, must perish from the cold. What then were the limits of the habitable world? For all such information geographers had to depend largely on the hearsay evidence submitted by travelers and sailors. How far had they traveled and what were the extremities of the world as they found them?

Most writers agreed that the habitable world must be confined to the northern temperate belt, thus far only loosely defined. Experience limited it further to only a small part of that zone, for it was generally agreed that no man had traveled further west than the Pillars of Hercules, and that India was the limit of habit-ability in the east. Both of these extremities, however, were of doubtful value. Even in Strabo's day, the exact location of the Pillars had not been fixed, and he went into elaborate detail on the probability of establishing reliable landmarks in the vicinity which would identify the spot for future geographers and travelers.[15] Timaeus had reported the existence of the Fortunate Islands beyond the Pillars, but most geographers were skeptical. And of course Plato had written about a gigantic land mass of continental proportions far to the west of the Pillars which he called *Atlantis*. But at the same time he admitted that this island continent had disappeared beneath the waters of Oceanus some three thousand years before his time, a circumstance which cast a shadow of doubt on the story.[16] As for the eastern extremity of the habitable world, men gave it a name but there was almost no single fact about the location of remote India and the Eastern Ocean that could be credited. However, Aristotle ventured to suggest that the western half of the temperate zone on the other side of the world might possibly be habitable, were it not for the impenetrable sea which filled it. So much for the length of the habitable world.

The breadth of the world, from north to south, was even more indefinite. The Island of Meroê, lying between the Atbara and the Nile, was well known, but further south places began to be a little cloudy.[17] Roughly speaking, the southern limits included the Island of the Fugitive Egyptians, the Island of Taprobane (Ceylon) and the cinnamon-producing country ("Cinnamon Land"); these three places were supposed to be about 3400 stadia (340 miles) south of Meroê. Here, too, Aristotle laid himself open to attack by suggesting that it was theoretically possible to have a corresponding temperate belt in the southern hemisphere; but, he added, if there was such a zone, there must be a corresponding set of winds to go with it.[18]

In the north, beyond Britain and Ierne (Ireland), the problem was even more complex; it concerned an island named Thule, identified, located and named by an astronomer-geographer named Pytheas who hailed from Massilia (Marseilles). Pytheas is a shadowy character whose dates and personality are unknown, and whose writings would have been completely forgotten as well as lost had it not been for some of the absurd statements he made. Some of them sounded so insane to such men as Eratosthenes and Strabo that instead of ignoring him completely, as is the custom in academic circles, the critics took another look at him and found that they were dealing with a creditable astronomer, a man worthy of their castigation.[19]

Thule, according to Pytheas, was six days' journey north of Britain and close to the frozen sea. From Thule northward, he reported, there was no longer a dis-tinction between earth, air and sea; instead there was a weird combination of the three, a kind of gelatinous suspension similar to a jellyfish, which of course made navigation, not to mention human life, impossible. Pytheas had seen some of the stuff when he visited the northern part of Britain to satisfy himself as to the limit of the habitable world. Now this was too much! Strabo called him an archfalsifier whose statements on any subject were not to be trusted. Polybius dismissed the whole story as "a tissue of fables." Consequently few people were impressed when Pytheas described with fair accuracy the western and northwestern coasts of

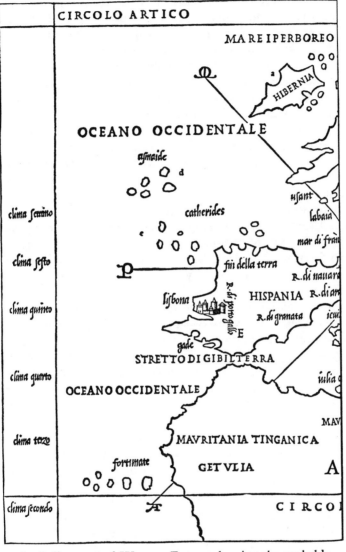

An Italian map of Western Europe showing the probable
location of the Fortunate Islands, first reported by Timaeus
about 352 B.C.

Europe including the Brittany peninsula, and the far-off British Islands. A few were less prone to ignore his statement that in the frigid region north of Thule the days were twenty-four hours long at the time of the summer solstice, for this was the kind of thing astronomers could figure out for themselves, and it fitted into their own scheme of thinking. However, a closer inspection of the alleged facts either in the region of the equator or in the desolate arctic region north of Britain was not a project which appealed to Greek philosophers. Certain astronomers and geometers avoided the issue of establishing precise geographical locations for the extremities of the habitable world. Instead, they generalized, and were content to limit their studies to its shape, favoring proportions. For example, most writers agreed that the habitable world was longer, from east to west, than it was wide, from north to south. Democritus said it was half as long again as it was wide; Dicaearcus agreed. Eudoxus said it was probably twice as long, and a few extremists such as Eratosthenes maintained it was *over* twice as long as it was wide. This sort of discussion, based on speculation only, added nothing to the cause of maps, but it is worth noting because in later estimates, when there were a few actual measurements to go by, geographers were sometimes prone to stretch their mathematics to fit a preconceived idea of proportion at the expense of common sense.

More practical-minded men of the day were not content to study their world on the basis of such philosophic jargon. They recognized the necessity of establishing an accurate way of measuring zones or climata, for as Strabo said, "it is impossible to determine whether Alexandria in Egypt is north or south of Babylon, or how much north or south of Babylon it is, without investigation through the means of the 'climata.' " [20] By investigation, Strabo meant the actual measurement of latitudes, imaginary lines across the earth's surface which would be parallel to each other and to the equator. "Now the practice of observing differences of latitude," he continued, "is not confined to a single method, but one method is used where the difference is greater, another where it is lesser." [21] There were perceptible differences, he pointed out, between the latitudes of Athens, Rhodes and Caria, but in dealing with differences of latitude of three or four thousand miles, there were pronounced differences in the length of seasons, in the vegetation and even in the animals and people. "Some peoples," he said, "flourish in spite of the latitude, because of training and habit."

When dealing with small differences in latitude, said Strabo, instead of depending on evidence visible to the naked eye such as the crops or changes in the atmosphere and temperature, "we observe the difference by the aid of sun-dials and dioptrical instruments." [22] Strabo did not indicate what these latter instruments were or how they were used, and if such tools of the map making trade were available and in use, the results did not show it. The known places in the habitable world, with respect to latitude, constituted a loosely wrought chain, weak in every link, whose principal source of strength was the equator, a reliable line of departure if nothing more. Latitudes were measured geometrically by means of "the shadow-catching sun-dial" or the simpler gnomon, and although the circle had been divided into 360 parts by the astronomers and geometers, latitude was not expressed in degrees and minutes of arc. Instead, it was expressed in ratios: the ratio between the height of the index or "style" and the length of the shadow it cast *on one of four days of the year.* The idea of finding the latitude of any place on *any* day of the year did not enter into the discussion of the general problem at all.

Another instrument for finding the latitude of different places, the astrolabe or star-measurer, was undoubtedly used by astronomers centuries before the Christian era, but was not described in such a way that it can be positively identified. In its simplest form and in the simplest terms, the astrolabe consisted of a plane circle of metal or wood, fixed or portable, whose perimeter was graduated into 60 or 360 equidistant parts. Pivoted at the center was a tube or solid arm (vane) which served both as a sight for the observer and an indicator of the angle sighted. It was used by astronomers both in a vertical and in a horizontal position, and could be adapted to measure angles in any plane whatsoever. It was used to measure the angular height of the sun or a star above the horizon as well as star angles of one kind or another.[23]

Regardless of how simple the model, the astrolabe was a vast improvement over the gnomon and sundial as an instrument for measuring angles. It was far more adaptable because it could be used to measure the angle of anything while the gnomon and dial were only sun-measurers. The data compiled by Egyptian and Chaldean astronomy is sufficiently complicated and accurate to indicate the existence of some such device as the astrolabe for measuring angles several thousand years before the development of Greek astronomy. Sixteen hundred years after the birth of Christ the astrolabe was still in use, and the only improvements in its construction were elaborations of the original design made to increase its usefulness and its accuracy.

Changes in latitude were also measured with the sand glass and clepsydra and expressed in terms of the longest day of the year. Certainly astronomers were familiar with the fact that the number of hours of daylight on the day of the summer solstice was a gauge of latitude. In fact, it was just another way of recording the angular height of the sun (the modern method, if the Nautical Almanac were added), because the length of the longest day in hours and minutes is directly proportional to the angular height of the sun. And Pytheas of Massilia, of all people, seems to have been the first to suggest this method of determining the limits of the various climata, that is, the latitude, as applied to the earth. The method gained favor among geographers and map makers and was commonly used as late as the sixteenth century when Tables of the Sun and improved instruments for measuring angles outmoded it.[24]

In many respects Strabo was an intellectual snob, and when it came to appraising the writings of his predecessors in the field of geography he felt that most of them were unworthy of his criticism and so passed them up. Among the few men of wide learning whom he considered worthy of his criticism were Eratosthenes and Hipparchus. Both were philosophers, according to Strabo's lights, and to be a philosopher was the first requisite to greatness. "Wide learning," he said, "which alone makes it possible to undertake a work on geography, is possessed solely by the man who has investigated things both human and divine —

knowledge of which, they say, constitutes philosophy." [25] Being a good Stoic, Strabo could not bring himself to marvel at the wide learning and accomplishments of these two men, but he paid them high tribute by criticizing their writings in minute detail.

A conventionalized map of the world was taking shape when Eratosthenes arrived in Alexandria to assume office as Librarian. There, in due course, he produced two mathematical works, one of them *On Means;* he founded a scientific

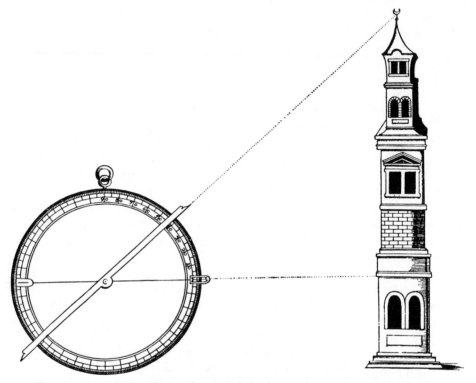

The simple astrolabe, dating from ancient times, was used to measure any angular height. Later it was graduated into 360 parts and developed into a precision instrument with many uses.

system of chronology; he wrote an astronomical poem *Hermes;* and most important of all he produced a *Geographica* in three books. With just cause he gave himself the appellation Philologos (in the sense of being the "friend of learning").[26]

Eratosthenes was not proud of his predecessors in the field of geography, and in his own work he undertook a revision of the fundamental principles of the subject, introducing at the same time some much needed physics (meteorology) and mathematics into the picture. Even Strabo, his worst critic, thought this was a commendable thing. He brought together the findings and conclusions of astronomers who were interested in the earth primarily as a celestial body and only incidentally as a place inhabited by human beings and other living creatures, adding to this material the practical findings of both mathematicians and philosophers. He drew freely from the store of data compiled by historians and geographers who had studied mankind in relation to its habitat. The result was a long step towards an intelligent, systematic conception of the earth and its occupants.

In regard to the universe, Eratosthenes accepted most of the theories curren' among astronomers from the time of Euclid and Aristotle, roughly 300 B.C. The earth was a sphere in the center of a spherical universe around which the celestial bodies revolved daily. The sun and moon had independent motions of their own. The horizon was the plane "from our station," to the heavens, bounding the hemisphere visible from the earth. The horizon was a circle, "for if a sphere be cut by a plane, the section is a circle." The "meridian" he defined as a circle passing through the poles of the spherical earth, and at right angles to the horizon, and therefore it, too, was a great circle. Also a great circle was the equinoctial or equatorial line, midway between the two poles of the earth's axis and in a plane at right angles to it. This was the line of equal day and night, halfway between the limits of the northern and southern tropics. Still another great circle was the zodiacal path or ecliptic representing the plane in which the sun apparently moved around the earth in the course of a year, a circle divided by the ancients into twelve equal parts or "signs" of 30° each. The amount of obliquity of this great circle to the equinoctial line had yet to be verified.[27]

Eratosthenes maintained, with Aristotle and others who believed in the relation between latitude and habitability, that the habitable part of the world formed "a complete circle, itself meeting itself; so that, if the immensity of the Sea did not prevent, we could sail from Iberia [Spain and Portugal] to India along one and the same parallel over the remainder of the circle," [28] that is, the remainder after subtracting the length of the inhabited world, a span which Eratosthenes estimated to be 7780 miles from ocean to ocean. Strabo agreed with him on this point, going on to say that by the inhabited world we mean that part which we inhabit and know. "It may be," he said, "that in this same temperate zone there are actually two inhabited worlds, or even more, and particularly in the proximity of the parallel of Athens" (37° 58' N.), approximately the same as Richmond, Virginia.[29]

Eratosthenes felt that there had been too much loose talk about the divisions of the world into continents by those, after the manner of Democritus, who chose to live on a diet of disputation, for if there be no accurate boundaries, "of stone posts, for example, or enclosures," it is impossible to distinguish such boundaries with any degree of accuracy.[30] Eratosthenes may have had in mind the *Periodus* written by Hecataeus of Miletus, a geographical description of the world incorporating all the countries known to the Greeks up to his time (the 56th Olympiad or 520 B.C.). Hecataeus had divided the habitable world into two great continents, Asia and Europe, and made them of equal size. He had also made a statement about the waters of the Nile, a perennial subject of discussion and speculation, to the effect that they were derived from the circumfluent ocean which overflowed periodically into all the rivers of the world. This was in contradiction to the current theory attributed to a priest in the temple of Athena which placed the source of the Nile on the frontier of Egypt between Syenê and Elephantine. Two high mountains, Crophi and Mophi, marked the place, and between them was an unfathomable abyss from which the waters rose to flood the land, half flowing north into Egypt and half into Ethiopia.[31] In the same irrational vein Ephorus, the author of a treatise *On Europe*, had divided the world into four parts: India, Ethiopia, the land of the Celts and the land of the Scythians, making no attempt to bound them. This sort of division was not satisfactory to Eratosthenes's way of thinking, nor did he approve of those writers who divided all of mankind into two groups, namely, Greeks and Barbarians. He thought it would be more sensible to divide them according to behavior, because not all Barbarians were bad any more than all Greeks were noble.[32]

Following a pattern established perhaps by Polybius and perhaps by Dicaearcus, Eratosthenes laid down a general map of the inhabited world. He began by limiting it to the northern hemisphere and to about one third of the belt lying mostly within the temperate zone. He first divided his world into a Northern Division and a Southern Division as Dicaearcus had done, running an east-west line or diaphragm parallel to the equator through familiar places that he supposed were in the same latitude. This time the eastern extremity was placed at the Sacred Promontory (the westernmost point of the Iberian peninsula), through the strait at the Pillars of Hercules. From there it ran the length of the Mediterranean, touching the Strait of Sicily, the southern capes of the Peloponnesus (Morea), Attica and the island of Rhodes, to the Gulf of Issus at the eastern end of the Mediterranean. From there it extended along the Taurus Range, "the capes and remote peaks of the mountain chain that form the northern boundary of India." With regard to India, Eratosthenes was uncertain, and thought there was room for further study of the region. For one thing, it ought to be moved further north on the maps. Strabo likewise deplored the dearth of knowledge concerning India and was scornful of writers who told of men without mouths, men with one eye (centrally placed), men whose fingers turned backwards and others who slept in their ears — presumably using them as a sleeping bag. That kind of talk reminded him too much of Pytheas.[33]

Naturally a man of such stature as Eratosthenes would not hesitate to set down specific dimensions for his habitable world. Its length, he said, was 7800 miles from Western to Eastern Ocean. The remaining two thirds of this belt, he said, was filled by the sea. The width of his habitable world, from the Cinnamon Land on the south to the Island of Thule on the north, was 3800 miles.

Strabo accused Eratosthenes of stretching the distance from east to west in order to satisfy the current conception that the length of the habitable world was more than double the breadth. He had added a bulge to the coast of Europe beyond the Pillars, "which lies over against Iberia and leans westward." He had also added various capes, and in particular that of the Ostimians (Brittany or specifically Pointe du Raz), and the adjacent islands, the outermost of which was Uxisamê (Ushant), which Pytheas had said was three days' sail from the Pillars. To this gross extension of the world Strabo retorted that all such places lay towards the north and belonged to Celtica, not Iberia, "or rather they are inventions of Pytheas." [34]

In addition to an east-west partition, Eratosthenes introduced a north-south line at right angles to it, a meridian running through the city of Alexandria. In the extreme south it intersected the parallel of the cinnamon-producing country, Taprobane and the Island of the Fugitive Egyptians. Going north it passed through Meroê, Alexandria, Rhodes, Byzantium, the mouth of the Borysthenes (Dnieper) River, and extended to the parallel of Thule, making a total breadth of 3800 miles. Strabo was willing to accept the distances between these places as they were set down by Eratosthenes with the exception of one, and that was from the Borysthenes to Thule, because, he explained, the sole authority on Thule and its location was the "archfalsifier" Pytheas. [35]

Much to Strabo's regret, Eratosthenes was neither orderly nor geometric in laying down additional lines to divide his world into convenient parcels. He drew his parallels through familiar places such as Meroê, Alexandria and Rhodes, instead of making them at equal distances from the equinoctial line and the Summer Tropic. Moreover, his north-south dividing lines (meridians) seemed to be based on little more than his own whims. There were nine of them, irregularly spaced. What Eratosthenes had done was to project his meridians north and south of the initial parallel, through places that were familiar, beginning on the west with Uxisamê and the Sacred Promontory and working eastward through the Pillars of Hercules (now the Strait of Gibraltar), Sicily, Rhodes and the Borysthenes, the Euphrates River, the mouth of the Persian Gulf, the mouth of the Indus River, the Tamarum (Tamus) Promontory at the eastern extremity of the Taurus range, and Coniaci Promontory (Cape Comorin). [36] In laying down his meridians, Eratosthenes was obliged to guess, and he did not guess well. Strabo did not trust his distances between meridians, for even though Hipparchus later suggested that simultaneous observations of lunar eclipses at different stations would help the situation, Eratosthenes and all other thinking men knew that there was no engine capable of marking the hours, minutes and seconds with any degree of accuracy. Nor was there any way of making simultaneous observations at two widely separated places. "The way things appear to the sight," said Strabo, "and the agreement of all the testimony are more trustworthy than an instrument." [37] Perhaps they were in Strabo's circle. It was much safer, he thought, to estimate east-west distances from the similarity or dissimilarity of the prevailing winds; the positions of the stars were also helpful. [38]

In general, the map of the world laid down by Eratosthenes was acceptable to Strabo, except that some of the distances were little more than approximations and the grid was much too arbitrary and irregular. Strabo felt that what was needed was a "metron" of some kind, a standard of measurement by which geometrical magnitudes could be reduced more accurately to linear measure and so represent the places on the map in something like their true relationship. At the same time he thought the geometers and astronomers were a little hard on Eratosthenes when they demanded that every measurement on his map should be precise, considering that he was drawing a map with convenient and practical divisions and not a geometrical design. He pointed out to his readers that Eratosthenes did not make his map grid with the aid of instruments such as the gnomon and sundial, and that in his text he often used the phrase, "in a line more or less straight"; therefore his critics should have been more tolerant.[39]

More important, in Strabo's estimation, were the sources used by Eratosthenes, which were not always reliable, and his ignorance about certain parts of the world. According to Strabo, he knew nothing about Iberia and Celtica and was vastly ignorant of Germania and Brettania. Less surprising was his lack of information concerning the countries of the Getans and Bastarnians, for in both cases there had been some question as to their precise location and the nature of their dominions. "Indeed," said Strabo, "in the case of the geography of the remote countries, we should not scrutinize him in the same way we do in that of the continental sea-board and of the other regions that are well known; nay, not even in the case of the nearer regions ought we to apply the geometrical test, but rather the geographical." [40]

Eratosthenes made a start towards an orderly portrayal of the habitable world, but his arbitrary network of parallels and meridians was far from satisfactory to his contemporaries and those who came after him. His world was a composite of divination and deduction, a smattering of geometry and a fair amount of applied astronomy, all of which added up to a state of confusion and a rather bad map. Places which had been investigated with reference to other places were few and far between; therefore, his intersecting lines were spaced irregularly and were of doubtful accuracy. Filling in the interstices involved considerable guesswork. If two places *appeared* to be about the same distance from the equator, if their climates and crops were essentially alike, it was sufficient evidence to establish them on the same parallel — it had to be — and the accurate determination of longitude was hopelessly beyond the realm of practicality.

His map was particularly offensive to Hipparchus, the astronomer and mathematician, who felt that there were much more sensible and scientific ways of dividing up the habitable world and the world as a whole.[41] In this vein he wrote a diatribe *Against Eratosthenes*, which was precisely what the title suggests.[42] In it he went to great pains to demonstrate what an incompetent, slovenly scholar he was dealing with, and to refute most of his geographical conclusions, though he himself was not a geographer. He criticized Eratosthenes for his total disregard of scientific precision in map making, even though it must have been apparent that in the absence of scientific data precision was out of the question. But Hipparchus made a suggestion in passing which was to alter the course of map making and one which was certainly logical in conception if not entirely practical at the time. Why not project all climata so that they would be really parallel with the equinoctial line, and lay down a series of them at equal intervals from the equator to the

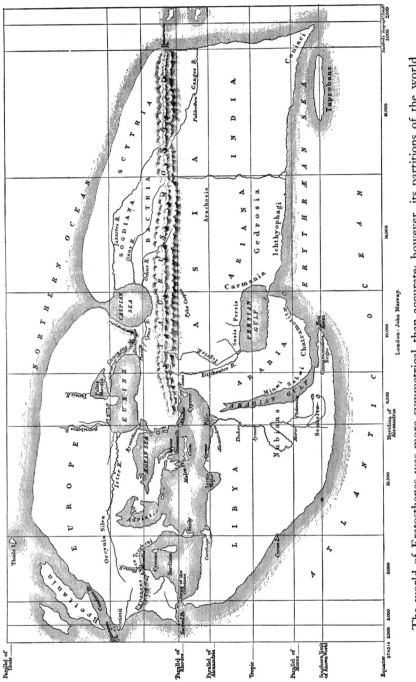

The world of Eratosthenes was more symmetrical than accurate; however, its partitions of the world were forerunners of our parallels and meridians.

poles? And why not construct a series of lines at right angles to the parallels, great circles passing through the two poles, equally spaced along the equator, thus forming an orderly, geometrical pattern or grid for the spherical earth?

In order to achieve this ideal, said Hipparchus, the parallels should be determined by astronomical observation only and the width of each parallel zone, belt or "clima" should be determined on the basis of the longest day of the year. Presumably this scheme would accomplish the same thing as a purely geometrical graduation. In practice, this method of laying down parallels and meridians was impossible because of the difficulties involved in getting from place to place and because travelers persisted in bringing home nothing but offhand accounts of what they had seen. Rarely ever was a merchant or politician interested in observing the stars or inquiring about the longest day of the year or any scientific matters whatsoever. Moreover, the system did not meet the requirements of a series of parallels equally spaced along the principal meridian, for it was discovered that the zone or clima in which the longest day of the year was between 14 and 15 hours, extended over 10° 32' of arc, while the zone in which the longest day was between 19 and 20 hours was only 2° 53' wide. As for a series of equally spaced meridians, it was nothing more than a beautiful ideal which might be realized when and if some device could be invented that would accurately mark the passage of the hours.[43]

This suggested mapping policy was not an original idea; on the contrary, Eratosthenes himself had seen the necessity of some such method of partitioning the world, and he no doubt appreciated the value of geometrical precision and scientific observation where map making was concerned. At the same time, he seems to have recognized the futility of trying to construct a scientific map on a foundation of speculation, and made the mistake of saying so. Most of the places on the earth had been located, and their relative positions fixed, solely on the basis of hearsay evidence and tradition. Nevertheless, in his critical exposé of Eratosthenes, Hipparchus insisted that the map of the world must be revised so that every important place would be located and set down on the map according to its latitude and longitude, both to be determined by astronomical observation.

After haranguing the multitudes with his scientific ideals and criticizing without stint the writings of his fellow scientists, Hipparchus proceeded with his map revision, and immediately got into deep water. Like all other cartographers before and after him, he was obliged to take on faith a certain amount of basic data, and apparently had no scruples about incorporating on his map some of the findings and conclusions of earlier writers. For instance, he accepted the figure of 25,200 miles for the earth's circumference calculated by Eratosthenes, which is rather strange in view of his low opinion of the man. He also condescended to accept the principal parallel laid down by Eratosthenes and approved by later writers, but he moved the Strait of Sicily towards the north, and made the parallel pass to the south of Syracuse, which were improvements. He likewise borrowed from Eratosthenes the principal meridian line running through Alexandria, Syenê and Meroê, Troas, Byzantium and the mouth of the Borysthenes. Eratosthenes had graduated his sphere into sixty parts of 6° each, but Hipparchus divided it into 360 parts and seems to have been the first to do so.[44]

Hipparchus established the precedent of describing various climata in terms of celestial phenomena, choosing intervals of 70 miles as conveniently spaced zones and ones which would produce perceptible changes in the heavens. To this end he plotted mathematically the changes in the stars that would appear at every degree of latitude (700 stadia to a degree) from the equator to the North Pole along the meridian of Alexandria. This data was culled from his own catalogue of 1080 stars, by far the most complete chart of the heavens that had yet been compiled. As a further check on the different parallels he calculated for each one the theoretical length of the solstitial day, the ratio between the height of the gnomon and the shadow it would cast, the height of the polestar, and in some cases the right ascension of other prominent stars as well. Among his other observations he noted that the cinnamon-producing country was the most southerly point above the equator at which the Little Bear never set; at Syenê, most of the seven stars of the Great Bear remained visible throughout the year; north of Byzantium Cassiopeia fell wholly within the celestial arctic circle. All such information, though interesting, was to all intents and purposes theoretical astronomy and at the time there was small hope of relating it to specific localities on the earth. Many places which actually existed had never been visited by astronomers, so that there was no way of checking the theoretical information against the existing facts, the celestial appearance for a given latitude against the alleged position of the place.[45]

The greatest contributions to cartography made by Hipparchus were those which at the time seemed only remotely connected with the subject and ones which were apparently beyond the scope of Strabo's studies. Hipparchus and Claudius Ptolemy, who flourished three hundred years after him, "remade celestial science," and laid the foundation of trigonometry, both plane and spherical. They computed tables of chords for the use of astronomers which served the same purpose as our table of sines, and so well were they compiled by Hipparchus and clearly developed by Ptolemy that for 1400 years they remained unsurpassed as mathematical standards. Hipparchus borrowed freely from the Babylonian and Assyrian schools of astronomy, but improved upon their methods of observation. He fixed the length of the tropical (solar) and sidereal years; the length of the various months and the synodic periods of the five known planets; he determined the obliquity of the ecliptic and of the moon's path; the place of the sun's apogee and the eccentricity of its orbit; all with unusual accuracy. He determined the positions of the stars by right ascensions and declinations. He studied the equinox and noted, in 130 B.C., its steady retrogression among the stars. On comparing his data with that compiled by Timocharis a century and a half earlier, he estimated the "precession" of the equinoxes as not less than 36 seconds and not more than 59 seconds a year. The actual value is 50 seconds! [46] "When we consider all that Hipparchus invented or perfected," wrote Delambre, "and reflect upon the number of his works, and the mass of calculations they imply, we must regard him as one of the most astonishing men of antiquity, and as the greatest of all in the sciences which are not purely speculative, and which require a combination of geometrical knowledge with a knowledge of phenomena to be observed only by diligent attention and refined instruments." [47] Hipparchus, so historians tell us, had everything but the refined instruments, but in view of some of the remarkable results he achieved, one begins to wonder about the instruments, which the experts say were nonexistent.

It is difficult to reconstruct the habitable world according to Strabo and his theories in regard to physical geography. He was primarily interested in a descriptive treatise, and most of his own ideas, none of which was original, are found in the critical comments he made on the writings of others. He flirted with the technicalities of astronomy and mathematics, but refused to get involved in the major issues. When he lacked information or when the going got too rough, he had a way of dismissing the subject as being "without value to the geographer," and he usually added, that if people were interested in knowing more about it they could go to Hipparchus! For this reason it is impossible to say just how much of a scientist he was. However, in his descriptions of places he often located them as Eratosthenes and Hipparchus would have done, using the stars as an index of distance. For instance, at Bernicê, on the Arabian Gulf, and in the country of the Troglodytes, north of the Caucasus, the sun was said to stand in the zenith at the time of the summer solstice and the longest day of the year had 13½ equinoctial hours; "and almost the whole of the Great Bear is also visible in the arctic circle, with the exception of the legs, the tip of the tail, and one of the stars in the square." [48] And if you sail into the Pontus Euxinus (Black Sea), "and proceed about 1400 stadia to the north, the longest day becomes 15½ equinoctial hours . . . there the arctic circle is in the zenith; and the star in the neck of Cassiopeia lies on the arctic circle, while the star on the right elbow of Perseus is a little north of it." [49]

The location of the remote regions of the habitable world were described in more general terms. Ceylon, for example, was said to be "considerably south of India," but nevertheless inhabited. "It rises opposite to" the Island of the Fugitive Egyptians and the cinnamon-producing country. A similar report was current in regard to the promontory of Iberia beyond the Pillars of Hercules. The "Sacred Promontory" (Cape St. Vincent), as it was called, lay on approximately the same parallel as the Pillars, Gades (Cadiz), the Strait of Sicily and Rhodes. Why? Because, "they say, the shadows cast by the sun-dial agree, and the winds that blow in either direction come from the same direction, and the lengths of the longest days and nights are the same; for the longest day and the longest night have fourteen and a half equinoctial hours." Moreover, the constellation of the Cabeiri was sometimes seen along the coast near Gades. Poseidonius reported that from a tall house in a city about 40 miles distant from these regions, he saw a star which he judged was Canopus itself. And because Canopus was also visible from the observatory of Eudoxus at Cnidus, which was not much higher than the dwelling houses slightly north of it, the obvious conclusion was that Cnidus and the other

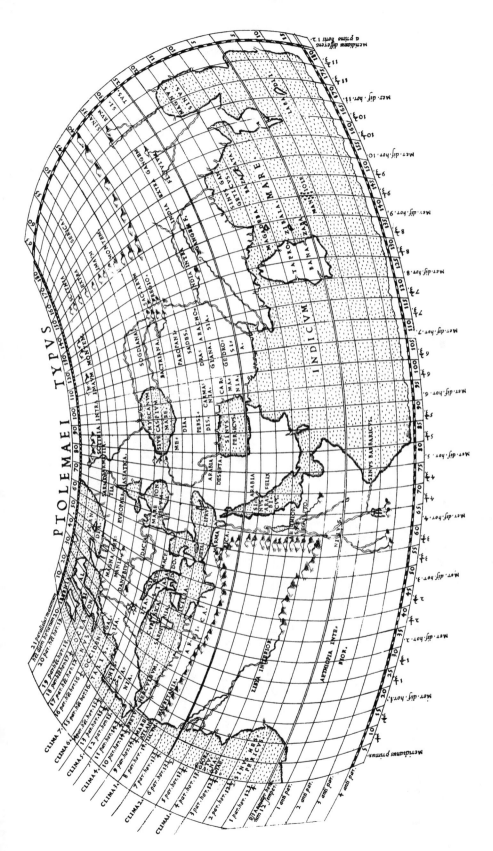

The world of Ptolemy according to a Venetian editor, 1561. Longitude is expressed in fractions of hours east of the Fortunate Islands while latitudes are designated by the number of hours in the longest day of the year.

The Romans had both general and topographical maps. The map above, one of few known specimens of Roman cartography, was drawn in the third century A.D. Though badly foreshortened, it nevertheless shows the elaborate network of roads studded with milestones that fringed the Mediterranean Sea. The above section, one of twelve, shows the area between Crete and the mouths of the Nile.

places including Rhodes and Gades must lic on the same parallel.[50] This kind of report, comprising a little geometry, a smattering of astronomy and a modicum of rather shrewd deduction, was commonly employed in the best scientific circles and was solemnly entered in the record for posterity to read.

Strabo's habitable world was a spherical quadrilateral bounded on the north by the arctic circle and on the south by the equator. It was "washed on all sides by the sea and like an island . . . the evidence of our senses and of reason prove this. But," he continued, "if anyone disbelieves the evidence of reason, it would make no difference, from the point of view of the geographer, whether we make the inhabited world an island, or merely admit what experience has taught us, namely that it is possible to sail round the inhabited world on both sides, from the east as well as from the west, with the exception of a few intermediate stretches. And, as to these stretches, it makes no difference whether they are bounded by sea or by uninhabited land; for the geographer undertakes to describe the known parts of the inhabited world, but he leaves out of consideration the unknown parts of it — just as he does what is outside of it." [51] So, reasoned Strabo, a geographer was justified in drawing two straight vertical lines as eastern and western limits of the world. Whether they fell in the ocean or on uninhabitable land made no difference. In this way he begged the issue and went on to something else, offering a few pointers on how to make a map.

The man who wishes to construct the most faithful representation of the earth, said Strabo, "must needs make for the earth a globe like that of Crates, and lay off on it the quadrilateral, and within the quadrilateral put down the map of the inhabited world." It should be a large globe, so that the inhabited part, "being a small fraction of the globe," may be on a large enough scale to be of practical value to the user, and so that all the important places can be drawn in, labeled and clearly understood. The globe, to be of adequate size, should be no less than ten feet in diameter! [52] But if a man found it impossible to construct a ten-foot globe, "or not much smaller," Strabo suggested that he sketch his map on a plane surface of at least seven square feet. "For it will make only a slight difference," he explained, "if we draw straight lines to represent the circles, that is, the parallels and meridians, by means of which we clearly indicate the 'Climata,' the winds and the other differences, and also the positions of the parts of the earth with reference both to each other and to the heavenly bodies — drawing parallel lines for the parallels and perpendicular lines for the circles perpendicular to the parallels, for our imagination can easily transfer to the globular and spherical surface the figure or magnitude seen by the eye on a plane surface." [53]

Strabo warned the prospective map maker that the transposition of the several meridians from a globe, where they all converged at the poles, to a plane surface, would make them more difficult to understand. But he added that in many instances it would be just as well to make the meridians straight lines on the map rather than compromise by using only slightly converging lines. So much for the construction of maps and globes.

Summarizing the progress of geography since the days of Eratosthenes, Strabo

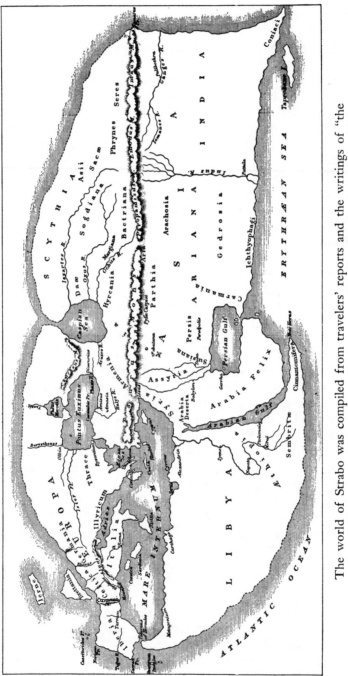

The world of Strabo was compiled from travelers' reports and the writings of "the ancients." It represented the sum total of cartographical knowledge before the Christian Era.

was encouraging. "In particular the writers of the present time," he said, "can give a better account of the Britons, the Germans, the peoples both north and south of the Ister, the Getans, the Tyregetans, the Bastarnians, and, furthermore, the peoples in the regions of the Caucasus, such as the Albanians and the Iberians." New information was available concerning Hyrcania and Bactriana by the writers of Parthian histories (Apollodorus of Artemita and his school), "in which they marked off those countries more definitely than many other writers. Again, since the Romans have recently invaded Arabia Felix with an army, of which Aelius Gallus, my friend and companion, was the commander, and since the merchants of Alexandria are already sailing with fleets by way of the Nile and of the Arabian Gulf as far as India, these regions also have become far better known to us of to-day than to our predecessors. At any rate, when Gallus was prefect of Egypt, I accompanied him and ascended the Nile as far as Syenê and the frontiers of Ethiopia, and I learned that as many as one hundred and twenty vessels were sailing from Myos Hormos to India, whereas formerly, under the Ptolemies, only a very few ventured to undertake the voyage and to carry on traffic in Indian merchandise." [54]

The publication, if it can be called that, of Strabo's *Geography* took place within the first twenty years of the Christian era. It brought to a fitting climax the first period in the history of cartography. The veil of superstition had been partly swept aside; geographers and cartographers at last knew what they were looking for. They also had at their command the theoretical means of finding it. The eyes of all scientists, as well as geographers, were still on "the high vault of the heavens," and it might well be added, "from whence came their help," for cartography had come to lean heavily on the findings of astronomy and what Strabo called physics.

CHAPTER III

The World of Claudius Ptolemy

G REAT CARAVANS and merchant fleets were moving, as Strabo said, in the first twenty years of the Christian era. The habitable world of 20 A.D. was a bigger world than the one he knew as a young man. Lines of communication and trade routes had lengthened and so had the hopes of man. Also moving were political and spiritual forces such as the world had never encountered, and no man could foresee the long interlude in store for geography and the budding science of cartography. Nor could any man anticipate that for the most part, the geographic heritage of the human race was to rest for more than 1200 years in the writings of two men: Strabo and Claudius Ptolemy: one furnishing the key to the past and the other a pattern for the future.

Almost nothing is known about Claudius Ptolemy the man. Neither his birthplace nor his dates have been positively established.[1] Certain early manuscripts indicate that he was born in Pelusium, while others favor the city of Ptolemais Hermii (Hermeiu), a Grecian city of the Thebaid. The legend that he was a member of the royal family of Egypt originated in the Middle Ages, and manuscripts of that period picture him in royal dress, complete with crown and mantle. However, the name Ptolemaeus was not uncommon in early Egypt, and there is no evidence that he was of royal blood. From his writings we learn that he intended to locate places on the earth with reference to the parallel of Alexandria, and Olympiodorus related in his scholia on the *Phaedo* of Plato that Ptolemy spent forty years making astronomical observations in the Pteron, a building which has been located both at Canopus and Alexandria. The last observations set down in Ptolemy's *Almagest* are for the year 141 A.D., and he is generally spoken of as flourishing about 150 A.D. He made observations during the reigns of Hadrian and Antoninus Pius. His earliest recorded observation was made in the eleventh year of Hadrian, 127 A.D., and his last was in the fourteenth year of Antoninus, 151 A.D. By deduction Ptolemy's dates have therefore been set at 90–168 A.D.

Ptolemy was a man of wide learning who possessed an exceptionally orderly mind and a remarkable gift of exposition. His original contributions to science may have been few, as some writers suggest, but he was never guilty of plagiarism. He improved most of what he copied and developed the ideas he borrowed. He repeated many of the important theories of his predecessors, but stated them better and more clearly. He usually gave credit where credit was due.

Although the name of Claudius Ptolemy is most frequently associated with geography and cartography, he wrote important works in a number of other fields including astronomy, astrology, music and optics.[2] He compiled a Table of Reigns, a chronological list of Assyrian, Persian, Greek and Roman sovereigns from Nabonasar to Antoninus Pius, a biographical history of kingship. His *Analemma* was a mathematical description of a sphere projected on a plane which greatly simplified the study of gnomonics, subsequently known as an "orthographic projection." His work entitled *Planisphaerium* (The Planisphere) described a sphere projected on the equator, the eye being at the pole, a projection later known as "stereographic." But his greatest works were his Syntaxis, known by the hybrid title of *Almagest*, and his *Geographia*. Both titles relate to map making, but while his predecessors combined their astronomy, mathematics and geography under the broad heading of philosophy, Ptolemy included in his *Almagest* all of his scientific theories and confined his *Geographia* to the subject of map making alone.

Ptolemy opened the thirteen books of the *Almagest* with a preface in which he commented on the distinction between theory and practice and the certainty of mathematical knowledge, "inasmuch as the demonstrations in it proceed by the incontrovertible ways of arithmetic and geometry." He told his readers that he intended to make use of the discoveries of the ancients in his discussions of the universe, but that he would explain in detail all such matters that had not been fully explained or treated in the past. In Book I he gave a general summary of the principles on which his Syntaxis or System was based.[3]

The heaven, said Ptolemy, is a sphere and moves according to the manner of a sphere. The earth is the center of the spherical heaven, and is a vast distance from the stars. The earth also is a sphere and does not move from its place in the center of the universe. As for the shape of the earth, it is not essential to consider either the mathematical or philosophical aspects of the problem because there is sufficient sensible evidence to prove that it is spherical. It is evident, for example, that the sun and moon and other celestial bodies do not rise and set at the same time for every observer on the earth; on the contrary, they rise earlier to those who live towards the east and later towards the regions in the west. And it is known that lunar eclipses are recorded at different times of day, with respect to midday at different places; in the Orient they are recorded later than they are in the Occident. Now if the earth were flat and shaped like a triangle or rectangle, the risings and settings of the heavenly bodies would occur simultaneously in all parts of the earth. There is other evidence. The further we go toward the North Pole the more stars in the southern sky are hidden, while new ones appear from under the northern horizon. Again, whenever we sail toward a mountain, and no matter from which direction we approach, it looms up out of the sea, getting larger and larger until its entire height is visible, whereas on sailing away from it the reverse process takes place until it finally disappears below the horizon. The ocean's surface, then, must be curved. In regard to the supposition that the earth rotates on its own axis, as some writers had said, Ptolemy was emphatic. He admitted that it was a convenient explanation of the behavior of the heavens, but nevertheless ridiculous.

Following the publication of the *Almagest*, divisions of the circle were no longer expressed in awkward fractions. In the ninth chapter of the first book, Ptolemy explained how to form a table of chords. He began with a circle whose circumference was divided into 360°. These he bisected. He divided the diameter into 120 equal parts, then divided the 60 parts of the radius into 60 equal parts and divided them again into 60 equal parts. In the Latin translation of the text these subdivisions became *partes minutae primae* and *partes minutae secundae* from whence our "minutes" and "seconds" of arc are derived. Neither the division of the circle into 360 parts nor the doctrine of chords was an original idea; the first may have originated in ancient Chaldea and was probably used by many of his predecessors. As for tables of chords, Theon of Alexandria reported that Hipparchus, whom Ptolemy called "a lover of labor and a lover of truth," had given the doctrine in twelve books and Menelaus had done the same in six. The remarkable part of Ptolemy's contribution was a few simple theorems which made it easy to find the value of each chord.[4]

In Book III of the *Almagest*, Ptolemy described how Hipparchus discovered the precession of the equinoxes. He also described the observations by which Hipparchus verified the eccentricity of the solar orbit. Ptolemy concluded this book with a clear exposition of the circumstances on which the equation of time depends. He also laid down the principle that for the best explanation of any kind of phenomena one should adopt the simplest hypothesis that it is possible to establish, provided that it does not contradict in any important respect the results of observation. In other words, never complicate an explanation if it is possible to make it simple. This avowed policy was a part of the credo adopted by Hipparchus, and centuries after Ptolemy it became the first law of the *philosophia prima* of Auguste Comte the French philosopher. Another principle expounded by Ptolemy and universally adopted by all science, was that in making investigations based on observations where great delicacy and precision are required, we should take our results from data acquired over a considerable interval of time, in order that the errors inherent in all observations (otherwise known as human frailty), even those made with the greatest care, may be reduced. In other words, repeat the observations many times; if necessary over a great number of years.[5]

Both Strabo and Ptolemy wrote extensive works which have been called geographical, but their approach to the subject was entirely different. Strabo was interested in the location of places and the compilation of an accurate world map, at least the habitable part of it, but he was even more concerned with man in relation to his environment: his history, his customs, the crops and domestic animals he raised, and the physical features peculiar to different regions of the world. But Ptolemy's approach to geography was strictly scientific and impersonal. He was interested in the earth, all of it, not just the habitable part; he tried to fit it into the scheme of the universe where it belonged. He was interested in the relation between the earth and the sun, the earth and the moon, in the scientific cause and effect of climate. And above all, he was concerned with a scientifically accurate portrayal of the spherical earth in a convenient, readable form. In other words, he was interested in a map of the world. More than any one of the ancients, Claudius Ptolemy succeeded in establishing the elements and form of a scientific cartography. With the publication of his *Geographia*, cartography as we know it parted company with geography as we are led to define it.

The *Geographia* is actually a general atlas of the world rather than a Geography, with a long textual introduction to the subject of cartography. Here for the first time were set down the duties of the map maker, his limitations and the nature of the materials he has to work with. The methods of mapping the world as they were outlined by Claudius Ptolemy, constitute the fundamental tenets of modern geodesy.

Ptolemy opened his introductory treatise by giving two valuable definitions which did much to shape the course of cartography, namely, *Chorography* and *Geography*.[6] The first, strangely enough, has remained essentially as Ptolemy phrased it for nearly two thousand years, but the second has caused no little trouble. Geography, its scope and limits, is no better defined today than it was in Strabo's age, and even that worthy writer at that early date could not make up his mind just what bypaths he should wander in and what difficult subjects he should leave in the hands of the "geometers," the astronomers and physical scientists. A recent definition calls geography "A bundle of specialisms without coherent unity." [7]

Ptolemy defined geography as, "a representation in picture of the whole known world together with the phenomena which are contained therein." Chorography, he said, differs from geography in that it is regional and selective, "even dealing with the smallest conceivable localities, such as harbors, farms, villages, river courses, and such like." [8]

The function of chorography, said Ptolemy, is to deal with a small part of the whole world, treating it exhaustively as a detached unit. Accordingly, it is not out of the province of chorography or unworthy of it to describe such detached units in minute detail; in fact the more details the better, even down to streets and public buildings. "Its concern is to paint a true likeness, and not merely to give exact positions and size." Chorography does not require mathematics, according to Ptolemy, at least not the spherical trigonometry required of geography, but it does need an artist, "and no one presents it rightly unless he is an artist." Modern cartographers take note!

As he proceeds to elaborate his definition of geography, it becomes apparent that Ptolemy conceived the primary function of geography as map making, and that to him geography was synonymous with cartography. "It is the prerogative of Geography" he said, "to show the known habitable earth as a unit in itself, how it is situated and what is its nature; and it deals with those features likely to be mentioned in a general description of the earth, such as the larger towns and the great cities, the mountain ranges and the principal rivers." No divergence from these fundamental matters should be made, except for "features worthy of special note on account of their beauty." [9] Having thus introduced an elastic "rider" into an otherwise rigid geographical code he went on to elaborate the task of the cartographer, which is to survey the whole of the world "in its just proportions," that is, to scale. He likened the problem to that of the painter who must first work out the outline of a figure in correct proportion before he fills in the minute details of feature and form. But he went on to say that cartography, in its broader aspects, does not require an artist. Cartography is concerned with the relation of distance and direction, and the important features of the earth's surface can be indicated by plain lines and simple notations, which are enough to indicate general features and fix positions. And for these reasons mathematics is an important part of cartography.

In cartography, said Ptolemy, one must contemplate the shape and size of the entire earth. Its position under the heavens is extremely important, for in order to describe any given part of the world one must know under what parallel of the celestial sphere it is located. Otherwise how can one determine the length of its days and nights, the stars which are fixed overhead, the stars which appear nightly over the horizon and the stars which never rise above the horizon at all. All such data must be considered as important to the study and mapping of the world. And, he added, "It is the great and exquisite accomplishment of mathematics to show all these things to the human intelligence." With the aid of astronomy and mathematics, Ptolemy concluded, the earth could be mapped as accurately as the heavens had been charted.[10]

Like his predecessors, Ptolemy proposed to confine his descriptions to "our habitable earth," and in order that they might correspond as much as possible to the earth itself, he would avail himself of all possible means of obtaining pertinent data. The first of these was as usual the great mass of information supplied by travelers and explorers. To be sure, if such men were more considerate and took observations as well as notes, it would be a relatively simple matter to describe with scientific accuracy the farthest limits of the habitable earth; but alas, they never do it. Of the men who were both interested and qualified, he complained, only Hipparchus, the astronomer, had recorded the elevation of the polestar at different places, and even *he* had supplied only a few such figures compared to the numerous places that were known to geographers; and as for places which are on the same meridian, extremely few had been recorded. East-west distances were based almost entirely on tradition, not because of indifference but because the necessary technical knowledge had been lacking in the observer. A few lunar eclipses had been observed simultaneously at two different places, such as the one observed in Arbella at the fifth hour and at Carthage at the second hour, but not enough of them to furnish any considerable data relative to the longitudes of places.[11]

Among the other resources that should not be overlooked in the mapping of the habitable earth, he said, were the celestial charts such as Hipparchus had plotted for various latitudes. All reliable tables of distances between well-known places should be given careful consideration, especially if the measurements were made either with surveying instruments, astronomical instruments or both. And while distances between places were important, it was also necessary to know in what direction they lay with respect to one another. Therefore, whenever possible, distances and directions should be checked by means of "meteorological instruments," by which Ptolemy presumably meant the gnomon and the astrolabe. Such instruments, if properly used, would help to establish geographic positions and, in theory, distances traveled.[12]

Ptolemy described how to make two instruments he himself had used to measure angles; in particular the arc between the tropics and the ecliptic. The first was an

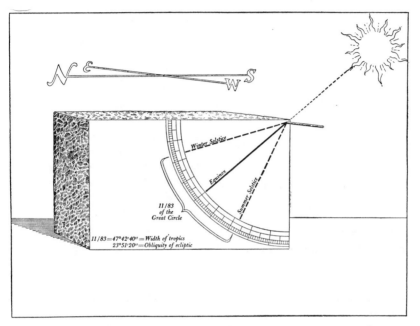

11/83
of the
Great Circle

11/83=47°42′40″=Width of tropics
23°51′20″=Obliquity of ecliptic

A replica of the polished stone block designed by Claudius Ptolemy for finding (1) the obliquity of the ecliptic, (2) the width of the Tropic zones, (3) the latitude of the observer and the stone.

astrolabe of brass, graduated on the outer circle into 360 parts, and each of these into as many subdivisions as there was room for.[13] Instead of using pin-hole sights, each end of the movable vane was fitted with a prism and a fine pointer to mark the degrees and minutes of arc. The instrument was attached to a pedestal, "a small and convenient column for its several uses." When the instrument was set up it was carefully adjusted so that the plane of the circle was perpendicular to the horizon, and a plumb line was dropped from the highest point of the instrument so that the proper graduations on the outer circle would correspond with the zenith and the horizon. "And after such a placement had been made we used to observe the advance of the sun to the north and to the south, moving the inside circle at middays until the lower prism was wholly shadowed by the whole of the upper prism. And when this was done the points of the needles would show us each time how many divisions from the zenith the center of the sun stood on the meridian line." [14]

A second piece of apparatus recommended by Ptolemy for finding the arc between the tropics was nothing more than a mural quadrant, a sundial tipped on its side. This instrument could be made of a block of wood or stone having one of its faces smoothed to a perfectly level surface. On this surface a quarter circle was drawn, with a pin or small right cylinder fastened at the center point. The circumference was divided into 90 parts or degrees and each degree subdivided into 30 minutes. The block was then upended and placed so that the pin, now projecting horizontally, lay in an east-west line, and the quadrant stood in the plane of the meridian. Then with wedges and a plumb line the block was carefully adjusted in place. Fixed in this position it was possible to measure the height of the sun in degrees and minutes without worrying about the length of the shadow, or the height of the shadow-casting pin. The sun indicated its own height without further calculation.[15]

The instrument was as effective as it was ingenious. By leaving the instrument in place for a year it was a simple matter to measure the arc between the two tropics. From observations of the sun's declination at the summer and winter solstices, or as Ptolemy said, "with the sun at the tropics themselves," he found that the arc between the two tropics "was always more than 47° 40', but less than 47° 45'. And with this the result is nearly the same ratio as that of Eratosthenes and as that which Hipparchus used. For the arc between the tropics turns out to be very nearly eleven out of the meridian's 83 parts." [16]

Ptolemy pointed out that it was easy to determine the latitude of any place where observations are made with this instrument. For the ratio of 11/83rds remains a constant, even though the angles of the two extremes will vary with the latitude of the observer. The latitude of the place of observation would be the midpoint between the two measured extremities, which is the equatorial point, another way of saying the arc between the midpoint and the zenith.

Ptolemy called attention to the fact that celestial observations for determining distances between places on the earth would not always be reliable, regardless of the instrument used, for overland journeys are almost never made as the crow flies. When traveling overland it is usually necessary to diverge from a straight line course in order to avoid inevitable land-barriers; and at sea, where winds are changeable, the speed of a vessel varies considerably, making it difficult to estimate over-water distances with any degree of accuracy. Nevertheless he concluded that the most reliable way of determining distances was by astronomical observation, and by no other method could one expect to fix positions accurately. Traditional information regarding distances should be subordinated, especially the primitive sort, for tradition varies from time to time, and if it must enter into the making of maps at all, it is expedient to compare the records of the ancient past with newer records, "deciding what is credible and what is incredible." In most cases disputes concerning distance and direction arose over who said it and in what connection. Was the story history or mythology? A story about a journey should sound right and sensible and be free of any mythological taint before it was admitted to the record and accepted as more or less authentic data. To say a place was "towards the summer sunrise" or "towards Africa," was not good enough, and yet that was the kind of information usually submitted by the untutored.[17]

Ptolemy devoted a great deal of space in his text to an exhaustive criticism of Marinus of Tyre, "the latest of the geographers of our time." Marinus, who flourished about 120 A.D., exerted considerable influence on the development of map making, but like Pytheas of Massilia, he never makes an appearance on the stage. He seems to have studied and made astronomical observations in Tyre, the oldest and largest city of Phoenicia, which even at that late date maintained important commercial relations with remote parts of the world. His treatise on geography, with its maps, should be ranked among the most important of the lost documents of the ancients, if for no other reason than that it was the foundation upon which Claudius Ptolemy built.[18]

Marinus, according to Ptolemy, was a man of parts who had found out many things which were not known before. He had read nearly all of the historians and had corrected many of their errors (presumably errors relating to the location of places as contained in travelers' itineraries). He had, moreover, edited and revised his own geographic maps, of which at least two editions had been published before Ptolemy saw them. The final drafts were nearly free from defects, and his text was so reliable, in Ptolemy's estimation, that "it would seem to be enough for us to describe the earth on which we dwell from his commentaries alone, without other investigations." Almost, but not quite! [19]

Ptolemy was both tolerant and gentle in his criticism of Marinus; both men had their own ideas of the incredible and at times there is little to choose between their conceptions of what made sense and what nonsense. But Ptolemy, having the advantage of the last word, felt constrained, when treating the errors of Marinus, to make suggested revisions, "more in keeping with the high caliber of the rest of his work and the man himself," dwelling only briefly on each kind of error he had made. In so doing, Ptolemy exposed his own credulity.

The most significant feature of the map of Marinus as seen through the eyes of Ptolemy was the growth of the habitable world and the changed attitude towards the uninhabited parts. Marinus was a good man in Ptolemy's estimation, but he had allowed himself to be led astray in his scientific investigations. The world had expanded, to be sure, but not as much as Marinus indicated on his map. Yes, Marinus had made mistakes, either because he had consulted "too many conflicting volumes, all disagreeing," or because he had never completed the final revision of his map. Whichever it was, the map needed correcting.[20]

Marinus placed the northern extremity of the habitable world at the parallel of Thule, which he designated as 63° above the equator, a meridian circle being equal to 360 degrees. The breadth of his world, then, from the equator to the parallel of Thule, was 3150 miles, each degree being equal to 50 miles. Marinus had taken the value of 18,000 miles for the earth's circumference established by Poseidonius, and there were no adverse comments from Ptolemy. But in the south he went too far, locating the country of the Ethiopians, Agisymba by name, and the promontory of Prasum, on a parallel well below the winter solstice (Tropic of Capricorn). Neither place was well known and Ptolemy had two reasons for doubting their location 24° below the equator. First, Marinus had said nothing about the appearance of the sky below the equator although he had taken the trouble to describe stars and their appearance in the region between the equator and the Summer Tropic. Second, he had introduced numerous north-south distances that were supplied by merchants and sailors, but both he and Ptolemy were doubtful about their accuracy, because in reckoning distances at sea there was usually only the elapsed sailing time to go on. And when necessary corrections had been made for the time the ship was hove to or anchored, the nature of the weather at different stages of the voyage, the strength and direction of the wind and unpredictable currents, a twenty-nine day voyage might mean almost anything in stadia or in degrees and minutes of arc.[21] However, both men apparently listened respectfully to the calculations of a certain seafaring man named Theophilus who estimated that a single day's sailing, "under favorable circumstances," was good for a hundred miles. On the whole, Marinus was dubious about the merchant class, because they were only intent on their business and, "through their love of boasting," had a tendency to magnify distances and other things. Ptolemy, too, had misgivings about this source of information, yet he concluded that in the absence of scientific data it was necessary to rely on the reports of travelers, and that on occasion it was fairly safe to do so.

If a geographer were obliged to fall back on the reports of travelers, he should exercise some discrimination in his choice of authorities, and Marinus did not do this, especially in regard to distances to the south. For example, he cited the military expedition of one Septimus Flaccus into the territory of the Ethiopians. Flaccus made a three-months' march from Garame to Agisymba (where the rhinoceros is found) and from his account Marinus made certain deductions about north-south distances in Africa. But, said Ptolemy, "it is ridiculous to think that a king should march through regions subject to him in a southerly direction when the inhabitants of those regions are scattered widely east and west, and ridiculous also that he should never have made a single halt that would alter the reckoning." [22] In another instance Marinus cited the sea voyage of an Indian traveler named Diogenes whose ship was driven for twenty-five days before a northerly gale down along the coast of the Troglodytes (the east coast of Africa). He finally made land at the promontory of Rhaptum close by the swampy sources of the Nile. What did this excursion mean to a map maker? Precisely nothing, in Ptolemy's opinion. Was the wind constant all that time, did the ship anchor or try to? Was the course due south or did it vary as the wind shifted? Diogenes did not say. If the region of the Winter Tropic really supported life and there were dark-skinned Ethiopians and rhinoceri living in that latitude, why, reasoned Ptolemy, were there no rhinoceri or Ethiopes in Syenê and cther places near the Summer Tropic, and why were there no elephants? Marinus was not there to answer.[23]

Marinus estimated that the habitable world extended over 15 hours of longitude or 11,250 miles at the equator. It was bounded on the west by the Fortunate Islands and on the east by three vaguely known places: Sera (Singan?), the Sainus River and Cattigara (Borneo?). Ptolemy said it was too long, that it was probably closer to 12 hours of longitude or 9000 miles at the equator. On analyzing this error, Ptolemy decided that Marinus was nearly correct in the distance between the Fortunate Islands and the Euphrates at Hierapolis (Membidj) but that he went wrong in his estimate of the distance from the Euphrates to the Eastern Ocean, or to Sera. Concerning that territory rumors thickened and distances lengthened. Instead of second- or third-hand accounts of travelers they were more often fourth- or fifth-hand, or else no one could remember exactly who said it or when. Marinus evidently submitted in evidence an account of a Macedonian trader who had journeyed thither and made some notes en route. But come to find out the man had not made the journey at all; he had sent one of his lackeys in his place, and the only information the fellow brought back was that it took him seven months to make the trip to the Far East. Ptolemy solemnly appraised this report and decided that the man had been forced to make a long circuitous march northward to avoid the Stone Tower (mountain), an obstacle that was said to block the eastward way of travelers.[24]

How could a scientist like Claudius Ptolemy soberly discuss various remote places, their distances and directions, in general terms such as "a few days' voyage" or "an overland march of four months," after stating flatly that mathematics and celestial observations were the principal tools of the map maker? The answer is to be found in his text. He admitted that mankind knew almost nothing about certain regions of the world and very little about others. He was therefore obliged, like every map maker before him, to take what information there was available from the most reliable authorities and dream of the time when travelers would take careful notes and astronomers could get around to different places and find out the truth about things. There is nothing incongruous in his methods or his text; he did the best he could with what he had to work with.

Marinus never completed the final revision of his map of the world, and his last effort, according to Ptolemy, lacked symmetry as well as more important things. He had not made the necessary corrections in the climata and the calculations of the zones in which the longest day of the year contains the same number of hours. Other errors had crept into the map because of the carelessness of copyists who followed the general layout but improvised on many small details, thereby magnifying the small errors of the original into serious faults on their copies. This situation Ptolemy considered as very unfortunate. Another fault in the Marinus text, which Ptolemy attempted to revise, was the arrangement of the information relative to various place names. In this connection Ptolemy made a suggestion and established a precedent. When a person wants to locate a place he needs to know two things about it: its latitude and longitude. Both figures, then, should be set down in the same place. Marinus had separated them, giving the latitudes of each place under his discussion of the parallels, and giving the longitudes in another part of the text. Never were the two positions given together. Ptolemy pointed out that in all worth-while geographical commentaries something was sure to be said about both latitude and longitude, and that it was important to know both figures at the same time; that in working with geographical data some valuable point might be overlooked if the reader has to skip back and forth in the text in order to locate the two factors which must be known in order to fix a geographical position.[25]

After appraising the work of Marinus, Ptolemy himself undertook the compilation of a geographical treatise and a series of maps which would contain the best elements of the Marinus plan. In addition, he proposed to add those things "which to him were not known, partly on account of history then unwritten . . ." In his own text, Ptolemy assured his readers that special attention had been given to an improved method of fixing political boundaries, and that the latitude and longitude of each place had been set down together, so that they could be seen at a glance.[26]

There are two ways of making a portrait of the world, he wrote; one is to reproduce it on a sphere and the other is to draw it on a plane surface. Each method has its advantages and disadvantages. "When the earth is delineated on a sphere, it has a shape like its own, nor is there any need of altering [it] at all." But it is not easy to provide space enough on a globe for all the details which should be included on it; moreover, if it is large enough to contain everything that should be drawn on it, the globe is too large for the eye to encompass. In order to see the far side of it, either the eye or the globe must be moved. Hence, if an individual wishes to construct a globe, he should first select the size he wants, keeping in mind that the larger it is, the clearer and fuller will be his pictorial description of the various places on the earth. Then having selected a sphere of suitable size and having determined the positions of the two poles, the globe should be suspended between two pivots connected by a semicircle. This semicircle should lie "a very little distance from the globe's surface," so that when the globe revolves it will almost touch it; and the semicircle should be narrow so that it will not obscure too many places. Then it is well to divide the semicircle into 180 parts, beginning the numbering at the equatorial line and working in both directions. In the same way the equinoctial line should be graduated, and the numbering should begin, not at the meridian of Alexandria but at the westernmost meridian, passing through the Fortunate Islands. From this point on, it was only a matter of "spotting" each place on the globe according to its latitude and longitude, previously determined by a comparative study of travelers' diaries, old wives' tales and the yarns of boastful mariners. It was that simple.[27]

If the second method of drawing the earth is used, that is, if the spherical earth is projected onto a plane surface, certain adjustments are necessary. Marinus had given the matter considerable thought, rejecting all previously devised methods of obtaining congruity on a flat map, yet, according to Ptolemy he had finally selected for his own use the least satisfactory method of solving the problem. He had laid out a grid of straight lines equidistant from one another for both his parallels of latitude and meridians of longitude. This was contrary to both truth and appearance, and the resulting map was badly distorted with respect to distance and direction, for if the eye is fixed on the center of the quadrant of the sphere which we take to be our inhabited world, it is readily seen that the meridians curve toward the North Pole and that the parallels, though they are equally spaced on the sphere, give the impression of being closer together near the poles.

Ptolemy was well aware that it would be desirable to retain a semblance of spherical proportions on his flat map, but at the same time he decided to be practical about it. He suggested a compromise projection whereby the meridians would be drawn as straight lines equidistant at the equator and converging at a common point — the North Pole. The parallels, however, would be laid down as arcs of circles having a common center at the North Pole. He suggested, as an additional compromise, that the parallel through Thule should be drawn parallel (literally) to the equatorial line, "so that the sides of our map which represent latitude may be proportionate to the true and natural sides of the earth." In addition, Ptolemy insisted on inserting the parallel through the island of Rhodes, because so many distances had been determined in relation to it that it had become a standard line of departure in map drawing and distance calculations.[28]

The meridians were to be spaced from each other "the third part of an equinoctial hour, that is, through five of the divisions marked on the equator." In other words, the total span of 12 hours, representing the length of the habitable world, was to be partitioned by a series of 36 meridians spaced 5° apart at the equator and converging at the North Pole. The parallel bounding the southern limit of the habitable world would be distant from the equator in a southerly direction only as far as the parallel through Meroê is distant in a northerly direction. Ptolemy laid down his parallels from the equator to Thule. There were 21 of them, spaced at equal *lineal* intervals. Each one was designated by (1) the number of equinoctial hours and fractional hours of daylight on the longest day of the year and (2) the number of degrees and minutes of arc north of the equator. For example, the first parallel of latitude north of the equator was distant from it "the fourth part of an hour" and "distant from it geometrically about 4° 15'." One other parallel was added south of the equator, identified with Rhaptum promontory and Cattigara and about 8° 25' distant from "The Line." The meridians for the southern hemisphere were extended from the equator at the same angle as those above it, but instead of converging at the South Pole they terminated at the parallel 8° 25' below the equator. All of the parallels north of the equator were located theoretically with the exception of three: Meroê, Syenê and Rhodes. The first was established traditionally as 1000 miles below Alexandria and 300 miles from the torrid zone; it was also known as the royal seat and principal metropolis of Ethiopia. Syenê was still considered as one of the very few scientifically located parallels because of the fact that it lay on the line of the Summer Tropic and was always included in any discussion of the parallels. Rhodes had become the most popular parallel of all and was located by common consent at 36° N.[29]

After giving detailed instructions on how to construct this simple conic projection with geometrical precision, Ptolemy concluded his remarks by saying that there was still a better way of picturing the habitable world. "We shall be able," he said, "to make a much greater resemblance to the known world in our map if we see the meridian lines that we have drawn in that form in which meridian

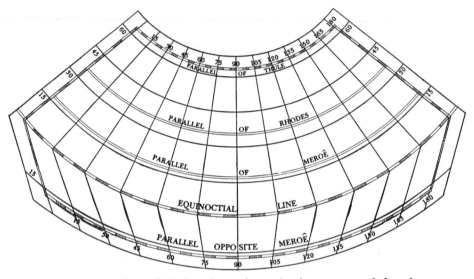

A reconstruction of Ptolemy's conic projection, suggested for the construction of a map of the habitable world. After a sixteenth-century copy.

lines appear on a globe. . . ." With that, he outlined the steps necessary to construct a modified spherical projection of the habitable quadrant of the earth; and as he said, the superior likeness resulting from such a projection was apparent. Also obvious was the fact that a spherical projection is basically more difficult to construct; not to mention the problem of maintaining distance and direction relationships when it came to "spotting" important places on the framework. "Since this is so," wrote Ptolemy, "even though for me both here and everywhere the better and more difficult scheme is preferable to the one which is poorer and easier, yet both methods are to [*sic*] me retained for the sake of those who, through laziness, are drawn to that certain earlier method." [30]

Book II of the *Geographia* opens with a prologue "of the particular descriptions," which is to say, the maps he was about to present, and a general statement of his map making policy. The latitudes and longitudes which have been assigned to well-known places are approximately correct since the traditional accounts concerning them agree. But the places that are little known, or about which there is considerable uncertainty, present a problem. About all one could do, Ptolemy thought, was to locate them as accurately as possible with reference to well-known places, inasmuch as it is advisable on a map of the entire world to assign a definite position to every known place, regardless of how little is known about it. This Ptolemy did in marginal notations, leaving spaces for any necessary corrections.

Each map was to be oriented so that north would be at the top and east at the right, because the better known localities of the world were in the northern

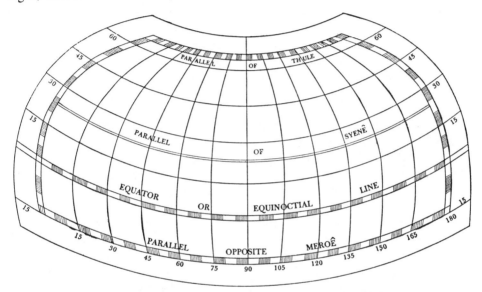

Ptolemy's modified spherical projection of the world, giving a superior likeness of the earth's surface on a sheet of paper. Though preferable to the conic projection, Ptolemy confessed that it was far more difficult to construct.

latitudes, and on a flat map they would be easier to study if they were in the upper right-hand corner. Three continents had taken shape: Asia, Europe and Libya. Of these, Europe was the most important, and should be separated from Libya by the Pillars of Hercules and from Asia by the river Tanais (Don) and by the meridian drawn through it to the *terra incognita* in the south. Libya, which lies next to the sea and extends eastward to the Gulf of Arabia, should next be inserted. It should be separated from Asia by the isthmus which extends from the interior of Heroöpoliticus to the Mediterranean and separates Egypt from Arabia and Judea. "Let us do this," Ptolemy said, "that we may not divide Egypt, in making a division of the continent, by the Nile, because continents are bounded more properly, where it is possible, by seas than by rivers." Finally Asia, occupying the balance of the habitable world, should be inserted.[31]

After outlining the continents, the various prefectures and provinces of the earth should be demarcated, but when doing this Ptolemy recommended spurning the "multitudinous farrago concerning the peculiar qualities of their inhabitants, except that, in the case of qualities renowned by general report, we make a short and suitable note on the religion and manners." In concluding his instructions, Ptolemy pointed out that anyone who cares to do so may make separate maps of the prefectures and provinces, or even groups of them, instead of trying to get them all on one sheet, giving each one its proper shape and size and preserving distance and directional relationships with the large map. He thought it would not matter a great deal if on these local maps we used parallel straight lines for meridians instead of curved, provided we kept the proper intervals between them in degrees and minutes of arc. Following his preliminary remarks, Ptolemy proceeded (in Chapter I of Book II) to the business of outlining the important subdivisions of the world, listing under each heading the important places within their boundaries and giving the latitude and longitude (east of the Fortunate Islands) of each one.

The lists of place names which follow are divided, geographically, into "Books" and "Chapters" but contain very little text or even the "short and suitable" notes on the religion and manners of the people which he suggested earlier. Yet this material constitutes Ptolemy's idea of a description of the habitable world. It is just as well, however, because there are parts of his text that are confusing and contradictory, and add no luster to Ptolemy's reputation as a careful scientist and reputable geographer. For example, he gives a descriptive summary in which he tells us that the habitable part of the earth is bounded on the south by the unknown land which encloses the Indian Sea and that it encompasses Ethiopia south of Libya, called Agisymba. On the west it is bounded by the unknown land encircling the Ethiopian gulf of Libya and by the Western Ocean which borders on the westernmost parts of Africa and Europe; on the north, "by the continuous ocean called Ducalydonian and Sarmantian which encompasses the British islands, the northernmost parts of Europe and by the unknown land bordering on the northernmost parts of Greater Asia; that is to say, on Sarmatia, Scythia and Serica." There are three seas surrounded by land. Of these, the Indian Sea is the largest, the Mediterranean (Our Sea) is next and the Caspian (Hyrcanian) is smallest. Among the most noted islands of the world are Taprobane, the Island of Albion ("one of the British Islands"), the Golden Chersonesus (the Crimea), Hibernia ("one of the British Islands"), Peloponnesus (Morea); then come Sicily, Sardinia, Corsica (also called Cyrnos), Crete and Cyprus.

In Book VIII of the *Geographia*, Ptolemy returned to the business of discussing maps and how to make them, and those writers who have argued that his text contained no maps neglected this "Book." In it Ptolemy said, "It remains for us to show how we set down all places, so that when we divide one map into several maps we may be able accurately to locate all of the well-known places through the employment of easily understood and exact measurements." [32]

Ptolemy went on to explain how the more common faults of map makers might be avoided. In a single map, for instance, embracing the entire earth, there is a tendency, he said, to sacrifice proportion, that is, scale, in order to get everything on the map. The better known regions have many place names, while the lesser known have few, and unless the map is carefully drawn it will have some crowded, illegible areas, and some where distances are unduly extended. Some map makers have a tendency to exaggerate the size of Europe because it is most populous, and to contract the length of Asia because little is known about the eastern part of it. And some surround the earth on all sides with an ocean, "making a fallacious description, and an unfinished and foolish picture."

The obvious way to avoid crowding, Ptolemy said, is to make separate maps of the most populous regions or sectional maps combining densely populated areas with countries containing few inhabitants, if such a combination is feasible. If several regional maps are made in order to supplement the general map of the world, they need not "measure the same distance between the circles," that is, be drawn to the same scale, provided the correct relation between distance and direction is preserved. Ptolemy repeated that it would not be too far from the truth if instead of circles we draw straight lines for meridians and parallels. As for his own policy, he said, "in the separate maps we shall show the meridians themselves not inclined and curved but at an equal distance one from another, and since the termini of the circles of latitude and of longitude of the habitable earth, when calculated over great distances do not make any remarkable excesses, so neither is there any great difference in any of our maps." These things being so, he continued, "let us begin the task of a division such as the following:

"We will make ten maps for Europe; we will make four maps for Africa; for Asia we will make twelve maps to include the whole, and we will state to which continent each map belongs, and how many and how great are the regions in each. . . ." The latitude of each place would be given as well as the length of the longest day in equinoctial hours. The longitudes would be determined from the meridian of Alexandria, either at sunrise or sunset, calculating the difference in equinoctial hours between Alexandria and point two, whatever it might be.

The authorship of the 27 maps which accompany the text of the *Geographia* is a favorite subject of dispute. Did Ptolemy do them himself, were they made by a draftsman working under his supervision or were they added, perhaps as late as 1450, by an energetic editor who thought the text needed some graphic emendation? It is clear from Ptolemy's text that he was supplementing his text and tables of distances (latitudes and longitudes) with maps — 27 of them, a general map of the world and 26 more, apportioned as he stated in Chapter II of Book VIII. Whether he had them made for him or whether he drew them with his own hand is a purely academic question. The proponents of the theory that Ptolemy made no maps for his *Geographia* base their case on a statement found on several manuscript codices of the work, to the effect that the maps were drawn by Agathodaemon of Alexandria. Perhaps they were; but internal evidence indicates that the text was written on the basis of maps already drawn or in the making. Moreover, the coverage of the maps, the projections on which they were drawn and the place names, all follow the text in every respect. There is no harm in attributing to Agathodaemon that which belongs to him, and the codices say that he "drew them according to the eight books of Claudius Ptolemy." However, this statement has never been dated nor is there anything known about the ghostly Agathodaemon. The earliest known manuscript of the *Geographia*, in the Vatopedi monastery of Mt. Athos, dates from the twelfth or thirteenth century. Therefore, all that can be said is that sometime between the years 150 and 1300 a man named Agathodaemon made a set of maps "according to the eight books of Claudius Ptolemy" — that and nothing more.[33]

The maps in Ptolemy's *Geographia*, or *Atlas of the World*, do not approach the ideals he expounded in his text. The first one, the general map of the habitable world, is laid down on the lazy man's projection he talked about, the modified conic instead of the spherical projection he recommended for a faithful delineation of the earth's surface.[34] The 26 regional maps, which in all extant manuscript copies bear a strong family resemblance, are laid down on the projection apparently used by Marinus in the form of isosceles trapezoids. The maps are usually about the same size but naturally the scales vary considerably, depending on the area, the number of legends, place names and conventional symbols used. And on each one the principal area is shown in full detail while the adjacent parts at the edges of the sheet are given in rough outline only; a device that is still as common as it is useful and practical. Also conspicuously modern is the lack of ornamentation on all of Ptolemy's maps. The early manuscript copies have none of the sea monsters, the ships and savages that were later introduced in the printed editions by map publishers of the sixteenth century. His method of differentiating land and water, rivers and towns, by means of either hachures or different colors, is strictly modern in conception; so much so that it is accepted at first glance without a thought being given to the origin of the technique.

The geographical errors made by Ptolemy in his text and maps constitute the principal topic of a vast literature, and are a perennial source of joy to scholars. Yet most of his errors arose from nothing more than a dearth of information. He lacked facts. The whole world lacked the fundamental data necessary to compile an accurate map. The only good reason for discussing a few of the glaring faults in the *Geographia* is that it was the canonical work on the subject for more than 1400 years. Geographers of the fifteenth and sixteenth centuries leaned on it so heavily, while ignoring the new discoveries of maritime explorers, that it exerted a powerful retarding influence on the progress of cartography. The *Geographia* was both a keystone and a millstone, a pioneering effort that outlived its usefulness. Yet few books have exerted a more profound and stimulating influence on the progress of civilization.[35]

Ptolemy made his first mistake when he chose to call the circumference of the earth 18,000 miles, following Poseidonius and Strabo instead of Eratosthenes. The length of his degree was 50 miles instead of 70; thus every calculation based on astronomical observation was too small. This initial error figured most conspicuously in his north-south distances where astronomical measurements were feasible.

Had there been a great many latitude observations made at different places the net result would have been a uniformly foreshortened world and the errors would not have been so disastrous; at least a semblance of relative proportion could have been established. As it was, Ptolemy admitted that all too few of such observations had been made, and distances were for the most part based on travelers' itineraries and later translated into degrees and minutes of arc, mathematical conclusions computed from gossip.

The importance of this fundamental error is well illustrated by his efforts to locate the equator on the map. The theoretical location of the line was well known to Ptolemy; none knew better how to determine it astronomically. But Ptolemy had not visited the equator, and his theoretical knowledge was of little help when it came to drawing it across his map. His best line of departure was Syenê, which was supposed to lie on the Summer Tropic. So he laid off the necessary 23° of arc below the Tropic of Cancer (Syenê) giving each degree a value of 50 miles. The result was that his equator was about 400 miles too far north. Below the equator there was little choice between what Marinus had to offer and the contributions of Ptolemy, because neither distances nor directions were reliable; no one had actually been there, and there was still a question as to whether the region would support life.

A second mapping policy which added nothing to the accuracy of Ptolemy's maps was his handling of east-west distances. Following Marinus, he established his prime meridian at the Fortunate Islands (now roughly the Canaries and the Madeira group), assuming that they lay further west than any point on the western coasts of Europe and Africa. Almost nothing was known about the Islands; however, both Marinus and Ptolemy placed their meridian 2° 30′ west of the Sacred Promontory (Cape St. Vincent), generally conceded to be the westernmost point of Europe, despite Pytheas. The line should have been close to 7° further west. To add confusion to the picture, Ptolemy computed his longitudes in two ways. Working eastward from the Fortunate Islands they were hypothetical and expressed in degrees and minutes of arc. But his factual meridians, distances contributed by travelers, were figured westward from Alexandria, the hub of the scientific world. These and many other features represent a futile attempt to reconcile scientific theory with a pitifully inadequate number of facts. His hypothetical map was excellent but his world of reality was faulty.

Ptolemy's knowledge concerning the fringes of civilization and the habitable world was broader than Strabo's, but in many respects it was confused. In the northern regions, for example, he had been ill-advised with regard to Ireland, and placed it further north than any part of Wales. Likewise, Scotland was twisted around so that its length ran nearly east and west. The Scandinavian peninsula was shown as two islands, Scandia and Thule. The northern coast of Germany beyond Denmark (Cimbrica Chersonese) was shown as the margin of the Northern Ocean, and running in a general east-west direction. The northern coast of Asia was not shown at all.

The southern limit of the habitable world had been fixed by Eratosthenes and

Strabo at the parallel through the eastern extremity of Africa (Cape Guardafiri), the cinnamon-producing country and the country of the Sembritae (Senaai). It also passed through Taprobane (Ceylon and, perhaps, Sumatra) usually considered the southernmost part of Asia. The extent of Africa below this parallel was a question.

Ptolemy recorded, following Marinus, the penetration of Roman expeditions to the land of the Ethiopians and to Agisymba, a region of the Sudan beyond the Sahara desert, perhaps the basin of Lake Chad, and he supplied other new information regarding the interior of North Africa, but most of it was extremely confusing. As to the source of the Nile, both Greeks and Romans had tried to locate it, but without success. The Emperor Nero had sent an expedition into Upper Egypt, and it had penetrated as far as the White Nile, about 9° N. latitude. But the source had not been reached. Ptolemy stated that the Nile arose from two streams, the outlets of two lakes a little south of the equator, which was closer to the truth than any previous conception, or any later one until the discovery of the Victoria and Albert Nyanza in modern times.

The eastern coast of Africa was better known than the western, having been visited by Greek and Roman traders as far as Rhapta (Rhaptum Promontory opposite Zanzibar?) which Ptolemy placed at approximately 7° S. To this he added a bay extending to Cape Prasum (Delgado?) at 15½° S. On the same approximate parallel he located the region called Agisymba, inhabited by Ethiopians and abounding in rhinoceri, supposedly discovered by Julius Maternus, a Roman general. This he took to be the southern limit of the world, while Thule remained the northern limit. Thus he extended the breadth of the world from less than 60° (Eratosthenes and Strabo) to nearly 80°.

According to Greek tradition, an extension of 20° in the width of the habitable world called for a proportionate increase in its length. Ptolemy extended the west coast of Africa with a free hand, and even though he reduced the bulge made by Marinus more than half, it was still way out of control. A more obvious place to stretch the length of the world was in Eastern Asia where there was every likelihood of additional territory yet unexplored. The silk trade with China had produced rumors of vast regions east of the Pamir and Tian Shan, hitherto the Greek limits of Asia. Ptolemy took little stock in the seven-months' journey to Sera and refused to follow Marinus who said the distance from the Stone Tower to Sera was 3620 miles, but he was, nevertheless, willing to cut the distance in half, on general principles.

Ptolemy's knowledge of the vast region from Sarmatia to China was better than that of previous map makers. He showed, for the first time, a fairly clear idea of the great north-south dividing range of mountains of Central Asia, which he called the Imaus, but he placed it nearly 40° too far east and made it divide Scythia into two parts: "Within Imaus" and "Beyond Imaus" (*Scythia Intra Imaum Montem* and *Scythia Extra Imaum Montem*). Asia and Africa were extended considerably to the east and south, far more so than on any previous maps, but not without cause. These distortions represented an actual extension of geographical knowledge and were doubtless based on exaggerated reports of distances traveled. All such information was of doubtful origin, and in laying down the coast line of Eastern Asia Ptolemy ran the line roughly north and south. Instead of continuing it to the Land of the Linae (seacoast China) he curved it around to the east and south, forming a great bay (*Sinus Magnus*), roughly the gulf of Siam. Continuing it around to the south until it joined *Terra Incognita* at the southern limit of the habitable world, he made a lake of the Indian Ocean (*Indicum Mare*). His eastward extension of Asia reduced the length of the unknown part of the world, between the easternmost point of Asia to the westernmost point of Europe, by 50° or 2500 miles. This mistake, coupled with his estimate of the circumference of the earth, was Ptolemy's greatest contribution to history if not cartography. The earth was only 18,000 miles around; Poseidonius had said it, Strabo substantiated it, and Ptolemy perpetuated it on his maps. More than 1300 years later this geographical understatement fired one Christopher Columbus with the dream of reaching the Indies by sailing westward, and to his royal sponsors, Ptolemy's Western Sea did not look too broad or too forbidding.

Many faults appear in Ptolemy's picture of Southern Asia, although for more than a century commercial relations between Western India and Alexandria had been flourishing. An important document entitled *The Periplus of the Erythraean* [Indian] *Sea* (*c.* 80 A.D.) [36] containing sailing directions from the Red Sea to the Indus and Malabar, indicated that the coast from Barygaza (Baroch) had a general southerly trend down to and far beyond Cape Korami (Comorin), and suggested a peninsula in Southern India. Ptolemy, apparently following Marinus, ignored this document or else he never saw it, because his India was unduly broadened and foreshortened. Eratosthenes, as reported by Strabo, reported that the southern capes of India lay opposite to Meroê. For the most part, the lands beyond the Ganges were not well known until a thousand years later when the brothers Polo first acquainted Western Europe with the existence of a number of large islands in that part of the world. And there were no good maps of the East Indian Archipelago until after the Portuguese voyages to the Indies. The legendary island of Taprobane, whose size had always been grossly overestimated, was not improved by Ptolemy, who extended it through 15° of longitude and 12° of latitude, making it about fourteen times as large as it really was and extending its southerly tip more than 2° below the equator.

Even in the more familiar territory of the Mediterranean basin, Ptolemy erred in many important cartographical details. His Mediterranean was about 20° too long, and even after correcting his lineal value of a degree it was still about 500 geographical miles too long. His *Mare Nostrum* from Marseilles to the opposite point on the coast of Africa was 11° of latitude (actually 6½°).

The best known parallel of latitude (36° N.) was not a parallel at all as he drew it.[37] Cleaving the habitable world from the Strait at the Pillars of Hercules to the Gulf of Issus, it passed through Caralis in Sardinia and Lilybaeum in Sicily (39° 12′ and 37° 50′ N.). Carthage was placed 1° 20′ south of the parallel of Rhodes; actually it is 1° north of it. Byzantium was placed in the same latitude as

Massilia, which made it more than 2° above its true position. This particular error threw the whole Euxine Pontus, whose general form and dimensions were fairly well known, too far north by the same amount, over 100 miles. His exaggeration of the Palus Maeotis (Sea of Azov), plus the fact that he switched its direction to north-south, brought its northern extremity, with the Tanais estuary, as high as 54° 30′, the true latitude of the south shore of the Baltic! However, he was apparently the first of the ancient geographers to have a fair conception of the relations between the Tanais, usually considered the northern boundary between Europe and Asia, and the Rha (Volga), which he said flowed into the Caspian. He was also the first geographer, excepting Alexander the Great, to return to the correct view advanced by Herodotus and Aristotle, that the Caspian was an inland sea without communication with the ocean.

It has been repeatedly pointed out that the distances set down in Ptolemy's tables for the Mediterranean countries, the virtual center of the habitable world, are erroneous beyond reason, considering the fact that Roman itineraries were accessible. But were they available to nonmilitary men such as Marinus and Ptolemy? It is very unlikely, in view of the secrecy attached to all maps and surveys of the Roman empire. If, as seems to be the case, Marinus depended for maritime distances largely on the writings of Timosthenes of Rhodes (the admiral of Ptolemy Philadelphus, who flourished about 260 B.C.), there must have been very little information available to a scientist and scholar such as Claudius Ptolemy, who seemed to have no motive except the advancement of learning to justify his investigations. And it is highly probable that Ptolemy the astronomer, who is usually discredited by geographers because of his methods and the kind of information he compiled, had no more standing among some of his influential contemporaries than he would today in the most approved geographical circles of the civilized world.

What about Ptolemy's fellow astronomers, and the fact that observation centers had long been established at Rome, Alexandria, Rhodes and Massilia? It is doubtful whether the distinguished astronomers who observed at those places were interested in anything but pure astronomy, or whether, as a group, they were sufficiently interested in the geographical application of their findings to overcome the difficulties of communication and transportation. So it is not so surprising that even in the better known parts of the world there was little pooling of information. Ptolemy mentioned only Marinus among his close contemporaries, though there must have been other scientists working in his time. Strabo cast doubt on the findings of all but a few geographers of his day and Hipparchus was wholeheartedly "Against Eratosthenes." What then could a man believe? In the light of present knowledge it is easy to look back at the gropings of science and wonder why the ancients did not always recognize sound facts when they were right under their noses. It is not so easy, perhaps, to understand the sifting and weighing of evidence that had to be done before a fact could be accepted for what it really was. Yet science has been built on skepticism and doubt, and often the greatest proponents of the scientific method have been the greatest doubters, except in the realm of mathematics where findings are usually more susceptible of proof.

In spite of the egregious errors on all of Ptolemy's maps, his atlas was an unsurpassed masterpiece for almost 1500 years. Its wealth of detail still constitutes one of the most important sources of information for the historian and student of ancient geography. This is especially true in the study of the earliest tribes that encompassed the Roman Empire in the first century of the Christian era, which were at that time barbarians, but which later bore the burden of civilization in Europe. To be sure, there are other geographical fragments, individual maps and charts, isolated examples of the best in Greek, Roman and Arabic cartography, but Ptolemy's *Geographia* is the only extant geographical atlas which has come down to us from the ancients. There is nothing in the literature to indicate that any other such systematic collection of maps was ever compiled, with the exception of the maps of Marinus, about which almost nothing is known.

Ptolemy departed from the standard Greek conception of the inhabited world. He abandoned the idea of a world encompassed by water (in the restricted sense employed by Homer), of a circumfluent "Oceanus" relatively close by. Instead, he recognized the possibility and probability of *Terra Incognita* beyond the limits of his arbitrary boundary lines. In other words, he left the matter open to further investigation. This attitude was an important step in the progress of cartography and an incentive to further exploration.

Claudius Ptolemy deserves a place among the scientific immortals of antiquity. He brought order out of a chaotic mass of facts and data representing the accretion of human thought from the time of primitive man. He was not an astronomer as opposed to a geographer, a mathematician rather than a cartographer; he was all of these and more; he was a great man, endowed with the ability to apply abstract principles to the particular problem at hand. He propounded a scientific method which is entirely modern in principle. He perfected the trigonometry invented by Hipparchus, and by the skillful application of its principles to celestial phenomena he systematized and rewrote the corpus of astronomy. By comparison, Ptolemy's accomplishments in the field of geography and cartography may not seem, at first glance, to be so important; but let us consider. He demonstrated more clearly than any of his predecessors, and in greater detail, the numerous feasible methods of applying the facts of astronomy to the study of the earth; he systematized the mapping of the earth's surface, and in his writings set forth the principles and techniques employed by modern geodesy.

Ptolemy made up the "dummy" of a systematic atlas of maps constituting the first orderly picture of the habitable world. The form of his atlas and the maps themselves are the prototypes of modern map making. Many of the legends and conventional signs he used are still employed by cartographers with only slight modifications. He originated the practice of orienting maps so that the north is at the top and the east to the right, a custom so universal today that many people are lost when they try to read a map oriented any other way. His map projections, the conical and modified spherical, as well as the orthographic and stereographic systems developed in the *Almagest*, are still in use. The listing of place names, either in geographical or alphabetical order, with the latitude and longitude of each place to guide the searcher, is not so different from the modern system of letters and numerals employed to help the reader, a little convenience that is standard on modern maps and Ptolemaic in origin.

If later cartographers and geographers had had Ptolemy's courage and critical faculties they would never have credited him with omniscience; but unfortunately this was not so, and Ptolemy has been published and quoted more than any other geographer before or since, to the detriment of both Ptolemy and the science of cartography. The single exception was, of course, Christopher Columbus, the dreamer and navigator, who pinned his hopes on Ptolemy and discovered a world — by accident.

CHAPTER IV

The Middle Ages

DURING the early Middle Ages, beginning in the year 300 A.D., cartography, like the Roman Empire, was converted to and encompassed by Christianity. As early as 150 A.D., Claudius Ptolemy, from his place in the Alexandrian Library, must have seen the signs and portents, the beginnings of unrest and corruption within the Roman Empire, the confusion and uncertainty among the masses.

Since the year 27 B.C., when Octavianus became Augustus Caesar, the Empire of the Romans had flourished. Even before the ink had dried on the text of Ptolemy's *Geographia*, the Mediterranean had become a Roman lake ringed by Roman provinces or territories which paid tribute to Caesar. *Mare Nostrum* was in reality "Our Sea" so far as Romans were concerned. An elaborate network of magnificent roads radiated from the shores of the Mediterranean and the Black Sea, passable, for the most part, all year round. Well marked and well policed, they extended across the inhabited world from Britain and Spain on the west to the Euphrates River on the east, an invitation to travel that was not ignored. The Mediterranean currently had been cleared of pirates, and coasting trade was brisk. In fact travel, either for business or pleasure, was safer in that region than it ever was again until the introduction of steam navigation. It was made still easier by a common language — Greek — spoken in all commercial towns, a system of laws that were universally binding, and a coin of the realm which was good as legal tender anywhere a sane Roman would care to go.[1]

But in spite of outward appearances, all was not well within the Empire. From beyond the frontiers there was constant pressure from the barbarians of Germany and Persia. Internally the situation was bad. Slowly but surely imperial power was being placed on a military basis, in spite of Marcus Severus Alexander's attempted revival of "constitutional" government. Intrigue, both civil and military, was the order of the day, and to the successful general, often provincial and untutored, went the spoils. For a time equestrians replaced senators; civil administration was absorbed by the army, which had the power to make and unmake emperors. Intellectual life began to totter, and Stoicism, the predominant philosophy of the Roman world, was obliged to compete with various Oriental cults that had crept in with other things exotic, brought from afar by traveling missionaries.

The people were ready for a new philosophy, or anything, in fact, that might help them forget their troubles, for all but the wealthy landowners were being crushed by heavy taxes. Labor and property were evaluated in terms of a unit of wheat-producing land. There was no recourse in the courts, now all but defunct, and there was little a freedman could do to escape the inevitable but flee the country, enter a monastery or become a serf on a large estate. Craftsmen and tradesmen were closely supervised and taxed to the hilt, so that there was no incentive to do good work, or any work at all, for that matter. Under the circumstances the masses lost interest in their government, their religion and life itself. Invasion by barbarians, far from being a nationalistic nightmare, might be a welcome relief from oppression. A new pagan cult from the Far East might be fantastic in concept and demanding of its adherents, but at least it would be a change.

The steady decline of the classical intellect and the growing despondency of the masses made Rome extremely vulnerable to the new thought and occult philosophies that were infiltrating the Empire. Missionaries of new sects, devotees, prophets and priests moved in, their progress unimpeded. All roads led to Rome, the mistress and protectress of cults, the center of Roman power, the tribune from which any preacher could hawk his religious wares. In addition to the dying religions of ancient Greece and Rome, bereft of much of their power, there came the worship of Cybele with its weird rituals, its frenzies and trances, its hymns and orgiastic dances. From Egypt came the worship of Isis, already highly organized, with a book of prayers, a code of liturgy and elaborate ceremonials. And out of nowhere, it seemed, came a new religion which was shortly recognized as a common and dangerous threat to all others: it was both feared and hated, and its followers were referred to as the "third race." It was called Christianity and revolved about the figure of a Nazarene named Jesus, called the "Anointed" (*Christos* in Greek).

The principal figure in this new religious movement had died ignominiously, crucified by the Jewish *Sanhedrin* (national council) with the tacit approval of Pontius Pilate, procurator of Judea, who objected to the seditious claims of the man Jesus. But the new faith had not died with Him, and His immediate followers, led by the ardent Apostle Paul, had spread His teachings and organized His followers. At first they had drawn their converts from the poorer classes — slaves, freedmen and laborers, with a smattering of wealthy and cultivated adherents. However, Christianity had flourished while other religions had waned, so that in the last decade of the second century men and women from all walks of life — senators and equestrians, distinguished pleaders and physicians, military and civil servants, judges and governors, had embraced the faith. Nothing save the army could approach the organization of the Church, and in spite of opposition and determined persecution, Christianity assimilated Hellenism; the despised and reviled "third race" became a nation within the Empire. Its churches were numerous and independent, governed by a board of elders (presbyters); it developed its own literature, beginning with the Gospels and apostolic writings of its leaders and prophets.

Early Christianity was easy to embrace. Its code was simple, rigid and uncompromising, but it promised much and demanded little — save faith — while the workaday world, in contrast, demanded much and offered nothing but mental confusion and physical fatigue. The stark realities of life, the myriad unsolved riddles of the universe, were no longer a challenge to the apathetic minds that had seen their government debased and their culture dragged through the muck. Christianity, therefore, predominated; it engulfed the best minds of Europe and bent them to its will. Scientific effort, though it did not die, was rendered comatose.

Much of the intellectual twilight of the early Middle Ages, beginning in 300 A.D., was caused by nothing more than man's preoccupation with his new-found road to glory and the sublime prospect of the hereafter. Such writers as Strabo and Ptolemy, Euclid and Archimedes were in disrepute. Human experience, close observation of natural phenomena, no longer mattered; recorded history was deprecated, and if it conflicted with the Holy Word it was branded as pagan and therefore untrue. The lamp of scientific knowledge, a tremulous flame at best, was obscured for a time by the blinding light of religious ecstasy.

Scientific doctrines in the early Middle Ages were considered irrelevant and unnecessary, if not altogether dangerous. Christianity could promote the arts and even literature with impunity, because these might properly be utilized as media for expressing its adoration. There was no such excuse for stimulating the development of science, including cartography. It was enough for mankind to draw both his mental and spiritual sustenance from the Church, and the Church, beginning with Lactantius (*c.* 300), declared that scientific pursuits were unprofitable. Some of the Church Fathers put it much stronger, vowing that the doctrines of science were dangerous as well as contrary to Scripture. When Pope Zachary (in 741) condemned at length the scientific views of Virgil (Virgilius), the learned Bishop of Salzburg, he pronounced them to be "a perverse and iniquitous doctrine." Resistance to obdurate thinkers such as Virgil, however, was not always so passive, and as the Christian Church grew in ecclesiastical and temporal power, unbridled thought which conflicted with theology was prosecuted with a zeal and determination that rivaled the fanaticism of Messius Quintus Traianus Decius, when he instituted the first general persecution of Christians.

Intellectual life in the Christian world of the Middle Ages was centered in the Church, led by such great Latin Fathers as Lactantius; Ambrose, Bishop of Milan; Jerome, who retired to Bethlehem and translated the Bible into Latin (the Vulgate); Augustine, Bishop of Hippo; Regius in Africa; Benedict, whose monastery at Monte Cassino was founded just at the time when the schools of Athens were closed by Justinian (529 A.D.). Some of the great scholars of the Latin Church, such as Jerome, were fascinated by and devoted to pagan learning, despite their profound ascetic convictions, and if they secretly pored over the works of pagan writers and worked out mathematical or astronomical problems, they could always hope for absolution by confessing their guilt and burying their doubts. The multitudes who had come to derive all comfort and hope from the Christian Church were strengthened by the never-ending chant of the Latin Fathers intoning with the mass a warning obligato against the flesh and the devil.

Such, in brief, was the background against which medieval cartography developed. What sort of maps did it produce, and who made them?

During the early Middle Ages (300–500 A.D.) pilgrimages were the fashion; it was a period of restless activity and movement. Many thousands of men and women moved back and forth across the face of Europe, either singly or in large groups, a likely source of new and increasingly accurate knowledge concerning the habitable world from Britain to the Orient. But travel, unfortunately, does not always broaden the mind, and in the case of the medieval pilgrim, travel did little to extend his mental horizon. Even when he wrote about what he saw his observations were usually innocent of geographic and cartographic knowledge, or even interest. Usually he was a solitary figure making his way to the Holy Land to do penance or merely to worship at one of the many shrines along the route. If so, he had eyes yet he failed to see anything but the Cross or the Holy Sepulchre before him, and if he had paused and looked, he would have failed to comprehend. Other pilgrims traveled to the East because it had become the center of the Church and the residing place of the emperor. Still others went in search of precious relics from Bethlehem and Calvary or objects related to the lives of the apostles. Vendors were there to meet them, and long after all authentic relics had been dispersed, the trade was brisk and lucrative. In addition to religious pilgrims, a large body of itinerant scholars was on the move; schools and universities were numerous throughout the Empire. But the intellectual pilgrim was more interested in wrangling or in comparing two versions of an important text than he was in what he saw around him. His contribution to cartography was of little consequence.

The first and most elementary form of geographical material furnished by the medieval mind came from the religious pilgrims of Europe in the form of guide books directing others how to get to sacred shrines and the historic sites of the Holy Land. Travel of any kind, the urge to be on the move, was a natural expression of the general unrest and insecurity which pervaded the Empire in the early Middle Ages. The devout Christian wanted to travel to the Holy Land, where he might see with his own eyes the objects of his devotion, where he might touch the ground on which his Saviour and the Apostles had walked.

The medieval guidebook was not a scientific document, but it was at least an indication that the medieval intellect, aside from the Church Fathers, was not entirely moribund. It was a contribution, though feeble, towards a descriptive geography that found expression in the Christian cartography of the tenth century. As guidebooks go, it was not a very useful article because it was written by untrained minds incapable of objective thought. The mind of the religious pilgrim was filled with the wonders of his dreams and the splendors he had seen. He filled his notebook with passages from the Scriptures, with the marvelous tales he had heard of visions, miracles, angels and demons. His contribution to an impoverished science was incidental.

Early records of religious pilgrimages are scanty, but there is rumor of a Gallic matron who trudged across Europe to the shrines of the Holy Land as early as 31 A.D. And lo, she returned bearing a shell filled with the blood of John the Baptist, murdered that year by Herod Antipas. There has been some doubt about the authenticity of the Gallic matron and her pilgrimage, but not so the Bordeaux Pilgrim.[2]

In 330 A.D. an anonymous traveler produced a manuscript under the title: *Itinerary from Bordeaux to Jerusalem*. This little work is the first known guide to the Holy Land via Southern Europe, the earliest pilgrims' Baedeker.[3] It could not have been a very helpful guidebook, for it contained no maps, and its directions are little more than an enumeration of place names and distances between; and only those places are listed which were on the beaten path between Bordeaux and Jerusalem. But the cities and towns listed by the man have a certain significance in that they represent a series of hostels or inns stretching across southern Europe and Asia Minor to the Holy Land. Pilgrimages were not a new thing in 330 A.D., nor were the roads, marked by mileposts, freshly built when the Bordeaux Pilgrim passed over them. From Arles to Milan he figured he had traveled 475 miles and had made 22 overnight "halts" for an average of 21½ miles a day. He also made an average of 3 "changes" a day, referring presumably to horses or donkeys. The total distance between Bordeaux and Constantinople according to the *Itinerary* was 2221 miles, with 112 halts and 230 changes.

As soon as he arrived in Judea, the Bordeaux Pilgrim began to make notes on historic landmarks such as the bath of Cornelius the Centurion; and at the third milestone beyond he saw the mountain Syna, "where there is a fountain, in which, if a woman bathes, she becomes pregnant." From here on his entries become more lengthy. As you come out of Jerusalem to go up Mount Sion, "on the left hand, below in the valley, beside the wall, is a pool which is called Siloe and has four porticoes; and there is another large pool outside it. This spring runs for six days and nights, but on the seventh day, which is the Sabbath, it does not run at all, either by day or night." Thereafter the Pilgrim goes from one historical site to another: the Mount of Olives marked by "a basilica of wondrous beauty," the tree Zacchaeus climbed in order to see Christ, the fountain of Elisha, the tomb of Rachel, wife of Jacob, and numerous others.

The *Itinerary* of the Bordeaux Pilgrim and a few of the later ones, such as those of Antoninus the Martyr and Saint Helena, were written before pilgrimages became a favorite form of religious penance. Although these early pilgrimages were made primarily "to seek after the footsteps of Jesus, and his disciples and the prophets," they set a pattern, blazed a trail, as it were, that centuries later was used by the crusading mutitudes who swarmed noisily eastward to liberate instead of visit the Holy Land. The medieval pilgrims' guidebook was also the forerunner of the "tourists' guide" to various parts of the world, an important adjunct of modern cartography.

Medieval cartography from 300 to 900 A.D. was predominantly Christian in origin and ecclesiastical in conception. It was a distillate of folklore, religious cosmography (a theological explanation of the universe and parts thereof), and an assortment of geographical statistics transcribed, with all the errors, from ancient

itineraries. The period was in every sense the Dark Age of science. Governed by divine revelation, all science was tested against an infallible Word and an infallible Church directed by that Word.[4] Theologians were obliged to study the universe in the process of explaining theology, but the science of ancient Greece and Rome was assiduously avoided. Ptolemy, Euclid and Strabo became the luxury of a select few, and though the more learned scholars doubtless subscribed to pagan theories such as the spherical shape of the earth, they kept very quiet about it. No minority could have been less popular or more subject to ostracism, if not persecution. The Latin Fathers did little to dispel the popular legends and folklore of the age, and a few, like Gregory the Great, through their personal popularity and influence, actually aided and abetted the cause of the storytellers. Gregory was a great popularizer, and through his *Dialogues*, which were widely read and narrated aloud, he contributed to the common (and often originally pagan) beliefs regarding angels and devils, relic worship, miracles, and the use of allegory in place of fact.

Much of the fabulous element that went into medieval maps, and that carried over into the seventeenth century, was contributed by an utterly shameless spinner of tall tales named Gaius Julius Solinus (fl. 250 A.D.) who was dubbed "Pliny's ape" by his enemies.[5] But Solinus was not even a good imitator of Pliny; he lifted only the nonsense from the *Natural History*, and the parts concerning geographical matters, passages concerning "Man," animals, trees and gems; in all about 700 extracts. He also borrowed freely, either directly or through Pliny, from Pomponius Mela, the earliest Roman geographer. With that material and a few fabrications of his own, Solinus published his gallery of wonderful things under the title *Collecteana rerum memorabilium*. It was an immediate success, and remained popular for over a thousand years. In the sixth century the work was revised and the title changed to *Polyhistor*. Solinus was copied and extracted by geographers and cosmographers long after his myths and marvels had been exploded, and his biological monstrosities adorned maps for the duration of the Middle Ages and for two hundred years beyond. Some of his imitators can be found in the writers of the popular medieval bestiaries, storybooks about animals. Solinus began to lose popularity only when man, in spite of threats and the fear of eternal damnation, shook the cobwebs out of his head and began to exercise his critical faculties with regard to natural phenomena in general and observed facts in particular.

Solinus was an unqualified success because he wrote for an age of superstition and awe. Ignorance and apathy supplied the superstition and Solinus the awe. He appealed to the masses, and because his writing did not conflict with Christian theology, the Latin Fathers did nothing to injure his reputation. On the contrary, he was cultivated. The people wanted fables, and the Church supplied or at least condoned them in the form of the *Collecteana* of Gaius Julius Solinus. Map makers used them because they made good illustrative material: it was easier to sell a map showing the marvels of the world, real or imaginary, than one that merely showed land forms and how to get from place to place.[6]

Solinus was fearless when it came to locating his supernatural marvels in familiar geographical settings. He told of people in Italy who sacrificed to Apollo by dancing barefooted on burning embers; he described the huge pythons of Calabria (a *compartimento* of Italy) that grew fat on the udders of milch cows, the lynxes there whose urine congealed into "the hardness of a precious stone, having magnetic powers and the color of amber." His statements concerning Greece were relatively conservative; its terrain and the natural history of the country were much too well known to permit free play of the imagination. But in the Black Sea region of Scythia and Tartary, Solinus felt more secure. There, he said, the dolphins were so spry that they were known to leap clear over the mainsails of passing ships. In the steppe regions were horse-footed men and those creatures, mentioned by Strabo, whose only apparel was their ears, and savages who lived back of the north wind, and the one-eyed men of ancient fables.

Asiatic Scythia was said to abound in gold and precious stones; there one could find the Gryphons, a fierce species of fowl that would tear an intruder to pieces. Among the wonders of Germany were the Hercynian birds, whose feathers glowed in the dark, and a creature resembling a mule, with such a long upper lip that he could feed only by walking backwards. The people of Ireland were described as uncivil, but the pasturage of the country was so rich and succulent that Irish cattle would burst if they were not restrained. In Ireland, it seems, there were no snakes. The people of Britain were noteworthy principally for their tattoos ("flesh embroidery").

The rivers around Mt. Atlas, according to Solinus, especially the Bambatum, swarmed with river horses and crocodiles. The Niger River boiled constantly from the immeasurable heat of the region — hotter than any fire. In Africa there were hyenas with unjointed backs, whose very shadows smote fear into the hearts of dogs so that they were rendered powerless to bark, let alone bite. In the innermost recesses of the Syrtis (in Libya) was the cockatrice or basilisk — a unique horror — a beast that crept along the ground like a crocodile by its forequarters while its hindquarters were suspended aloft by two wings or lateral fins. His bite, nay, even his breath was fatal. Only weasels could overcome him. Then there were the dog-headed Simeans of Ethiopia, and an obscure race of men who had a dog for a king. Also in Ethiopia was a coastal tribe whose people had four eyes apiece. The ants along the Niger were as big as mastiffs. In the Land of Silk (Western China), the silk was combed off the leaves of the trees that produced it.

In addition to the animals from Pliny's zoo, some of the gruesome characters found on medieval maps are the men without noses (located in furthest Africa); men without heads, whose eyes and mouths are in their chests; the Crook-legs of the desert (who slide instead of walk). Located in India there are the men with eight toes on each foot, others (in the mountainous regions) with dog's heads and talons for fingers (who bark instead of talk). There, too, are the men with only one leg, but with a foot so large that it is often shown doubling as a parasol. Thus spake Solinus!

The system of the universe set forth by Strabo and Ptolemy was perpetuated throughout the darkest years of the Middle Ages by a few pagan writers such as Macrobius who flourished about 400 A.D. To be sure, it was pagan science in an attenuated form, edited and expurgated in many respects, but the sources of information are apparent. And when Macrobius borrowed from fanciful writers such as Pliny, he was far more discriminating than Solinus. Even the Latin Fathers helped, indirectly, to keep pagan science alive. Instead of burning seditious writings they stored them in the libraries of their convents and monasteries where they served as horrible examples of man's frailty. There, too, they could be studied, renounced and disproved. So the earth was a sphere, was it? "Can any one be so foolish," wrote Lactantius, "as to believe that there are men whose feet are higher than their heads, or places where things may be hanging downwards, trees growing backwards, or rain falling upwards?" Chrysostom and Augustine wrote in the same caustic vein. "Men go abroad to admire the heights of mountains and study the circuits of the stars, and pass themselves by." Even more scathing in his criticism was Cosmas, the converted merchant and traveler who renounced all profane knowledge of the world in favor of that gleaned solely from the Holy Scriptures and certain other carefully selected sources. "I open my stammering and unready lips," he wrote, "trusting in my Lord that He would vouchsafe me of His spirit of wisdom." [7]

Cosmas of Alexandria, surnamed Indicopleustes, flourished during the sixth century. His conversion to Christianity followed a successful career as a traveling merchant. He had sailed the Red Sea and the Indian Ocean, he had traded at the market places of Abyssinia and Socotra, Western India and Ceylon. As a climax to this unusually broad and worldly experience he embraced Christianity and became a monk; and about 548 A.D., in the solitude of a Sinai cloister he wrote, besides his memoirs, an explanation of the universe entitled *Christian Topography* (*Topographia Christiana*). His chief object was to demolish the false and heathen doctrine of a spherical earth, and to vindicate at the same time the Scriptural account of the earth and its place in the universe. Cosmas did not shirk his task, and in order to disprove the pagan writers he cited nearly seventy of their authorities, damning the best and most reliable ones with vigor and feeling. After tearing down the writings of Greek infidels such as Plato, Aristotle, Eudoxus and Ptolemy he proceeded to construct his own cosmography based on the Scriptures and the writings of the Holy Fathers. The text was illustrated by diagrams and the earliest known maps of Christian origin.[8]

Cosmas had no time or sympathy for men like Saint Basil who avoided the issue of whether or not the earth was a sphere. Some writers openly declared that it did not matter so far as faith was concerned whether it was a sphere, a cylinder or a disc. But this sort of rationalizing was not good enough for Cosmas. There had to be an answer to the question, and he, Cosmas, found it in the words of the Apostle Paul when he declared that the first Tabernacle was a pattern of this world, for the first "had ordinances of divine service and a worldly sanctuary; for there was a tabernacle made; the first wherein was the candlestick, and the table and the shew-bread, which is called the Sanctuary."[9] In calling it *worldly*, Cosmas explained, Paul was indicating "that it was, so to speak, a pattern of the world, *wherein was also the candlestick*, by this meaning the luminaries of heaven, *and the table*, that is, the earth, *and the shew-bread*, by this meaning the fruits which it produces annually. . . ." The same reasoning was applied to the shape of the world, for the Scripture said thou shalt make the table in length two cubits and in breadth one cubit.[10] This indicated to Cosmas that the flat earth was twice as long, from east to west, as it was broad. Moreover, the earth was suspended, as Job said, on nothing, but was founded on God's stability. Above it the vault of heaven was fastened or "glued" to the earth along its extremities.[11] The heavenly vault was divided into two strata, the lower being the firmament, the dispensation of angels and men. From the firmament to the arch of the second heaven was the kingdom of the blessed into which Christ had entered.[12]

There was only one *face* of the earth according to Cosmas, namely, that which we dwell on. How could we use the God-given power to tread on scorpions and serpents if we walked upside down? How could a spherical earth such as men boast of hold bodies of water such as lakes, rivers and oceans?

The sun rises slightly south of east, said Cosmas, moving south and west during the day, and retracing its course behind the great mountains of the north, the source of darkness "even to the ocean beyond our earth, and thence to the land on the other side of our ocean." This fact was proved by the furniture of the

Tabernacle, where the candlestick, placed to the south of the table of shew-bread, typified the heavenly bodies shining on the earth. The molding that Moses put around the table of shew-bread signified the ocean encompassing our present world, and by a "crown of a palm's width" beyond the molding, was indicated the former world of the patriarchs on the other side of the ocean, where man lived before the flood.[13]

The world, said Cosmas, is divided into two parts, present and antediluvian. It contains four great seas or gulfs: Mediterranean, Persian, Arabian and Caspian. The four extremes of the world are occupied by four nations. In the east are the Indians, in the south the Ethiops, in the west the Celts, in the north the Scythians. On his map of the world, Cosmas showed the earth surrounded by an unnavigable ocean and beyond it another earth (*Terra ultra Oceanum*) in which the Paradise of Adam was located, and where man lived before the Flood. The earth is enriched by four rivers whose headwaters are in Paradise. Somehow they cleave a passage through or under the Ocean Sea and spring up in the earth proper. "Of these the Pheisôn (Pison) is the river of India, which some call Indus *or* Ganges. It flows down from regions in the interior, and falls by many mouths into the Indian Sea. . . . The Gêon (Gihon or Nile) again, which rises somewhere in Ethiopia and Egypt, and discharges its waters into our gulf by several mouths, while the Tigrês and Euphrates, which have their sources in the regions of Persarmenia, flow down to the Persian Gulf. Such then, are our opinions on these points."

Cosmas, like all good Christian geographers, shrank from the idea of an inhabited part of the world in the Antipodes, separated from Christianity by an ocean belt near the equator. The theory of such a region, found in some of the pagan writings of the early Greeks, was impossible on two counts. In the first place, the region, if indeed there was land there, would be uninhabitable because of the withering heat. In the second place, the inhabitants could not possibly be descended from Adam, since the Ark of Noah carried the sole survivors of the great Flood. The subject of the Antipodes and the possibility of inhabitants in that region became an important theological issue, ably debated by Isidorus of Seville in the sixth century. Two hundred years later Virgil of Salzburg with Basil and Ambrose agreed that even though it was a delicate subject, it was not necessarily closed to the Church. Cosmas was most emphatic on the subject. Pagans, he said, "do not blush to affirm that there are people who live on the under surface of the earth. . . . But should one wish to examine more elaborately the question of the Antipodes, he would easily find them to be old wives' fables. For if two men on opposite sides placed the soles of their feet each against each, whether they chose to stand on earth or water, on air or fire, or any other kind of body, how could both be found standing upright? The one would assuredly be found in the natural upright position, and the other, contrary to nature, head downward. Such notions are opposed to reason, and alien to our nature and condition." [14]

The geographical statistics compiled during the Dark Age of medieval thought were spotty and in general unreliable. They reviewed in a disorderly way the theories on the size of the world, the continents and various countries, that had been set down centuries before by Hipparchus, Eratosthenes and Ptolemy. Nothing new was added except confusion and theology. One such contribution, a statistical summary of the world, was made about one hundred years after Cosmas (650 A.D.) by an anonymous student of Ravenna.

The anonymous Ravennese found a place in history because his manuscript survived and was copied, unfortunately, by other writers. He was little more than a compiler of old, pre-Christian itineraries, though he used, in addition,

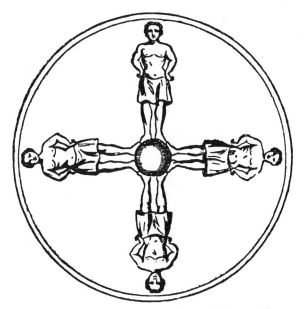

"If two men on opposite sides [of the earth]
placed the soles of their feet against each
. . . how could both be found standing
upright?" — Cosmas, 535 A.D.

several new tables of distances gleaned from "Gothic Cosmographies" brought into the Roman Empire by the Teutonic conquerors from the north. But in the use of his material, the Ravennese was about on a par with his contemporaries. For instance, he confused Claudius Ptolemy with the "King of the Macedonians in Egypt." The blunders in his spelling of place names can be laid to his copyists, perhaps, but in most respects he showed a decided lack as a student.[15]

In addition to his scientific faults and lack of originality, the Ravennese went to considerable trouble to infuse a generous quantity of extraneous material into his tables of distances. He began his text with a rhapsody on the immensity of God's world. Who has measured the height of heaven, the breadth of the earth, or the depth of the abyss? As for himself, he said, "though not born in India, nor

brought up in Scotland, — though I have never travelled over Barbary, nor examined Tartary, — yet I have gained a mental knowledge of the whole world and
the dwelling-places of its various peoples, as that world has been described in
books under many emperors." The world he visualized stretched from Britain
to India, and was divided into twelve parts, beginning in the east, even as the
day itself was divided. Between the two extremities were the lands of the Persians,
the Arabs, Ethiops, Moors, Spaniards, Aquitanians and others. Upon them blew
the "six winds of the treasuries of God." West of Scotia (Ireland) was an im-
passable tract, the Northern Ocean, beyond which no land had been discovered.
But to pry into this vast unknown would be blasphemous for any Christian.
Likewise, it was ordained that no mortal man should penetrate to the hidden Paradise of God, located in the furthest East.

As for the mountains behind which the sun and moon disappear, what man is
impudent enough to question their existence? It is perfectly clear that the Creator
did not wish mortal man to know their whereabouts; He therefore made them
inaccessible. After concluding his prefatory remarks on cosmography, the
Ravennese proceeded to set forth his tables of distances, giving as his chief source
of information the name of Castorius, a nebulous character who had at one
time compiled a cosmography of the Empire (*Cosmographus Romanorum*). His
discourse on the habitable world closed with a coasting guide or *periplus* of the
Mediterranean and a summary of the important islands within and beyond the
"Roman Sea." In his entire text there is only one indication of an active imagination and possibly an original idea of importance concerning longitude. "If," he
said, "by the horologium of metal [clock or sundial] we can discern accurately
each part of the day in the reckoning of hours, how much more can prudent and
wise men reckon what countries are to be taken into account as they go over the
world hour by hour?" [16]

World maps of the Middle Ages fall into three general groups, depending on
their shape: circular, rectangular, and oval; in all other respects there is little
choice between them. The shapes of the first two groups were based on sound
Scriptural foundations. "It is He that sitteth upon *the circle of the earth*, and the
inhabitants thereof are as grasshoppers; that stretcheth out the heavens as a cur-
tain, and spreadeth them out as a tent to dwell in." [17] This was sufficient docu-
mentation for the flat disc conception of the world. In case there were those
who had not read Cosmas and absorbed his ingenious parallel between the Table
in the Tabernacle and the earth, there was another passage of Scripture which
did just as well to verify a world of straight lines, either a square or a rectangle.
"And He shall set up an ensign for the nations, and shall assemble the outcasts
of Israel, and gather together the dispersed of Judah *from the four corners of
the earth*." [18]

Having established the shape of the world, each according to his choice of
Scriptural text, early medieval geographers floundered in a morass of tradition
and half-proved facts. For the most part they adopted a motif for the interior of
their world after the system of Eratosthenes, exaggerated and shorn clean of any

scientific principles he contributed. The Ganges River marked the eastern extremity of the habitable world, and the Sahara Desert the southern limit. The Roman Empire embraced most of terra firma, or at least all of it that was worth inhabiting. The existence of an Ocean Sea surrounding the habitable world was confirmed for Cosmas by the undulated border on the table of shew-bred, and for others by remnants from earlier Greek geographers such as Eratosthenes. The Caspian was an inlet of the Northern Sea and Scandinavia an island to the north of Germany.

The only survivals of map making from the old Roman Empire are the maps of Claudius Ptolemy, a few fragments, and one known as the Peutinger Table, named after its discoverer, which is predominantly a road map. But there are at least ten classical references to others in works written by Varro, Vitruvius, Suetonius, Pliny, and others.[19] However, all of the maps referred to in these texts are lost. From all that was written about them at the time, it would seem that in contrast to the early Christian maps of the Middle Ages, they were not lacking in geographic details; the information they supplied was plentiful, whether it was correct or not.

The eight or nine maps that can be dated with fair accuracy between 500 and 800 A.D. are sadly lacking in detail and display a primitive conception of the world that belies their surroundings and the probable knowledge of the men who made them. The rectangular world map of Cosmas, for example, was made by a traveled man, a man of the world. It is a mere outline of his theological conception of the world, entirely lacking in practical information; not even the author could have used it to get from place to place, nor could he use it to demonstrate the most elementary political boundaries. Was it used only as an allegorical picture of the world, a figurative illustration of a thesis? Or did Cosmas think his readers were so stupid that they would be deceived by his primitive explanation of the world they lived in? Cosmas did not say.

A second world map of the period is in the library of Albi, in Languedoc. It is bound in with an eighth century manuscript containing the cosmographies of Orosius and of Julius Honorius. The execution is extremely crude; in fact it is so bad that the numerous geographical errors it contains may be the faults of the bad artist who made it rather than the information he had to work with. The habitable world is shown as an oblong with rounded corners surrounded by the ocean. The land shown includes only the Mediterranean region or what he considered the extent of the old Empire; Asia is reduced to nothing but a fringe of land to the east of the Mediterranean. Though the map is obviously of Roman origin, Italy too is poorly drawn. The Nile and the Red Sea are shown flowing into the Mediterranean. The west wind (Zephyrus) blows from the south; the Ganges River is in south Africa. But with all its faults, the Albi map, drawn about 750 A.D., remains one of the oldest cartographic pictures of Latin Europe in the Middle Ages.[20]

Among the interesting maps that are mentioned in the writings of the period but which have disappeared without a trace, there was the picture of the world painted by Bishop Theodulf of Orleans (788–821) on the wall of his house. Anastasius tells how Pope Zacharias, who stamped out the geographical heresies of Virgil, had a map of the world designed for his own use, and during his reign it adorned one of the chambers of the Lateran Palace. Einhardt (770–840), the friend and biographer of Charlemagne, described, among the wonders of the emperor's library, three "tables" of silver and one of gold. On one of the silver tablets was engraved the "entire circuit of the earth," divided into three continents. The other two contained detailed plans of the cities of Rome and Constantinople. Even the anonymous Ravennese claims to have designed "with wondrous skill" a picture of all the lands he described.

More than 600 maps and sketches made between 300 and 1300 A.D. have survived the ravages of time. They have been unearthed in many strange places and under curious circumstances. They range in size from an inch or two, such as the schematic picture of the world in the *Etymologies* of Isidorus of Seville, to five feet or more in diameter, such as the beautiful map in Hereford cathedral (1275 A.D.). But regardless of size and the quality of the draftsmanship, it is impossible to trace in them a developmental process, a progression of thought whereby a few basic ideas or facts were added to and improved upon. It is also impossible to classify medieval maps in a sensible way or to grade them according to accuracy and utility. Even the "types" of maps that show similar characteristics cannot be traced to prototypes other than the accepted Scriptural sources, the universally popular myths of the age and the garbled Graeco-Roman fragments of a better day. Copies of maps seldom showed improvement over the original in the way that Ptolemy's maps were perfected by his editors. The maps of the Spanish priest Beatus, for example, first appeared in his *Commentary on the Apocalypse*, written in 776 A.D. During the next five hundred years they were copied many times, probably by representative intellectuals of the clergy, yet the only changes made in them were trivial additions of decorative features and some of the marvelous creatures created by Pliny and Solinus. Such additions to maps which were schematic or allegorical in the first place have little if any historical significance in the scheme of a developing science.[21]

"It is improbable," wrote one historian, "that much of essential worth developed in antiquity was ever destroyed."[22] This may or may not be true, but during the Middle Ages, at least, a great deal that was of essential worth became sequestered in the monasteries and convents, and for a time, science and scientists had to move out of Western Europe. Constantinople took over the custody of ancient learning while Western Europe basked in the aura of sanctity shed by the Latin Church. Her libraries and museums became the repository of ancient civilization and culture, and science was thereby kept alive. A few hardy souls of Western Europe did their bit to keep the torch burning. In the first half of the twelfth century, for instance, Adelard of Bath spent a summer on the coasts of Wales and Ireland studying the flux and reflux of the tides and working out a theory of their behavior. And Duns Scotus, at the end of the thirteenth century, worked a whole winter in a monastery in Paris, calculating with charcoal on a whitewashed wall the precession of the equinoxes, employing both Greek and Arabic mathematics.[23] But in spite of a handful of scholars such as Adam of Bremen, Pope Sylvester II, Albertus Magnus and Roger Bacon, who accepted the hypothesis of a spherical world as a fact, the authors of medieval maps, most of whom were monks, relied on the Scriptures and little else for guidance in outlining the inhabited world. What they produced was a number of rough sketches and allegorical pictures designed to edify and entertain the multitudes, or to support some theological doctrine.

In addition to the circular and rectangular maps whose shapes were documented by Holy Scripture there were a few oval maps that had to stand on their own. One such map was produced by Henry (Canon Heinrich) of Mainz (c. 1110 A.D.) and is found in his *Imago Mundi*.[24] A variation of the oval world is sometimes found in the form of two cones united at their bases. Matthew Paris (1195–1259) went back to the ancient Greek conception of the military cloak-shaped (*chlamys extensa*) world. Nearly all medieval map makers seem to have agreed that the habitable part of the world was surrounded by the Ocean Sea: "Let the waters under the heaven be gathered together unto one place, and let the dry land appear: and it was so." [25] There were differences of opinion as to the extent and precise nature of the ocean. Some believed it was a narrow band surrounding a comparatively large earth; others believed that it was extensive in breadth, but all believed it was not to be probed, even though it might be navigable. The secrets of the sea belonged to the Almighty and were not to be tampered with.[26]

One of the reasons for this irrational fear of the Ocean Sea was the existence, somewhere beyond the horizon, of Paradise. There was no question about the reality of it, it was merely a question of locating it precisely. Usually it was placed in the Far East: "The Lord God planted a garden Eastward in Eden . . . and he placed at the East of the garden of Eden, Cherubims, and a flaming sword, which turned every way, to keep the way of the tree of life." Isidorus of Seville was the principal authority on Paradise; he pictured it on the mainland in the Far East, but surrounded it by a fiery wall in case adventurers should become too curious about it. Some located it on an island in the remote East, encircled by mountains that could not be scaled. Others avoided locating it accurately by drawing effigies of Adam and Eve and the Garden of Eden in the general vicinity, usually the East.

Ranulf Higden, the Benedictine monk, devoted a long chapter of his *Polychronicon* to the subject of Paradise. Sir John Mandeville (c. 1360) wrote on the subject in his book of travels. He had not actually visited Paradise, nor even tried to, because he felt himself unworthy, but he wrote without hesitation about worthier travelers than himself who had been there and described what they saw. Columbus thought he must have reached the earthly Paradise when he hit the flood of the Orinoco River in the Gulf of Paria, sweetening the ocean as only the fountain springing from the tree of life could do.[27]

Paradise, then, was in a general sense the eastern extremity of the world, either an island apart from the earth or a portion of the mainland. The western extremity was Britain or the Pillars of Hercules with nothing but ocean beyond. As for the northern extremities, a group of Irish wanderers in search of solitude were supposed to have visited Thule in 795 A.D. They reported that in the summer the setting sun, "not only at the solstice, but for many days in the year, seems merely to hide itself behind a little mound, so that there is no darkness to hide a man from doing what he liked, even from picking lice out of his clothes." The open sea remained the northern limit of Asia until the middle of the thirteenth century.[28]

The southern extremity of the medieval world was the subject of an endless controversy, chiefly because of the Antipodes. Both Solinus and Juba visualized a long curve of coast line from the Atlantic Ocean sweeping south and east without interruption to the Indian Ocean, an easy maritime route. Some maps recognized in a vague way the existence of land south of the Indian Ocean, but it was generally considered uninhabitable on account of the extreme heat. And it was uninhabited because God, "hath made of one blood all nations of men for to dwell on all the face of the earth. . . ."[29] There were, of course, map makers such as Lambert of St. Omer, who qualified their statements regarding the land below the equator. Lambert described the "region of the south" as "temperate in climate, but unknown to the sons of Adam, having nothing which belongs to our race." It was separated from the world of Adam, he said, by the equatorial sea and was invisible to the human eye. The Antipodes, said Lambert, always received the full force of the sun's rays, and in spite of the equatorial ocean there was no passage to or from it. The region was inhabited, not by humans, but by strange creatures called Antipods whose anatomy was distorted by the ghastly climate. "For when we are scorched with heat," he wrote, "they are chilled with cold; and the northern stars, which we are permitted to discern, are entirely hidden from them." In addition to the Antipodes, Lambert suggested the existence of two or more unknown continents, earth islands, one in the northern hemisphere and one in the southern, out in the Ocean Sea somewhere.[30]

The circular or wheel map of the medieval world was usually divided into three parts by a T-shaped partition, a T within an O. This popular figure of the world was probably conceived in the fifth century B.C. by Ionic philosophers. The earliest T–O maps of the Middle Ages were produced by Isidorus of Seville, and they are typical of all the others. The T within the O produced a world divided into a half (by the cross of the T) and two quarters. The half segment (east) at the top of the map represented Asia, the lower left Europe and the lower right Africa. These segments also represented, according to Isidorus, the divisions of the earth apportioned to the three sons of Noah: Shem, Japheth and Ham, respectively. The T separating the boundaries between the three continents also represented three of the principal waterways of the world. The upright running east and west to the center of the world was the Mediterranean Sea. The northern half of the cross was the Don River, and the southern half the Nile.[31]

Place names for the three continents varied considerably; some maps bore the Biblical names only; others had explanatory inscriptions stating, for instance, that Asia was named after a Queen Asia, "of the posterity of Shem, and is inhabited by 27 peoples; that Africa is derived from Afer, a descendent of Abraham, and has 30 races in 360 towns"; and that Europe, named from the Europa of mythology, "is inhabited by the 15 tribes of the sons of Japhet and has 120 cities." Other maps give definite localities for the Twelve Tribes of Israel and the abiding places of the Twelve Apostles.

Regardless of experience and all knowledge to the contrary, the most important city regionally was located in the center of the habitable world. In ancient Greece, Ionic philosophers placed Greece in the center of their world map and Delphi in the middle of Greece. The Hindus had their Merou, the Persians their Kangdiz, the Arabs their Aryne (Aren, Arim or Arin). It was therefore inevitable that the Christian map maker should place Jerusalem in the geographic center of the world: "This is Jerusalem: I have set it in the midst of the nations and countries that are round about her." [32] The Holy City appeared in the center of the world on the Sallust maps, T–O designs of about 1110 A.D. But there are earlier textual references to its central location. The Vulgate translation of the Bible calls the city the umbilicus of the world (*umbilicus terrae*). Two hundred years after the Sallust maps Marino Sanuto called it the *punctus circumferentiae.* There it remained in the center of the world until about 1450 when map makers were forced to shift it to the east. The discoveries of Marco Polo and other explorers made it necessary to enlarge Asia, to move Jerusalem or to ignore the discoveries.[33]

Remnants of ancient classical geography crop up on medieval maps without any apparent reason. But obviously there was no compendium of geographical data on which a map maker could draw. Nor was there any scientific or philosophic group in Europe dedicated to the gathering and checking of cartographical data. Ancient landmarks were indicated on maps whether they existed at the time or not. Troy and Carthage were pictured as contemporaneous with Rome and Jerusalem. The Labyrinth of Crete and the Colossus of Rhodes were indicated as though they were still there. Most place names, in fact, were confused and badly located. Delphi was sometimes mistaken for Delos; Corinth seldom resembled an isthmus: Potomos was moved to the middle of the Black Sea; Gades (Cadiz) became a large island in the middle of the Strait of Gibraltar; Palestine appeared in the interior of Africa.

The *climata* or zones of Ptolemy's day came back briefly in the Middle Ages, distorted and unrelated to practical cartography. Ambrosius Aurelius Macrobius (fl. 410) used a series of climate sketches to illustrate his *Commentary on the Dream of Scipio.* Some of his map sketches show five and some seven zones or climate belts; others show his conception of the two earth islands of the Eastern Hemisphere. His ocean covers most of the surface of his world, and the landmasses are reduced to small spots. The ecliptic is seldom seen on medieval maps, any more than parallels and meridians, but there are at least two zone sketches which show it. One was done by the Abbess of Herrade, of Landsberg, in her

Garden of Delights (*c.* 1180). A second one was made by John Halifax of Holy-wood (Sacro Bosco) about 1220 A.D.[34]

In addition to important cities such as Rome, Antioch, Jerusalem and Con-stantinople, many Biblical sites are found on the maps of the Middle Ages, often accompanied by figures and pictorial sketches. The Ark is often shown resting on the mountains of Ararat. The Tower of Babel and the lighthouse tower of Pharos at Alexandria are common landmarks. The destruction of Sodom and Gomorrah and the site of the sojourn in Egypt, marked by the Pyramids ("Joseph's Barns"), were always popular. The passage through the Red Sea, a well-charted thoroughfare, and the partition of the Promised Land into Twelve Tribes, were desirable additions when there was room enough to show them.

The fables of Pliny and Solinus, sanctioned by such eminent authorities as Augustine and bolstered by their association with the deeds of Alexander the Great, were always popular map material. Other myths, such as the legend of Saint Brendan (Brandon or Brandan) found their way onto maps and remained there for centuries. Saint Brendan (*c.* 484–578) was an Irish monk who undertook a voyage in search of Paradise, which he assumed was an island somewhere in the Atlantic. After a long series of stirring adventures he found an island of great beauty and fertility. To Saint Brendan it was Paradise, the "Promised Land of the Saints." It was later designated "Saint Brendan's Island." The legend was perpetuated in Latin, French, English, Saxon, Flemish, Irish, Welsh, Breton and Scottish Gaelic. The island itself was located on maps and charts for nearly 1200 years, or until as late as 1759. On a map of 1435 it was associated with Madeira. Martin Behaim (1492) located it west of the Canaries and close to the equator. Later it was moved about 100 miles west of Ireland, and eventually it ended up in the West Indies. Several expeditions were sent out by the Portuguese over a period of nearly two hundred years (1526–1721) to locate it, but the terrestrial Paradise of Saint Brendan was finally conceded to be a mirage.[35]

Nearly as mobile as Saint Brendan's Island was the mythical kingdom of Prester John. About 1150 A.D. a rumor spread through Europe that somewhere in Asia there was a powerful Christian emperor named Presbyter Johannes (with the court title of "Gurkhan"), who had founded the kingdom of Kara Khitai. He had broken the power of the Musselman in his own domain after a fierce and bloody fight. The mysterious Priest-King became a symbol of hope in a Christian world beset by Mongol hordes. Pope Alexander III resolved to make contact with Prester John, and his first step was to address a letter to him (dated 27 September, 1177). The Pope's physician was dispatched to deliver the letter in person. He never returned.[36]

Pope Innocent IV was even more determined than his predecessor, and decided to convert the barbarians instead of trying to conquer them. Dominican and Fran-ciscan missionaries as well as civil ambassadors of peace plodded back and forth between the Pope, the King of France and the Mogul Khan. These travelers soon learned that His Highness Presbyter Johannes and the Christian kingdom in deep-est Asia were probably myths. But the popular fancy was not easily dispelled, and instead of allowing their bubble to be punctured, the people merely transferred the kingdom of Prester John to Africa — specifically Abyssinia. No one knew very much about Abyssinia. A few die-hards like John de Plano Carpini and Marco Polo persisted in the belief that Prester John still reigned in all his splendor deep in the heart of the Orient. On the larger map in Higden's *Polychronicon* the empire of Prester John was located in lower Scythia within the limits of Europe, but on the map of Marino Sanuto it was placed in further India. It was moved again to Central Asia and ended up in Abyssinia. The legend persisted, however, and four hundred years after Pope Alexander III wrote his letter to Presbyter Johannes, Abraham Ortelius, a Dutch map publisher issued a separate map entitled: *Presbiteri Iohannis sive Abissinorvm Imperii Descriptio*. In the upper left corner of the map is a decorative cartouche adorned with the coat of arms of Prester John and a long, genealogical record which traces his royal ancestors back to none other than King David.[37]

The Biblical characters Gog and Magog assumed an important place in the cartography of the Middle Ages. Not only did these characters exist as realities in the medieval mind, they also constituted a dire and ever-present threat to the safety and welfare of the Christian world.[38] According to Aethicus of Istria, a narrator of great tales, Gog and Magog, "and twenty-two nations of evil men," were driven by Alexander the Great back to the very shores of the Northern Ocean. There they were imprisoned on a peninsula behind the Caspian gates and a wall of iron erected with divine aid by Alexander. Rumor had it that Prester John, in a letter to one Manuel Comnenus, wrote that besides Gog and Magog, the region was inhabited by the Anie, Agit, Azenach, Fommeperi, Befari, Agrimandri, Casbei, Alanei and other nations; that these cannibals, who ate their own dead as well as their enemies, were imprisoned behind lofty mountains towards the north.

In this same letter, Prester John expressed the fear in the hearts of all Europeans that eventually, in the days of Antichrist, Gog and Magog with their evil companions would burst forth and spread desolation over all Christendom, that they would overrun the abodes of the saints "as well as the great city of Rome." The dread of this event overshadowed Western Europe for many years. So real was it that Roger Bacon, an enlightened man, recommended the study of geography so that the proper authorities might anticipate the time of the outbreak and the probable direction of the invasion. The belief in Gog and Magog was also widespread in the Orient. There are notices of them in the Koran and in the ninth century an eastern khalif sent out an expedition to locate the ramparts of the evil ones. The report of this expedition was set down in good faith by the Arabian geographer Edrisi. Gog and Magog and their rampart prison became a stock feature of medieval cartography.

Some of the decorative features on medieval maps survived for centuries in one form or another, modified and adapted to the current styles in map making. One of these was the symbolic treatment of the winds. On a tenth century map of the world in the Royal Library of Turin the four wind-blowers are human figures seated on Aeolus bags that bear a striking resemblance to nineteenth-century cannon. With one hand they hold trumpets or horns, and with the other they squeeze the wind out of the bags. This symbol was a remnant of Greek mythology, taken from Homer, who wrote of Aeolus the son of Hippotes, god and father of the winds and ruler of the island of Aeolia. In the *Odyssey* Aeolus entertained Odysseus and gave him a fair wind to hasten his journey and a sealed bag containing the unfavorable winds. Odysseus's crew, of course, opened the bag without permission and the results were disastrous. Figures of the wind-blowers, with or without their Aeolus bags, were popular as late as the seventeenth and eighteenth century. On some maps they appear as heads of old men, on others as cherubs; in some cases the facial expression of the wind-blower and the size of the blast emerging from his mouth told the reader a great deal about the wind without further explanation. For example, the north wind was often an old, grotesque character who looked very unhappy while blowing a gale. Zephyrus ("Zephyr"), the west wind, was often shown as a cherub with what appeared to be a gentle breeze blowing from his lips.

To the majority of Christian worshipers the Crusades (1096–1270) were a God-given opportunity to liberate the Holy Land from the power of the infidel. To the science of cartography they were the first step towards a permanent enlargement of the habitable world. The rumored wealth of the Indies, of Cathay and India, became a known fact. "When one remembers that missionaries like Plano Carpini, and traders like the Venetian Polos, either penetrated by land from Acre to Peking, or circumnavigated southern Asia from Basra to Canton, one realizes that there was, about 1300, a discovery of Asia as new and tremendous as the discovery of America by Columbus two centuries later." [39]

The events leading up to the revision of The Map were many. They began with the invasion of Western Europe by barbarian hordes who descended from the north to conquer and plunder and remained to become militant defenders of the Christian faith. They brought with them the blood of Vikings; they had fearless eyes with which to see as well as the knowledge and experience necessary to travel safely over long distances. They infiltrated, transfused and invigorated Christianity. The Church, in turn, tooled its theology to its new converts, so as to bridle and direct their energies.

The problem was to effect a clerical reform in the fighting layman, to consecrate his baser instincts, to give him an ideal, a noble purpose to fight for. The answer was a Crusade, a large-scale penitentiary pilgrimage under arms, "with the one additional object of conquering the goal of the pilgrimage." [40] Chivalry taught the layman to defend the right, but the object of the Crusade was to attack what was wrong, namely, the possession by "infidels of the Sepulchre of Christ." The Crusades represent the offensive side of chivalry. To the majority of people, the religious motive of the Crusades was all in all. Imbued with a spirit of revivalism, the masses were ready and eager to fight to the death for the liberation of the city of Jerusalem and the Holy Sepulchre. Famine and pestilence in 1094 and 1095 added to the ranks of the first Crusaders, so that it was "no wonder that a stream of emigration set towards the East, such as would in modern times flow towards a newly discovered gold-field — a stream carrying in its turbid waters much refuse, tramps and bankrupts, camp-followers and hucksters, fugitive monks and escaped villains, and marked by the same motley grouping, the same fever of life, the same alternations of affluence and beggary, which mark the rush for a gold-field today." Palestine became a kind of Botany Bay where cutthroats were sent to do penance.[41]

The Church went about the business of sanctifying the means of gaining its end, which was a militant diffusion of Christianity over the whole known world. It was thinking in terms of empire, a universal Church which would inevitably rule the Holy Land. The question was how to transport a fighting force to the East and keep it properly supplied. Military reconnaissances of the routes to Egypt were made for the Crusaders, and guidebooks were available in large numbers, compiled in advance for the annual flood of pilgrims that journeyed every Easter to the Holy Land where they could bathe in the Jordan River, gather palms and see the miracle of fire at the Sepulchre. But in spite of careful planning and preparation, it was necessary for Pope Urban II to rely on outside help in order to launch the First Crusade. In so doing he brought into play a force which soon transformed the Crusades from a religious enterprise into big business, a force which inspired a corrupted papacy to cry Crusade when there was no Crusade. That force was the love of gain.

In September, 1096, the Genoese were solicited by His Holiness "to go with their galleys to Eastern parts in order to set free the path to the Lord's Sepulchre." Sensing a substantial profit in the transaction, the Italians agreed. In the course of time they moved an army of at least 150,000 men, and possibly twice that many, from the southern ports of France to the eastern shores of the Mediterranean, and all during the First Crusade they cruised the coast of Syria carrying arms and provisions to bearers of the cross. They were also in a position to lend a hand in the sieges of Antioch and Jerusalem. At first the situation amounted to little more than a convenient solution to a problem in logistics, but as time and warfare progressed, the Crusading states in the eastern Mediterranean came to depend more and more on the maritime and commercial powers. Pisa and Venice as well as Genoa became interested in the proceedings, but strictly from a commercial point of view. The cost of Crusading rose sharply.

Genoese ships were at Jaffa in 1099, and the same year Dagobert, Archbishop of Pisa, led a fleet from his home port to the Holy Land. The following year, 1100, a Venetian fleet of 200 sail dropped anchor in the port of Jaffa and offered assistance in return for freedom from all tolls and a one-third share in each town they helped to conquer. Each year thereafter new privileges were granted to the Italians and each year greater concessions were demanded in return for supplies and siege artillery. They received tracts of land along the waterfront immune from taxation of any kind. Within a walled compound they set up shop with warehouses and a flourishing bazaar, an independent constabulary and other civic conveniences. Trade was so brisk and profits so high that soon the

Hospitalers and Templars, and even the lowly religious pilgrims, began to peddle merchandise. Holy shrines were all but forgotten and trade became the chief interest of Europeans in the East. "By the time of the Second Crusade the Provençal cities like Marseilles and Barcelona had entered the lists. All Latin Europe which touched the Mediterranean waxed fat on the Oriental trade." [42] In 1124 the Venetians helped the Regent Eustace to capture Tyre in return for certain privileges — freedom from taxation, one fourth of the city of Jerusalem in fee simple, baths and ovens in Acre, and in Tyre itself, one third of the city and suburbs, their own court of justice and their own church. The Venetians maintained their position in Palestine, and their quarters, with those of the Genoese, remained as privileged commercial franchises in an otherwise feudal state. Under Pope Innocent III the Fourth Crusade was planned in the spring of 1200 against Egypt, by then the center of Mohammedan power. The following year envoys went to Venice to negotiate for passage to Egypt. The Venetians were more interested than ever. From Egypt they could easily reach the Red Sea, the wealth of India and the commerce of the Indian Ocean. However they did not allow themselves to be carried away by their enthusiasm. They promised help and ships, for which they were to receive 85,000 marks and the cession of half of the conquests of the Crusaders. That the Crusade never reached Egypt was no fault of the Venetians.

While the Mediterranean bustled with trade and political intrigue, Genoa and Venice sought new markets for the flood of eastern merchandise that was pouring into their warehouses. From Venice a great trade route was pushed northward over the Brenner Pass and up the Rhine to Bruges, an avenue along which municipal development — in Lombardy, Germany and Flanders — took place, where the great towns of the Middle Ages sprang to life, where the trade of the East and the south of Europe made contact with the ramifying activities of the Hanseatic League in the north. The habitable world was soon extended as far as the North Sea and the Baltic.

During the thirteenth century the whole of Europe was Christian; part of Asia Minor had been converted, and there was a Christian kingdom in Palestine. A strong missionary movement, a product of the Crusades, had begun, a peaceful attempt to conquer Moslem souls in opposition to the violent tactics of Holy Warfare. The prospects were good among the Mongols, where there were already many Christians. A peaceful invasion by missionaries and diplomats began in the direction of the empire founded by Genghiz Khan; a kingdom stretching from Peking on the east to the Euphrates and Dnieper on the west. The movement was launched by Pope Innocent IV whose object was twofold. First, he hoped to convert the Great Khan and his people to Christianity. Second, he hoped by judicious inquiry to learn the whereabouts of Presbyter Johannes and eventually to make contact and possibly an alliance with the great Christian empire in further Asia, if such an empire existed. A third object, though it was never alluded to directly, was to sound the depths of Oriental wealth that had captured the imagination and whetted the appetites of all Europe.

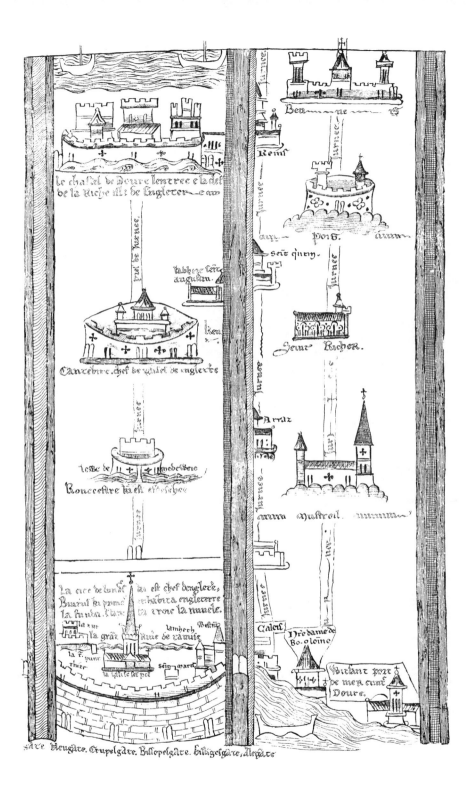

This medieval road map guided religious pilgrims from London to Jerusalem.
Dover Castle (*upper left*) and Calais (*lower right*) mark the channel crossing.

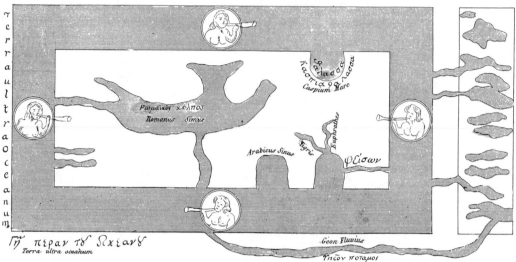

The world of Cosmas, about 548 A.D., was patterned after the Tabernacle.
Four great rivers in Paradise supply the waters of the earth.

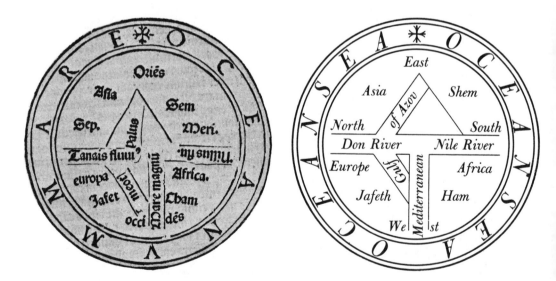

The world of Isidore, Bishop of Seville (570–636 A.D.) was extremely simple.
The T–O map at left, from his *Etymologies*, is explained by diagram at right.

The emissaries sent out by Innocent IV were missionaries, of course, but there was a difference. They were learned men instead of religious zealots, trained diplomats and skillful observers who knew the specific gravity of gold and the difference between a precious jewel and a false one. First to go was Friar John de Plano Carpini, a companion and disciple of Saint Francis of Assisi. Loaded down with gifts, he set out from Lyons, then the residence of the Pope, on Easter day, 1245. Accompanied by an interpreter, Benedict the Pole, Carpini crossed the Dnieper, the Don and the Volga rivers. At the Volga the two men began the second leg of their journey, "so ill," Carpini wrote, "that we could scarcely sit a horse; and throughout all that Lent our food had been nought but millet with salt and water, and with only snow melted in a kettle for drink." On the feast of Saint Mary Magdalene (July 22) they reached the imperial camp called Sira Orda ("Yellow Pavilion"), near Karakorum and the river Orkhon, having ridden through bitter weather nearly 3000 miles in 106 days. There they found ahead of them between three and four thousand envoys and deputies from all parts of Europe and Asia, all bearing tribute and homage to His Imperial Highness. For all their pains, Carpini and his companion were dismissed, finally, with a curt letter in Mongol, Arabic and Latin which did little more than assert to whom it might concern that the Khan's office was the scourge of God. All was not lost, however, because Carpini produced a long, detailed account of his journey, the earliest important Western work on Northern and Central Asia, Russian Europe and other regions of the Tartar Empire.[43]

The second of a long series of missions to the Great Khan was undertaken by William of Rubruquis, another Franciscan friar (c. 1215–1270). Friar William was sent out by Louis IX ("Saint Louis") after His Majesty had failed, diplomatically, in an exchange of envoys with the Mongol leader of Armenia and Persia. Great emphasis, therefore, was placed on the fact that Friar William was about to make an extremely informal, friendly call on the Tartar prince Sartak. In 1252 Friar William crossed the Black Sea from Constantinople and landed at Sudak in the Crimea, then an important trans-shipping point between the Mediterranean and the southern part of Russia. Fitted with horses and wagons to cross the steppes, the friar's party visited the "courts" or nomad camps of Sartak and Batu his father. They were detained at the Volga by Batu, who finally referred them to the Great Khan himself in the remote regions of Mongolia near Karakorum. There they arrived December 27, 1253, and there they remained until about the 10th of July, 1254. On the return journey the party again visited Batu's camp and did not reach Tripoli until August 15, 1255.

The account of this mission, written by William of Rubruquis, is rated as one of the best travel narratives in existence, despite the limitations of his dragoman or interpreter and his own dog-Latin. He was a keen observer and gathered a remarkable mass of information concerning the Asiatics, the geography and ethnology of the region, the manners and customs of the people as well as their language and religion. Diplomatically his mission, like others before and after him, was a failure, but his detailed report on Asia was an important contribution to the mass of information which was slowly confirming the existence of a great continent lying beyond the old limits of the habitable world.[44]

The diplomatic success of the three Venetian brothers Polo in their dealings with the Great Khan was as spectacular as their approach was informal. Maffeo, Marco and Nicolo were merchants, working in and around the Crimea and Constantinople. From the Crimea a series of chances and speculative transactions brought them first to the court of Barka Khan at Sarai, then to Bolgher (Kazan), and eventually across the steppes to Bokhara. There they fell in with envoys of the great Khan Kublai, who convinced the Polos that it would pay them to visit the Lord of Lords and see some of the wonders of Cathay (China). They found Kublai either at Khanbaligh ("the Khan's city," that is, Peking) which he had just rebuilt, or at his summer retreat at Shangtu, north of the Great Wall.[45]

Kublai Khan gave the Polos a reception without precedent. He listened eagerly to their amazing descriptions of the Latin world, its customs, its culture and its Christian religion. Kublai was not particularly interested in the hereafter or the ultimate fate of his soul, but like other monarchs who used organized religion as a means of gaining a political end, he perhaps saw a way of taming his barbarian Mongols. He sent the Polos home as his personal envoys to the Pope, and gave them letters to His Holiness requesting that a group of educators be sent to his court to teach the people about the western arts and about Christianity. This mission marked the beginning of an open-door policy in Asia which lasted about a hundred years, or to the middle of the fourteenth century. It might have lasted longer if the Christian Church had responded in good faith. As it was, the Khan fell back, eventually, on Buddhism as a civilizing agent.

After two years at home the Polos started back to Cathay empty-handed. Pope Clement IV had died and no one had replaced him. Moreover, Nicolo's wife had died and left their fifteen-year-old son Marco to shift for himself. So the brothers Polo took young Marco along to China. At Lajazzo on the Cicilian coast, the last outpost of European merchants trading in Asia, the Polos learned of the elevation of a new Pope who called himself Gregory X. They hurried back to Acre and there obtained from His Holiness a papal reply to Kublai. They were not so fortunate when it came to a tangible response to the Khan's request for educators. Instead of the hundred teachers he asked for, the Pope was able to enlist only two men, both Dominicans, and before the first leg of the journey to Mongolia was over, the two had grown weary of the hardships and turned back.

The three brothers and young Marco went on alone, starting from Acre about November, 1271. They followed a long, circuitous route, apparently abandoning at the last minute a plan to go by way of the Persian Gulf and the Indian Ocean. After traversing Kirman and Khorasan they moved on through Balkh and the hills of Badakshan. They ascended the upper Oxus through Wakhan to the plateau of Pamir, so called for the first time by young Marco. These regions, incidentally, were hardly described again by any European traveler till the expedition of Lieutenant John Wood in 1838.[46] Crossing the Pamir, the Polos descended through Kashgar, Yarkand and Khotan (Khutan), a region thereafter unknown to Europe until after 1860. Next the travelers reached the vicinity of Lop-Nor (next visited by Prejevalsky in 1871). They crossed the Gobi Desert to Tangut, the extreme northwestern part of China, then so called. Welcomed by the Khan's people, the Polos were at last escorted into his presence at Shangtu, in the spring of 1275. By this time young Marco ("the young bachelor") was a seasoned traveler and about twenty-one years old.

Kublai took a special interest in the young man and was fascinated by his ability in learning the numerous languages of the empire. Finding Marco discreet as well as clever, Kublai began to use him in the public service. One mission took the young man through the provinces of Shansi, Shensi and Szechuen and the borders of Tibet, to the remote province of Yunnan, called Karajang by the Mongols, and into Northern Burma (Mien).[47] For three years Marco governed the great city of Yangchow, just within the Great Wall. As he rose in the Khan's favor, Marco was sent more often on distant missions; in the course of time he traversed the greater part of the Mongol empire besides taking an important part in civil administration. The Polos, one and all, soon amassed great wealth, according to European standards, and contrary to the Great Khan's wishes they wanted to take it back to Venice where it could be converted into European affluence. Moreover, they were dubious about their future security if the Khan should happen to meet with an untimely death. The opportunity came unexpectedly.

In 1286, Arghun, Khan of Persia, lost his favorite wife, whose last wish was that her place should be taken only by a lady of her own Mongol tribe. Ambassadors were sent to Peking to look for a suitable bride for their ruler. The request was courteously received by Kublai Khan, and Cocacin (Kukachin), a girl of seventeen, was selected. Warfare among some of the tribes residing between Peking and Tabriz made the return trip to Persia a hazardous overland journey, so Arghun's envoys proposed to return home by sea. And having met the Polos, they begged Kublai Khan to let the Venetians escort them. The Khan reluctantly consented. The party sailed from Zaiton or Amoy Harbor in Fukien, early in 1292, handsomely equipped for the long journey and bearing friendly greetings from Kublai Khan to the Pope, and to the kings of France, Spain and England. There was a long delay in the journey when the Polos reached the coast of Sumatra and another in the southern part of India, so that two years elapsed before their ship arrived in Persia. Meanwhile two of the envoys had perished along the way and the prospective bridegroom Arghun Khan had died. After delivering the young lady into the safekeeping of Arghun's brother, the Polos continued on to Venice, probably by way of Tabriz, Trebizond, Constantinople and Negropont. There they arrived about the end of 1295.

Marco Polo wrote his *Book* while languishing in the prison of Genoa, following a political altercation between Venice and Genoa. There, too, he acquired the nickname *Marco Millioni*, because of his frequent use of astronomical figures in describing his experiences and the marvels of Cathay. But in spite of his faults and the weaknesses of his editors and translators, Marco Polo emerges as the greatest traveler and explorer of the Middle Ages. He unrolled the map of Asia to its eastern limits and traced a route across it, "naming and describing kingdom after kingdom which he had seen." He was "the first to speak of the new and brilliant court which had been established at Peking; the first to reveal China in all its wealth and vastness, and to tell of the nations on its borders; the first to tell more of Tibet than its name, to speak of Burma, of Laos, of Siam, of Cochin-China, of Japan, of Java, of Sumatra and of other islands of the archipelago, of the Nicobar and Andaman Islands, of Ceylon and its sacred peak, of India but as a country seen and partially explored; the first in medieval times to give any distinct account of the secluded Christian Empire of Abyssinia, and of the semi-Christian island of Sokotra, and to speak, however dimly, of Zanzibar, and of the vast and distant Madagascar." At the same time, "he carries us also to the remotely opposite region of Siberia and the Arctic shores, to speak of dog-sledges, white bears and reindeer — riding Tunguses." [48]

While the principal contribution of the Polos was in the realm of geography and cartography, they also did much to aid the cause of Christianity. By their diplomacy and tact they succeeded in gaining the confidence and respect of the Mongol Khan, where thousands before them had failed. The apostles of Christianity who later traveled eastward found a smooth path and a fertile field, so that by 1350 the Mongol world had been so well worked that Christian missions and Christian bishops were established from Persia to Peking, and from the Dnieper River to the fastness of Tibet.

The militant diffusion of Christianity in the crusading era produced a change in the course of history which was entirely unpredicted. Christianity furnished the fringes of civilization with a deity and a theology, but in so doing its apostles were exposed to an entirely new world, hitherto beyond their comprehension. The old fables were exploded, but for a while they were replaced by equally fantastic tales contributed by Christian pioneers who had seen with their own eyes the marvels of the world beyond the horizon. Not only the Polos of Venice but Monte Corvino and Friar Odoric (d. 1331) probed the interior of China; Jordanus had traveled in India and Pascal in Central Asia.[49] These and other ambassadors of Christianity had returned home and made their reports. The merchants of all countries produced tangible evidence of wealth in Asia and parts of Africa in the form of fine textiles, gold, silver and precious gems. The general upheaval in Europe caused by the Crusades disrupted the complacency of man and broadened his mind in spite of himself. The average European had either marched in a Crusade or knew someone who had. Religion was still important but fanaticism was on the wane. Man was torn from ancestral customs and ancestral homes. He saw and heard new things, and consequently began to think new thoughts. He learned how to tolerate and compare, and how to criticize. He was presented with new food for scientific thought and poetic imagination. He began to study geography and write history as well as poetry. He learned about new plants and fruits: sugar and maize, lemons, apricots and melons. New processes of spinning and weaving came from the Orient; he learned how to make muslin and damask. He learned some very handy tricks of warfare — the most important being the fascinating effect of gunpowder when used against an enemy. He added new words to his vocabulary such as "tariff" and "corvette." After the Crusades, European man was never quite the same again.

Once having tasted the sweets of the Orient, the Christian Church was not to be put aside or stopped by the death of a Kublai Khan or because the Mongols finally chose to follow the teachings of Mohammed instead of Jesus Christ. Nor were merchants and kings content to let Asia go by default merely because the borders were closed and overland travel was brought to a halt. The "Indies," a generic term which sometimes included Asia, India and the Malayan Archipelago, became the goal of civilization in general and Western Europe in particular. They remained the most cherished commercial prize in the world for more than two hundred years after the discovery of North and South America. The burning question was how to get there when both the overland route across Asia and the Red Sea route were closed. The answer to that question was the answer to many others; and it was the search for a water route to the Indies that ultimately unrolled the map of the world to the south and to the west, revealing the continent of Africa and the important island groups of the Atlantic.[50]

During the Crusades, France dominated the European scene and became the most considerable power in Europe. But because of the enormous carrying trade entailed by the Holy Wars, the republics of Venice and Genoa steadily rose in power as well as maritime skill. Genoese ships, in particular, roamed the Mediterranean at will, carrying the world's merchandise, seeking new markets and likely spots along the coast to fortify and colonize. About 1270, just before the second journey of the Polos and while the Seventh Crusade was in progress, a Genoese fleet under Lancelot Malocello sailed out through the Strait of Gibraltar and after a cruise of some length rediscovered the Fortunate Islands. The accounts of this cruise are vague, and it is not clear whether their islands corresponded to the Canaries *and* part of the Madeira group or only the Canaries. However the approximate position of Malocello's discovery was close enough to warrant naming the islands according to the Greek, Roman and Phoenician designation. In 1291 Tedisio Doria, a prominent Genoese, conducted a great expedition in search of a water route to the Indies, the object of which was strictly commercial. With Ugolino de Vivaldo in command of a second galley, Doria sailed south along the west coast of Africa beyond Gozora (Cape Nun in 28° 47′ north latitude) far into the dread Sea of Darkness or the "Green Sea of Gloom" as the Moslems called it. Almost certainly before the outbreak of the Hundred Years' War (1338) the Madeira group and probably several of the Azores were discovered by Italian seamen. By 1345 the Madeiras were named, all except the Formigas.[51]

An interesting sidelight on the course of maritime exploration in the Atlantic Ocean concerns Diniz, the "Laborer-King" of Portugal and founder of the National University at Lisbon. In 1317 Diniz began the task of creating a navy. He promptly imported one Emmanuel Pezagno from Genoa and bestowed upon him the title of Lord High Admiral of Lusitania. Also imported to serve under the Lord High Admiral were twenty Genoese mariners who were to act as pilots and captains as well as instructors to the Lusitanean fleet. The terms of the original contract stated that the admiral and his successors were bound to *maintain* this number of Genoese officers in Portuguese service. The Portuguese marine, then, which became the foremost maritime power of the world a hundred years later, was founded and perpetuated by a cadre of Genoese navigators.[52]

After a detailed survey of the Canaries was made in 1341 under the leadership of Nicoloso de Recco of Genoa and a mixed crew, Portugal allowed the islands to go almost by default to Spain, whose Don Luis obtained from Pope Clement VI a grant to the Fortunate Islands and the title of Prince of Fortune as a vassal of the Apostolic See. With the title went the privilege of paying a yearly tribute of 400 gold Florentine florins. The transfer of title to the Canaries also marked the entry of Catalan, Castilian and French navigators into the field of Atlantic exploration and colonization. In 1346, on the feast of Saint Lawrence (August 10), a Catalanian vessel under Jacme Ferrer left Majorca to search for the River of Gold (supposedly the Western Nile) and in the course of time his ship apparently rounded Cape Bojador which represented the jumping-off-place, the "Finisterre" of the habitable world to the south. And in 1364 French mariners from Rouen and Dieppe sailed far below Cape Bojador, and soon established a flourishing coastal trade between Cape Verde and the Bight of Benin in the Gulf of Guinea. This commerce, it is said, lasted over fifty years and was abandoned only because of civil war at home.[53]

Several factors combined to make Portugal the greatest maritime and colonizing power in Europe during the period of discoveries (1415–1499). Its people comprised a mixture of Moors and Mozarabs in the south, Galicians in the north, Jews and foreign Crusaders everywhere. The Portuguese had fallen heir to the best and worst qualities of mankind; the most highly developed culture was combined with the most primitive barbarity. The result was a people of unusual courage, ingenuity and greed. They had inherited the best in science from the Arabs, and had acquired by purchase the navigational skill developed in Italy. Situated on the southwesternmost tip of Europe, with a long coast line and fine harbors, Portugal was an ideal training ground for mariners who could sail "outside." And in the fifteenth century the ability of Portuguese seamen to navigate was a matter of stark necessity as well as a technical accomplishment. Intercourse by land between Portugal and other European countries was effectively blocked by Aragon and Castile. Portuguese goods, therefore, were moved by sea to England, Flanders and the Hanse towns in Northern Europe. Any new markets would have to face the ocean. Moreover, the crusading spirit was still strong in Portugal. "To make war upon Islam seemed to the Portuguese their natural destiny and their duty as Christians." The Order of Christ founded by Diniz, on the dissolution of the Templars, was both wealthy and powerful, and under the direction of Prince Henry the Navigator, the vast resources of that Order were consecrated to the maritime expansion of Christianity.

Henry of Portugal, Duke of Viseu and Governor of Algarve, surnamed the "Navigator" (1394–1460), was the third son of John (João) I and Philippa, daughter of John of Gaunt. It is doubtful whether Dom Henry ever sailed beyond the sight of land, but without question he was the foremost patron of the art of navigation up to his time. His enthusiasm for maritime exploration has been attributed to many causes, some without foundation; but certain facts about him can hardly be denied, even in the absence of documentary evidence.[54] Azurara, the historian, gave five reasons why his Lord Infante Dom Henry was moved to order a search for the lands of Guinea. First, he wanted to find out something about that part of the world beyond the islands of Canary and Cape Bojador, "for that up to this time, neither by writings, nor by the memory of man, was known with any certainty the nature of the land beyond that Cape." To this end, a charter was issued October 22, 1443, prohibiting anyone from making a voyage beyond Cape Bojador without his permission. No one in Christendom, read the charter, knew about the region, "nor did they know whether there were people there or not, nor in the sea charts and maps was anything beyond Cape Bojador depicted except what seemed good to the makers." Dom Henry, therefore, had sent fourteen expeditions to bring back full details, and had ordered a chart made of the coast and any islands that might be discovered.[55]

Second, if there happened to be colonies of Christians beyond the Cape and safe harbors to anchor in, it was likely that many unusual kinds of merchandise might be brought into the kingdom in exchange for Portuguese goods, and at a great profit "to our countrymen," wrote Azurara. A third reason was that if the Moors in Africa were as numerous and powerful as they were said to be, and if there were no Christians among them, it would be sensible for the said Lord Infante, "as every wise man is obliged by natural prudence," to learn the strength of the enemy and the extent of his power.

The fourth reason, said Azurara, was that during the thirty-one years the said Lord Infante had warred against the Moors, "he had never found a Christian king, nor a lord outside this land, who for the love of our Lord Jesus Christ would aid him in the said war. Therefore he sought to know if there were in those parts any Christian princes, in whom the charity and the love of Christ was so ingrained that they would aid him against those enemies of the faith." More specifically, Prince Henry wanted information about the land of Prester John and about the Indies. And the fifth reason was Henry's great desire "to make increase in the faith of our Lord Jesus Christ and to bring to him all the souls that should be saved. . . ."[56]

If the charter of 1443 meant what it said, it indicated a desire on the part of navigators to do a little exploring on their own without reporting back to Prince Henry; in other words, they had to be restrained in the interests of the kingdom. But Azurara, on the other hand, seemed to think none dared to sail beyond Cape Bojador, because mariners still believed that beyond that point "there is no race of men nor place of inhabitants; nor is the land less sandy than the deserts of Libya, where there is no water, no tree, no green herb — and the sea so shallow that a whole league from land it is only a fathom deep, while the currents are so terrible that no ship having once passed the Cape, will ever be able to return." [57]

In all things, Prince Henry was an energetic leader, and seems to have carried out successfully the five purposes listed by Azurara, with the exception of locating Prester John and enlisting his support in warring against the Moors. He wanted facts about the coast of Guinea (that is, Africa) and the Western Ocean. About 1415 the first of a series of exploring expeditions began, under the command of John De Trasto. There were many sorties against the Moors along the coast and colonizing ventures in the Madeiras and Canaries, but every sea captain who left port under the flag of Prince Henry was encouraged as well as ordered to round Cape Bojador and report back on what he found. And each returning captain was questioned sharply by Dom Henry; the charts were studied and plans were made to refit for sea at the earliest opportunity. In 1419 Dom Henry was made governor of the kingdom of Algarve in the southernmost province, and the settlement of the "Infante's Town" (*Villa do Iffante*) began at Sagres, close to Cape St. Vincent. There a naval arsenal was constructed and there Prince Henry spent a great part of his life.

In 1434, after many captains had failed, one of Henry's ships, commanded by Gil Eannes, rounded Cape Bojador, and the following year Affonso Gonçalvez Baldaya, the king's cupbearer, sailed fifty leagues beyond. By 1436 Portuguese navigators had almost reached as far south as Cape Blanco. In 1441 Prince Henry, whose maritime projects had been scoffed at as costly and absurd, hit pay dirt. That year Antam Gonçalvez brought back from beyond Bojador a load of slaves and gold dust from the coast of Guinea. From then on co-operation from court officials and skeptical navigators was never lacking. That same year Nuno Tristam pushed south as far as Cape Blanco. Volunteer merchants and seamen promptly forgot the perils of the Sea of Darkness and journeyed from Lisbon, Lagos and other distant towns to offer their services to Prince Henry.

In 1442, Tristam reached the Bay or Bight of Arguim, which was soon fortified and made the center of slave-raiding forays. Between 1444 and 1446 more than thirty ships bearing the license of Prince Henry sailed for Guinea. Tristam and Diniz Diaz reached the Senegal in 1445, and the same year Diaz rounded Cape Verde. In 1446 Alvaro Fernandez sailed beyond the cape at Dakar to a point 110 leagues beyond Cape Verde, or almost to Sierra Leone.

This was probably the most southerly point reached by Portuguese explorers until 1460, the year Henry the Navigator died. But many important side explorations were made. For instance, John Fernandez spent seven months among the natives of the Arguim coast and returned to Portugal with the first trustworthy European account of the Sahara region. Alvise Cadamosto, a Venetian navigator in the service of Prince Henry, visited the Madeiras and Canaries, and coasted the West Sahara area in 1455. He explored the Senegal River, which, he reported, had already been traversed about sixty miles up. He explored the mouth of the Gambia and while there observed the "Southern Chariot" (Southern Cross) in the heavens. The following year he sailed again for Henry. After doubling Cape Blanco on his way down to the Senegal and parts south, his ship was blown offshore by violent gales. One such ill wind literally drove him to the discovery of the Cape Verde Islands. After exploring Boavista and Santiago he returned to the African coast and visited the Gambia, the Rio Grande and Geba rivers.[58]

Henry the Navigator was both resourceful and diplomatic in financing his maritime enterprises, especially in the early years when his government watched the funds trickle away and waited time and again for something to return. Dom Henry was Grand Master of the Order of Christ and his ships sailed under its flag. He made no bones about using the revenues of the Order to finance his expeditions or its name to gain the official recognition of Pope Eugenius IV, when discoveries were made in behalf of Christendom. Later, when his exploring voyages began to pay off, he graciously bestowed upon the Order many privileges in the newly discovered lands, including the tithes of Saint Michael in the Azores and one half of its sugar revenues; the tithe of all merchandise from Guinea; the ecclesiastical dues collected at Madeira, and other perquisites. The arrangement proved mutually satisfactory to the parties concerned.

Prince Henry bore the title of "protector of Portuguese studies." Actually he was more of a "patron" or sustaining buttress. He is said to have founded a professorship of theology and perhaps one in mathematics and one in medicine at the University of Lisbon; likewise in 1431 he is said to have provided living quarters for both teachers and students. Some have said that he founded a school of navigation and cartography, but João de Barros, the historian, says merely that Henry employed one Master Jacome from Majorca and certain Arab and Jewish mathematicians to instruct his captains and pilots more fully in the art of navigation and the making of charts and nautical instruments. There was also a Master Peter, who inscribed and illuminated maps for the Prince. Cadamosto, one of his captains, reported that in his day (1455), Portuguese caravels were the best sailing ships afloat, and Pedro Nunez (Petrus Nonius, 1492–1577), Portuguese mathematician and geographer, wrote that Henry's navigators were well instructed and well supplied with the instruments and rules of astronomy and geometry, "which all map-makers should know." Henry the Navigator may never have founded a school where formal instruction was given in mathematics, astronomy, navigation, and map making, but he most certainly did the next thing to it. Whether his men learned their lessons in a classroom or on the deck of a caravel makes little difference. He saw to it that his ships were well equipped and his men well informed, and when they reported a new discovery he expected a full, detailed report with charts to back it up. His most important contribution to map making was his revival of scientific method: training his men to apply mathematics and astronomy to their navigation and the charting of strange waters. His persistence and inspiring leadership brought fame to the Portuguese marine and fortune to the crown. Under Alphonso V the Gulf of Guinea was explored, and under John II (1481–1495) the fortress of São Jorge da Mina (Elmina) was founded in 1481–1482 for the protection of the Guinea trade. In 1482 Diogo Cam (Cão) discovered the Congo and in 1486 reached Cape Cross (21° 50′ S.).

The climax of Portuguese explorations along the west coast of Africa came in 1488. It was a triumph great enough to satisfy even Dom Henry, had he lived to see it. In August, 1487, Bartholomeu Diaz de Novaes, a cavalier in the household of King John II, sailed from Lisbon with three ships. His course was the same as usual — south, and if possible, further south. He sailed past Cape Cross and on to Diaz Point, south of Angra Pequena or Lüderitz Bay (26° 38′ S.) where he erected a monument on shore. From there, according to Barros, he ran to the south before strong winds for thirteen days, whereupon the weather grew stormy and the wind freshened to gale force. After things had cleared somewhat he set his course to the east for several days, looking for the coast he had lost but knew must be there. Failing to sight it he finally turned north, and so hit the southern coast of Cape Colony at Mossel Bay (*Bahia dos Vaqueiros*) half way between the Cape of Good Hope and Port Elizabeth. The date was February 3, 1488. Coasting eastward, he passed Algoa Bay (*Bahia da Roca*). At this point Diaz began to have trouble with his crew, who had had enough for one trip, but he persuaded them to sail on to the estuary of the Great Fish River (*Rio do Iffante*). Here he could plainly see the northeasterly trend of the coast. It was enough. The great land mass of Africa could be rounded; the Indian Ocean, enclosed as an inland sea since Claudius Ptolemy and the second century, was open water to the south; an ocean route to the Indies was found at last.[59]

Charts and the Haven-Finding Art

NAVIGATION," wrote Thomas Blundeville, "is an Art which teacheth by true and infallible rules, how to governe and direct a Ship from one Port to another, safely, rightly and in shortest time: I say heere safely so farre as it lyeth in mans power to performe. And in saying rightly, I meane not by a right line, but by the shortest and most commodious way that may be found. . . ." In order to accomplish this feat safely and commodiously, Blundeville and others recommended certain standard equipment. "Item, an universall Horologe, or Diall, to know thereby the houre of the day in every Latitude, and a Nocturnall able to know thereby the houre of the night." For long voyages he recommended a "Topographicall instrument to describe thereby [that is, trace] those strange Coasts and Countries" one might encounter. Also desired was a "Mariners compasse," and last of all a mariner's "Carde" or chart, by means of which, with the aid of "certaine Tables made of purpose," you could tell what way your ship had made.[1]

The kind of a chart Blundeville had in mind and the one he went on to describe was a sheet of paper with nothing on it but a series of wind roses, a large one in the center connected with the others by radiating lines or rhumbs. It was a chart on which to lay off a course and plot the distance and direction of the day's run at sea. It was essentially the same in function and design as the modern "ocean" or "small scale plotting chart." On the modern version graph paper is used and the wind rose of Blundeville's day has been replaced by the modern compass rose graduated numerically from 1 to 360 degrees.[2]

A second kind of chart, and the one with which this story is concerned, was the *portolano* or harbor-finding chart, originally designed to accompany the early coast pilots (peripli). Which came first in the history of navigation is a question. The coast pilot was a book designed to aid mariners in negotiating stretches of coast line and intricate harbor approaches; it described the location of reefs and shoals and prominent points along the shore from which a mariner could get a bearing. The portolan chart was a supplement that evolved from the need of more graphic descriptions of navigational hazards and from the inadequacy of words to describe the various situations a pilot might encounter in the course of routine coastwise sailing. The portolan chart, then, was a coastal chart conceived by seafaring men and based strictly on experience with the local scene, that is, with the coasts and harbors actually used by navigators to get from one place to another. This was in contrast to the early maps of the world as a whole, and of countries and provinces, which were projected academically and geometrically for the use of a small group of scholars. From the fragmentary documents that have survived, we know that in the early stages, the evolution of the mariner's chart ran a course parallel to the development of general geographical maps and that except for certain distances between places contributed by inquisitive fellows such as Strabo, Marinus and Ptolemy, chart makers had very little in common with geographers and the men who struggled to map the world.

The history of sea charts and their makers is even more difficult to trace than maps and the men who compiled them, for next to professional lawbreakers, no group of people in the history of mankind has been more reluctant to keep records than professional sailors. They were philosophers without benefit of school tie, mathematicians of necessity rather than conviction, astronomers without an observatory other than the deck of a ship. They kept their knowledge to themselves.

The men who went "down to the sea in ships" and ventured forth upon great waters, surrounded themselves with an air of mystery that was both pleasant and convenient. Neither deep-sea fishermen nor merchant skippers ever had any desire to dispel it. On the contrary, they carefully fostered it, traditionally refusing to divulge by what magic means they were able to navigate from place to place. A shorter route between two ports, or between a fishing ground and home, was money in the pocket in ancient times, even as it is today. In the beginning, mariners made their own charts, by dint of hard labor and at the peril of their own lives. Such trade secrets as they contained were guarded with care, and early sea charts were either worn out from constant use or were destroyed — willfully and with malice aforethought. And why not?

Historians tell us that before the invention of the mariner's compass, navigation was restricted to coastwise sailing, and some go so far as to say it was also limited to daylight hours. It is an interesting supposition and fits the popular and attractive theory that navigation burgeoned, as it were, with the compass rose. But it is a theory unsupported by evidence and one that is contrary to the nature of seafaring men who, like the ant and the bee, seem to have undergone few if any mutations in the past three thousand years or more. Fishermen follow the fish, regardless of life and limb, and fish migrate. Furthermore, who ever heard of a fisherman abandoning a prize school of fish because he lacked a compass or because it was getting dark?

The first important chapter in the history of sea charts and navigation concerns the Phoenicians and their maritime activities some twelve hundred years before the birth of Christ. Much is known about this remarkable people, their history as a nation, their commerce and religion. But the subject of their maritime accomplishments is another matter. They left no records and no charts, only their mark. What they did, where they cruised and where they may have sailed, is recorded only in fragmentary texts and incidental references made by more or less disinterested persons. However, the mark they left on the coasts and islands of the Mediterranean was deep and indelible, and there is little doubt that later developments in navigation and the evolution of accurate sailing charts are the by-products of Phoenician sea lore.

The Phoenicians were an offshoot of one of the Semitic tribes who called themselves Canaanites.³ Sidon, the "first-born" of Canaan is classed (Genesis X) as one of the descendents of Ham. In their early struggle for existence the Phoenicians occupied a modest portion of Syria on the coast between the Eleutherus River (Nahr el-Kebīr) on the north and Mount Carmel on the south. Theirs was the land of Canaan. In the Old Testament and on ancient Assyrian tablets, the inhabitants were also called Sidonians. Herodotus tells a story of the founding of Tyre (Sur, Surru or Sarra) 2300 years before his time, that is, about 2756 B.C. "Tyre," said Strabo, "is wholly an island, being built up nearly in the same way as Aradus [Ruad]; and it is connected with the mainland by a mole, which was constructed by Alexander when he was besieging it; and it has two harbours, one that can be closed and the other, called 'Aegyptian' harbour, open. The houses here, it is said, have many stories, even more than the houses at Rome, and on this account, when an earthquake took place, it lacked but little of utterly wiping out the city. The city was also unfortunate when it was taken by siege by Alexander; but it overcame such misfortunes and restored itself both by means of the seamanship of its people, in which the Phoenicians in general have been superior to all peoples of all times, and by means of their dye-houses for purple, for the Tyrian purple has proved itself by far the most beautiful of all; and the shellfish are caught near the coast; and the other things requisite for dyeing are easily got; and although the great number of dye-works makes the city unpleasant to live in, yet it makes the city rich through the superior skill of its inhabitants." ⁴

The Phoenicians were essentially a seafaring nation though the ramifications of their commercial enterprises extended far inland and exerted considerable influence in the great trading centers of the world. Their sailors were called "red men" because of their skin, weathered and sunburned from constant exposure to the elements. They mastered many of the "secrets of the sea" and the more important secrets of the heavens, but just how much they knew about the sea and the universe as a whole, and how far they were able to develop the science of navigation, history does not say. Certainly the Phoenicians never said. Their skill and their willingness to sail where others dared not go gave them a peculiar power over more powerful nations bordering on the Mediterranean who depended on them to transport their merchandise and fight their naval engagements for them. They were indispensable to the great political powers. Sennacherib, Psammetichus, Necho, Xerxes and Alexander all depended on them to maintain their supply lines and transport their legions. It was all the same to the Phoenicians. They knew what they had and guarded their secrets concerning trade routes and discoveries, their knowledge of winds and currents, with their lives. The influence of sea power began to manifest itself at an early date, and the Phoenicians were cordially detested in Greece if not elsewhere. They were also feared.

One of the few fleeting glimpses of sea life in the Phoenician world comes from Xenophon, and to anyone familiar with the sea and the men who sail it, it is an important piece of documentary evidence as to the ability of Phoenician navigators to get around. In the *Oeconomicus*, Ischomacus, the Greek, discoursing on the advantages of orderliness, says:

> The best and most accurate arrangement of things I think I ever saw, was when I went to look at the great Phoenician ship. For I saw the greatest quantity of tackling separately disposed in the smallest stowage. You know that a ship comes to anchor or gets under way by means of many wooden instruments and many ropes, and sails by means of many sails, and is armed with many machines against hostile vessels, and carries about with it many arms for the crew, and all the apparatus which men use in a dwelling-house, for each mess. Besides all this, the vessel is filled with cargo which the owner carries for his profit. And all that I have mentioned lay in not much greater space than would be found in a chamber large enough conveniently to hold ten beds. All things too lay in such a way that they did not obstruct one another, so that they needed no one to seek them, could easily be got together, and there were no knots to be untied, and cause delay if they were suddenly wanted for use. I found the mate of the steersman, who is called the prow's man, so well acquainted with the place of each article, that even when absent he could tell where everything lay, and what their number was, as one who has learnt to read could tell the number and order of the letters in the name of Socrates. I saw this man examining, at an unoccupied time, everything that is of use on board a ship; and on my asking him the reason, he replied, Stranger, I am examining whether anything is deficient or out of order; for it will be no time to look for what is wanting, or put to rights what is awkwardly placed, when a storm arises at sea.[5]

There is little agreement among the historians who have dealt with the navigational accomplishments of the Phoenicians, and in the absence of documentary evidence some amazing inconsistencies have arisen. These are worth examining. The one statement which has been most universally accepted is that early navigation among the Phoenicians (no dates are mentioned), was cautious and timid, and restricted to coastwise sailing in sight of land. Later, we are told, the Phoenicians became bolder, and instead of creeping along close to shore, they sailed from headland to headland (always assuming such were available), taking a bearing whenever they came abreast of a new promontory. Following this general introduction to the subject it is customary to discuss the fragmentary allusions to their more spectacular voyages, either real or alleged, trimming the Phoenicians' sails to fit the historian's appraisal of the evidence and his personal opinion as to how much of their original timidity they had overcome. Actually it is not necessary to hold the Phoenicians responsible for the humble origin of navigation, when mankind first took to water, because there is evidence of a Cretan (Minoan) sea power centered at Cnossus in remote antiquity — possibly as early as 3000 B.C. So it is doubtful whether the Phoenician sailors were ever a part of the timidity era of navigation.[6]

The limited coastwise navigation of the Phoenicians prior to the invention of the compass is difficult to reconcile with the colonial empire established in the Mediterranean at the height of their power, about 850 B.C. From Sidon and Tyre on the coast of Syria they moved out towards the west in their armed merchant-men. Homer knew of them plying Greek waters before his time. Later they established a number of trading stations on the islands of the Aegean and in the Isthmus of Corinth. There, among other things, they gathered the mollusk from which they extracted murex, the purple dye used in their flourishing textile in-dustry. They did not settle in the Adriatic but they sailed it from one end to the other. Later they occupied the southern coast of Sicily and the western shore of the toe of Italy at Temesa and Medma. Eventually they took Melite (Malta), Gaulos (Gozo), Cossyra (Pantellaria), Lampas (Linosa), Lopedusa (Lampedusa), lying between Sicily and the African coast. Sardinia and Corsica were partially colonized, but it was in the west that they found trade and exploration most to their liking. From the Gulf of Sidra to Tangier, the African coast was theirs; likewise the Balearic Islands. Carthage and Utica, situated on the Bay of Tunis, dominated the western Mediterranean and became the center of their commercial activities. The wealth of Spain poured into Tarshish, the region of Tartessus in the southwest. There the Phoenicians controlled rich mines of silver and other metals, not to mention a lucrative fishing monopoly. Beyond the Pillars of Hercules they built a seaport town near the mouth of the Guadalquiver which they called Gadeira or Gades (Cadiz). From their ocean port they worked the African coast line southward, founding Lixus (El-Araish), and ventured as far as the Subur (Seboo, Sebou) River. They found the Canary Islands, about sixty miles off the African coast.[7]

Carthage, according to Strabo, was founded by Dido, who brought a host of people from Tyre. The move was a great success; so much so that according to Strabo, even to his day the best part of Continental Europe and also the adjacent islands were occupied by Phoenicians. Moreover, they gained possession of "all that part of Libya which men can live in without leading a nomadic life," in other words, all but the desert. They not only developed Carthage into a rival of Rome, but also waged three wars against the Romans. Although the Phoenicians were finally wiped out, they had, up to the time of their encounter with Scipio Aemilia-nus, "Three hundred cities in Libya and seven hundred thousand people in their city [Carthage]." After the second war with the Romans, Strabo reported, the Phoenician naval power was limited by treaty to twelve ships. "But at Byrsa, the acropolis of Carthage, where the military had taken refuge, there were stores of seasoned timber and a great many skilled ship-builders in hiding." While the Romans patrolled the outer harbor the Phoenicians went to work, and in two months they had built 120 decked ships, dug a canal to the sea and sailed forth to battle. "But though Carthage was so resourceful," wrote Strabo, "still it was captured and razed to the ground."[8]

Thus far the exploits of the Phoenician fleet do not have the sound of a primi-tive effort undertaken in an unfamiliar medium. From Tyre and Sidon in Syria they maintained regular communication with their colonies at the western end of the Mediterranean 2200 miles away. Shore crawling and island hopping may have been in vogue, but even so, there are still some long stretches between points and islands to be accounted for. From Mizratah to Benghazi, across the Gulf of Sidra, is 250 miles as the crow flies. From Cagliari on Sardinia to Bizerte on the African coast is 120 miles. From Malta to Alexandria it is 820 miles and to Port Said 940 miles. Strabo explained some of these riddles when he said the Phoenicians were "philosophers in the sciences of astronomy and arithmetic, having begun their studies with practical calculations and with night-sailings . . . and if one must believe Poseidonius, the ancient dogma about atoms originated with Mochus, a Sidonian, born before the Trojan times." In another place he said that the Little Bear had not been marked as a constellation until the Greeks learned about it from the Phoenicians who used it for purposes of navigation.[9]

Aside from the unanswered question as to how the Phoenicians sailed from place to place, the most controversial subjects relate to their monopolistic commerce in tin and amber and their alleged circumnavigation of Africa. There is no question about the fact that tin arrived in the eastern markets or that the Phoenicians brought it in their ships. According to Ezekiel, some of it came from Spain. "Tarshish was thy merchant by reason of the multitude of all kind of riches; with silver, iron, tin, and lead, they traded in thy fairs."[10] More tin came from the Cassiterides or Tin Islands (probably the Scilly Islands, 30 miles west-southwest of Land's End), which Strabo said were ten in number, lying near each other in the high sea to the north of the port of the Artabrians (Cape Finisterre in northwest Spain). "One of them is a desert, but the rest are inhabited by people who wear black cloaks, go clad in tunics that reach to their feet, wear belts around their breasts, walk around with canes, and resemble the goddesses of Vengeance in tragedies. They live off their herds, leading for the most part a nomadic life. . . . Now in former times," Strabo continued, "it was the Phoenicians alone who carried on this commerce (that is, from Gades), for they kept the voyage hidden from everyone else. And when once the Romans were closely following a certain ship-captain in order that they too might learn the markets in question, out of jealousy the ship-captain purposely drove his ship out of its course into shoal water; and after he had lured the followers into the same ruin, he himself escaped by a piece of wreckage and received from the State the value of the cargo he had lost."[11] After long perseverance the Romans found the way to the Cassiterides, and Publius Crossus inspected the mines himself. He found the tin close to the surface and the people friendly. The only drawback was the journey thither, across "a wider sea than that which separates Britain from the continent"; probably the Bay of Biscay.

Amber or "electrum" was sold by the Phoenicians to the Greeks and Romans in great quantities. Most of the ancient writers agree that it came from the Baltic, where it is now almost exclusively obtained, especially the promontory of Samland. Tavernier (1605–1689) said that in his time amber was found exclusively on the coast of Ducal Prussia, cast up by the sea, and that the gathering of it was a monopoly of the Elector of Brandenburgh. Pliny said it was brought from the shores of Northern Germany to Pannonia. There the inhabitants passed it on to the Veneti at the head of the Adriatic, who carried it into Italy. In the

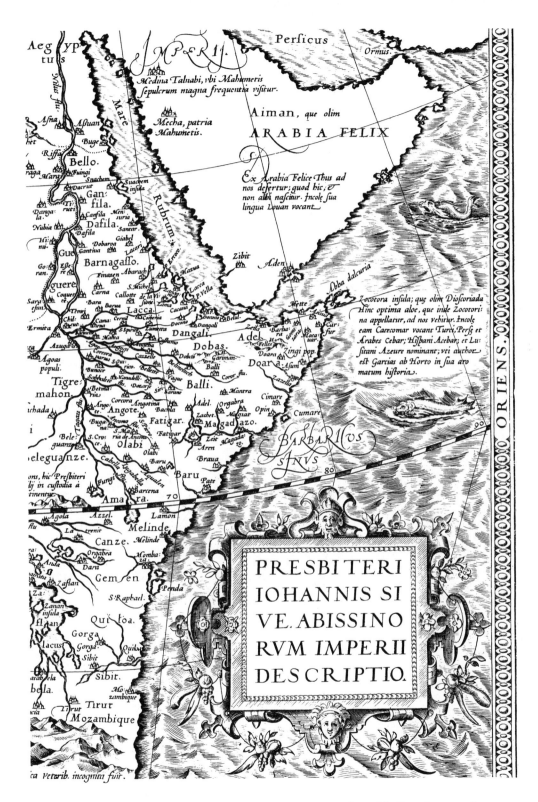

The mythical kingdom of Prester John was perpetuated on this Dutch map of 1573.

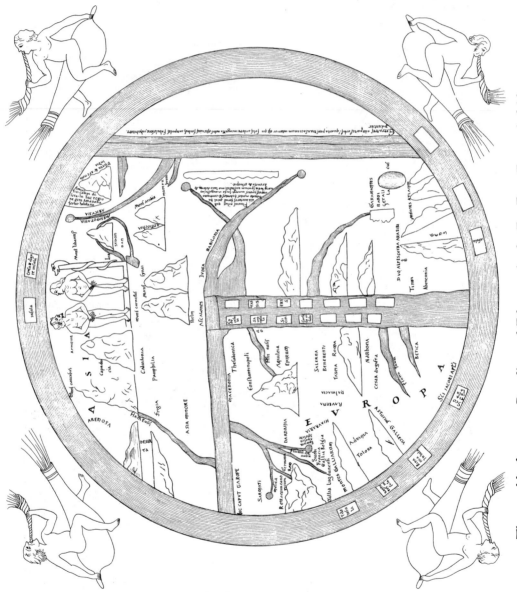

The world of 900 A.D. Paradise and Eden are in the Far East. Four wind blowers are releasing the winds of the earth from their Aeolus bags.

Middle Ages there was a commercial route from the Upper Vistula to Southern Germany, which, passing through Thom and Bresslau, reached the River Waas, and from there descended the Danube. The question is — where did the Phoenicians get their amber? Did they make the long voyage up the coast of Europe and around into the Baltic, or did they buy it at trading stations established by some unexplained means at the head of the Adriatic? The Phoenicians did not say.[12]

The story of the circumnavigation of Africa by the Phoenicians concerns Necho, King of Egypt, a son of Psammetichus who reigned from 616 to 600 B.C. The project was the result of Necho's impatience and frustration. He wanted a canal dug to connect the Nile with the Red Sea. The work was begun, but many things went wrong. After 120,000 laborers had died in the cause, an oracle came to the rescue of the remainder and suggested to Necho that it would be best to give up the project, which he did. But the king grew restless and after conducting a series of military depredations with armed vessels in the Red Sea and the Mediterranean, he invaded Syria. His contacts with the Phoenicians in that region doubtless inspired him with the idea of connecting the Red Sea and the Nile the hard way. At any rate, according to Herodotus he sent out a fleet manned by Phoenicians, with orders to sail from the Red Sea southward until they rounded Africa, assuming that it could be done. From there they were to return to Alexandria by way of the Western Ocean and the Pillars of Hercules.[13]

Herodotus went on to say that the Phoenicians sailed for the southern sea; and when autumn came they put in, beached their ships and sowed the land. After the harvest they resumed their voyage, and "so after two years had passed, it was in the third that they rounded the Pillars of Hercules and came to Egypt." Now Herodotus did not question the credibility of the voyage as a whole, but he discounted it on the basis of a single point: the one point, incidentally, which confirms the story. The Phoenician sailors reported "what some believe, though I do not," said Herodotus, that when they rounded Africa and set a course to the west and north, they had the sun on their right hand. This meant, of course, that they were sailing below the equator.[14]

The arguments against the marvelous exploits of the Phoenicians are legion. Voyages as long as from Cadiz to the southern Baltic, or from the Red Sea to Gibraltar by way of the Cape of Good Hope did not seem too fantastic to talk about in the days of the ancients, but today they do imply the existence of sound ships, skillful sailing, and navigational aids such as instruments and charts that the Phoenicians were not supposed to have. Rennell, for example, states that the mean rate of sailing for Phoenician ships was thirty-five miles a day, but he does not give a satisfactory explanation of how he arrived at such a figure. Other critics list numerous insuperable difficulties connected with a primitive attempt to round Africa which are supposed to prove the impossibility of such a voyage. Yet the Phoenicians were faced with no more hazards than Christopher Columbus, who accomplished the theoretically impossible with perhaps no more to work with than the Phoenicians had.[15]

The Phoenicians left no charts for historians to criticize. The Greeks and Romans did no better, for although there are a few fragmentary textual allusions to their geographical maps, nothing at all was written, apparently, concerning navigational charts, that is, coastal maps for the use of seafarers. The "charts" of Marinus, written about by Ptolemy, were charts in name only and represent a translator's choice of words; and even though they are concerned with distances between places, many of which were over water, they cannot be considered as navigational aids in any sense of the word.

One of the principal clues to the existence of mariner's charts as early as the fourth or fifth century B.C. is a coast pilot or periplus: *"Scylax of Caryanda, his circumnavigation of the sea of the inhabited part of Europe and Asia and Libya."* This document is in effect a pilot of the Mediterranean Sea, similar to the modern textual descriptions issued for the use of mariners the world over. And like our modern pilots, the periplus of Scylax was written to accompany a chart of some kind, a chart which no longer exists.

The periplus of Scylax is the oldest and most complete coast pilot which has survived.[16] Its language is simple and its descriptions, although too brief, were no doubt lucid enough for the wary navigator of ancient times who probably relied as much on his senses and experience as he did on someone else's description. No bearings are given and few linear distances between ports; distances are usually reckoned according to the number of days of sailing. These reckonings, incidentally, give the lie to those historians who expound the timidity and caution of ancient navigators. For example, Scylax wrote, "The sailing along Libya from the Canopic mouth [of the Nile] in Egypt to the Pillars of Hercules, reckoning being made according to that used in Asia and in Europe [that is, 50 miles for an average day's run], takes 74 days *if one coast round the bays.*" This statement implies that there was a shorter way — sailing across the bays in a straight line, ignoring the historians who would have the boats run up on the beach every night at sundown, assuming that there was always a beach at hand. Night sailing is frequently mentioned. Scylax said, "In this region is the Greek city of Massilia and port, also the Massilian colonies Taurois, Olbia and Antium. The coasting of this bit from the river Rhodanus to Antium [the Rhone to Anzio] *takes four days and four nights*"; and again, "From Carthage hither to the Pillars of Hercules with most favorable navigation is a *seven days and seven nights sail.*" Clearly it was a much longer sail if the wind was not favorable or the weather was foul. A night's sail can mean only one thing — just what it says. And if a ship were under sail four days and four nights crossing the Ligurian Sea from Antipolis (Nice) to the island of Elba, her skipper was neither coasting nor was he at a loss to know how to navigate a ship.

A second document of ancient times, dating from the fourth or fifth century A.D., is a periplus entitled *Stadiasmus, or circumnavigation of the great sea* (that is, the Mediterranean and the Black Sea). This coast pilot, likewise designed to be used with a chart, reads much more like a modern pilot than the periplus of Scylax. In his preface, the anonymous author said, among other things, that he would give numerous distances that separate Europe and Asia; that he would indicate distances between the important islands and their relation to the mainland, how many and how large they were. He would describe how they look to the navigator and with what winds they can be safely approached. The entries in the *Stadiasmus* are brief and to the point and nearly always there is a comment on the presence or absence of fresh water. "From Antiphrae to Derra," says the *Stadiasmus*, "there is anchorage during the summer, and the place has water — 90 stadia." And again, "From Phoenicus to Hermaea, 90 stadia; anchor with the cape on your right; the place has water in a tower." Another entry reads, "From Hermaea to Leuce Acte, 20 stadia; hereby lies a low islet at a distance of two stadia from the land; there is anchorage for cargo boats, to be put into with west wind; but by the shore below the promontory is a wide anchoring-road for all kinds of vessels. Temple of Apollo, a famous oracle; by the temple there is water." [17]

Regardless of the *Stadiasmus* and other fragments of sailing directions, there is no true mariner's chart known which was made during the first thousand years of the Christian era, and yet there must have been some. A sea chart is mentioned by Raymond Lull in his *Arbor scientiae* which dates from the crusade of Saint Louis in 1270 A.D., but the earliest specimen extant is at present the chart of Petrus Vesconte dated 1311. This priority claim, however, is open to debate, as there are several specimens known which might be construed as sea charts if a scholar felt the urge to prepare a brief in their behalf.[18]

At the outset, sea charts, by their very nature, were destined to be removed from the academic realm and from general circulation. They were much more than an aid to navigation; they were, in effect, the key to empire, the way to wealth. As such, their development in the early stages was shrouded in mystery, for the way to wealth is seldom shared. There is no doubt that the complete disappearance of all charts of the earliest period is due to their secret nature and to their importance as political and economic weapons of the highest order.

The development of charts took place in three general phases. First came surveys of the local scene in numerous localities, charts of a harbor, an island or a short stretch of coast line. The second phase, not necessarily in sequence, involved the charting of large bodies of water and long reaches of coast line, such as the Mediterranean Sea, its islands and important harbors, the Black Sea and the Sea of Azov, the Caspian Sea and the Indian Ocean. This kind of chart, embodying a great many smaller ones of the local scene drawn to various scales, was slow to evolve and slower yet to accept revision of any kind. The third and final phase in the mapping of the "seven seas" began when a universally acceptable prime meridian of longitude was fixed, when the linear value of a degree of arc was more or less agreed upon, when continents were linked by an uninterrupted series of charts, with accurately measured oceans between them. All this took time — about 2000 years if we choose to ignore the Phoenicians and say that it could not have happened because there are no records to prove it.

The early hydrographers made several important contributions to the science of cartography. From the very beginning these men were utterly practical in their approach and there was nothing academic about what they produced. Their charts were designed as "aids to navigation," and on them there was no room for theory. They treated in a simple, direct way the problems which concerned navigators and ignored the rest. The safest place for a navigator and his ship is deep water — beyond soundings. It is when he heads for shore that he inevitably heads for trouble. Then he wants an accurate picture of the coast line he is approaching, with the location of prominent points from which he can check his position in relation to his chart. He must know the location of reefs and shoals and submerged rocks before he gets to them, not after. He wants to know distances from place to place, and above all he must know *direction*. *Distances* are important on sea charts, but *direction* is even more so. Arriving late at a destination may be inconvenient or even hazardous, but without an accurate knowledge of direction a navigator will never arrive at all.[19]

The mathematicial expression of direction was developed by the astronomers of remote antiquity, but a scheme for expressing it either orally or on a map or chart in conventional terms was slow in developing, especially one that was universally acceptable to all nations. Chart makers gave *direction* to cartography by evolving the wind rose; they "quartered" the winds before the compass quartered the globe. The requirements of navigators were met by a chart projection that made possible directional navigation, that is, laying out a straight-line course and sailing it on the curved surface of the ocean.

Direction, to the average man who lived prior to the Christian era, was elementary and based on the needs of his daily existence, which were for the most part limited. "Towards the darkness" was north and "towards the light" referred, in a general way, to the south. At the same time the heavens were divided, according to Heracleitus, into four quarters: the Bear (north), morning (east), evening (west), and "the region opposite the Bear" (south). Slightly more complicated were the terms used by Poseidonius and Polybius, as recounted by Strabo. Besides "the darkness" and "the light," the "equinoctial rising" and "equinoctial setting" (east and west respectively), four intermediate directions were introduced: "summer sunrise," "summer sunset," "winter sunrise" and "winter sunset" (roughly northeast, northwest, southeast and southwest). But, as Strabo pointed out, such terms "are not absolute, but relative to our individual positions; and if we shift our position to different points, the positions of sunset and sunrise, whether equinoctial or solstitial, are different." [20]

It was perfectly natural for the ancients to think of direction in terms of the winds and the places from which they were supposed to blow. Winds as well as the sun were associated with good and evil; they brought with them blessed rain and accursed floods, heat and drought as well as temperate growing weather. They were life and death, wealth and privation. In describing the winds, the ancients displayed a primitive sort of meteorology. Aristotle and his sect, wrote ßlundeville, "doe define the Winde to bee an exhalation hot and drie, engendred in the bowels of the Earth, and being gotten out, is carried side-long upon the face of the Earth." He does not have a vertical motion, "because that whilest by his heate hee striveth to mount up and to passe through all the three Regions of the Ayre, the middle Region by his extreme cold, doth alwayes beate him backe, so as by such strike, and by the meeting of other exhalations rising out of the Earth, his motion is forced to be rather round then [*sic*] right." [21]

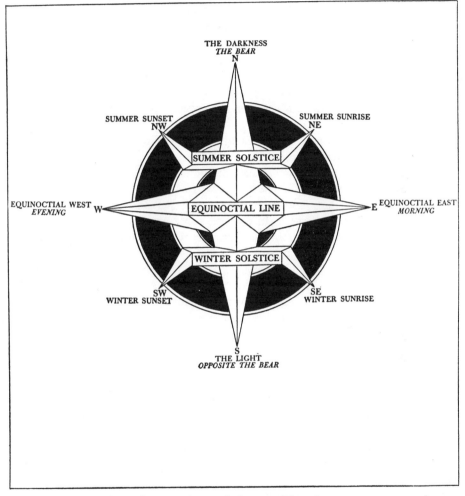

A reconstruction of an ancient wind rose. Directions were not precise and their modern equivalents are only approximate.

Apparently there were only four winds commonly known to ancient civilization, although people must have been aware of others. "And upon Elam will I bring the four winds from the four quarters of heaven, and will scatter them toward all those winds. . . ." (Jeremiah XLIX. 36). They blew from the north, east, south and west. "And after these things I saw four angels standing on the four corners of the earth, holding the four winds of the earth. . . ." (Revelation VII. 1). Homer wrote of only four winds: Boreas, Eurus, Notus, and Zephyrus. Strabo observed, "there are some writers who say that there are only two principal winds, Boreas and Notus; and that the rest of the winds differ from these only by a slight variation of direction — Eurus blowing from the direction of the summer sunrise [northeast], Apeliotes blowing from the direction of the winter sunrise [southeast], Zephyrus from the direction of summer sunset [northwest], Argestes from the direction of winter sunset [southwest]." There was, in fact, a looser distinction between the east and west winds than there was for the north and south, for directions related to the sun, such as the "summer sunrise" and the "winter sunrise," were transitory. Even the two most commonly used names, Zephyrus and Eurus, were applied loosely to winds ranging from northwest to southwest and northeast to southeast, or better than 46° of arc. Additional confusion arose when writers described a wind that blew from a specific place. Homer said that Boreas and Zephyrus blow from Thrace, though he did not imply that they originated there.

In the vicinity of the Mediterranean there were certain winds that did not seem to blow from any one of the principal quarters of the sky. These were usually given local names and sometimes were personified according to the weather they brought with them. In Greece, for example, the cold east wind of springtime and the balmy east wind of autumn were two different persons, one evil and the other good. The Euroaquilo of Crete and the Skiron of Athens were strictly local winds. Euroaquilo (a combination of Eurus and Aquilo), is mentioned in connection with the voyage of Saint Paul (Acts XXVII. 12–14) "And whereas it was not a commodious haven to winter in, the greatest part gave counsel to sail thence, if by any means they might reach Phenice, to winter there; which is a haven of Crete, looking towards the south-west and north-west . . . But not long after there arose against it a tempestuous wind, called Euroaquilo."

Like Euroaquilo, there were other names that described wind direction in a rather loose way. Greco was a wind of the Middle Ages that was used in Italy to designate the northeast. Greco was also used in Spain, even though it did not blow from Greece. Septentrio replaced Boreas and Arctos as the north wind, but the name was applied loosely, referring to the region of the seven stars of the Plow or Great Bear. The name Meridies for the south wind, used in place of Notus or Auster, referred to the direction of the midday sun. Oriens and Occidens (east and west) were also called Levante and Ponente in Italy.[22]

Strabo recognized two fixed winds, Boreas and Notus (north and south) and two moveable winds, Eurus and Zephyrus (east and west). Hippocrates said there were six winds, but there is some uncertainty as to where they blew from. Aristotle seems to have been the first to suggest a subdivision of the four cardinal winds into three parts, making a wind rose of twelve.

According to Vitruvius, Eratosthenes modified the circle of twelve winds, reducing it to eight. This scheme was carried out in the Tower of the Winds at Athens, built about 100 B.C. The building has eight flanks facing the eight winds, each adorned with an emblematic figure in relief and labeled Boreas, Kaikias, Apeliotes, Euros, Notos, Lips, Zephuros and Skiron. In his *Natural History*, Pliny mentioned two systems, one of four winds and one of twelve. "The Moderne sailers of late daies," he wrote, "founde out a meane betweene both: and they put unto that short number of the first, foure winds and no more, which they tooke out of the later. Therefore every quarter of the heaven hath two winds apeece. From the equinoctiall sunne-rising bloweth the East wind *Subsolanus:* from the rising thereof in Mid-winter, the Southeast *Vulturnus.* The former of these the Greekes call *Apeliotes*, and the later *Eurus*. From the mid-day riseth the South wind [*Auster*]: and from the sunne-setting in Mid-winter the Southwest, *Africus.* They also name these two *Notus* and *Libs*. From the equinoctiall going downe of the Sunne, the West wind *Favonius* commeth, but from that in Summer season, the North-west *Corus;* and by the same Greekes they are tearmed *Zephyrus* and *Argestes*. From the North-waine or pole Arctike, bloweth the North wind *Septentrio:* betweene which and the Sunne-rising in the Summer, is the Northeast wind *Aquilo*, named *Aparctias* and *Boreas* by the Greekes." [23]

The rose of twelve winds is found in Seneca and later writers down to the sixteenth century and the *Margarita Philosophica* of Georgius Reisch, but with Latin names appended. At the beginning of the ninth century, Charles the Great revised the wind rose which, in the Teutonic languages, gave names to only the four cardinal points, and devised from the old Latin winds a twelve-point rose with Frankish names.

This nomenclature for the twelve-point rose was carried over to the eleventh century, surviving in a single manuscript, since burned. But it appears again in the literature of the fourteenth century with variations which indicate that a system of sixteen winds was current at the same time. Commenting on the Frankish names applied to this wind rose, Oronce Finé pointed out in his *De Mundi Sphera* that in any wind rose, if the names of the intermediate winds were compounded from the four cardinal winds, as in Charlemagne's system, monosyllabic terms would have to be used for the four cardinal points; simple names such as Nord, Est, Sund and Oëst. This was done, and Flemish mariners, especially those who dwelt in Bruges, adapted the Frankish names of the winds. Moreover, there is a persistent rumor that the names of the thirty-two points of the compass as they are still used throughout the world, were framed by the pilots of Bruges.

The Latin rose of twelve winds was accepted throughout the Roman Empire from Egypt to Spain and was common throughout the Middle Ages. Most of the fifteenth and sixteenth century editions of Ptolemy's *Geographia* give the rose of twelve winds. The transition from the twelve wind rose to the thirty-two, with eight primary winds subdivided into half-winds and again into quarter-winds, began with a simplification process. The twelve winds were reduced to eight, and colloquial names were substituted for the cardinal points. Oriens became Levante and Occidens became Ponente. Ostro (Italian form of Auster) was substituted for Meridies. Garbin or Lebex became Africo with Libeccio, Labetes or

Le Bex as synonyms. In his *Instrvction Novvelle . . . touchant l'art de nauiguer*, Antwerp, 1581, Michiel Coignet gave his impression of the current names of the eight winds in Italian and French:

Tramontana	— *Nort*	Mezzodi	— *Sud*
Griego	— *Nortest*	Garbino	— *Sudoëst*
Levante	— *Est*	Ponente	— *Oëst*
Syrroccho	— *Sudest*	Maistro	— *Nortoëst*

Portuguese mariners seem to have been quick to adopt the Flemish designations of the winds in preference to the Italian. In the *Arte de navegar* of Pedro de Medina (Valladolid, 1545) the Flemish names are given on roses of four, eight, twelve and thirty-two points. Roderigo Zamorano, in his *Compendio del arte de navegar* (Seville, 1588) also used the Flemish names.[24]

The modern compass is a combination of the ancient rose of the winds (*Rosa ventorum*) and a magnetized needle. The wind rose evolved separately, and was no more than a convenient way of partitioning the circular horizon. Names of winds were used to express direction instead of numerals or degrees of arc. The naming of the winds was as natural and elementary as the naming of the stars. It was likewise natural that the wind rose should eventually be used in connection with that greatest of all instruments for finding direction — the compass needle.

The origin of the magnetized needle of iron or steel is obscure, to say the least. Every country with any patriotism and a shred of evidence has claimed the invention for its own, but the earliest use of the compass needle is implied rather than clearly stated. This is unfortunate, since so many other claims and counterclaims of exploration and discovery are based on whether or not there were compasses to steer by. In the absence of documentary evidence regarding the early use of the compass, all voyages such as those of the Phoenicians must remain doubtful — and yet . . .

The earliest references to the subject deal with the loadstone, an iron ore called magnetite; also known as "adamant" and in Latin as *Magnes*. This mineral "hath two marvellous great and secret properties or vertues, the one to draw steele or iron unto it, and the other to shew the North and South part of the world." [25] The first of these virtues was known to the ancients of eastern and western civilization. The attractive power of the loadstone appears in the writings of Plato and Euripides; it is also found in early Chinese writings. In a Chinese dictionary finished in A.D. 121, the loadstone is defined as "a stone with which an attraction can be given to a needle." Lucretius (*c.* 98–55 B.C.) wrote of the same phenomenon and on the behavior of the magnet produced by touching iron with the loadstone.

In the Nordic sagas there are numerous references to the *Leidarstein*, in German Leitstein (loadstone), a word similar in formation to *Leistern* meaning the guiding, or polestar. There is also a "gloss" in the Saga of Floki, the discoverer of Iceland (874) which says that the reason Floki carried ravens to help him determine the direction of land, was that "in northern lands those who sailed the

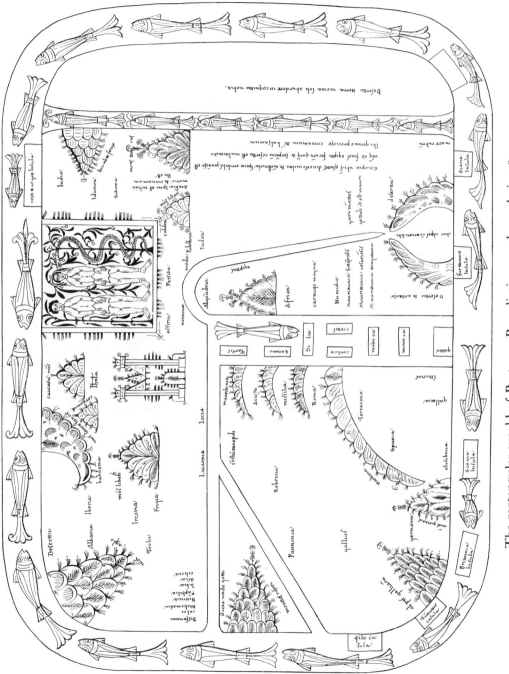

The rectangular world of Beatus, a Benedictine monk, made in 787 A.D.

The world of Andrea Bianco, 1436 A.D., was still surrounded by the Ocean Sea.
Paradise is in the East (*top*). To the left of it are the tribes of Gog and Magog,
held in check by Alexander the Great.

ORBIS TERRARVM EX MENTE POMPONII MELAE DELINEATVS A P. BERTIO.

Christianissimi   SEPTENTRIO   Regis Geographo

Life on Antichthon, below the equatorial ocean, was impossible, said the Church, because the Ark with all survivors of the Flood landed north of it on Mt. Ararat.

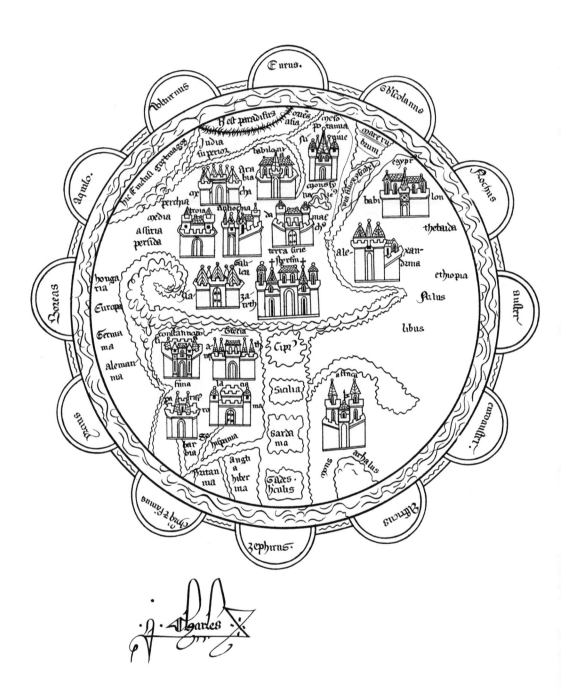

A map of the world made in the time of Charles V, between 1364 and 1372.
The world is surrounded by twelve winds.

sea had not the load-stone." The date of the gloss has been established as *c.* 1225 A.D. Moreover, the loadstone is found in various parts of Norway, and it is not unlikely that the Vikings used its attractive powers in navigating strange waters — possibly as early as 1000 A.D. when, legend says, they reached North America and discovered Wineland or Vinland.[26]

Although there are various kinds of magnetite, the small deposits of polar-magnetic ore are by no means common. Besides the Scandinavian countries, there are deposits in the Urals. Blundeville, writing at the beginning of the seventeenth century, said that those loadstones are considered best "which are found in the East Indies upon the Coast of China, and Bengala, which is no shell but a whole stone of sanguine Colour like to Iron, and is firm, massy, and heavy, and will draw or lift up the just waight of it selfe in Iron or Steele . . . such stones are commonly sold for their waight in silver." [27]

Several of the early sagas of the Faröe Islands (170 miles northwest of the Shetlands), colonized by the Danes, mention the loadstone floating in a container. This sort of apparatus, either a floating piece of loadstone or magnetized needle, was the primitive form of mariners' compass and was used throughout the Mediterranean and in the Baltic as early as the twelfth century. Guyot de Provins, writing about 1190 A.D., expressed the wish that the Holy Father, like the polestar (*la tresmontaine*), would remain immovable in the heavens and guide the sailor to a safe harbor. But when the moon and stars are hidden by clouds or darkness, the poet continues, the sailor can use an unfailing means of fixing and steering his course. All he has to do is put into a basin or bowl of water a straw pierced by a needle that has first been rubbed with an ugly brown stone which draws iron unto itself. The point of this floating needle will always turn towards the polestar. Another writer of the same period put it another way, saying that even when obscured by mist or storm, the polestar continues to guide the sailor by remote control, because like a magnet it has the power to attract iron. And if an iron needle is attached to a piece of cork and rubbed with a loadstone and the whole thing is floated in water, the needle will always point to the north.[28]

One Brunetto Latini, in a work written about 1260 A.D., said that Roger Bacon had shown him a magnet, a stone, black and ugly, to which iron fastened itself. And if a needle were rubbed with the stone and then floated on a straw, it would always point towards *the star*. Bacon himself described some such device in his *Opus Minus*, written in the second half of the thirteenth century. But the earliest definite mention of the use of the mariner's compass in the Middle Ages is found in the writings of an Englishman, Alexander Neckam of St. Albans, who was born in 1157. He joined the Augustinian Order and taught at the University of Paris from 1180 to 1187. In a treatise entitled *De Utensilibus*, Neckam mentioned a needle carried on shipboard, which, when balanced on a pivot and allowed to come to rest, showed mariners their direction even when the stars were obscured. In a second work, *De naturis rerum*, he wrote, "Mariners at sea, when, through cloudy weather in the day which hides the sun, or through the darkness of the night, they lose the knowledge of the quarter of the world to which they are sailing, touch a needle with a magnet, which will turn round till, on its motion ceasing, its point will be directed towards the north." [29]

In 1269 there appeared "a small work attributed to one Petrus Peregrinus, a pretty erudite book considering the time." It was indeed a pretty erudite little manuscript, as Gilbert said, but whether it owed its origin to the writings and opinions of Friar Roger Bacon the Franciscan, as some have said, is a question. These men were contemporaries, and both were far ahead of their times so far as original research and careful observation of facts were concerned. Petrus Peregrinus (Pierre de Maricourt) was a practical man who got his name from the village of Maricourt in Picardy. The appellation Peregrinus or Pilgrim came from his having visited the Holy Land as a member of one of the crusading expeditions of the times. In 1269 he was in the engineering corps of the French army then besieging Lucera in Southern Italy, a city which had revolted against the authority of Charles of Anjou, their French taskmaster. Peregrinus was in charge of fortifying the camp, laying mines and constructing offensive weapons such as battering rams and catapults. In the midst of the siege Peregrinus conceived a beautiful solution to a perpetual motion machine which operated on the principle of magnetic attraction. With success and immortality in sight, he sat down and wrote to a friend at home named Picard, telling him not only the story of his marvelous machine, but all about the properties of the loadstone — most of which he, himself, had discovered. His letter of 3500 words, a masterpiece of exposition, and not his perpetual motion machine, gave him the immortality he well deserved. Referring to Petrus Peregrinus, Bacon said, "I know of only one person who deserves praise for his work in experimental philosophy, for he does not care for the discourses of men and their wordy warfare, but quietly and diligently pursues the works of wisdom. Therefore, what others grope after blindly, as bats in the evening twilight, this man contemplates in all their brilliancy because he is a master of experiment."

In his experiments with the loadstone, Petrus Peregrinus was the first to assign a definite position to the poles of a loadstone, and to give directions for determining which is north and which south. He proved that unlike poles attract and similar ones repel. He established by experiment that every fragment of a loadstone is a complete magnet. He was the first to pivot a magnetized needle and surround it with a graduated circle. He determined the positions of objects by their magnetic bearings as is done today in compass surveying. In his perpetual motion machine was the germ of an engine driven by a magnet!

In Part II of his letter, Peregrinus described two compasses; the first was for measuring the azimuth of the sun, the moon or any star. This was actually a floating loadstone attached to a horizontal astrolabe, so to speak, with a wooden or metal vane to measure the degrees. In the second chapter he described "The construction of a better instrument for the same purpose:" [30]

> Select a vessel of wood, brass or any solid material you like, circular in shape, moderate in size, shallow but of sufficient width, with a cover of some transparent substance, such as a glass or crystal. It would be even better

to have both the vessel and the cover transparent. At the center of this vessel fasten a thin axis of brass or silver, having its extremities in the cover above and the vessel below. At the middle of this axis let there be two apertures at right angles to each other; through one of them pass an iron stylus or needle, through the other a silver or brass needle crossing the iron one at right angles. Divide the cover first into four parts and subdivide these into 90 parts, as was mentioned in describing the former instrument. Mark the parts north, south, east and west. Add thereto a ruler of transparent material with pins at each end. After this bring either the north or the south pole of a lodestone near the cover so that the needle may be attracted and receive its virtue from the lodestone. Then turn the vessel until the needle stands in the north and south line already marked on the instrument; after which turn the ruler towards the sun if day-time, and towards the moon and stars at night, as described in the preceding chapter. By means of this instrument you can direct your course towards cities and islands and any other place wherever you may wish to go by land or sea, provided the latitude and longitude of the places are known to you.

As to the source of the magnet's power or "vertue," there were differences of opinion. Pointing as it did to the polestar, it was not too fantastic to suppose as some did that the heavens were the source of attraction, and in particular the North Star. Others, according to Peregrinus, "who were but poor investigators of nature," believed that the power of the loadstone was derived from the veins of ore where the stones were quarried. This theory was all right for those that came from Norway in the far north, but it did not apply when loadstone was actually found in many different parts of the earth. Peregrinus concluded that, "since the lodestone points to the south as well as to the north; it is evident that . . . not only from the north pole but also from the south pole rather than from the veins of the mines virtue flows into the poles of the lodestone." [31]

The loadstone and the magnetized needle were considered fickle in their behavior and were badly maligned by most writers up to the time of William Gilbert of Colchester, a London physician. Gilbert wrote, in his *De Magnete*, 1600, the first scientific treatise on the principles of electricity and magnetic attraction. He tested by repeated experiments every statement that had been made on the subject and afterwards rewrote the literature on the magnet. His greatest contribution to science in general and cartography in particular, was the statement and proof that the spherical earth is magnetic and itself a magnet. His work was done so carefully and thoroughly that no material advance in the science of magnetism was made until 1785 when Charles Augustin de Coulomb established the law of magnetic action. [32]

Gilbert discussed, one by one, the "figments and falsehoods which in the early time no less than nowadays were by precocious sciolists and copyists dealt out to mankind to be swallowed." For example, it was said that a diamond would destroy the magnetic power of the loadstone, but Gilbert proved by experiment that this was not so; that actually the stone would attract iron through the thickest diamonds. He also experimented with a thick barrier of hides, but found that in spite of popular opinion the magnetic force would penetrate the skins undiminished.

Gilbert was equally contemptuous of some of the other peculiarities attributed to the loadstone. "If pickled in the salt of a sucking fish," some said, "there is a power to pick up gold which has fallen into the deepest wells." There were said to be "various kinds of magnets, some of which attract gold, others silver, brass, lead; even some which attract flesh, water, fishes." Stories were current of "mountains in the north of such great powers of attraction that ships are built with wooden pegs, lest the iron nails be drawn from the timber." The loadstone was also credited with marvelous occult powers: it was a prime tool in the hands of burglars because it could draw bars and open locks; it was an effective love potion with "the power to reconcile husbands to their wives, and recall brides to their husbands." But as Gilbert pointed out, "it is very easy for men of acute intellect, apart from experiment and practise, to slip and err." But not he.[33]

Another popular myth that had been "spread abroad and been accepted — even as evil and noxious plants ever have the most luxurious growth," was that onions and garlic destroyed the power of the loadstone and of the compass needle. For this reason, said Gilbert, "Steers-men, and such as tend the Mariners Card are forbid to eat Onyons or Garlick, lest they make the Index of the Poles drunk." In all seriousness Gilbert tested the powers of onions and garlic with as much care as he conducted his other experiments. "But when I tried all these things," he wrote, "I found them to be false: for not onely breathing and belching upon the Loadstone after eating of Garlick, did not stop its vertues: but when it was all anoynted over with the juice of Garlick, it did perform its office as well as if it had never been touched with it: and I could observe almost not the least difference, lest I should make void the endeavours of the Ancients." To further substantiate his laboratory findings, Gilbert inquired into the matter at first hand, questioning several Marines as to their opinion on compass variation caused by garlic fumes. He was told, with emphasis, by those hardy souls that seamen "would sooner lose their lives, then [*sic*] obstain from eating Onyons and Garlick." [34]

The box compass invented and described by Peregrinus had a pivoted needle revolving around a graduated disc similar to an astrolabe, but about forty years later, the wind rose and the pivoted needle were used in combination on the coastal chart of Petrus Vesconti. In fact, 1302 is the traditional date of the "invention" of the mariners' compass by an unknown navigator of Amalfi. But the "invention" consisted merely of mounting the *rosa ventorum* upon the magnetic needle, where it rests today. For at about that time, the end of the thirteenth century, the wind rose of eight principal winds, with subdivisions of half-winds and quarter-winds, was fitted with a metal cap for a pivot, and two or more magnetic needles were fastened on the under side, a design and mechanical contrivance that has changed very little in six hundred years of navigation. The earliest known compass card marked with the initials of the names of winds is that ascribed to Jachobus Giraldis (1426), in the Biblioteca Marciana in Venice.

The "points" of the compass and the rose itself, were transposed to sea charts, with lines (rhumbs) radiating from each of the thirty-two points which were supposed to give a navigator his sailing direction.[35]

Early Italian compass roses with eight principal winds or compass points were marked with Gothic capitals, using the initials of the Italian winds. However, there were variations of this scheme, for instead of marking the east point with an L for Levante, that point was more frequently marked with a cross. The west point, Ponente, was sometimes indicated by a setting sun. There were other variations on the Italian compass rose introduced at different times and in different localities, but there were three points that remained constant: G for Greco (northeast), S for Scirocco (southeast) and M for Maestro (northwest).

The most variable point on all compass cards as far as designation and symbol are concerned, was north, now universally indicated by a fleur-de-lis. In the pre-compass era, the names used for north on maps and charts were derived from various sources. Some came from astronomy. Others were taken from the names of the winds which were supposed to blow from the north, such as Boreas, Hyperboreas, Aquilo and Tramontana. These not only symbolized the wind that blew from the north, but also the North Pole Star (Stella Tramontana). As a result, after the invention of the compass the letter T was commonly used to denote the north point. But there were other symbols used as well, such as a star or a group of seven stars (Septentrio). Some map makers used a narrow dart-like triangle extending from the center of the rose to the northern edge; others used a trident.

The fleur-de-lis, or "Prince of Wales' feathers" as sailors used to call it, was a late addition to the compass rose, and has never been found in the wind rose of a map or chart prior to the year 1500. As a decorative motif and heraldic emblem the fleur-de-lis is ancient, dating back at least to Byzantine times and probably to ancient Egypt, where it evolved from the lotus ornament. It was adopted by the early kings of France, by the dukes of Anjou and by the Bourbons. Just how it became a part of the compass rose, no one knows, but one of the less fantastic theories is that the fleur-de-lis is nothing more than a glorification of the T for *Tramontana*. However, there is an equally sensible explanation which steers closer to the development of the rose of the winds itself. The fleur-de-lis in its present conventional form has often been attributed to Clovis, the founder of the Frankish monarchy. The design is said to have been used instead of a sceptre at the proclamation of Frankish kings. It is possible that when Flemish mariners adopted the Frankish names for the winds they also adopted the heraldic symbol of the Franks and, centuries later, applied it as a sort of trade-mark to the wind rose of Charlemagne.[36]

Prior to 1600, sea charts, both manuscript and printed, were often beautifully colored, and the compass rose was the artist's big chance. There he could take liberties and embellish to his heart's content a figure which was an attractive design to start with. He used brilliant colors and sometimes gold and silver leaf. But there was also a method in some of his coloring. He designated the principal winds, the half-winds and the quarter-winds with different colors. For example, on Italian charts of the fifteenth century the principal winds were done in gold, the half-winds in green and the quarter-winds in red. Moreover, these three colors were carried out in the rhumbs or loxodromes radiating from the central compass rose across the chart, which made it easier for the navigator to follow a given line from the compass rose to some other point on the chart.

From the earliest days, the compass needle did not always point true north, but for a long time no one suspected the reason. Some of the Mediterranean pilots blamed it on the compass makers and faulty workmanship. This is not surprising, because at the time compass steering first came into general practice, magnetic declination in mid-Mediterranean was almost negligible and was for the most part ignored. In the thirteenth century the declination was slightly westward. In 1350 it was zero, and slightly eastward from then to 1655. Gradually, by comparing notes and keeping careful logs, it began to dawn on pilots and navigators that declination or variation of the needle was a reality and that on some voyages it was appreciable enough to reckon with, if a captain wanted to make port.

General acceptance of the fact came slowly and reluctantly, varying, no doubt, with the locale in which compass variation was observed. In some places it was appreciable and consequently easy to accept as a fact, but in other places, where the variation was only slight, it was much easier to dismiss the whole thing by blaming the man who had hammered out the needle or placed it on the card. And there were a few die-hards like Pedro de Medina, an able navigator of wide experience, who flatly denied the existence of declination, saying that if the compass did not show the pole, the fault lay in the construction of the instrument and nothing else, except careless observation on the part of the men using it. All agreed, however, that if the needle did not point to true north, something should be done to correct the fault. An irreverent helmsman might give the binnacle a kick or two accompanied by a few lusty curses when the mate had his back turned, but it never helped. A more effective way of "adjusting" the compass was to set the needle slightly askew beneath the card to compensate for the amount of declination observed in a given place. Instrument makers soon began to do this before selling their instruments, so that for the time and place of origin, the compass, at least on the face of it, did not vary from true north. In the Levant, compasses that were manufactured in Sicily, Genoa or Venice had their needles set three quarters of a point to a point eastward. Instruments made in Spain, Portugal, France and England had the needle set half a point to the east. This sort of practice usually took care of the situation temporarily, especially when a compass was to be used only on short cruises, but as Gilbert pointed out, it was a sloppy thing to do and tended to obscure the facts which lay behind the mystery of variation.[37]

The real test of the theory of compass declination came when men began to navigate the Western Ocean or "Ocean Sea." Then the compass began to act very strangely. On his first voyage in 1492, Columbus noted that far from pointing true north, his compasses showed a declination most of the time, depending on the longitude, and that rarely ever did they point true north as they did at a point 2½° east of Corvo in the Azores, where, he reported, there was "no variation." Credit for making the first fundamental observations concerning the declination of the compass needle is not universally conceded to Columbus, although the facts were established about that time, and were certainly apparent to such explorers as Cabot and Verrazzano who sailed across the Western Sea. But few navigators other than Columbus had the task of quieting the panic and suppressing the mutiny in a superstitious crew when word got around that the compass was misbehaving. In addition to all their other woes, an erratic compass was a little more than they could stand. Columbus added to his own navigational problems by carrying both Flemish and Genoese compasses, and while the Genoese needle, or wire, was set in line with the north point of the card, the Flemish needle was probably offset to the east of north by three quarters of a point (8.4°) as was the custom.[38]

The next important discovery in connection with the magnetic needle was made, history says, by Robert Norman, an English instrument maker. In a little book, *The Newe Attractive*, 1581, Norman described a phenomenon he had observed some years earlier in manufacturing compass needles. It was customary to balance the needle before magnetizing it and Norman noticed that a needle which was perfectly balanced in a horizontal position before it was magnetized would become off balance the minute it was stroked with a magnet or loadstone. Interested by this strange phenomenon, Norman devised a dip-needle mounted against a graduated circle and pivoted to swing in a vertical arc instead of horizontally. With this instrument he more or less confirmed the terrestrial source of magnetic attraction. He also originated a series of observations which led to the discovery that magnetic declination varies instead of being constant for any given place. But the official announcement of this fact was made by Henry Gellibrand, professor of mathematics at Gresham College, in his *Discourse Mathematical on the Variation of the Magneticall Needle together with its admirable Diminution lately discovered*, 1635.

What Gellibrand did was to interpret correctly the results obtained by some of his colleagues who failed to see what they themselves had discovered. For instance, William Borough, in his *Discourse on the Variation of the Compass or Magneticall Needle*, 1581, gave the declination at Limehouse for October, 1580, as 11° 15' E., approximately. In 1622 Edmund Gunter, professor of astronomy at Gresham, repeated the experiment and found the declination to be only 6° 13'. Inevitably Borough was blamed for an error he did not make. Eleven years later, in 1633, a third observation resulted in a still smaller value for the declination at Limehouse. Now in spite of the fact that in the short space of fifty-three years the change in declination at that particular place was more than seven degrees, Gellibrand did not feel sure enough of his data until the midsummer of 1634 to report that Gilbert and other authorities notwithstanding, magnetic declination was not fixed but was changing constantly and at an appreciable rate each year.[39]

Magnetic variation was of practical importance in maritime circles and numerous wild theories cropped up as to why it should not remain constant. In 1530, long before the discovery of Gellibrand, Alonzo de Santa Cruz constructed the first chart showing, to the best of his knowledge, the various zones of the world where the declination of the compass had been observed and the amount of the declination within each zone.[40] But in spite of all such scientific research, magnetic declination, not to mention the theory of what made it change, remained a mystery for many years. However, Edmund Halley made a major contribution to the subject. In 1698 he was commissioned captain of the *Paramour*, pink, and sailed in her on an extensive cruise whose sole purpose was to gather more information concerning the facts of terrestrial magnetism. The voyage was a long one – two years – and the *Paramour* sailed far below the equator, as far as Latitude 52° S. The results of Halley's observations were published in the form of a chart of the world "Shewing the Variations of the Compass in the Western & Southern Oceans as Observed in ye Year 1700 by his Ma[ties] Command by Edm. Halley." On the chart were plotted lines of equal variation (isogonic lines) representing the various bands or zones on the earth's surface within which magnetic variation was supposed to be uniform.[41] Besides giving cartographers a precedent and a pattern for recording magnetic data, the publication of Halley's chart created a mild furore in scientific circles and stimulated other explorers to make similar observations in various parts of the world, if only to prove Halley wrong. As for the annual change in magnetic variation, there was grave doubt among the learned, and as late as 1757, Don Jorge Juan, in his *Compendio de Navegacion*, refers to the change of variation, "which sailors have not believed and do not now believe."

The development of navigation as a science and sea charts as a navigational aid went hand in hand from the beginning. A new development in one inevitably produced an improvement in the other. All mariners felt the need of better charts and were outspoken about it. Martin Cortes lamented that wise men could not seem to produce charts that were accurate. Wise men, among them cartographers, were well aware of the problems involved, but solving them was another matter.

Michiel Coignet of Antwerp, a wise man and a chart maker, put his finger on the chief problem when he pointed out, in 1581, that under existing conditions and with the map projections then available, there was no sense in laying off a course on a chart according to compass direction as it appeared on the chart. The rhumb lines radiating from the compass rose might be straight lines on the chart, but the same rhumbs applied to the spherical surface of the ocean would produce a series of spiral curves that would take a navigator precisely nowhere.[42] The problem, then, was to lay down a chart on which a straight-line compass course would be something a navigator could follow to his destination, wherever it was. How then, could a spiral rhumb line be straightened out and presented on a sheet of paper so that compass direction would be preserved against all odds as a straight line? The answer came from Gerard Mercator (the latinized form of De Cremer or Kremer), a cartographer, engraver and instrument maker.[43]

Mercator was more than a toolmaker. Born and reared in Rupelmonde in East Flanders, he had studied in the best schools of the Netherlands. He took a master's

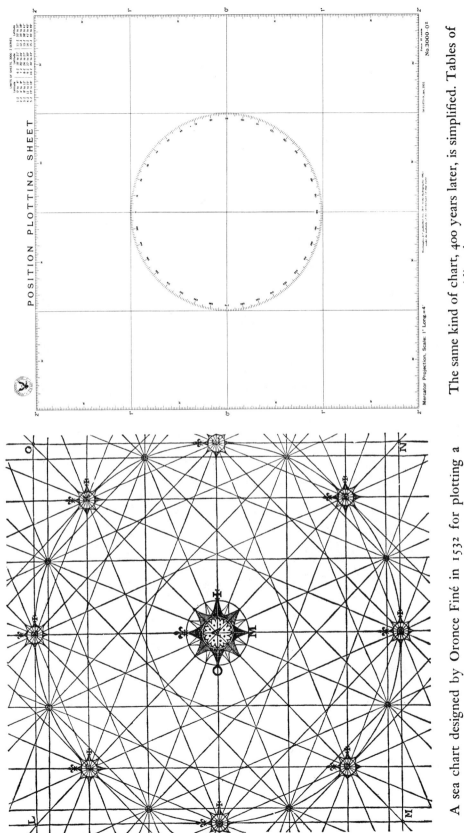

The same kind of chart, 400 years later, is simplified. Tables of meridional parts are unnecessary.

A sea chart designed by Oronce Finé in 1532 for plotting a ship's course in deep water.

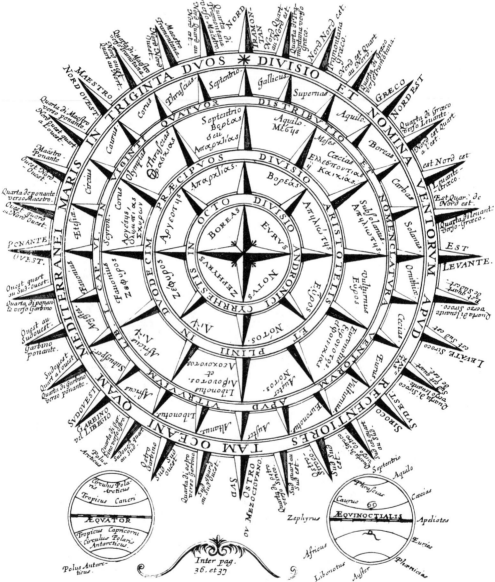

A seventeenth-century composite wind rose showing the evolution of *direction* from Homer's four-wind rose to the 32-point card found on modern compasses.

degree at the University of Louvain and private lessons in advanced mathematics from Gemma Frisius. He would have made a great teacher of mathematics himself if he had not tried to mix theology, that is, the Mosaic doctrine being taught at Louvain, with his scientific approach to the study of Aristotle. One did not question the harmony between the Church and Aristotle at Louvain, so Mercator withdrew from the teaching profession and for a time went into retirement at Antwerp. When he finally returned to Louvain, he settled down to the business of making a living with his hands as well as his brain. His instruments were beautifully wrought; his celestial and terrestrial globes, in various sizes to suit the customer's pocketbook, were handsome to look at and ingeniously made. A celestial globe, one of a pair made for the Emperor Charles V, was made of crystal with the constellations etched on its surface with a diamond. Suspended inside the globe was a terrestrial globe of wood, covered with an elaborately engraved map of the world on paper gores. This sort of craftsmanship brought Mercator the necessary sanction of royalty, and he became both famous and prosperous.

Mercator had been in the map and chart business for thirty years by the time he was ready to tackle the problem of formulating a map projection suitable for navigators. He was no novice at mathematics and apparently had tried out every projection known to cartography including those proposed by Claudius Ptolemy. His object in creating a new one was to straighten out the spiral rhumbs, to make a practical straight-line projection that would distort distance and shapes of land masses as little as possible. It was a large order!

Mercator began by straightening the meridians of the globe, so that instead of converging at the poles they were parallel vertical lines extending to infinity. In so doing he produced a distortion of east-west distances which increased steadily from the equator, where there was no distortion, to the poles, where distortion was at a maximum. Moreover, in straightening his meridians, he necessarily distorted his directions; they were pulled to one side. But direction was the one factor he wished to retain. Therefore, to bring the *direction* of his rhumbs back where it belonged, he stretched the distance factor still more by separating, or lengthening, every degree of latitude in the same proportion he had distorted his meridians to make them parallel. Thus, near the equator the distortion of distance (for latitude and longitude) was negligible, while near the poles the parallels and meridians were so badly distorted and elongated that even though compass direction was preserved, distances indicated on the chart – in any direction – were hopelessly exaggerated. Distortion of the distance factor, of course, meant a bloating of all land masses in the higher latitudes towards the poles, so that islands such as Greenland and Spitzbergen, as well as the continental land masses above the arctic, appeared inflated almost beyond reason. However, Mercator did what he set out to do, and laid down a chart with compass points and rhumb lines headed in the right direction. That was enough for one man. Mercator's intentions were of the best, and as a mathematician and chart seller he was interested in making life easier for the navigator. But he was dealing with an opinionated fraternity, many of whom were uneducated and superstitious. They wanted to get home from a cruise, and it seemed much simpler to use the means at hand than trust to a new and unproved scheme devised by a former college professor who was by no means a master of exposition. There were enough "gross errors and absurdities" in the common sea chart without adding any more. So Mercator's straight-line projection got off to a slow start.[44]

Nearly thirty years later, in 1597, William Barlowe summed up the existing chart situation in *The Navigator's Supply, &c.* The most commonly known sea chart, "in ordinarie use with Saylers," was a chart laid down on a projection of equidistant straight lines. "Of these," wrote Barlowe, "I need not write anything, they are so commonly known, and their imperfection in long voyages so manifest." And yet, he added, there is one chart, and a straight-line chart at that, "very artificial and regular, which being well understoode, redresseth the errors of the other; and (as farre as I can discerne) will so satisfie the navigator's expectation, as no carde [chart] hitherto invented was ever comparable with it, neither, (as I thinke) any that shall be hereafter will in all respects surpass it." This "carde," which Barlowe said had been in print for at least thirty years, was of course Mercator's chart, "resembling ordinarie Sea Cardes, save that the degree of the *Meridians* in it doe proportionally encrease from the *Equator* toward each *Pole*, upon good reason and firme *Demonstration*, thereby showing the true Position of any place in respect of any other; which the usuall Cardes in a far distance cannot doe, being yet the very principall point that the Navigator desireth." [45]

"But," Barlowe continued, "a cloude (as it were) and thick myste of ignorance doth keep [this chart] hitherto concealed; and so much the more, because some who were reckoned for men of good knowledge, have by glauncing speaches (but never by any one reason of moment) gone about what they coulde to disgrace it." In addition to professional jealousy there was another reason for the mist of ignorance surrounding the Mercator chart. Mercator had laid down his projection with compass dividers and protractor — mechanically. The finished product was a fine piece of descriptive geometry, but it did not give a navigator any numerical data that would help him find his position at sea. If the distance between the degrees of latitude increased from the equator to the poles, and if the increase represented a certain proportion, how much did it represent in linear distance, something a sailor could measure and plot? If distances became increasingly distorted from the equator to the poles, how much of a correction in leagues, or nautical miles, would a man have to make in order to find his actual position in a given latitude? These were practical questions and important ones. They involved the motion of points in a straight line. If a mariner were sailing a straight-line course and his line kept moving away from him, as it were, or continued to stretch as he sailed into the higher latitudes, how much had his line stretched at any given latitude and exactly where was he on that line? Edward Wright told him.

Wright was a professor of mathematics at Caius College, Cambridge; a colleague of Henry Briggs, also a brilliant mathematician, and of John Napier, baron of

Merchiston in Scotland, who invented logarithms. Unlike some great mathematicians, Wright strove to reassure rather than confuse his students. He was interested in all phases of navigation; he invented a sea quadrant and an astronomical ring for use at sea. In 1599, thirty years after the first appearance of Mercator's chart, Wright published a work entitled *Certaine Errors in Navigation,* . . . Instead of scaring the life out of sailors with a learned treatise punctuated with mathematical symbols, he led up to the technicalities of the Mercator projection with what he considered a "popular" approach. His explanation went something like this:

Suppose the spherical earth to be represented by a balloon covered with a network of parallels of latitude and meridians equally spaced. Let the balloon be placed inside a cylinder whose inside diameter is such that the equator of the sphere just touches the walls of the cylinder. Then let the balloon be inflated. As it expands, the curved meridians become straightened and flattened against the walls of the cylinder. At the same time, each successive parallel finally comes to rest against the walls of the cylinder. This process goes on to infinity, because the polar regions and the poles themselves can never be pressed against the walls. If the balloon remains against the sides of the cylinder, and the cylinder is unrolled and flattened, the impress is a Mercator projection of the world.[46]

Wright's mathematical explanation of the projection and how to correct distortion of distance was by no means as popular as the simplified version above, but it was his great contribution to the science of cartography — that and his table of "meridional parts." Cartographers had been searching for a conformal projection, which, even though it distorted shape and distance, would do it systematically; and if distortion had to be increased, conformity (or scale) would be preserved within a given area. Mercator drew the picture and Wright computed a table, giving a numerical value to each succeeding "meridional part" as the meridians were straightened and the parallels widened. In other words, he computed for each degree of ascending latitude the proportional change in scale which would take place at each parallel. Correcting the scale of the chart between two or more parallels was the same as correcting the distortion of distance produced when the chart was projected. Wright, then, gave mariners the key to Mercator's chart and told them how to plot a course upon it. Other projections may display greater accuracy of size or shape, yet these are often merely intended to be looked at or studied while "the Mercator projection is meant seriously to be worked upon, and it alone has the invaluable property that a course from any point desired can be laid off with accuracy and ease. It is, therefore, the only one that meets the requirements of navigation and has a world-wide use, due to the fact that the ship's track on the surface of the sea under a constant bearing is a straight line on the projection."[47]

The invention of a geometrically accurate and "conformal" projection, the answer to a mariner's prayer, was too important to have only one claimant. Wright, for instance, credited Martin Cortes with having suggested a projection similar to Mercator's in the second chapter of his *Breve Compendio de la esfera y*

de la arte de navigar, 1551, but no such proposal is to be found in the text. Mercator's claim to immortality is substantiated by the existence of a single copy of his
chart of 1569 preserved in the Imperial Library in Paris. A facsimile of it was
published by Jomard in his *Monuments de la geographie.* William Barlowe was
probably the first man to give a clear description of how to lay out a chart geometrically, though he made no claims for himself as author of the Mercator
scheme.[48]

Edward Wright's *Certaine Errors* may properly be considered the first practically correct treatise on navigation and in most respects it marked the turning
point in scientific chart construction. Wright was a little sensitive on the subject
of his indebtedness to Mercator, for in his preface, he says that it was "indeed by
occasion of that mappe of Mercator," that he conceived the idea of correcting
"so many gross errors and absurdities in the common sea chart. But the way
how this should be done," he adds, "I learned neither of Mercator nor of any
else." [49]

Wright himself made a chart of the world projected in the manner of Mercator
which was printed about the time his book was finished. But instead of accompanying the *Certaine Errors* as a folding plate, it came out first in Richard
Hakluyt's *Principall Navigations,* London, 1598. Why, we do not know. A Dutch
engraver, Jodocus Hondius, worked with Wright on his chart, and after hours
worked on one of his own, which he printed and published in Holland in 1597 (a
year before Wright's came out) together with an explanation that was more than
faintly reminiscent of Wright's own text, but without benefit of quotation marks
or any mention of Wright. He explained this extraordinary coincidence in a letter
to Wright. "I was purposed," he said, "to have set this forth under your name:
but I feared that you would be displeased therewith, because I have but rudely
translated it into Latine." [50]

Regardless of its authorship, the chart projected by Mercator and perfected
by Wright has not yet outlived its usefulness after three hundred and fifty years.
It has surpassed all others in simplicity and utility. Its parallels and meridians are
at right angles to one another. With a protractor it is possible for a navigator to
measure on any meridian the angle his course makes with any other meridian. A
compass course can be laid off on it from the compass rose to any part of the
chart and the course sailed with confidence. With a table of meridional parts,
the distance factor can be corrected for any latitude, but even without the table,
a mariner can be sure of the rhumb he is sailing, and that eventually he will
arrive at his destination if he sails it long enough. The Mercator chart is "conformal," which means that distortion, wherever it occurs, is proportional in every
respect; shapes, therefore, are not distorted within narrow belts, and if the scale
of any such latitude belt is enlarged or reduced, it will fit exactly the corresponding area on any Mercator chart. Extreme distortion of distance and size, the chief
fault of the projection, occurs in the latitudes with which mariners are least concerned — the polar regions.[51]

There is no such thing as an ideal, all-purpose map or chart; every projection must sacrifice accuracy and tolerate distortion of one kind or another. However, as an aid to navigation, the Mercator chart has never been approached, let alone surpassed. It did not come into general use in the author's lifetime, and there is little evidence as to when it was adopted as a standard, as it is today. However, about the year 1630, when the French seaport of Dieppe was the principal emporium for the sale of nautical charts and coast pilots, most of the charts for sale there were drawn on a Mercator projection.[52]

The search for documentary evidence of charts made before 1300 A.D. yields nothing. Then suddenly come several copies of a full-blown chart of the Mediterranean and the Black Sea, with not a shred of evidence as to who made it or how it evolved. But it was much too accurate and detailed to be the work of any one man or any one group of navigators, nor could it represent the surveys of any one generation; the area is much too large and the details too complex. For three hundred years, from 1300 to 1600, this early chart of unknown origin was copied and recopied with few alterations or improvements. In effect it was a standardized picture of the Mediterranean, and as such it might have caused great confusion in maritime circles, but for the fact that it was amazingly accurate. And even though The Chart lacked parallels and meridians and apparently was not laid down on any particular projection, Nordenskiöld has pointed out the striking similarity between the outlines of this chart and a modern one of the same area on a Mercator projection. Could it be that some ancient chart maker solved the riddle of the conformal projection and either purposely covered up his tracks or lost his co-ordinates because of a copyist who felt that they only cluttered the picture? It is highly probable.[53]

The standard portolan or harbor-finding chart was in most cases perpetuated by chart makers and navigators of Catalonia in northeastern Spain and in Italy. In fact, internal evidence seems to indicate that the standard chart originated in Genoa as a compilation of smaller charts of limited stretches of coast line sailed and charted by local fishermen and the skippers of small, coastwise traders. The Chart was nearly always drawn on parchment, either on a whole skin or in sections (leaves) glued to thin boards in the form of a portolan atlas. It was always executed with great care and the lines were fine and sharp. Nearly all copies were colored, following a conventional pattern and using black, red, green, blue, yellow and sometimes gold and silver foil. The Red Sea was nearly always reddish brown. Rhodes was usually colored red and spotted with a white cross. Place names were usually lettered in black, but a few were arbitrarily colored red. The red did not indicate size or commercial importance, but the presence of a good safe harbor where water and stores could be obtained.

Although portolan charts were designed solely for the use of mariners, the wind rose does not appear on the earliest ones. A Catalan portolan atlas dated 1375 has a single wind rose, and Pinelli's portolan charts were laid down against a background of wind roses connected by intersecting rhumb lines or loxodromes, forming a basic grid on which the copyist could work and along which the navigator could sail with impunity. Here too the colors were conveniently standard-

ized. The eight principal winds and rhumb lines were drawn in black; the half-
winds in green and the quarter-winds in red.[54]

Scale graduations were indifferently drawn on a ribbon-like strip resembling a
tape measure, and in view of the care with which The Chart itself was executed,
it seems unlikely that any one, including the draftsman, had much faith in it. The
wind roses and loxodromes were always drawn carefully and cleanly, and on
surviving copies these have remained straight and true in spite of shrinkage and
centuries of aging.

Islands and coastal cliffs are often drawn in perspective and exaggerated in size,
for emphasis. Shoals are indicated as they are on modern charts. Coastal details are
never slighted, but details of the interior such as mountain ranges, cities and
inland roads are often neglected or omitted altogether. Place names are usually so
numerous along the coasts that they are difficult to decipher. The language of
The Chart is almost always Latin, though there are a few whose legends are in
Catalan and certain others can be traced to the ancient Italian dialects of coastal
towns.[55]

Compass roses indicating both true and apparent north were slow in getting on
sea charts. The earliest known rose to indicate compass variation appeared on a
map in the *Cosmographiae introductio* of Apianus printed at Ingolstadt in 1529.
Among sea charts, variation was first indicated in the *Caertboeck vande Mid-
landtsche Zee* of Willem Barentszoon, Amsterdam, 1595.[56]

The more complete portolan atlases of the fourteenth and fifteenth centuries
contained (1) a world map, usually oval; (2) charts of a local character, such as
individual harbors and short stretches of coast line; (3) separate charts of the
Adriatic, the Aegean and sometimes the Caspian; (4) The Chart of the Mediterranean (standard). Frequently the atlas contained sketchy sailing directions,
calendars — both astronomical and astrological — and sometimes tables of lunar
cycles. For the sailor of the Middle Ages, all such data constituted his *Nautical
Almanac*, with medical and astrological counsel thrown in for good measure. In
1436, Andrea Bianco, commander of a Venetian galley, produced a portolan atlas
containing, in addition to the customary tables, directions for computing dead
reckoning, both when tacking and when running before the wind. And in the
upper corner of one of his charts is a traverse-table (*toleta de marteloio*) and
brief instructions (*raxon de marteloio*) on how to use it.[57]

One of the most prolific chart makers of the sixteenth century was Battista
Agnese, who flourished between 1536 and 1564. His charts and portolan atlases,
dated and signed, are all that is known about him, and his place in the history of
cartography has been the subject of considerable debate. Nevertheless, the exquisite draftsmanship and rubrication of his charts is equal to the best art work
of his time. About 60 of his atlases containing an average of 10 charts each are
known, and he may have done as many as 100. It is difficult to imagine a volume
of charts drawn on vellum, never a cheap commodity, rubricated in beautiful
colors as well as silver and gold, being used at sea. It would have been the gross-
est extravagance. Moreover, the scale of the Agnese charts is so small that it

would be impossible to lay off a course on any one of them. But even if the scale were large enough and the owner extravagant enough to carry such beautiful things to sea, these charts would still be of little practical value, because they are actually maps drawn in the manner of portolan charts, with much more land than water on them, especially the later ones.[58]

There was no originality in Agnese's cartographical work, as far as we know; but in addition to the artistic merit of his maps, they are important historical compilations, showing many new discoveries. In addition, he revived the custom of drawing in land forms against a background grid of parallels and meridians. Agnese was resourceful and enterprising if nothing more. His earlier atlases are devoted to the Mediterranean and Black Sea as were most portolans, but his later charts cover many of the discoveries made by the Spanish and Portuguese in the New World and Far Eastern Asia.

Historians have spent many hours trying to find out where he got his information on new discoveries, but Agnese himself did not say. He was apparently the first to show on a map the discoveries of Francisco de Ulloa in 1539–1540, as well as those of Marcos de Niza in what is now Arizona and New Mexico.[59]

The roster of charts and chart makers who flourished before 1500 contains many gaps. It really constitutes a "Survivors List" without special significance. However, thanks to the relatively small number of survivors, we have at least a clue to the methods used at different periods, the quality of the charts produced, and a suspicion of how much important material has been lost. A few portolan charts got into print before the year 1500, the oldest known being the work of Albinus de Canepa — a single chart printed on parchment. The only known copy is in the Milan Library. They were by no means universally popular, even though many of them stemmed, or were copied direct, from manuscript portolans. As late as 1612, one editor wrote, "Amongst manie Pilots there is an opinion, that they had rather use the written Cardes then [*sic*] such as are printed, esteeming the written Cardes are much better and perfecter. . . ." Even after a hundred and fifty years there was still a demand for copies of the standard hand-drawn chart of the Mediterranean, and chart publishers were still struggling to establish their products as safe and reliable aids to navigation.[60]

Chart making became big business with the discovery of a New World across the Western Sea. By 1500 Columbus had completed three voyages to the west; Cabot had discovered the North American mainland; Ojeda, Nino and Guerra, Pinzon and Diego de Lepe had probed the coast of South America. That year Pinzon was said to have spotted Cape St. Augustine, and Cabral reached the coast of South America. Enough wealth was trickling back to Europe to make the New World, whether it was a part of Asia or "Terra Sanctae Crucis," interesting to European monarchs. Queen Isabella considered that part of the world her own private preserve. In her court America was known officially as "Las Indias." Expeditions to the west, ordered by the Spanish government, were fitted out at Seville, Cadiz and Palos, and their commanders were compelled to take their departure from one of the three, having first obtained the necessary royal sanction.

A school for Basque pilots from the Biscay region was established, where hydrography and navigation were foremost on the curriculum.[61]

By decree of January 20, 1503, the "Casa de la Contratación de las Indias" was formed. The Casa, as it was later called, functioned as a sort of combination Board of Trade and Hydrographic Office for the purpose of regulating overseas commercial relations, with special reference to the New World. Foreign commerce had become almost synonymous with the art of navigation, and for this reason the Casa was given the authority to examine and grant licenses to pilots and masters, to supervise the charting of all new regions and to establish navigation laws for the regulation of ships sailing the great Western Sea. "Its jurisdiction is as large," wrote Veitia Linaje, "as its territory is boundless; its authority is so extraordinary that it has supplied the place of a Council, and has acted as such not only in reference to revenues and military affairs, with orders passing directly from the King to it; its wealth is such that none in Europe can compare with it; its credit so high that no private person could equal it; its preeminence is such that it had the appointment of all officers including admirals of the Royal fleet, and the civil magistrates; it gave passes to ships sailing to all ports, and the dispatching of advice boats with only its own owners." Such was the Casa de Contratación.[62]

By decree of August 8, 1508, a separate geographical or cosmographical department of the Casa was created, perhaps the first Hydrographic Office in history. One of its chief functions was to organize under a supervisory junta the charting of the New World. In spite of all regulations and precautions, merchants, adventurers and gentlemen of fortune were sailing thither and yon, disregarding the rights of Spain and her claims in the western world. Trade routes were being established that were perhaps better and more lucrative than those established by pilots sailing under orders of the House of Castile. If a merchant failed to get a license to sail from a Spanish port he merely took his ship to a foreign port, and after fitting out, he sailed without a license — his monarch knew not where. As for charts, there was doubtless an illicit traffic in them at all important seaports; not in standard, out-of-date products, but the latest thing compiled last month by a friend of a friend, that could be bought (only by a friend, of course) for a price. Charts went underground.

In order to maintain a semblance of control over the charting of new territory, the Spanish government ordered the creation of a master chart (Padron Real). Its compilation was to be supervised by a junta or commission of pilots headed by a Pilot-Major, who, in 1500, was Amerigo Vespucci. Also members of the commission were such celebrated navigators as Juan Diaz de Solis and Vincente Yañez Pinzon. Ostensibly this master chart was designed only to avoid confusion among chart makers and costly errors among those pilots who were sailing the Western Sea. Too many false reports and incorrect data were being added to charts and there was no way of checking the authenticity and accuracy of information when a large proportion of it was coming in through questionable sources. But very few people were fooled by this noble enterprise. Veitia Linaje said the official charts compiled by the Casa were kept in a coffer with two locks and two keys — one for the Pilot-Major and one for the Cosmographer-Major. After Sebastian Cabot, one of the many foreign experts employed by the Spanish government, tried to sell the fabulous "Secret of the Strait" to England and Venice, and when the minions of Charles V began to boast about a shorter route to the Molucca Islands, the disguise was dropped. His Majesty issued an order forbidding all strangers (that is, foreigners) to hold the rank of pilot or mate.

Meanwhile work on the Padron Real progressed. It was probably a large-scale chart hung on the wall of the old Alcazar in Seville. The chart was supposed to embrace "all the lands and isles of the Indies until then discovered and belonging to the Crown." And all pilots were enjoined to trace on their chart "every land, island, bay, harbour, and other thing, new, and worthy of being noted." As soon as a pilot landed in Spain he was to turn over his chart, properly annotated, to the Pilot-Major. No pilot could use any but a copy of the official government chart, under penalty of a 50 doblas fine. In 1527 the Padron Real became the Padron General, committed to the care of the president and judges of the Casa de Contratación, and verified (edited) by the Pilot-Major and the official government cosmographers of the Casa twice a year. At one stage the chart was revised twice a month, the Pilot-Major meeting with the other pilots, chart makers and cosmographers.[63]

In addition to being under rigid government control, the commercial chart publishers also had to sit back and watch the operation of a tidy little monopoly in chart selling. Juan Vespucci, nephew of Amerigo, and Juan Diaz de Solis were entrusted with the supervision of the Padron Real.[64] They were also authorized to control the sale of all copies at a price fixed by the Casa. It was a pernicious monopoly in more ways than one. In the first place, inferior copies and counterfeits could be obtained — cheap. In the second place, the Casa got only a small percentage of the new information that came in. Privately financed expeditions sailing without licenses were finding out many interesting things about the New World, about which they said nothing to the Casa. No one in government circles knew where these expeditions sailed from until it was too late. Stories of precious cargos of hardwoods and dyewoods and Indians for the slave market were persistently cropping up, but when official enquiries were made, all was silence. A third evil arose directly from the monopoly enjoyed by the Pilot-Major and his colleagues. "You should know," wrote Teodosio, "that all maps and nautical instruments have to be examined by the Pilot-Major in the following manner:

> Whenever the pilot or master is about to undertake a voyage to the Indies, he must show his implements to the Pilot-Major, that the latter may see whether they are in working order; by which [implements] are meant the map, compass, astrolabe, and sailing directions. And as the Pilot-Major, besides being the colleague of the cartographer, is his great friend, if any other person has constructed the map or instrument, the Pilot-Major, seeing that it is not the work of his companion, declares the same at once unfit for use, and refuses his certificate, on the plea that those implements must be

examined again thoroughly. He then keeps the map and instruments at his house for a long time, and finally gives neither his approbation nor leave to use them, however good they may be. The reason is that he does not want any other than his companion to construct naval objects. And as that is known, no one cares to make such things, however perfect they might be, as no one would buy them, for fear of the enmity of the Pilot-Major and of his companion. I speak as an eye-witness.[65]

In spite of threats and promises, this first large-scale attempt to chart the coasts and harbors of the New World was a magnificent failure. But the Padron Real and its management illustrates a trend in the history of cartography and the importance of sea charts in world affairs. Navigators were reluctant to put down on paper what they had discovered, with the result that printed maps and charts were always scarce and there was often a lag of from two to twenty years between the date of a new discovery and the time it became incorporated on the map. At the same time, map and chart publishers were frequently cut off from their only reliable source of information — the men who made the discoveries, the navigators who had been there and seen for themselves.

While Spain and Portugal busied themselves with the wealth of the Indies and quarreled over their rights and privileges in the New World, Dutch ships dutifully beat their way back and forth between Lisbon and the northern ports of Europe and the British Isles, trans-shipping the wealth of the East. In so doing, Dutch skippers learned the coast and harbors, the prevailing winds and currents, the reefs and shoals of Western Europe as they were never known before. Charts and sailing directions (coast pilots) were vital tools of their trade, and it was logical that the Dutch should produce the first systematic collection of navigational charts bound together in book form. This sea atlas was compiled and published by Lucas Janssz Waghenaer (or Wagenaer) of Enckhuysen in the Zuyder Zee, under the title *Spieghel der Zeevaerdt (The Mariner's Mirror)*.[66]

As a collector of maritime duties in his home port, Waghenaer had not covered himself with glory, and was asked to resign. When he applied to the Commissioners of the States General for a loan of five hundred gulden to launch his publishing venture, the commissioners said no, even though the entire population of the town supported his request. Somehow the money was raised, eventually, and in 1584 the first volume of the *Spieghel* was published with the "permission" or "privilege" of His Majesty and the Council of Brabant. In spite of its getting off to a bad start, Waghenaer's sea atlas was printed by Christopher Plantin in Leyden, one of the best in the business. There were twenty-three double-page folio charts in this first volume, engraved on copper by Joannes a Doeticum (Jan Van Doet) from Waghenaer's original and improved drafts. They covered the navigation of the western coast of Europe from the Zuyder Zee to Cadiz.[67] And, incidentally, Plantin used a specially fine grade of paper for the plates that he had bought originally for the printing of the great Spanish Antiphonal. The success of the *Spieghel der Zeevaerdt* was unprecedented and immediate. In response to its popularity Waghenaer issued a second volume, also printed by Plantin. This time the volume was dedicated to the States of Holland, and that body hurriedly granted the author a pension of five hundred pounds. A second edition of the completed work appeared the following year, and by that time foreign publishers began to show interest. Lord Charles Howard of Effingham, Lord Admiral of England, drew the attention of Her Majesty's Privy Council to Waghenaer's publication, which body decided it was the answer to a long felt want. After due deliberation and consideration of all factors relative thereto, the work being "esteemed by the chief personages of the grave counsell worthy to be translated and printed into a language familiar to all nations," Anthony Ashley was commissioned to translate the text and place names into English. *The Mariners Mirrovr*, "First made & set fourth in divers exact sea-charts, by that famous navigator Luke Wagenar of Enchuisen," was published in London in 1588. The charts, entirely re-engraved, were among the first copperplates done in England. They were engraved by foreign mercenaries, however, such as Jodocus Hondius, Johannes Rutlinger, Augustine Ryther (who illustrated the fracas with the Spanish Armada) and Theodore de Bry, one of the most prolific and successful European engravers.

The title of the English edition became *The Mariners mirrovr wherin may playnly be seen the courses, heights, distances, depths, soundings, flouds and ebs, rising of lands, rocks, sands and shoalds, with the marks for th'entrings of the harbouroughs, havens and ports of the greatest part of Europe* . . . The author's name eventually became synonymous with any volume of sea charts, and in England a "Waggoner" was just that. In France it was called a "Charettier." [68]

There were no striking innovations on Waghenaer's charts, with the possible exception of perspective elevations of prominent headlands to guide the navigator to port. In some respects they did not come up to the standard of excellence established by Italian and Catalan chart makers a century earlier. But Waghenaer's atlas was an unusually timely publication. It reached the market when European powers and the Queen of England needed it. It contained not only working charts but concise sailing directions for a hotly contested area: the entire western coast of Europe, the Baltic, the North Sea and the English Channel. So that by the time Lucas Janssz Waghenaer received his license to print from King Philip II and the States of Holland and Zeeland, and sheets of the atlas were ready, his market was ready-made. Moreover the *Spieghel* was practical in every sense of the word. In addition to the charts and sailing directions, Waghenaer gave his readers a table of the sun's declination for four years and a catalogue of Dutch geographical place names with the Spanish, French and English equivalents. The *Spieghel* contained the first printed literature on sailing the east coast of Sweden as far as Stockholm.

Waghenaer published a second sea atlas in 1592 under the title *Thresoor der Zeevaerdt* (*The Treasure of Navigation* or *Mariners' Treasury*). This was an improved volume newly edited and published at Leyden by Plantin's son-in-law François van Raphelingien. By this time Waghenaer's reputation was firmly established, and both the States General and the States of Holland gave him proper recognition and appropriate grants of money, for services rendered "and the services which are still to be expected from him." In the *Thresoor*, the sailing directions were much more detailed than in the *Spieghel*, especially with regard to Northern Europe. Descriptions of the Shetland and Faeroe Islands, for instance, and the coast of North Russia as far as Waigatsch and Novaja Zemblija are minutely described. Along such a northern route, the author says, one might be able to sail to the rich lands of China, taking about a quarter as long as the Spanish and Portuguese who have to take the long way around the Cape of Good Hope.[69]

For a hundred years after the first publication of the *Spieghel der Zeevaerdt*, "Waggoners" of all sorts and sizes were issued throughout Europe. Waghenaer's own publication went through many editions and there were many imitations of varying quality. There were six editions of Willem Jansszoon Blaeu's *'t Licht der Zeevaerdt* (The Light of Navigation) published between 1608 and 1629, and twelve editions of his *Zeespiegel* (Mirror of the Sea) between 1623 and 1658. Titles were dramatic and fully as promising as any modern panacea. There was *The Fierie Sea-Columne* of Jacob Colom; *The Lightning-Columne or Sea-Mirrour* of Pieter Goos; *The Clear-Lighted North-Star or Sea Atlas* of Johannes van Loon. But in spite of strong competition, "Waggoners" by the original author were foremost in popularity during the sixteenth and seventeenth centuries and the early part of the eighteenth. All Dutch, French, English, Scandinavian and German navigators sailing between the Canaries and Spitzbergen used Waggoners. In France, by order of Richelieu, pilots had "to give proof of their knowledge of the nautical instruments and of the Dutch books of sailing directions."[70]

England's answer to the Dutch monopoly on charts and sea atlases came with the publication of *The English Pilot. Part I. Describing the sea coasts, capes, headlands, bays, roads, harbours, rivers and ports, together with the soundings sands, rocks and dangers in the southern navigation upon the coasts of England, Scotland, Ireland, Holland, Flanders, Spain, Portugal, to the straights-mouth, with the coasts of Barbary, and off to the Canary, Madera, Cape de Verd, and Western Islands*. London, for R. & W. Mount & T. Page, 1715. The English charts covered the same territory as the Dutch Waggoners but were not so well engraved. Sources of information were in many cases doubtful, but *The English Pilot* was a strong bid for a share of the chart publishing trade. The government made it stronger by forbidding further importation of Dutch charts and atlases into England. *The English Pilot* came out in four "Books," the fourth "Describing the West-India navigation from Hudson's-bay to the River Amazones."[71]

Exploration and chart making achieved world-wide proportions at the beginning of the seventeenth century and with the founding of East India Companies by Holland, England, France, Denmark, Scotland, Spain, Austria and Sweden. Subsidized in part by royalty and in part by private enterprise, these corporations, with immeasurable wealth as a prize, contributed more towards the mapping of the seven seas than any other organized effort in history. Large-scale exploitation of the Indies and the formation of East India companies was begun by the Dutch.

The long years of internal political strife endured by the Netherlands reached a climax in 1579 when the Northern and Southern Netherlands were divided into Holland and Belgium. Two years later Philip II of Spain annexed Portugal, and in order to appease the gentry (*hidalgos*) and make them happier over their lot in life, he committed a serious blunder. He cut the Dutch off from their European coastal trade and presented the exclusive shipping rights in those waters to the Portuguese. The Dutch were faced with imminent ruin, but Philip underestimated his opponent. Neither Philip nor the Dutch realized that this decision in favor of the Portuguese was to mark the beginning of a vast and mighty Dutch empire.

Dutch navigators, already familiar with the waters of the North Sea and the Baltic, vainly probed for a northern route to the Far East that would circumvent the Spanish and Portuguese armadas. In 1594 Willem Barents left Amsterdam with two ships in search of a northeast passage. He completed two voyages and died of exposure on a third, but it was no use; the passage could not be found. In desperation the Dutch decided to fight their way to the Spice Islands and the Malay Archipelago by way of the coast of Africa and the Cape of Good Hope. The first expedition sailed under Cornelius Houtman, April 2, 1595. Houtman's book of sailing instructions had been compiled by none other than the explorer Jan Huyghen van Linschoten, a veteran world traveler at thirty-two. Two years and four months later the fleet returned, battered and weary, but with a pay load aboard. And in Houtman's pocket was a treaty signed by the Sultan of Bantam in Java. From then on events moved rapidly. Independent companies designated as "Van Ferne" — of the distant seas — were formed, and in another five years sixty or seventy Dutch ships, armed to the gunwales, had made the long voyage to Hindustan and the Indian Archipelago.

The situation in Eastern waters rapidly got out of hand, and the government was powerless to control or protect the armed merchantmen flying the Dutch flag. It was a chaotic free-for-all, with the government taking the short end of the purse. In order to suppress the fighting over prizes and to establish a united front against foreign powers, the States General decided to organize one great Dutch East India Company. This organization, founded in 1602, was granted full power to govern all Dutch nationals in the Far East, to prosecute the war with Spain and Portugal and to regulate trade. A capital of nearly 6,500,000 florins was raised by national subscription, in shares of 3000 florins. A general Directorate of sixty members was chosen from local boards throughout the United Netherlands, thus insuring to the home government a full share of all profits.

From the time of its founding until its dissolution in 1798, the Dutch East India Company wielded unprecedented power in the Far East. Its headquarters were in Batavia, Java, and its principal colony was at the Cape of Good Hope. But the Dutch were not alone in the Indian Ocean or in the Pacific, and conviviality on the high seas was conspicuously lacking. Queen Elizabeth chartered the English East India Company in December 31, 1600 (the price of pepper had gone up at a frightful rate), and in addition, there were always Spain and Portugal, not to mention the lesser intruders, whose armed ships might be just below the horizon.[72]

The powerful English East India Company constituted the principal threat to Dutch control of the Indies, and in 1613 the Dutch suggested that the English might like to talk things over before further blood was spilled. Ever confident in its own superiority, the Queen's navy refused to co-operate, and it was six years (1619) before a "treaty of defence" was arranged. This alliance, designed to prevent further disputes between the Dutch and English merchantmen was without doubt the shortest if not the least sincere diplomatic gesture of amity in history. After the affair had been solemnly proclaimed throughout the Far East, the two fleets cautiously approached each other at sea. The yards were manned and every ship broke out its bunting. Salutes were exchanged, after which the guns were quickly reloaded with ball and grape, and for the space of one hour the two fleets lay hove to while the treaty was signed and sealed. Immediately after the ceremony, all sails were trimmed and all ships hurriedly stood away from one another and prepared to resume hostilities. Thus ended the Treaty of Defence.

The keen and violent rivalry for the East India trade called for better ships and better men to sail them. It also demanded better charts. The office of Hydrographer or Cosmographer to one of the East India companies was one of great importance and prestige, and rival nations spared no expense to procure the services of the very best men. At the same time, merchant skippers and their navigators, spurred on by the promise of fat bonuses, grew increasingly bold and unscrupulous in their search for new islands and shorter trade routes, snug harbors and secret watering places. So it was that the Far East was scanned, studied and charted. Some of these "new discoveries" seem relatively unimportant in retrospect, but not so New Zealand, located and explored by Abel Tasman in the *Heemskirk* in 1642, or the continent of Australia, which was pretty well charted by the Dutch between 1616 and 1665.

Until the seven seas had been thoroughly explored and a semblance of trade balance had been established among maritime nations, chart making and chart publishing were divided among three general groups. Private enterprise was first and foremost, represented by the merchant class, the East India Companies that went about their devious ways with or without the sanction of their several governments. Their cartographical activities are beautifully illustrated by the "Secret Atlas" of the Dutch East India Company which came to light in the collection of Prince Eugene of Savoy in Vienna.[73] This remarkable lot of 180 maps, charts and views was made for the exclusive use of the Company by the best cartographers in Holland. Included in the collection, and of the utmost importance, was a series of consecutive survey charts, which, when pieced together, show the fairway through the Indian Archipelago, the route to India along the coast of Africa and through the Indian Ocean, and the best course to China and Japan. In addition there were many single charts on a larger scale which showed in detail the small islands and atolls that played an important part in the hit-and-run battles on the high seas. There are Columbo on Ceylon, Bantam, Makassar, Atjeh and the Portuguese stronghold of Goa; Ternate and Makian and the strategic outpost of Mauritius. Fortified with such wonderful aids to navigation and by the knowledge that the man on the bridge knew what he was doing and where he was going, Dutch seamen could well shift their cutlasses and sing with feeling their morning song, *"Hier zeilen wy met God verheven"* — "Now we sail with God exalted." [74]

The second class of chart publishing was government sponsored. Such charts differed widely in accuracy and the amount of authentic information they contained, and their value was usually in direct proportion to the closeness of the government to the operations of the merchant class. Government-made or government-controlled charts were of course never issued to the public until the information they contained had become common knowledge or, in the case of new island possessions, until the outposts had been firmly secured and adequately garrisoned.

Commercial chart makers and publishers, an offshoot of the book trade, were obliged to bring up in the rear. They had to subsist on the scraps of information tossed to them by the merchant combines (often sadly out of date) and on whatever information they could pick up by bribe, theft or purchase. Consequently they were always behind the times and frequently guilty of perpetuating false rumors and incorrect data. Rarely was a commercial chart publisher able to hit the market with something that was really new. When it happened, there was usually a weak government official involved or a loosemouthed seaman in combination with an overdose of ardent spirits. To make up for the deficiency in information and yet stay in business, the talents of the engraver and colorist were called upon. Published charts were without doubt beautiful, skillfully engraved and embellished in the best tradition. Figures of ships and sea monsters, palm trees and heraldic emblems were supposed to draw the attention of the customer and make him happy about his purchase, at least until he got home. But neither fantasy nor art could hide for long the fact that commercial chart makers just did not have the information and consequently could not possibly produce independently a sheet that would be of the slightest use to a navigator.

In the eighteenth century it became apparent that it would be mutually beneficial if private enterprise and government officialdom united in an effort to produce better charts. Most of the "secrets of the sea" were no longer secret and yet too many ships and valuable cargoes were lost because of inadequate or conflicting information. In England, prior to the issue of Admiralty charts, masters were instructed "to provide such charts and instruments as they considered necessary for the safe navigation of the ship," leaving the details and the selection of the best charts up to the masters. Real progress was made only after the patronage of the East India Company had been extended in support of the British Navy and the mercantile marine, and their Hydrographer, Alexander Dalrymple, began to direct the work of improving charts. In 1795, he was made the official Hydrographer to the Admiralty, the first of a long succession of able nautical surveyors. After the war ended in 1815, the Admiralty took over the chief responsibility of surveying the important coasts of the world, whether or not they were British possessions, and by that time other nations were ready and for the most part willing to co-operate on an international scale. [75]

CHAPTER VI

The Map and Chart Trade

BETWEEN 1440 and 1500 A.D., three of the most important events in modern history occurred. Printing by means of movable types was introduced to European civilization; Ptolemy's *Geographia* was multiplied by the printing process; the New World was discovered by Christopher Columbus.

In 1440, or thereabouts, while Portuguese mariners under Henry the Navigator were probing the African coast beyond Cape Bojador, a young German in Strassburg was putting the finishing touches on an invention potentially far more valuable than black slaves or gold dust. John Gutenberg was a secretive fellow and kept his affairs to himself, but like many another genius, he was eventually forced to borrow money and before long word leaked out that the young man who came and went so silently was cutting separate letters of the alphabet in wood and, after arranging them into words and sentences, was "printing" an entire page of writing in one operation, just as you would a picture, and doing it far quicker than any mortal scribe could do it by hand. The news brought loud protests from the craft guilds, whose tightly knit membership was dedicated to the mutual protection of handicrafts and the monopoly of consumer goods. It was a bad thing, they said, this printing of words on a machine. It would put men out of work; the scribes, the painters and goldsmiths who made a living copying and decorating manuscripts would starve. And if unscrupulous and seditious writers used the printing press to further their evil ends, it might well turn out to be an instrument of the devil himself.

In spite of the clamor, Gutenberg went ahead with his plans and finally produced enough "types" to do business on a small scale. His first attempts were modest enough, small commissions of job printing such as single sheet calendars (for the year 1448) and an elementary schoolbook (the *Donatus*). There may have been earlier jobs, but if so they are lost. Next came a propaganda pamphlet warning all Christendom of an impending Moslem threat to the strategic island of Cyprus. But the job that established the printing press commercially, if not Gutenberg himself, was nothing more than a receipt issued by the Church as an acknowledgment of cash contributions solicited throughout the various parishes of Europe. Following an inflexible and lengthy form, the copying of these receipts by hand was a tedious process which consumed most of the profits, and any machine that could strike off thousands of them, identical in every respect, was a priceless invention indeed. So thought Johann Fust, a goldsmith of Mainz, who on two occasions had loaned Gutenberg money — at six percent.

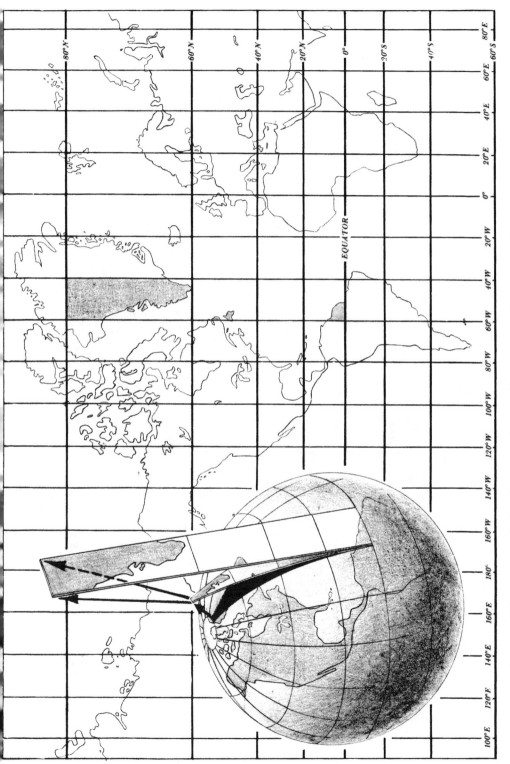

A gore of the globe peeled and projected according to the scheme devised by Gerard Mercator.

The title page of the first sea atlas, in English: *The Mariner's Mirror*.

The printing and selling of books struck Johann Fust as a sound investment, even big books containing many pages, books such as the Bible.[1]

The first, or "Gutenberg," Bible though printed by Gutenberg was taken over by Fust before it got as far as the bindery, probably as a foreclosure on unpaid loans. And with the unbound sheets went Peter Schoeffer who had worked with Gutenberg. Schoeffer, an able craftsman, soon devised a method of making types in metal by first cutting the characters in a mold or matrix and then casting them individually. As a reward for this remarkable display of ingenuity, Schoeffer was made a partner in the printing house of Fust and received his master's only daughter, Christina, in marriage. There was nothing secretive or even reticent about the activities of the partners Fust and Schoeffer. They signed and dated their publications, and seldom failed to offer their customers an impromptu eulogy on the glorious art of printing and the city of Mainz that they claimed had spawned it.[2]

The success of the printing press and of printed books was not immediate. For one thing, the reading public of Europe was limited more or less to the Church, the professions and a handful of intellectuals. And even in the Church there was some doubt as to whether a *printed* book was a proper object to be admitted to a holy sanctuary. As a piece of ecclesiastical apparatus it was without precedent and therefore suspect, even though the words it contained might be sacred enough. But once these scruples were overcome the new printing industry derived most of its revenue from churches, monastery libraries and parish priests. By 1480, 111 towns in Europe boasted printing presses. Germany had 22 (4 of them in Mainz); Italy had 49; France and Holland 8; Belgium and Austria-Hungary 5; Spain 6; England and Switzerland 4.[3]

Humanity was beginning to show the first symptoms of an unquenchable thirst for knowledge. By the year 1500 more than 238 towns in Europe and England had one or more printing presses, that is, printer-publishers who had made a book and impressed upon it the place in which it was made and the date of publication. People became interested in reading, and it was generally conceded that someday one might find a book in some place besides a church, monastery or school. The list of authors selected for publication expanded, and in addition to sacred literature and textbooks, several histories and biographies, medical and legal tomes and many of the Greek and Latin classics began to appear in print. Cicero and Caesar, Aristotle and Plutarch, Cato and Josephus were revived, published and presumably read. The fables of Aesop, the tall tales of Pliny and Solinus, the salacious stories of Giovanni Boccaccio furnished the lighter reading of the age, together with those marvelous compendiums to suit all tastes: the *Chronicles of England* and the *Nuremberg Chronicle*.

Publishers of books were quick to learn some of the likes and dislikes, the foibles and fancies of the public. They discovered, for example, that readers were susceptible to an attractive book, neatly printed on good paper; that it was good business to strive for the beauty achieved by the scribes and painters who copied and illuminated books for the Church and for the wealthy. Color printing, usually in red and blue, was popular. Fust and Schoeffer used it successfully and other printers followed their example. Publishers found that their readers liked clean-cut letters, types resembling as nearly as possible the stylized handwriting of the region. And they discovered that readers from every walk of life had a weakness for pictures of any kind, good, bad or indifferent.[4]

Illustrators, engravers of wood and metal, had been turning out their wares long before Gutenberg and other printers cut their first movable types, in Europe as early as 1406. The first wood block pictures like the first wooden letters of the alphabet were for the most part crude affairs, limited in subject matter to religious scenes and characters. However, there was considerable demand for them at country fairs, markets and other gathering places, and the competition was strong enough to encourage engravers to perfect the art of carving pictures on blocks of wood and transferring them with ink to a sheet of paper.

Line engraving on stone and metal, a very ancient form of art, was developed in Europe not by budding illustrators but by goldsmiths who made a living decorating gold and silver objects with chasing.[5] Plate printing from metal evolved because Italian craftsmen often wanted to keep a record of their ornate designs. To do this they first filled the incised lines they had made on a pitcher or piece of jewelry with a gummy black ink; then after wiping the surface clean they pressed against it a sheet of dampened paper, thus transferring the design in black to a white background. The application of this technique to picture engraving was natural enough, and from 1450 or earlier, half the goldsmiths and goldsmith-painters of Central Germany and the Upper and Lower Rhineland had worked at copperplate printing, turning out prints with religious subjects to sell in the market places.[6] By the time the first books were printed in Europe, the stage was set to illustrate them, either with pictures or with maps. What sort of maps were there to publish?

The revival of scientific thought in the latter half of the fifteenth century came with a surge, stimulated by travel and exploration. Man began to scrutinize again the world he lived in, to dream of the world beyond his doorway instead of dwelling exclusively on the hereafter. He was interested in descriptions of far-away lands, in the habitable world beyond the horizon, in a system of the universe — what makes the world go round. But who was there to tell him?

Pliny and Solinus could still tell an interesting story, after a thousand years or more. The *Natural History* and the *Polyhistor* were popular staples of the publishing fraternity, as were the elementary treatises of Pomponius Mela and Sacro Bosco. But these ancient texts, with their diagrams of the universe and the heavenly bodies, their monstrosities and astrology, were no longer good enough; they entertained but left too many things unexplained. Not so the *Almagest* and the *Geographia* of Claudius Ptolemy.

Before the year 1500 A.D. and in the first sixty years of printing, when paper and vellum were costly and buyers were scarce, not less than seven folio editions of Ptolemy's *Geographia* were published, expensively illustrated and rubricated, and supplemented, in most cases, with maps. And up to the year 1570, when the

Theatrum Orbis Terrarum of Ortelius was published, most of the cartographical publications of importance were editions of Ptolemy's *Geographia*.[7] Such works were either complete copies of the text and maps or their compilers used Ptolemy's text as a foundation on which to build their own descriptions of the world. The *Geographia*, in short, became the canonical work on the subject of cartography during the whole period of the great geographical discoveries, and the prototype of almost all geographical atlases from the invention of printing to the development of modern cartography. To be sure, there were other atlases, augmented with the very latest geographical data, and new discoveries were tentatively set forth on "new" maps, but always there was Ptolemy for an anchor to windward, a solid buttress on which a publisher could lean with impunity. When introducing a new atlas to the public, it was always a good idea to add to the title page the fact that the work was "After the original maps of Claudius Ptolemy," or at least "After the manner of Ptolemy." The name of Ptolemy alone gave a new atlas a mantle of respectability as well as authenticity. It is a curious fact that even after the text and maps of the *Geographia* were outmoded, in the sixteenth and seventeenth centuries, they were printed with all their faults as a preface to concepts which contradicted entirely the principles laid down by Ptolemy. It was a matter of blind reverence, bad editing, or a carefully conceived plan of introducing new ideas to a skeptical world; probably a little of each. Even more puzzling is the fact that as late as the middle of the sixteenth century, long after Diaz and Vasco da Gama had shown by rounding Africa that the Indian Ocean was not an enclosed sea like the Caspian, the old Ptolemaic map was reprinted and published often side by side with maps showing the very latest discoveries.

More important to the history of cartography than the life of the man Ptolemy, is the career of his text and maps, for they are the patterns from which modern cartography evolved. Whether Marinus of Tyre was a better man than Ptolemy, whether *he* was actually the man who contributed so much to cartography, are questions which have never been answered and probably never will be. It may be that Marinus designed the form and content of a systematic portrayal of the world, but there is no evidence pro or con that his contributions to cartography were any greater than those made by Ptolemy. Ptolemy's text and maps survived and were published, which is the important fact of history making.

If the *Geographia*, or *Cosmographia* as it was arbitrarily dubbed, was first printed in 1472 and the earliest known manuscript copy of the text and maps dates from the twelfth or thirteenth centuries, what kind of copy did the printer have to work with? Was the latest manuscript anything like the original which must be dated about 150 A.D.? If so what is the evidence? Actually the burial of Ptolemy's work during the Dark Ages was not complete. According to at least one authority, the principal source of information used by Paulus Orosius (fl. 415 A.D.) in his *De miseria mundi* was Claudius Ptolemy. Likewise, Jordanes the historian of the Goths (fl. 550 A.D.) referred to Ptolemy as *"orbis terrae descriptor egregius"* in his *De Origine Actibusque Getarum* (551 A.D.). Both Ptolemy and Marinus are mentioned by Arabic geographers between the eighth and fifteenth centuries, but the

Arabs do not mention any other Greek or Roman geographers, or any of their works.[8]

As for the purity of the text and likeness of surviving manuscript maps to Ptolemy's originals, the best piece of evidence is negative. After a thousand years of copying and recopying, no trace of pagan or Christian influence is found either in the maps or text. The best of the early manuscripts and the best printed editions contain no mythology, nor do the maps show any of the fanciful, allegorical figures which characterized the map productions of the Middle Ages. The assumption, therefore, is that not only was the work of Ptolemy kept alive but it was copied many times over between the years 200 and 1200 A.D., arriving at the printers in 1472 in just about the same form as it was written — with one or two exceptions.[9]

The *Geographia* was originally written in Greek, and at the beginning of the fifteenth century very little Greek was studied in western Europe, even among the learned. A translation into Latin was begun by Emanuel Chrysoloras, a Byzantine scholar who set up in Italy as a teacher of Greek, but it was finished by one of his pupils, Jacobus Angelus, who seems to have been responsible for changing the title of the *Geographia* to *Cosmographia*. Probably all of the oldest Latin texts of the *Geographia* stem from the Angelus version, finished about 1410 A.D. (it was dedicated to Alexander V, who was Pope from 1409 to 1410); Angelus also provided Latin titles and legends for the maps.

A second scholar of the fifteenth century named Dominus Nicolaus Germanus (usually called Nicolaus Donis or Donnus Nicholaus Germanus) a Benedictine from Reichenbach edited a manuscript edition of the *Geographia*, based on the Latin of Jacobus Angelus. Donis did for the maps what Angelus did for the text. An ardent admirer of the Alexandrian geographer, he approached the task with great humility and profuse apologies to the author and his own patron, Pope Paul II. He ventured to improve the maps by redrawing them on the same difficult spherical projection recommended, and later abandoned, by Claudius Ptolemy himself.

Being fully aware, wrote Donis, that Ptolemy the Geographer depicted the earth with the greatest skill, it would have been folly to attempt a new approach to the task and any person endeavoring to do so should justly be convicted of ignorance or rashness, for Ptolemy alone, "even including the many excellent geographers who flourished before him, first discerned a method by which he could represent the several localities of the entire earth in a picture." Donis did not claim to have found anything in Ptolemy's maps that should be corrected or amended. But he assured his readers that if any man familiar with maps cared to sit down with a calm mind and compare the maps of Ptolemy with those he, Donis, had prepared, he would certainly find merit in the new ones, even though they varied a little from Ptolemy's picture.

Donis read the Ptolemaic text very carefully, and when he came to Chapter XXIV of Book I, where Ptolemy challenged all map makers who were not too lazy to draw their maps on his spherical projection, if they possessed sufficient mentality, he rose to the bait and began to reflect "by what means we ourselves might obtain some glory." He concluded that the best way to do it was to redraw Ptolemy's maps, altering nothing but the projection. In no copy of the text, however, either Greek or Latin, did he find good descriptions of different regions, "how many and what kinds of peoples may be found, what towns, cities, rivers, harbors, lakes and mountains, or under what place in the heavens they lie, or in what direction they face." The copyists had evidently failed to insert many of the small details which Donis said he had found in Ptolemy's writings, such as the boundary lines between provinces and countries. Donis reduced the size of the picture, that is, the map of the world, "which heretofore was too large and exceded the common size of books" to a size that would make it more acceptable to those wishing to study it. But in all other respects, he left the maps strictly alone.

Donis did a lot for the maps, and his redrawings on the Ptolemy-Donis projection furnished the pattern for the printed editions of the atlas which followed. In most editions the spherical projection is not apparent at first glance, because the meridians and parallels are not carried across the map; they are merely indicated by graduations on the margins. The map outlines themselves do not have curved lines, with the exception of the world map, but are generally in the form of an isosceles trapezoid. Aside from the modified projection itself, the only other changes made during the transfer of the maps from handwritten parchment to wood block and copperplate were those necessitated by the transposition of colored areas on the manuscripts, denoting boundaries and physical features, to black and white, shaded or hachured for pictorial clarity. Map making taught engravers many tricks! [10]

A conspicuous exception to the above editions, and one of the earliest printed editions of the *Geographia*, is an Italian translation of the text in rhyme (*terza rima*) done by Francesco Berlinghieri and published in Florence c. 1478. The book is undated. This is by no means the most important rendering of the text, though it is the first of several poetical versions. But the maps are said to be the first ones printed from copper plates and the projection seems to be the only faithful reproduction of the one employed by Ptolemy, with equidistant parallels and meridians. Also printed in this edition was Ptolemy's catalogue or index of geographical place names with their longitudes and latitudes, arranged alphabetically instead of geographically, as they were in the original. [11]

While European printers and publishers were struggling with the problem of how to handle a book containing both text and maps, keeping both within the realm of practicality and usefulness, certain men were looking beyond the limits of Ptolemy's habitable world. In 1482 a map was published showing Greenland. In 1485 the travels of Marco Polo were published in Latin, a book which Christopher Columbus read and annotated. By 1491, this same Christopher Columbus, a map and chart seller, had secured the royal ear, and on the strength of evidence found on Ptolemy's maps, on Martin Behaim's globe and on a chart of the world by Paolo Toscanelli, was trying to sell a fantastic scheme to their Royal Highnesses Ferdinand and Isabella of Spain. Nine years and three voyages later, the discoveries in the Western Sea were laid down on a great chart of the world painted by Juan de la Cosa on an oxhide for all to see and contemplate. With other members of the crew, La Cosa had been forced by Columbus to sign an affidavit stating that Cuba was not an island but part of the mainland of Asia. Whether the great land barrier explored by Columbus and drawn by La Cosa was Asia or a New World, time and further exploration would tell.[12]

The chart of the world drawn by Juan de la Cosa was the first of a long series of publications summarizing the latest discoveries in the Western Sea. Every year from 1500 on, at least one new map or chart appeared. Some were never printed; others were engraved on wood and copper. A few such maps were published separately, but more often they were bound in with a treatise on cosmography or a narrative of an exploring expedition.[13] Geographical information was no longer the exclusive property of a small group. Travel and exploration, even across the Western Sea, became more or less commonplace, and most world travelers wrote about what they saw. Often these writers were merely trying to inspire awe or make money, but a certain number, stimulated by royal command, were bent on "selling" the New World to potential colonists in the Old. It was the greatest real-estate venture of all time.

From the very beginning, the printing of maps and charts presented certain physical problems that have dogged publishers ever since and that have never been completely solved. First there was the matter of size. How large should a map be? The larger the better, as Ptolemy had pointed out and later cartographers had discovered. The larger the map the more details could be shown, and the more place names and legends could be legibly printed. On a very small map, especially of a large area, not only outlines but practically all details including legends were either lost completely or were so small that they were useless for all practical purposes. But large maps, beyond a given size, had certain drawbacks. They were awkward to handle and costly to publish. The ingenious Richard Hakluyt devised what he thought was a good system of rolling and unrolling large maps, but even with a system, he pointed out, "most dwelling-houses are not spacious or light enough to contain a large map fully spread out." [14] In addition, as all map publishers discovered, the high cost of copper, the time and expense involved in having the plates engraved and printed also tended to limit map sizes — and still do. However, there were a few large-scale maps produced in the early 1500's. One such map was compiled and published by Martin Waldseemüller in 1507. It was the first map to bear the name *America*. One of the most important maps of all time, its existence was known only by what the author wrote about it until the year 1900, when a single copy was found.[15]

Waldseemüller, who was probably born at Radolfszell on Lake Constance, studied at the University of Freiberg. Later he became a clergyman in the diocese of Constance and was finally appointed Canon of St. Dié in the Vosges Mountains. His interests were broad and his friends learned; in fact St. Dié was an unusual little town. A small group of men including Waldseemüller comprised the Gymnasium Vosagense, a kind of literary salon devoted to the study of philosophy, cosmography and cartography. Canon Walter Ludd, secretary to the Duke of Lorraine, was the guardian angel of the group. Ludd set up a printing press in St. Dié for the express purpose of publishing his own effusions, and, incidentally, the writings of other members of the Gymnasium. Martin Waldseemüller and Philesius Ringmann did the printing.

Ringmann and Waldseemüller spent considerable time prowling through the libraries of Strassburg and Basel, collating various manuscripts and maps for a proposed edition of Ptolemy's *Geographia*, but the discoveries of the Spanish and Portuguese were too important to ignore, and Waldseemüller was fascinated by the dramatic figure of Amerigo Vespucci. So Claudius Ptolemy was brushed aside and a little book, *Cosmographiae Introductio* was written and published instead. The book consisted of four parts. The first was Waldseemüller's outline of the principles of cosmography according to the best tradition, dealing with geometrical theorems, definitions of the globes, circles, axes and climata; the divisions of the earth, the principal winds, the seas and islands and the various distances from place to place. But in addition to the old routine facts he made a proposal in his text which was a new idea. Commenting on the new territories described by Vespucci in his *Quatuor Navigationes*, referred to as the fourth continent (*quarta orbis pars*), Waldseemüller suggested that it be christened America in honor of the (alleged) discoverer. Moreover, he followed up his proposal by printing the name America in the region of South America on the two maps made to accompany his *Introduction to Cosmography*.[16]

Waldseemüller compiled a large map: *Universalis Cosmographiae Descriptio in Plano*, which was supposed to comprise the third part of the *Cosmographiae*, but it is doubtful whether a copy was ever bound up with the book. It was printed from twelve wood blocks on stout paper and each sheet measured 18 by 24½ inches. Pasted together they would make a map of about 36 square feet. Here was another problem for map publishers to solve. The text, printed in octavo size, was written to explain, among other things, the large-scale map. In order to bind the two together, each sheet would have to be folded at least once and probably twice, making a cumbersome volume and weakening the map sheets at the folds. Yet if the book were bound separately, the map would lack a protective covering and inevitably the two would become separated, if not lost.[17]

The little book and the big map were popular. Two editions were published the first year (1507), one in April and a second in August. In 1508 Waldseemüller wrote his copartner Ringmann that the map had been sold far and wide, and in a later publication he stated that 1000 copies had been sold.[18] Both text and map were reprinted and "adapted" many times, and each reprinting drove home the suggestion that the New World should bear the name America. Such is the power of the printed word that by the time Waldseemüller became convinced that Amerigo Vespucci was not the man to honor, it was too late to do anything about it. He deleted the name America in his later map publications, but offered no substitute in its place. The name persisted, and in 1538 Gerard Mercator clinched the matter on his large-scale map of the world. Carrying the idea a step further, according to the latest discoveries and his own inclination, Mercator subdivided the New World into "North America" (*Americae pars septentrionalis*) and "South America" (*Americae pars meridionalis*). And so it is today.[19]

About 1550 bookseller-publishers began to switch from woodcut illustrations, title pages and maps to copperplate engraving. This change of policy automatically centered the map making and map publishing business in the Netherlands, which then boasted the best line engravers in the world. This was especially true of Antwerp, the great commercial center and capital of Western Europe. Her craftsmen were turning out thousands of prints of religious scenes, illustrating the Bible and the lives of the saints, to be sold in the local market and exported to the Jesuit missions in South America. Specialties had developed within the craft; some men worked on title pages and decorative borders for books; others engraved ornate patterns for artists and architects; still others worked on maps and charts; some branched out and became printsellers and distributors. Engravers in the principal cities of the Netherlands were highly organized craftsmen, members of the guild of Saint Luke. All were well-trained men with high standards of workmanship. Family dynasties sprang up among them, whose members trained the young; fathers and sons, uncles and cousins, brothers and relatives by marriage mastered the same techniques, and, too frequently, the same designs. Guild members participated in the same religious rites and festivals, they contributed to a common fund; hours of work, terms of admission and rules governing apprenticeships were fixed by the members, while "wardens" supervised the quality of the goods produced.[20]

Two of the greatest figures in the history of cartography flourished during this period, when the Netherlands led the world in map making. One was Gerard Mercator, cartographer, engraver and scientist; the other was Abraham Ortelius, map seller and publisher. Technically the two were competitors; actually they were friendly collaborators; together they wrote an important chapter in history, each contributing according to his background and particular talents. Ortelius lived and worked at Antwerp while Mercator was in Duisburg, sixty miles away.

The name Mercator has become synonymous with a navigational chart and a map projection; as a result his numerous other accomplishments have been all but forgotten.[21] Yet for fifty-seven years he was the foremost cartographer of Europe and perhaps did more than any other one man to raise map making from a low art form to an exact science. Mercator drew and engraved his first map in 1537, three years after he set up shop in Louvain. It was a small-scale map of Palestine, and like most of his later maps was published separately (*Terrae Sanctae descriptio*). Only one copy has survived.[22] Next he was commissioned by a group of affluent merchants to make an accurate map of Flanders. This he did, not only the surveying and leveling but the drafting and engraving as well. After three years of grueling labor the finished map (*Exactissima Flandriae descriptio*) was published in 1540 at Louvain.[23] As the title indicates, this was not an artistic conception of the country, but an exact survey, drawn to scale. It was such an improvement over all previous maps of Flanders that it attracted wide attention and brought the author a commission, through Cardinal Granvelle, Prime

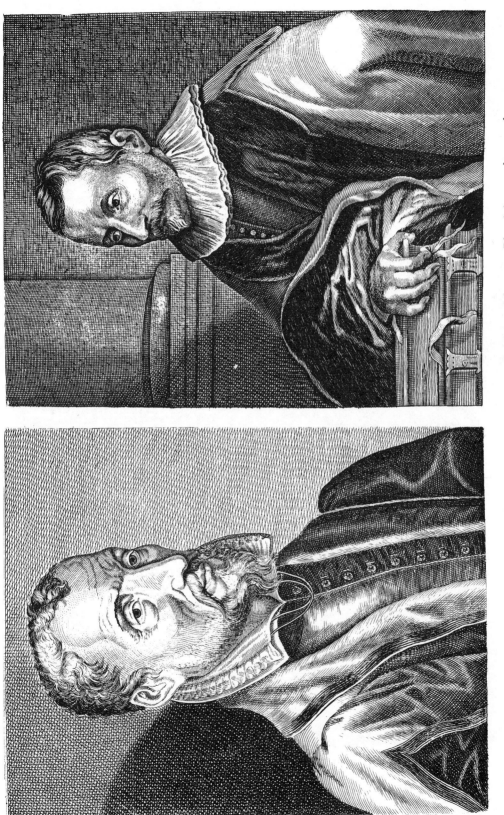

Christopher Plantin of Antwerp, printer of atlases as well as books.

Balthasar Moretus, Plantin's grandson and successor.

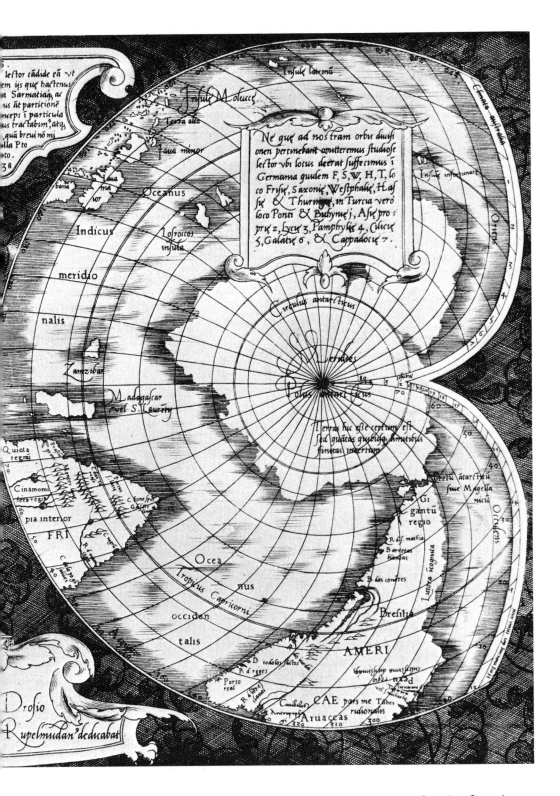

Mercator's map of 1538, naming North America and South America for the first time.

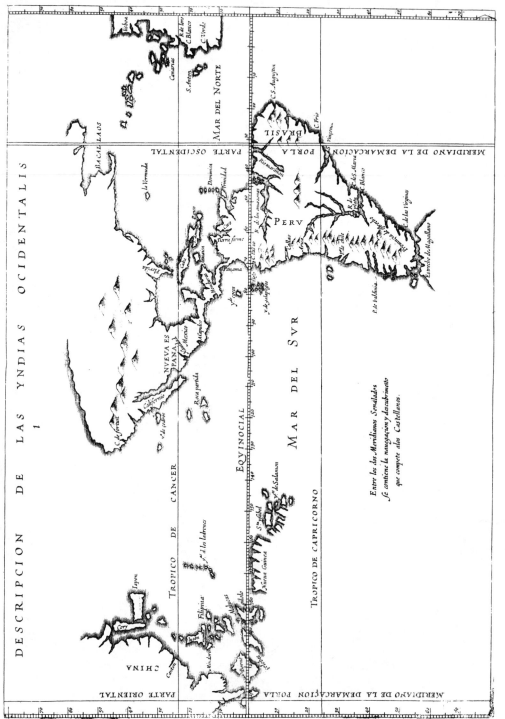

The Line of Demarcation as it appeared on a map of the New World in 1622.

Minister to Charles V, to make a terrestrial globe for His Majesty. Mercator finished it in 1541 and dedicated it to Granvelle. When he delivered the globe he took along a little treatise on the use of it (*Libellus de usi globi*). The Emperor was so pleased with his globe that he ordered Mercator to make him a set of surveyors' instruments to take along on his military campaigns; these consisted of a small quadrant, an astronomical ring, a sundial (probably pocket size), and various drafting instruments such as compass and dividers.[24]

In 1538 Mercator made a map of the world in two hemispheres, drawn on an unusual double cordiform projection used earlier by Orontius Finé and Bernard Sylvanus. Only two copies of this map, rediscovered in 1878, have survived. It was on this map that the names "North America" and "South America" were introduced. Contrary to popular opinion, Mercator did not believe that Asia and North America were joined at any point; he subscribed to the more advanced theory that the ocean lay between the two, and that there was a northwest passage to Asia above the furthest extremity of North America. This belief, demonstrated on his map of the world, was perpetuated by other map makers who copied him. It was a tantalizing theory, and one worthy of consideration by such navigators as Drake, Frobisher, Davis and others.[25]

Mercator's career very nearly came to an abrupt end in 1544 when he was imprisoned as a heretic by the Regent Mary, Queen Dowager of Hungary. A fierce reactionary against the Protestant Reformation, Mary was violent when it came to the Anabaptists and their excesses. She thought all heretics should be exterminated, and so ordered it. A wholesale slaughter ensued, "care being only taken that the provinces were not entirely depopulated." The imperial edict issued at Brussels condemned all heretics to death. Repentant males were executed by the sword; repentant females were buried alive; the obstinate of both sexes were burned at the stake. The charge: Lutheran heresy. Mercator was one of forty-three condemned at Louvain, and was saved only by the intercession of his parish curate, a clever man and shrewd debater.[26] Thereafter Mercator had nothing more to do with political and religious controversies. In 1552 he had just about decided to move out of Louvain when he was approached by George Cassander, who had been ordered by the Duke of Juliers, Cleves and Berg, to organize a university at Duisburg. Cassander offered Mercator the chair of cosmography. The plans for the university did not materialize, but Mercator nevertheless moved his family to Duisburg and became cosmographer to the Duke instead. Soon after, he completed a celestial sphere (*cosmos*) and presented it to Charles V with a written *Declaratio*, outlining a theory already advanced, concerning the determination of longitude by measuring magnetic declination.

In 1552 Mercator began work on a large-scale map of Europe, engraved on six sheets, which he finished in 1554.[27] The immediate importance of the map was greater than any of his previous efforts. Europe had been poorly mapped, even though there were many artistic specimens of alleged surveys available for sale. He drew his information from many sources, but the net result was a general increase in accuracy for almost every part of the continent. The length of the

Mediterranean Sea, for example, was given as 62° by Ptolemy. Mercator shortened it to 58° on his globe of 1541, and further reduced it to 53° on his new map. In addition, he moved Cape Finisterre and the adjacent coast of Spain 15° to the east. A reduced copy of the map was published by his son Rumold. In 1563 he undertook the difficult assignment of making a survey and map of Lorraine at the request of Duke Charles. It took him two years, and the hardships of making the survey, which he directed in person, almost killed him. The map was finished in 1564 (*Lotharingiae descriptio*) but it is doubtful whether it was ever published. The same year, in spite of his poor health, he engraved a map of the British Isles drawn by his friend William Camden in England.[28]

In the midst of a busy life as a cartographer whose work was much in demand, Mercator took the time to compile and publish (Cologne, 1569) a Latin manuscript of 450 folio pages on the subject of chronology, a work which was badly needed after the confusion of the Middle Ages. Even as Mercator's book was coming from the press, scientists were working on the reformation and correction of the Julian Calendar, a task which was completed thirteen years later by order of Pope Gregory the Thirteenth. Mercator's approach to the subject was scientific enough. He tried to revise the dates of important historical events by making calculations on the basis of the solar and lunar eclipses mentioned by historians. He also compiled a catalogue of events, with their dates, in tabular form, according to the systems of the Assyrians, Persians, Greeks and Romans. The book was not universally accepted, in spite of the care and work that went into it; the Italians were enthusiastic in their praise, but it was severely criticized in France.

With just cause, Mercator was a great admirer of Ptolemy's writings, not as they had been edited and interpreted, but Ptolemy unvarnished. Like many other map publishers, Mercator brought out an edition of the maps in the *Geographia*, which was published in 1578. But instead of presenting Ptolemy with improvements by Mercator, he tried to reproduce the maps in their original form. The twenty-seven map reproductions, engraved on copper, are considered the best in existence. Six years later he printed the text of the *Geographia*, after collating five different versions, and purging it of interpolations, alterations and corruptions that had crept in.[29]

Mercator's friend Abraham Ortel or Ortels, better known as Ortelius, had not been fortunate enough to acquire an academic background, yet he was highly regarded by the scholars of Europe. He was born in Antwerp in 1527 and died there in 1598. When he was twenty, Ortelius became a member of the guild of Saint Luke as an illuminator of maps (*äfsetter van kaertën*). Seven years later his father died and the young man was faced with the problem of supporting his mother and two sisters. To increase his earnings he began to buy maps on the side. His sisters mounted them on linen and Abraham colored and sold them at the fairs at Frankfurt and other cities. Soon he began to travel abroad, both to find new markets for his Netherlands maps and to bring back foreign publications. He visited France and Italy, selling his beautifully colored maps and buying up copies of the best available maps of foreign cities and countries. One of his first and best customers was Aegidius Hooftman, of Antwerp, a canny merchant who prospered while others failed. Hooftman studied the sea, the tides and the winds, trying to figure out the best routes for his ships and the best times to send them on their way to foreign ports. He bought every chart he could lay his hands on, and every map. Europe, as usual, was in a turmoil, and Hooftman followed the wars on his maps, trying to work out the shortest and safest ways to transport his merchandise overland and what the freight rates would be. His office was strewn with maps and charts of all sizes and descriptions. They were a nuisance to handle and yet they were a vital asset to a man whose business was foreign commerce. Like others before and after him, Hooftman grumbled about his maps, the balky ways of the big ones that had been rolled up a long time, and the eyestrain a man suffered from trying to decipher the print on the very small ones. Hooftman aired his woes one day to his friend Radermacher, who was also a friend of Ortelius, and Radermacher suggested that they ask Ortelius to gather together as many reliable maps as possible of the Netherlands, Germany, France and Italy and any other surveys that might be available, but only maps that were printed on one sheet of paper. Then Hooftman or Ortelius could have the collection bound up like a book and it could be used and stored conveniently.[30]

When Hooftman and Radermacher spoke about a "sheet" of paper, they had a definite size in mind. All paper was made by hand in those days, and the size of the "sheets" so made was limited by the efficiency and convenience with which a frame of wet pulp could be handled by the papermakers. Years of experience proved that an average man could handle a loaded frame 28 inches long and 24 inches wide; larger ones were too heavy and awkward to handle. These dimensions, of course, varied slightly from time to time and from place to place, but they were the average limit. When larger maps were made they were engraved on more than one plate and printed on two or more sheets of paper.[31]

Ortelius made up a volume of about thirty maps, uniform in size, and had it bound for Hooftman. By the time he had completed the order he had decided to make up similar volumes for general sale. Apparently his friend Mercator encouraged him to go ahead with the idea. Up to this time he had put his name as publisher on no more than three maps, but he knew many people in the book trade and many map sellers throughout Europe who could supply him with maps for a general collection such as the one he had made up for Hooftman. First, however, he talked with his friends about the problems of publishing such a book. He talked with Radermacher about the best projections to use, especially the heart-shaped projection originated by Orontius Fineus (Oronce Finé); he also inquired from Mercator and other engravers about having large-scale maps reduced to the size of his proposed atlas. Then began the work of collecting and editing the maps, getting the permission of cartographers to use their publications; engraving the plates and having the whole thing printed, with title page, dedication and table of contents. The compilation of the material took about ten years. Fortunately one of the best printing houses in Europe was in Antwerp and Christopher Plantin, the proprietor, was a good friend of Ortelius.[32]

In spite of the splendid support Ortelius received from his friends and colleagues, it was not a good time to launch a new enterprise of any kind. Charles V had abdicated in 1556 and the seventeen provinces of the Netherlands, like Spain, had passed to his son Philip II. Calvinism had taken root in the northern provinces (commonly called Holland), but the southern provinces (now Belgium) remained Catholic. The atmosphere was tense with fear lest the Spanish Inquisition should come to the Netherlands, bringing with it bloodshed and torture. In 1567 the Duke of Alva had arrived with 20,000 Spaniards. William of Orange fled with many of his followers. The Council of Blood was created, and the estates of those who failed to appear before the tribunal were confiscated. The Netherlands seethed with revolt. Talk of any kind was dangerous; anything in writing was more so, and printing of every description was scrutinized minutely by the authorities.

In a letter from a map seller in Lisbon, Ortelius was cautioned about the kind of material he could send to Spain without getting into trouble. He would have to avoid all pictures and engravings that might offend the Church, and any that might be considered obscene, because the Inquisitor examined all such things as well as books. Bible pictures were safe, and engraved portraits of distinguished Catholics, all except Erasmus, who was considered a heretic. And by implication Ortelius was warned not to send maps that bore the coats of arms of the wrong families or any other decorative symbols that might have political significance. All in all it was a delicate situation for a vendor of the graphic arts or for a publisher of illustrated books. Nevertheless, on May 20, 1570, the first edition of the first modern geographical atlas was issued from the press, compiled and edited by Abraham Ortelius and published in Antwerp by Egidius Coppens Diesth. It bore the Latin title: *Theatrum Orbis Terrarvm* (Theater of the World).[33]

The atlas exceeded everyone's expectations, including the publisher's. It was made up of sheets folded once ("in folio") and contained 35 leaves of text and 53 copperplate maps, most of them engraved by Francis Hogenberg. A remarkable feature of the *Theatrum* was the editor's catalogue of authorities (*catalogvs avctorvm tabvlarvm*), containing 87 names of geographers and cartographers whose works he had consulted or copied. This list not only established a high precedent in the ethics of map publishing, it also publicized the names of many cartographers who might otherwise have remained obscure or entirely unknown at home or abroad. In short, it was a "Who's Who in Cartography" both past and present.[34]

The first printing of the *Theatrum* was soon exhausted and in three months a second edition came out with a few minor changes. The table of errata was gone and some necessary changes had been made in the text. Four new names had been added to the list of authorities; a few pages of text had been reset and the whole had been lengthened by three pages. That edition, too, was soon exhausted. With all its faults, the *Theatrum Orbis Terrarvm* was a complete success, commercially and otherwise. Granted that some of the maps bore traces of the Ptolemaic tradition and others were little better than artistic conceptions; nevertheless the collection as a whole was fairly comprehensive, and above all it was well documented. It was a new kind of publication, a portrait of the world done up in one volume on a series of maps reduced to a convenient size, attractively decorated and neatly engraved. People liked it. Its interest was universal; it was an international publication compiled by a diplomat and scholar. On the ornamental title page, instead of the usual three human figures denoting the continents of the world, there were now four, "and thus in this book we have America for the first time admitted into the realm of symbolism as the equal of the other three parts of the globe." The general plan of the volume and the selection of maps were as ancient as Ptolemy's *Geographia* and as modern as any twentieth-century geographical atlas. First there was a general map of the world (*Typvs orbis terrarvm*), followed by maps of the four known continents: America, Asia, Africa and Europe. Then followed separate maps of the various countries and the smaller political divisions within them, including many which have long been extinct.[35]

Public response to the *Theatrum* was prompt and for the most part favorable. Letters began coming in to Ortelius referring to "your most beautiful *Theatrum*." Some of the praise was ecstatic, such as the letter received from one Petrus Bizarus. "Ortelius, you, the everlasting ornament of your country, your race, and the universe, you have been educated by Minerva. . . . By the wisdom she has imparted to you, you unfold the secrets of nature, and declare how this stupendous frame of the world has been adorned with countless towns and cities by the hand and labour of men, and by the command of kings . . . Hence all extol your Theatrum to the skies and wish you well for it. . . ." More to the point was the letter from Gerard Mercator at Duisburg. "I have examined your 'Theatrum,' " he wrote, "and compliment you on the care and elegance with which you have embellished the labours of the authors, and the faithfulness with which you have preserved the production of each individual, which is essential in order to bring out the geographical truth, which is so corrupted by mapmakers." Maps published in Italy, he continued, were especially bad. Hence Ortelius deserved great credit for having selected the best descriptions of each region and collected them in one manual which could be bought at a small cost, kept in a small space, and even carried about wherever one pleased. Mercator hoped Ortelius would add some recently published maps to his collection, such as one of Hungary by the Vienna bookseller, Johann Maior, "for your work will (I believe) always remain saleable, whatever maps may be reprinted by others."

By the simple expedient of being honest with his readers, and inviting criticism and suggestions, Ortelius made his *Theatrum* a sort of co-operative enterprise on an international basis. He received helpful suggestions from far and wide, and cartographers stumbled over themselves to send him their latest maps of regions not covered in the *Theatrum*. From Spire he received a map of Moravia sent by a friend and colleague who thought it would add to the usefulness of the volume. And from an emissary of Cardinal Espinosa he received a letter suggesting that the Cardinal's home town, Martimuñoz, which was not on the map of Spain, be added to the map, and would Ortelius then please send two copies (colored) of the *Theatrum* to His Eminence, bound in leather and decorated in gold. From Rome came a letter enclosing a map of Siena and environs with a little book summarizing the history of the city, which the author, Caesar Orlandius, said Ortelius was welcome to abridge. Orlandius added, "I think your work ought to be speedily reprinted, as all copies which arrive here are at once bought, notwithstanding the booksellers daily raise the price, and Franciscus Tramezzinus lately sold a copy for ten gold crowns, whereas four months ago it only fetched eight." [36]

The *Theatrum* was, in fact, "speedily reprinted" several times. A third edition in Latin and a Dutch edition were published in 1571; and the following year a German and a French edition came out. Suggestions for corrections and revisions, always friendly, kept Ortelius and his engravers busy altering plates for new editions. Within three years he had acquired so many new maps that he issued a supplement (*Additamentum*) of 17 maps which were afterwards incorporated in the *Theatrum*. When Ortelius died in 1598, at least 28 editions of the atlas had been published in Latin, Dutch, German, French and Spanish. These do not include the separate printings of the *Additamentum* or abridgments of the *Theatrum* published by others. The last edition was published by the House Plantin in 1612, fourteen years after the author's death, edited by Balthasar Moretus of the Plantin firm. [37]

While Ortelius basked in well-earned glory, enjoying the prosperity of a successful editor and publisher, his friend Gerard Mercator went about the laborious business of surveying land, drawing maps and engraving plates on his own account. He remained the friend and adviser of Ortelius, sharing valuable information and the gossip of the map world with the younger man. In 1580 he wrote Ortelius from Duisburg, telling him how glad he was to hear that he had obtained a good description of China. Mercator had just heard that a new map of France had been published; and a friend had just loaned him a large-scale map of the world drawn on vellum. It was rather roughly drawn and distances were not accurate; but Cathay and Mangi were especially well described, and he had thought about contracting that part of the East as far as the Ganges and redrawing it for Ortelius, but as long as the latter already had found a map of China he would wait to see how it looked in print before offering him another. Ortelius had written Mercator the news that Sir Francis Drake had been sent out on a new naval expedition, and Mercator wrote back that he had heard from England that Captain Arthur Pitt had been dispatched to explore the northern coasts of Asia even beyond the promontory of Tabis, probably in order to meet the returning fleet which had sailed through the strait of Magellan to Peru, the Moluccas and Java. Mercator suspected that this fleet had returned on a course to the west and north of Asia by way of the strait which surrounds the northern coasts of America, a route already explored by Frobisher. This letter and others like it illustrate how commercial map makers tried to keep posted on the latest developments in world exploration without benefit of inside information. [38]

Mercator, too, had plans for publishing a general collection of his maps which could be bound up in convenient book form. Sentimental historians have said that he postponed the publication of his atlas in order to give his friend Ortelius a clear field, but actually he was not ready with his collection when he died in 1594, twenty-four years after the appearance of the first edition of the *Theatrum*. He had planned a work on heroic proportions to be published in three parts or numbers. The second part was published first (Duisburg, 1585), consisting of 51 maps of France, Germany and the Netherlands (*Gallia* and *Germania*) with elaborate descriptive text in Latin. The third part was published next (Duisburg, 1590), comprising 23 maps of Italy, Slavonia, Candia and Greece. The first part was published last by his son Rumold, in 1595, a year after Mercator died. The maps, laid out by Gerard, include Iceland and the polar regions, the British Isles (dedicated to Queen Elizabeth), the Scandinavian countries, Prussia, Livonia, Russia, Lithuania, Transylvania, the Crimea, Asia, Africa and America. The title selected for this collection of maps represents the first use of the word "Atlas" in connection with a geographical work. It read: *Atlas sive Cosmographicae meditationes de fabrica mundi et fabricati figura* ("Atlas, or cosmographical meditations upon the creation of the universe, and the universe as created"). In the dedicatory epistle, Rumold explained that this was the title his father had chosen for his publication. A genealogical tree in the introductory text gave the ancestry of Atlas, the mythological character who led the Titans in their war against the god Jupiter, and was therefore condemned to support the heavens on his shoulders.[39]

In 1602 the three parts of the Mercator *Atlas* were brought out together in one volume for his heirs. This was really the first edition of the complete work and was published at Dusseldorf by Bernard Busius. Neither Gerard Mercator nor his son Rumold lived to see the great popularity of the *Atlas*, but their maps were perpetuated, after a fashion, by Jodocus Hondius, an engraver and map seller who bought the plates and thereby made himself both rich and famous. Hondius was born at Wacken, Flanders, in 1563. His parents moved to Ghent when he was very young and there he learned drafting, engraving, type founding and the art of making and decorating mathematical instruments. He fled to London in 1584 when Ghent was stormed, like many another Flemish craftsman. He would engrave anything, but specialized in maps, charts and globes. He made globes that were larger than any that had been made before. He worked with Ryther and De Bry on the charts for the English edition of Wagenaer's *Mariner's Mirrour*. He married Colette Van der Keere, whose family were printers and engravers of Ghent. In 1595 he moved to Amsterdam and set up shop. His own maps were closely "adapted" from Edward Wright and such eminent explorers as Drake and Cavendish. He borrowed only the best.[40]

The Mercator plates were a gold mine to an opportunist such as Hondius, and he made the most of them. He acquired fifty additional maps and published them together with the Mercator maps at Amsterdam in 1606 under Mercator's title. The text for the work was written for him by Peter Montanus. The following year, 1607, more maps were added and the third edition of Mercator (the second of Hondius) was published. The same year a pocket-size edition was issued with all the plates re-engraved on a very small scale. This was called *Atlas Minor Gerardi Mercatoris à I. Hondio*. . . . The Mercator-Hondius atlases, major and minor, gradually superseded the Ortelius atlas and one edition followed another for nearly fifty years, printed in Latin, French, Dutch and German. When Hondius died in 1611, his son Hendrick and his son-in-law Jan Jansson carried on the publishing business.[41]

Neither the *Theatrum* of Ortelius nor the Mercator-Hondius *Atlas* had things entirely its own way in the field of commercial map publishing; it was too much of a good thing. But for many years these atlases were more successful than any others. The first serious competitor to the *Theatrum* was published in Antwerp by Gerard de Jode in 1578, eight years after the first edition of Ortelius under the title *Specvlvm Orbis Terrarvm*. This atlas contained 65 maps and was a respectable job of printing, but it never approached the popularity of the *Theatrum*, which was already widely known throughout the world. One edition of the de Jode atlas seems to have been enough to satisfy the public demand for a considerable length of time, because it was not reprinted for fifteen years. Between 1593 and 1613 it appeared on the market in various stages of alteration, with eighteen new maps signed by Cornelis de Jode, the author's son. The title was eventually changed to *Specvlvm Orbis Terrae*.[42]

About 1575 an Italian collection of maps entered the publishing field, but it was in no sense a competitor to the Dutch and Flemish atlases. Italian maps were not popular in Europe, though many publishers were forced to rely on them in the absence of better ones.[43] Ortelius needed them to fill out his collection, but Mercator said that maps published in Italy were especially bad. The Italian atlas, containing about one hundred maps (the few known copies vary), was published at Rome without a date and by persons unknown, with the title *Geografia tavole moderne di geografia de la maggior parte del mondo*. . . . The only name attached to the volume is that of Antonio or Antoine Lafreri, who probably did the elaborate title page. Little is known about Lafreri except that he, with his uncle Duchet, founded a celebrated *atelier* for copper engraving at Rome in 1540. The Lafreri or Roman atlas, as it is sometimes called, is extremely rare, and regardless of the merit of the maps it contains, it is interesting because of its title page. In addition to a conventional border design, the artist used, apparently for the first time, the figure of Atlas with the terrestrial globe on his shoulders as a symbol of the contents of the volume. No one knows whether it was this figure, used hundreds of times by later publishers, or Mercator's running title beginning with the word Atlas, that was responsible for use of the word as a synonym for a map collection.[44] *Theatrum*, *Speculum* and other catchwords were tried and later abandoned. And just as the name *Waggoner* was universally adopted as a synonym for a volume of sea charts, *Atlas* became a generic term for a collection of maps, charts or plans bound together in one or more volumes.

Collections of specialized maps, charts, and plans were published before and after the *Theatrum* of Ortelius, but they lacked the universal interest and importance of the first world atlas. However, they contributed a vast amount to the record of the local scene and eventually found their place in the overall picture. In 1528, for instance, an Italian named Benedetto Bordone brought out an atlas of the important islands of the world (*Libro di Benedetto Bordone. Nel quale si ragiona de tutte l'isole del mondo con li lor nomi antichi & moderni . . . .* This useful volume, containing 111 maps and plans, was published at Venice. A second edition came out in 1534 with the title changed to read *Isolario di Benedetto Bordone.*[45] The earliest atlas devoted primarily to the New World was published at Louvain in 1597 by Corneille Wytfliet. It contained 19 maps. This work was very popular and was reissued a second time the first year. Seven editions were printed between 1597 and 1611. "It is as important in the history of the early cartography of the new world as Ptolemy's maps are in the study of the old."[46] Also published about this time were numerous "descriptions" of the East and West Indies, which are primarily atlases with a certain amount of descriptive text. Atlases featuring plans of the principal cities and fortresses of the world (usually the two were synonymous) were fairly common, and some of these combined both important cities and important islands.[47]

National atlases were a logical development in the progress of commercial map publishing, and several such collections appeared before 1600. Christopher Saxton, surveyor and topographical draughtsman, made the first systematic survey of the counties of England and Wales, thanks to a wealthy patron (Thomas Seckford), Her Majesty the Queen and the Privy Council. Saxton's atlas took five years to compile (1574–1579), and would have taken much longer if the Privy Council had not granted him special privileges and issued injunctions ordering Mayors, Justices of Peace and other officials "to see him conducted unto any towre, castle, high place or hill, to view that country . . . and that at his departure from any town or place that he hath taken the view of, the said towne do set forth a horseman that can speak both Welsh and English to safe-conduct him to the market-towne."[48] The finished survey contained 35 maps beautifully colored and worthy to be called the Elizabethan atlas. The ornamental title page features Queen Elizabeth, patron of geography and astronomy, flanked by Strabo and Ptolemy. Perhaps the rarest of all sixteenth century atlases was the collection of maps of France published at Tours in 1594 by Maurice Bouguereau under the title *Le Théâtre François, où sont comprises les chartes générales et particulières de la France*. It was a small atlas (about 15½ by 10 inches) and contained only 16 maps. It is important chiefly because of its rarity (probably not more than six copies are known) and because it is the first strictly French atlas.[49]

Nearly all of the best-selling atlases, originally published in folio or quarto (the "sheet" folded twice), were reduced in size sooner or later to fit the pocket and pocketbook of the average man. The great atlases, as one publisher expressed it, were masses of geographical information, but with two defects. "The first is that they are priced so that many scholars are unable to afford them. The second is that because of their grandeur . . . they are, so to speak, nailed up in the book-case, usually adorned with a very appropriate binding . . . one shows them in one's library rather as a decorative ornament than a useable book. This I tell you is what I have learned from experience, and I know individuals who have never profited from the money these atlases have cost them." [50] Over thirty pocket-size *Epitomes* of the *Theatrum* of Ortelius were published in Dutch, French, Latin, Italian, German and English. The Mercator *Atlas* was first re-produced on a small scale in Venice by Girolamo Porro. Thereafter at least seventeen editions were published, the last one in 1651. The same principle was applied to other works originally printed with large-scale maps. John Speed, the English cartographer, compiled a series of maps after the surveys of Christopher Saxton and John Norden and published them first in folio and later in reduced form in a little atlas entitled *England, Wales, Scotland and Ireland described and abridged with ye historic relation of things worthy memory from a farr larger volume by John Speed*. London, 1627. The pocket atlas became firmly established in the map world. It was "Everyman's" version of the famous cartographers, and more often than not the little atlas was printed by the same presses and engraved by the same artists who did the mammoth volumes that only the wealthy could afford. [51]

Map publishing in the grand manner reached its peak in Amsterdam about the time Jodocus Hondius died and left a going map concern in the hands of his son and his son-in-law. But it was not Hondius the younger or Jan Jansson who was responsible for the magnificent maps and atlases published in Amsterdam about this time; it was a rival of theirs named Willem Janszoon Blaeu (1571–1638), whose career began as a joiner's apprentice. As a young man, he visited the little island of Hveen or Hven, a Danish possession in the Sound, eight miles south of Elsinore. Of all the small islands to shape a man's career, this was it, for it was the leasehold of Tycho Brahe the great astronomer. Ensconced in his palatial observatory at Uraniborg and surrounded by the best instruments that money could buy, Brahe dispensed great learning to his students and apprentices, regarding them coldly down the length of a copper alloy nose which replaced the original one lost in a duel. Young Blaeu stayed at the observatory two years, according to Brahe's day-book, studying astronomy, geography and the construction of precision instruments under the master. [52]

In 1596, Blaeu returned to Amsterdam and set up as a maker of maps, globes and instruments. Apparently he was successful as a manufacturer and vendor of maps, because in 1600 or thereabouts he opened his own establishment and began to do printing and engraving as well. The records of the Amsterdam guilds tell nothing about his activities, but in 1605 the States General passed a resolution proposing that he be granted a sum of money for printing and publishing a *Nieuw Graetbouck* or seaman's guide which was to include tables of the sun's declination for that year as well as charts, an important and profitable commission for any printer. [53] His first cartographic efforts were a pair of globes, made in 1599 and 1602. His first sea chart (*Pascaerte*) was published in 1606, "at the sign of the golden sun-dial," a trade-mark he later used on many of his title pages and on the shingle above his shop. However, not all of Blaeu's maps were signed and few were dated. The plates were used over and over again, and like most map makers, Blaeu probably had a few whose origin was not openly discussed. Complaints were made about his propensity for borrowing information from other maps, disregarding the fact that cartographers were supposed to be protected by a "privilege" or octroi. Rivalry was keen, especially in Amsterdam, where the Hondius-Jansson and Blaeu firms claimed infringements on each other's publica-

The earliest woodcut picture of a cartographer at work. From Paul Pfintzing's *Methodus Geometrica*. Nürnberg, 1598.

tions at one time or another. In 1608, for example, Blaeu made a special plea to the States of Holland and Friesland for protection against the vultures who were pirating his maps, asserting that he could support his family by honest means, with God's mercy, if certain persons would desist from copying all his newest maps before the ink on them was dry.[54]

This sort of appeal was universally the map maker's lament whenever and wherever maps were made. And in the sixteenth and seventeenth centuries, the first important period of commercial map publishing, there was a certain amount of plagiarism, a tremendous amount of publishing zeal and not a little professional jealousy among the gentry. Because of the high cost of copper and its amazing adaptability when doctored by an expert, many map plates had long and check-ered careers. They were bought, begged and stolen; they were patched, spliced, added to, erased and otherwise altered until their original owners would never have recognized them. Maps are known which were made from two plates, one ten or more years older than the other. Many are known whose titles were altered or completely changed, with the names of new cartographers and en-gravers replacing the originals. In some cases such alterations were legitimate, and were made because a plate was sold, but more often because a zealous publisher wished to give the impression that he was offering an entirely new publication.

A certain amount of co-operation was expedient in the map making fraternity, even between such rivals as Jansson and Blaeu who operated in the same town. Travel was expensive and generally unreliable, and accurate geographic informa-tion was hard to get. Like Ortelius, all map makers had to depend on foreign publishers for maps of foreign countries. It was therefore mutually profitable for them to exchange maps with one another when a new survey would be un-profitable if not impossible to make. Moreover, publishing centers were widely scattered. Surveys were made in Italy and the finished maps engraved in Holland. Dutch cartographers and engravers worked in France, England and other foreign countries. Ideas and copper plates went back and forth across Europe and the English Channel. Map titles and legends as well as the language of the map were frequently changed to fit the occasion and place of publication. But in spite of the bonds that united the cartographers of the world, every man reserved the right to denounce a colleague as a thief and an ingrate when a breach of etiquette was discovered, as when a cartographer "scooped" a rival with a choice bit of con-fidential information acquired from a seaman just returned from the Indies. Such bursts of temperament were fairly common, and we find two map men working peacefully together for a time and then suddenly one of them accusing the other of horrible crimes. Later we find them completely reconciled and again collaborat-ing on a new map or series of charts. Map men, too, were human.

Finances were of course a problem among map and chart sellers, but there were ways around that difficulty. Some men were fortunate enough to acquire patrons, usually from among royalty, who considered it amusing and fashionable to sponsor painters, sculptors, musicians and cartographers. Map publishers in turn were able to reward a duke for his generosity by dedicating a map or atlas to His Magnificence or by displaying on a map the ducal coat of arms and perhaps a miniature profile of his country estate. Others received government subsidies; either outright grants of money or pensions in return for services rendered. Orte-lius was given the title of Geographer to His Majesty Philip II of Spain after having been pronounced clean of Protestant taint by his friend Montanus.[55] And Mercator so pleased His Majesty Charles V that he was honored with the title of *Imperatoris Domesticus* or member of the royal household, with numerous per-quisites and prerogatives. John Speed, historian and cartographer, was commis-sioned by Fulk Greville, first Lord Brooke, to survey England, "whose beautie and benefits," Speed wrote, "not a farre off, as Moses saw Caanan from Pisgah, but by my own travels through every province . . . mine eyes have beheld; and whose Climate, temperature, plenty and pleasures make it to be as the very Eden of Europe." [56] Willem Blaeu, on the other hand, was favored by the States General of Holland, who gave him their business and usually a cash advance with each commission. In 1608 they granted him the sum of 200 guilders for the dedication and presentation of a book of sea charts *Het Licht der Zeevaert* (The Light of Navigation) describing the coasts and harbors of the Northern, Eastern and Western Seas. This publication was doubtless nothing more than a current issue of the Dutch "Waggoner" which had become standard equipment aboard ship, because Blaeu drew freely from Waghenaer and Barentszoon in the compilation of his charts. In 1623 he received an even more important commission from the States General in the form of an exclusive right, for a period of ten years, to the publication of "Tables of the declination of the sun and of the most important planets, with the different uses of the North Star calculated anew for the use of all navigators by Willem Jansz. Blaeuw [*sic*]." This meant that he had the monopoly on the official Dutch equivalent of the "Nautical Almanac and Ephemerides," a contract that allowed him to expand his publishing activities considerably.[57]

Willem Blaeu's first atlas of maps came out in 1631, entitled *Appendix Theatri Ortelii et Atlantis Mercatoris*. Just as earlier map publishers had leaned on the name of Ptolemy, Blaeu used Ortelius and Mercator, either to give his atlas an air of authenticity or because he had borrowed freely from their maps. It is possible, of course, that he announced a supplement to their atlases in deference to their fame, but it is not likely. The volume contained 103 maps with text in Latin. Only 7 maps are dated, and only 27 bear the names of the original cartographers. Many are signed by Blaeu.[58]

Aside from his publishing activities, Blaeu was keenly interested in science and did not forget his early training under Tycho Brahe. He is said to have built a huge seven-foot wooden quadrant trimmed with brass, which was installed on the roof of the tower of Leyden. In 1633 the Directors of the Dutch East India Company made Blaeu the head of their department of hydrography. At the time of his appointment, he said, "I requested them to charge all pilots and masters who sailed for India to observe all eclipses, in whatever part they might be seen, and this has been done." Blaeu, in other words, was a highly respected man of science, who held the title of Map Maker to the Republic, yet many of his maps and charts are far from scientific achievements. As one historian has pointed out, none of his charts is laid down on a Mercator projection, though other chart makers had been using it for many years. The majority of his maps are drawn without parallels or meridians; a few have parallels, but usually there are no meridians. The answer is that he probably made two kinds of maps and charts: one for the carriage trade, pretty things with bright colors and gold leaf to please the eye and decorate the home; and one for seamen and officialdom who knew and demanded the best in scientific documents. Blaeu was not stupid or uninformed; he was a shrewd business man who gave his customers what they wanted. His working maps and charts were worn out or were destroyed as a safety measure, while his beautiful maps and atlases, because they were usually locked up in a gentleman's library and never disturbed, have survived.[59]

The year before he died, in 1637, Willem Blaeu and his two sons, Joan (or John) and Cornelius, moved their plant into larger quarters in the Blumengracht, "near the third bridge and the third alley." The business prospered. The building stood near the canal with a 150-foot frontage on a cross street; it was 75 feet wide. "Fronting on the canal," wrote a contemporary, "is a room with cases in which the copper plates are kept, from which the Atlases, the Books of the Cities of the Netherlands and foreign countries, also the Mariners' Atlas and other choice books are printed, and which must have cost a ton of gold. Next to this first room is a press room used for plate printing, and opening upon the cross street referred to above is a place where the type, from which impressions have been made, are washed; then follows in order the room for book printing, which resembles a long hall with numerous windows on either side. In the extreme rear is a room in which the type and certain other materials used in printing are stored. Opposite this store room is a stairway leading to a small room above which is set apart for the use of the proof-readers, where first and second impressions are carefully looked over, and the errors corrected which have been made by the typesetters. In front of this last designated room is a long table or bench on which the final prints are placed as soon as they are brought from the press, and where they are left for a considerable time. In the story above is a table for the same purpose just indicated, at the extreme end of which, and over the room occupied by the proof-readers, is the type foundry wherein the letters used in the printing of the various languages are molded." [60]

Blaeu employed the best pressmen, engravers, scribes and colorists in the Netherlands. His types were clean and well cut; his paper, bearing his own watermark, was heavy and of good quality. In addition to geographical books he published astronomical works and miscellaneous publications, usually in folio size. The Blaeu establishment boasted nine flat bed presses for letter press printing named after the Nine Muses, and six presses for copperplate printing. The number of presses was unusual but their quality was even more so. Willem Blaeu had designed them himself, making the first substantial improvements in the moving parts that had been made since the invention of printing. In 1683, Joseph Moxon summed up the situation in these words, "There are two sorts of presses in use, viz., the old fashion and the new fashion," the "new fashion" being Blaeu's press. The improvements in the "new fashion" were simple enough, but no one had thought of them before, small details that made a big difference and tended to eliminate chronic backache as an occupational disease of printers. In a very few years Blaeu's improved printing press was standard equipment in Europe, and was reluctantly accepted by English printers who were at first skeptical.[61]

The best known publication of the Blaeu press was their great Atlas Major in twelve volumes, in many respects the most beautiful geographical work ever published. It served as eloquent testimony to the prosperity of the Blaeu firm after thirty years of map publishing. John and Cornelius had increased the good will and fixtures of the plant to a considerable extent, and were able, respected men in their own right. No house engaged in foreign commerce was allowed to send marine charts to India, or have them carried there by ships' captains, unless they

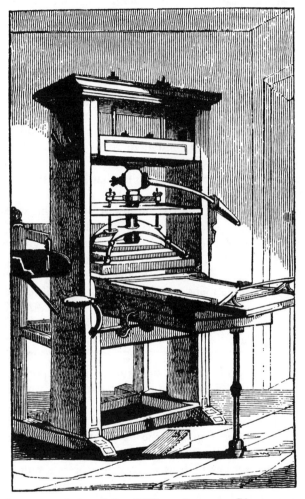

The printing press designed by Willem Janszoon Blaeu, map and chart publisher, embodying the first major improvements since the invention of printing.

were made by the Blaeus. In 1670, when John Blaeu was appointed Map Maker in Ordinary to the Dutch East India Company, he was instructed to examine the journals (log books) of their pilots and to correct their maps whenever possible. John Blaeu, Counsellor and Magistrate, was a man of consequence in Amsterdam.[62]

The acquisition of plates for a twelve-volume atlas was a slow process, and naturally many of the plates had been used before. Willem Blaeu's "Appendix" to Ortelius and Mercator was enlarged to two volumes in 1635 and issued with text in Latin, Dutch and French. Three years later the French edition had grown to three volumes (*Le Théâtre dv Monde, ou Novvel Atlas*) and contained nearly three hundred maps. Every edition thereafter was a little larger than the preceding one until in 1662 the collection had grown to about six hundred. It was published in that year by John Blaeu under the title *Atlas Maior sive Cosmographiae Blaviana* with text in Latin. It was issued in 1663 in 12 volumes with the text in French, and again in 1667. The copies that have survived are usually found as they were published, in full vellum bindings tooled with gold; all edges of the sheets are gilt. It never was and never will be a poor man's book. Special copies were made up for statesmen and royalty, colored and bound to order. A copy of the complete atlas was bound in royal purple and presented by the Blaeus to the Sultan Mohammed IV. He was so impressed by the tremendous coverage of the maps and their innate beauty that he ordered the text and map legends translated into Turkish.[63]

European map publishers of the sixteenth and seventeenth centuries may not have had access to the best and latest geographical information, and might not have used it if they had. But in the absence of facts they gave their customers just about every conceivable substitute in the form of fine engraving, pictorial views, ships and sea monsters, heraldic emblems, portraits of important personages and exquisite coloring. Since maps were made to be beautiful, the pattern necessarily changed from time to time with the current conception of beauty. Obviously a utilitarian sheet such as a map or chart had its limitations as a background for artistic display, but there were ways and means, as the public soon discovered.

Commercial maps had to have titles describing the area portrayed. Often such titles were brief and to the point, but more frequently they were long, rambling descriptions — running titles in every sense of the term. They included the kind of information usually found on the title page of a book: the author (cartographer), the place of publication and the date. At times the dedication of the map was included in the title, as well as the name of the engraver. All such information, running at times as high as seventy-five or one hundred words, gave the map maker a point of departure, an outlet for artistic expression. Like the craftsman who embellished the title pages of books, map makers resorted at first to standardized designs, working them into an enclosed area known as a cartouche.

The name, principle and use of the cartouche have become corrupted during the course of time. Scroll-like figures were used by the Egyptians to enclose inscriptions on tablets and pillars. Later the cartouche referred to an oval formed by a rope knotted at one end, a design used to enclose the arms of the Pope or members of royal families. In this, its proper form, the cartouche is found on very old maps, sometimes topped by a cardinal's hat or some other symbol of the clergy. But when different schools of engraving sprang up in Europe, during the latter

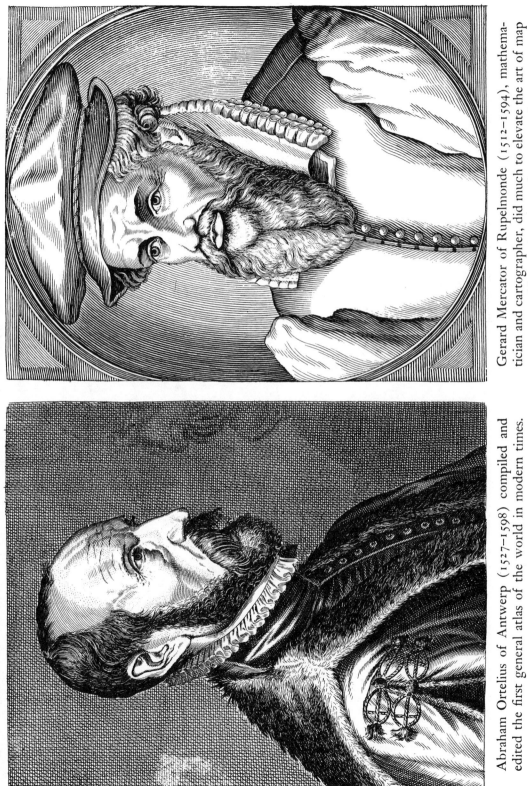

Gerard Mercator of Rupelmonde (1512–1594), mathematician and cartographer, did much to elevate the art of map making to the status of an exact science.

Abraham Ortelius of Antwerp (1527–1598) compiled and edited the first general atlas of the world in modern times.

This seventeenth-century view of Taioan (Tainan) Formosa, by a Dutch artist, shows the fortress of Zelandia guarding the harbor. From "The Secret Atlas" of the Dutch East India Company.

Also found in "The Secret Atlas" is this remarkable view of Manila Bay as it looked in 1647. In the foreground is the Dutch fleet of Pieter de Goyer.

The interior of an eighteenth-century map seller's shop.

The various steps in preparing and engraving a copper plate are illustrated
in this scene from Diderot's *Encyclopédie*, 1751–1765.

part of the sixteenth century, in the days of Ortelius and Wytfliet, characterized by new and increasingly ornate designs, the oval knotted rope underwent remarkable transformation. It was an age of allegory and emblematic pedantry. The formalized, academic style of Italian engraving was transmitted to the northern countries including the Netherlands. The most popular ornamental designs consisted of heavy strap-work or roll-work, simulating leather shields with rolled edges cut in intricate patterns. They were adopted by architects, furniture designers and monumental sculptors. Map makers of all countries used them as all-purpose border designs for titles, dedications, legends of various kinds and heraldic emblems. Engravers made up patterns of this strap-work in every conceivable combination. In the course of time the motif and the cartouche were modified, but never wholly abandoned.[64]

The heavy Dutch scroll cartouches of the early maps became less formal after 1600 but hardly less formidable. Sphinxes, sirens and cherubs were worked into the design, with their extremities terminating in strap-work, fluted columns or clusters of fruit. On the Blaeu maps the cartouches were further modified, and in addition to the formal cartouche the artists included realistic perspective views of villages and towns, hunting and fishing scenes, artistic groupings of the flora and fauna of the locality shown on the map. Human figures as well as naked cherubs were used in the design. There were hawking scenes, boar hunts, tournaments and battle scenes. The costumes, drawn with great care, are still a favorite source of historical information on the subject.[65]

The development of conventional signs and symbols on maps was slow, and varied widely in different countries. Mountains at first were indicated by crude, overlapping lumps or "molehills," and no attempt was made to indicate the height or extent of a range. They all looked alike. As time went on, they were drawn more carefully, often in perspective, so that variations in height were clearly indicated as well as passes, roads and foothills. Elaboration of conventional signs usually depended on the ability of the artist and engraver, and the desire of the cartographer to make himself clear. On the better maps, cities and towns were shown by dots, small circles or by a miniature perspective view, complete with towers, fortifications and flying pennants. Parishes were usually indicated by a cross, the larger ones by a miniature church. Occasionally maps were much more informative, and in the table of legends, symbols were given for vineyards, gold, silver and tin mines, iron and lime deposits, et cetera. The treatment of coast lines varied widely, depending on the cartographer and the people for whom the map or chart was intended. The simplest treatment was to shade the coast with fine lines (hachures) to make the coast line stand out. On the better maps, important stretches of coast were drawn in perspective, showing beaches, dangerous rocks and shoals. Anchorages were indicated by a cross or by a tiny anchor, and shoals were indicated by stippling.

Political boundaries were indicated by dotted lines, single or double. Many roads followed watercourses and received no special treatment; others were indicated by double lines as they are today. Rivers, large and small, were not handled with skill. They were shown either as single wavy lines or double wavy lines, depending on the size; they were either big rivers or small, and seemed to meander aimlessly across many a map until they came to the town or city they were supposed to flow through.

The art of coloring or limning was well established centuries before cartographers produced anything worthy of a painter's talents. Colorists no doubt had their trade secrets, but there was no great mystery about their general methods; in fact they were common property. Books were written on the subject, revealing that the secret of success lay in the ingredients used and the care with which the colors were applied. Ortelius discovered that beautiful coloring sold maps, and later publishers found that color on a map could serve a double purpose. It could make a map beautiful to look at, and it could be used more effectively than any other device to set off or differentiate adjacent political areas, land forms and bodies of water as well as prominent physical features that should be emphasized such as forests, lakes and river valleys, not to mention differences in topography.

In 1573 an Englishman named Richard Tottill wrote *A very proper treatise, wherein is briefly sett forthe the art of Limming, which teacheth the order in drawing & tracing of letters, vinets, flowers, armes and imagery, & the maner how to make sundry sises or grounds to laye silver or golde uppon.*[66] In this treatise, gleaned from the recipe books of ancient European artists, we learn that the hen's egg was one of the most important ingredients in the artist's paint box. The egg white was a favorite "size" and was also used as a glaze in place of shellac or varnish. To preserve egg whites for an indefinite time, "without corrupting or putting of arsenic to them," Tottill advised straining them through a linen cloth without breaking them; then adding an equal amount of the best white vinegar. Let stand for two days; then pass the mixture through a linen cloth without beating or stirring. Let stand five days. Strain again and bottle with a good stopper.[67]

To make an "embossed ground" to lay gold or silver leaf upon, you should make a fine powder of "Venice cerese," white lead, chalk (or the plaster from an old image). Then grind them with the white of an egg and a little water on a painter's stone. This "size" should be well tempered: "thicke standing" and should be allowed to get "clammy and rotten" in a moist, dark place. The older, clammier and rottener this size gets, the better.[68] Egg yolk was used to make white letters on a black field in the following manner. The yolk of a "newe layde egge" was ground on a painter's stone and a little water added. This liquid was used with a pen to trace the letters on paper or parchment. When dry, the field and letters were covered with black ink. After the ink was dry the lettered area, covered with dried egg yolk, was rubbed with a woolen cloth, revealing white letters on a black field.[69]

Tottill used two kinds of black. One he called Sable or Fume black. This was nothing more than lampblack, obtained by holding "a burnynge torche" under a basin until the bottom was black. The black was scraped off and tempered with white of egg or gum water, that is, gum arabic and water. But to make "an excellent black like Velvet" you "take Hartes horne, and burn it to cole on a Coliars harth, then put it in a shel to drie in a shadowy place. And when you wil occupye the same, grynde parte thereof againe with the glayze, or with gumme water: and work it forthe."

To diaper with gold or silver on top of colors, you should take "the joyce of garlike" and draw with it the design you wish to lay over the colors. "Then take and lay the gold upon it, and presse it downe lightly with an Hares tayle, & let it dry halfe a day or more. Then rubbe of [*sic*] the golde which cleveth not to the garlike." In regard to varnishing over colors or over gold and silver, Tottill was lyrical; he said, "As the daye becometh more light and brighter by the shining of the sonne, even so all colours that are vernished do shewe furth a better glosse or luster, and become more brighter by the shyning of the same. . . ." [70]

William Salmon, writing a hundred years later, was more lucid on the subject of coloring, and went into greater detail for the uninformed reader. "Limning," he wrote, "is an Art whereby in water colours, we strive to resemble Nature in every thing to the life. The Instruments and Materials thereof are chiefly these 1. *Gum* [*Arabic*] 2. *Colours*. 3. *Liquid Gold and Silver*. 4. *The Grindstone and Muller*. 5. *Pencils*. 6. *Tables to Limn in*. 7. *Little glass or China-dishes*." Salmon listed seven "principal" colors: white, black, red, green, yellow, "blew," and brown, out of which are made mixed or compound colors. [71] Instead of egg white for a size, Salmon recommended gum arabic diluted with spring water, a substance which later came into general use as an adhesive, a component of ink, and an important ingredient in textile printing. In map coloring it was used chiefly as a size on which to lay gold leaf. To keep water colors from sinking into the paper, Salmon prescribed alum-water (eight ounces of alum to a quart of "fair" water). This solution, he said, "will add a lustre unto them, make them shew fairer, and keep them from fading." [72] In lieu of gold leaf he suggested the following golden liquor: "Take a new laid Egg, through a hole at one end take out the white, and fill up the Egg with Quick-silver two parts, Sal-armoniak [ammonium chloride] finely powdered, one part; mix them all together with a Wire or little stick: stop the hole with melted wax, over which put an half Egg-shell: digest in horse-dung for a month, and it will be a fine golden coloured Liquor." [73]

The embellishment of maps and charts, always more or less conventional, became even more so in the seventeenth century, both as to color and the treatment of symbols. This fact is demonstrated by Salmon's instructions for drawing the four principal winds. To indicate Eurus, the east wind, "draw a youth with puffed and blown cheeks (as all the other winds must be), wings upon his shoulders, his body like a Tauny Moor, upon his head a Red Sun." Zephyrus, the west wind, should be a youth with a merry look, holding in his hand a swan with wings outspread as though he were about to sing. On the youth's head should be a garland of all sorts of flowers. Zephyrus still had a good reputation, "because it cherisheth and quickneth, bringing life." Boreas, the north wind, should be drawn like an old man, "with a horrid, terrible look; his hair and beard covered with snow, or the hoar-frost; with the feet and tail of a Serpent." Auster, the south wind, was drawn, "with head and wings wet, a pot or urn pouring forth water, with which descend frogs, grasshoppers, and the like creatures which are bred by moisture." [74]

About 1700, a little book was published in England by one John Smith entitled *The Art of Painting in Oyl, to which is added the whole art and mystery of colouring maps.* This book contains a chapter on "The Whole Art and Mystery of Colouring Maps, and other Prints, in Water-Colours." Such a chapter was indicated, the author felt, because he had seen no authentic treatise on the subject, and because map coloring was an excellent recreation "for those Gentry, and others, who delight in the Knowledge of Maps; which by being coloured, and the several Divisions distinguished one from the other by Colours of different Kinds, do give a better Idea of the Countries they describe, than they can possibly do uncoloured." [75]

A basic ingredient of Smith's colors for maps was what he called tartar-lye, made in the following way: take two ounces of the best white tartar (that is, wine stone or argol), which Smith described as a stony substance that sticks to the sides of wine casks and is sold by druggists. Wrap the tartar in paper, wet it thoroughly and fuse in hot coals; then douse it in water and break up with your fingers. This solution was added in various proportions to the pigments. [76] Also used was gum water made of gum arabic, which served as a binder. In regard to the colors themselves, Smith had some definite ideas as to quality. "Copper-Green," made from verdigris, should come from Montpelier; all other varieties, he said, would fade. To get a "stone color" you should use liquor of myrrh, made by mixing one ounce of the best powdered myrrh in one pint of tartar-lye. Boil till the myrrh is dissolved. Let settle and decant. [77]

To make a good crimson color, buy a half ounce of good cochineal. Take thirty or forty grains and bruise to a fine powder in a galley-pot. Then add just enough tartar-lye to wet it. Add at once a half spoonful of water, and you will get a delicate purple mixture. Scrape a very little alum into the mixture and it will turn from purple to crimson. Strain through a fine cloth. It looks "most noble" when used at once. Blue bice (azurite blue) was recommended because it needed only a little "tempering" with gum water, but, "when Men design to be curious, they may use, instead thereof, Ultramarine, which is the best and most glorious of all Blues, but vastly dear . . . It needs only to be tempered in a very small Galley Pot with a little Gum Water." To make "a most pleasant Grass-Green," take a lump of gamboge; poke a hole in it. Put in some copper green (malachite green) and stir with a pencil. It will turn from a "willow" to a "grass-green." [78]

The colors being prepared, says Smith, "you may proceed to colour your maps." You should note the political divisions, whose boundaries are indicated by dotted lines. Between Spain and Portugal, for example, there are mountains. Color them first, using tincture of myrrh and a fine camel's-hair brush fixed in a duck quill. Then if there are any trees shown, dab every one with the point of a fine brush, using grass green (that is, copper green tempered with gamboge). Next color the principal cities and towns with red lead, "that the eye may more readily perceive them." Trace the boundaries of the provinces, using a duck quill dipped in copper green. Use a different color on each province, making sure that no two adjacent provinces are colored the same, "for then you could not distinguish them." [79]

Color the seashore and all the lakes, if there be any, with thin indigo. And if there are any ships, color the water shaded at the bottom with the same indigo, painting the hull of the ship with umber, the sails with tincture of myrrh, and the flags with vermillion or blue bice; and if the ships are represented as firing their guns, the smoke should be colored with very thin bice. The border of the map should be colored either yellow or red lead or crimson; "none but those three Colours serving well for this Purpose." Clouds may be painted sometimes with tincture of myrrh, and in some cases, a very thin Crimson, and, "for Variety, you may do some with thin Ivory-Black." Sea waves should be colored with indigo.

Land should be colored with a very thin yellow shaded with orpiment (arsenic trisulphide, also called "Kings Yellow"). For variety, do parts of it light green, shaded with deeper green. Rocks must be done with tincture of myrrh; trees may be done with copper green, grass green and some with thin umber. Houses may be done with red lead; the tiles with vermilion or bice to represent blue slate. Do castles with tincture of myrrh and thin red lead. Color spires and pinnacles with blue. "And," Smith concludes, "if your Paper be good, and bear the Colours well, without suffering them to sink into it, all that are here mentioned will be fair and pleasant to the Eye; and it is the Fairness of the Colours that is most esteemed in this Art of Map-Painting: But if the Paper be not good and strong, no Art can make the Colours lie well; therefore in buying Maps, chuse those that are printed on the strongest and thickest Paper." [80]

Between 1650 and 1700 there were eighteen map making centers in Europe. Line engraving and picture drawing were so thoroughly developed that in all of these cities it was taught well, and the technique of map reproduction was universally good.[81] All that map publishers lacked was good maps to copy. Nearly all of Europe and parts of Asia and Africa had been surveyed after a fashion, but all too few of the standard maps were based on trigonometric surveys. And for every map compiled from a survey there were a hundred copies, forgeries and adaptations, all bearing a strong family resemblance to the original (with all its faults), and usually containing a vast amount of misinformation. Progress in the *science* of cartography was in abeyance, and the Old World was badly in need of new surveys. The situation was further complicated by the endless discoveries in the New World. The map of the habitable world needed enlarging in all directions — how much, no man knew. Where did new places belong in relation to other places? Who had verified distances and directions across the Western Sea? European monarchs had staked out possessions in foreign lands, yet not one of them could locate what he claimed. Thus cartography, the art of making maps, was forced to turn again to science before further progress could be made, and science was ready with many of the answers.

The Latitude

BY THE MIDDLE of the sixteenth century there were two established methods of finding the latitude on land and at sea. The first was to determine the height of the sun above the horizon at the place of observation; the second was to determine the height of the polestar. Both methods required the use of angle-measuring instruments; and in each case, having determined the observed height of the celestial bodies, the observer had to make certain corrections, aided by mathematical tables computed for the purpose. The theoretical requirements, both as to instruments and mathematical tables, were fully appreciated by the ancients, and the only scientific contributions to the subject made in the next 2000 years were improvements: instruments that would measure fractions of seconds of arc and mathematical tables that were correspondingly accurate.

The quadrants, sextants and octants, developed throughout the centuries, were little more than segments of the ancient astrolabe, refined and adapted to meet the special requirements of surveyors and navigators. The modern Nautical Almanac, with its complex and multifarious tables that make it possible to find the latitude at any hour of the day or night, is nothing more than the sum total of ancient astrology, streamlined and perfected by astronomical instruments, including telescopes. Necessity mothered most of the inventions that led to their present state of perfection, and at no time in history was the need more urgent than in the latter part of the fifteenth century and for the next hundred years, the age of great explorations and discoveries. During that period the astrolabe, varying only slightly from the one described by Claudius Ptolemy in the second century, was standard equipment among geographers and mariners.

There was no limit to the size of the astrolabes used by astronomers. Some of them were mammoth, several feet in diameter, made of iron or brass, trussed and braced and installed as permanent fixtures in the towers of European observatories. Portable astrolabes, designed for travelers and mariners, had the disadvantage of being small and therefore less accurate for celestial observations than large, stationary ones. The graduations were naturally closer together on the circumference and slight errors in angle measurements were magnified to a dangerous extent when used in distance calculations or in navigation. These instruments were commonly made of brass or wood and in many cases the workmanship was of the finest; but regardless of the precision that went into their construction, they were no more accurate than the men using them. On a rolling deck at sea it was almost impossible to hold such an instrument with one hand, adjust the rule or alidade with the other while sighting on the horizon and a celestial body at the same time. João de Barros, the historian, reported that when Vasco da Gama reached the bay of St. Helena on his first voyage round the Cape of Good Hope in 1497, he went ashore and set up a large wooden astrolabe to get his bearings. He had been unable to get a trustworthy meridian altitude of the sun from the deck of his ship with his portable instrument.[1] The mariner's astrolabe was stripped of all frills. The outer circle of the disc was quartered by crossed lines repre-senting the horizon and the zenith. Half of the upper hemisphere was graduated into 90 degrees. The alidade or vane was fitted with two sights and the instru-ment was held aloft by a ring in the top while the observation was being made. It was not very satisfactory and there were many complaints. Master John, one of the pilots of Cabral's fleet, reported that errors of four or five degrees were almost unavoidable.

In his *Exercises*, London, 1594, Thomas Blundeville described three kinds of astrolabes he had seen. The first was designed by Johann Stöffler (Stofflerus or Stofflerinus) the German astronomer and teacher of mathematics. Blundeville said that for the previous hundred years or thereabouts, this instrument had been held in great esteem and was also the most expensive to buy. It was apparently a universal astrolabe or armillary requiring the use of several sets of tables in order to solve any kind of problem. The second type was designed by Reinier Gemma Frisius (Gemma the Frisian), the Dutch physician and astronomer. His was an instrument that required only one table for all latitudes; he called it the *Catholicon*, because it was a universal astrolabe. "Of very late yeares," said Blunde-ville, "one of our owne Countreymen, a Gentleman of Redding besides London, called M. *Blagrave*, hath greatly augmented the said *Catholicon*, and hath thereby as it were newly inuented a third kinde of Astrolabe, which he calleth the Mathe-maticall Iewell, whereby are to be wrought more Conclusions than by any other one Instrument whatsoever, for which his most excellent invention used therein, he deserveth great commendation. . . ."[2]

Blundeville, like many another practical man before him, was aware of the numerous defects in the various kinds of astrolabes available to astronomers and cartographers. Large ones, he remarked, were certainly more accurate than small ones, yet, "they are subject to the force of the winde, and thereby ever mooving and unstable, are nothing meete to take the Altitude of any thing, and especially upon the Sea." In order to overcome this defect, the Spaniards commonly made their astrolabes narrow and heavy, frequently of brass. They were usually not more than five inches in diameter and weighed at least four pounds; the lower part was built thicker than the upper part near the ring or handle to provide additional stability. Most English pilots, however, preferred an astrolabe about seven inches across, "very massive and heavie, not easie to be mooved with every wind, in which the spaces of the degrees be the larger; and thereby the truer." When taking the altitude of the sun or any star, "be it wandering or fixed," Blundeville advised, "I would wish you to use the Mariners heavy and massive Astrolabe, which in mine opinion for that purpose is the fittest and most assured

The cross-staff or Jacob's staff, a crude instrument, was used for centuries to measure the height of the sun. Its chief fault lay in the fact that the observer was usually blinded by the sun's rays.

Instrument of all others; and to finde out all other conclusions, by help of Master Blagrave his Iewell, or rather by helpe of the Celestiall Globe . . ."[3]

Martin Cortés (fl. 1551), geographer and writer on navigation, described a mariner's astrolabe in some detail. His was made of copper or tin, about ¼ inch thick and 6 or 7 inches in diameter. It was circular except at one place on the limb where a projection (shoulder) was provided for a hole and ring by which the astrolabe could be suspended. A plumb line extending from the point of suspension to the opposite side marked the vertical line, and from it the horizontal line and center were derived. The face of the instrument having been well polished, the upper left quadrant was graduated into degrees. The pointer or rule was made of the same metal and finished to the same thickness; it was about 1½ inches wide, and its length was equal to the diameter of the circle. The center of the rule was bored, and a line was drawn across its full length, which was appropriately called "the line of confidence." Small plates were fitted at either end of the rule, exactly over the line of confidence; these were bored, and the holes served as sights. The rule moved up and down on a pinion the size of a goose quill. The instrument was held with the right hand and sighted on the sun or a star with the left. The reading was taken directly from the upper left quadrant only. Eventually the opposite quadrant (lower right) was also graduated, so as to give a double reading. Aboard ship it was commonly a three-man job to take a sight with the astrolabe, regardless of the size or weight of the instrument. One

The back-staff was an invention of John Davis of Sandridge, who described
it in a book entitled *The Seamans Secrets* published in 1607.

man held the instrument by a ring passed over his thumb, while he stood with his
back braced against the mast; the second man took the sight, measuring the altitude of the sun or star, and the third man read off.[4]

The cross-staff was an instrument used by ancient astronomers for determining
latitudes and the angle between two stars; it was later adapted by mariners for
measuring altitudes at sea. Its simplicity suggests that it may have antedated the
astrolabe as a device for measuring angles, although it was widely used by the
Spanish and Portuguese navigators as late as the fifteenth and sixteenth centuries,
and was probably introduced to them by the celebrated navigator and cartographer Martin Behaim ("Boehm" or "the Bohemian"). The earliest known description of the cross-staff was written by Levi ben Gerson, a learned Jew of Bañolas
in Catalonia, and was dedicated to Pope Clement VI in 1342. Gerson called the
instrument "*baculus Jacob*" (Jacob's staff). George Purbach, the Austrian astronomer, called it "*virga visoria*" or sighting stick and Regiomontanus called it
"*radius astronomicus.*" The Portuguese and Spanish seamen called it the "*balle-
stilla*" or "*balestilha*" also "*baculo de São Tiago*" (staff of Saint James, patron
saint of pilgrims), because of its shape. The French called it the "*arbalète*" or
"*arbalestrille*" because it looked similar to a cross-bow. In England it was the cross-
staff. It was an instrument that belonged to no one and was apparently used by
all; through a series of alterations and adaptions it became the modern sextant.[5]

"The Crosse Staffe," wrote Edmund Gunter, "is an instrument well known to our Seamen, and much used by the ancient Astronomers and others, serving Astronomically for observation of altitude and angles of distance in the heavens, Geometrically for perpendicular heights and distances on land and sea." There were five parts to the instrument: the staff, the cross and three sights. The staff or "yard" was simply a stick of wood about 1¼ inches square and of varying length. Blundeville described one about 27 inches long but Gunter preferred one 36 inches long, so that he could also use it for linear measure as well. The cross, "transom" or "transversary," was usually about 1¼ inches thick and 2½ inches wide.[6] On Blundeville's instrument it was about 12 inches long and on Gunter's a little over 26 inches. The cross or transom was pierced in the center with a square hole or mortise, cut so that the piece would fit snugly on the staff but would at the same time slide freely at right angles back and forth along it. Larger instruments were possible, of course, but as Gunter pointed out, the ratio between the length of the staff and the length of the cross should be about 360 to 262.

The cross-staff was fitted with three peephole sights in the form of plates (pinnules); one at either end of the transom, and one on the near end of the staff which served as an "ocular" or eyepiece. In taking the altitude or angular height of the sun or of a star, the trick was to line up the three sights simultaneously: the ocular and the upper sight of the transom on the sun or star, the ocular and lower transom sight on the horizon. This feat was accomplished by sliding the transom backward and forward on the staff until the three sights were in line. Meanwhile, says Blundeville, the end of the staff should be held close to the "upper point of your cheeke bone, keeping your legs close together."[7]

In its simplest form, the cross-staff was not graduated. After making an observation, the instrument was laid on a table or sheet of paper and the observed angle was computed from a tracing. Later the top side of the staff was graduated so that the measured angles could be read off at a glance. When multiple vanes or transoms were added in order to measure smaller angles, and more than one angle at the same time, the sides of the staff were also ruled off. The instrument developed by Edmund Gunter had four sets of graduations; one served "for measure and protraction," another for the observation of angles, a third to determine "the meridian of a Sea-chart, according to *Mercators* projection from the Equinoctiall to 58 gr. [degrees] of latitude." The fourth was designed "for working of proportions in severall kindes."

An obvious defect in both the astrolabe and cross-staff was that in making solar observations the observer had to look directly into the sun. Even when the sights of the instruments were fitted with smoked glass there was still enough glare on a bright day to blind the observer; consequently, great errors in angle measurement were the rule rather than the exception. It took several centuries to solve the problem of glare in making solar observations, either with an astrolabe or cross-staff, and the solution came from an ingenious mariner with a practical turn of mind who got tired of peering into the eye of the sun in order to find his latitude. The man was an Englishman, John Davis of Sandridge in Devonshire, who described his invention, the back-staff, in a little book entitled *The Seamans Secrets*, which was published in London, 1607.[8]

The original back-staff consisted of a staff and transom, the latter in the form of a "halfe crosse," riding, as it were, on top of the yard. The functioning of the instrument, Davis pointed out, was contrary to that of the cross-staff, because the observer worked with his back to the sun, sighting the horizon through a horizontal slit at the far end of the staff. The angle of the sun was caught by moving the transom until the sun cast a shadow from the upper tip of the transom down onto the surface of the sight at the far end of the staff. Thus a simultaneous

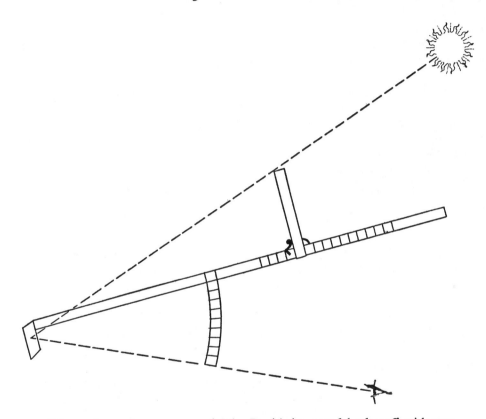

The conjectural appearance of John Davis's improved back-staff with two sliding transoms, designed and described but apparently never built.

alignment of sun and horizon was possible without moving the eye. But the use of the instrument was limited, as it was first designed, to observations of the sun, and then only when it was not more than 45° above the horizon. But Davis was not through.

"Finding by practise the excellencie of the Crosse Staffe above all other instruments to satisfie the Seamans expectation," wrote Davis, "and also knowing that those instruments whose degrees are of largest capacitie are instruments of most certaintie, I have very carefully laboured to search a good and demonstrable meane how a cross staffe might be proiected, not only to contain large degrees, but also to avoid the vncertaintie of the sight, by disorderly placing of the staffe to the eye." Moreover, he assured his readers that the improved instrument he had recently invented and tried at sea, would work as well below the equator as above it.[9]

This second staff was a yard long, fitted with two "halfe crosses" or transversaries, a straight one 14 inches long riding above the staff, at right angles to it, and a curved one in the form of a sector suspended below the staff, also on a slide. Davis promised a full description of this instrument, an elaborated back-staff, in a separate publication (which he never wrote), but temporarily he assured his public that, "it hath a large demonstration with manifold uses." Davis had a low opinion of the quarter circle as an instrument for making observations at sea, but he admitted that it was "an excellent instrument vpon the shore, to performe any Astronomical observations." Nevertheless, in spite of his opinion, Davis's improved back-staff, with sector transom, was the forerunner of an instrument which became known in England as "Davis's quadrant," and in France the *quartier Anglais*.

The English quadrant was developed by John Davis, probably with the help of Edward Wright of Cambridge, who was also applying his mathematical skill to the improvement of navigational charts. The improved instrument was a divided quadrant or quarter circle, actually the old back-staff with refinements. The sector transom, originally on a slide, was moved to the near end of the staff and fastened there. A second staff or brace was added to make it rigid. The straight upper transom of the old back-staff was replaced by a second sector transom; this, too, was reinforced and fastened at the far end of the staff. There were still three pinnule sights; one of them fixed at the far end of the staff as before, and two on slides, one on each of the two sectors. Now, instead of sliding the transoms back and forth, the pinnule sights were moved up and down on their sectors to make the necessary angle adjustments. When the instrument was in use, the observer would make a coarse adjustment of the upper slide before attempting to line up his sights. Then placing the instrument to his eye he would make a fine adjustment with the sliding sight on the lower sector. The angular height of the sun or star under observation would be equal to the sum of the angles indicated on the two sectors.[10]

The first refinement in the English quadrant came from France. Two years before John Hadley described his first quadrant, a Frenchman named Pierre Bouguer, professor of Hydrography at Croissic, and a member of the Académie Royale de Bordeaux, submitted a paper to the Académie Royale des Sciences entitled "De la methode d'observer exactement sur mer la hauteur des astres." The paper was published by the Académie as one of their prize essays for the year 1729. As an introduction to his description of an improved instrument for the determination of latitude, Bouguer reviewed the various instruments which were then in use by scientists and mariners of the world at large, outlining in simple language their several defects. He classified all such instruments into two general groups. The first included all portable instruments which were best adapted to the use of astronomers on land, such as the astronomers' quadrant ("quarter circle"), the astrolabe, the astronomical ring, the hemisphere of Michiel Coignet, and so on. These instruments, Bouguer pointed out, carry their horizon with them, as it were, either in the form of a plumb line and bob or a suspension ring, so that they will always assume a vertical or horizontal position, as required. His second group included such instruments as the cross-staff of Gemma Frisius (*bâton astronomique*) and Davis's back-staff, which depend on a visible horizon and are therefore best adapted to the use of navigators, who in theory always have a horizon to work with. All such instruments, as Bouguer said, must suffer the in-

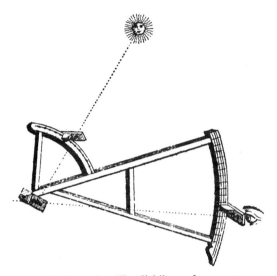

"Davis's" or the "English" quadrant was a
logical refinement of the back-staff and the
forerunner of the modern sextant.

dignity of being tossed around on an unstable deck and blamed for errors they do not make.[11]

As illustrations of the first group of instruments, Bouguer demonstrated to his colleagues several with ring suspensions, that depended on their dead weight and the accurate placement of the ring to maintain a level position. The simple astronomical ring was a circular metal band pierced near the top with a small hole and graduated on the inside where the sun's light would fall. In spite of its limited usefulness, the ring was popular with astronomers and with a certain number of navigators, who frequently used it as a check against the latitude obtained with the astrolabe. The same was true of the half circle, which was used in the same way and for the same purposes as the astronomical ring. Bouguer ascribed the invention of the half circle to M. Maynier, Royal Professor of Hydrography at Havre de Grace. Bouguer had not actually seen the instrument, but had read a description of it. Apparently two variations of the quarter circle were in use during Bouguer's time, made of flat metal and utilizing the pinhole principle of the ring and half circle. One was suspended by a single radius, and the other had a spirit level attached, for the purpose of establishing a horizon which might not exist, either on land or sea. Bouguer referred to these instruments as a method of supporting an instrument by its center of gravity, and in concluding his essay he described an ingenious device, an astronomical ring, which,

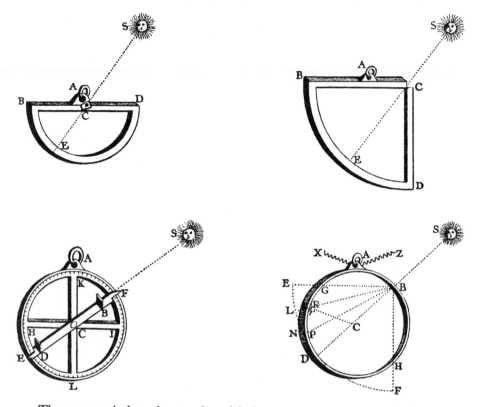

The astronomical quadrant and semicircle were not as popular as the astronomical ring for measuring angular heights. However, all were used far into the eighteenth century for measuring the height of the sun.

like a compass binnacle, was designed to maintain its level in all kinds of weather. The ring was fixed to a circular wooden plate which floated in a tub of water or oil. The tub was swung in gimbals fastened to a sturdy frame. The theory was that the shocks caused by a heavy sea would be taken up first by the gimbals, then by the fluid in the bath, so that the floating instrument would always remain plumb. Here then, was a fine solution to the problem of finding latitude; it was foolproof, almost. By means of a series of diagrams and complex equations, Bouguer demonstrated that even though the floating ring might be a splendid idea, it would not work as well as the inventor supposed, and unlike a floating compass, a ring could not be used to measure the latitude if it bobbed up and down and was out of plumb first one way and then another. Man himself, Bouguer concluded, is the best suspension device of all for taking sights at sea.[12]

Many French pilots depended on the cross-staff for finding the latitude, but Bouguer thought it was unsatisfactory because it was often poorly graduated, and when the transom became worn it fitted loosely on the staff, causing great errors in angle measurement. For his part, Bouguer favored the *quartier Anglais* of Davis and Wright, and as he proceeded to demonstrate, only a few alterations

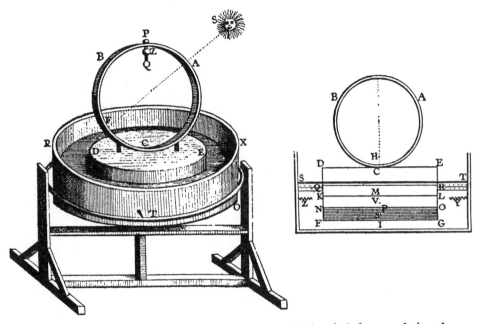

A floating astronomical ring, the bath suspended in gimbals, was designed for use at sea. Its faults were pointed out by the French scientist Pierre Bouguer.

were necessary to make it an ideal instrument for use at sea. The two arcs or sectors, for example, were unnecessarily complicated, he thought, and much precious time was lost in adjusting the pinnules and aligning the sights, so that a midday observation too frequently turned out to be several minutes after the hour. Why not combine the two arcs, asked Bouguer. Even if it made the instrument a little unwieldy to carry around, it would nevertheless be easier to graduate and much easier to use. He proposed to graduate his quarter circle into degrees *and* minutes by means of transversals.

What Bouguer proposed was a back-staff in the form of a quadrant, with a few new wrinkles added. The quadrant was to have three pinnule sights: one fixed at C and one fixed at E. All angle adjustments could be made with one movable sight F attached to the graduated arc ED. The cross-pieces within the quadrant were only to give the instrument extra strength and rigidity. Bouguer's instrument had two sights E and F fitted with small convex lenses, so ground that they would both focus on the pinnule at C. The pinnule C was important, because it contained a new reflection feature. From the eye of the observer, P represented the mortise by which the pinnule was attached to the apex of the instrument, as it was on the English quadrant. MN represented a slit about 1⅔ inches

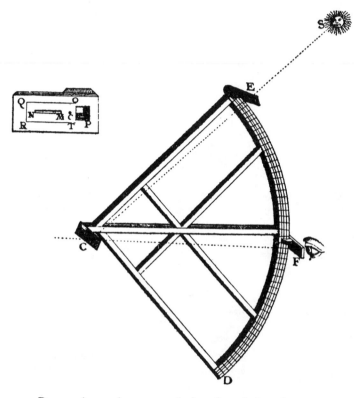

Bouguer's quadrant was designed to bring the sun
down to the horizon so that the observer could see
both sun and horizon simultaneously.

long for scanning the horizon. C was the point where the sun's rays should be brought to a focus, and the rectangle QRTO represented the shadow cast by the pinnule at E on the large diagram. Thus in an area of about 2 by 3 inches, the observer could, without moving his eye, fix his horizon through the slit and adjust his movable sight until he had a sharp pin point of light on a line with his horizon, both enclosed in a rectangular shadow. A lens of the proper focal length at E, Bouguer warned, was absolutely essential; with only a pinhole sight there would be a penumbra from the sun's rays which would mar the accuracy of the observation.

Tracing the genealogy of the modern sextant in direct descent from the primitive cross-staff is literally impossible. The scientific activity of the late seventeenth and early eighteenth centuries was widespread, and the problems were so universal and simple that many simultaneous discoveries and inventions were made. Scientific bodies such as the Royal Society in England, the Académie Royale des Sciences in France, the Académie Royale de Belgique and the American Philosophical Society were active, and members of one society were frequently corresponding members of others. Each learned body had a pretty good idea of what was going on in the others, and it was inevitable that a certain amount of duplication of ideas should occur, one way or another. International rivalry was keen, and occasionally there was unpleasantness, but in general the effect on the progress of science was beneficial.

The invention of the reflecting quadrant is a case in point. Who first had the idea, no one knows. In 1669 Jean Picard used a quadrant equipped with telescopes in place of the customary pinhole sights, but his instrument was an improved design of a quadrant already in use by the Danish astronomer Tycho Brahe. As for the reflecting feature of the quadrant and sextant, several independent ideas were thrown into the scientific hopper before anything very practical emerged. In a paper read before the Royal Society on March 23, 1691, Edmund Halley said, "Being sensible of the great advantage of Telescope sights in observing of objects on shore, I have long thought if it might be possible to contrive an instrument for doing the same thing in those observations the seamen use to take their Latitude, there being no thing more desirable than to attain a reasonable certainty in this affair. At length I presume I have attained what will with all possible exactness perform the thing required: that is to make a sea Quadrant wherein both the Horizon and object shall both be seen distinctly and enlarged, at one view in the common focus of a Telescope." [13]

Halley went on to describe what might be called a collapsible reflecting quadrant. In conclusion, he made an interesting remark. "The Instrument I proposed some time since, to observe with Telescope sights at Sea, and wherin I found Dr. Hook [Robert Hooke] had gone before me." It seems, actually, that Hooke had beaten Halley, for in the Journal Book of the Society is the following statement: "Dr. Hook said that he had long since invented such an Instrument as this, that he made the same Object glass serve for both Objects . . ." Moreover, in 1678 the innocent Halley had proudly lugged a two-foot quadrant all the way to Dantzig so that he could show Joannes Hévélius, the astronomer, how cleverly he had applied telescopes to the instrument, not knowing that Hooke and Hévélius had been for some time embroiled in a dispute as to which of the two was entitled to priority honors for having had the idea first. It must have been an interesting meeting! [14]

It also appears that at a meeting of the Royal Society held on the 11th of March, 1672, one Isaac Newton, Lucasian professor at Cambridge, then thirty years of age, was elected to the Society. A paper was read to the members describing one of his inventions, a reflecting telescope. Neither his invention nor his later work was greeted with unrestrained joy. He became embroiled with his scientific colleagues, whose strongest case against the man was that he was young and they were advanced in years, a condition often confused with superior mentality. One of his bitterest opponents was Lucas, professor of mathematics at Liège, against whom Newton defended himself stoutly, but with his back to the wall. He wrote to Oldenburg, one of the Secretaries of the Society, who was then writing the Transactions, "if I get free of Mr. Lucas's business, I will resolutely bid adieu to [research] eternally, excepting what I do for my private satis-

More than one third of the deck space on this sixteenth-century ship is given over to the navigator and his swinging chair designed for determining latitude at sea. It was never used.

faction, or leave to come out after me; for I see a man must either resolve to put out nothing new, or to become a slave to defend it." [15]

In view of his numerous troubles, it is not surprising that the world heard nothing about Newton's invention of a reflecting instrument for measuring angles until Edmund Halley died. In 1742, a description of such an instrument, an octant, in Newton's handwriting, was found buried in Halley's papers, and was later printed in the *Philosophical Transactions* of the Royal Society. Newton's chief interest at the time was the measurement of star distances and distances between stars and the moon, for which purpose his octant was well suited; "and though the Instrument shake, by the Motion of your Ship at Sea," he wrote, "yet the Moon and Star will move together, as if they did really touch one another in the Heavens; so that an Observation may be made as exactly at Sea as at Land. And by the same Instrument," he added, "may be observed, exactly, the Altitudes of the Moon and Stars, by bringing them to the Horizon; and thereby the Latitude, and Times of Observations, may be determined more exactly than by the Ways now in Use." [16]

Before Newton's design for a reflecting quadrant was published, John Hadley, country gentleman and vice-president of the Royal Society, produced an instrument "for taking angles" that was destined to become the pattern of the modern sextant. He described it in a communication to the Society dated May 13, 1731. [17] His brother George later testified that it was built during the summer of 1730. Why did he testify, and why was the date important? Because across the Atlantic "a poor glazier of Philadelphia" named Thomas Godfrey finished work on a similar quadrant in that same year of grace, and had it ready for a trial at sea in November.

After reading about Hadley's new instrument in the *Transactions* of the Royal Society, James Logan of Philadelphia suddenly remembered young Godfrey and his sea quadrant, "to which he had fitted two pieces of looking-glass in such a manner as brought two stars at almost any distance to coincide," an instrument that was practically the same as Hadley's first design. In May of 1732 Logan wrote to Edmund Halley, who was then astronomer-royal, describing the instrument in detail.

By the time the matter was brought before the Royal Society at a meeting on January 31, 1734, Logan had transmitted two valuable sworn affidavits which were read to the members. They proved that Godfrey's quadrant had gone aboard the sloop *Truman*, John Cox, in the hands of G. Stewart, mate, on November 28, 1730, bound for Jamaica, and that in August, 1731, it was taken by the same master and mate on a trip to Newfoundland. Logan apologized to the Society for his neglect in not bringing the matter to their attention at an earlier date, but as he explained, he was a very busy man and was unaware of any competitors in the field. No great damage was done, however, and the Society graciously acknowledged Godfrey's claim to share honors equally with Hadley. It was just another one of those unaccountable instances where two men working independently, an ocean between them, arrived at the same point in their thinking at just about the same time. [18]

The reflecting quadrant, octant or sextant, was not strictly the invention of one man or two. It was the logical development of the old cross-staff into an instrument which would measure celestial angles under any conditions, on land or sea, with a fair degree of accuracy. What Godfrey and Hadley did was combine the best features of many instruments and optical principles into a single measuring device. In it were features contributed by Halley and Hooke, Hévélius and Picard, Newton, Bouguer, Davis, and probably dozens of others. The time was right for an instrument that would anticipate the handicaps of weather, tempestuous seas and human frailty. The instruments designed by Godfrey and Hadley came close to solving the problem of angle measurements.

In describing his invention, Hadley said his instrument was designed "to be of

Use, where the Motion of the Objects, or any Circumstance occasioning an Unsteadiness in the common Instruments, renders the Observations difficult or uncertain." Hadley called it, properly, an octant or eighth part of a circle, "having on its Limb . . . an Arch of 45 Degrees, divided into 90 Parts or half Degrees; each of which answers to a whole Degree in the observation." It had an index or radius, "moveable round the Center, to mark the Divisions," that is, record the angle. Near the center of the movable radius a plane mirror ("speculum") was fixed perpendicular to the plane of the instrument, set at an angle which would be "most convenient for the particular Uses the Instrument was designed for." The mirror would make an angle of about $65°$ with the movable radius when the radius showed $00°$ $00'$ $00''$ on the graduated limb. A second mirror was fixed to the frame of the octant, also perpendicular to the plane of it and set in such a way that when the movable index registered $00°$ $00'$ $00''$ the second mirror would be parallel with the first and facing in the opposite direction, that is, towards the eye of the observer.

A telescope was fixed along one radius of the octant and parallel to it, so placed that half of the rays which would normally pass through the objective of the telescope were intercepted by the fixed mirror; the other half were free to pass through to the observer. Up to this point Hadley's first "quadrant" was essentially the same in principle and design as Newton's, but one or two noteworthy refinements had been added which later became standard among instrument makers. For example, there was a frame which turned on a pin, into which plates of dark glass of varying shades could be fitted. Thus the intensity of the light coming from the sun to the observer could be reduced, either by changing the shade of dark glass or by swinging the darkened plate around so that some of the light from the sun would be cut off before it reached the first mirror. A similar improvement was made in the mirror attached to the radius of the instrument. To facilitate adjustments, the mirror was attached not to the framework itself, but to a circular plate which turned on a pivot and was connected by a series of gear teeth to a worm adjustment thumbscrew. A third improvement was made in the movable index. Instead of having a tapering fiducial edge running close to the graduated limb from which to take the reading, the movable index was slotted at the distal end and the rectangular cut was tapered inwards on all four sides. The index was in this way centered all the way down from the point of rotation of the index to the etched line crossing the limb at the slot, where the reading was taken.

Hadley used a filar micrometer in the ocular of his telescope attachment in the form of three cross hairs, two of which were horizontal and parallel to each other; the third was fixed vertically, thus allowing the observer to make a finer adjustment during the observation, and in a vertical and horizontal plane simultaneously. Hadley cautioned that the limb of the instrument should be graduated with extreme care, because in a reflecting instrument of this kind, the angle of incidence being equal to the angle of reflection, all errors would be doubled.

Hadley summed up the advantages of his quadrant when he pointed out that

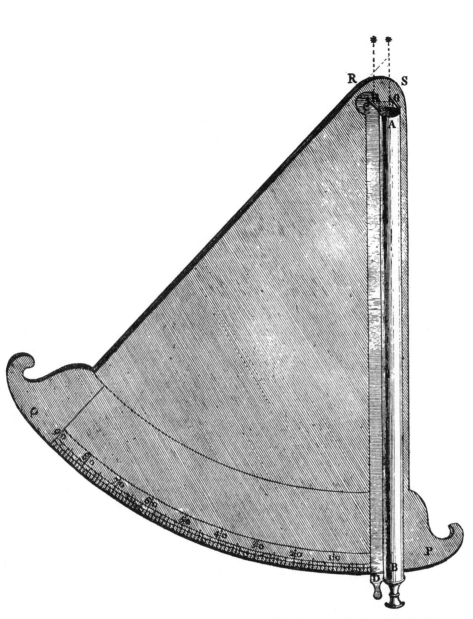

Isaac Newton's design for a reflecting octant, discovered after his death, was first described and published in 1742.

a supporting pedestal for the instrument was not an important consideration, because in using it no more steadiness was required than it would take to peer through the telescope with which it was equipped. If the instrument vibrated for any reason, all parts of the instrument and both objects under observation, such as the sun and the horizon, would vibrate as one, and could still be brought together in the ocular of the telescope, especially if the telescope were powerful enough to produce a magnification of four or five times.[19]

Hadley's second quadrant (that is, "octant") was designed with the mariner's needs in view, and differed from his first instrument chiefly in the placement of the mirrors and the telescope with respect to the graduated limb and the movable index. This arrangement, with the index moving across the limb like the pendulum of a clock, and the telescope set transversely across the radii, is essentially the same as the parts on the modern sextant. Hadley also added a third mirror and two sights, a peephole ocular and a rectangular objective equipped with cross hairs, to replace the telescope. It was then possible to observe the sun with one's back to it, in other words, when the angular height of the sun was more than 90°. This was the octant which was tried out on board the *Chatham*, yacht, August 30, 31, and September 1, 1732, in pursuance of an order made by the Right Honourable the Lords Commissioners of the Admiralty. It was an instrument "intended chiefly for taking Altitudes of the Sun, Moon and Stars, from the visible Horizon, either forwards or backwards." The wooden model Hadley demonstrated to the Society was later reproduced in brass by Mr. J. Sisson. It was made with an adjustable standard or "single Stem" as Hadley called it, which could be raised or lowered; and instead of a ball and socket, it was fitted with two arcs so that the octant could be tilted forward or backward.

During the trials of Hadley's quadrant, the Admiralty was represented by Mr. James Young, Master Attendant at Chatham; also present were the Reverend Sir Robert Pye, Robert Ord and Hadley's two brothers, all members of the Royal Society. Observations were made while the *Chatham* was at anchor in the mouth of the Medway near Sheerness eleven miles east-northeast of Chatham. The weather was boisterous and at times clouds made it necessary to suspend observations. All data, such as the sun's altitude at various hours and the distances of numerous stars from each other and from the horizon, were checked against Mr. Flamsteed's data compiled at the Observatory at Greenwich; a watch was used for keeping time. By and large the results were good. The errors of observation, tabulated after the trials were completed, in most cases were less than plus or minus one minute of arc and frequently as small as plus or minus 30 seconds.[20]

In 1732 Hadley wrote a second paper for the Royal Society describing "A Spirit Level to be fixed to a Quadrant for taking a Meridional Altitude at Sea, when the Horizon is not visible." As he pointed out to his fellow members, the necessity of seeing a horizon in order to find the latitude of a ship at sea had always presented such difficulties that any method of determining it without the aid of a horizon would be a help, even if the method should be liable to an error of a few minutes of arc. Hadley therefore proposed, as a solution to the problem,

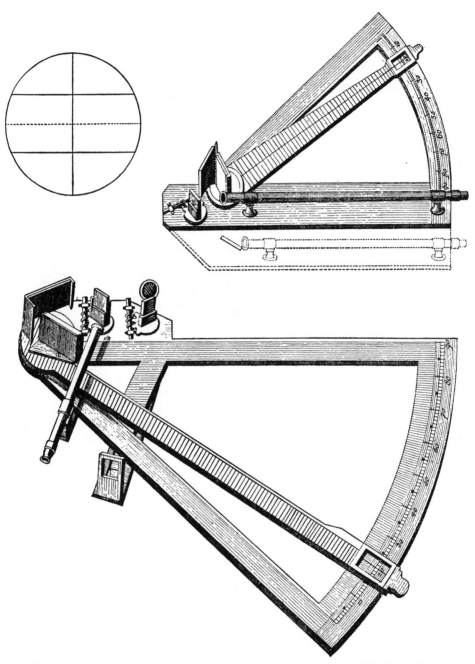

Two designs for a reflecting octant were made by John Hadley. The second (*bottom*) was tested at sea in 1732.

a quadrant fitted with a rather complex spirit level, bent into an arc and fastened to the base of the instrument. He gave minute instructions as to the proper bore to be used in the glass tube of the level, how it should be filled and the whole thing adjusted. But here again was a two man instrument, for Hadley proposed a finely graduated tube which would require the full attention of one man while the observer was getting the altitude. Hadley made no great claims for his level attachment, however, and concluded his discussion of its merits by saying that the normal amount of error to be expected in rough weather was about seven or eight minutes of arc, but that in a calm sea and with a moderately skillful observer it might be considerably less.[21]

The perpetuation of star data over a period of several thousand years is one of the amazing facts of history. All such information constituted the elements of a particular kind of publication which became known as an "almanac." Originally a monopolistic production of the priestly cult, it later became the journal of scientific astronomy, a compendium of facts and figures about the heavens. After the invention of printing, astronomy retained for its own purposes all such scientific data as star distances and their right ascensions, the declinations of the sun and the moon and of the fixed stars, the prediction of solar and lunar eclipses. At the same time, the proponents of astrology adapted to their own purposes information concerning the zodiac, the passage of the seasons, and so on, embellishing it with their own cabalistic signs and symbols. The application of star data and the astronomical almanac to the making of maps is difficult to trace. When map makers needed the heavens badly enough they used them; and without the adaptation of the astronomical almanac and tables of the sun the development of cartography would have come to an abrupt standstill.

In addition to the corpus of astronomy, which was to all intents and purposes fixed and permanent, both astronomers and map makers, from the earliest times, were dependent on tables of ephemeral data to supplement their observations and calculations. Such tables were necessary because of the irregularity of the calendar year, the oblique track of the sun across the sky and the celestial changes caused by the precession of the equinoxes. At what stage in the history of cartography tables of the sun and of the fixed stars were applied to the study of terrestrial latitude, history does not say. Ibn Junis (*c.* 950–1008) compiled in Egypt the Hakimite Tables of the planets and observed at Cairo. Nasir ud-din (1201–1274) drew up the Ilkhanic Tables and determined the constant of precession at 51″. Ulugh Beg (1394–1449), a grandson of Tamerlane, founded an observatory about 1420 A.D., at Samarkand, where he redetermined the positions of most of Ptolemy's stars. His Tables were foremost among astronomers for two centuries. Arab astronomy, transported by the Moors to Spain, flourished temporarily at Cordova and Toledo. The Toletan Tables, drawn up by Arzachel in 1080, took their name from the latter city. Also published in Toledo were the Alfonsine Tables, compiled in 1252 under the direction of Alphonso X of Leon and Castile ("Alphonso the Wise"), patron of the arts and sciences. The Alfonsine Tables appeared in Europe about the time a Yorkshireman named John Holywood (Sacro Bosco)

J. D. Cassini (1625–1712) used them to determine longitude.

Galileo Galilei (1564–1642) discovered Jupiter's satellites.

Isaac Newton (1642–1727) announced, before it was proved, that the earth is flattened at the poles.

Christian Huygens (1629–1695), Dutch scientist and inventor, discovered and formulated the physical laws governing the behavior of the pendulum.

published a textbook of spherical astronomy under the title *De Sphaera Mundi,* a book that went through fifty-nine editions, coming as it did at a time when Europe was hungering for scientific data.[22]

The earliest known tables of the sun's declination, whose use by map makers and mariners can only be conjectured, came from Robert Anglès de Montpellier, compiled for the years 1292–1295. Nearly two hundred years later the *Almanach Perpetuum* of Abraham Zacuto, a Spanish Jew, was published, though its appearance in print did not come until 1496.[23]

Most commonly associated with printed tables of the sun's declination, is the name of Johann Müller (Joh. de Monteregio) of Königsberg. Regiomontanus, as he was also called, studied in Vienna under Georg Purbach (Peurbach), an eminent Austrian astronomer who died in the process of revising some of the important errors and omissions in Ptolemy's *Almagest.* His pupil continued the work, which had begun as a joint enterprise, and in addition struggled with a revision of the Alfonsine Tables. He went to Rome in search of better translations of the *Almagest* than were available in Germany, accompanied by Cardinal Bessarion. But Rome got too warm for him after he had openly criticized the translation of Ptolemy done by George of Trebizond, and he left the Holy City without delay. At Nuremberg, with the financial aid of his wealthy patron and student, Bernhard Walther, Regiomontanus built the first modern European observatory and equipped it with improved instruments of his own design. The two men collaborated on the publication of a series of popular calendars, and at Walther's house they printed the New Theories concerning the planets (*Theoricae planetarum novae*) written by Purbach. And in 1474 they printed a volume of Tables (*Ephemerides*) calculated by Regiomontanus for thirty-two years (1474–1506). In this volume the method of "lunar distances" for determining the longitude at sea was recommended and explained.[24]

Neither the *Almanach Perpetuum* of Zacuto nor the two works of Regiomontanus (the *Ephemerides* and the *Tabula directionum*) furnished explanations to go with their tables, and finding the latitude by taking the meridian altitude of the sun or by the method of equal altitudes, was no mean feat. Moreover, the publications of Zacuto and Regiomontanus were cluttered with extraneous data and astrological symbols which interested navigators and map makers not at all. The man of the sixteenth century world, whose subsistence depended on a knowledge of the latitude, wanted a short, concise and simple explanation of the facts and how to get them. A solitary example of such a publication exists, compiled by an anonymous Portuguese, and printed about 1509, probably in Lisbon. This little twenty-four page pamphlet contained the following useful information: (1) The calculation of the latitude from the height of the sun; (2) the regiment of the polestar; (3) a list of the latitudes of known places; (4) the regiment for evaluating the course traversed by a vessel; (5) a calendar and nautical tables for a bissextile year. As a sort of appendix to this compact body of useful information, the author or compiler threw in the *De Sphaera Mundi* of Sacro Bosco, translated into Portuguese. The *Regimento do estrolabio e do quadrante,* as it was called, is the earliest known prototype from which two standard publications were derived: the manual of navigation and the nautical almanac. Neither of the two is strictly for nautical use alone, and both contain the elements of astronomy and mathematics necessary for the development of geodesy.[25]

The first known Spanish Manual was issued in 1519 by Don Martin Fernandez de Enciso under the title *Suma de Geografia*. In Portugal, all other early writers on cosmography, astronomy, and navigation were eclipsed by Pedro Nunes, whose *Tratatado da Sphera* was published in Lisbon in 1537. This work, also, was a compendium of navigation; it included translations into Portuguese of Sacro Bosco's *De Sphaera mundi*, Georg Purbach's *Theoricae novae planetarum* and Book I of Claudius Ptolemy's *Geographia*. Nunes, however, was a scientist, and he added his own valuable contribution to the steadily growing mass of data concerning the earth and its relation to the heavens.

Two other Spanish works on the sphere and on navigation in general were very popular in the sixteenth century. The *Arte de Navegar* was written by Pedro de Medina and published at Valladolid in 1545. It was reprinted at least twelve times in the first hundred years and was translated into French, Italian and English. The second work of importance, and one which exerted an even greater influence on the progress of navigation and applied astronomy, was the *Breve compendio de la sphera y de la arte de nauegar* of Martin Cortés, Seville, 1551. The popularity of this manual was enhanced by Richard Eden, who translated the book into English (London, 1561) ten years after its first publication. This translation was reprinted by John Tapp in London, 1609, with improved tables of the sun's declination computed for the years 1609 to 1625. He gave as the maximum declination of the sun (the obliquity of the ecliptic) 23° 30'. He also listed the declinations of the principal stars and the times of their meridian transits. In this volume, Eden stated that the cross-staff was in most common use for determining latitude, but that he himself favored Wright's (that is, Davis's) sea quadrant for the purpose.[26]

In 1581 Michiel Coignet of Antwerp published a small treatise in French, *Instruction nouvelle des points plus excellens et necessaires, touchant l'art de nauiguer, ensemble vn moyen facile et tres sur pour nauiguer Est et Oest*, wherein he exposed the errors of Medina. He, too, published tables of the sun's declination and observed the gradual decrease in the obliquity of the ecliptic (precession). He also described a cross-staff (redescribed by Edmund Gunter) equipped with three transversals.

The maritime commerce of Portugal in the early fifteenth century stimulated the progress of navigational aids. An observatory was established at Sagres (a peninsula four miles southeast of Cape St. Vincent), chiefly to get more accurate tables of the declination of the sun. King John II, who ascended the throne in 1481, continued the astronomical research begun by Prince Henry, and appointed his two personal physicians, Roderick and Joseph, as well as Martin de Bohemia (Martin Behaim), from Fayal, to act as a committee on navigation. Among their other activities they calculated tables of the sun and made certain improvements in the astrolabe. The early *Ordenanzas* of the Spanish Council of the Indies outline the course of instruction prescribed for pilots at that time. It included a knowledge of Sacro Bosco's *De Sphaera Mundi*, the spherical triangles of Regiomontanus, the *Almagest* of Claudius Ptolemy, and such technical matters as the use of the astrolabe, the correction and adjustment of scientific apparatus and a general course in astronomy, with emphasis on the movements of the heavenly bodies.[27]

Of printed almanacs, beginning with the *Kalendarium novum* of Regiomontanus, there was no end in Europe. They combined astronomical data furnished by scientists with prognostications and planetary influences on human organs and on life in general furnished by astrologers. Out of the sum total of information contained in these popular Annuals, mariners and map makers gleaned little more than tables of the sun's declination, the rough elements of a few star positions and, in some cases, tables for determining latitude from the polestar. The inevitable cleavage between the scientific and the occult came in 1679 and in France. The *Connoissance des temps* appeared under letters patent from His Majesty Louis XIV, dated March 24 of that year.

The first edition of the French counterpart of the *Nautical Almanac* appeared anonymously, but was actually the compilation of the Abbé Jean Picard of Villé in Anjou, one of the foremost astronomers and mathematicians in France. The publication was advertised in the following terms:

> This little book is a collection of holy days and festivals in each month. The rising and setting of the moon, when it is visible, and of the sun every day. The aspects of the planets as with respect to each other, the moon and the fixed stars. The lunations and eclipses. The difference of longitude between the meridian of Paris and the principal towns in France. The time of the sun's entrance into the twelve signs of the zodiac. The true place of the planets every fifth day, and of the moon every day of the year, in longitude and latitude. The moon's meridian passage, for finding the time of high water, "as well as for the use of dials by moonlight." A table of refraction. The equation of time [this table is strangely arranged, as though the clock were to be reset on the first of every month, and the explanation speaks of the "premier mobile"]. The time of twilight at Paris. The sun's right ascension to hours and minutes. The sun's declination at noon each day to seconds. The whole accompanied by necessary instructions.

Picard edited the first five years of the *Connoissance des Temps*, and in 1684, when he died, the publication was continued by divers members of the Académie Royale des Sciences, principally by J. J. François de Lalande. The title was changed slightly from time to time; from 1762–1767 it was *Connoissance des Mouvemens Célestes;* for the year 1787, the title was *Connoissance des temps, ou exposition des mouvemens des astres.* In June, 1795, the Bureau des Longitudes took over the publication of the *Connoissance des Temps* and has continued its publication without interruption since then. In 1797 the book was supplemented by a second publication, *l'Annuaire*, issued by the Bureau des Longitudes, which contained, besides the annual calendar, certain astronomical and meterological data, physical tables, and often a variety of newly acquired scientific facts.[28]

The *Connoissance des Temps* apparently failed to come up to expectations, because even the French historians say that it was not as popular in France as the British *Nautical Almanac*, first published under the supervision of Nevil Maskelyne (1732–1811), who in 1765 succeeded Nathaniel Bliss as astronomer-royal. The first number of the *Nautical Almanac*, for 1767, was issued in 1766, and for forty-five years thereafter Maskelyne edited the publication. Each year new tables were added, such as the lunar tables compiled by Johann Tobias Mayer of Göttingen, purchased in final form from his widow. The lunar distances printed in the *Nautical Almanac* proved so popular that in France the Académie Royale de Marine had them copied (for 1773 and thereafter), retaining Greenwich time for the three-hourly intervals. The French, however, retained their own method of clearing lunar distances. Since 1903 the *Nautical Almanac* has been published in two forms, a large, unabridged edition for astronomical observatories, and a smaller edition for navigators. A second periodical, "Tables requisite to be used with the Nautical Ephemeris," was first compiled by Maskelyne in 1766 for the convenience of seamen. It sold 10,000 copies at once and was reprinted in 1781 and again in 1802, edited by William Wales.[29]

The German *Astronomische Jahrbuch* was first published in Berlin, 1776, but the Spaniards, despite their leadership in navigation during the sixteenth and seventeenth centuries, did not publish their first almanac until November 4, 1791. It was calculated at Cadiz for the year 1792 and printed at Madrid. The compilers freely acknowledged their indebtedness to both the *Nautical Almanac* and the *Connoissance des Temps*. The American *Ephemeris*, an entirely independent work of high repute, first appeared in 1849.[30]

With a reliable set of tables and an accurate instrument for measuring angles, the sun will give an observer his latitude on any day of the year. But — "What if the Sun do not shine at noon, nor perhaps all . . . day?" Then, as Blundeville said, "you must tarry untill night that some starre appeare, which you perfectly know . . ." Such a star was found in the constellation Ursa Minor, the Little Bear, which had been used for thousands of years to determine the height of the pole (that is, latitude) and to tell the passing hours of night. The constellation was well known to Thales in the seventh century B.C. and was mentioned later by Eudoxus and Aratus. The Phoenicians named it *Phoenice*. Ptolemy charted eight stars and Hévélius twelve in the constellation. Two of the stars, corresponding in position to the "Pointers" in the Great Bear, are considerably brighter than the others, and have been known for ages as "The Guards." These are β (Kochab), the principal guard and γ (Gamma). They have pointed the way to mariners and kept them out of trouble because they are often visible when the other stars in the Little Bear, including Polaris, are obscured.[31]

Among ancient astronomers there was a certain amount of confusion with regard to the two Bears. Thales, according to Callimachus, observed the Little Bear (α *Ursae Minoris*) or Little Dipper, and was said to have used the small stars

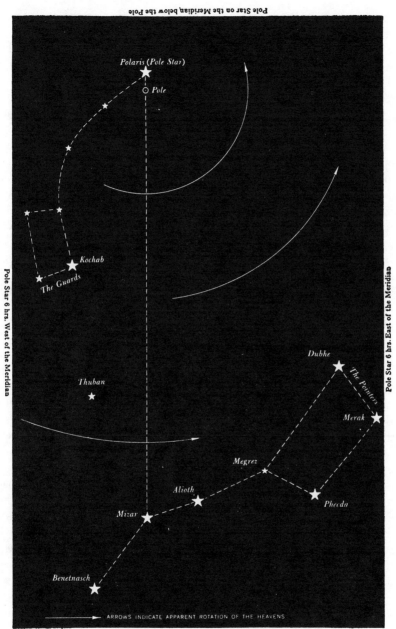

Polaris (Pole Star)

○ Pole

Kochab

The Guards

Thuban

Dubhe

The Pointers

Merak

Megrez

Alioth

Phecda

Mizar

Benetnasch

ARROWS INDICATE APPARENT ROTATION OF THE HEAVENS

Pole Star on the Meridian above the Pole

The two Bears (The Great Dipper and Little Dipper) have
been used for hundreds of years to tell the hour of the night
and the latitude. This diagram, after Lecky, shows how they
appear to the observer as they rotate together counterclockwise.

of the Wain or Great Bear (also "Big Dipper") for finding the pole, "that being the method by which Phoenician navigators steer their course." But according to Aratus, the Greeks sailed by the Great Bear and the Phoenicians by the Little Bear. At any rate, it was common knowledge that the Bear or Bears marked in a general way the north pole of the earth's axis, and, as Homer put it, that they had no part in the daily baths in Oceanus like the other constellations.

"As regards the north pole," wrote Hipparchus (about 380 B.C.), "Eudoxus is in error in stating that 'there is a certain star which always remains in the same spot, and this star is the pole of the universe;' for in reality there is no star at all at the pole, but there is an empty space there, with, however, three stars near to it [probably α and κ of Draco and β of the Little Bear], and the point at the pole makes with these three stars a figure which is very nearly square, as Pytheas of Massilia stated." [32] This statement represented one side of a warm discussion as to the position of the extreme northern constellations but there was something to be said on the other side. There were various discrepancies between the star data compiled by the ancient astronomers of Egypt and Chaldea and observations made by Hipparchus and his contemporaries. Maunder pointed out that the heavens described by Aratus in 270 B.C. represent observations made approximately 2500 years earlier, in or near latitude 40° N. At that time, because of the precession of the equinoxes, Polaris was a considerable distance from the celestial pole, so far, in fact, that in 2700 B.C. the Chinese considered α Draconis as the polestar. Ptolemy knew about precession and corrected the star catalogue of Hipparchus by adding 2° 40′ to the celestial longitudes, in order to allow for precession, while the latitudes remained unaltered. In view of these facts, it is no wonder there was some confusion when it came to comparing notes that ranged over a period of two or three thousand years. Had there been some carelessness along the line? Or did the fixed stars actually have a movement around the pole of the ecliptic (precession) of about one degree in 100 years? [33]

Hipparchus, of course, was correct when he said there was no star at the pole of the universe, and at the time he said it the evidence was much more apparent than it is today, when Polaris is only about one degree away from it. This being so, the Little Bear, including Polaris, described a circle around the celestial pole in the course of a day and night, a circle which varied slightly from year to year. In the fifteenth century Polaris was about 3° 30′ away from the pole, and in determining the latitude from the height of the polestar, corrections had to be made according to the position of the star, that is, whether it was above, below or to one side of the celestial pole. Moreover, the Little Bear, *A Buzina* or *Il Cornu*, as he was called by the Portuguese and Italian sailors, had a reputation as a good timekeeper, swinging as he does around the pole each night, his tail pinioned to the top of the universe by the star Polaris. But here again, if he was to tell the time of night, allowance had to be made for the difference between *sidereal* time (star time) and *mean* time (clock time). Each night at the same hour (by the sandglass or clock) the Guards were in a slightly different position, because the sidereal day is three minutes and fifty-six seconds shorter than the mean solar day.

Every fifteen days the Little Bear lost about an hour, and the Guards were not where they should have been.

Regardless of the timekeeping ability of the Little Bear, what mariners and cartographers were principally interested in was the position of Polaris, as indicated by the Guards, with respect to the celestial pole, at any hour and on any night the stars were visible. Was Polaris above the pole (upper transit) or directly below it (lower transit) or was it on a level with the pole on either side of it? Only when the star was at three o'clock or nine o'clock (halfway between upper and lower transit) would the altitude of the star correspond to the height of the pole.

The correction or "rectification" of the polestar as a necessary step in determining latitude must have been fully appreciated by the ancient astronomers, but

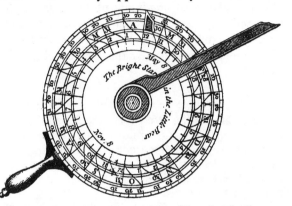

An eighteenth-century nocturnal, a simple instrument that would give the observer the hour of the night and the position of the star Polaris with respect to the celestial pole.

what they did about it is a question. The earliest recorded data on the subject seem to be the writings of Raymond Lull (Lulli, Lully, or Lulle), of Palma in Majorca, about 1235 A.D. He seems to have been the inventor of a simple instrument called a "nocturnal" that in one operation made the necessary corrections for telling the hour of the night and the position of Polaris with respect to the celestial pole. Lull's nocturnal was a tabular wheel or volvelle consisting of three discs of varying diameter fastened together and made to revolve around a central hole through which the observer peered. The outer circle was divided into the days and months of the year; the next smaller disc contained the hours and minutes of the day, and the inner disc consisted of a figure of a little man, an effigy of Kochab, with a hole in his midriff. His head, feet and extended arms marked the four quarters of the circle but instead of referring to compass points, they were labeled Head, Foot, East Arm and West Arm. Four intermediate points on the disc were marked East Shoulder, West Shoulder, Line below East Arm, Line below West Arm. To make a correction of the polestar, having measured its angular height, the observer held the nocturnal aloft, sighting the star through the hole in Kochab's middle. The Kochab disc was then turned until his head pointed towards Kochab the "Guard." The top of the outer (calendar) disc was kept directly over Polaris while the hour disc was turned until the hour of 12 corresponded with the date on the outer disc. The observer then read off the position of the polestar with respect to the pole. In later nocturnals, the effigy of Kochab was replaced by numerical graduations. Martin Cortés devised an inner disc on which Kochab was replaced by the figure of a trumpet or horn representing the constellation, so that the observer could sight on the guards with a miniature of the Little Dipper, showing each star in its proper location with respect to the Guards.[34]

The earliest known written directions for correcting the polestar appeared in the *Regimento do estrolabio e do quadrante* of 1509, under the generic heading "The Regiment of the North Star." The same instructions were used in varying forms by all writers and compilers of books on navigation and cosmography. The "Regiment" said in simple language what the Nocturnal computed by revolving two discs. For example:

This is the Regiment of the North Star

When the Guards are on the West Arm the North Star stands above the Pole one degree and a half [Altitude minus 1.5° = Latitude].

When the Guards are on the line under the West [Arm] the North Star is above the Pole three degrees and a half [Altitude minus 3.5° = Latitude].

When the Guards are at the Foot, the Star is 3 degrees above the Pole [Altitude minus 3° = Latitude].

When the Guards are on the Line below the East Arm the Star is above the Pole half a degree [Altitude minus 0.5° = Latitude].

And when you take the altitude of the Star, and the Guards are in some one of these four positions where the Star is above the Pole, from the altitude that you take of the Star, you should know, you subtract as many degrees as the Star is above; and the degrees which remain are as many as you are removed from the equator.

These are the Four Positions in which the North Star is below the Pole

When the Guards are on the East Arm, the Star is below the Pole one degree and a half.

When the Guards are on the Line above the East Arm the Star is three degrees and a half below the Pole.

When the Guards are at the Head, the Star is below the Pole three degrees.

When the Guards are on the Line over the West Arm the Star is below the Pole half a degree.

Similar directions follow for *adding* these corrections to the altitude in order to obtain latitude.[35]

Blundeville employed the same principle to make his "Rectifier," but changed the relative positions of the three discs. His calendar disc was innermost; the angle disc, graduated from zero degrees to 3½ degrees, was next larger; and the hour disc was on the outside circle. He also converted the instrument into something more permanent and portable. It should be made, according to Blundeville, "upon a smooth piece of board of firme wood, or upon a piece of polished plate of brasse, or Lattin, [that is, latten] being sixe or seven inches broad, having a handle." Instead of giving directions in terms of Kochab's anatomy, Blundeville furnished "a little table, made according to the Mariners rule, touching the eight principall rombs" through which Polaris swung in the course of twenty-four hours.[36]

	The Rombes or windes		The degrees and minutes of the declination of the Load-starre from the Pole		
	West		0	37	
	South-west		2	50	Aboue the
	South		2	24	Pole
If the	South-east	Then the	0	34	
guards	—————	Loadstarre			
be	East	is	0	37	
	North-east		2	50	Beneath the
	North		2	24	Pole
	North-west		1	34	

The principles involved in the rectification of Polaris are the same as they were six hundred years ago. The radius of the circle described by the star has become smaller and hence the amount of correction is smaller. In 1492 the star was 3° 39' off the pole, the *Regimento* of 1509 gave it as 3° 30'. In 1556 Martin Cortés said it was off 3°; Blundeville (1622) called it 2° 50'. Bowditch's *Navigator* for 1802 gives it as 1° 42'. In 1940 the distance was 1° 02'. The nocturnal is an instrument no longer in use at sea, but the 1948 edition of the *American Nautical Almanac* contains four "Tables" relating to Polaris; these tell how to find the latitude by an observed altitude of the star, and how, with a table of azimuths, the position of the star with respect to the pole may be determined.

CHAPTER VIII

The Longitude

SCIENTIFIC cartography was born in France in the reign of Louis XIV (1638–1715), the offspring of astronomy and mathematics. The principles and methods which had been used and talked about for over two thousand years were unchanged; the ideal of Hipparchus and Ptolemy, to locate each place on earth scientifically, according to its latitude and longitude, was still current. But something new had been introduced into the picture in the form of two pieces of apparatus — a telescope and a timekeeper. The result was a revolution in map making and a start towards an accurate picture of the earth. With the aid of these two mechanical contrivances it was possible, for the first time, to solve the problem of how to determine longitude, both on land and at sea.

The importance of longitude, the distance of a place east or west from any other given place, was fully appreciated by the more literate navigators and cartographers of history, but reactions to the question of how to find it varied from total indifference to complete despondency. Pigafetta, who sailed with Magellan, said that the great explorer spent many hours studying the problem of longitude, "but," he wrote, "the pilots content themselves with knowledge of the latitude, and are so proud [of themselves], they will not hear speak of the longitude." Many explorers of the time felt the same way, and rather than add to their mathematical burdens and observations, they were content to let well enough alone. However, "there be some," says an early writer, "that are very inquisitive to have a way to get the longitude, but that is too tedious for seamen, since it requireth the deep knowledge of astronomy, wherefor I would not have any man think that the longitude is to be found at sea by any instrument; so let no seamen trouble themselves with any such rule, but (according to their accustomed manner) let them keep a perfect account and reckoning of the way of their ship." What he meant was, let them keep their dead reckoning with a traverse board, setting down the ship's estimated daily speed and her course.[1]

Like the elixir of life and the pot of gold, longitude was a will-o'-the-wisp which most men refused to pursue and others talked about with awe. "Some doo understand," wrote Richard Eden, "that the Knowledge of the Longitude myght be founde, a thynge doubtlesse greatly to be desyred, and hytherto not certaynly knowen, although Sebastian Cabot, on his death-bed told me that he had the knowledge thereof by divine revelation, yet so, that he myght not teache any man. But," adds Eden, with a certain amount of scorn, "I thinke that the good olde man, in that extreme age, somewhat doted, and had not yet even in the article of death, vtterly shaken off all worldly vayne glorie." [2]

Regardless of pessimism and indifference, the need for a method of finding the longitude was fast becoming urgent. The real trouble began in 1493, less than two months after Columbus returned to Spain from his first voyage to the west. On May 4 of that year, Pope Alexander VI issued the Bull of Demarcation to settle the dispute between Spain and Portugal, the two foremost maritime rivals in Europe. With perfect equanimity His Holiness drew a meridian line from pole to pole on a chart of the Western Ocean one hundred leagues from the Azores. To Spain he assigned all lands not already belonging to any other Christian prince which had been or would be discovered west of the line, and to Portugal all discoveries to the east of it; a masterful stroke of diplomacy, except for the fact that no one knew where the line fell. Naturally both countries suspected the worst, and in later negotiations each accused the other of pushing the line a little in the wrong direction. For all practical purposes, the term "100 leagues west of the Azores" was meaningless, as was the Line of Demarcation and all other meridians in the New World laid down from a line of reference in the Old.

Meanwhile armed convoys heavily laden with the wealth of the Indies ploughed the seas in total darkness so far as their longitude was concerned. Every cargo was worth a fortune and all the risk involved, but too many ships were lost. There were endless delays because a navigator was never sure whether he had overreached an island or was in imminent danger of arriving in the middle of the night without adequate preparations made for landing. The terrible uncertainty was wearing. In 1598 Philip III of Spain offered a perpetual pension of 6000 ducats, together with a life pension of 2000 ducats and an additional gratuity of 1000 more to the "discoverer of longitude." Moreover, there would be smaller sums available in advance for sound ideas that might lead to the discovery and for partially completed inventions that promised tangible results, and no questions asked. It was the clarion call for every crank, lunatic and undernourished inventor in the land to begin research on "the fixed point" or the "East and West navigation" as it was called. In a short time the Spanish government was so deluged with wild, impractical schemes and Philip was so bored with the whole thing that when an Italian named Galileo wrote the court in 1616 about another idea, the king was unimpressed. After a long, sporadic correspondence covering sixteen years, Galileo reluctantly gave up the idea of selling his scheme to the court of Spain.[3]

Portugal and Venice posted rewards, and drew the same motley array of talent and the same results as Spain. Holland offered a prize of 30,000 scudi to the inventor of a reliable method of finding the longitude at sea, and Willem Blaeu, map publisher, was one of the experts chosen by the States General to pass on all such inventions. In August, 1636, Galileo came forward again and offered his plan to Holland, this time through his Paris friend Diodati, as he did not care to have his correspondence investigated by the Inquisition. He told the Dutch authorities that some years before, with the aid of his telescope, he had discovered what might be a remarkable celestial timekeeper — Jupiter. He, Galileo, had first seen the four satellites, the "Cosmian Stars" (*Sidera Medicea*, as he called them), and had studied their movements. Around and around they went, first on one side of the planet, then on the other, now disappearing, then reappearing. In 1612, two years after he first saw them, he had drawn up tables, plotting the positions of the satellites at various hours of the night. These, he found, could be drawn up several months in advance and used to determine mean time at two different places at once. Since then, he had spent twenty-four years perfecting his tables of the satellites, and now he was ready to offer them to Holland, together with minute instructions for the use of any who wished to find the longitude at sea or on land.[4]

The States General and the four commissioners appointed to investigate the merits of Galileo's proposition were impressed, and requested further details. They awarded him a golden chain as a mark of respect and Hortensius, one of the commissioners, was elected to make the journey to Italy where he could discuss the matter with Galileo in person. But the Holy Office got wind of things and the trip was abandoned. In 1641 after a lapse of nearly three years, negotiations were renewed by the Dutch scientist Constantine Huygens, but Galileo died a short time after and the idea of using the satellites of Jupiter was set aside.[5]

In the two thousand year search for a solution of the longitude problem it was never a foregone conclusion that the key lay in the transportation of timekeepers. But among the optimistic who believed that a solution could somehow be found, it was agreed that it would have to come from the stars, especially for longitude at sea, where there was nothing else to observe. It might be found in the stars alone or the stars in combination with some terrestrial phenomenon. However, certain fundamental principles were apparent to all who concerned themselves with the problem. Assuming that the earth was a perfect sphere divided for convenience into 360 degrees, a mean solar day of 24 hours was equivalent to 360 degrees of arc, and 1 hour of the solar day was equivalent to 15 degrees of arc or 15 degrees of longitude. Likewise, 1 degree of longitude was the equivalent of 4 minutes of time. Finer measurements of time and longitude (minutes and seconds of time, minutes and seconds of arc) had been for centuries the stuff that dreams were made of. Surveys of the earth in an east-west direction, expressed in leagues, miles or some other unit of linear measure, would have no significance unless they could be translated into degrees and minutes of arc, fractional parts of the circumference of the earth. And how big was the earth?

The circumference of the earth and the length of a degree (1/360th part of it) had been calculated by Eratosthenes and others but the values obtained were questionable. Hipparchus had worked out the difference between a solar day and a sidereal day (the interval between two successive returns of a fixed star to the meridian), and had plotted a list of 44 stars scattered across the sky at intervals of right ascension equal to exactly one hour, so that one or more of them would be on the meridian at the beginning of every sidereal hour. He had gone a step further and adopted a meridian line through Rhodes, suggesting that longitudes of other places could be determined with reference to his prime meridian by the simultaneous observation of the moon's eclipses. This proposal assumed the existence of a reliable timekeeper which was doubtless nonexistent.

The most popular theoretical method of finding longitude, suggested by the voyages of Columbus, Cabot, Magellan, Tasman and other explorers, was to plot the variation or declination of the compass needle from true north. This variation could be found by taking a bearing on the polestar and noting on the graduated compass card the number of points, half and quarter points (degrees and minutes of arc) the needle pointed east or west of the pole. Columbus had noted this change of compass variation on his first voyage, and later navigators had confirmed the existence of a "line of no variation" passing through both poles and the fact that variation changed direction on either side of it. This being so, and assuming that the variation changed at a uniform rate with a change of longitude, it was logical to assume that here at last was a solution to the whole problem. All you had to do was compare the amount of variation at your place of observation with the tabulated variation at places whose longitude had already been determined. It was this fond hope that induced Edmund Halley and others to compile elaborate charts showing the supposed lines of equal variation throughout the world. However, it was by no means that simple, as Gellibrand and others discovered. Variation does not change uniformly with a change of longitude; likewise, changes in variation occur very slowly; so slowly, in fact, that precise east-west measurements are impractical, especially at sea. And, too, it was found that lines of equal variation do not always run north and south; some run nearly east and west. However, in spite of the flaws that cropped up, one by one, the method had strong supporters for many years, but finally died a painful, lingering death.[6]

In addition to discovering Jupiter's satellites, Galileo made a second important contribution to the solution of longitude by his studies of the pendulum and its behavior, for the application of the swinging weight to the mechanism of a clock was the first step towards the development of an accurate timekeeper.[7] The passage of time was noted by the ancients and their astronomical observations were "timed" with sundials, sandglasses and water clocks but little is known about how the latter were controlled. Bernard Walther, a pupil of Regiomontanus, seems to have been the first to time his observations with a clock driven by weights. He stated that on the 16th of January, 1484, he observed the rising of the planet Mercury, and immediately attached the weight to a clock having an hour-wheel with fifty-six teeth. By sunrise one hour and thirty-five teeth had passed, so that the elapsed time was an hour and thirty-seven minutes, according to his calculations. The next important phase in the development of a timekeeper was the attachment of a pendulum as a driving force. This clock was developed by Christian Huygens, Dutch physicist and astronomer, the son of Constantine Huygens. He built the first one in 1656 in order to increase the accuracy of his astronomical observations, and later presented it to the States General of Holland on the 16th of June, 1657. The following year he published a full description of the principles involved in the mechanism of his timekeeper and the physical laws governing the pendulum. It was a classic piece of writing, and established Huygens as one of the leading European scientists of the day.[8]

By 1666 there were many able scientists scattered throughout Europe. Their activities covered the entire fields of physics, chemistry, astronomy, mathematics, and natural history, experimental and applied. For the most part they worked independently and their interests were widely diversified. Occasionally the various learned societies bestowed honorary memberships on worthy colleagues in foreign countries, and papers read in the various societies were exchanged with fellow scientists in foreign lands. The stage was set for the transition of cartography from an art to a science. The apparatus was at hand and the men to use it.

Pleading for the improvement of maps and surveys, Thomas Burnet made a useful distinction between the popular commercial map publications of the day and what he considered should be the goal of future map makers. "I do not doubt," he wrote, "but that it would be of very good use to have *natural* Maps of the Earth . . . as well as civil. . . . Our common Maps I call *Civil*, which note the distinction of Countries and of Cities, and represent the Artificial Earth as inhabited and cultivated: But natural Maps leave out all that, and represent the Earth as it would be if there were not an Inhabitant upon it, nor ever had been; the Skeleton of the Earth, as I may so say, with the site of all its parts. Methinks also every Prince should have such a Draught of his Country and Dominions, to see how the ground lies in the several parts of them, which highest, which lowest; what respect they have to one another, and to the Sea; how the Rivers flow, and why; how the Mountains lie, how Heaths, and how the Marches. Such a Map or Survey would be useful both in time of War and Peace, and many good observations might be made by it, not only as to Natural History and Philosophy, but also in order to the perfect improvement of a Country." [9]

These sentiments regarding "natural" maps were fully appreciated and shared by the powers in France, who proceeded to do something about it. All that was needed was an agency to acquire the services and direct the work of the available scientific talent, and someone to foot the bills. The agency was taken care of by the creation of the Académie Royale des Sciences, and the man who stood prepared to foot the bills for better maps was His Majesty Louis XIV, king of France.

Louis XIV ascended the throne when he was five years old, but had to wait sixteen years before he could take the reins of government. He had to sit back and watch the affairs of state being handled by the queen-mother and his minister, Cardinal Mazarin. He saw the royal authority weakened by domestic troubles and the last stages of the Thirty Years' War. Having suffered through one humiliation after another without being able to do anything about it, Louis resolved, when he reached the age of twenty-one, to rule as well as reign in France. He would be his own first minister. Foremost among his few trusted advisors was Jean Baptiste Colbert, minister for home affairs, who became, in a short time, the chief power behind the throne. Colbert, an ambitious and industrious man with expensive tastes, contrived to indulge himself in literary and artistic extravagances while adding to the stature and glory of his monarch. As for the affairs of state over which he exercised control, there were two enterprises in particular which entitle Colbert to an important place in the history of France. The first was the establishment of the French Marine under a monarch who cared little for naval exploits or the importance of sea power in the growth and defense of his realm; the second was the founding, in 1666, of the Académie Royale des Sciences, now the Institut de France.[10]

The Académie Royale was Colbert's favorite project. An amateur scientist, he realized the potential value of a distinguished scientific body close to the throne, and with his unusual skill and seemingly unlimited funds he set out to make France pre-eminent in science as it was in the arts and the art of war. He scoured Europe in search of the top men in every branch of science. He addressed personal invitations to such figures as Gottfried Wilhelm von Leibnitz, German philosopher and mathematician; Niklaas Hartsoeker, Dutch naturalist and optician; Ehrenfried von Tschirnhausen, German mathematician and manufacturer of optical lenses and mirrors; Joannes Hévélius, one of Europe's foremost astronomers; Vincenzo Viviani, Italian mathematician and engineer; Isaac Newton, England's budding mathematical genius. The pensions that went with the invitations were without precedent, surpassing in generosity those established by Cardinal Richelieu for the members of the Académie Françoise, and those granted by Charles II for the Royal Society of London. Additional funds were available for research, and security and comfort were assured to those scientists who would agree to work in Paris, surrounded by the most brilliant court in Europe. Colbert's ambition to make France foremost in science was realized, though some of the invitations were declined with thanks. Christian Huygens joined the Académie in 1666 and received his pension of 6000 livres a year until 1681, when he returned to Holland. Olaus Römer, Dutch astronomer, also accepted. These celebrities were followed by Marin de la Chambre who became physician to Louis XIV; Samuel Duclos and Claude Bourdelin in chemistry; Jean Pecquet and Louis Gayant in anatomy; Nicholas Marchant in botany.[11]

In spite of the broad scope of its activities, the avowed purpose of founding the Académie Royale, according to His Majesty, was to correct and improve maps and sailing charts. And the solution of the major problems of chronology, geography and navigation, whose practical importance was incontestable, lay in the further study and application of astronomy.[12] To this end, astronomical observations and conferences were begun in January, 1667. The Abbé Jean Picard, Adrian Auzout, Jacques Buot and Christian Huygens were temporarily installed in a house near the Cordeliers, the garden of which was taken over for astronomical observations. There the scientists set up a great quadrant, a mammoth sextant and a highly refined version of the sundial. They also constructed a meridian line. Sometimes observations were made in the garden of the Louvre. On the whole, facilities for astronomical research were far from good, and there was considerable grumbling among the academicians.

As early as 1665, before the Académie was founded, Auzout had written Colbert an impassioned memorandum asking for an observatory, reminding him that the progress of astronomy in France would be as nothing without one. When Colbert finally made up his mind, in 1667, and the king approved the money, events moved rapidly. The site chosen for the observatory was at Faubourg St. Jacques, well out in the country, away from the lights and disconcerting noises of Paris. Colbert decided that the Observatory of Paris should surpass in beauty and utility any that had been built to date, even those in Denmark, England and China, one which would reflect the magnificence of a king who did things on a grand scale. He called in Claude Perrault, who had designed the palace at Versailles with accommodations for 6000 guests, and told him what he and his Académie wanted. The building should be spacious; it should have ample laboratory space and comfortable living quarters for the resident astronomers and their families.[13]

On the 21st of June, 1667, the day of the summer solstice, the members of the Académie assembled at Faubourg St. Jacques, and with great pomp and circumstance made observations for the purpose of "locating" the new observatory and establishing a meridian line through its center, a line which was to become the official meridian of Paris. The building was to have two octagonal towers flanking the southern façade, and eight azimuths were carefully computed so that the towers would have astronomical as well as architectural significance. Then, without waiting for their new quarters, the resident members of the Académie went back to work, attacking the many unsolved riddles of physics and natural history, as well as astronomy and mathematics. They designed and built much of the apparatus for the new observatory. They made vast improvements in the telescope as an astronomical tool; they solved mechanical and physical problems connected with the pendulum and what gravity does to it, helping Huygens get the few remaining "bugs" out of his pendulum timekeeper. They concentrated on the study of the earth, its size and shape and place in the universe; they investigated the nature and behavior of the moon and other celestial bodies; they worked towards the establishment of a standard meridian of longitude for all nations, the meridian of Paris running through the middle of their observatory. They worked on the problem of establishing the linear value of a degree of longitude which would be a universally acceptable constant. In all these matters the Académie Royale des Sciences was fortunate in having at its disposal the vast resources of the court of France as well as the personal patronage of Louis XIV.

An accurate method of determining longitude was first on the agenda of the Académie Royale, for obviously no great improvement could be made in maps and charts until such a method was found. Like Spain and the Netherlands, France stood ready to honor and reward the man who could solve the problem. In 1667, an unnamed German inventor addressed himself to Louis XIV, stating that he had solved the problem of determining longitude at sea. The king promptly granted him a patent (brevet) on his invention, sight unseen, and paid him 60,000 livres in cash. More than this, His Majesty contracted to pay the inventor 8000 livres a year (Huygens was getting 6000!) for the rest of his life, and to pay him four sous on every ton of cargo moved in a ship using the new device, reserving for himself only the right to withdraw from the contract in consideration of 100,000 livres. All this His Majesty would grant, but on one con-

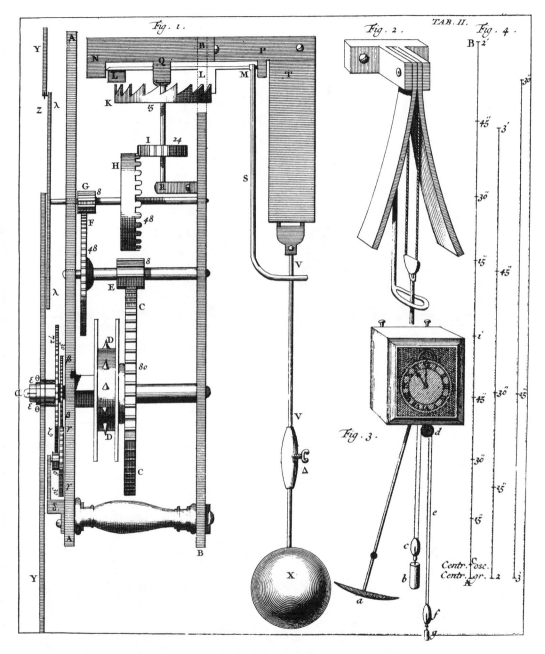

A versatile and ingenious scientist, Huygens built, and in 1657 perfected, the first reliable pendulum clock, revolutionizing astronomy and making it possible for the first time to determine longitude. The works shown above would be familiar to any clock maker today.

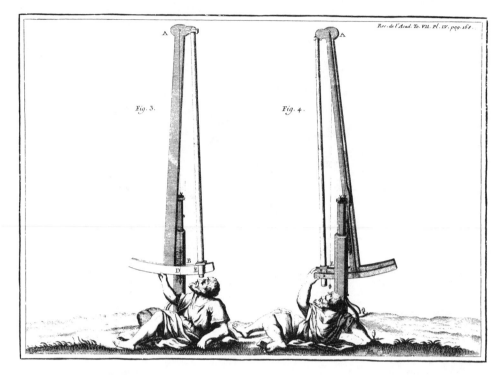

Picard's zenith sector, used to measure small angles.

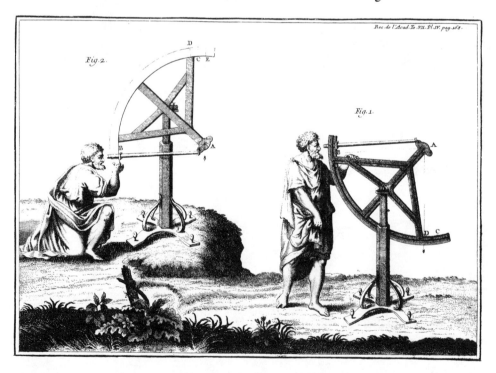

The surveyor's quadrant designed by Jean Picard, fitted with telescope sights
instead of the usual pin-hole alidades.

dition: the inventor must demonstrate his invention before Colbert, Abraham Duquesne, Lieutenant-General of His Majesty's naval forces, and Messrs. Huygens, Carcavi, Roberval, Picard and Auzout of the Académie Royale des Sciences.[14]

The invention proved to be nothing more than a variation on an old theme, an ingenious combination of water wheel and odometer to be inserted in a hole drilled in the keel of a ship. The passage of water under the keel would turn the water wheel, and the distance traversed by the ship in a given period would be recorded on the odometer. The inventor also claimed that by some strange device best known to himself his machine would make any necessary compensations for tides and crosscurrents of one kind and another; it was, in fact, an ideal and perfect solution to the longitude problem. The royal examiners studied the apparatus, praised its ingenuity and then submitted their report to the king in writing. They calmly pointed out, among other things, that if a ship were moving with a current, it might be almost stationary with respect to the water under the keel and yet be carried along over an appreciable amount of longitude while the water wheel remained motionless. If, on the other hand, the ship were breasting a current, the odometer would register considerable progress when actually the ship might be getting nowhere. The German inventor departed from Paris richer by 60,000 livres and the members of the Académie went back to work.[15]

In 1669, after three years of intensive study, the scientists of the Académie Royale had gathered together considerable data on the celestial bodies, and had studied every method that had been suggested for the determination of longitude. The measurement of lunar distances from the stars and the sun was considered impractical because of the complicated mathematics involved. Lunar eclipses might be all right except for the infrequency of the phenomenon and the slowness of eclipses, which increase the chance of error in the observer. Moreover, lunar eclipses were utterly impractical at sea. Meridional transits of the moon were also tried with indifferent success. What the astronomers were looking for was a celestial body whose distance from the earth was so great that it would present the same appearance from any point of observation. Also wanted was a celestial body which would move in a constantly predictable fashion, exhibiting at the same time a changing picture that could be observed and timed simultaneously from different places on the earth. Such a body was Jupiter, whose four satellites, discovered by Galileo, they had observed and studied. The serious consideration of Jupiter as a possible solution of the longitude problem brought to mind a publication that had come out in 1668 written by an Italian named Cassini. While the members of the Académie continued their study of Jupiter's satellites with an eye to utilizing their frequent eclipses as a method of determining longitude, Colbert investigated the possibilities of luring Cassini to Paris.

Giovanni Domenico Cassini was born in Perinaldo, a village in the Comté of Nice, June 8, 1625, the son of an Italian gentleman. After completing his elementary schooling under a preceptor he studied theology and law under the Jesuits at Genoa and was graduated with honors. He developed a decided love of books, and while browsing in a library one day he came across a book on astrology. The work amused him, and after studying it he began to entertain his friends by predicting coming events. His phenomenal success as an astrologer plus his intellectual honesty made him very suspicious of his new-found talent, and he promptly abandoned the hocus-pocus of astrology for the less dramatic study of astronomy. He made such rapid progress and displayed such remarkable aptitude, that in 1650, when he was only twenty-five years old, he was chosen by the Senate of Bologna to fill the first chair of astronomy at the university, vacant since the death of the celebrated mathematician Bonaventura Cavalieri. The Senate never regretted their choice.[16]

One of Cassini's first duties was to serve as scientific consultant to the Church for the precise determination of Holy Days, an important application of chronology and longitude. He retraced the meridian line at the Cathedral of Saint Petronius constructed in 1575 by Ignazio Dante, and added a great mural quadrant which took him two years to build. In 1655 when it was completed, he invited all the astronomers in Italy to observe the winter solstice and examine the new tables of the sun by which the equinoxes, the solstices and numerous Holy Days could now be accurately determined.

Cassini was next appointed by the Senate of Bologna and Pope Alexander VII to determine the difference in level between Bologna and Ferrara, relative to the navigation of the Po and Reno rivers. He not only did a thorough job of surveying, but wrote a detailed report on the two rivers and their peculiarities as well. The Pope next engaged Cassini, in the capacity of a hydraulic engineer, to straighten out an old dispute between himself and the Duke of Tuscany relative to the diversion of the precious water of the Chiana River, alternate affluent of the Arno and the Tiber. Having settled the dispute to the satisfaction of the parties concerned, he was appointed surveyor of fortifications at Perugia, Pont Felix and Fort Urbino, and was made superintendent of the waters of the Po, a river vital to the conservation and prosperity of the country. In his spare time Cassini busied himself with the study of insects and to satisfy his curiosity repeated several experiments on the transfusion of blood from one animal to another, a daring procedure that was causing a flurry of excitement in the scientific world. But his major hobby was astronomy and his favorite planet was Jupiter. While he worked on the Chiana he spent many evenings at Citta della Pière observing Jupiter's satellites. His telescope was better than Galileo's and with it he was able to make some additional discoveries. He noted that the plane of the revolving satellites was such that the satellites passed across Jupiter's disc close to the equator; he noted the size of the orbit of each satellite. He was certain he could see a number of fixed spots on Jupiter's orb, and on the strength of his findings he began to time the rotation of the planet as well as the satellites, using a fairly reliable pendulum clock.[17]

After sixteen years of patient toil and constant observations, Cassini published his tables (*Ephemerides*) of the eclipses of Jupiter's satellites for the year 1668, giving on one page the appearance of the planet in a diagram with the satellites grouped around it and on the opposite page the time of the eclipse (immersion) of each satellite in hours, minutes and seconds, and the time of each emersion.[18]

Cassini, then forty-three years old, had become widely known as a scholar and skilled astronomer, and when a copy of his *Ephemerides* reached Paris Colbert decided he must get him for the Observatory and the Académie Royale. In this instance, however, it took considerable diplomacy as well as gold to get the man he wanted, for Cassini was then in the employ of Pope Clement IX, and neither Louis XIV nor Colbert cared to offend or displease His Holiness. Three distinguished scholars, Vaillant, Auzout and Count Graziani, were selected to negotiate with the Pope and the Senate of Bologna for the temporary loan of Cassini, who was to receive 9000 livres a year as long as he remained in France. The arrangements were finally completed, and Cassini arrived in Paris on the 4th of April, 1669. Two days later he was presented to the king. Although Cassini had no intention of staying indefinitely, Colbert was insistent, and in spite of the remonstrances of the Pope and the Senate of Bologna, Cassini became a naturalized citizen of France in 1673, and was thereafter known as Jean Dominique Cassini.[19]

Observations were in full swing when Cassini took his place among the savants of the Académie Royale who were expert mechanics as well as physicists and mathematicians. Huygens and Auzout had ground new lenses and mirrors, and had built vastly improved telescopes for the observatory. With the new instruments Huygens had already made some phenomenal discoveries. He had observed the rotation period of Saturn, discovered Saturn's rings and the first of the satellites. Auzout had built other instruments and applied to them an improved filar micrometer, a measuring device all but forgotten since its invention by Gascoyne (Gascoigne) about 1639. After Cassini's arrival, more apparatus was ordered, including the best telescopes available in Europe, made by Campani in Italy.[20]

One of the first important steps toward the correction of maps and charts was the remeasurement of the circumference of the earth and the establishment of a new value for a degree of arc in terms of linear measure. There was still a great deal of uncertainty as to the size of the earth, and the astronomers were reluctant to base their new data on a fundamental value which might negate all observations made with reference to it. After poring over the writings of Hipparchus, Poseidonius, Ptolemy and later authorities such as Snell, and after studying the methods these men had used, the Académie worked out a detailed plan for measuring the earth, and in 1669 assigned Jean Picard to do the job.

The measurement of the earth at the equator, from east to west, was out of the question; no satisfactory method of doing it was known. Therefore the method used by Eratosthenes was selected, but with several important modifications and with apparatus that the ancients could only have dreamed of. Picard was to survey a line by triangulation running approximately north and south between two terminal points; he would then measure the arc between the two points (that is, the difference in latitude) by astronomical observations. After looking over the country around Paris, Picard decided he could run his line

nearly northward to the environs of Picardy without encountering serious ob-
structions such as heavy woods and high hills.[21]

Picard selected as his first terminal point the "Pavillon" at Malvoisine near
Paris, and for his second point the clock tower in Sourdon near Amiens, a
distance of about thirty-two French leagues. Thirteen great triangles were surveyed between the two points, and for the purpose Picard used a stoutly reinforced iron quadrant with a thirty-eight inch radius fixed on a heavy standard.
The usual pinhole alidades used for sighting were replaced by two telescopes with
oculars fitted with cross hairs, an improved design of the instrument used by
Tycho Brahe in Denmark. The limb of the quadrant was graduated into minutes
and seconds by transversals. For measuring star altitudes involving relatively acute
angles, Picard used a tall zenith sector made of copper and iron with an amplitude
of about 18°. Attached to one radius of the sector was a telescope ten feet long.
Also part of his equipment were two pendulum clocks, one regulated to beat
seconds, the other half-seconds. For general observations and for observing the
satellites of Jupiter, he carried three telescopes: a small one about five feet long
and two larger ones, fourteen and eighteen feet long. Picard was well satisfied
with his equipment. In describing his specially fitted quadrant, he said it did the
work so accurately that during the two years it took to measure the arc of the
meridian, there was never an error of more than a minute of arc in any of the
angles measured on the entire circumference of the horizon, and that in many
cases, on checking the instrument for accuracy, it was found to be absolutely
true. And as for the pendulum clocks he carried, Picard was pleased to report
that they "marked the seconds with greater accuracy than most clocks mark the
half hours." [22]

When the results of Picard's survey were tabulated, the distance between his
two terminal points was found to be 68,430 toises 3 pieds. The difference in latitude between them was measured, not by taking the altitude of the sun at the
two terminal points, but by measuring the angle between the zenith and a star
in the kneecap of Cassiopeia, first at Malvoisine and then at Sourdon. The difference was 1° 11' 57". From these figures the value of a degree of longitude
was calculated as 57,064 toises 3 pieds. But on checking from a second base line of
verification which was surveyed in the same general direction as the first, this
value was revised to 57,060 toises, and the diameter of the earth was announced
as 6,538,594 toises. All measurements of longitude made by the Académie Royale
were based on this value, equivalent to about 7801 miles, a remarkably close
result.[23]

In 1676, after the astronomers had revised and enlarged his *Ephemerides* of
1668, Cassini suggested that the corrected data might now be used for the determination of longitude, and Jupiter might be given a trial as a celestial clock.
The idea was approved by his colleagues and experimental observations were
begun, based on a technique developed at the Observatory and on experience
acquired by a recent expedition to Cayenne for the observation of the planet Mars.
The scientists were unusually optimistic as the work began, and in a rare burst

of enthusiasm one of them wrote, "*Si ce n'est pas -là le véritable secret des Longitudes, au-moins en approche-t-il de bien près.*"

Because of his tremendous energy, skill and patience, Cassini had by this time assumed the leadership of the scientists working at the observatory, even though he did not have the title of Director. He carried on an extensive correspondence with astronomers in other countries, particularly in Italy where the best instruments were available and where he and his work were well known. Astronomers in foreign parts responded with enthusiasm when they learned of the work that was being done at the Paris Observatory. New data began to pour in faster than the resident astronomers could appraise and tabulate it. Using telescopes and the satellites of Jupiter, hundreds of cities and towns were now being located for the first time with reference to a prime meridian and to each other. All of the standard maps of Europe, it seemed, would have to be scrapped.[24]

With so much new information available, Cassini conceived the idea of compiling a large-scale map of the world (planisphere) on which revised geographical information could be laid down as it came in from various parts of the world, especially the longitudes of different places, hitherto unknown or hopelessly incorrect. For this purpose the third floor of the west tower of the Observatory was selected. There was plenty of space, and the octagonal walls of the room had been oriented by compass and quadrant when the foundation of the building was laid. The planisphere, on an azimuthal projection with the North Pole at the center, was executed in ink by Sédileau and de Chazelles on the floor of the tower under the watchful eye of Cassini. The circular map was twenty-four feet in diameter, with meridians radiating from the center to the periphery, like the spokes of a wheel, at intervals of 10°. The prime meridian of longitude (through the island of Ferro) was drawn from the center at an angle "half way between the two south windows of the tower" to the point where it bisected the circumference of the map. The map was graduated into degrees from zero to 360 in a counterclockwise direction around the circle. The parallels of latitude were laid down in concentric circles at intervals of 10°, starting with zero at the equator and numbering both ways. For convenient and rapid "spotting" of places, a cord was attached to a pin fastened to the center of the map with a small rider on it, so that by swinging the cord around to the proper longitude and the rider up or down to the proper latitude, a place could be spotted very quickly.

On this great planisphere the land masses were of course badly distorted, but it did not matter. What interested the Académie was the precise location, according to latitude and longitude, of the important places on the earth's surface, places that could be utilized in the future for bases of surveying operations. For this reason it was much more important to have the names of a few places strategically located and widely distributed, according to longitude, than it was to include a great many places that were scientifically unimportant. For the same reason, most of the cities and towns that boasted an astronomical observatory, regardless of how small, were spotted on the map.

The planisphere was highly praised by all who saw it. The king came to see it with Colbert and all the court. His Majesty graciously allowed Cassini, Picard and de la Hire to demonstrate the various astronomical instruments used by the members of the Académie to study the heavens and to determine longitude by remote control, as it were. They showed him their great planisphere and explained how the locations of different places were being corrected on the basis of data sent in from the outside world. It was enough to make even Louis pause.[25]

What effect the king's visit had on future events it is difficult to estimate, but in the next few years a great deal of surveying was done. Many surveying expeditions were sent out from the Observatory, and the astronomers went progressively further afield. Jean Richer led an expedition to Cayenne and Jean Mathieu de Chazelles went to Egypt. Jesuit missionaries observed at Madagascar and in Siam. Edmund Halley, who was in close touch with the work going on in France, made a series of observations at the Cape of Good Hope. Thevenot, the historian and explorer, communicated data on several lunar eclipses observed at Goa. About this time, Louis-Abel Fontenay, a Jesuit professor of mathematics at the College of Louis le Grand, was preparing to leave for China. Hearing of the work being done by Cassini and his colleagues, Fontenay volunteered to make as many observations as he could without interfering with his missionary duties. Cassini trained him and sent him on his way prepared to contribute data on the longitudes of the Orient. Thus the importance of remapping the world and the feasibility of the method devised by the Académie Royale began to dawn on the scholars of Europe, and many foreigners volunteered to contribute data. Meanwhile Colbert raised more money and Cassini sent more men into the field.

One of the longest and most difficult expeditions organized by the Académie Royale was led by Messrs. Varin and des Hayes, two of His Majesty's engineers for hydrography, to the island of Gorée and the West Indies. It was also one of the most important for the determination of longitudes in the Western Hemisphere, involving as it did the long jump across the Atlantic Ocean, a span where some of the most egregious errors in longitude had been made. Cassini's original plan, approved by the king, was to launch the expedition from Ferro, on the extreme southwest of the Canary Islands, an island frequently used by cartographers as a prime meridian of longitude. But as there was some difficulty about procuring passage for the expedition, it was decided to take a departure from Gorée, a small island off Cape Verde on the west coast of Africa, where a French colony had recently been established by the Royal Company of Africa.[26]

Before their departure, Varin and des Hayes spent considerable time at the Observatory, where they were thoroughly trained by Cassini and where they could make trial observations to perfect their technique. They received their final instructions in the latter part of 1681, and set out for Rouen equipped with a two and a half foot quadrant, a pendulum clock, and a nineteen foot telescope. Among the smaller pieces of apparatus they carried were a thermometer, a barometer and a compass. From Rouen they moved to Dieppe, where they were held up more than a month by stormy weather and contrary winds. With time on their hands, they made a series of observations to determine the latitude and longitude of the city. The two men finally arrived at Gorée in March, 1682, and there they were joined by M. de Glos, a young man trained and recommended by Cassini. De Glos brought along a six foot sextant, an eighteen foot telescope, a small zenith sector, an astronomical ring and another pendulum clock. Although the primary object of the expedition was to determine longitudes by observing the eclipses of the satellites of Jupiter, the three men had orders to observe the variation of the compass at every point in their travels, especially during the ocean voyage, and to make thermometrical and barometric observations whenever possible; in short, they were to gather all possible scientific data that came their way. From Gorée the expedition sailed for Guadeloupe and Martinique, and for the next year extensive observations were made. The three men returned to Paris in March, 1683.[27]

Cassini's instructions to the party were given in writing. They furnish a clear picture of the best seventeenth century research methods and at the same time explain just how terrestrial longitudes were determined by timing the eclipses of the satellites of Jupiter. The object was simple enough: to find the difference in *mean* or *local* time between a prime meridian such as Ferro or Paris and a second place such as Guadeloupe, the difference in time being equivalent to the difference in longitude. Two pendulum clocks were carried on the expedition, and before leaving they were carefully regulated at the Observatory. The pendulum of one was adjusted so that it would keep *mean* time, that is twenty-four hours a day. The second clock was set to keep *sidereal* or *star* time ($23^h\ 56^m\ 4^s$).[28] The rate of going for the two timekeepers was carefully tabulated over a long period so that the observers might know in advance what to expect when the temperature, let us say, went up or down ten degrees in a twenty-four hour period. These adjustments were made by raising or lowering the pendulum bob to speed up or slow down the clock. After the necessary adjustments were made, the position of the pendulum bobs on the rods was marked and the clocks were taken apart for shipping.

Having arrived at the place where observations were to be made, the astronomers selected a convenient, unobstructed space and set up their instruments. They fixed their pendulum bobs in position and started their clocks, setting them at the approximate hour of the day. The next operation was to establish a meridian line, running true north and south, at the place of observation. This was done in several ways, each method being used as a check against the accuracy of the others. The first was to take a series of equal altitude observations of the sun, a process which would also give a check on the accuracy of the clock which was to keep mean time. To do this, the altitude of the sun was taken with a quadrant or sextant approximately three (or four) hours before apparent noon. At the moment the sight was taken the hour, minute and second were recorded in the jog. An afternoon sight was taken when the sun had descended to precisely the same angle recorded in the morning observation. Again the time was taken at the instant of observation. The difference in time between the two observations divided by two and added to the morning time gave the hour, minute and second indicated at apparent noon. This observation was repeated two days in succession, and the difference in minutes and seconds recorded by the clock on the two days (always different because of the declination of the sun) divided by two and added to the first gave the observers what the clock did in twenty-four hours; in other words, it gave them mean time. A very simple check on the arrival of apparent noon, when the sun reaches the meridian, was to drop a plumb line from the fixed quadrant and note the shadow on the ground as each observation was taken. These observations were repeated daily so that the observers always knew their local time.

The second pendulum clock was much simpler to adjust. All they had to do was set up a telescope in the plane of the meridian, sight it on a fixed star and time two successive transits of the star. When the pendulum was finally adjusted so that 23^h 56^m 4^s elapsed between two successive transits, the job was done. The latitude of the place of observation was equally simple to determine. The altitude of the sun at apparent noon was taken with a quadrant and the angle, referred to the tables of declination, gave the observers their latitude. A check on the latitude was made at night, by observing the height of the polestar.

With the meridian line established, and a clock regulated to keep mean time, the next thing was to observe and time the eclipses of the satellites of Jupiter, at least two of which are eclipsed every two days. As Cassini pointed out, this was not always a simple matter, because not all eclipses are visible from the same place and because bad weather often vitiates the observations. Observations called for a very fussy technique.

The most satisfactory time observations of Jupiter, in Cassini's opinion, could be made of the immersions and emersions of the first satellite. Six phases of the eclipse should be timed: during the immersion of the satellite (1) when the satellite is at a distance from the limb of Jupiter equal to its own diameter; (2) when the satellite just touches Jupiter; (3) when it first becomes entirely hidden by Jupiter's disc. During the emersion of the satellite (4) the instant the satellite begins to reappear; (5) when it becomes detached from Jupiter's disc; (6) when the satellite has moved away from Jupiter a distance equal to its own diameter. To observe and time these phases was a two-man job: one to observe and one to keep a record of the time in minutes and seconds. If an observer had to work alone, Cassini recommended the "eye and ear" method of timing observations, which is still good observational practice. The observer begins to count out loud "one-five-hundred, two-five-hundred, three-five-hundred" and so on, the instant the eclipse begins, and he continues to count until he can get to his clock and note the time. Then by subtracting his count from the clock reading, he has the time at which the observation was made.

The emersion of the satellite, Cassini warned, always requires very careful observation, because you see nothing while you are waiting for it. At the instant you see a faint light in the region where the satellite should reappear, you should begin counting without leaving the telescope until you are sure you are seeing the actual emersion. You may make several false starts before you actually see and can time the actual emersion. Other observations worth using, according to Cassini, were the conjunctions of two satellites going in opposite directions. A conjunction was said to occur when the centers of the two satellites were in a straight perpendicular line. In all important observations requiring great accuracy, Cassini recommended a dress rehearsal the day before and at the same hour, so that if the instruments did not behave or the star was found to be in a difficult position, all necessary adjustments would have been made in advance.[29]

In addition to the observations for the determination of longitude, all expeditions sent out from the Paris Observatory were cautioned to note any variation

The planet Jupiter showing the six positions of the first satellite used
by seventeenth-century astronomers to determine the difference in
longitude between two places.

in the functioning of their pendulum clocks. This did not mean normal variations caused by changes in temperature. Such variations could be predicted in advance by testing the metal pendulum rods: determining the coefficient of expansion at various temperatures. What they were watching for was a change caused by a variation in gravity. There were two reasons involved, one practical and one theoretical. The pendulum was an extremely important engine, since it was the driving force of the best clocks then in use. And too, the whole subject of gravitation, whose leading exponents were Christian Huygens, Isaac Newton and Robert Hooke, was causing a stir in the scientific world. The idea of using the pendulum experimentally for studying gravitation came from Hooke, and the theories of Newton and Huygens might well be proved or disproved by a series of experiments in the field. What no one knew was that these field trials would result in the discovery that the earth is not a perfect sphere but an oblate spheroid, a sphere flattened at the poles.

What effect, if any, did a change of latitude produce in the oscillations of a pendulum if the temperature remained unchanged? Many scientists said none, and experiments seemed to prove it. Members of the Académie had transported time-keepers to Copenhagen and The Hague to try them at different latitudes, and a series of experiments had been conducted in London. The results were all nega-tive; at every place a pendulum of a given length (39.1 inches) beat seconds or made 3600 oscillations an hour. However, there was one exception. In 1672, Jean Richer had made an expedition to Cayenne (4° 56′ 5″ N.) to observe the opposi-tion of Mars. On the whole the expedition was a success, but Richer had had trouble with his timekeeper. Although the length of the pendulum had been carefully adjusted at the Observatory before he sailed, Richer found that in Cayenne his clock lost about two minutes and a half a day, and that in order to get it to keep mean time he had to shorten the pendulum (raise the bob) by more than a "ligne" (about $\frac{1}{12}$ of an inch). All this was very trying to Cassini, who was a meticulous observer. "It is suspected," he wrote, "that this resulted from some error in the observation." Had he not been a gentleman as well as a scholar, he would have said that Richer was just plain careless.[30]

The following year, 1673, Huygens published his masterpiece on the oscillation of the pendulum, in which he set down for the first time a sound theory on the subject of centrifugal force, principles which Newton later applied to his theoreti-cal investigation of the earth.[31] The first opportunity to confirm the fallacy of Richer's observations on the behavior of his timekeeper came when Varin and des Hayes sailed for Martinique (14° 48′ N.) and Guadeloupe (between 15° 47′ and 16° 30′ N.). Cassini cautioned them to check their pendulums with the greatest possible care and they did. But, unfortunately, their clocks behaved badly, and they, too, had to shorten the pendulums in order to make them beat mean time. Cassini was still dubious, but not Isaac Newton. In the third book of his *Principia* he concluded that this variation of the pendulum in the vicinity of the equator must be caused either by a diminution of gravity resulting from a bulging of the earth at the equator, or from the strong, counteracting effect of centrifugal force in that region.[32]

The discoveries made by the Académie Royale des Sciences set a fast pace in the scientific world and pointed the way towards many others. The method of finding longitude by means of the eclipses of Jupiter's satellites had proved to be feasible and accurate, but it was not accepted by foreign countries without a struggle. Tables of Jupiter's satellites were finally included in the English *Nautical Almanac* and remained there in good standing for many years, along with tables of lunar distances and other star data associated with rival methods of finding longitude. It was generally conceded, however, that Jupiter could not be used for finding longitude at sea, in spite of Galileo's assertions to the contrary. Many inventors besides the great Italian had come up with ingenious and wholly impractical devices to provide a steady platform on shipboard from which astronomical observations could be made. But the fact remained that the sea was too boisterous and unpredictable for astronomers and their apparatus.

England made her official entry in the race for the longitude when Charles II ordered the construction of a Royal Observatory, for the advancement of navigation and nautical astronomy, in Greenwich Park, overlooking the Thames and the plain of Essex.[33] In England things moved slowly at first, but they moved. The king was determined to have the tables of the heavenly bodies corrected for the use of his seamen and so appointed John Flamsteed "astronomical observator" by a royal warrant dated March 4, 1675, at the handsome salary of £100 a year, out of which he paid £10 in taxes. He had to provide his own instruments, and as an additional check to any delusions of grandeur he might have, he was ordered to give instruction to two boys from Christ's Hospital. Stark necessity made him take several private pupils as well. Dogged by ill health and the irritations common to the life of a public servant, Flamsteed was nevertheless buoyed up by the society of Newton, Halley, Hooke and the scientists of the Académie Royale, with whom he corresponded. A perfectionist of the first magnitude, Flamsteed was doomed to a life of unhappiness by his unwillingness to publish his findings before he had had a chance to check them for accuracy. To Flamsteed, no demand was sufficiently urgent to justify such scientific transgression.

Flamsteed worked under constant pressure. Everybody, it seemed, wanted data of one sort or another, and wanted it in a hurry. Newton needed full information on "places of the moon" in order to perfect his lunar theory. British scientists, as a group, had set aside the French method of finding longitude and all other methods requiring the use of sustained observations at sea. They were approaching the problem from another angle, and demanded complete tables of lunar distances and a complete catalogue of star places. Flamsteed did as he was told, and for fifteen years (1689–1704) spent most of his time at the pedestrian task of compiling the first Greenwich star catalogue and tables of the moon, meanwhile reluctantly doling out to his impatient peers small doses of what he considered incomplete if not inaccurate data.[34]

The loudest clamors for information came from the Admiralty and from the waterfront. In 1689 war broke out with France. In 1690 (June 30) the English fleet was defeated by the French at the battle of Beachy Head. Lord Torrington, the English admiral, was tried by court-martial and acquitted, but nevertheless dismissed from the service. In 1691 several ships of war were lost off Plymouth because the navigators mistook the Deadman for Berry Head. In 1707 Sir Cloudesley Shovel, returning with his fleet from Gibraltar, ran into dirty weather. After twelve days of groping in a heavy overcast, all hands were in doubt as to the fleet's position. The Admiral called for the opinion of his navigators, and with one exception they agreed that the fleet was well to the west of Ushant, off the Brittany peninsula. The fleet stood on, but that night, in a heavy fog, they ran into the Scilly Islands off the southwest coast of England. Four ships and two thousand men were lost, including the Admiral. There was a story current, long after, that a seaman on the flagship had estimated from his own dead reckoning that the fleet was in a dangerous position. He had the temerity to point this out to his superiors, who sentenced him forthwith to be hanged at the yardarm for mutiny. The longitude had to be found! [35]

There was never a shortage of inventive genius in England, and many fertile minds were directed towards the problem of finding longitude at sea. In 1687 two proposals were made by an unknown inventor which were novel, to say the least. He had discovered that a glass filled to the brim with water would run over at the instant of new and full moon, so that the longitude could be determined with precision at least twice a month. His second method was far superior to the first, he thought, and involved the use of a popular nostrum concocted by Sir Kenelm Digby called the "powder of sympathy." This miraculous healer cured open wounds of all kinds, but unlike ordinary and inferior brands of medicine, the powder of sympathy was applied, not to the wound but to the weapon that inflicted it. Digby used to describe how he made one of his patients jump sympathetically merely by putting a dressing he had taken from the patient's wound into a basin containing some of his curative powder. The inventor who suggested using Digby's powder as an aid to navigation proposed that before sailing every ship should be furnished with a wounded dog. A reliable observer on shore, equipped with a standard clock and a bandage from the dog's wound, would do the rest. Every hour, on the dot, he would immerse the dog's bandage in a solution of the powder of sympathy and the dog on shipboard would yelp the hour.[36]

Another serious proposal was made in 1714 by William Whiston, a clergyman, and Humphrey Ditton, a mathematician. These men suggested that a number of lightships be anchored in the principal shipping lanes at regular intervals across the Atlantic ocean. The lightships would fire at regular intervals a star shell timed to explode at 6440 feet. Sea captains could easily calculate their distance from the nearest lightship merely by timing the interval between the flash and the report. This system would be especially convenient in the North Atlantic, they pointed out, where the depth never exceeded 300 fathoms! For obvious reasons, the proposal of Whiston and Ditton was not carried out, but they started something. Their plan was published, and thanks to the publicity it received in various periodicals, a petition was submitted to Parliament on March 25, 1714, by "several Captains of Her Majesty's Ships, Merchants of London, and Commanders of Merchantmen," setting forth the great importance of finding the longitude and praying that a public reward be offered for some practicable method of doing it.[37] Not only the petition but the proposal of Whiston and Ditton were referred to a committee, who in turn consulted a number of eminent scientists including Newton and Halley.

That same year Newton prepared a statement which he read to the committee. He said, "That, for determining the Longitude at Sea, there have been several Projects, true in the Theory, but difficult to execute." Newton did not favor the use of the eclipses of the satellites of Jupiter, and as for the scheme proposed by Whiston and Ditton, he pointed out that it was rather a method of "keeping an Account of the Longitude at Sea, than for finding it, if at any time it should be lost." Among the methods that are difficult to execute, he went on, "One is, by a Watch to keep time exactly: But, by reason of the Motion of a Ship, the Variation of Heat and Cold, Wet and Dry, and the Difference of Gravity in Different Latitudes, such a Watch hath not yet been made." That was the trouble: such a watch had not been made.[38]

The idea of transporting a timekeeper for the purpose of finding longitude was not new, and the futility of the scheme was just as old. To the ancients it was just a dream. When Gemma Frisius suggested it in 1530 there were mechanical clocks, but they were a fairly new invention, and crudely built, which made the idea improbable if not impossible.[39] The idea of transporting "some true Horologie or Watch, apt to be carried in iourneying, which by an Astrolabe is to be rectified . . ." was again stated by Blundeville in 1622, but still there was no watch which was "true" in the sense of being accurate enough to use for determining longitude.[40] If a timekeeper was the answer, it would have to be very accurate indeed. According to Picard's value, a degree of longitude was equal to about sixty-eight miles at the equator, or four minutes by the clock. One minute of time meant seventeen miles — towards or away from danger. And if on a six weeks' voyage a navigator wanted to get his longitude within half a degree (thirty-four miles) the rate of his timekeeper must not gain or lose more than two minutes in forty-two days, or *three seconds a day*.

Fortified by these calculations, which spelled the impossible, and the report of the committee, Parliament passed a bill (1714) "for providing a publick reward for such person or persons as shall discover the Longitude." It was the largest reward ever offered, and stated that for any practical invention the following sum would be paid: [41]

£10,000 for any device that would determine the longitude within 1 degree.
£15,000 for any device that would determine the longitude within 40 minutes.
£20,000 for any device that would determine the longitude within 30 minutes (2 minutes of time or 34 miles).

As though aware of the absurdity of their terms, Parliament authorized the formation of a permanent commission — the Board of Longitude — and empowered it to pay one half of any of the above rewards as soon as a majority of its members were satisfied that any proposed method was practicable and useful, and that it would give security to ships within eighty miles of danger, meaning land. The other half of any reward would be paid as soon as a ship using the device should sail from Britain to a port in the West Indies without erring in her longitude more than the amounts specified. Moreover, the Board was authorized to grant a smaller reward for a less accurate method, provided it was practicable, and to spend a sum not to exceed £2000 on experiments which might lead to a useful invention.

For fifty years this handsome reward stood untouched, a prize for the impossible, the butt of English humorists and satirists. Magazines and newspapers used it as a stock cliché. The Board of Longitude failed to see the joke. Day in and day out they were hounded by fools and charlatans, the perpetual motion lads and the geniuses who could quarter a circle and trisect an angle. To handle the flood of crackpots, they employed a secretary who handed out stereotyped replies to stereotyped proposals. The members of the Board met three times a year at the Admiralty, contributing their services and their time to the Crown. They took their responsibilities seriously and frequently called in consultants to help them appraise a promising invention. They were generous with grants-in-aid to struggling inventors with sound ideas, but what they demanded was results.[42] Neither the Board nor any one else knew exactly what they were looking for, but what everyone knew was that the longitude problem had stopped the best minds in Europe, including Newton, Halley, Huygens, von Leibnitz and all the rest. It was solved, finally, by a ticking machine in a box, the invention of an uneducated Yorkshire carpenter named John Harrison. The device was the marine chronometer.

Early clocks fell into two general classes: nonportable timekeepers driven by a falling weight, and portable timekeepers such as table clocks and crude watches, driven by a coiled spring. Gemma Frisius suggested the latter for use at sea, but with reservations. Knowing the unreliable temperament of spring-driven timekeepers, he admitted that sand and water clocks would have to be carried along to check the error of a spring-driven machine. In Spain, during the reign of Philip II, clocks were solicited which would run exactly twenty-four hours a day, and many different kinds had been invented. According to Alonso de Santa Cruz there were "some with wheels, chains and weights of steel: some with chains of catgut and steel: others using sand, as in sandglasses: others with water in place of sand, and designed after many different fashions: others again with vases or large glasses filled with quicksilver: and, lastly, some, the most ingenious of all, driven by the force of the wind, which moves a weight and thereby the chain of the clock, or which are moved by the flame of a wick saturated with oil: and all of them adjusted to measure twenty-four hours exactly." [43]

Robert Hooke became interested in the development of portable timekeepers for use at sea about the time Huygens perfected the pendulum clock. One of the most versatile scientists and inventors of all time, Hooke was one of those rare mechanical geniuses who was equally clever with a pen. After studying the faults of current timekeepers and the possibility of building a more accurate one, he slyly wrote a summary of his investigations, intimating that he was completely baffled and discouraged. "All I could obtain," he said, "was a Catalogue of Difficulties, *first* in the doing of it, *secondly* in the bringing of it into publick use, *thirdly*, in making advantage of it. Difficulties were proposed from the alteration of *Climates*, *Airs*, *heats* and *colds*, temperature of *Springs*, the nature of *Vibrations*, the wearing of Materials, the motion of the Ship, and divers others." Even if a reliable timekeeper were possible, he concluded, "it would be difficult to bring it to use, for Sea-men know their way already to any Port. . . ." As for the rewards: "the Praemium for the Longitude," there never was any such thing, he retorted scornfully. "No King or State would pay a farthing for it."

In spite of his pretended despondency, Hooke nevertheless lectured in 1664 on the subject of applying springs to the balance of a watch in order to render its vibrations more uniform, and demonstrated, with models, twenty different ways of doing it. At the same time he confessed that he had one or two other methods up his sleeve which he hoped to cash in on at some future date. Like many scientists of the time, Hooke expressed the principle of his balance spring in a Latin anagram; roughly: *Ut tensio, sic vis,* "as the tension is, so is the force," or, "the force exerted by a spring is directly proportional to the extent to which it is tensioned." [44]

The first timekeeper designed specifically for use at sea was made by Christian Huygens in 1660. The escapement was controlled by a pendulum instead of a spring balance, and like many of the clocks that followed, it proved useless except in a flat calm. Its rate was unpredictable; when tossed around by the sea it either ran in jerks or stopped altogether. The length of the pendulum varied with changes of temperature, and the rate of going changed in different latitudes, for some mysterious reason not yet determined. But by 1715 every physical principal and mechanical part that would have to be incorporated in an accurate timekeeper was understood by watchmakers. All that remained was to bridge the gap between a good clock and one that was nearly perfect. It was that half degree of longitude, that two minutes of time, which meant the difference between conquest and failure, the difference between £20,000 and just another timekeeper. [45]

One of the biggest hurdles between watchmakers and the prize money was the weather: temperature and humidity. A few men included barometric pressure. Without a doubt, changes in the weather did things to clocks and watches, and many suggestions were forthcoming as to how this principal source of trouble could be overcome. Stephen Plank and William Palmer, watchmakers, proposed keeping a timekeeper close to a fire, thus obviating errors due to change in temperature. Plank suggested keeping a watch in a brass box over a stove which would always be hot. He claimed to have a secret process for keeping the temperature of the fire uniform. Jeremy Thacker, inventor and watchmaker, published a book on the subject of the longitude, in which he made some caustic remarks about the efforts of his contemporaries. [46] He suggested that one of his colleagues, who wanted to test his clock at sea, should first arrange to have two consecutive Junes equally hot at every hour of every day. Another colleague, referred to as Mr. Br . . . e, was dubbed the Corrector of the Moon's Motion. In a more serious vein, Thacker made several sage observations regarding the physical laws with which watchmakers were struggling. He verified experimentally that a coiled spring loses strength when heated and gains it when cooled. He kept his own clock under a kind of bell jar connected with an exhaust pump, so that it could be run in a partial vacuum. He also devised an auxiliary spring which kept the clock going while the mainspring was being wound. Both springs were wound outside the bell by means of rods passed through stuffing boxes, so that neither the vacuum nor the clock mechanism would have to be disturbed. In spite of these and other devices, watchmakers remained in the dark and their problems remained unsolved until John Harrison went to work on the physical laws behind them. After that they did not seem so difficult.[47]

Harrison was born at Foulby in the parish of Wragby, Yorkshire, in May, 1693. He was the son of a carpenter and joiner in the service of Sir Rowland Winn of Nostell Priory. John was the oldest son in a large family. When he was six years old he contracted smallpox, and while convalescing spent hours watching the mechanism and listening to the ticking of a watch laid on his pillow. When his family moved to Barrow in Lincolnshire, John was seven years old. There he learned his father's trade and worked with him for several years. Occasionally he earned a little extra by surveying and measuring land, but he was much more interested in mechanics, and spent his evenings studying Nicholas Saunderson's published lectures on mathematics and physics. These he copied out in longhand including all the diagrams. He also studied the mechanism of clocks and watches, how to repair them and how they might be improved. In 1715, when he was twenty-two, he built his first grandfather clock or "regulator." The only remarkable feature of the machine was that all the wheels except the escape wheel were made of oak, with the teeth, carved separately, set into a groove in the rim.[48]

Many of the mechanical faults in the clocks and watches that Harrison saw around him were caused by the expansion and contraction of the metals used in their construction. Pendulums, for example, were usually made of an iron or steel rod with a lead bob fastened at the end. In winter the rod contracted and the clock went fast, and in summer the rod expanded, making the clock lose time. Harrison made his first important contribution to clockmaking by developing the "gridiron" pendulum, so named because of its appearance. Brass and steel, he knew, expand for a given increase in temperature in the ratio of about three to two (100 to 62). He therefore built a pendulum with nine alternating steel and brass rods, so pinned together that expansion or contraction caused by variation in the temperature was eliminated, the unlike rods counteracting each other.[49]

The accuracy of a clock is no greater than the efficiency of its escapement, the piece which releases for a second, more or less, the driving power, such as a suspended weight or a coiled mainspring. One day Harrison was called out to repair a steeple clock that refused to run. After looking it over he discovered that all it needed was some oil on the pallets of the escapement. He oiled the mechanism and soon after went to work on a design for an escapement that would not need oiling. The result was an ingenious "grasshopper" escapement that was very nearly frictionless and also noiseless. However, it was extremely delicate, unnecessarily so, and was easily upset by dust or unnecessary oil. These two improved parts alone were almost enough to revolutionize the clockmaking industry. One of the first two grandfather clocks he built that were equipped with his im-

John Harrison's first marine chronometer, "No. 1," and his prize-winning "No. 4" which solved the problem of determining longitude at sea.

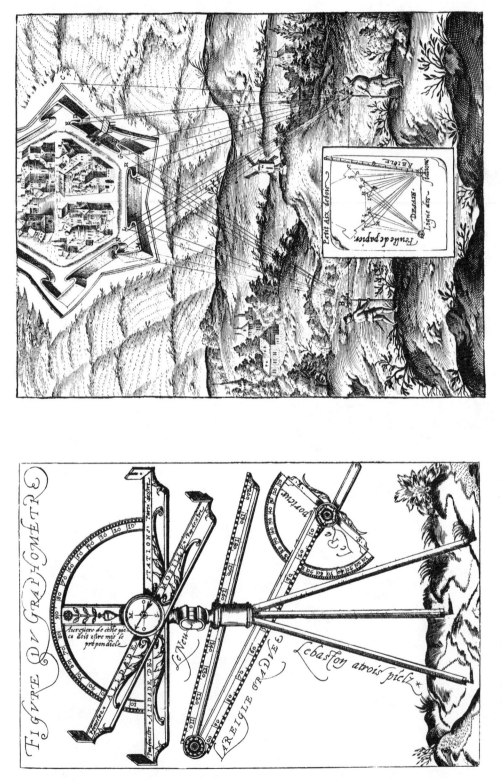

A sixteenth-century surveying scene showing the construction of the instruments and their use in the field.

proved pendulum and grasshopper escapement did not gain or lose more than a second a month during a period of fourteen years.

Harrison was twenty-one years old when Parliament posted the £20,000 reward for a reliable method of determining longitude at sea. He had not finished his first clock, and it is doubtful whether he seriously aspired to winning such a fortune, but certainly no young inventor ever had such a fabulous goal to shoot at, or such limited competition. Yet Harrison never hurried his work, even after it must have been apparent to him that the prize was almost within his reach. On the contrary, his real goal was the perfection of his marine timekeeper as a precision instrument and a thing of beauty. The monetary reward, therefore, was a foregone conclusion.

His first two fine grandfather clocks were completed by 1726, when he was thirty-three years old, and in 1728 he went to London, carrying with him full-scale models of his gridiron pendulum and grasshopper escapement, and working drawings of a marine clock he hoped to build if he could get some financial assistance from the Board of Longitude. He called on Edmund Halley, Astronomer Royal, who was also a member of the Board. Halley advised him not to depend on the Board of Longitude, but to talk things over with George Graham, England's leading horologist.[50] Harrison called on Graham at ten o'clock one morning, and together they talked pendulums, escapements, remontoires and springs until eight o'clock in the evening, when Harrison departed a happy man. Graham had advised him to build his clock first and then apply to the Board of Longitude. He had also offered to loan Harrison the money to build it with, and would not listen to any talk about interest or security of any kind. Harrison went home to Barrow and spent the next seven years building his first marine timekeeper, his "Number One," as it was later called.

In addition to heat and cold, the archenemies of all watchmakers, he concentrated on eliminating friction, or cutting it down to a bare minimum, on every moving part, and devised many ingenious ways of doing it; some of them radical departures from accepted watchmaking practice. Instead of using a pendulum, which would be impractical at sea, Harrison designed two huge balances weighing about five pounds each, that were connected by wires running over brass arcs so that their motions were always opposed. Thus any effect on one produced by the motion of the ship would be counteracted by the other. The "grasshopper" escapement was modified and simplified and two mainsprings on separate drums were installed. The clock was finished in 1735.

There was nothing beautiful or graceful about Harrison's Number One. It weighed seventy-two pounds and looked like nothing but an awkward, unwieldy piece of machinery. However, everyone who saw it and studied its mechanism declared it a masterpiece of ingenuity, and its performance certainly belied its appearance. Harrison mounted its case in gimbals and for a while tested it unofficially on a barge in the Humber River. Then he took it to London where he enjoyed his first brief triumph. Five members of the Royal Society examined the clock, studied its mechanism and then presented Harrison with a certificate stating that the principles of this timekeeper promised a sufficient degree of accuracy to meet the requirements set forth in the Act of Queen Anne. This historic document, which opened for Harrison the door to the Board of Longitude, was signed by Halley, Smith, Bradley, Machin and Graham.

On the strength of the certificate, Harrison applied to the Board of Longitude for a trial at sea, and in 1736 he was sent to Lisbon in H.M.S. *Centurion*, Captain Proctor. In his possession was a note from Sir Charles Wager, First Lord of the Admiralty, asking Proctor to see that every courtesy be given the bearer, who was said by those who knew him best to be "a very ingenious and sober man." Harrison was given the run of the ship, and his timekeeper was placed in the Captain's cabin where he could make observations and wind his clock without interruption. Proctor was courteous but skeptical. "The difficulty of measuring Time truly," he wrote, "where so many unequal Shocks and Motions stand in Opposition to it, gives me concern for the honest Man, and makes me feel he has attempted Impossibilities." [51]

No record of the clock's going on the outward voyage is known, but after the return trip, made in H.M.S. *Orford*, Robert Man, Harrison was given a certificate signed by the master (that is, navigator) stating: "When we made the land, the said land, according to my reckoning (and others), ought to have been the Start; but before we knew what land it was, John Harrison declared to me and the rest of the ship's company, that according to his observations with his machine, it ought to be the Lizard — the which, indeed, it was found to be, his observation showing the ship to be more west than my reckoning, above one degree and twenty-six miles." It was an impressive report in spite of its simplicity, and yet the voyage to Lisbon and return was made in practically a north and south direction; one that would hardly demonstrate the best qualities of the clock in the most dramatic fashion. It should be noted, however, that even on this well-worn trade route it was not considered a scandal that the ship's navigator should make an error of 90 miles in his landfall.

On June 30, 1737, Harrison made his first bow to the mighty Board of Longitude. According to the official minutes, "Mr. John Harrison produced a new invented machine, in the nature of clockwork, whereby he proposes to keep time at sea with more exactness than by any other instrument or method hitherto contrived . . . and proposes to make another machine of smaller dimensions within the space of two years, whereby he will endeavour to correct some defects which he hath found in that already prepared, so as to render the same more perfect . . ." The Board voted him £500 to help defray expenses, one half to be paid at once and the other half when he completed the second clock and delivered same into the hands of one of His Majesty's ship's captains. [52]

Harrison's Number Two contained several minor mechanical improvements and this time all the wheels were made of brass instead of wood. In some respects it was even more cumbersome than Number One, and it weighed one hundred and three pounds. Its case and gimbal suspension weighed another sixty-two pounds. Number Two was finished in 1739, but instead of turning it over to a sea captain appointed by the Board to receive it, Harrison tested it for nearly two years under conditions of "great heat and motion." Number Two was never sent to sea because by the time it was ready, England was at war with Spain and the Admiralty had no desire to give the Spaniards an opportunity to capture it.

In January, 1741, Harrison wrote the Board that he had begun work on a third clock which promised to be far superior to the first two. They voted him another £500. Harrison struggled with it for several months, but seems to have miscalculated the "moment of inertia" of its balances. He thought he could get it going by the first of August, 1741, and have it ready for a sea trial two years later. But after five years the Board learned "that it does not go well, at present, as he expected it would, yet he plainly perceived the Cause of its present Imperfection to lye in a certain part [the balances] which, being of a different form from the corresponding part in the other machines, had never been tried before." Harrison had made a few improvements in the parts of Number Three and had incorporated in it the same antifriction devices he had used on Number Two, but the clock was still bulky and its parts were far from delicate; the machine weighed sixty-six pounds and its case and gimbals another thirty-five.[53]

Harrison was again feeling the pinch, even though the Board had given him several advances to keep him going, for in 1746, when he reported on Number Three, he laid before the Board an impressive testimonial signed by twelve members of the Royal Society including the President, Martin Folkes, Bradley, Graham, Halley and Cavendish, attesting the importance and practical value of his inventions in the solution of the longitude problem. Presumably this gesture was made to insure the financial support of the Board of Longitude. However, the Board needed no prodding. Three years later, acting on its own volition, the Royal Society awarded Harrison the Copley medal, the highest honor it could bestow. His modesty, perseverance and skill made them forget, at least for a time, the total lack of academic background which was so highly revered by that august body.[54]

Convinced that Number Three would never satisfy him, Harrison proposed to start work on two more timekeepers, even before Number Three was given a trial at sea. One would be pocketsize and the other slightly larger. The Board approved the project and Harrison went ahead. Abandoning the idea of a pocket-size chronometer, Harrison decided to concentrate his efforts on a slightly larger clock, which could be adapted to the intricate mechanism he had designed without sacrificing accuracy. In 1757 he began work on Number Four, a machine which "by reason alike of its beauty, its accuracy, and its historical interest, must take pride of place as the most famous chronometer that ever has been or ever will be made. It was finished in 1759.[55]

Number Four resembled an enormous "pair-case" watch about five inches in diameter, complete with pendant, as though it were to be worn. The dial was white enamel with an ornamental design in black. The hour and minute hands were of blued steel and the second hand was polished. Instead of a gimbal suspension, which Harrison had come to distrust, he used only a soft cushion in a plain box to support the clock. An adjustable outer box was fitted with a divided arc so that the timekeeper could be kept in the same position (with the pendant always slightly above the horizontal) regardless of the lie of the ship. When it was finished, Number Four was not adjusted for more than this one position, and on its first voyage it had to be carefully tended. The watch beat five to the second and ran for thirty hours without rewinding. The pivot holes were jeweled to the third wheel with rubies and the end stones were diamonds. Engraved in the top-plate were the words "John Harrison & Son, A.D. 1759." Cunningly concealed from prying eyes beneath the plate was a mechanism such as the world had never seen; every pinion and bearing, each spring and wheel was the end product of careful planning, precise measurement and exquisite craftsmanship. Into the mechanism had gone "fifty years of self-denial, unremitting toil, and ceaseless concentration." To Harrison, whose singleness of purpose had made it possible for him to achieve the impossible, Number Four was a satisfactory climax to a life-time of effort. He was proud of this timekeeper, and in a rare burst of eloquence he wrote, "I think I may make bold to say, that there is neither any other Mechanical or Mathematical thing in the World that is more beautiful or curious in texture than this my watch or Time-keeper for the Longitude . . . and I heartily thank Almighty God that I have lived so long, as in some measure to complete it." [56]

After checking and adjusting Number Four with his pendulum clock for nearly two years, Harrison reported to the Board of Longitude, in March 1761, that Number Four was as good as Number Three and that its performance greatly exceeded his expectations. He asked for a trial at sea. His request was granted, and in April, 1761, William Harrison, his son and right-hand man, took Number Three to Portsmouth. The father arrived a short time later with Number Four. There were numerous delays at Portsmouth, and it was October before passage was finally arranged for young Harrison aboard H.M.S. *Deptford*, Dudley Digges, bound for Jamaica. John Harrison, who was then sixty-eight years old, decided not to attempt the long sea voyage himself; and he also decided to stake every-thing on the performance of Number Four, instead of sending both Three and Four along. The *Deptford* finally sailed from Spithead with a convoy, November 18, 1761, after first touching at Portland and Plymouth. The sea trial was on.

Number Four had been placed in a case with four locks, and the four keys were given to William Harrison, Governor Lyttleton of Jamaica, who was taking passage on the *Deptford*, Captain Digges, and his first lieutenant. All four had to be present in order to open the case, even for winding. The Board of Longitude had further arranged to have the longitude of Jamaica determined *de novo* before the trial, by a series of observations of the satellites of Jupiter, but because of the lateness of the season it was decided to accept the best previously established reckoning. Local time at Portsmouth and at Jamaica was to be determined by taking equal altitudes of the sun, and the difference compared with the time indicated by Harrison's timekeeper.

As usual, the first scheduled port of call on the run to Jamaica was Madeira. On this particular voyage, all hands aboard the *Deptford* were anxious to make the island on the first approach. To William Harrison it meant the first crucial test of Number Four; to Captain Digges it meant a test of his dead reckoning against a mechanical device in which he had no confidence; but the ship's company had more than a scientific interest in the proceedings. They were afraid of missing Madeira altogether, "the consequence of which, would have been Inconvenient." To the horror of all hands, it was found that the beer had spoiled, over a thousand gallons of it, and the people had already been reduced to drinking water. Nine days out from Plymouth the ship's longitude, by dead reckoning, was 13° 50' west of Greenwich, but according to Number Four and William Harrison it was 15° 19' W. Captain Digges naturally favored his dead reckoning calculations, but Harrison stoutly maintained that Number Four was right and that if Madeira were properly marked on the chart they would sight it the next day. Although Digges offered to bet Harrison five to one that he was wrong, he held his course, and the following morning at 6 A.M. the lookout sighted Porto Santo, the northeastern island of the Madeira group, dead ahead.

The *Deptford's* officers were greatly impressed by Harrison's uncanny predictions throughout the voyage. They were even more impressed when they arrived at Jamaica three days before H.M.S. *Beaver*, which had sailed for Jamaica ten days before them. Number Four was promptly taken ashore and checked. After allowing for its rate of going (2⅔ seconds per day losing at Portsmouth), it was found to be 5 seconds slow, an error in longitude of 1¼' only, or 1¼ nautical miles.[57]

The official trial ended at Jamaica. Arrangements were made for William Harrison to make the return voyage in the *Merlin*, sloop, and in a burst of enthusiasm Captain Digges placed his order for the first Harrison-built chronometer which should be offered for sale. The passage back to England was a severe test for Number Four. The weather was extremely rough and the timekeeper, still carefully tended by Harrison, had to be moved to the poop, the only dry place on the ship, where it was pounded unmercifully and "received a number of violent shocks." However, when it was again checked at Portsmouth, its total error for the five months' voyage, through heat and cold, fair weather and foul (after allowing for its rate of going), was only 1ᵐ 53½ˢ, or an error in longitude of 28½' (28½ nautical miles). This was safely within the limit of half a degree specified in the Act of Queen Anne. John Harrison and son had won the fabulous reward of £20,000.

The sea trial had ended, but the trials of John Harrison had just begun. Now for the first time, at the age of sixty-nine, Harrison began to feel the lack of an academic background. He was a simple man; he did not know the language of diplomacy, the gentle art of innuendo and evasion. He had mastered the longitude but he did not know how to cope with the Royal Society or the Board of Longitude. He had won the reward and all he wanted now was his money. The money was not immediately forthcoming.

Neither the Board of Longitude nor the scientists who served it as consultants were at any time guilty of dishonesty in their dealings with Harrison; they were only human. £20,000 was a tremendous fortune, and it was one thing to dole out living expenses to a watchmaker in amounts not exceeding £500 so that he might contribute something or other to the general cause. But it was another thing to hand over £20,000 in a lump sum to one man, and a man of humble birth at that. It was most extraordinary. Moreover, there were men on the Board and members of the Royal Society who had designs on the reward themselves or at least a cut of it. James Bradley and Johann Tobias Mayer had both worked long and hard on the compilation of accurate lunar tables. Mayer's widow was paid £3000 for his contribution to the cause of longitude, and in 1761 Bradley told Harrison that he and Mayer would have shared £10,000 of the prize money between them if it had not been for his blasted watch. Halley had struggled long and manfully on the solution of the longitude by compass variation, and was not in a position to ignore any part of £20,000. The Reverend Nevil Maskelyne, Astronomer Royal, and compiler of the *Nautical Almanac,* was an obstinate and uncompromising apostle of "lunar distances" or "lunars" for finding the longitude, and had closed his mind to any other method whatsoever. He loved neither Harrison nor his watch. In view of these and other unnamed aspirants, it was inevitable that the Board should decide that the amazing performance of Harrison's timekeeper was a fluke. They had never been allowed to examine the mechanism, and they pointed out that if a gross of watches were carried to Jamaica under the same conditions, one out of the lot might perform equally well — at least for one trip. They accordingly refused to give Harrison a certificate stating that he had met the requirements of the Act until his timekeeper was given a further trial, or trials. Meanwhile, they did agree to give him the sum of £2500 as an interim reward, since his machine had proved to be a rather useful contraption, though mysterious beyond words. An Act of Parliament (February, 1763) enabling him to receive £5000 as soon as he disclosed the secret of his invention, was completely nullified by the absurdly rigid conditions set up by the Board. He was finally granted a new trial at sea.[58]

The rules laid down for the new trial were elaborate and exacting. The difference in longitude between Portsmouth and Jamaica was to be determined *de novo* by observations of Jupiter's satellites. Number Four was to be rated at Greenwich before sailing, but Harrison balked, saying "that he did not chuse to part with it out of his hands till he shall have reaped some advantage from it." However, he agreed to send his own rating, sealed, to the Secretary of the Admiralty before the trial began. After endless delays the trial was arranged to take place between Portsmouth and Barbados, instead of Jamaica, and William Harrison embarked on February 14, 1764, in H.M.S. *Tartar*, Sir John Lindsay, at the Nore. The *Tartar* proceeded to Portsmouth, where Harrison checked the rate of Number Four with a regulator installed there in a temporary observatory. On March 28, 1764, the *Tartar* sailed from Portsmouth and the second trial was on.

It was the same story all over again. On April 18, twenty-one days out, Harrison took two altitudes of the sun and announced to Sir John that they were forty-three miles east of Porto Santo. Sir John accordingly steered a direct course for it, and at one o'clock the next morning the island was sighted, "which exactly agreed with the Distance mentioned above." They arrived at Barbados May 13, "Mr. Harrison all along in the Voyage declaring how far he was distant from that Island, according to the best settled longitude thereof. The Day before they made it, he declared the Distance: and Sir John sailed in Consequence of this Declaration, till Eleven at Night, which proving dark he thought proper to lay by. Mr. Harrison then declaring they were no more than eight or nine Miles from the Land, which acordingly at Day Break they saw from that Distance." [59]

When Harrison went ashore with Number Four he discovered that none other than Maskelyne and an assistant, Green, had been sent ahead to check the longitude of Barbados by observing Jupiter's satellites. Moreover, Maskelyne had been orating loudly on the superiority of his own method of finding longitude, namely, by lunar distances. When Harrison heard what had been going on he objected strenuously, pointing out to Sir John that Maskelyne was not only an interested party but an active and avid competitor, and should not have anything to do with the trials. A compromise was arranged, but, as it turned out, Maskelyne was suddenly indisposed and unable to make the observations.

After comparing the data obtained by observation with Harrison's chronometer, Number Four showed an error of 38.4 seconds over a period of seven weeks, or 9.6 miles of longitude (at the equator) between Portsmouth and Barbados. And when the clock was again checked at Portsmouth, after 156 days, elapsed time, it showed, after allowing for its rate of going, a total gain of only 54 seconds of time. If further allowance were made for changes of rate caused by variations in temperature, information posted beforehand by Harrison, the rate of Number Four would have been reduced to an error of 15 seconds of loss in 5 months, or less than $\frac{1}{10}$ of a second a day. [60]

The evidence in favor of Harrison's chronometer was overwhelming, and could no longer be ignored or set aside. But the Board of Longitude was not through. In a Resolution of February 9, 1765, they were unanimously of the opinion that "the said timekeeper has kept its time with sufficient correctness, without losing its longitude in the voyage from Portsmouth to Barbados beyond the nearest limit required by the Act 12th of Queen Anne, but even considerably within the same." Now, they said, all Harrison had to do was demonstrate the mechanism of his clock and explain the construction of it, "by Means whereof other such Time-keepers might be framed, of sufficient Correctness to find the Longitude at Sea. . . ." In order to get the first £10,000 Harrison had to submit, on oath, complete working drawings of Number Four; explain and demonstrate the operation of each part, including the process of tempering the springs; and finally, hand over to the Board his first three timekeepers as well as Number Four. [61]

Any foreigner would have acknowledged defeat at this juncture, but not Harrison, who was an Englishman and a Yorkshireman to boot. "I cannot help thinking," he wrote the Board, after hearing their harsh terms, "but I am extremely ill used by gentlemen who I might have expected different treatment from. . . . It must be owned that my case is very hard, but I hope I am the first, and for my country's sake, shall be the last that suffers by pinning my faith on an English Act of Parliament." The case of "Longitude Harrison" began to be aired publicly, and several of his friends launched an impromptu publicity campaign against the Board and against Parliament. The Board finally softened their terms and Harrison reluctantly took his clock apart at his home for the edification of a committee of six, nominated by the Board; three of them, Thomas Mudge, William Matthews and Larcum Kendall, were watchmakers. Harrison then received a certificate from the Board (October 28, 1765) entitling him to £7500, or the balance due him on the first half of the reward. The second half did not come so easily.

Number Four was now in the hands of the Board of Longitude, held in trust for the benefit of the people of England. As such, it was carefully guarded against prying eyes and tampering, even by members of the Board. However, that learned body did its humble best. First they set out to publicize its mechanism as widely as possible. Unable to take the thing apart themselves, they had to depend on Harrison's own drawings, and these were redrawn and carefully engraved. What was supposed to be a full textual description was written by the Reverend Nevil Maskelyne and printed in book form with illustrations appended: *The Principles of Mr. Harrison's Time-Keeper, with Plates of the Same.* London, 1767. Actually the book was harmless enough, because no human being could have even begun to reproduce the clock from Maskelyne's description. To Harrison it was just another bitter pill to swallow. "They have since published all my Drawings," he wrote, "without giving me the last Moiety of the Reward, or even paying me and my Son for our Time at a rate as common Mechanicks; an Instance of such Cruelty and Injustice as I believe never existed in a learned and civilised Nation before." Other galling experiences followed.[62]

With great pomp and ceremony Number Four was carried to the Royal Observatory at Greenwich. There it was scheduled to undergo a prolonged and exhaustive series of trials under the direction of the Astronomer Royal, the Reverend Nevil Maskelyne. It cannot be said that Maskelyne shirked his duty, although he was handicapped by the fact that the timekeeper was always kept locked in its case, and he could not even wind it except in the presence of an officer detailed by the Governor of Greenwich to witness the performance. Number Four, after all, was a £10,000 timekeeper. The tests went on for two months. Maskelyne tried the watch in various positions for which it was not adjusted, dial up and dial down. Then for ten months it was tested in a horizontal position, dial up. The Board published a full account of the results with a preface written by Maskelyne, in which he gave it as his studied opinion "That Mr. Harrison's Watch cannot be depended upon to keep the Longitude within a Degree, in a West-India Voyage of six weeks, nor to keep the Longitude within Half a Degree for more than a Fortnight, and then it must be kept in a Place where the Thermometer is always some Degrees above freezing." (There was still £10,000 prize money outstanding.) [63]

The Board of Longitude next commissioned Larcum Kendall, watchmaker, to make a duplicate of Number Four. They also advised Harrison that he must make Number Five and Number Six and have them tried at sea, intimating that otherwise he would not be entitled to the other half of the reward. When Harrison asked if he might use Number Four for a short time to help him build two copies of it, he was told that Kendall needed it to work from and that it would be impossible. Harrison did the best he could, while the Board laid plans for an exhaustive series of tests for Number Five and Number Six. They spoke of sending them to Hudson's Bay and of letting them toss and pitch in the Downs for a month or two as well as sending them out to the West Indies.

After three years (1767–1770) Number Five was finished. In 1771, just as the Harrisons were finishing the last adjustments on the clock, they heard that Captain Cook was preparing for a second exploring cruise, and that the Board was planning to send Kendall's duplicate of Number Four along with him. Harrison pleaded with them to send Number Four and Number Five instead, telling them he was willing to stake his claim to the balance of the reward on their performance, or to submit "to any mode of trial, by men not already proved partial, which shall be definite in its nature." The man was now more than ever anxious to settle the business once and for all. But it was not so to be. He was told that the Board did not see fit to send Number Four out of the kingdom, nor did they see any reason for departing from the manner of trial already decided upon.

John Harrison was now seventy-eight years old. His eyes were failing and his skilled hands were not as steady as they were, but his heart was strong and there was still a lot of fight left in him. Among his powerful friends and admirers was His Majesty King George the Third, who had granted Harrison and his son an audience after the historic voyage of the *Tartar*. Harrison now sought the protection of his king, and "Farmer George," after hearing the case from start to finish, lost his patience. "By God, Harrison, I'll see you righted," he roared. And he did. Number Five was tried at His Majesty's private observatory at Kew. The king attended the daily checking of the clock's performance, and had the pleasure of watching the operation of a timekeeper whose total error over a ten week's period was 4½ seconds.[64]

Harrison submitted a memorial to the Board of Longitude, November 28, 1772, describing in detail the circumstances and results of the trial at Kew. In return, the Board passed a resolution to the effect that they were not the slightest bit interested; that they saw no reason to alter the manner of trial they had already proposed and that no regard would be paid for a trial made under any other conditions. In desperation Harrison decided to play his last card — the king. Backed by His Majesty's personal interest in the proceedings, Harrison presented a petition to the House of Commons with weight behind it. It was heralded as follows: "The Lord North, by His Majesty's Command, acquainted the House that His Majesty, having been informed of the Contents of the said Petition, recommended it to the Consideration of the House." Fox was present to give the petition his full support, and the king was willing, if necessary, to appear at the Bar of the House under an inferior title and testify in Harrison's behalf. At the same time, Harrison circulated a broadside, *The Case of Mr. John Harrison*, stating his claims to the second half of the reward.[65]

The Board of Longitude began to squirm. Public indignation was mounting rapidly and the Speaker of the House informed the Board that consideration of the petition would be deferred until they had an opportunity to revise their proceedings in regard to Mr. Harrison. Seven Admiralty clerks were put to work copying out all of the Board's resolutions concerning Harrison. While they worked day and night to finish the job, the Board made one last desperate effort. They summoned William Harrison to appear before them; but the hour was late. They put him through a catechism and tried to make him consent to new trials and new conditions. Harrison stood fast, refusing to consent to anything they might propose. Meanwhile a money bill was drawn up by Parliament in record time; the king gave it the nod and it was passed. The Harrisons had won their fight.

CHAPTER IX

Survey of a Country

DURING the seventeenth century, the heyday of Dutch and Flemish cartography, France had her share of commercial map publishers, and a few of them were successful. Like Hondius, Jansson and the Blaeus, the map makers of France offered their public little that was new. They followed the Ptolemaic tradition, leaning heavily on ancient itineraries and hearsay evidence, reworking old material and older plates. At their best, French maps lacked luster; the beautiful engraving and elegant coloring of the Dutch and Flemish masters were lacking, and by comparison, they were drab and uninteresting. As a result, the French public showed a preference for the maps and atlases published in Amsterdam and Antwerp, and there was no market for a French counterpart of the great ten- and twelve-volume atlases from across the border.

About the time the Académie Royale des Sciences was founded, the old school of geographers, many of whom had worshiped at the shrine of the ancients, had begun to languish. Yet, strangely enough, one of the last survivors, a scholarly devotee of classical geography named Nicolas Sanson (d'Abbeville), played an important part, indirectly, in the reformation of geography and cartography. He taught the young. Sanson was an antiquarian by nature and a cartographer by necessity. He studied the ancients, and drew maps to illustrate their history. And in order to indulge his taste for history he allowed some of his maps to be published, but only to keep body and soul together. He married young and soon discovered that the business of living required more and more of his time. From then on he made and published many maps, mostly concerned with ancient history, but his heart was not in the production end of the business. In desperation he turned over to his creditors all of his worldly possessions and moved to Paris in 1627, taking with him what proved to be his only financial asset — a map he had compiled of ancient Gaul, superior in every way to any that were on the market. The map saved him. Richelieu saw it and was impressed, both by the work itself and the burning enthusiasm of its maker. He arranged to have Sanson presented to His Majesty Louis XIII, and the king promptly succumbed to the geographer's personality and zeal. Sanson tutored his monarch in geography, and in return for his services was appointed Engineer to the Province of Picardy. Later the king presented him with a brevet of Geographer-in-Ordinary, a position carrying a stipend of 2000 livres a year. On the side, Sanson continued to compile maps.[1]

Sanson raised three sons, Nicolas, Guillaume and Adrien, all of whom became geographers, trained in the classical tradition by their father. Also trained by the elder Sanson were Pierre du Val, who later published several creditable geographical works, and Claude Delisle, a talented historian with a remarkable flair for teaching. Sanson and Delisle shared many interests. Both men appreciated the close relationship between geography and history, and the "tutoring" they did for each other, if it could be called that, was doubtless more of an exchange of ideas, at which Delisle was no novice. Like Sanson, Claude Delisle had sons, four of them. And like Sanson's sons, the four Delisles received from their father a thorough background in history. Simon-Claude, the second son, chose history for his lifework; the other three chose science, and ultimately were elected members of the Académie Royale des Sciences. Joseph-Nicolas and Louis became astronomers and Guillaume climaxed his career as "Premier Géographe du Roi," the first man in France to be granted that important title.

Guillaume Delisle decided at the tender age of nine to concentrate on the geographical aspects of history, which to him meant making maps. He might well have carried on in the Sanson tradition, letting his elders have the say, except for two things. One was a natural critical faculty which was considered unbecoming in one so young. The other was that in addition to his regular teachers, he was exposed to the scientific teachings of Jean Dominique Cassini and the Académie Royale des Sciences. Delisle was shocked to learn that even the most highly respected geographers, including Nicolas Sanson himself, had been guilty of perpetuating false information regarding the earth and its inhabitants, that the facts of history had been misrepresented, that geography and cartography needed a thorough overhauling on the basis of scientific facts and accurate observation. Was Japan an island? What sort of a country was Moscovie — was it as cold as people said? Was the Mediterranean as long from east to west as Ptolemy had said it was? These and thousands of other questions needed to be answered in the light of new information or by scientific methods which would lead to such information. Guillaume Delisle, with almost no practical experience behind him, undertook a complete reform of a system of geography that had been in force since the second century, and by the time he was twenty-five he had very nearly accomplished his purpose.[2]

Cassini tutored Delisle. He demonstrated the great planisphere laid out on the floor of the Observatory tower, pointing out that it was no longer necessary to rely on travelers' tales in order to locate the various places on the earth. He gave the young geographer an infusion of scientific skepticism and a taste of scientific method, both of which were badly needed in the profession. Cassini's teachings bore fruit, and while the younger Sansons continued to publish maps from their father's old plates, with almost no revisions, Delisle made a fresh start. In 1700 he published simultaneously a map of the world, separate maps of Europe, Asia and Africa, a celestial globe and a terrestrial globe. Though far from perfect, these productions contained the elements of scientific maps, and the number of improvements was large enough and sufficiently spectacular to establish Delisle as a new kind of geographer, a man who might make Ptolemy's dreams come true. With the endless data coming into the Observatory added to his own surveys,

Guillaume Delisle soon shocked the geographical world out of its complacency and drew the attention of foreign kings and potentates to the fact that they knew as little about their own domains as Louis XIV knew about his. He also won for himself (in 1702) a place in the Académie Royale. In the course of time he published more than a hundred maps of various parts of the world. He reduced the length of Asia, and for the first time in history, gave the Mediterranean Sea its proper length of 41°. He shifted land masses and moved islands to the consternation of his elders, but all such radical changes were made on the basis of informa-

A gentleman surveyor of the sixteenth century rode in style. A dial recorded the revolutions of the carriage wheels while the surveyor and his assistant sketched the road and countryside with the aid of a portable compass.

tion usually obtained by astronomical observation or actual surveys. Though he worked independently, Delisle was in a sense the unofficial geographer-reporter or interpreter for the Académie Royale, to the mutual advantage of both parties.[3]

Among the royal visitors who called on Guillaume Delisle was Peter the Great, who wanted to meet the foremost geographer in Europe and tell him in person what he could about the land of the Moscovites. He hoped, perhaps, that in return, Delisle could shed some light on the precise limits of Moscovia (Muscovy), about which very little was known. The Czar also met Joseph-Nicolas and Louis Delisle, Guillaume's two brothers. Having seen for himself the unlimited possibilities of astronomy as it was being applied to cartography, the Czar Peter invited Joseph Delisle, with the approval of Catherine, to come to Russia and organize a school of astronomy at St. Petersburg. Joseph was not interested at first, but after a second invitation he consented to go, and with him went his brother Louis. The arrangement was ideal from the standpoint of the Czar, and it proved to be a boon to geography in general. The Delisles were treated handsomely, and in their turn the two astronomers proved capable ambassadors of good will as well as expert technical advisors. They organized a school of astronomy, prepared an elementary text for the students, showed them how to make their own apparatus, and with great solemnity distributed prizes for meritorious accomplishment. They also found time to probe the vastness of Russia, making extensive marches into the interior for the purpose of gathering physical and geographical data. Louis visited and explored the coasts of the Arctic Ocean, Lapland and Archangel, making astronomical observations wherever he went in order to determine the precise location of important places. He traversed Siberia as far as the peninsula of Kamchatka, and embarked with Vitus Bering on a voyage of exploration. But the fatigue and bitter cold were too much for him and he had to be set ashore at the port of Avatcha (Avacha), where he died a few months later.

After nearly twenty-two years in Russia, Joseph-Nicolas returned to France. With him he brought hundreds of maps and charts and reams of scientific notes that he and his brother had compiled. It was a priceless collection, the first comprehensive report to reach Europe on one of the most inaccessible parts of the world, and a region about which Europeans knew almost nothing. Delisle offered it to France and Louis XV promptly bought it for deposit in the Dépôt de la Marine and paid Delisle a stipend of 8000 francs to act as custodian of the collection.[4]

While the belated reform of geography by French scientists and explorers was gratifying enough to the government, there were other matters that were more urgent. One of them was the map of France. Though the Académie Royale des Sciences had been founded for the improvement of geography and cartography in general, Colbert considered that the lack of an adequate map of the kingdom was a national disgrace. To the harried Secretary in charge of home affairs, an accurate, large-scale map of the country was of the utmost importance. It was a necessity of peace as well as war. Colbert's job was to restore the exhausted resources of France and to try at the same time to keep abreast of the insatiable appetite of Louis XIV for building and conquest.

Colbert always needed money, and struggled manfully to find new sources (revenue that would stem the flood of rising debts. He was forced to sacrifice many things to support the pomp of Versailles. He tried to introduce new industries against the opposition of municipal bodies and the bourgeoisie, who were terrified by any innovation. It was obvious to all Frenchmen that Colbert's burning desire to make France prosperous was only a means of making Louis XIV and the state more powerful. Colbert called for unity of effort, at the same time keeping private initiative in subjection and under suspicion. As a result, France was a miniature Europe, studded with provincial customhouses, senseless levies, sundry systems of weights and measures, and many other concrete indications of disunity and independence. Against this solid front of tradition, indifference, civil resistance and conceit, Colbert strove for the internal improvement of the country — without a map to aid him.

He probed the kingdom from one end to the other, looking for undeveloped resources to encourage trade. He made Marseilles and Dunkerque free ports. He engineered the great *Canal du Midi* across France. He knew the country needed more canals, more roads, new bridges and dikes, but no man could say where they should be built because he did not know the topography of the country. Roads could not be built without first knowing something about distances and directions between cities and towns. Colbert's whole economic program as well as his political career depended on a map that was nonexistent. Moreover, no geographer had yet conceived a method of compiling a survey that would meet Colbert's exacting demands.[5]

In 1663, three years before the first meeting of the Académie Royale, Colbert made the initial step towards the mapping of France. In an "Instruction" sent out to the Maîtres des Requêtes, field commissioners in the provinces, Colbert ordered that the maps of each province or *généralité* be examined to determine whether or not they were adequate and accurate. If such maps were wanting or if they were deficient in scale or accuracy, capable surveyors were to be employed to make new ones, immediately and without interference. If qualified men were not available locally, His Majesty would refer the matter to Sieur Nicolas Sanson, Geographer-in-Ordinary, who would delegate trained men to make the surveys. Colbert's directive brought little more than grumbling from the hinterland and in spite of Sanson's best efforts the desired maps were not forthcoming.[6]

Louis was not disposed to postpone his military plans merely because he lacked good maps. In 1667 he launched his first campaign designed to extend the frontiers of France. The War of Devolution, in which he laid claim to Flanders in the name of his wife Marie Theresa, was conducted by Michel le Tellier, Marquis de Louvois, Secretary of State for War, who had organized and equipped the French army in spite of Colbert's protestations of poverty. Turenne conquered Flanders in less than three months. England, the United Provinces and Sweden formed a triple alliance at The Hague in January, 1668, to prevent the occupation of the Netherlands, but Louis was able to preserve his conquest in Flanders by signing a treaty at Aix-la-Chapelle. Louis's object was to ruin the Netherlands as a financial threat and a military power in order to annex to French Flanders the rest of the Catholic Netherlands alloted to him by secret treaty. Colbert produced the money, Louvois furnished the army and de Lionne took care of the conniving that resulted in the necessary alliances. Meanwhile Colbert's own program was more or less brushed aside by everyone except Colbert and his scientists.[7]

The problem of mapping France was discussed at the first meeting of the Académie, and in May, 1668, Pierre de Carcavi, the King's Librarian and Colbert's spokesman, appeared before that body with a message. Monseigneur Colbert desired that the members direct their efforts without delay towards the making of maps of France more accurate than those which were then available. He further desired that the members should prescribe the manner in which this purpose might best be accomplished. The Académie resolved to discuss the matter at their next meeting, and as it was deemed advisable to have the counsel of the most able geographers, the presence of M. Sanson was requested at the meeting to be held on Wednesday, May 30. At the second meeting the entire problem was discussed at length, and after listening to Sanson, the Académie decided to make a trial survey of Paris and environs, in order to test several methods that had been suggested, as well as the accuracy of various pieces of apparatus.

In June of 1668, there was another meeting of the Académie in the King's Library, at which M. de Carcavi announced that since the last meeting of the company, one David du Vivier had presented himself as a candidate to make the survey of Paris. Du Vivier was brought in and questioned, after which he unrolled one of his own maps to show the assembly what he could do. Apparently the Académie was favorably impressed, because it was moved that du Vivier be appointed to make the trial survey under the immediate direction of Abbé Jean Picard and Gilles Personne de Roberval, inventor and mathematician. Picard watched the work closely, and in July, 1669, he reported on a reconnaissance journey he had made with Jean Dominique Cassini to Mareil-en-France in order to check Vivier's measurement of effectual angles. They had found that the quadrants he was using were not accurate enough to measure angles closer than a few minutes of arc. Picard had therefore ordered the alidades of the quadrants removed and replaced by telescopes fitted with filar micrometers. While Vivier continued with his surveying in the vicinity of Paris, Picard began running his meridian line northward from the city for the determination of the length of a degree.[8]

Picard's line between Sourdon and Malvoisine, a distance of thirty-two leagues to the north and south of Paris, was calculated to tie in with the preliminary surveying (leveling) being done by Vivier. The base line was measured on the actual road between Paris and Fontainebleau, between the mill at Villejuif and the flagpole at Juvisy. From this base, Picard began running a chain of great triangles northward. Triangulation was continued during the summer of 1669 and the meridian line was finished in 1670. Meanwhile Picard and his assistants had furnished Vivier with a series of precisely measured angles in the vicinity of Paris. The line itself, with triangles extending on either side of it, was the beginning of an accurate survey of France as well as a meridian line for the measurement of the earth. And the whole operation demonstrated to Picard's satisfaction the utility of proceeding independently with the two operations preliminary to mapping: the establishment of a chain of triangles and topographic surveying on the ground. This conclusion has since been borne out by cartographers of all nations, and the method has become standard practice among scientific map makers.

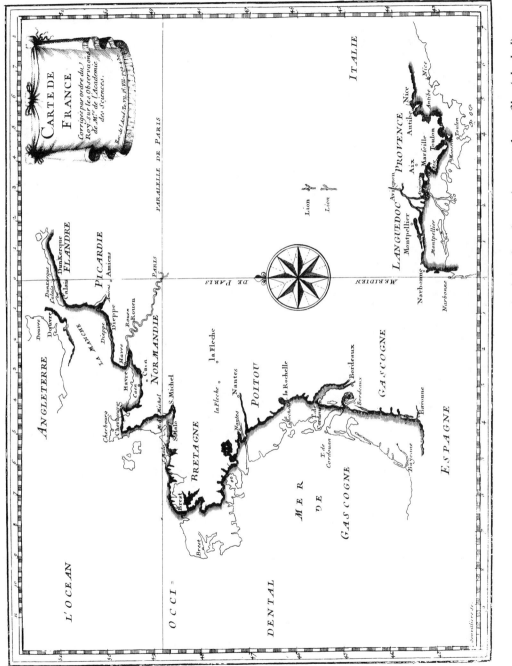

The resurvey of France under Cassini and Picard resulted in the above improved profile (*shaded*).

Triangulation in France (*above*). Picard's meridian line (*below*).

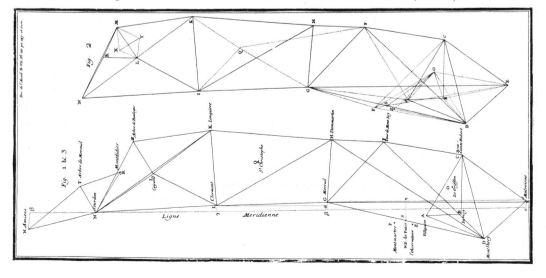

The engraving of Vivier's map was begun in 1671 and was in process for nearly seven years, the work being done by F. Delapointe. It was finally published under the title *Carte Particuliere des environs de Paris. Par Messrs. de l'Académie Royale des Sciences. En l'Année 1674. Gravée par F. de la Pointe en l'an 1678.* The finished product was in 9 sheets, each one measuring 45 by 41 centimeters. The scale was 1:86,400 or 1 ligne to 100 toises. The area covered extends from Mantes to La Ferté-sous-Jouarre and from Pont-Sainte-Maxence to Milly-en-Gâtinais. Not only the surveying of the ground but the engraving of the map was a laboratory experiment in methods and technique. For instance, instead of using the conventional "molehill" effect to indicate topography, a device dating back to the earliest Ptolemaic manuscripts, Delapointe tried out a new system, using short scratches or "hachures" to indicate land contours. On later maps these hachures were refined, and from them evolved the contour lines of modern cartography. Contour lines (isobaths) in the modern sense were first used on a chart of the Merwede by a Frenchman, M. S. Cruquires in 1728, and again by Philip Buache, also French, on a chart of the English Channel made in 1737.[9]

Even while Vivier's map was being engraved, Picard and his colleagues were making plans for the extension of the Paris survey, and Colbert gave them his wholehearted support, passing on to the Académie what money he could divert from the royal coffers without causing alarm. The prospects were never good. Louis XIV crossed the Rhine in June, 1672; the United Provinces, with only Brandenberg and Spain on their side, were occupied in a matter of days. The victorious march of Condé and Turenne was stopped finally, by the broken dikes of Muiden. William of Orange, the stadtholder, preached resistance unto death. Under the circumstances, a large-scale mapping program was out of the question, but the Académie did what it could. Its activities were largely confined to observations made at isolated spots throughout the kingdom, where the latitude and longitude were in doubt. The astronomers had a plan, even if His Majesty did not. Everywhere they went they took their instruments, and when feasible their pendulum clocks, checking their data with the information on the best available maps. In every spot they were able to make valuable corrections.[10]

When Queen Maria Theresa learned what was going on, she gave the project her official sanction and ordered that these scattered observations be applied without delay to the compilation of a unified map of France. From 1679 to 1685 the Académie made better progress, and presumably received a little more financial support. Working independently along the Atlantic was a group of engineers detailed to revise the existing charts of the coast and harbors of the country. But like Vivier, they worked on isolated areas, and needed a certain number of positions accurately fixed by astronomical observations. The astronomers from the Académie furnished them with the information necessary to co-ordinate their detailed surveys, later published in atlas form as *Le Neptune François*. In 1679 Picard and de la Hire worked at Brest, Nantes and points between, checking the latitude and longitude of each place. The following year they worked up the coast from Bayonne to Bordeaux and as far north as Royan at the mouth of the

Gironde. In 1681 the astronomers established numerous points on the Manche peninsula including Cherbourg. From there the two separated; Picard moved south to Mont-Saint-Michel and Saint-Malo. La Hire moved north to Calais and Dunkerque, and while working the channel coast he measured the distance between the French coast and Dover. Varin and des Hayes, on their way to Gorée, made observations at Rouen and Dieppe.

The results of these and other reconnaissance surveys were finally plotted on a map compiled by Gabriel la Hire of the Académie Royale. The contours of the coast between the points of observation were filled in from the surveys previously made by Her Majesty's engineers. The results were startling, and when the new outline of France was superimposed on a map made by Sanson in 1679 for the Dauphin, they were even more so. The new longitudes were figured from the meridian of Paris, and corrections varied from a few minutes (towards the east) in the region of Calais and Havre, to more than a degree and a half on the peninsula of Bretagne. The latitudes, too, varied widely; in some localities the astronomers moved them north and in others to the south; but all of them were shifted.[11]

The revised outline map of France made a good beginning, but it also emphasized how much remained to be done in the interior. In 1681 Picard wrote a memorandum on the subject for Colbert's information. The project of mapping France by provinces, he said, might sound well on paper, but it would take forever. And even if the separate maps were actually completed, sooner or later all the pieces would have to be brought together within a general framework. Therefore, why not make the skeleton first and fill it in afterwards? If the framework of triangles were projected for the entire country, a "traverse" survey should be made first, running close to the meridian of Paris. But, he pointed out, this traverse had already been partly surveyed, and the meridian line for the determination of the length of a degree could easily be extended north and south to the extremities of the kingdom. Working east and west from this line it would then be relatively easy to establish an uninterrupted chain of great triangles, the more the better, throughout the country. After establishing a series of accurately fixed points, the detailed topographic surveying could be done, time and money permitting.[12]

Picard's plan sounded logical and feasible to Colbert, and he passed it on to the king. Louis XIV was interested, and called in J. D. Cassini to explain just how longitude was determined by means of Jupiter's satellites and how he and Picard and the other members of the Académie proposed to map France with a telescope and pendulum clock. Cassini explained everything to the king's satisfaction, and the following spring His Majesty paid a visit to the Observatory to see all these things for himself. The king was convinced when he saw the work being done by the Académie, and though Picard died the same year, his plan did not die with him. In June of 1683 Colbert announced that Picard's meridian line was to be extended at both ends to the extremities of the country, and that J. D. Cassini was to direct the work. The extension of the line would serve a double purpose. It would furnish a line for the remeasurement of the circumference of the earth about eight times longer than the original line surveyed by Picard. And it would provide the necessary base line for all future surveying operations in France. Each objective was dependent on the other.[13]

The great survey of France had its ups and downs. Colbert, sponsor of the project and champion of the Académie Royale, died in 1683, and after that things were never quite the same. He was succeeded by the Marquis de Louvois, who assumed the duties of Director of His Majesty's fortifications and protector of the Académie. A good politician, Louvois announced that he intended to carry on in Colbert's footsteps, developing public works and directing his efforts towards any project that would contribute to the glory of his monarch and the good of France. But Louvois was a professional soldier who was far more interested in the king's plans for territorial expansion than in the internal improvement of the country, and war soon absorbed all of his time and energy.

Louvois died in 1691, and for a time there was hope that work on the meridian of Paris as well as the map of France might be continued. But war had eaten far into the royal treasury, and instead of receiving a subsidy to continue the work, the king's pensioners began to receive only part of their salaries, and for a while it was doubtful whether the Académie Royale would survive the financial crisis. However, in 1699, things began to look better. The Académie was completely reorganized and its members took a new lease on life. In 1700 they were ordered to continue work on the meridian line, thanks to the intercession of Count Pont-chartrain and Abbé Bignon, President of the Académie.[14]

By this time the scientific world had become preoccupied with a growing suspicion that the earth was not a perfect sphere. But if it was spheroidal, was the long axis through the poles or in the plane of the equator? A great deal hinged on the answer to the question. If, as some said, it were a sphere, the value of a degree would be the same for both latitude and longitude; but if the earth turned out to be a spheroid, numerous calculations would have to be altered and many a line would have to be resurveyed. The map of France was involved, but every scientist knew the issue was bigger than that. Isaac Newton was on trial. His theory of universal gravitation hinged on the actual shape of the earth, which many savants, including Picard, stoutly maintained was a perfect sphere. The gravitational theories of Huygens and Newton called for an earth flattened at the poles, and the evidence brought back by Richer, Varin and des Hayes regarding the behavior of their pendulums in low latitudes seemed to verify their theories, but the proof was by no means conclusive. At the same time there were several reputable scientists who had presented evidence that seemed to indicate that the earth was a spheroid elongated at the poles.

Work on the extension of Picard's meridian line was begun in August, 1700, in the vicinity of Bourges. With Cassini was his son, Jacques, as well as other assistants. The party finished the southern end of the line at Collioure in 1701. When it came time to measure a degree of arc over this new portion of the meridian line, the linear value was found to be greater than Picard's value for a degree measured further north. If both measurements were accurate and the length of a degree of latitude diminished towards the poles, the inference was that the earth was elongated towards the poles, a prolate spheroid. Cassini had nothing to say on the subject, and further proof depended on the measurements yet to be made at the northern extremity of the line, in and around Dunkerque. The difference in the south was so small that it might have been caused by human error or a defect in the apparatus. Picard's value for a degree was 57,060 toises and Cassini's party had obtained 57,097 toises.

Jean Dominique Cassini did not live to finish the northern extension of the meridian line. His eyes failed, and like Galileo, he spent the last years of his life in darkness. When he died in 1712, his son Jacques succeeded him as pensioner in the Académie Royale. With Maraldi and de la Hire the younger, Jacques Cassini projected a plan for running the northern extension of Picard's line, but once again surveying operations were postponed, this time because of the War of the Spanish Succession. In June, 1718, the survey finally got under way. A chain of 28 triangles was run from the Paris Observatory to Dunkerque, of which 9 were Picard's and 19, extending from Montdidier to the sea, were new. Again the results were in favor of a spheroid elongated towards the poles. Jacques Cassini calculated the length of a degree between Paris and Dunkerque as 56,960 toises. He summarized his findings in a report to the Académie stating flatly that the earth was a prolate spheroid. Instead of settling the dispute, Cassini's report merely added fuel to the fire, as it was entirely opposed to the theoretical conclusions of Huygens and Newton. However, the report was by no means a total loss. It emphasized the need of a still more decisive test, a survey and measurement of two arcs widely separated; one as near as possible to the equator and one close to the Arctic Circle.[15]

From 1718 to 1733 there was another lapse in surveying operations relative to the map of France, but in the interval the Académie acquired a new champion. In 1730, Philibert Orry, Comte de Vignori, became Comptroller-General of finances, and shortly thereafter was elevated to the position of Minister of State and Director of Fortifications, with supervisory control over the arts and manufactures. With some of Colbert's appreciation and enthusiasm, he took over the patronage of the arts and sciences. His wisdom and foresight would have carried him far, but for his unfortunate personality. A bachelor with extremely bad manners and a sharp tongue, Orry had the temerity to insult a Mme. d'Étoiles whose star was in the ascendency, and later, as La Pompadour, she successfully accomplished his political ruin. Meanwhile Orry gave the Académie his support, encouraging the astronomers to go ahead with the mapping of France. Louis XV, an amateur scientist, had studied geography under Guillaume Delisle and was easily persuaded to support the project. In 1733 Jacques Cassini read a paper to the Académie summarizing the progress of the map of France to date. He pointed out that a great many observations had been made throughout the country and the latitude and longitude of numerous places had been redetermined. In addition to a skeleton outline of the country and a fairly accurate set of charts of the Atlantic coast, there was a fine topographic map of the environs of Paris in print; but that was all. More research was needed, more triangles must be surveyed and the length of a degree needed verification before the great map itself could be compiled.

Through his minister, Orry, Louis XV gave the astronomers the nod and authorized them to continue their surveying. Having bisected France with a meridian line running through the Paris Observatory from Dunkerque to the Spanish border, the astronomers decided to run a perpendicular to the meridian through the Observatory from the Atlantic coast to the eastern boundary at "Fortlouis" near Strassburg. The alleged purpose of this move was to furnish surveyors with another measured base line, but every scientist in the land knew better. With perfectly straight faces the astronomers began to run the western half of the line between the Observatory and Saint-Malo, while the scientific world waited impatiently to see what was going to happen. If the length of a degree on the perpendicular line (in the latitude of Paris) should satisfy the requirements of a sphere, then Huygens and Newton would be wrong and many of the previous measurements and theoretical calculations would have to be revised.[16]

Jacques Cassini began the survey in June, 1733. With him went his son, César François (Cassini de Thury), Maraldi, the Abbé de la Grive and Chevalier. Normally they would have run the line to Granville on the parallel of Paris, but because the position of Saint-Malo, a little to the south, had been previously fixed by astronomical observation, they surveyed a small triangle to get down to it. When the survey of the perpendicular was finished, a degree of longitude was measured along its length by observation of the satellites of Jupiter. Instead of measuring 37,707 toises as it would have on a spherical earth, the line was only 36,670 toises, short by 1037 toises. In other words, it appeared that the degrees of latitude diminished in length towards the poles more rapidly than they would on a perfect sphere. When the eastern half of the perpendicular was run the following year, the astronomers got the same result. It was then that Louis XV ordered a decisive test made to settle the shape of the earth once and for all.[17]

Two expeditions were dispatched from Paris, the object being to survey two arcs, one as near as possible to the equator and the other near the Arctic Circle. The first survey was begun in Peru in 1735 under the direction of Louis Godin, Pierre Bouguer and Charles Marie de la Condamine. It took them ten long years to survey an arc between Tarqui and Cotchesqui, after establishing a base line near Quito at the northern terminus. In spite of hardships, difficult terrain and a quarrel between Bouguer and de la Condamine, the value of the toise established by the expedition, known thereafter as the "toise of Peru," became a standard of linear measure in France. The second party surveyed an arc near the Gulf of Bothnia under the leadership of Pierre Louis Moreau de Maupertuis, Alexis Claude Clairault, Charles Étienne Louis Camus, Pierre Charles Lemonnier and Reginaud Outhier. The hardships were just as great as they were in Peru. Because of ice conditions, the islands in the Gulf of Bothnia could not be used for trigonometrical stations and the expedition had to go into the forests of Lapland, beginning at Tornea and running their arc northward to Kittis mountain. The net result of the two expeditions was proof that the earth was not a sphere, that it was a spheroid flattened at the poles.[18]

A second perpendicular to the meridian of Paris was surveyed in 1735 on the parallel of Orléans. Only the western half of the line was run, however, as the primary object was to check on the accuracy of the charts for the coast of Bretagne currently published in *Le Neptune François*. Cassini de Thury and Maraldi directed the operations. They discovered serious errors in even the best charts of the region, and rather than try to patch up the old surveys they decided to run a new chain of triangles linking Cherbourg, Nantes and Bayonne, in reality a new meridian line nearly parallel to the meridian of Paris. At the same time Jacques Cassini and Lacaille worked the coast of Manche and Pas de Calais and Saint-Valery, north to Dunkerque. After checking all important points along the Atlantic coast, the astronomers moved back to Bayonne. In 1738 they began a chain of triangles across the southern boundary of France from Bayonne to Antibes on the Mediterranean, fifteen miles southwest of Nice. Cassini de Thury and Lacaille surveyed the mouths of the Rhône.

By this time there was no longer any doubt about the general shape of the earth, and the conclusion that it was flattened at the poles meant that the meridian of Paris had to be resurveyed. Cassini de Thury and Lacaille completed the job in 1740 after nearly two years of the most exacting work. Meanwhile Maraldi surveyed a new chain of triangles along the eastern frontier of France, taking his departure from Nice. By the early part of 1740 he had surveyed the line northward through Strassburg to Spire. Cassini de Thury spent part of the summer of 1740 making a triangulation of the northern frontier, working towards the east, and finally closed with Maraldi's chain in the vicinity of Metz. The Abbé Outhier completed the survey of Normandy and Bretagne in 1739. France was now enclosed by an uninterrupted chain of 400 triangles surveyed from 18 fundamental bases. This was the framework Picard had asked for, a proper foundation for a large-scale national map.[19]

The first cartographic publication resulting from these eight years of surveying was an engraved map compiled by Maraldi and Cassini de Thury on one sheet and published in 1744. It was little more than an outline map of France but it contained all the triangles surveyed under the direction of the Académie Royale des Sciences up to 1740. A much more complete map in 18 sheets was presented to the Académie by Cassini de Thury at a meeting in 1745. He explained to his colleagues that this map was designed to accompany a *Description Géométrique de la France* which was even then in process (*sous presse*). The text was to contain, among other things, the value of the angles of all the triangles and the lengths of each side.

The 18 sheets (undated) when joined, formed a map of France on a scale of 1:878,000, and included additional surveys made between 1740 and 1744. It contained nearly 800 uninterrupted triangles terminating in 19 measured base lines representing a total of 100,000 toises. Though primarily an outline map and a base for future topographical surveys, Cassini pointed out that within the various tri-

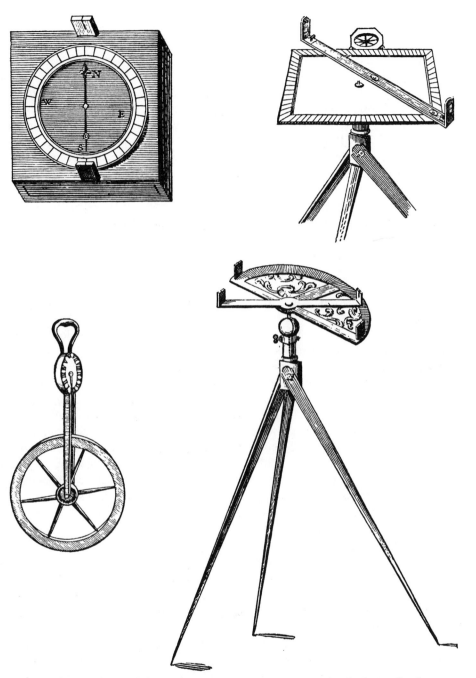

The tools of the eighteenth-century surveyor were simple but effective. In the field he used a portable box compass with alidade, a plane table equipped with compass and alidade, a perambulator (odometer) for measuring irregular lines such as the course of a river, and a semicircle for measuring angles.

angles there were, incidentally, many cities, towns, villages, chateaux and other important landmarks that had been located geometrically in the course of the survey. He also called attention to the fact that since the start of the survey there had been numerous topographic plans made of local regions that now might well be added to the larger map. The province of Languedoc, for instance, had been surveyed by the Royal Society of Sciences of Montpelier. The dioceses of Bayeux and Sens had been accurately mapped by the Abbé Outhier. And in addition, there were scattered patches of the landscape that had been surveyed in detail for one reason or another, such as the king's forests, the various theaters of war; the encampments of the king's armies and the battlefields along the frontier. All such regional surveys were suitable for inclusion on the skeleton map of France. But Cassini de Thury was not willing to vouch for the accuracy of such inclusions. In the process of compiling the outline map of the principal triangulation, he and his assistants had tried to use some of the local maps of the different provinces to trace the courses of the important rivers. But they had uncovered so much conflicting information on them that they were obliged to warn their readers that the location, size and course of all rivers should not be taken too seriously.[20]

In 1746 Cassini de Thury was sent to Flanders to make a triangulation survey in conjunction with the topographic surveying being done by the engineers attached to the army. The triangulation was completed but the topographic surveying was interrupted by the military operations then in progress. However, the resulting plans were impressive enough to make Louis XV want more of the same, preferably of his dominion in France. He ordered Cassini de Thury to formulate a plan for the continuation of a large-scale topographic survey of France and present it to Machault, who had succeeded Orry as Comptroller-General of finances. Machault not only agreed to put up the necessary 40,000 livres per year, but also agreed to augment this sum if necessary in order to hurry the work along. In 1750 leveling operations were begun for the compilation of a map such as Colbert had dreamed of over eighty years before, and Cassini de Thury was now determined to see it executed. With good reason the project became known as the *Carte de Cassini*, for, regardless of its early origin and the numerous scientists such as Picard who contributed to its development, it was Cassini de Thury more than any other one man who kept the survey moving against all odds. In 1756, when funds for the project were suspended, he rounded up a group of capitalists who agreed to finance the map in exchange for a proprietary interest in the published sheets, and under this new arrangement the work progressed even faster. It was not long before the government again showed an interest in what was going on and resumed control of the project. The provinces began to make voluntary contributions to the cost and Cassini de Thury had the satisfaction of seeing the work almost finished before he died of smallpox in 1784.[21]

The *Carte de Cassini* or *Carte de l'Académie* was finished in 1789 at a total cost of 700,000 livres. It was drawn to a scale of 1:86,400 (*"une ligne pour cent toises"*), and engraved on 180 sheets, by far the most ambitious mapping project ever attempted by any country, a veritable *"chef-d'œuvre de géodésie."* [22] The sheets, if joined, would make a map 33 feet high and 34 feet wide. The sheets were bound up in atlas form, preceded by an *Avertissement ou Introduction à la Carte Générale et Particulière de France*, dated 1755. The first sheet was the map of Paris and environs, and so many proofs of it were pulled to satisfy the demand of the public in general and collectors in particular that the plate, in spite of re-touching, was worn out before the last sheets came from the press. In 1789, shortly after the printing was finished, Cassini de Thury's son, Jacques-Dominique Cassini, paid his respects to the National Assembly of the revolutionary govern-ment and demonstrated the handsome work, showing La France newly partitioned into *départements*. The National Assembly approved of the *Carte de Cassini*. They liked it so well, in fact, that they practically confiscated the project and took over the production and publication of the map sheets. The value of the map as a military and political asset of the utmost importance was immediately recognized by the new government, and revision of the work was begun without delay.

The *Carte de Cassini* is important historically because it was the first general topographic map of a whole country based on extensive triangulation and topo-graphic surveys. It taught the rest of the world what to do and what not to do. The French developed the essential technical details of geodesy, leaving noth-ing but refinements of apparatus and methods for later generations to struggle with. Their map was the prototype of many derivatives drawn to various scales according to specific needs. However, a good peacetime map is not necessarily an adequate military survey, and by 1802 the necessities of war brought out the inadequacies of the Cassini map. A new survey was proposed, but nothing hap-pened. It was again proposed in 1808, this time by Rigobert Bonne, geographer, and Napoleon Bonaparte. No action was taken, however, till 1817, when work was begun on the *Carte de France de l'Etat Major* on a scale of 1:80,000. This map, which was not finished until 1880, furnished the base for the *Carte de la France* published by the Service Vicinal on a scale of 1:10,000 in 596 sheets, and a general map prepared by the Ministère des Travaux Publiques on a scale of 1:200,000 in 80 sheets.[23]

The first proposal for a co-operative mapping venture of any kind came from César François Cassini de Thury and was addressed to England. In October, 1783, the French Ambassador, Comte d'Adhémar, presented to Mr. Charles James Fox, then one of His Majesty's principal Secretaries of State, a Memoir written by the French astronomer. Cassini, who was then Director of the Paris Observatory and a member of the Royal Society of London, pointed out the advantages that would accrue to astronomy if the difference in latitude and longi-tude between the two most famous observatories in Europe were precisely measured. There was a difference of opinion between the French and English astronomers that amounted to nearly eleven seconds for the longitude and fifteen seconds for the latitude. Who was right? Cassini suggested that the matter could be settled to the satisfaction of all if the English scientists would make a trigono-metric survey from London to Dover, or more precisely, from Greenwich Observatory to the coast. He, Cassini, had reconnoitered the English coast with his telescope from the French side in the vicinity of Calais, and had spotted several prominent points that would be suitable for surveying stations. Moreover, they were points that were also clearly visible from Dover Castle, a point that would figure prominently in any cross-channel survey.[24]

Cassini's proposal was received by the Royal Society with mixed emotions. In due time, the Reverend Nevil Maskelyne, Astronomer Royal, replied in a paper read before the Society to the effect that if M. Cassini had first made himself acquainted with the splendid work of Dr. Bradley in this connection he would not have hazarded such a rash opinion as to the amount of error in the latitude and longitude of the Greenwich Observatory. Some of the other astronomers of the Royal Society doubtless felt the sting of Cassini's implications and would have gladly debated the question at length. But not so Major General William Roy. When he was approached by the President, Sir Joseph Banks, to make the survey for the government on behalf of the Royal Society, he must have chuckled to himself, because he had many times been tempted to do some such thing with or without official orders or sanction.[25]

General Roy had been a military engineer for over thirty-five years, and was making maps and sketches before the Engineers were officially recognized as gentlemen and fit to be included in the Army List. As early as 1747 he was employed under orders of the Duke of Cumberland to carry out a plan for the subjugation of the Scottish clans. The first step was to map the Highlands and make surveys for a system of roads that would connect the remote regions of Scotland with the rest of civilization. He received his commission as practitioner-engineer in 1755. Four years later he was a captain in the Corps of Engineers, and in 1783 was Director and lieutenant colonel of the Royal Engineers as well as major general in the regular Army List.

General Roy liked surveying and was a profound believer in maps and their importance. The Scottish rebellion of 1745 and the battle of Culloden the following year convinced the government of the importance of exploring and mapping the inaccessible Highlands. After the Treaty of 1763 the British government for the first time began to consider the advisability of a general survey of Britain such as the French were making, to be executed at public expense. Roy was to have had charge of the survey, but as he said himself, profound peace throughout the land was first necessary. Twelve years elapsed and nothing happened. The "American War" delayed the project, and no official action was taken until the Treaty of 1783 was signed and sealed. Meanwhile, General Roy roamed the countryside when time permitted, studying the contours of the land and planning for the location of base lines. In 1783 he surveyed, for his own amusement, a base line of 7744.3 feet across the fields from the Jews-Harp, near Marybone to Black-Lane near Pancras, at the same time fixing the positions of steeples and other prominent points around London in relation to the Royal Observatory. He wanted first to give the public and particularly British officialdom a gentle hint in regard to the forgotten project of 1763 and second, to check on the accuracy of earlier surveys made by the "lovers of astronomy" in and around London. He thought he might read a paper before the Society and prod them a little about the survey when, lo and behold, along came the Memoir from Cassini. When Sir Joseph Banks invited him to make the survey from London to Dover, General Roy accepted with alacrity. Perhaps this would lead to the general map of Britain he had dreamed of and hoped for.[26]

The first step in the survey from London to Dover was to establish an accurately measured base line. On April 17, 1784, General Roy led a delegation including Sir Joseph Banks, Mr. Henry Cavendish and Dr. Charles Blagden, to look at Hounslow Heath, an open stretch of country convenient to London and the Royal Observatory at Greenwich. It was unusually flat, and the only preparatory work required was to clear it of numerous furze bushes and anthills. A detail of soldiers was chosen by General Roy to do the heavy work rather than a party of civilian helpers, both to cut down the cost of the operation and to insure the maximum protection in the field for the elaborate equipment that was to be used.[27]

As soon as the site was agreed upon, Roy placed an order with Jesse Ramsden, instrument maker, for the best engineer's chain that could be made, one hundred feet long exactly. While Ramsden was working on it, Roy and his assistants looked around for the best deal (fir or pine) rods in the land. What they wanted was a piece of New England white pine, which was usually straight-grained, lighter and less likely to warp than most pine. They found such a piece, an old mast, at His Majesty's Yard at Deptford, but when they began to cut it up they found it was riddled with shot holes and could not be used. Finally a piece of Riga (Scotch pine) was selected and from it three rods were cut measuring 20 feet 3 inches long from the extremities of their bell-metal tips, and 2 by 1¼ inches thick. They were finished with all the care of precision instruments, as it was assumed that they would furnish the standard against which the expansion and contraction of the steel chain, caused by temperature changes, could be checked. Roy was very much pleased with them. He was also very proud of a pedigreed 42-inch graduated brass scale with a vernier attachment that would measure thousandths of an inch. It had been made by Jonathan Sisson for George Graham the watchmaker. Later James Short, another instrument maker, had bought it, and General Roy bought it at the sale of Short's instruments. When Roy checked it against the standard scale kept at the Royal Society (at 65° F.) it was precisely the right length.[28]

Seldom if ever had there been a line measured with such care as the base on Hounslow Heath. The first rough measurements with a taut cord were begun on June 16, 1784, and the base line, a little over five miles long, was not finished until the last day of August. The actual measurement of the line was to be made first with Mr. Ramsden's chain and then with the deal rods, and there was every hope of keeping the accuracy of each measurement to within a few thousandths of an inch. Every day the chain and rods were checked for expansion and contraction; temperature changes were noted around the clock and the apparatus was carefully protected each night against sharp changes of temperature and humidity.

The rods, in particular, received a maximum of loving care. They were enclosed in wooden cases, carefully braced on all sides, with a thermometer close at hand to check their temperature. Yet in spite of all precautions, they soon began to register variations in humidity, and at the end of a twenty-four-hour period they sometimes varied in length as much as $\frac{1}{30}$ of an inch. "Considering how much time and labour had been bestowed in obtaining what we had every reason to conclude were the best deal rods that ever were made," wrote Roy, "it was no small disappointment now to find, that they were so liable to lengthen and shorten by the humid and dry states of the atmosphere, as to leave us no hopes of being able, by their means, to determine the length of the base to that degree of precision we had all along aimed at." More than half of the base had been measured when Roy decided that regardless of how careful he was in making corrections for expansion and contraction of the rods, he knew the line would not be accurate enough for the projected survey. He figured it would be off by at least two feet in the overall distance, and this was too much.[29]

Roy had just about decided to try rods of cast iron when Lieutenant Colonel Calderwood came out to the Heath to see what was going on. He suggested trying glass rods, preferably solid. Roy liked the idea and ordered one made, but after several tries the glass blowers announced that a solid rod one inch in diameter and twenty feet long was more than they could handle. Mr. Ramsden finally produced rods of glass tubing, carefully made and more carefully measured against the standard used during the entire survey. Trussed in wooden cases, the glass tubes showed a total contraction and expansion of not more than .279 inches, an amount easily calibrated. By this time the season was getting late. There were numerous delays; there were many important visitors to be shown around, including His Majesty the King. And when the surveyors came to the crossing of the old Roman road from Staines to London, there was trouble because of the endless stream of traffic passing to and fro. For these reasons the steel chain was finally abandoned and the survey was finished with the glass rods alone. The military detail was dismissed on August 31, and Roy announced to his colleagues that the base line, after throwing out "some useless decimals," was 27,404.7219 feet at sea level. This figure was later reduced, after numerous corrections were made, to 27,404.0137.[30]

Nearly three years elapsed between the survey on Hounslow Heath and the beginning of the triangulation between London and Dover. This time the delay could not be laid to government; instead it was caused by "the instrument." Roy tried unsuccessfully to be patient. "It was little expected," he wrote, "that nearly three full years would have elapsed before, even in this country, an instrument could be obtained for taking the angles"; yet such was the case. Evidently Picard's iron quadrant fitted with telescopes was not good enough for Roy and his colleagues; they had ordered from Mr. Ramsden an instrument of a different kind, and one that had infinite possibilities if it could be built to their exacting specifications. It was to be a combination of transit telescope for measuring vertical angles and a graduated circle (instead of a quadrant), also fitted with a telescope for measuring horizontal angles. Its chief claim to superiority would lie in its capacity to measure fractional seconds of arc, and the precision factor gave Mr. Ramsden some trouble.

In the spring of 1787 Ramsden thought the instrument would soon be ready, and there was considerable excitement among the members of the Royal Society. Dr. Blagden postponed a vacation tour of Germany, and Sir Joseph Banks began corresponding with the French Académie through the Marquis of Carmarthen, the French Ambassador, concerning the details of the combined operation across the channel and the part to be played by the French scientists. Meanwhile General Roy let none of his colleagues forget that while the forthcoming events were important in themselves, the chief and ultimate object "has always been considered of a still more important nature, namely, laying the foundation of a general survey of the British Islands." He had, in fact, compiled a map of the proposed disposition of the triangles, 12 to 18 miles to a side, from Greenwich to the coast, from coast to coast across the channel, and the series on the French side in the vicinity of Calais and Dunkerque, with an eye to future surveys.[31]

Mr. Ramsden finally delivered "the curious instrument" for observing the angles of the triangles, on the 31st of July, 1787, and it was immediately installed at the surveying station set up at Hampton Poor-House. There was great rejoicing in the Royal Society. Roy described the instrument as "a great theodolet [*sic*], rendered extremely perfect; having this advantage in particular, which common theodolets have not, that its transit telescope can be nicely adjusted by inversion on its supports; that is to say, it can be turned upside down, in the same manner that transit-instruments are, in fixed observatories." The instrument was essentially a graduated brass circle three feet in diameter, fitted with a great many gadgets designed for fine adjustment of the moving parts and promising the greatest possible accuracy in observations. It was equipped with two achromatic telescopes of 36-inch focal length, with double object glasses of 2½-inch apertures. The axis of the transit telescope was hollow, and attached to it at an angle of 45° (to the line of vision) was a perforated "illuminator" for throwing light from a small lantern onto the cross hairs (filar micrometer) during night observations. Larger lanterns were built into the frame of the instrument for illuminating the brass circle. The instrument with all its fittings weighed about 200 pounds. It was a beautiful piece of craftsmanship, a precision machine if there ever was one, but how well it would perform remained to be seen.

Hopes for the instrument ran so high that Roy and his assistants were confident that, working with such large triangles, they could measure for the first time the spherical excess of the triangles they were about to survey. All surveyors were well aware of the fact that on a spherical or spheroidal surface the sum of the three angles of a triangle always exceeds 180°, the amount of excess being in proportion to the length of the sides. However, the French had worked with relatively small triangles, and the excess was not appreciable. Roy was in for a disappointment with regard to spherical excess, for "notwithstanding the goodness of our instrument," he later wrote, "and the pains taken in using it, we have frequently failed in bringing out an excess: and indeed the results have even sometimes been in a small way defective." He experimented with the instrument in various ways, changing the zero, for instance, to try to get greater accuracy, but there was still considerable doubt as to the shape of the earth and the amount of spherical excess he might expect to measure, so he finally gave it up as a bad job. Besides, the "French Gentlemen" were waiting on the coast.[32]

The triangulation across the Channel was to be conducted at night, for greater accuracy, and as the rainy season was close at hand, it was decided to go ahead with that part of the survey, even though only the first ten stations inland had been surveyed from Hampton Poor-House to Wrotham Hill. The French delegation led by Jacques Dominique, Comte de Cassini, Mechain and Le Gendre arrived at Dover September 23, and after two days of conferences all details were arranged. The Duke of Richmond, Master General of His Majesty's Ordnance, furnished artillerymen, fireworks and scaffolding to be used for signaling between Greenwich Observatory, Shooter's Hill and Dover Castle. Fixed white lights and "reverberatory lamps" (blinkers) were chosen for signals on both sides of the Channel. The two principal triangles were to be measured from signal towers erected at four stations, Dover Castle and Fairlight Head on the English side, Cape Blancnez and Montlambert on the French coast. Never had such great triangles been attempted. From Fairlight Down to Montlambert was 47 miles and to Blancnez 48 miles. For the most part the weather was bad, but at Calais and Dover, on the few important nights, it was clear, so that with the aid of the powerful white lights and Mr. Ramsden's theodolite they were able to intersect with great accuracy Blancnez and Montlambert, "vulgarly" known as Boulemberg, "and thereby to establish for ever, the triangular connection between the two countries." [33]

The base line of verification on Romney Marsh, between Ruckinge and High Nook, was measured between October and December under Lieutenant Bryce of the Royal Artillery; it was extremely hard work in dirty weather. The glass rods were dispensed with and only Ramsden's steel chain was used, because during the survey on Hounslow Heath it was found that the difference in error between the two had amounted to not more than one half inch for the 27,404.7 feet, not enough to make an appreciable difference in the final calculations. The decision was further justified when it was discovered that the two base lines "measure each other reciprocally within a few inches of the truth." [34]

In addition to the two base lines measured on the English side of the Channel, a total of 45 great triangles were eventually surveyed between the meridian of Greenwich Observatory and the meridian of Paris extended to the North Sea coast in the vicinity of Dunkerque. The completed survey would have yielded conclusive results except for certain doubtful factors. First there was the problem of converting the French toise into the English league. Then, having found, geodetically, the linear distance between the two meridians, it was necessary to convert this value into degrees, minutes and seconds of arc. Here the scientists again became involved in the precise length of the degree and the shape of the earth. In addition, the geodetic results failed to coincide with the astronomical findings in several respects. Roy was particularly dissatisfied with the difference in clock time between the two meridians. Maskelyne had published a value of 9^m 30.5^s obtained astronomically, but according to the trigonometrical survey the difference was only 9^m 19^s.[35] Roy argued that if the difference in time were as great as Maskelyne said it was, the earth would have to be extremely prolate instead of quite flattened at the poles. As for the difference in latitude between the two observatories, Maskelyne was very doubtful whether the survey would throw much light on the matter, "because of the uncertainty we are still under about the true figure and dimensions of the earth. . . ." To be sure, a series of observations had been made, whereby the height of the polestar in its eastern and western azimuths had been measured and a small table of figures had been specially prepared, giving the exact times when the polestar was east and west of the pole. And on these occasions Roy had borrowed from the Board of Longitude the "praemium watch" made by John Harrison to clock the star. From their corrected tables of data Roy and his associates fixed the difference in latitude at $2°$ $11'$ $35''$ which was later altered by Mudge to $2°$ $19'$ $51''$.[36]

Regardless of the questions that remained unanswered, the combined operations between Greenwich and Paris had a profound effect on the future of map making. It was the first project of the kind conducted on British soil, and the triangulation exposed a multitude of errors on the best maps of England. In addition, Roy prophesied that all the longitudes on the great map of France would be affected by the new data.[37] From Strassburg to Ushant, for instance, there was probably a total error of from 17 to 20 seconds of time. As to future operations, Roy ventured a few predictions in passing. He was sure that because of the problem of terrestrial refraction and in hot weather the "tremulous motion or boiling in the air," that early morning or, better still, night surveying, would be universally adopted in the future. He was also convinced that with the aid of a theodolite such as Jesse Ramsden had constructed, it was possible to determine differences in longitude by angular measurements taken from the polestar alone, without regard to differences in time. This method, he concluded, "may be said to be a new mode of surveying," and should be adhered to in the future.[38]

Roy persisted to the last in an effort to launch a general survey of Britain. He spoke of his king as his "most gracious and beneficent Sovereign, the Patron of the Sciences." In his report, he said it would be a pity to have all those fine and expensive instruments laid up in storage, and he felt it incumbent upon himself to recommend that this splendid beginning should be continued and gradually extended over the whole island. "Compared with the greatness of the object," he wrote, "the annual expence to the publick would be a mere trifle not worthy of being mentioned." The honor of the nation was concerned, "in having at least as good a map of this as there is of any other country." And if, while the map of England was in progress, the same sort of experiments were carried on by the East India Company on the coast of Coromandel and in Bengal, "every thing would then be done that Britain could do within her own dominions, in regard to the determination of the figure and dimensions of the earth." To clinch the point, Roy included in his report a list of stations and secondary triangles surveyed incidental to the project just concluded, data that he thought might well be used at some time in the future to improve some of the existing maps, especially those of the country around London. These he grouped into two series, one of thirty-five and one of thirty-seven triangles. Also listed were 15 prominent objects in and near London, with their bearings and distances from the center of the dome of Saint Paul's cathedral. The inference was clear enough. Here, without additional cost to the realm, was a good start towards a better map of England and the capital city of London.[39]

Neither the government nor the British public was quick to take the hint. General Roy saw the triangulation through, and afterwards spent long hours with his men compiling the results of the survey and writing a detailed report of all that had happened. But his health failed, and before his report had gone to press he died. All interest in the survey and in the mapping of the British Isles, "seemed to expire with the General." [40] The project was saved, however, by the Duke of Richmond, Master General of the Ordnance, who bought from Jesse Ramsden a theodolite similar to the one used by General Roy, but incorporating several improvements. Having acquired such a magnificent precision instrument, His Grace was naturally interested in trying it out, and in 1791 he persuaded His Majesty to give the order for the continuation of the national survey. Apparently His Grace was anxious to sever connections with the Royal Society, because he returned their instruments, depending thereafter on his improved theodolite and two surveyor's chains made for the Master General of the Ordnance by Ramsden. He may also have decided that it might be wise to have all surveying and mapping activities centered in the army while France was in a state of revolution, not knowing when there might be trouble.[41]

From 1791, the survey of Britain became a military project without outside support. The Board of Ordnance was continued as the Ordnance Survey, a government office with responsibility for all standard maps of the country. Its headquarters were located with the Ordnance in the Tower of London. Working from Roy's triangulation of the southeastern counties, the surveying, on a scale of one inch to the mile (1:63,600), was begun, for strategic reasons, in Kent and part of Essex. Officers of the Royal Artillery, trained at Woolwich, the Royal Military Academy, were considered most eligible to conduct the survey, and Lieutenant Colonel Edward Williams was chosen to direct the work, assisted by Captain William Mudge and Mr. Isaac Dalby, a civilian expert who later became a professor of mathematics at Woolwich. Detailed plans of strategic areas were furnished by the officers and men of the Royal Engineers. Colonel Williams died in 1798 and was succeeded by Mudge, now a major. In 1805 a special Corps of Royal Military Surveyors and Draughtsmen was created. Its complement was trained by and for the Ordnance Survey, and the result was that the standard of work was improved considerably. Although this Corps was abolished in 1817, it was

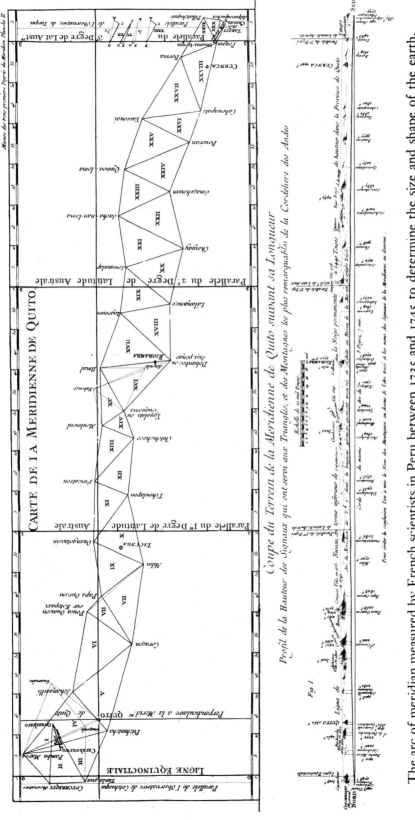

The arc of meridian measured by French scientists in Peru between 1735 and 1745 to determine the size and shape of the earth.

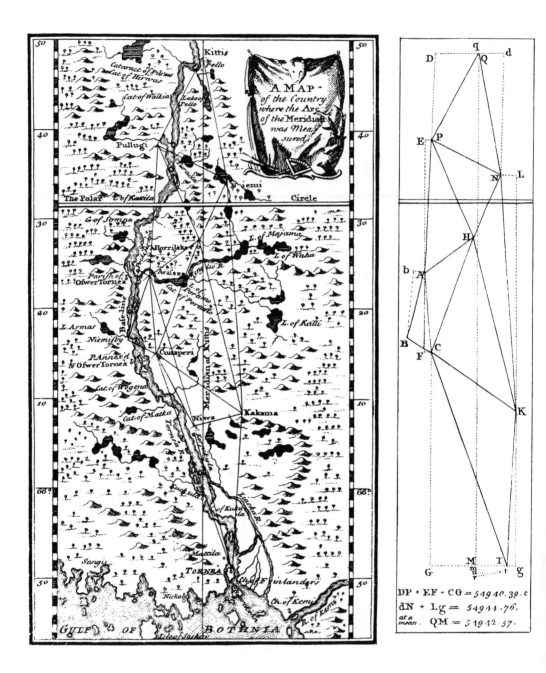

In 1736 Louis XV despatched a second expedition, this time to the arctic.
Under Maupertuis, Clairault and others a meridian line was surveyed northward from the Gulf of Bothnia to Kittis.

re-established in 1823 by Brevet Major Thomas Frederick Colby of the Royal Engineers, who was chief executive officer of the Survey from 1809 and Director-General from 1820 to 1848. In 1824 this body became the 13th (Survey) Company of Royal Engineers.[42]

As the work of the Survey progressed, a certain amount of friction developed within the organization, and the public at large was not entirely co-operative. Prejudices existed against surveyors, traceable to the Norman Conquest and England's first tax survey recorded in the Domesday Book. Landowners stoutly denied the right of a surveyor to trespass on a private estate, and in the early years of the Survey many of the small streams and enclosed estates were skirted to avoid trouble, and inevitably other areas were bypassed because a detail of surveyors did not care to get their feet wet or push through acres of thorny bushes. In 1801, soon after the first map sheets of the Survey were engraved and published, there was a clamor from the public for more and better maps of all parts of the country. Influential citizens organized pressure groups and demanded that their counties and parishes be mapped right away, out of turn if necessary. Certain gentlemen of Lincolnshire and Rutlandshire went a step further and guaranteed to pay for a certain number of copies of the finished map if the government would survey their lands immediately. These gentlemen were interested first, in the problem of draining their fens and second, in spotting new hunting and fishing grounds. In answer to popular demand, the Ordnance Survey added many civilian surveyors to its roll and the topographic mapping of scattered districts was farmed out under contract.[43]

In 1825 the survey of England ceased abruptly, and Lieutenant Colonel Colby moved his entire staff to Ireland, where many knotty administrative problems had arisen. A cadastral survey was urgently required for purposes of defining boundaries and levying taxes. Instead of the inch to a mile scale, Colby recommended a scale of six inches to a mile (1:10,560), and it was so ordered. This time Parliament anticipated a few of the problems in advance, and an Act was passed by the House of Commons defining the principal object of the Survey, prescribing the legal method of determining boundaries and granting surveyors the power to enter any lands for purposes of surveying. At the same time it prohibited the removal or destruction by landowners of any apparatus used by the surveyors. The six-inch map of Ireland was finished in 1840, and the Ordnance Survey returned to England. The success of the Irish Survey was apparent from the clean, accurate sheets that were published shortly after, and permission was soon granted to continue the unfinished map of England on the same scale.[44]

The results obtained by the Ordnance Survey and the scope of its activities were spectacular, yet for the most part it was nothing but grueling work in all kinds of bad weather and over every conceivable kind of terrain. In view of the nature of the work and the obstacles that had to be surmounted, the results were even more remarkable, and have seldom been equaled for accuracy. In the autumn of 1791 General Roy's base line on Hounslow Heath was remeasured, just to make sure, and the second measure of the five-mile base varied from the first by only

2¾ inches. In the principal triangulation of Great Britain and Ireland there were 218 stations. The number of observed bearings was 1554. Many of the sides of the principal triangles were long. Sixty-six of them were more than 80 miles on a side, and 11 were more than 100 miles long. The longest, from Sea Fell to Sheir Donard, was 111 miles. Yet in spite of the great length of the sides of the triangles, the average amount of correction of the observed angles was no more than 0.6″. When the measured length of the base line on Salisbury Plain was checked by computation from the Irish base line 350 miles away, the two values differed by only 5 inches! [45]

Most of the surveying, the triangulation as well as the topographic work, was done with the 36-inch theodolite belonging to the Duke of Richmond, and occasionally the original used by General Roy was borrowed from the Royal Society. In addition, the Survey used an 18-inch theodolite, also by Ramsden, and a 24-inch instrument made by Troughton and Simms. As the work progressed, numerous refinements in technique contributed to the accuracy and efficiency of the Survey. Thomas Drummond, who had studied mathematics and chemistry under Brand and Faraday, joined the Survey under Colby in 1820. In a short time his inventive genius had solved one of the most serious problems of all surveyors — how to make accurate observations over long distances in murky weather. One of his inventions was the limelight ("Drummond Light"), a light of great intensity produced by directing an oxyhydrogen flame against a cylinder of lime. His second invention was an improved heliostat, an instrument combining a mirror and two telescopes, whereby the sun's rays could be converged and focused in a given direction. Both inventions proved to be a great boon to mankind, and the Drummond Light was for many years after a favorite lighthouse fixture, producing as it did a very white beam. [46]

The Ordnance Survey proved and disproved several important map making theories. First and foremost, it demonstrated to the world that there is no such thing as a perfect, all-purpose map or chart. The one-inch map of Great Britain never suited the Admiralty; the scale was too small; on the other hand, many people felt it was unnecessarily large and much too expensive to produce. But for a cadastral survey, the six-inch scale of the map of Ireland seemed none too great, and when it was finished, the six northern counties of England and all of Scotland were surveyed on the same scale, by order of the Treasury. These sheets were later reduced to the one-inch scale for inclusion on the general map of the kingdom. While working in Lancashire and Yorkshire the Survey was called upon to make 23 plans of parishes and townships, at the expense of the landowners, on a scale of 26⅔ inches to 1 mile for the computation of tithes. Yet when it came to a plan of London on a scale of 60 inches or 5 feet to a mile, it was decided that the scale was not large enough to solve the problem of house drainage in the area. Dissatisfaction and confusion arose throughout the land, with the Ordnance Survey in the middle. [47]

In 1851 and 1852 three select committees and one royal commission deliberated on the question of what scale was best suited for a national map of Great Britain.

Fourteen Blue Books on the subject were presented to Parliament. Foreign experts were called in to advise the government and the directors of the Ordnance Survey. Keeping in mind the needs of their own countries, the majority of them decided tentatively in favor of a scale somewhere between 20 to $26\frac{2}{3}$ inches to a mile. In 1853 a statistical conference was held at Brussels to discuss the problem of national surveys. Present were 26 delegates from the principal states of Europe. All voted in favor of a scale of 1:2500 or about $25\frac{1}{3}$ inches to a mile, for an adequate national topographic survey. They also recommended a supplementary map on a scale of 1:10,000 or about $6\frac{1}{3}$ inches to a mile, very close to the scale of the Ordnance Survey. In spite of the recommendations of the conference, the whole of England was finally mapped on a scale of 1:2500, a scale later adopted by the principal powers of Europe. This scale had the incidental advantage that a square acre of ground was equal to a square inch on the map.

There was little resemblance between the Ordnance Survey of 1900 and the map of England projected without guile by General William Roy in 1789. The average annual cost of the Survey during its first twenty years of operations was less than £3000. Between 1875–1885 it rose to about £180,000 a year, and between 1885–1895 it was closer to £228,000. The original project called for a single map on a one-inch scale, about 100 sheets. The first completed survey (1851) contained more than 108,000 sheets drawn to scales ranging from 10 and 5 feet to a mile for cities and towns, down to 25,344 inches, 6 inches, 1 inch, $\frac{1}{4}$ inch and $\frac{1}{10}$ inch for larger areas and the country as a whole. The principal maps of the Survey are (1) a general map of the country on a scale of 1 inch to a mile, (2) county maps on a scale of 6 inches to a mile, (3) cadastral or parish plans of the whole country on a scale of $25\frac{1}{3}$ inches to a mile, (4) plans of towns of more than 4000 population on a scale of 1:500 or 10.56 feet to a mile. On this last scale London would require a map more than 300 feet long and 200 feet wide.[48]

While France and England struggled with the problem of making a national topographic survey, the rest of Europe watched the proceedings with interest and profit. The fundamental importance of accurate maps and charts and their bearing on good government was slowly gaining recognition throughout the civilized world. Not only governments were beginning to see the light, but private citizens as well. The merchant and manufacturer, the agriculturalist and the professional man began to think of maps in terms of prosperity and security instead of just another burden to be borne by the taxpayer. Government surveyors began to assume the role of emissaries in the cause of civic improvement and national solidarity instead of trespassers against the personal rights and civil liberties of the small landholder. The pioneering efforts of Colbert, the Cassinis and William Roy began to bear fruit, and the mapping of a country was now generally conceded to be the responsibility of the central government rather than the commercial publisher. However, international mapping projects of any size were still suspect and remained so for many years – which was an almost insurmountable barrier to an accurate portrayal of the world as a whole.

Regardless of wars and political intrigue, there was a certain amount of co-operation among the scientists of Europe. The universal affinity of such men, not towards each other but towards the common cause, did wonders where statesmen failed. The scientific academies of France, England, Belgium, Denmark and other countries were keenly interested, not so much in an accurate topographic survey of their several countries, but in the larger issues related to the mapping of the earth's surface. So interested were they in determining the true size and shape of the earth, in the laws of gravitation, and in the further acquisition of information regarding the behavior of pendulums, that international disputes were swept aside or winked at. They knew full well that the only hope of getting the information they wanted was to pool their resources and work together. Each European state might map the territory within its own boundaries but only international scientists could map the world. François Arago and Jean Baptiste Biot worked with the Spaniard Don Rodriguez on the extension of the Paris-Dunkerque meridian to Barcelona and Formentera in the Balearic Islands. Arago proposed that Yarmouth (Great Yarmouth) should be made a European sector station, and form the northern terminal of the grand combined Anglo-French-Spanish meridian. There were other tentative gestures made towards an international scientific effort. Denmark started the publication of a topographical survey in 1766 under the auspices of the Academy of Science of Copenhagen. In 1816, Heinrich Schumacher, the Danish astronomer, wrote to the Ordnance Survey on behalf of the king of Denmark, requesting the loan of Ramsden's great theodolite in order to check several observations for latitude. It was sent over in 1819 and set up at Louenberg. Both Denmark and England profited by the results of the observations.[49]

Following the inauguration of the French and English surveys, other countries began to investigate the state of their own surveys and maps. What they found was neither good nor sufficient. In most cases, the history of national mapping efforts followed the same general pattern, usually dating from the sixteenth century and the advent of commercial map publishing. In every case the work was delayed, sometimes for many years, by internal strife, war with the outside world, lack of funds and universal indifference to the importance of accurate maps and charts. The oldest map of Denmark, for example, was probably executed about the middle of the sixteenth century under Christian III by Professor Jerdanns, a mathematician, and was published in Georg Braun's *Theatrum Orbum*. After a lapse of one hundred years, the Royal Mathematician Johann Meyer was ordered by Christian IV to survey the duchies of Schleswig and Holstein (1638–1648) and by 1652 more than thirty-seven general and special maps of the regions had been produced. Meyer was then ordered to make a general survey of the entire kingdom. He made little progress with the work, through no fault of his own, and in 1658, because of war with Sweden, work on the survey was suspended altogether. Under Christian V a new attempt was made (1681–1687) to complete a survey and census of the kingdom, under the direction of Jens Dinesen, professor of mathematics at the University of Copenhagen. This survey was to have been accompanied by a map, but only a beginning was made.[50]

In 1742 the Royal Danish Scientific Society was founded, and friendly relations with foreign scientific bodies were soon established. The need for better maps of the country was frequently discussed at the meetings of the Society and finally, acting on the suggestion of Peter Hofod, professor of mathematics at the Odense Gymnasium, Frederick V authorized in 1757 the survey of one bailiwick every year (there were eight provinces divided into eighteen bailiwicks) at royal expense. Hofod was placed in charge of the survey, and when he died in 1761 he left behind him a complete map of the bailiwick of Copenhagen and rough drafts of the entire map.

The first triangulation of Denmark was begun, by royal decree of June 26, 1761, following a plan outlined by the Royal Scientific Society. A general survey was first made on the basis of a series of parallel lines, with reference to which all objects were located. Then and only then, positions were tested and corrected by means of trigonometrical surveys and astronomical observations. The survey began in 1762 with only two men working in the field. Under Thomas Bugge, professor of astronomy, a base line of 14,515 ells (a Danish "ell" equals 24.7 inches) was run west of Copenhagen from Ting Hill to Brondby Hill (1764–1765). Later a belt of triangles of the first order was commenced in the vicinity of Copenhagen and gradually extended throughout the country from Skagen to the Elbe. The detailed measurements for the national topographic map were completed about 1820 on a scale of 1:20,000. The map sheets were engraved and published over a period of years, from 1766 to 1834.[51]

By a royal resolution dated January 20, 1808, the Danish General Staff was established. Prior to that date the only maps prepared for the exclusive use of the army were military sketches used for training maneuvers. After appraising the existing maps of the country prepared by the Scientific Society, the General Staff decided that they were inadequate for military purposes. An independent survey was begun for a "Military Geographical Map," using the Scientific Society's maps as a base and laid down on the same scale (1:20,000). The principal improvements in the military map were the details furnished by plane-table surveying between fixed points. Several additional surveys on various scales were started before the General Staff received orders in 1830 to publish a "Military Topographical Map of the entire country." This survey was to be based on the triangulation established by the Scientific Society and executed on the scale of 1:20,000. The scale was to be reduced for publication to 1:80,000. In order to insure uniformity, a manual of instructions was issued by the General Staff: *The Art of Topographical Drawing.* By 1843 all national mapping activities formerly in the hands of the Royal Danish Scientific Society were transferred to the War Department where they have since remained.[52]

Early maps of Scandinavia are rare. Olaus Magnus, Archbishop of Upsala, made a crude small-scale map which was published in Venice in 1539 and again at

Basel in 1567. Charts of the coastal regions appeared in several Dutch coast pilots such as Waghenaer's *Speculum Nauticum* and similar collections.

Duke Charles (later Charles IX of Sweden, 1550–1611) was interested in locating the boundaries of his domain, and after the peace of Tusina (1595) had his surveyors run the eastern line of the country. Andrew Bure, Sweden's first noteworthy maker of maps, published a map of Lapland in 1611, the earliest map engraved in Sweden. In 1626 he produced the first separate map of Sweden in six folio sheets. Under the direction of Bure, who was given the title of General Mathematician, a Corps of Surveyor-Geometers (one for each province) was organized in 1634. This body was ordered to prepare adequate maps of the provinces as well as plans of ports, mines and towns. Between 1650 and 1660 nine official maps were made by the Corps and published in Amsterdam by the brothers Blaeu.

A number of revised provincial maps of Sweden were published in the early part of the eighteenth century, and the Bureau of Land Surveying made several new general maps of the country between 1739 and 1747. However, the earliest trigonometric extension in Sweden was laid out between 1758 and 1761 from Cimbrishamn along the coast to the boundary of Norway. A modern survey was established in 1805 when Major General G. W. af Tibell, who had labored under Napoleon I on a map of the Italian Republic, promoted the organization of the Swedish Field Survey Corps. The object of the Corps, stated in a royal letter dated April 16, 1805, was to compile, in time of peace, comprehensive military maps of the kingdom based on trigonometric and astronomical observations, accompanied by topographic, statistical and military descriptions. The scale for the field work and preliminary map was to be 1:20,000, and any special maps required were to be reduced from the original survey to a scale of 1:100,000. In 1806 the Field Surveying Corps took over the duties of the Royal Fortification Corps and the mapping activities of the army at large. This body was later merged, in 1811, with the Fortification Corps and was called the Royal Engineer Corps; its activities were divided into fortification and field survey brigades. The topographic section was organized separately in 1831 and in 1874 all mapping activities, under the direction of the Topographical Division of the General Staff, were confined to the War Department.[53]

Sweden's General Topographic Map (including Lapland) on a scale of 1:100,000 was begun in 1815. For several years the sheets remained in manuscript, their contents secret. And when, in 1826, the order was given to print the map, it was specified that the sheets were to be engraved on copper by officers of the Corps who had first sworn to secrecy and who would be held responsible for the information contained on the map during the entire process of engraving and printing. The finished map was printed in 4 colors on 232 sheets. In 1857, when the King permitted the publication and general distribution of the map, 20 sheets were too obsolete to be published and 11 more had to be first corrected from new field observations. In addition to the map itself, field notes were made on a scale of 1:20,000 for the southern parts of the country and 1:50,000 for the northern regions. Special topographic maps of important passes and positions were made on a scale of 1:10,000 and 1:20,000, the latter being used for a map of Stockholm.[54]

Early maps of Norway are rare, although a few partial surveys were made prior to 1700. One of the earliest dated maps (1661) is a survey of the bailiwick ("Amt") of Bahus, adjacent to the inlet of Ide. Another, dated 1696, was a land and boundary map of the South Mountain range. Bailiwick maps were made in 1704 and in 1706; the Norwegian clergy were required to prepare a description of their parishes for use in a statistical and topographical description of Norway which was to be compiled by the royal historiographer. The work was never finished. Like many another country, Norway intended to have a national map long before the first line was actually surveyed, but up to 1746 only a few of the southern dioceses had been mapped in any kind of detail — a scale of about 1:100,000. In addition, sporadic mapping projects were initiated in the latter half of the eighteenth century, stressing statistical material, boundaries, soils and natural resources of one kind and another. All such material was forgotten until Christian Joachim Pontoppidan, artist-cartographer, made good use of it in his general maps of Scandinavia and Northern and Southern Norway (1781–1806).

The need for a national topographic survey patterned after those being made by neighboring countries, was apparent in Norway. Wars with Denmark and Sweden were all too frequent, and the needs of the General Staff had to be met if Norway were to survive. The launching of a Norwegian topographic survey is attributed to the Mathematical Military School, where topography and map making were an important part of the curriculum. The survey, primarily a military project, was ordered in 1773, and from then on there was considerable doubt as to what government agency should administer its affairs. The geographical survey of the Interior Department was first merged with the Topographic Section of the General Staff, and in 1828 the official name of the survey was the Combined Topographic and Hydrographic Survey. In 1833 the name was changed to the Royal Norwegian Geographical Survey, and later it became the Norwegian Geographical Institute.[55]

The principal topographic product of the Institute was a map of Norway on a scale of 1:100,000 in 54 sheets, and a general map on a scale of 1:400,000. In 1815, a year after Norway and Sweden were united under a common king, Charles XIII resolved to carry out topographic surveys of both countries, using the same scale and the same projection. However, the two countries failed to come to an agreement on such matters as the form and size of the map sheets to be used, and the choice of a common prime meridian, which Sweden had selected five degrees west of Stockholm. As a result, Sweden and Norway had separate topographic surveys and maps.[56]

Except for the information brought back to Europe by the Polos, the oldest geographical data on Russia consisted of descriptions of real estate compiled in the middle of the thirteenth century during the Mongolian occupation. The first general map (manuscript) of the Russian Dominions was compiled in the middle of the sixteenth century by order of the Czar of Moscow and was known as "The

Great Drawing." [57] Apparently this map was not for general circulation. During the next two hundred years maps of "Moscovie" or "Moscovia" appeared in the numerous popular atlases of Europe, but no serious attempt was made to survey the country until 1720. At that time Peter the Great issued an order ("ukase") for thirty young men to be sent from the Naval Academy into the various provinces to make surveys, compile maps and prepare detailed geographical descriptions. These young "Geometers" were to make their surveys by districts, determining the latitudes of the various cities as they went along, but taking the longitudes from old maps and catalogues. The work was done under the supervision of the Senate and the maps were edited by the chief clerk of that body.

In 1726 the Empress Catherine I ordered all the maps prepared by the Naval Geometers transferred to the Academy of Sciences for correction and revision. And about this time the two Delisles, Joseph-Nicolas and Louis, arrived from Paris and were placed in charge of the Russian surveys. In addition to establishing a school of astronomy, the Delisles organized, in 1739, a special Geographical Department within the Academy of Sciences, later directed by the Academician Heinzius. In 1745 the Geographical Department published an atlas containing 1 general map and 19 special maps, 13 of which represented European Russia on a scale of about 1 inch to 32 miles and 6 of Asiatic Russia on a smaller scale. The general map, on 2 sheets, covered the whole empire on a scale of about 1 inch to 103 miles. Following the general procedure worked out by the Académie Royale des Sciences in France, various astronomical expeditions, many of them under the supervision of the Delisles, were sent out to all parts of Russia over a period of sixty years or more, with very satisfactory results. Special training courses were made available for government surveyors, and Constantine's Survey Institute and the Survey Department of the Senate were organized for the purpose.[58]

Peter the Great laid the foundation for a military topographic survey of Russia by establishing the post of Quartermaster-General, whose duty it was to collect all pertinent information for the War College. In 1763 the Empress Catherine II established the General Staff, subject to orders of the Quartermaster-General. The formation of an Imperial Depot of Maps was the first step towards a Military Topographical Division of the General Staff, in reality, a central State Depot of Maps and Plans. In 1812 it became the Military Topographic Depot, first under the Minister of War and later (1816) under the Chief of the General Staff, Topographic Section. The year 1816 also marked the beginning of the first systematic scientific triangulation of the country, which was opened with a survey of the government of Wilna (Vilna). The average length of the sides of the triangles was 11 miles and the accuracy of the work left little to be desired, the probable error of observation being ± 0.62″. Under the direction of Professor W. G. Struve, a survey of Liefland was made (1816–1819), and in the process, a base line 6½ miles long was measured on the ice of Lake Vir Yarvi. The line was so accurately measured that it was later used as part of the great degree measurement made along the western boundary of Russia, usually considered one of the most accurate in the Eastern Hemisphere.[59]

The first important publication of the Topographic Section of the Russian General Staff consisted of a great map of European Russia on a scale of 1:126,000 in 792 sheets, including a topographic map of Poland in 59 sheets on the same scale. Original field minutes for this map were taken on scales of 1:21,000 and 1:42,000. Other surveys included a topographic map of the Caucasus on a scale of 1:210,000 in 77 sheets; a topographic map of European Russia on a scale of 1:420,000 in 154 sheets; Asiatic Turkey on a scale of 1:840,000; the military districts of Turkestan on a scale of 1:1,680,000; Western Siberia on a scale of 1:210,000; Central Asia on a scale of 1:4,200,000 and various other surveys.

These first Russian topographic surveys exerted a powerful influence on the mapping activities of other European nations. The accuracy and zeal shown by the Russian surveyors, plus the vast extent of the European territory controlled by the Czar, placed Russia in an important position in scientific and political circles. Several international co-operative ventures were launched on a small scale, with mutual benefit to all concerned. In 1835 a series of triangles was surveyed for the purpose of establishing a connection with the Swedish triangles near Stockholm. Working simultaneously, the Russian and Swedish topographers established chains of triangles on both banks of the Sea of Alend. Later Danish geographical engineers continued the chain to the coasts of the Skaane and the Isle of Seland, and eventually the triangulation of Norway was linked with that of Sweden. Thus a geodetic connection was established between the three principal Scandinavian observatories at Stockholm, Christiana and Copenhagen. A more ambitious co-operative project failed to materialize because of international political complications. In 1826 the French government proposed that the Russian government take part in the measurement of the 48th north parallel of latitude, a line that would connect the surveys of the French, Bavarian and Austrian engineers, and continue it from Chernovitz in Bukovina to the Volga or possibly the Ural River. If completed, this line would have given European scientists an uninterrupted arc extending over 48 degrees of longitude, of which 18 would have been on Russian soil.[60]

In spite of the political turmoil in Europe during the eighteenth century, and the constantly changing political boundaries, other topographic surveys were instituted and in some cases finished. In 1767 Count Joseph Ferraris, an Austrian general, was made Director General of Artillery in the Netherlands. Under his leadership a topographic survey of the Austrian Netherlands was immediately begun on the same scale as the French *Carte de Cassini*. The map was finished in 1777. A map of Mecklenberg-Strelitz on 9 sheets was finished in 1780 and one of Mecklenberg-Schwerin on 16 sheets in 1788. Surveys of Bohemia, Moravia and Silesia were well under way by 1730, varying widely in scientific accuracy and utility. In this same period surveys of Lombardy and Transylvania were begun. General land and topographic surveys of the several states that later comprised Austria-Hungary and the German Empire were prosecuted independently and later reorganized on a grand scale.[61]

A survey of the Tyrol was begun in 1760 and a map of the region was published between 1769 and 1774 on 23 sheets drawn to a scale of one Vienna inch to ⅓ German mile. This survey was later extended over Vorarlberg and republished with additions in 1783. Beginning in 1762, triangulation was begun in Austria and Northern Italy, the object of which was to connect with the French surveys and especially the meridian of Paris. Maps resulting from this triangulation were published in Milan in 1796. By the end of 1787 Emperor Joseph II had seen to it that every Austrian province was mapped, although there was little continuity or uniformity in them, and there was as yet no general topographic map of the entire monarchy. A new survey was in order, and under Emperor Francis II it was begun. The administration of Austrian surveys, as with other European countries, shifted from time to time. The General Staff issued maps for military purposes from 1792 to 1800, and after the inauguration of the Cis-alpine Republic in 1800 a Ministry of War (*Dipartimento della guerra*) was established at Milan. Attached to this Department was a Deposito della Guerra, similar to the French Dépôt de la Guerre, whose function was to collect and preserve maps, plans and related topographic material. At the same time a Military Topographical Corps ("Engineer Geographers") was formed, to which officers of the Engineer Corps (*Corps du Génie*) of the Franco-Italian army were attached. The duties of the corps were to make a detailed topographic survey of the Republic, to draw plans and plot strategic lines of operation leading to surrounding states. In March, 1802, the "Cis-alpine" became the "Italian" Republic.[62]

The scope of the surveying and mapping done by Austria was vast. A trigonometric net of triangles in Lombardy was connected with the triangulation of Piedmont and of Romagna and extended to the Adriatic. More than 125 map sheets on various scales resulted, published between 1814 and 1839. From the time of the first triangulation, ordered in 1762 by the Empress Maria Theresa, to the completion of the survey of the entire empire in 1860, Austria played an important part in the geodetic operations conducted throughout Europe. And at the suggestion of General Baeyer a union of the Central European states was effected in 1861 for the sole purpose of combining all large-scale geodetic operations. The Mittel Europäische Gradmessung, later (1867) shortened to Europäische Gradmessung, was a clearinghouse to which European states were glad to contribute. The only exceptions were Servia, Montenegro, Greece, Turkey, and England, whose geodetic operations were by then completed.[63]

Under Joseph II, the provinces of Marmaros, Banate, Sclanonia, Banal and Transylvania were surveyed between 1768 and 1790. The maps in themselves were good enough, but they were not laid down on an accurately surveyed base of triangles, and when the cartographers tried to put the sheets together, the distortion close to the borders made the job impossible. Under Francis II an entirely new survey of the monarchy was ordered, and in spite of war with Napoleon the work went on intermittently, suspended when hostilities broke out and resumed after each declaration of peace.

The mapping of Switzerland presented some of the most difficult problems known to the science of cartography. Lineal distances from place to place were meaningless, just as a line map fails to give a correct picture of the country. Waldseemüller, who made the earliest map of the country of the Helvetians, published in the 1513 Strassburg edition of Ptolemy, gave it up as a bad job. He concentrated his efforts on the cities and towns, filling the map with profiles of castles, monasteries, churches and other prominent buildings. When it came to a representation of topography, he solved the problem by scattering across his map a series of interrupted, undulating super-molehills, dismissing the problem by indicating to his readers that the terrain is all bad, but that some parts of it are a lot worse than others. In short, a sensible portrayal of Switzerland's topography involved a difficult surveying problem and an artistic presentation of the facts on paper. Small wonder, therefore, that the earliest known relief map of any region (1667) should be a representation of the canton of Zurich.[64]

The heroic task of making a topographic survey and map of Switzerland fell to the lot of General Guillaume Henri Dufour (1787–1875). Under his personal supervision the work was begun in 1830 and the first sheet was published in 1842. Thirty-four years later the entire survey, on a scale of 1:100,000, was finished and the last of the 25 sheets came from the press. Soon after, the map appeared in atlas form, published at Berne. Far from being a pioneering effort that would require immediate revision, the Dufour atlas proved to be a model of accuracy and artistic delineation, not only for future map makers of Switzerland, but for cartographers at large. The sheets of the atlas were used as a basis for later surveys on different scales, and on the sheets of Switzerland's new survey references were made to the corresponding sections and subsections of the original Dufour map. The art work and conventional signs on the new map were almost identical with those on the Dufour originals. The lettering and bench marks (figures denoting heights), prominent buildings, roads, boundaries and forests were printed in black. Small slopes and passes, ravines and narrow defiles that could not be shown by equally spaced contour lines were printed in brown hachures. Black hachures were used to indicate rocky prominences and precipices, the general effect being a pictorial representation by oblique lighting. Horizontal surveys were shown in bronze and water was indicated by shades of blue.[65]

Under the direction of the Federal Topographic Bureau of the General Staff at Berne, a new, enlarged topographic survey of Switzerland was projected. The mountain regions were surveyed on a scale of 1:50,000 (119 sheets) and the valleys on a scale of 1:25,000 (442 sheets). The survey was placed under the personal supervision of a colonel of the Corps of Military Engineers in 1868. The sheets of the new map were adjusted to those of the Dufour map so that one sheet of the Dufour map (scale of 1:100,000) was equal to 16 sheets of the large scale (1:50,000) sections and 64 sheets of the smaller scale (1:25,000) sections on the new map. In addition to the topographic series, a general map of the Confederation of Switzerland on 4 sheets, drawn to a scale of 1:250,000, was launched, patterned after the Dufour atlas.[66]

Centuries before the organization of the constitutional German Empire in 1870, the twenty-six states from which it was derived had made many maps of their several territories. And long before the organization of the German State Survey (*Landes-Aufnahme*), most of the twenty-six territories were among the pioneers who helped to raise the status of map making from a fine art to an exact science. Leading the German procession were the kingdoms of Bavaria, Saxony and Württemberg as well as the grand duchy of Baden.

Württemberg was first mapped by Johann Stöffler of Tübingen (1452–1531), a mathematician and astronomer. The quality of his work cannot be appraised because the maps he drew were destroyed when the university burned in 1534. However, one of his pupils, a monk at the convent of Tübingen, named Sebastian Münster, produced a map (in manuscript) whose chief claim to fame is that it is the oldest one on record. The oldest *published* map of the region appeared at Tübingen, a woodcut printed on common letter paper. About 1570, 22 plates, beautifully executed on parchment, were made by George Gadner and copied by Abraham Ortelius in his *Theatrum* of 1575.[67]

Plans for the first trigonometric survey of Württemberg were submitted to Duke Carl in 1793 by a self-appointed reformer of cartography named Bohnenberg. The proposed map was to be patterned after the Cassini map of France, and though the total state appropriation was only 600 florins (about $300), the balance was underwritten by the publishers. The first sheet of Bohnenberg's map appeared in 1798 and the "Tübingen" sheet in 1800. This survey was eventually extended into Baden and Hesse and printed on 60 sheets; the scale was 1:86,400. Bohnenberg became director of Württemberg's land survey in 1803 and held the position until 1831.

The oldest known survey of any part of Saxony is a map of the district of Schwarzenberg made by George Oder in 1531 on a scale of about 1:26,000. A land survey of Saxony conducted between 1550 and 1600, sponsored by the Elector August, seems to have been a monopoly of the Oder family.[68] August, like European rulers up to the end of the eighteenth century, tried to prevent the publication of special maps of his country, and it was only after long, tedious negotiations that Johann Griginger, rector of Marienberg, was allowed to bring out the first published map of Saxony in Prague, 1568. Ortelius copied it, and for over 200 years it stood, with all its faults, as the basis on which all maps of Saxony were reproduced. Triangulation of Saxony began in 1781 and detailed surveys in 1785, on a scale of 1:12,000, each sheet of 24 Dresden inches representing 1 square mile. In 1819 a Topographic Atlas of Saxony (24 sheets on a scale of 1:57,600) was ordered engraved on copper. In 1861 it was replaced by a new topographic map on a scale of 1:100,000, on 28 sheets.[69]

A map of Upper and Lower Bavaria was made as early as 1523, but a later one, made by Peter Apian (Petrus Apianus) has been called a masterpiece of the times, and it was without doubt considerably ahead of the times in scientific accuracy. Material for the survey was gathered by Apian and his assistants between 1554 and 1563 by traversing the country and making astronomical and trigonometric observations. The map was drawn on a scale of 1:50,000 and consisted of 40 sheets covering 484 square feet. Although the original is lost, a copy reduced to a scale of 1:144,000 in 25 sheets was published in 1568, a map which was the prototype of all maps of Bavaria for the next 200 years.

Topographical map sheets of Bavaria were introduced by Rigobert Bonne (1727–1794), a military engineer attached to the French army of occupation. The importance of his surveys was appreciated by Joseph I, king of Bavaria, who decided to institute a thorough topographic survey of the country. Negotiations were opened with the French Republic for the loan of French engineers to do the work, and a Topographic Bureau was established at Munich. A series of false starts was made and a collection of mediocre maps resulted, after which the General Staff of the War Office took over the Topographic Bureau. Between 1820 and 1830 maps of Upper and Central Franconia were made, comprising the principalities of Anspach and Bayreuth. Additional sheets of the mountains of Southern Bavaria came out between 1825 and 1835.[70]

No one country can claim distinction for having originated the idea of a national survey. All nations foresaw the importance of detailed maps on a large, workable scale for the defense of the realm and the development of trade and national resources. All that can be said is that some were more successful than others in circumventing the political intrigue, professional jealousy and public lethargy that forever dogged the nations of Europe. The task was endless, and even when work in the field was not stopped by lack of funds, it suffered the ever-present blighting influence of war, either within a country's borders or at its back door. And too, there was always the age-old question — to map, or not to map? The better the map the more useful it would be to an enemy and the more likely to be stolen. In the end, however, the advantages outweighed the risks.

Thousands of maps embracing what is now the United States of America were made between 1500 and 1800. They ranged from crude, conjectural sketches to accurately made surveys of limited areas. Nearly every country in Europe had a part in the mapping of the New World, but no such thing as a scientific national survey existed in the United States before 1800. Scientific mapping of the nation by triangulation and astronomical observation began after the acquisition of the territory west of the Mississippi River, the purchase of Louisiana in 1803.[71] Once again history repeated itself, in that a learned body was indirectly responsible for spurring a government into scientific activity. As early as 1796 Thomas Jefferson pointed out to his colleagues in the American Philosophical Society the importance of the territory west of the Mississippi River and the necessity of exploring it in the interests of national defense and the future welfare of the nation. Thus, when the time came to take possession of the Territory of Louisiana, Jefferson negotiated, in 1803, a confidential grant of money by Congress for the purpose of exploring the new purchase. Meriwether Lewis, Jefferson's private secretary, and Captain William Clark of the United States Army were sent by President Jefferson to explore the new territory and survey a route to the Pacific Ocean.[72] From then until 1880 rarely a year went by without at least one military reconnaissance party being in the field or about to embark on an expedition into the wilds of the interior. Yet the country was so vast, and according to the best reports so much of it was uninhabitable, that few, if any, seriously considered an intensive topographic survey of the whole.

In 1880 the area of the United States was approximately 3,025,600 square miles, with a population of 50,155,983, an average of less than 17 to a square mile. This area was composed of 38 States and 8 Territories; the "Indian Territory," the Territory of Alaska, purchased from Russia in 1877, and the District of Columbia. But, wrote Captain George Wheeler in 1885, "the United States has thus far organized no systematic topographic survey of any portion of its territory. An act of Congress for a geological survey has been passed, and works of a trigonometric or topographic character for specified purposes (notably those of the Coast and Lake Surveys, that of the Mississippi River and the various works to the west of it) have been carried on. . . . While the professional work performed especially by the Coast and Lake Surveys of the United States has been of the first order of merit, yet in the line of progress towards systematic and final results, the United States is in arrears of fourteen other nationalities." When the day comes, Wheeler added, "the co-operation of the General and State governments will prove advantageous; the former producing the skeleton basis, with such added details including all natural features, with means of communication and all principal economic or artificial details, as are first most needed for its uses, and the States clothing this skeleton with full and complete minor economic topographic details, the cadastral survey included." [73]

The principal difficulty of making an intensive topographic study of the United States before 1800 had been caused by the fact that there was so much to be done in a hurry, without precedent and before the central government was properly organized. The boundaries of the country were poorly defined and much of the interior was a dark mystery filled with unknown perils. However, according to Captain Wheeler, who was as energetic and insistent as England's General Roy, "the topographic survey lies at the foundation of all that constitutes finally an exact knowledge of physical geography, and no such survey is complete until all the natural and artificial features, are mathematically measured, recorded, and delineated. . . ." [74]

Lacking the incentive of European countries to keep abreast of belligerent neighbors and defend her boundaries, the loosely united Federal government, composed of delegates from the several colonies, failed to see the importance of mapping the new country as a whole. A conspicuous exception was President Jefferson, who proposed a survey of the Atlantic coast to aid navigators and provide scientific data for future mapping activities. Congress authorized the "Survey of the Coast" on February 10, 1807, placed it under the jurisdiction of the Treasury Department and appointed a Swiss scientist, Professor Ferdinand Rudolph Hassler as superintendent. Trouble ensued. The Survey was transferred to the Navy Department; Congress now and then failed to provide the necessary funds to carry on the work; shipowners failed to receive the promised navigational charts from the Survey and demanded a congressional investigation. Hassler, who was trained in Europe, intended to place the mapping of the United States on a sound scientific basis. He ordered instruments from England in 1812 but did not get them until 1816, after the war was over.[75]

After 1843, the Survey was given a more stable organization and provided with funds which were more nearly adequate. The expansion of the country and the acquisition of island dependencies increased the duties of the Coast Survey, bringing under its surveillance more than 100,000 miles of coast line. In 1878, with still no national topographic survey in the offing, the duties of the Coast Survey were increased still further. Accurate maps of the wild West were urgently needed, and the only department of the government that was properly organized and tooled to meet the emergency, to provide the necessary connecting triangles between the old territory and the new, was the Coast Survey. On June 20, 1878, Congress enlarged the scope of the Coast Survey to cover inland topography as well, and since July 1, 1903, the organization has borne the name of the Coast and Geodetic Survey, under the Department of Commerce and Labor (now the Department of Commerce).

Among the aids to navigation published by the Coast and Geodetic Survey are *Coast Pilots*, *Notices to Navigators*, *Current Tables* and *Inside Route Pilots* describing inland waterways along the Atlantic and Gulf coasts. The compilation of hydrographic surveys and the publication of nautical charts constitute the principal functions of the Survey. Such charts are usually limited to a coastal strip about three miles inland, showing only the most prominent landmarks rather than detailed topography. Four distinct series of charts are published. Three series are so delineated that they overlap, giving an uninterrupted chart of the coast. The fourth, on scales varying from 1:5000 to 1:40,000 are "Harbor Charts" for local navigation. The first series ("Sailing Charts") varies in scale from 1:600,000 to 1:4,500,000, and is designed to aid navigators approaching the coast from deep water. The second series ("General Charts of the Coast") varies in scale from 1:180,000 to 1:400,000 and the charts cover more limited areas, being used chiefly for coastwise navigation. The third series ("Coast Charts") is in scales varying from 1:80,000 to 1:100,000. They are detailed and necessarily cover limited stretches of coast line.[76]

Almost as old as the Coast and Geodetic Survey is a second government mapping agency which evolved more or less from the expedition of Lewis and Clark. This was the Corps of Topographical Engineers, organized March 3, 1813. This body, later consolidated with the Corps of Engineers of the Army under the War Department, furnished a nucleus, the only proper agency, in the opinion of Captain Wheeler, for organizing and executing an adequate topographic survey of the nation. The Corps was charged with military topographical reconnaissance, exploration and survey at a time when the population, both white men and red, was in dire need of military discipline. It was kept so busy exploring and policing the interior that it had neither the time nor the funds to do anything else. After 1863 its duties were broadened to include the "planning and construction of works for the improvement of rivers and harbors; the trigonometric, hydrographic, and topographic survey of the northern lakes; the astronomical determination of boundaries and initial points; the topographic surveys and reconnaissances of the Interior, and of the Western Territory, &c." Although the administration of all topographic surveys in the United States up to 1869 was vested in the War Department, after 1879 "general topography as an integral quantity was stricken from the list of things appropriated for by the Government."

A third mapping agency established within the United States government was the Geological Survey. Prior to its establishment, various temporary organizations within the Department of the Interior had operated off and on in the regions west of the Mississippi River. There was the "Geological and Geographical Survey of the Territories," the "Geological Exploration of the Black Hills" and others, all controlled "by the theoretical considerations of the geologist," to use Captain Wheeler's words. But the "Geological Exploration of the 40th Parallel" and the "Geographical Survey of the Territory West of the 100th Meridian" were mammoth projects assigned to the Engineers. This last survey, according to Wheeler, "proceeded from almost a diametrically opposite standpoint, giving due weight to the astronomic, geodetic, and topographic observations, with map delineations of all natural objects, means of communication, artificial and economic features, the geologic and natural history branches being treated as incidental to the main purpose." The above, Wheeler concluded, "may be considered as the only organized, systematic, *topographic* work with a practical basis ever begun in the United States." [77]

When the Geological Survey was constituted, March 3, 1879, under the Department of the Interior, its function was to furnish closer co-ordination between government agencies assigned the job of classifying the public lands and "the examination of the geological structure, mineral resources, and products of the national domain." It was to supersede all of the earlier geological and geographical surveys. Limited at first to the land west of the 100th meridian, the field of the Geological Survey was eventually extended over the entire country. Publications of the Survey included technical monographs, professional Papers, water-supply papers and numerous publications on the mineral resources of the United States. As originally planned, all topographic mapping by the Geological Survey was incidental to the production of geological surveys, but because of the public demand for topographic maps funds for this purpose were voted by Congress in 1889. Today less than 7 per cent of the topographic maps produced by the Geological Survey are prepared for the use of Federal geologists. In fact the Survey presents "the anomalous situation of a bureau which has developed an originally subsidiary function into a major service concerned for the most part with broad public needs."

Most of the topographic mapping of the United States has been taken over by the Geological Survey instead of the General Staff of the War Department. The country has been divided into quadrangles bounded by parallels of latitude and meridians of longitude. These quadrangles are mapped on three different scales, exceptions being made in the case of maps compiled for special purposes. The scale selected for each quadrangle is based on "that which is best adapted to general

A night scene in an eighteenth-century observatory.

A view of the Royal Observatory at Greenwich, 1785.

The Observatory of Paris, 1785, from the rear.

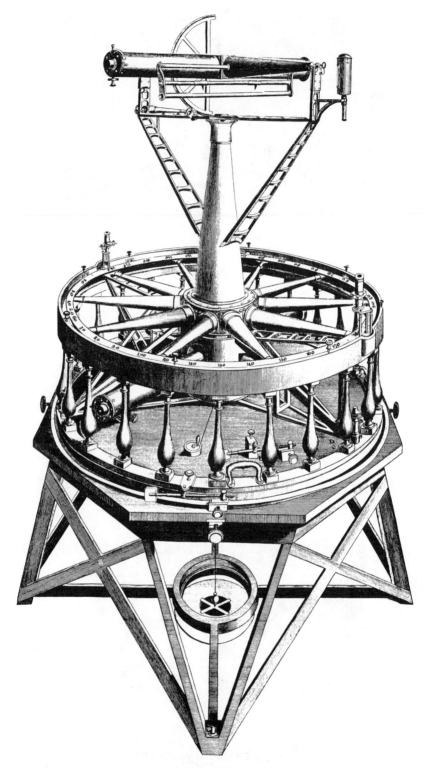

Jesse Ramsden's theodolite, built for the Royal Society, made possible the first accurate triangulation of England.

use in the development of the country. . . ." Of the three general types of maps published by the Survey, the first are those which represent problem areas of *great* public importance, such as mineral development, land reclamation and irrigation. These sheets are published either on a scale of 1:31,680 (one inch to a half mile) or 1:24,000 (1 inch to 2000 feet). Areas which present problems of *average* importance, such as the basin of the Mississippi and its tributaries, are mapped on a scale of 1:62,500 (one inch to nearly a mile). Areas in which there are *less important* problems such as the desert region of Arizona and New Mexico, are mapped on a scale of 1:125,000 (one inch equal to nearly two miles). This large-scale topographical survey has been in progress since 1882, and according to the description on the verso of one of the 1947 sheets "the published maps cover slightly more than 47 percent of the country, exclusive of outlying possessions." Apparently there has been a lack of agreement when it came to decide what areas were of *great, average* or *minor* importance, for another authority goes on to say that of this 47 or 48 per cent of the country, "only about one-half is mapped adequately according to modern needs and standards." [78]

The numerous mapping agencies of the United States government are widely scattered among various departments and bureaus. Overlapping of government surveys, under the circumstances, is unavoidable, and economy is impossible. In all, there are twenty-seven branches of the Federal Government concerned either directly or indirectly with the making of maps and charts. The work accomplished varies from year to year according to the needs of the times and in direct proportion to the amount of money appropriated by Congress for surveys and maps. The emphasis on certain kinds of maps is constantly shifting. The mapping activities of the Department of State and the Corps of Engineers (War Department) for example, were increased a hundredfold in the past eight years, to meet the necessities of war. What will happen to them in the next ten years is problematical. Yet the fact remains that the United States, with all its wealth and technical skills, does not yet know itself cartographically, and has yet to produce a topographic survey of the entire country based on uninterrupted triangulation and astronomical observations and a complete series of maps that are adequate "according to modern needs and standards." [79]

CHAPTER X

Survey of a World

NINETY years ago, within the memory of living man, world cartography was in many respects similar to French cartography in the days of Louis XIV. The attitude of mankind towards a unified survey of the world was essentially provincial. Surveys and maps of foreign parts would be expensive, and rather than stand the cost, the brotherhood of man was for the most part content to settle for a good map of the local scene and let the rest of the world take care of itself. As a matter of fact, many countries, because of apathy and the prohibitive cost of an instrumental survey, had failed to produce anything that resembled an accurate topographic map of their own territory. Consequently as late as 1885 it was estimated that not more than 6,000,000 square miles, less than one ninth of the land surface of the globe, had been surveyed or was in the process of being surveyed. The remaining eight ninths, inhabited by more than 900,000,000 people, was unfamiliar or entirely unknown to the world at large, a *terra incognita* from a cartographical point of view.[1]

The old antipathy of the lord of the manor, the local politician and the small landowner for the surveyor-intruder persisted on an international scale. But unlike the provinces and *departements* of England and France that were ultimately subject to the law of the land or the edict of a ruler, the several countries of the world at large were still free to decide whether or not they chose to participate in an international mapping project, and whether they should permit the surveyors of a foreign power to trespass on their territory, regardless of the universal aspects of the enterprise. With few exceptions, of which the United States was one, topographic surveying on a large scale had become one of the accepted activities of the military caste of all nations. The motives, real or alleged, of foreign powers that chose to launch an international mapping project were immediately suspect. International mapping, or topographic surveys of any kind, had definite military implications, with invasion and conquest a logical and never-to-be-forgotten aftermath. So it was that "up to the year 1857, most of the map results were held a secret and kept entirely within the custody of the Government" that made them. After that time, for some mysterious reason, it was possible to purchase copies of the best topographic map sheets of foreign countries, usually for a modest price. Equally mysterious was the universal practice of stopping all map sales the minute war was declared, when it must have been obvious to all concerned that the General Staff of the opposing power had long since acquired the information it desired.[2]

In 1885 there were twenty "systematic duly organized topographic works in existence," representing a small fraction of the earth's surface. Of these, fourteen (Prussia, Saxony, Bavaria, Austria-Hungary, France, Switzerland, Holland, Dutch East Indies, Italy, Sweden, Norway, Russia, Belgium and Denmark) were from the beginning administered by their War Departments. The remaining six (The United Kingdom, Spain, India, Württemberg, Baden and Portugal) were assigned to other departments of the government, but in every instance the work was executed under the direction of an army officer, either from the General Staff or the Military Engineers. This was precisely as it should be, in the opinion of Captain Wheeler, for topographic maps meet the requirements of the military strategist and commander, "and thus very properly through the centuries, topography has grown up a permanent unvarying essential of the military profession." And, he continued, "one of the results of modern civilization in its quest after habitable lands . . . will naturally be, to gradually subject the temperate regions, at least, to the analysis of a minute topographical survey, the value of such data having already become so well fixed in the polity of the older civilized nations." [3]

In addition to the basic topographic or "mother surveys" in progress throughout the world, there were, in 1885, thirty-five countries engaged in active geological research, systematic study and reconnaissance leading to the preparation of geological maps. These surveys were generally under the jurisdiction of any one of a number of civil departments of the government, such as Interior, Public Works, Commerce, Industry, Public Instruction, and so forth. The maps produced under the direction of the various Geological Surveys represent the first important offshoot of the basic topographic survey, whereby a specialized class of information is superimposed on the base map. With an accurate picture of the terrain before them the geologists of the world were able for the first time to study the earth systematically, and apply some of their theoretical abstractions to the development of natural resources. It was possible to trace the outline of geological formations, to classify and map the soil, to outline the probable location of valuable mineral deposits, and in general to plot the maximum utilization of the land. Spot locations of important mineral deposits are found on Dutch and Flemish maps of the seventeenth century, and in the middle of the eighteenth century the French Académie Royale des Sciences began to publish maps in connection with geological studies, plotting either by hachures or color applied by hand important differences in the earth's crust with an eye to more efficient and economical use of the soil. With the development of large-scale topographic maps, geology came into its own. The groundwork was laid; distances and directions, contours and elevations were no longer problematical and the scientists concerned were able to devote full time to the close examination of the earth. [4]

A third class of national survey supported by public funds was fairly well developed by 1885; this was the Hydrographic Survey, the charting of the coasts and harbors of the world. At that time nineteen governments were conducting such coastal surveys (both domestic and foreign) as well as charting the islands that were concerned with their colonial interests or that lay across the path of their merchant fleets. With the exception of Portugal and the United States, all of these countries had seen fit to delegate the administration of their Hydrographic Surveys to the Navy Department or the Marine Ministry. In Portugal the topographic, geologic and hydrographic surveys were grouped under one head. In the United States the duties normally performed by a Marine Survey were divided between the Hydrographic Office, with a civilian head, administered by the Navy Department, and the Coast and Geodetic Survey, also with a civilian head, under the Treasury Department.[5]

The importance of any one of these Hydrographic Surveys and the duties it performed depended on the interest of the country in maritime affairs. Thus the Surveys of England, France and Holland took the lead in hydrographic research. The chief purpose of all such nautical surveying was to produce the best possible charts for the use of navigators, to serve as an advance guard for the merchant fleets, and for the navies in time of war. In Great Britain the Hydrographic Office was established as a department of the Admiralty under Earl Spencer, by an order in council issued in 1795. From a humble beginning, one hydrographer (Alexander Dalrymple), one assistant and a draftsman, the British Admiralty eventually became one of the chief sources of supply for the maritime world, furnishing charts and hydrographic information to all nations. The very nature of the work performed by the various Hydrographic Surveys precluded isolation and secrecy, and from the beginning, the benefits to be derived from international co-operation were apparent to all countries. In this case it was not a matter of uniting in the common cause of science, it was a union of the seafaring men of the world against the common perils of the deep. Moreover, the seas were so vast that little headway could be made in nautical surveying without the combined effort of every ship and every nation that sailed them. The nautical surveyors of the world were a roving lot, working wherever they were allowed to cruise, sometimes protected by the beneficial nature of their task and at other times by the convincing appearance of their naval armament.[6]

Sixty years ago the cartographer who set out to compile a map of the world had as many problems to solve as the map maker of 1550, but they were different. He had to work from numerous isolated surveys without a connecting framework. Although the scientific principles of topographic surveying had been fairly well standardized throughout the world, the end products, the maps produced by various nations, were far from standardized. Foremost among the problems remaining to be solved by cartographers was the selection of a point or line of departure for a world map, a universal prime meridian of longitude.

From the earliest days to the year 1880 or thereabouts, the selection of a prime meridian was based on patriotism, whim, convenience or misconception. Ptolemy chose the Fortunate Islands for the simple reason that they were considered the westernmost extremity of the habitable world, further west than any point on the coast of Europe or Africa. Christopher Saxton (1584), the English cartographer, chose the island of St. Mary in the Azores. John Davis (1594) chose St. Michael's in the same group, because he thought there was no compass variation on that meridian. Ortelius, Jansson and Blaeu used Isla del Fuego (Fogo) in the Cape Verde group. Blaeu later proposed the peak of Teneriffe in the Canaries, and the Dutch followed. In 1634 Louis XIII decreed the island of Ferro (Hierro) in the Canaries as the prime meridian to be used on all French maps, and so it remained until about 1800.

John Seller's map of Hertfordshire (1676) was the first to use the prime meridian of London, and the Ordnance Survey under General Roy established it specifically through the center of the dome of Saint Paul's cathedral. About 1794, after the Royal Observatory at Greenwich had been properly "located," the meridian of Greenwich, first used on John Carey's *New Map of England and Wales*, became the standard for Great Britain. Other prime meridians used between the sixteenth and nineteenth centuries, were Toledo, Cracow, Uranibourg, Copenhagen, Goes (Ter-Goes), Pisa, Augsberg, Rome, Ulm, Tübingen, Bologna, Rouen, St. Petersburg, Washington and Philadelphia. Every country had its favorite prime meridian; some had two, one for general land maps and another for marine charts. On the latter, Greenwich was most commonly used, because of the widely circulated Admiralty charts. It was adopted by India, Prussia, Austria, Russia, Holland, the United States, Sweden, Norway and Denmark. French charts used the meridian of Paris; Spain used Cadiz; Russia used Pulkowa; Italy used Naples. At one time or another Spain has had eleven different prime meridians within her borders. And in 1881 there were no less than fourteen different prime meridians being used on topographic survey maps alone.[7]

As early as 1800 Pierre Simon Laplace (1749–1827), the astronomer and mathematician, pointed out to his fellow men the wisdom and utility of a single prime meridian for the scientific determination of geographical longitudes. "It is desirable," he wrote, "that all the nations of Europe, in place of arranging geographical longitude from their own observatories, should agree to compute it from the same meridian, one indicated by nature herself, in order to determine it for all time to come. Such an arrangement would introduce into the science of geography the same uniformity which is already enjoyed in the calendar and the arithmetic, and, extended to the numerous objects of their mutual relations, would make of the diverse peoples one family only."[8]

Directly related to the problem of establishing a universal prime meridian was the reckoning of time. Again, the desirability of a time standard for the world was apparent to all scientists, and in 1828 Sir John Herschel, astronomer, proposed the adoption of a uniform system based on the equinoctial ("mean") hours used by the ancient astronomers, whereby the day of the equinox was taken as a standard and divided into twenty-four equal parts. Forty years later Sir Henry James of the Royal Military Engineers made the same proposal, carrying the idea a step further by suggesting that the Greenwich Observatory be established as the standard meridian for the timekeeping world. However useful these suggestions may have seemed at the time, considerable agitation was necessary before they were adopted.

Another source of confusion in the map world of the 1880's was the scale on which maps and charts were drawn. There were as many different scales used in map making as there were countries making maps. Some countries used two or three different scales, designed to suit the agencies for whom the maps were compiled. Based on ancient and venerated systems of linear measure, these scales were as much a part of the tradition of a country as the language itself, and were not to be discarded lightly. Confusion was the inevitable consequence. The scale of the provincial or county map often had to be converted into the unit of measure adopted by the central government before it could be incorporated in a national survey. Commercial map publishers who aspired to financial success did what they could to cope with the situation. When issuing a map of a foreign country they indicated the scale in the most common unit of linear measure used in that country. But they never lost sight of possible domestic scales, and usually furnished an equivalent scale in units common to their native land.

In an effort to make everyone happy, map publishers often gave several equivalent scales, sometimes as many as eight or ten, for a single map. For example, a map of Turkey published in London in 1810 gave the scale in Turkish *Miles*, Turkish *Agash, Parasangs* of Persia and British *Miles.*[9] In the same atlas the map of Barbary gave the scale in *Sea Leagues, Day's Journeys in a Level Country, Day's Journey in a Mountainous Country* and *British Miles.* The map of Switzerland gave the scale in *Swiss Leagues, Common Miles of Italy, Common Miles of Germany, Common French Leagues* and *British Statute Miles.* The value of the "league" in different parts of Europe caused a great deal of trouble. It varied in length but was used as a unit of linear measure in Sweden, Denmark, Norway, England, France, Poland, Switzerland and the Netherlands, to mention a few.

In an effort to eliminate some of the confusion of this kind it was customary, though by no means a universal practice, to state the number of leagues, miles or stadia in a degree, thus giving a universal unit of measure that would presumably be familiar to all readers. For instance, the scale would read, "British Miles 69½ to a Degree," or "Wersts of Russia 105 in a Degree." All would have been well except for the fact that the value of a degree of longitude and of latitude in terms of linear measure was still a matter of doubt in every European country, and few cartographers had made the necessary astronomic and trigonometric observations to determine the exact value of the local unit of measure in terms of arc.

A third source of confusion in the compilation of world maps was the promiscuous use of conventional signs and symbols among cartographers. On the topographic maps published in Europe alone there were, in 1885, no less than 1148 delineated objects represented by names, abbreviations or conventional signs and symbols. A certain number were represented by color. About 140 symbols were related to natural features, starting with alkaline flats, alluvium, beaches, chasms, deltas, and ending with sand dunes, shoals, steppes, volcanoes and willows. About 330 symbols and signs referred to commerce and communication, either natural or improved. In connection with communication there were always the railroads, and on some maps a distinction was made between single and double track; then there were culverts, bridges, repair shops and turntables and on rivers there were bridges, fords and ferries. Seventy-one different symbols were used in connection with agriculture, such as areas under cultivation with a distinction made between groves, orchards and vineyards; every crop had a symbol or a sign. Sixty-five different symbols were used to denote manufacturing of various kinds and 18 were used for mining. One hundred and eighteen "technical" signs and symbols were in use, of which 65 related specifically to military operations, such as forts, arsenals, navy yards, trenches and towers. There was little if any uniformity in the methods used to denote such fundamental details as boundary lines, bench marks, compass points and contours.[10]

Numerous systems of indicating topographic relief (orography) were in use. After the publication of Vivier's map of the environs of Paris in 1674, the map world began to elaborate on the crude hachures he had introduced, replacing the ancient "molehill" symbol for hills and mountains. Yet after more than one hundred years cartographers were still experimenting with different ways of portraying elevations, and in no part of the world was there any semblance of standardization. Jean Louis Dupoin-Triel, a French topographical engineer, used horizontal curves (contour lines) to indicate elevations on a map published in 1791. Two other Frenchmen experimented with the use of contour lines at about the same time. General Noizet de St. Paul, one time Director of Fortifications in France, suggested their use in connection with large-scale planning and construction. Rigobert Bonne, cartographer and member of the commission for planning the atlas of France, proposed that the terrain be expressed by equidistant curves, but the idea was rejected by his colleagues. A few years later a German topographer, Johann George Lehmann, introduced a method of hill shading based on contours described as "full straight line hachures normal to the adjacent contour of least level and of thickness corresponding to the slope." Another modified system was originated by General Friedrich Müffling, a Prussian officer, utilizing broken and sometimes wavy lines. However, "the present state of development of topographic methods was, in 1830, still in its infancy. The brilliant idea of the Swiss engineer du Carla [and others], to express 'differences of altitude and variation in form of the earth's surface' by equidistant curves, has long battled for recognition, the necessity of sufficient level and altitude determinations, conditioned thereby, delaying its practical introduction. Between 1830 and 1840, the first attempts in this new direction of terrain representation were published, but it took until the years 1840 and 1850 before this idea was fully appreciated, and still some Governments pay no attention to the use of equidistant curves." The method was first used on the survey and original drawings of the beautiful atlas of Hesse-Cassel (1835), but when the sheets were published, the engravers discarded the contour lines for hachures. In all, more than 80 different systems of indicating hills and mountains were tried out at one time or another, employing various combinations of contours and shading as well as colors of different shades. For this reason a detailed "key" or legend was always necessary to let the reader know just what the map maker meant when he used a hachure, a contour line or a tint.[11]

A perennial source of confusion to the map compiler is now and always will be the orthography used on maps and charts in different parts of the world. Yet no thinking person would deny the importance of words as they are used on a map to give names to places or to explain in a note or legend what the map is all about. The cartographer of the nineteenth century had to cope with several alphabets involving hundreds of different characters in order to decipher the most elementary data on foreign maps. Among the more commonly used were Arabic, German, Greek, Hebrew, Russian, Chinese and Japanese; and even though the cartographer might familiarize himself with the various alphabets, he seldom mastered enough of the languages themselves to be of much help. Also related to the problem of orthography was the spelling of place names. Should the name be written Moskva, Moscua, Moschia, Moscou, Moskau or Moscow? Perhaps it should be Muskau or Mockba instead? Which would be most widely understood, Marseilles, Massiglia, Marsella, Massillia, or Massalia? To the classical scholar Lugdunum Batavorum might have some significance, but for a popular map Leyden or Leiden would be better; or perhaps the French form Leyde or even Leida. The ancient city of Lutetia or Lutetia Parisiorum might also be correctly spelled Parigi in Italian or Paris if you lived there, but what did the map world want? These and other questions of policy, resulting from the hundreds of independent surveys being made throughout the world, made it literally impossible to compile a map that could be read and properly interpreted in any part of the globe. The evolution of an international mapping policy and technique was next in order.

The first step in such a mapping policy was taken, indirectly, by French scientists when they laid down the principles of the metric system. Their objective was the establishment of a universal system of weights and measures. It is doubtful, however, whether at the outset they themselves fully appreciated the important contribution they were making to the science of cartography. Their chief purpose was to bring order out of chaos in their own country, as far as weights and measures were concerned.[12]

The idea was to utilize some unit in nature as a standard of linear measure. The first suggestion in this regard came, during the latter part of the seventeenth century, from Jean Picard, Gabriel Mouton and Christian Huygens. Why not use as a standard the length of a pendulum that beats one second? The same general idea was later phrased by Cassini, du Fay and La Condamine, and the scheme might eventually have been adopted, except for the fact that continued experiments had just about proved that the length of the pendulum that beats seconds varies in different latitudes. Consequently any such standard of linear measure would have to be adjusted to latitude and perhaps longitude, as well as temperature and barometric pressure, and all scientists agreed that there was much to be learned about gravitation before accurate tables could be compiled for the rectification of the pendulum.

Although the pendulum was abandoned and the proposed revision of weights and measures was set aside, nature was approached a second time in 1790. On May 8 of that year it was decreed by the National Assembly that the Académie Royale des Sciences should take steps towards the establishment of a decimal system of linear measure whose fundamental unit would be based on a "natural" standard. Two commissions composed of members of the Académie worked on the problem, and on March 19, 1791, a comprehensive report was submitted, in which the principles of the *metric* system were formulated. The basic unit was to be the *meter* — one ten-millionth part of the terrestrial meridian quadrant or one forty-millionth part of a great circle meridian. A week later, March 26, the report was approved, and by decree of the National Assembly the metric system was adopted.

Under the direction of Jean Baptiste Delambre and Pierre François Méchain, five commissions were appointed to carry out the arduous task of establishing the precise length of the meter. Jacques Dominique Cassini, Méchain and Delambre were to remeasure the difference in latitude between Dunkerque and Barcelona along the meridian already established, while Monge and Meusnier surveyed and measured the base lines in this connection. Borda and Coulomb were to carry out a series of experiments with the pendulum in different latitudes; Tillet, Brisson and Vandermonde were to make an intensive study of ancient measures for comparison purposes. The fifth commission, composed of Lavoisier and Haüy, was to conduct a series of experiments with distilled water to establish the precise weight of the gram and kilogram.

Elaborate precautions were taken to make every measurement as accurate as possible, and a great deal of time was consumed by the surveying parties. Meanwhile came the Revolution, and every intellectual in the land found himself under the scrutiny of the new government. Then for a time it was Citizen Méchain and Citizen Delambre; Citizen Laplace and Citizen Haüy. Those who failed to pass muster went to jail or to the guillotine. However, somehow the work progressed, and just as the Republic took over the mapping of France, the new government eventually saw to it that the metric system was established. In fact the Convention announced on August 1, 1793 (1 Fructidor An II) that the system would be made obligatory in about a year. Actually it was two years (1795) before a complete, verified, report was ready, and a glossary was issued, defining the *mètre*, *kilomètre*, *centimètre* and *millimètre*. That same year, on September 1 (1 Vendémiare), the metric system was made compulsory in the commune of Paris.[13]

On September 25, 1798 (25 Vendémiare An VII), scientists from various European nations gathered in Paris to take part in the ceremony of fixing the value of the fundamental unit of measure. Acting on the report of van Swinden, the length of the meter was fixed at 443 lignes — (440/1.000) with certain qualifications. At the same time a standard of the meter in platinum was deposited in the National Archives. On December 10, 1799 (19 Frimaire An VIII) the law was passed making the gram and meter standard units of weight and measure. The adoption of the metric system by law was one thing and the acceptance of it by the people was another. In France an interim adjustment was necessary, and in 1812 a system of *mesures transitoires* was instituted to ease the country into something new.[14]

The effect of the metric system on cartography was almost immediate. From it a reliable attempt to express scale in the universal language of numbers evolved in the form of the "natural" or fractional scale, one unit on the map being equal to

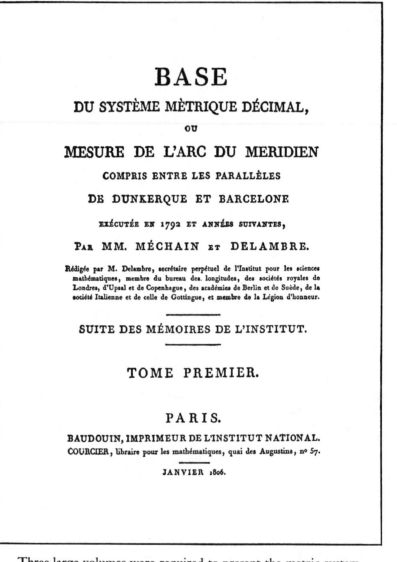

BASE

DU SYSTÈME MÈTRIQUE DÉCIMAL,

ou

MESURE DE L'ARC DU MERIDIEN

COMPRIS ENTRE LES PARALLÈLES

DE DUNKERQUE ET BARCELONE

EXÉCUTÉE EN 1792 ET ANNÉES SUIVANTES,

PAR MM. MÉCHAIN ET DELAMBRE.

Rédigée par M. Delambre, secrétaire perpétuel de l'Institut pour les sciences mathématiques, membre du bureau des. longitudes, des sociétés royales de Londres, d'Upsal et de Copenhague, des académies de Berlin et de Suède, de la société Italienne et de celle de Gottingue, et membre de la Légion d'honneur.

SUITE DES MÉMOIRES DE L'INSTITUT.

TOME PREMIER.

PARIS.

BAUDOUIN, IMPRIMEUR DE L'INSTITUT NATIONAL.
COURCIER, libraire pour les mathématiques, quai des Augustins, n° 57.

JANVIER 1806.

Three large volumes were required to present the metric system of weights and measures to the scientific world. This is the title page of volume one.

X units on the ground or "in nature." This new fractional scale (Representative Fraction or R. F. scale) did not tell the whole story; it merely stated the relative size between the map and the area of the earth it depicted. It had to be supplemented by more specific information, such as the fact that the unit expressed by the numerator referred to an inch, ligne or centimeter, and that the number in the denominator referred to leagues, miles or kilometers. Nevertheless it was a convenient way of expressing scale and one that could be universally understood.

The "natural" or fractional scale appeared as early as 1806 in a revised edition of the *Atlas National de la France*, edited by P. G. Chanlaire, with the statement that *"les cartes sur la même Échelle de un sur le papier a 259,000 sur le terrain."* This information was supplemented by the explanation that one ligne was equal to three hundred toises.[15] The phraseology accompanying the fractional scale varied as time went on. In some cases, such as on Gray's maps of the United States, the scale referred specifically to "nature" when giving the representative fraction, but after the R. F. scale had become almost universally adopted by geographers and map makers, the explanatory statement was taken for granted and only the fraction, such as 1:100,000 or 1/86,400 was considered necessary to tell the story. In this respect, R. F. scale was ideally suited to the expression of the metric system as it was used on maps and charts; 1:100,000 representing, let us say, one centimeter on the map to one kilometer on the ground, or 1:50,000 representing 1 centimeter to five hundred meters.[16]

The adoption of the metric system by foreign countries was slow. Even in France it was accepted reluctantly; so much so that in 1837 a law was passed prohibiting the use of any other system of weights and measures. Belgium, Holland and Greece adopted it and eventually most of the other European states. The system became the *legal* system in Europe except for Great Britain, Denmark, Russia and Montenegro. In fact, the metric system probably did more than any one thing to induce international co-operation and interest in determining the shape of the earth, the length of a degree and the creation of an international mapping project. By accepting it as a standard, the various countries were forced to investigate the older systems of measure in use beyond their borders that had been used to determine latitude and longitude, and to get together on comparative values. A systematic series of comparisons of linear measure was instituted at the Ordnance Survey Office at Southampton in 1866, and many countries found it best to co-operate in the common cause. Cartography was rapidly expanding, sweeping political boundaries aside; in order to map a country according to modern standards of precision it was first necessary to map, at least in outline, the world in its entirety.[17]

On May 20, 1875, a "General Conference of Weights and Measures" convened at Paris. The result of the meeting was an international agreement ratified and signed by Germany, Austria-Hungary, the Republic of Argentine, Belgium, Denmark, the United States, France, Italy, Peru, Portugal, Russia, Sweden, Norway, Switzerland, Turkey and Venezuela. Two years later (1877) a permanent international bureau of weights and measures was established (Comité International), with headquarters in the pavillon of Breteuil in the commune of Sèvres. Also installed were the official standards, such as the platinum meter and the gram. Subsequently the standard of platinum was replaced by a rod of platinum-iridium alloy with a cross section shaped like an H. Thirty identical copies of this standard were made and distributed to the various signatories of the international agreement. Forthwith the following values were handed down as official: [18]

One legal meter	= 3.28086933	feet
One international meter	= 3.2808257	feet
One toise	= 6.39453348	feet

The simple act of establishing the length of the meter, of setting the figures down in cold print, had a remarkable effect on the map world. It should have settled the matter once and for all, but instead it fanned the flame of the old controversy as to the shape of the earth: was it prolate or oblate? If it were prolate, how flat was it at the poles? Many able scientists were still doubtful about the results already obtained and demanded further proof. What they did not know was that the difference between the polar circumference and the equatorial circumference was very slight, about twenty-six miles, and that the smallest errors in measuring arcs, either of latitude or longitude, would be enough to alter considerably the shape they were dealing with. Yet all were aware by now that the earth was not a perfect sphere. A few were weighing the possibility that they were dealing with an ellipsoid with three unequal axes, a theory advanced by Karl G. J. Jacobi, and one that could not be ignored. Longer arcs would have to be surveyed, and the behavior of the pendulum would have to be re-checked as well as the laws of gravitation. Science took another step towards the standardization of map making.[19]

During the nineteenth century the surface of the earth was well scratched by surveyors in an effort to determine its shape. At first they were disjointed efforts, relatively short arcs of parallels and meridians, hardly long enough to bring out a slight change in the length of a degree at different latitudes, and scarcely accurate enough to suit the requirements of the scientific world. A few arcs overran national boundary lines, but for the most part they were run from independent initial points and bases with initial level points starting from separate zeros or datum planes. Triangulation and leveling operations were carried on independently according to the technique and standards of accuracy established by individual countries. It is significant, however, that in no instance were the findings of history ignored, not even the pioneering efforts of Hipparchus, and in groping for a method and an answer, each historical measurement of a degree was carefully reviewed.

After Hipparchus and Poseidonius, scientists re-examined what seems to have been the first degree measurement in Europe, made between Paris and Amiens by the celebrated French physician ("the modern Galen") Jean Fernel. His meridian line was measured over the ground by counting the number of revolutions of a moving carriage wheel. His celestial observations were made with a triangle used as a quadrant, and the results he obtained later proved to be very close to the truth. Never to be ignored was the work of Willebrord Snell (or Snellius),

Dutch astronomer and mathematician, who was a professor of mathematics at the University of Leyden. In 1615 he executed a survey to determine the shape of the earth and the length of a degree, using a technique of his own, whereby his base line was surveyed by triangulation instead of using an odometer or a perambulator. His line, measured on the frozen meadows near Leyden between Alkmaar and Bergen-op-Zoom, was naturally much straighter than Fernel's, although his results were not proportionally more accurate. His astronomical observations were made with a quadrant and semicircle. An Englishman, Richard Norwood, contributed his bit to the cause by surveying a line between London and York, partly with a chain and partly by pacing. His observations of the difference in the meridian height of the sun between the two stations were made with a quadrant, between 1633 and 1635, and the resulting "quantity of a Degree in our English Measures," was a fair result. From 1669, when Jean Picard measured the length of a degree using wooden rods and an iron quadrant, rarely a year went by without at least one new announcement concerning the length of the degree and the shape of the earth. In 1838 Friedrich Wilhelm Bessel introduced the method of least squares applied to the calculation of a series of triangles and after he had published the results of his surveys in East Prussia, the way was cleared for operations on a grand scale and a result that would be acceptable to the scientific world.[20]

The ultimate objective of all geodetic operations was to plot without interruption the curvature of the earth's surface. That being impractical if not impossible because of the prohibitive cost, the next best thing was to plot the curve of the longest possible surveyed lines, both arcs of meridians and arcs of parallels. This was done on a modest scale at first. The network of triangles in Greece was united with those of Italy and Bosnia; the Italian triangulation from Palermo north through Rome and Rimini was extended to unite with the triangulation of Central Europe and southward to Tunis; the meridian of Vienna was extended southward to Malta. The triangulation of Britain was extended northward to Saxavord in the Shetland Islands and southward to the Isle of Wight. Three other small arcs of meridian in central Europe figured in the early nineteenth century measurements of a degree; one in Hanover was run between Göttingen and Altona, a second one in Denmark was run between Lavenburg and Lyssabel, and a third, in Prussia, extended from Trunz to Memel. By further combining the work already done and enlisting the co-operation of the nations concerned, two great arcs of meridian were eventually produced. The first combined the English, French and Spanish surveys, from Saxavord in the north to Greenwich, across the English Channel to Dunkerque, from there southward through France to Barcelona, down through Spain and terminating at Formentera, a line extending over 22° of latitude. The second arc, run by the combined surveys of the Russians and Scandinavians, began at Hammerfest, Norway, the northernmost town of Europe (Lat. 70° 40' 7" N.) and terminated at Ismail in Bessarabia, on the northern arm of the Danube, an uninterrupted line extending over 25½° of latitude.[21]

Three great arcs of parallel were similarly stretched across Europe and European Asia for the purpose of making longitude measurements. The first, proposed in 1857 by the German astronomer Friedrich G. W. Struve, was executed by Russia, Prussia, Belgium and England and ran from the island of Valentia (or Valencia) off the west coast of Ireland (Lat. 51° 55′ 8″ N.; Long. 10° 19′ W.) to Orsk in Russia on the Ural River, a span of 69 degrees. The second arc, executed by France, Piedmont and Austria, ran the parallel from the mouth of the Gironde in France through Turin and Milan to Fiume, an extension of the original French survey. The third arc, also of French origin, was a resurvey of the parallel from Brest to Strassburg.[22]

In addition to these great arcs, there were many scattered lines and chains of triangles in Europe, surveyed in connection with national mapping projects. And on the fringes of civilization there was the arc of parallel surveyed in North America by Charles Mason and Jeremiah Dixon to determine the boundary between Maryland and Pennsylvania; the old arc of meridian run in Peru by Bouguer and La Condamine; the meridian arc in Lapland surveyed by Maupertuis, Clairault, Camus, and Lemonnier; the arc of meridian begun in Punnae in India by Colonel Lambton and extended by Captain George Everest; the controversial arc of meridian at the Cape of Good Hope measured in 1752 by Lacaille and remeasured by Sir Thomas Maclear over one hundred years later. There was, in fact, a wealth of material available for the definitive study of the shape of the earth and the length of a degree. This was especially true in Central Europe, where there were extensive, though unco-ordinated, chains of triangles across Sweden, Norway, Denmark, Germany, Switzerland and Italy. Within the area bounded by the meridians through the observatories of Bonn and Trunz and the parallels of Palermo and Christiania (12° of longitude and nearly 22° of latitude), equal to about 38,000 German square miles, were more than thirty astronomical observatories equipped with the best instruments and manned by competent observers. However, a unifying agency was needed to get the best results.[23]

On June 20, 1861, the Prussian government placed its stamp of approval on a project for unifying the degree measurements of Central Europe submitted by General Johann Jacob Baeyer of the Prussian General Staff. According to his estimate, at least ten arcs of meridian and even more arcs of parallel could be measured without much trouble within that area. It would then be possible to adjust the belts of triangles already surveyed along selected quadrilaterals and to compare the astronomic and trigonometric measurements made by all of the nations involved. Thus the largest possible arcs of great circles could be measured, and in time it would perhaps be possible to establish a single datum level for all Europe, and as the revision of the various topographic surveys progressed the myriad differences between field and map delineation would be eliminated, "and the conventional illustration of the ground for all Europe be made uniform"[24]

With General Baéyer at its head, an organization for a "Central European degree-measurement" was instituted, and in 1862 a conference of delegates from the several European nations met at Berlin to discuss the general problem, on invitation of the Office of Foreign Affairs. Two years later the first general conference was held, and after several additional countries joined the movement, the name was changed to "The European Degree-Measurement," and a Central Bureau was established at Berlin, supported by the Prussian government. However, by 1886 the scope of activities was so broadened that co-operating states began to make contributions to the maintenance of the Central Bureau and the name of the organization was again changed to "The International Earth-measurement" or "International Geodetic Association" (*Internationale Gradmessung*). The Central Bureau became affiliated with the Prussian Geodetic Institute, located after 1892 on the Telegraphenberg near Potsdam. Between 1897 and 1906 twenty-one countries were listed as members of the association, and general conferences were held every three years.[25]

Every country involved in geodetic operations has evolved an elaborate technique and precise instruments for making earth measurements, none of which is flawless. The results obtained in each case have approximated a constant, but a single value for the flattening of the earth at the poles would obviously be highly desirable. No such universal standard has yet been established. In their published report on the length of the meter (1810) Méchain and Delambre submitted eight different figures based on shapes ranging from a sphere to an oblate spheroid with a flattening of 1/150, the curvature at that time being far from certain. However, within the last hundred years the range of estimates, based on the best available data, has narrowed. Clarke's value of 1/294.26 for the flattening (1858) represented the maximum reciprocal and Harkness's 1/300.20, announced in 1891, was the minimum estimate.[26]

Since 1849 (Airy's estimate), no fewer than thirteen values, based on the most precise measurements, have been set forth, each one having its merits and its faults. Yet because of the international aspects of the problem, a universal standard, at least for use in general discussions, was indicated. At a meeting held in Madrid, October, 1924, the Congress of the International Geodetic and Geographical Union discussed the matter at great length. The Executive Committee then proposed the adoption of Hayford's estimate of 1910, based entirely on results of the U. S. Coast and Geodetic Survey — assuming a semimajor axis of 6,378,388 kilometers, the reciprocal of the flattening was given as 1/297. There were dissenting voices in the Congress; Hinks objected on the grounds that Hayford's determination was based, not on European degrees measurements, but on observations and measurements made entirely within the United States and between latitudes 25° and 50° N. The objections were overruled, however, and Hayford's figure was adopted as the international standard. The establishment of a standard was one thing and the application of it to actual surveys was another. Today there are no fewer than seven different values for the spheroid in use in various parts of the world, no one of which is Hayford's.[27]

While geodesy and geophysics pursued the geoid, making pendulum observations, computing polar co-ordinates, determining the intensity of gravity and otherwise contributing scientific data relevant to the mapping of the world.

geographers everywhere were busying themselves with some of the less abstract but equally important issues yet to be settled. In 1871, almost before the smoke of the Franco-Prussian War had cleared, an International Congress assembled at Antwerp to discuss the unsolved problems relating to geography, cosmography and commerce. Because of the recent unpleasantness, the atmosphere was tense; French delegates felt called upon to protest their natural love of peace, and gestures of amity between the various delegates from nineteen widespread countries were tentative if not furtive. Nevertheless the gestures were made and the international ice was broken. All nations had been invited to exhibit maps and charts, both historical and up-to-date, and several responded. Tribute was paid to the memory and accomplishments of Abraham Ortelius and Gerard Mercator and plans were made to meet again in Paris.[28]

No great issues were solved at the first International Geographical Congress, but many questions were posed and discussed. How should cosmography and geography be taught, and what should be the scope of these subjects? What was the best projection to use in compiling general maps and atlases of the world? Could a uniform orthography be established for use on maps and in geographical treatises? Would it not be feasible to adopt a prime meridian for the entire world? Was there an ice-free ocean at the North Pole? Should the decimal system, now generally adopted by the scientific world, be extended to the division of the quarter circle from whence it was derived, and would such a division be wise in view of the sexigesimal division of the day into hours and minutes? How could the Congress promote the establishment of a central organization for the compilation and publication of geographical studies? [29]

The second International Geographical Congress met at Paris in 1875, and a third meeting took place at Venice in 1881. By that time many of the problems discussed at the first two meetings had crystallized and the world at large began to take an active interest in the proceedings. Twenty-nine countries, counting India and the British colonies as two, were represented. Among the delegates was a high percentage of officials and military engineers actively engaged in topographic surveying, either at home or in the outposts of civilization. The exhibits of maps and charts were lavish, and the discussion of common problems was less restrained than in the first two meetings. A comparative criticism of the maps submitted by various nations was the order of the day, and an international jury awarded prizes for the best cartographic work submitted in various categories.[30]

High on the agenda of the Third International Geographical Congress was the establishment of a universal prime meridian and a uniform standard of time. It was voted that within a year an international commission be appointed to consider an initial meridian, not only for longitude but for hours and dates as well. Hitherto all such standards had been arbitrarily selected by the various nations of the world to suit their own convenience, and were "at variance, often by many minutes, with true local time" at all such places. Under the circumstances, scientific map making on an international basis was practically impossible. A resolution was passed by the Congress that, "Whereas it is practicable, by referring the time of all places on the globe to a limited number of meridians suitably chosen, to create a time system for the world so nearly uniform that the minute and the second shall be everywhere the same, and the time of places widely differing in longitude shall differ only by entire hours — a system of great simplicity, and likely to be conducive to the convenience of all mankind . . ." It was thereupon resolved "that this Congress approves and recommends to the favorable consideration of the Governments of all nations, as well as to all scientific associations, chambers of commerce, boards of trade, and telegraphic and transportation companies, a time system of the world . . ." [31]

The proposed time system called for the establishment of twenty-four standard meridians, distant from each other fifteen degrees of longitude or one hour of time, to which the local time (clock time) at all places on the earth should be referred. The prime meridian for the system was to be "the meridian situated in longitude one hundred and eighty degrees, or twelve hours distant from the meridian of Greenwich, which prime meridian passes near Behrings Straits and lies almost wholly on the ocean." This meridian was also to be used to mark the change of date as well as time, "The diurnal change of count in the monthly calendar [the civil day] to begin when it is midnight on this prime meridian, and the same change to take place for the several meridians successively, until the circuit of the globe has been completed from east to west." The hour of the day at any place, such as twelve o'clock noon, was to be reckoned at the moment the mean sun passed the nearest standard meridian, "the minute and second to be the same at all times and for all places throughout the day." The hours of the day were to be numbered without interruption from one to twenty-four, and the old division of the day into halves of twelve hours each was to be abandoned. Time zones would be established (standard hour meridians), fifteen degrees apart, these to be designated by letters of the English alphabet, omitting J and V. The zero meridian was to be lettered Z, and the balance lettered from east to west, beginning with A. [32]

The proposals and resolutions made during the meetings of the Third International Geographical Congress were subsequently altered in various respects. After further discussion it was found that a majority of those concerned with time reforms favored a prime meridian passing through the center of the transit instrument of the Greenwich Observatory rather than one near the Behring Straits a half a world away. Likewise, the lettering of time meridians and zones was ultimately voted down. In fact there were enough controversial issues in connection with time reform to warrant an international meeting for the sole purpose of settling differences of opinion and the fundamental issues relative to international time recording. In this category was a plan submitted by one of the French delegates for a metric division of both time and arc as well as the calendar, a drastic step that was worthy of debate but one that many of the delegates felt was "as yet perhaps somewhat premature." [33]

No country in the world was more vitally interested in time reform than the United States. In 1880, thanks to a rapidly expanding system of railroads from coast to coast, timekeeping had become a serious problem. The boundary between Canada and the United States was 3987 miles long, a span of more than 57 degrees of longitude. In the absence of a national or international standard, it was customary for each railroad to keep its own time and establish its own time zones across the continent. Many a railroad station was graced with three or four clocks, each set according to a different zone, and in some cases, when more than one road used the same terminal, it was not uncommon to find clocks set according to the dictates of three or more corporations as well as the location of the sun at different cities. Rapid transportation and the development of telegraphic communication brought out the necessity for a uniform system of timekeeping on a continental, if not a world basis.

Plans for an International Meridian Conference to be held in Washington were authorized by an act of Congress passed on August 3, 1882. All nations were

Adoption of the metric system inspired the invention of a new kind of clock. The inventor of the above watches was a proponent of the decimal division of time and the calendar.

invited to appoint delegates to fix upon a universal prime meridian "as a common zero of longitude and standard of time reckoning throughout the globe." Meanwhile the railroads took independent action. A general "Time Convention of Railway Superintendents and Managers" met at St. Louis, Missouri, April 11, 1883. In a series of resolutions, the delegates approved in principle a suggestion made in 1869 by Professor Charles David of Saratoga, New York, that a national time standard be established, based on one hour differences. In formulating their resolutions, they also took into consideration a series of resolutions adopted in 1875 by the American Meteorological Society, as well as suggestions made by the American Metrological Society, the American Society of Civil Engineers, the Royal Society of Canada and various other learned societies. The resolution read as follows:[34]

> *Resolved*, That this convention recommends the adoption of the following as the future standards for the use of the railway lines of the country:
>
> 1st. That all roads now using Boston, New York, Philadelphia, Baltimore, Toronto, Hamilton, or Washington time as standard, based upon meridians east of those points or adjacent thereto, shall be governed by the 75th Meridian or Eastern time (4 minutes slower than New York time).
>
> 2nd. That all roads now using Columbus, Savannah, Atlanta, Cincinnati, Louisville, Indianapolis, Chicago, Jefferson City, Saint Paul, or Kansas City time, or standards based upon meridians adjacent thereto, shall be run by the 90th Meridian time, to be called Central Time (one hour slower than Eastern Time and nine minutes slower than Chicago Time).
>
> 3rd. That west of the above-named sections the roads shall be run by the 105th and 120th meridian times, respectively two and three hours slower than Eastern Time.

Time referred to the 105th meridian and adopted for use between it and the 120th meridian was designated as Mountain Standard Time and time referred to the 120th meridian for use between it and the coast was designated as Pacific Standard Time. The same resolutions were adopted at the General Time Convention held at New York City, April 18, 1883, and the system was approved for adoption by the Association of American Railroad Superintendents, May 28, 1883. In October of that year roads aggregating 78,158 miles had agreed to the adoption of these standards. The system went into general effect November 18, 1883.

Twenty-five countries responded to the presidential invitation to attend the first International Meridian Conference, which opened in Washington, D. C. October 22, 1884. After long and careful deliberation the following resolutions were passed with very few dissenting votes:

> Resolved:
>
> I. That it is the opinion of this Congress that it is desirable to adopt a single prime meridian for all nations, in place of the multiplicity of initial meridians which now exist.
>
> II. That the Conference proposes to the Governments here represented the adoption of the meridian passing through the center of the transit instrument at the Observatory of Greenwich as the initial meridian for longitude.
>
> III. That from this meridian longitude shall be counted in two directions up to 180 degrees, east longitude being plus and west longitude minus.
>
> IV. That the Conference proposes the adoption of a universal day for all purposes for which it may be found convenient, and which shall not interfere with the use of local or other standard time when desirable.
>
> V. That this universal day is to be a mean solar day; is to begin for all the world at the moment of mean midnight of the initial meridian, coinciding with the beginning of the civil day and date of that meridian; and is to be counted from zero up to twenty-four hours.

VI. That the Conference expresses the hope that as soon as may be practicable the astronomical and nautical days will be arranged everywhere to begin at mean midnight.

VII. That the Conference expresses the hope that the technical studies designed to regulate and extend the application of the decimal system to the division of angular space and of time shall be resumed, so as to permit the extension of this application to all cases in which it presents real advantages.[35]

The plan for establishing twenty-four world time zones of 15° each was ultimately accepted by almost every nation except Holland. Beginning with the meridian of Greenwich (zero longitude) as the center of the first zone, the world was divided into twenty-four time belts, each one hour or 15° apart, and numbered east and west of Greenwich from one to twelve. Thus Greenwich time would be uniformly used within a belt 7½ degrees of longitude east and west of the prime meridian, while the 12th zone, centered on the 180th meridian, would include the area 7½ degrees on either side of it, and have a time difference of twelve whole hours. For the sake of convenience, certain exceptions have since been made in laying down the meridian boundaries of the time zones. Several of them have been bent one way or another so as to include an island group or to follow a country's north-south boundary line. For example, the eastern boundary of Zone 2 (Long. 142° 30′ W.) is bent eastward 7½ degrees from the equator southward to the Tropic of Capricorn, or to the western boundary of Zone 3, in order to include the Marquesas Islands, the Low (Tuamotu) Archipelago and Pitcairn Island. It is brought back again in a straight horizontal line just below Pitcairn Island, about Lat. 26° S. Following this same line northward, it is again bent away from the meridian about 2½° eastward at Lat. 59° 30′ so as to follow the eastern boundary of Alaska (Long. 141° W.), and returns to its original position just above the 70th parallel. The tendency is for the time zones to follow international boundary lines, especially when a country has long been using the time indicated by an adjacent zone. In other words, the meridians marking the boundaries of the various time zones have yielded to the custom of the country whenever possible, thereby promoting harmony and a more general acceptance of international "legal" clock time.[36]

According to the original plan for the establishment of standard time throughout the world, the time adopted for each zone would be uniform throughout the zone and would vary from the clock time kept in the two adjacent zones by one whole hour. This rule has been modified in numerous localities to fit the needs or demands of a country. Thus Central Australia has a time zone which keeps time that is 9 hours 30 minutes fast on Greenwich mean time instead of 9 hours or 10 hours, and the Hawaiian Islands keep clock time which is 10 hours 30 minutes slow on Greenwich. In the same way, certain small islands and island groups are so isolated that they have chosen to keep clock time which corresponds to their longitude east or west of Greenwich. Thus, the island of South Georgia, which straddles the zonal boundary marked by Long. 37° 30′ (2 hours slow on Greenwich), keeps time which is 2 hours 7 minutes slow on Greenwich Civil Time.

Chatham Island, which is normally 12 hours fast on Greenwich, keeps time which is 12 hours 15 minutes fast. In the light of history, it is logical to suppose that other modifications will be made from time to time as governments rise and fall and world conditions change. It is also a foregone conclusion that no system of time keeping will ever be devised that will seem satisfactory to all factions of the human race.[37]

Other departures have been made from the plan for a universal standard time. Both Canada and the United States use four time zones, Eastern, Central, Mountain, and Pacific, which zones are respectively 5, 6, 7, and 8 hours slow on Greenwich. European countries, with the exception of Holland, are divided into three time zones keeping (1) Greenwich time, (2) Mid-European time (1 hour fast), (3) Eastern European time (2 hours fast). However, as of today, the terms Greenwich Civil Time (G.C.T.), Weltzeit (W.Z.) and Universal Time (U.T.) all refer to time measured from Greenwich beginning at mean midnight, and hours numbered from one to twenty-four. For the average citizen, however, time is still nothing more than what the clock says, and for him that is enough. In general, the time kept by the town hall clock has been so regulated by his government that even without benefit of sextant or telescope the sun always seems to be high overhead at noon and is certainly totally absent at midnight.

After centuries of groping, of trial and error, the stage was finally set for the unveiling of an accurate picture of the world. All that remained was to produce it. The shape and size of the earth were pretty well established; topographic surveying and geodetic methods had reached a high state of accuracy; international science had established a uniform "natural" system of weights and measures; a standard system of keeping time and measuring longitude had been established. The ultimate goal of cartography, a standard map of the world, was just around the corner.

The science of cartography reached maturity about 1890, when, for the first time in history, mankind was mentally prepared and scientifically equipped to think and act in terms of global cartography. The event took place at Berne, Switzerland, in 1891, when a young man named Albrecht Penck, professor of geography at the University of Vienna, stepped up to the platform and read to the Fifth International Geographical Congress a plan for an International Map of the World to be executed on a scale of 1:1,000,000 (1/M). Fortunately for the author, the time and the audience were right. The delegates listened and were interested. The desirability of such a map was apparent to most of those present, and doubtless several of them wondered why they had not thought of it before. As it was originally presented, Penck's proposal resolved itself into three general cartographic problems: (1) the division of the surface of the earth into a certain number of sheets, all drawn on the same scale and preferably on the same projection, a projection such that when all the sheets were put together they would completely cover a sphere one million times smaller than our globe; (2) reduction of the distortion suffered by every spherical surface projected or developed on a plane to the barest possible minimum, this to be accomplished by the size of the proposed scale; (3) calculations of a technical nature in connection with the actual construction of the map, and estimates of the probable cost of organizing and printing the map as well as the probable remuneration from the publication.[38]

Inevitably there were objections to the scheme, and a series of heated discussions followed. Some said flatly that the scheme was impossible; others said the cost would be prohibitive; still others maintained that the technical difficulties connected with standardization were insurmountable. Action was postponed until the next international meeting, scheduled to be held at London in 1895. Meanwhile the International Geographical Congress passed a series of resolutions favoring the plan, and placed the matter in the hands of a committee representing ten different countries, with instructions to report at the next meeting. Neither the resolutions nor the committee made much headway. The resolutions passed by the delegates, independent scientists whose connections with their respective governments were only incidental, lacked official sanction and no one was bound by them. The committee was too large (twenty members) to function effectively, and its members were so widely scattered across the globe that little could be accomplished. Eventually three of Switzerland's leading scientists were chosen by the committee to act as a subcommittee and advise the International Congress what steps were necessary to launch the International Map. Under the leadership of Professor Eduard Brückner, a detailed report was drawn up outlining the principal items on which agreement was necessary before further progress could be made, and presenting clearly the problems that would immediately arise because of the differences in cartographic technique and usage.[39]

Brückner's report was read and discussed at the Sixth International Geographical Congress. More resolutions were passed and the technical problems were gone over in minute detail both at home and abroad. But instead of clarifying issues and removing obstacles, the situation seemed to go from bad to worse. Moreover, international politics began to cloud the issue. It was inevitable; for if topographical surveys had become the exclusive responsibility of governments because of excessive costs and legal complications, mapping on a world-wide scale would certainly require the full backing of the governments concerned and necessitate delicate diplomatic negotiations. A case in point was the selection of a prime meridian for the International Map. As one of the French commissioners put it, the choice of a prime meridian was one of the most important, one of the most delicate, if not one of the most irritating points to be settled. Numerous and sundry meridians of departure were suggested, most of which were offered without reason except political jealousy, a perverted streak of patriotism or intellectual jaundice. The problem was to find a neutral prime meridian, and the only one available was the ocean. However, the high seas left something to be desired: namely, a fixed observatory from which observations and measurements could be made. A perfect impasse resulted when French delegates insisted on using the meridian of Paris and English geographers, to emphasize the virtues of the meridian of Greenwich, countered by stoutly refusing to accept the metric system as the official system of measurements on the proposed map. This sort of thing was repeated many times before all of the countries involved came to terms. Still there was no official sanction of the project from any quarter.

In 1904 Professor Penck went to Washington, along with 798 members and associate members of the Eighth International Geographical Congress. For the third time he addressed the delegates on the subject of an International Map of the World. The situation had taken a turn for the better and Penck now had something concrete to offer in evidence, namely three trial maps compiled essentially according to the standards proposed for the International Map, and covering nearly 10,000,000 square miles. France had led the way by producing a series of map sheets covering trouble spots in the Antilles, Persia and China, compiled under the direction of the General Staff on a uniform scale of 1:1,000,000, each sheet limited by parallels and meridians rather than political boundaries. The sheets were so drawn that they could be incorporated without important revision into a general map of the world on the same scale. Thirty-one sheets had been produced, 20 more were in progress and 6 more were in the planning stage.[40]

The second series exhibited by Penck was the work of the cartographic division of the Prussian General Staff and comprised a part of Eastern China. Twenty-two sheets had been planned on a scale of 1:1,000,000, the sheets limited by parallels and meridians. Of these, 2 were now ready for inspection; and as Penck demonstrated, they were so drawn that they too could readily become a part of an International Map. The third series, planned by the Intelligence Division of Britain's War Office, was to be a large map of Africa on 132 sheets, projected on the same scale and drawn according to the proposed specifications for the International Map. Eighteen sheets had already been published. These three great mapping projects would ultimately cover a large part of the surface of the earth, "a whole continent, Africa, and very large part of another, Asia, and parts of America." The sheets already published showed none of the terrible distortion that some of the delegates had anticipated when the modified conic projection had been selected by vote of the Congress. In fact, here was a concrete demonstration that an International Map of the World was feasible, expert opinions to the contrary. To be sure, there were variations in execution that would have to be reconciled, but they were by no means insurmountable. France had used Paris as a prime meridian of longitude; Germany had taken the meridian of Long. 4° E., and England had used the meridian of Greenwich. However, in most details the three countries had conformed to the standards tentatively accepted by the Congress, limiting each sheet to an area bounded by 4° of latitude and 6° of longitude; coloring the water blue, shading the mountains brown or gray, and so on.

In summarizing the progress already made towards the realization of an International Map, Penck made a special plea to the countries of the Western Hemisphere, especially the United States, for a series of maps of the New World on a scale of 1:1,000,000, the minimum required for practical purposes, pointing out the glaring need of map material in this part of the world. Tactfully he called attention to the splendid work already done by the Coast Survey (United States Coast and Geodetic Survey) and the Geological Survey, but at the same time he said, "there is such a want of general maps that a visitor to the United States is much at a loss what map to take as a companion.

"I studied this question seriously," he continued, "when fitting myself out for the excursion of the congress, and finally I found that the best general maps of the United States are made in Germany, and I chose the maps of the new Stieler Atlas as companions . . . they contain as much as the scale can afford. This is 1:3,700,000. But this scale is far from being sufficient for containing such details as a traveler wishes to know [let alone a citizen of the country], and it is far too little to give the impression of the grandeur of the country." [41]

At the Ninth International Geographical Congress held at Geneva, July, 1908, the American delegate, Doctor David T. Day, presented several resolutions drawn up in advance by Henry Gannet of the U. S. Geological Survey. The substance of these resolutions was a recommendation that the Congress make a serious effort to come to an agreement on the essential details of the plan for an International Map, that these details be submitted to the various nations with a request for an international conference empowered to act upon them. "The resolutions were passed, a committee was appointed, and the details of a plan were worked out and adopted." Thereupon the British government issued invitations to Austria-Hungary, France, Germany, Italy, Japan, Russia, Spain and the United States to send delegates to an international conference in November, 1909, with power to act upon details for a standard international map of the world. All countries responded, with the exception of Japan, and twenty-two delegates assembled at the British Foreign Office for a series of discussions. One by one the salient points in the resolutions passed by the International Congress were debated in English, French or German, as the spirit moved. But this time the delegates were determined to reach an agreement, and so they did, on every important point. The resolutions were approved unanimously and signed by the delegates of the eight powers represented. Copies were sent through the usual diplomatic channels to all governments which had not been represented, and their official replies were in almost every case favorable. A second International Conference on the International Map was held in Paris, December, 1913. Thirty-five countries were represented. In eight days of intensive work four sub-committees succeeded in drawing up a complete guide to the conventional signs and colors to be used on the map as well as all standards previously adopted at the London conference. This information, in the three official languages decided upon — French, German, and English — was published in the following year in a pamphlet entitled *Carte du Monde au Millionième, Comptes Rendus des Séances de la Deuxième Conférence International.* Paris, Service Géographique de l'Année, 1914. Accompanying this publication was a separate cover containing several additional documents relating to the map, including a conventional sign sheet and a conventional layer system. The printing of this document was finished successfully, but before copies could be distributed World War I had begun.[42]

The International Map, better known as the 1/M Map (1 inch = 15.78 miles) was designed to be the ultimate in accuracy and practicality, shorn of embellish-

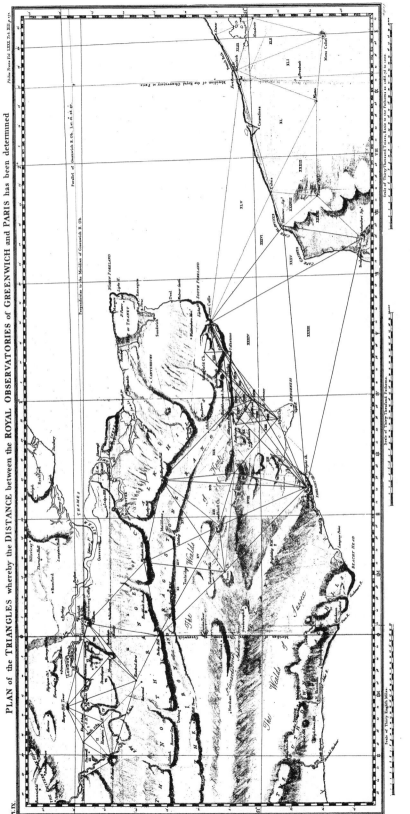

Pl. IX.

PLAN of the TRIANGLES whereby the DISTANCE between the ROYAL OBSERVATORIES of GREENWICH and PARIS has been determined

The English Channel, showing the chain of great triangles surveyed under the direction of General William Roy between the meridians of Greenwich and Paris.

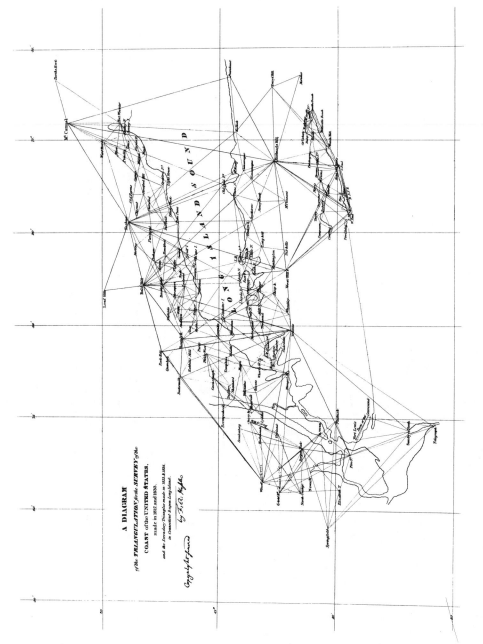

The first mapping operation of the United States Coast Survey (now the U. S. Coast and Geodetic Survey) was made in the vicinity of Long Island Sound under the direction of Ferdinand Rudolph Hassler, first Superintendent of the Survey.

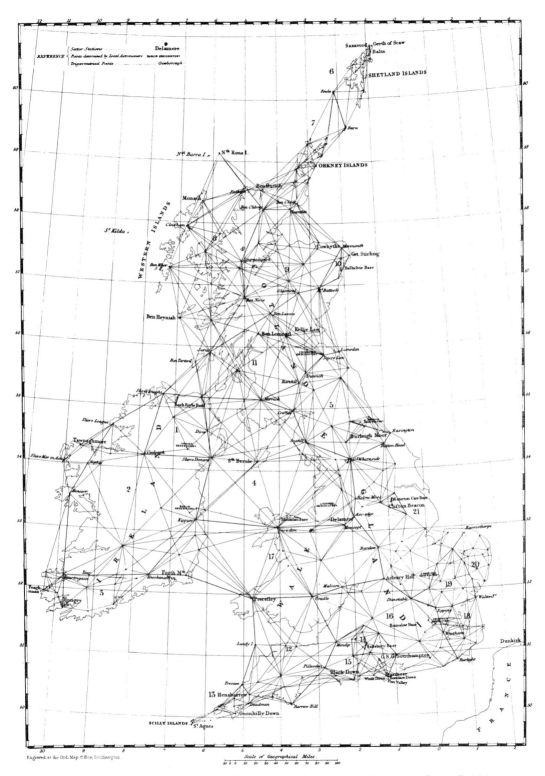

Results of Britain's Ordnance Survey are shown on this map of the British Islands published in 1858.

Only the shaded areas of Europe and Asia were mapped topographically in 1885.

ment and nonsense. It was to be a map that could be "read" by any contributing nation or in any nation possessing the key to its system. It was to be a basic map in every sense of the word, a topographic picture on which any amount of specialized information, geographical, geological, political or economic, could be superimposed merely by overprinting. The base map itself would show such elementary features as streams and larger water bodies, towns and cities, railroads and highways, political boundaries and topography. By arbitration, the fundamental objections raised by France and England had been settled; the prime meridian of the $1/M$ map was to be the center of the transit instrument at Greenwich Observatory and the metric system was to be the official system of measure for expressing both distances and altitudes above sea level, with the proviso that when expressing distances, the local units of measure (English feet or Russian versts) might also be included on the map by the country responsible for mapping the area. Latitudes were to be measured, and the sheets of the map numbered, from the equator. Political boundaries were to be ignored. Each sheet was to cover an area 4 degrees in latitude by 6 degrees in longitude; however, north of Lat. 60° N. and south of Lat. 60° S. it would be permissible to join two or more adjoining sheets of the same zone, so that the combined sheet would cover 12, 18, or more degrees of longitude. Each sheet was to bear the French heading CARTE INTERNATIONALE DU MONDE AU 1 000 000°, and under it a translation of the heading in the language of the country publishing the sheet.[43]

In regard to the projection, the following resolutions were passed:

(a) It is necessary that the projection should fulfil the following conditions:

(i) The meridians should be straight lines;
(ii) The parallels should be arcs of circles of which the centres should lie on the prolongation of the central meridian (London, 1909).

(b) In view of the fact that on the scale proposed several suitable projections differ but little from each other, and that the contraction and expansion of the paper on which the map is printed effect all lengths on the map, and prevent it from being in fact exactly either orthomorphic or equivalent, it is not necessary to lay great stress upon the selection of a projection which has the best properties as to conformity or equivalence. It is therefore agreed to select a projection which can be easily constructed, and permits every sheet to fit exactly together with the four sheets adjoining its four sides.

A modified polyconic projection, with the meridians as straight lines, satisfies these two conditions (London, 1909).

The map was to be a hypsometric map, that is, the successive altitudes would be indicated by a system of color tints; consequently a color chart was necessary for every contributing nation. There was a possibility, however, that editions of the map might be published without color tints. The rules for delineating contours (principal and auxiliary) were carefully stated. "There is perhaps nothing which more strikingly distinguishes . . . maps of one nationality from another, than the manner in which valleys, hills and mountains are represented, whether it be by drawing the shapes of mountains, as in Chinese maps, or by covering the paper with dashes, sometimes called hachures, which show the way the water runs, or by horizontal lines that delineate the contours of the slopes, or by shading with high light and shadow, as if the map were a relief model." Realizing this fact, a serious attempt was made at the Paris conference to harmonize the various methods in current use, but no system of showing relief was to be used if the information was not sufficient to justify it. Underwater features were to be shown by the same system of contour intervals as land features, while shading was decided upon to bring out minor features that could not be adequately represented by contours.

Adequate rules were provided for the spelling and transliteration of names on the 1/M map. The Latin alphabet was to be used exclusively, and each sheet of the map was to have an explanatory table showing the Latin characters which best represented, in the three official languages of the map, the phonetic value of the letters used on the sheet.[44] This was not the easiest policy to define, nor was it easy for the various countries to interpret. Equally difficult to decide upon was the spelling of place names, which was to be entirely in Latin characters. The spelling would be that used on the official maps of the country or countries represented on the sheet. Florence would be spelled *Firenze*, Flushing would be *Vlissingen*, Vienna, *Wien*, and so on. Even though there would be no Arabic, Greek, Persian, Russian or Turkish script on the map, the transliteration of all such languages presented many a knotty problem. There are many consonants in Eastern alphabets that have no precise equivalents in the Roman alphabet; and, too, there is a general absence of vowels in the written language, making it often impossible to decide upon the probable native form from a European rendering. In fact, transliteration in many instances was not "a reversible process with the data and characters usually available." Countries having no alphabet, but having a post or customs service in which the Latin alphabet is used, were to adopt the spelling used by those services. Colonies and protectorates were to use the spelling of the governing country.[45]

The sheets of the 1/M map will be arranged in the following way. Sixty sheets will belt the earth at the equator and 22½ sheets will cover the distance from the equator to the pole. The execution of the circular sheet covering the polar regions north of the 88th parallel was delegated to the United States. To represent the entire world according to the plan of the 1/M map 2642 sheets would be required, but since three fourths of the earth's surface is ocean, the 1/M map or atlas, according to early estimates, would never contain more than 1500 sheets, and probably less, even including the oceanic islands. By 1934 the estimated number of sheets had been reduced to 840.

The progress of the International 1/M map is the history of cartography repeated with all its ramifications, a record of man's innate aversion to change, his preoccupation with his own back yard. At the Paris conference in 1913, a Central Bureau was instituted, and by general agreement it was established at the Ordnance Survey Office at Southampton, England. Here the affairs of the International Map were to be handled for all nations. Almost before the Bureau was opened for business World War I broke out. The official booklet containing the Resolutions of the International Map Committee and the rules for compiling and printing the 1/M map was off the press, but had not yet been distributed. Work on the 1/M map itself came to an abrupt halt. Yet the necessity and the objective of such a map were now more than ever apparent.[46]

It is paradoxical that even though a state of perfect peace is necessary, as General Roy pointed out, to produce an accurate topographical survey of a country, "it happens that if a country has not actually been surveyed, or is but little known, a state of war generally produces the first improvements in its geography. . . ."[47] Without doubt World War I stimulated the production of maps on a scale of 1:1,000,000 as well as other scales, but there were battles to be fought, and maps were urgently needed. Conformity to international mapping standards, no matter how desirable it might be, was set aside in favor of the immediate needs of the armed forces. At the outbreak of the war only 8 sheets of the International Map had been published. "For practical purposes, the *Carte Internationale du Monde au Millionième* was so incomplete that it was of very limited use."[48] Every country did the best it could, and Germany and Austria-Hungary did better than most, being far better prepared in advance. Many countries were forced to compile a "provisional" series of maps of the European theater of war, so named in deference to the International Map; some of its principles and standards were followed and others were ignored. Of the many good European maps available in 1914, very few were suitable for military purposes without revision. Maps on large scales embodied so much detail that a photographic reduction was not practical, while maps on smaller scales, even though they were enlarged photographically, had to be filled in with the desired information, a technique not recommended where accuracy is required.

"War and its aftermath," wrote Colonel Close, "had a generally depressing effect upon all international schemes."[49] The 1/M map should be included in this category. The Central Bureau at Southampton was closed in 1914 for the duration, and its reorganization followed the third International Conference in Paris in 1919. In December of that year a circular letter was dispatched to all nations concerned, asking them to furnish the Central Bureau with a progress report on what sheets, if any, had been prepared or published during the war. Communication between nations was still badly disrupted and apparently several letters failed to reach their destination. A second letter was tried in October, 1920, and the last reply was received by the Central Bureau in March, 1921.[50]

Eight years later the Annual Report of the Central Bureau, noting progress on the 1/M map to the end of 1929, indicated that only 81 sheets had been published in conformity with the resolutions and standards established at the Paris conference. Of these 33 were of Europe, 33 of Asia, 5 of Africa, 5 of North America, 3 of South America, 2 of Australia. By 1931 there were 4 more sheets of Europe, 2 of Africa, 8 of North America and 2 of Australia, 16 sheets added in two years. There was an increasing tendency to issue "provisional" and irregular sheets, and sheets that covered very little land. "Thus eight of the European sheets together do not make more than a half a sheet of land, the four sheets published by the United States amount to perhaps 1½; and the two Australian sheets first published did not make together an eighth of a sheet." [51]

Much of the prewar enthusiasm was lacking; governments failed to support the 1/M map and hundreds of sheets have since been credited to "Private Societies, etc." These include 25 sheets of the Near East compiled during World War I by the Royal Geographical Society and 49 sheets of the Provisional Series of Europe, also compiled by the Royal Geographical Society and reproduced by the Ordnance Survey. Forty sheets of the "Croquis du Sahara" were produced by the Service Géographique de l'Année in France. Fifty sheets of Brazil were published by the Club de Eugenaria do Rio de Janeiro to celebrate the centenary of the country. The American Geographical Society has been responsible for a complete coverage of Latin America and the West Indies, "remarkable examples of private enterprise supplanting official effort."

By 1921 most of the 35 governments that had taken part in the Paris conference of 1913 resumed work on their part of the 1/M map and the official Resolutions, reprinted in French and English, were incorporated in the Annual Report of the International Congress of that year. The latest progress report on The Map was issued in 1938. At that time Europe, excluding the U.S.S.R., with the exception of the Malta sheet (I.33) had been published. However "Provisional Editions" only, sheets which failed to conform to standard, were available for Albania, Austria, Bulgaria, Denmark, Estonia, Germany, Greece, Hungary, Irish Free State, Italy, Rumania and Yugoslavia. The only published sheets of the U.S.S.R. were unlayered Provisional Editions. These covered most of Russia in Europe and were prepared during World War I by the Geographical Section of the British General Staff. "In many cases these sheets were actually compiled and drawn at the Royal Geographical Society. They are now obsolescent."

India, Siam, French Indo-China and Japan were "nearly" covered; Iran and Iraq were nearly covered, but the sheets were Provisionals, and did not conform in every respect. Saudi Arabia was about half covered, but some of the sheets were Provisionals. Burma, the Dutch East Indies and the Malay States were covered by Permanent Editions. Egypt was the only country in Africa fully covered by Permanent sheets; other regions were partly covered, mostly by Provisionals. The British West African colonies were covered by the series "Croquis du Sahara." The southeastern block of Australia (13 sheets) was completed and New Zealand had published 3 sheets. [52]

The Western Hemisphere was not well represented on the 1/M map in 1938. Canada had published 3 sheets and the United States had produced only 4. In South America, the Argentine and Brazil were the only countries that had compiled sheets of their own territories. Central and South America had been nearly covered by the 1:1,000,000 map compiled under the direction of the American Geographical Society. Although it was an "unofficial" map in the strictest sense, many if not all of the sheets had been made so as to conform with the Resolutions. It would seem that the Central Bureau at Southampton was reluctant to recognize this invaluable contribution, completed in 1945, for in the Report made by Captain Sanceau he said, "it is doubtful whether the publishers have obtained their material for the territory of any given country from that country or obtained the approval of that country to their compilation for its territory. In the circumstances these sheets are listed as Provisional Editions and fill a very considerable gap." [53]

The history of the International 1/M map represents an unfinished attempt to map the world in such a way that all nations could read it and interpret it correctly. Perhaps this objective is beyond the realm of practicality, human nature being what it is, an ideal that hardly comes within the province of the workaday world. Let us consider it a side issue and assume that despite the fact that we are not yet in possession of a standard map of the entire world there are nevertheless enough good maps to go around without worrying about minor technicalities; that to all intents and purposes the world has been well mapped. Let us then examine the evidence, limiting ourselves to the cartographic record of the Allied nations from 1937 to 1947.

As of 1937, there were six primary Departments of the United States Government engaged in the publication of maps and charts, no one of which was financed or equipped to furnish the Army and Navy with adequate maps and charts to fight a war on foreign soil, or within the territorial limits of the United States, for that matter. Within the War Department, the Corps of Engineers was the unit authorized and equipped, theoretically, to compile military maps for the General Staff. Actually this vital function was in the hands of the Engineer Reproduction Plant, a unit of the Corps derived from three small agencies of earlier years: the Central Map Reproduction Plant, the Central Photographic Laboratory and the Engineer School Press. Staffed by able cartographic engineers in search of a budget, the ERP was often obliged to do odd jobs entirely unrelated to cartography, and to prepare maps of a nonmilitary nature for other departments. Yet the ERP was the agency which was to bear the map making load in World War II, the agency from which the Army Map Service evolved. The archives of the War Department, sources of cartographic data, consisted of a collection of maps housed in the library of the War College and the maps and field notes of long-forgotten engineers stored in the basement of the Munitions Building. The poverty of this bulwark of national defense, the Corps of Engineers, is unbelievable. In 1938, sensing that trouble was ahead, its Engineer Reproduction Plant compiled a Strategic Map of the United States on a scale of 1:500,000 and printed it on 87 sheets. This urgent preliminary to a national war effort was made possible, not by a War Department appropriation, but by WPA funds and WPA personnel. [54]

The miracle of the Army Map Service, how it grew from an almost defunct branch of the War Department to the largest and one of the most efficient mapmaking agencies in the world, is another story. "Within its walls hummed an industrious refrain, challenging the war's most pathetic condemnation — 'Too little and too late.'" The challenge was there, but not the answer to it. The fundamental data in many instances were not to be had by gift, theft or purchase. A map is no better than the sources from which it is compiled, and too often the sources were not to be had, at least so far as the Allied nations were concerned. No amount of synthesis, scientific or artistic, no amount of high-speed printing on fine paper could remedy the fundamental lack, the basic objective of cartography — an accurate survey of the ground. Without base maps to work from the Army Map Service might just as well have started with a dream or an impressionistic painting and worked out the details by differential calculus. The first rude jolt suffered by the United States and her allies came when it was discovered that, alas, the world had not been mapped after all.

The second blow came when the armed forces and their geographical aides discovered that much of the "antiquated" material relegated to such repositories as the Library of Congress was a potent source of information, that in the absence of anything better, a map published in 1880 or even 1860 was to be treated with respect. Historical cartography suddenly became current and highly desirable. Every scrap of information was carefully scrutinized before it was discarded, and every map. The libraries of the country, both public and private, were scoured in a frantic search for cartographic data. The War College library was found to be pathetically inadequate. Sea captains, missionaries, businessmen and tourists who had traveled abroad were interviewed by the General Staff. Their diaries, journals, even their snapshots were carefully studied. "There were many regions for which no source material was available. A co-operative program was arranged with the Army Air Forces for the procurement of aerial photography to fill these gaps. Countless sorties were flown over both enemy and friendly territories for reconnaissance and photographic purposes. In fact, the primary purpose of the early bomber raids of the war was to obtain photography suitable for map-making." [55]

Speed was the dominant theme in the colossal mapping program launched by the Army Map Service. Everything depended on it. The location and construction of war plants, the location and distribution of strategic materials, the mobilization and movement of troops, all depended on maps that had not yet been compiled. The situation with regard to the European battlefield was even worse. One by one the countries whose map collections could have shown the way were lost to the Axis so that by the time the United States entered the war the archives of Britain and the United States were the principal sources of cartographic information. Thanks to perfect co-operation between the British and American Intelligence officers a joint mapping program was laid out, care being taken to avoid duplication of effort. Each country assumed responsibility for mapping certain areas of the world and source material was flown back and forth in an endless stream. Miraculously the job was done and the war was won, but no chapter in the history of World War II better illustrates the provincial attitude of the United States, the utter indifference towards the outside world, quite so graphically as the cartographic record of the past ten years.

"Accurate surveys of a country are universally admitted to be works of great public utility, as affording the surest foundation for almost every kind of internal improvement in time of peace, and the best means of forming judicious plans of defence against the invasions of an enemy in time of war, in which last circumstances their importance usually becomes the most apparent." [56] Thus spoke General William Roy in 1785, and surely every statesman and military leader today would respond with a loud "Amen." The time has come when the United States must take a careful inventory of her natural resources, a closer look at her needs in the field of internal improvement. The wealthiest nation on the face of nature must have a thorough understanding of her organic structure, and in order to do this she must have maps of every description second to none. She owes it to herself. A step in the right direction would be to combine all government mapping agencies into one, and place them under the direction of the newly created Department of National Defense, thus avoiding costly duplication of effort and conflicting spheres of influence and activity.

As for the world at large, it is impossible to know a country well, to understand its social, economic and political problems, without adequate maps of the area. We cannot hope to negotiate a world peace without a thorough knowledge of every part of the world, without world maps, complete and on as many scales as are necessary to give us a thorough understanding of what we are talking about. Maps are synonymous with strategy and strategy wins wars. Strategy also wins peace if not prosperity. But until such time as man can, without restriction or fear, sail up to his neighbor's shore, travel across or fly over his dominion, the map of the world must wait and cartography go impeded.

Notes

INTRODUCTION

1. Hooke wrote the Preface for Robert Knox: *An historical relation of Ceylon* . . . London, 1681. Reprinted Glasgow, 1911.
2. G. V. Schiaparelli: *I precursori di Copernico nell' antichità*, Pubbl. del R. Osservatorio di Brera, No. iii (1873); and *Le sfere omocentriche di Eudosso, di Callippo e di Aristotele*, Pubbl. del R. Osservatorio di Brera, No. ix (1873). The title of his later paper is *Origine del sistema planetario eliocentrico presso i Greci* (n.p., 1898).
3. *Aristarchus of Samos the ancient Copernicus. A history of Greek astronomy to Aristarchus* . . . by Sir Thomas Heath. Oxford, The Clarendon Press, 1913.
4. Many of the ideas on this subject originated in a remarkable paper by Johann Georg Kohl entitled "Substance of a lecture delivered at the Smithsonian Institution on a collection of the charts and maps of America." (In the *Smithsonian Institution Annual Report*, 1856. Washington, 1857, pp. 93–146.) This discourse is by far the most lucid and thought-provoking contribution to the subject of map economy and historical cartography, a classic of its kind. Further remarks on the subject have been made by Lloyd A. Brown in *Notes on the care and cataloguing of old maps*, Windham, 1941; also in a paper by the same author, "Special Reference Problems in Map Collections," in *The reference function of the library*, edited by Pierce Butler (Chicago, University of Chicago, 1943, pp. 144–62).
5. The technical term for a parchment or papyrus which has been scraped or washed clean and used again (usually crossways to the original writing) is *palimpsest*. There are also double palimpsests, skins that have been used three times. The discovery and study of palimpsests represents the acme of bibliographic sleuthing, as several extremely important "lost" manuscripts have been discovered beneath the legible writing on early manuscripts; these have been successfully transliterated with the aid of chemicals and infrared light. For example, the fifth-century *Codex Ephraemi* in the Bibliothèque Nationale, containing portions of the Old and New Testaments in Greek, is covered with the writings of Ephraem Syrus in a twelfth-century hand.
6. *The principal navigations, voyages, traffiques & discoveries of the English nation*, by Richard Hakluyt. Reprinted Glasgow, The Hakluyt Society, 1903. Extra Series, Vol. II, p. 180.
7. For further information concerning the functions of the Casa de la Contratación and the establishment of a master chart of the world (Padron Real) under the direction of Juan de Fonseca, the reader should consult Hubert Howe Bancroft's *Central America*, San Francisco, 1882–1887, Vol. I, pp. 270, 280, 282, 297, 330; Henri Harrisse, *The discovery of North America*, London, 1892, pp. 256–68, 329–30, 417, 421, 436, 671, 682–83, 690, 739; Edward Luther Stevenson, "The Geographical Activities of the Casa de la Contratacion," in *Annals of the Association of American Geographers*, 1927, Vol. XVII, No. 1. Other titles are listed in the Bibliography.
8. Woodes Rogers (d. 1732), sea captain and onetime governor of the Bahamas, led an exciting life. Some of his biographers have taken exception to the appella-

tion "pirate" which inevitably was attached to him after his marauding expedition in 1708–1709. He cruised as captain of the *Duke* and commander in chief of the *Duke* and *Duchess*, private men-of-war, fitted out by merchants of Bristol to sail against the Spaniards in the South Sea. William Dampier, who later made a name for himself, sailed as master of the *Duke* and pilot of the expedition. The journal of Woodes Rogers was published under the title *A cruising voyage round the world* (London, 1712). A second edition was published in 1718.

CHAPTER I

1. For further details regarding the ancient city of Alexandria see J. P. Mahaffy, *A history of Egypt under the Ptolemaic dynasty*, London (1914), pp. 8, 58, 59, 64, and map after Botti, p. 262; *The Geography of Strabo* translated by H. L. Jones, London, Loeb Classical Library, 1917, Vols. I, p. 93, VIII, pp. 23 ff.; article "Alexandria, The Ancient City," by David G. Hogarth, *Encyclopaedia Britannica*, 11th edition.

2. The principal authority on Strabo, his lineage, his background and training, is Strabo himself. All references to Strabo in this book were taken from the Loeb Classical Library edition of his *Geography*, London, 1917, translated by Horace Leonard Jones, in eight volumes. Citations refer to volume and page of this translation. For a summary of Strabo's career, culled from his own text, see Vol. I, pp. xi–xxviii.

3. See Mahaffy, *op. cit., passim.*

4. *Ibid.*, pp. 13, 100, 102b for details of this remarkable structure. The principal authority on the subject of the lighthouse is Hermann Thiersch: *Pharos, antike, Islam und Occident; ein beitrag zur architekturgeschichte* . . . Leipzig and Berlin, 1909. The term *pharology* has come to denote the science of lighthouse construction, taking its name from the light on Pharos.

5. Strabo, *op. cit.*, Vol. VIII, p. 25.

6. *Ibid.*, Vol. VIII, p. 31.

7. *Ibid.*, Vol. VIII, p. 35.

8. *Ibid.*, Vol. VIII, p. 65.

9. *Ibid.*, Vol. VIII, p. 41.

10. *Ibid.*, Vol. VIII, pp. 34–35.

11. For further information on the origin, development and destruction of the great Library at Alexandria, see Henry R. Tedder's article under "Ancient Libraries. Alexandria," in *Encyclopaedia Britannica*, 11th edition; Octave Delepierre, *Historical difficulties and contested events*, London, 1868, pp. 32–39; the article "Alejandria" in *Enciclopedia universel illustrada* . . . IV, pp. 383; Octave Delepierre, "Le canard de la bibliothèque d'Alexandrie," in *Miscellanies* of the Philobiblon Society, London, 1860–61, Vol. VI; Strabo, *op. cit.*, Vol. I, p. 259; Mahaffy, *op. cit.*, pp. 61, 62, 85, 242.

12. Strabo, *op. cit.*, Vol. I, pp. 51, 53.

13. *Ibid.*, Vol. I, pp. 25, 27.

14. *Ibid.*, Vol. I, p. 23.

15. See Eduard Meyer, "Aegyptische Chronologie," in Abhandl. der Berlin Akad., 1904, pp. 38 ff.; also James Henry Breasted's *A history of the ancient Egyptians*, London, 1920, p. 35. The bibliography appended to this work is invaluable for a comprehensive study of Egyptian early history.

16. For further information on the subject of ancient astrology see A. Bouché-Leclercq, *L'Astrologie grecque*, Paris, 1899, both text and bibliography; R. C. Thompson, *Reports of the magicians and astrologers of Nineveh and Babylon*,

2 vols., London, 1900; Bouché-Leclercq, *Histoire de la divination dans l'antiquité*, Paris, 1879, Vol. I, pp. 205–57; the article "Astrology" by Morris Jastrow in *Encyclopaedia Britannica*, 11th edition.

17. See E. W. Maunder, "Snake forms in the constellations," *Knowledge & Scientific News*, New Series, Vol. I, no. 9, London, 1904, pp. 227–30.

18. For a historical survey of ancient astronomy see J. S. Bailly, *Histoire de l'astronomie ancienne*, 5 vols., Paris, v.d. 1775–1787; J. B. J. Delambre, *Histoire de l'astronomie ancienne*, Paris, 1817; also his histories covering the astronomy of the Middle Ages, modern astronomy and astronomy of the eighteenth century; R. Grant, *History of physical astronomy*, London, 1852; G. C. Lewis, *An historical survey of the astronomy of the ancients*, London, 1862.

19. A good, brief summary of the progress made by Greek astronomers during this period will be found in the article "Astronomy" by Agnes Mary Clerke in *Encyclopaedia Britannica*, 11th edition.

20. Strabo, *op. cit.*, Vol. I, p. 3.

21. For a discussion of this point see Victor Brérard, *Did Homer Live?* translated by Brian Rhys, London and Toronto [1931]. An extensive but selective bibliography on Homer will be found appended to the article "Homer" by David B. Monro in *Encyclopaedia Britannica*, 11th edition. Strabo quotes Homer frequently throughout the entire text of his *Geography*. *Quotations* used in this text are taken from the English edition of Strabo.

22. Strabo, *op. cit.*, Vol. I, p. 5.

23. For an excellent, detailed summary of Homer's geographical references gleaned from the *Odyssey* and *Iliad*, see E. H. Bunbury's *A history of ancient geography*, 2 vols., London, 1879, Vol. I, pp. 31–84.

24. Strabo, *op. cit.*, Vol. I, p. 17.

25. E. H. Bunbury, *op. cit.*, Vol. I, p. 85.

26. For a detailed description of the ancient city of Miletus see T. Wiegand's "Vorläufige Berichte über die ausgrabungen in Milet," in *Sitzungsberichte* of the Berlin Academy, 1900. Thales is generally considered the founder of physical science among the Greeks. See E. H. Bunbury, *op. cit.*, Vol. I, pp. 120 ff.

27. Strabo, *op. cit.*, Vol. I, p. 23.

28. Anaximander's dates, according to Apollodorus, are 611–547 B.C. For details of his philosophy and contributions to learning, see the histories of the Ionian School by Mallet and Ritten; see also "Dissertation sur la philosophie d'Anaximandre," in *Mémoires de l'académie des sciences de Berlin*, 1815; J. Burnet's *Early Greek philosophy*, London, 1908; A. W. Benn's *The Greek Philosophers*, London, 1914; A. Fairbanks's *The First Philosophers of Greece*, London, 1898.

29. Anaximenes of Miletus flourished in the latter half of the sixth century B.C. For further information about him and his philosophy see the general references cited in Note 28 above.

30. Hecataeus, the historian-philosopher, flourished between the sixth and fifth centuries B.C. For surviving fragments of his writings see K. W. Müller's *Fragmenta historicorum Graecorum*, 4 vols., Paris, 1848–1853, Vol. I; E. H. Bunbury, *op. cit.*, Vol. I, pp. 134–55.

31. Pythagoras was probably born in Samos about 582 B.C. For a detailed account of his school of philosophy, see Eduard Zeller's *Outlines of the history of Greek philosophy*, translated from the German by S. F. Alleyne and Evelyn Abbott, New York, 1890; see also his other writings on the subject; also Theodor Gomperz: *Greek Thinkers*, Vol. I, London, 1901; G. J. Allman's *Greek Geometry from Thales to Euclid*, Cambridge, 1889; James Gow's *A Short history of Greek mathematics*, Cambridge, 1884; Sir G. C. Lewis, *op. cit.*; T. L. Heath, *op. cit.*, pp. 94–120.

32. T. L. Heath, *op. cit.*, pp. 190–224; G. V. Schiaperelli, *Le sfere omocentriche di Eudosso* . . . ; A. J. Letronne, *Sur les écrits et les travaux d'Eudoxe de Cnide* . . . Paris, 1841.

33. Aristotle (384–322 B.C.) was born at Stagira on the Strymonic Gulf. The best edition of his works, by Bekker and Brandis, was published in Berlin, 1831–1870. See also J. W. Blakesley's *Life of Aristotle*, London, 1839; T. L. Heath, *op. cit.*, pp. 190–248.

34. T. L. Heath, *op. cit.*, pp. 300 ff.

35. *Ibid.*, p. 301 and notes.

36. *Ibid.*, p. 302; see also his references, pp. 301–02 *n*.

37. *Ibid.*, p. 304, quoting and presumably translating from Plutarch's *De facie in orbe lunae*.

38. Plato's *Phaedo*, translated by H. N. Fowler, Loeb Classical Library edition, London, 1914, p. 375. See also *Selections illustrating the history of Greek Mathematics*, translated by Ivor Thomas, Loeb Classical Library, 2 vols. London, 1939. Vol. I, pp. 387–405.

39. T. L. Heath, *op. cit.*, p. 147, follows Aristotle's *De caelo*.

40. Modern equivalents of ancient units of linear measure have caused great confusion in the scientific world. The Attic *stadium*, in particular, has received more than its share of attention from classical scholars, with indifferent results. For further information on the deductions of these writers see E. H. Bunbury, *op. cit.*, Vol. I, pp. 209–11, and the works cited by him. See also the *Oxford Dictionary* under "Stadium"; *Smith's Dictionary of Greek and Roman Antiquities*, p. 893; *Webster's Unabridged Dictionary* under "Measure."

41. T. L. Heath, *op cit.*, p. 147 *n* gives Heath's sources on this figure.

42. An edition of all surviving fragments of Eratosthenes's writings was issued by Gottfried Bernhardy: *Eratosthenica, composuit Godofredus Bernhardy*, Berlin, 1822; poetical fragments were issued by E. Hillier, Leipzig, 1872; geographical fragments by G. C. F. Seidel, Götingen, 1789, and by Dr. H. Berger, Leipzig, 1880. See also E. H. Bunbury, *op. cit.*, Vol. I, pp. 615–66; G. C. Lewis, *op. cit.*, pp. 141–206.

43. See Ivor Thomas's *Selections* . . . Vol. II, pp. 267–73. This excerpt is from Cleomedes, *On the circular motion of the heavenly bodies*. See also T. L. Heath, *op. cit.*, pp. 114, 147, 339–40 for a critical commentary on Eratosthenes.

44. Until the expedition of Jean Richer to Cayenne in 1672. (See Chapter VIII.)

45. For further information on Poseidonius see Eduard Zeller's *Philosophie der Griechen*, Vol. I, pp. iii, 570–84; T. L. Heath, *op. cit.*, pp. 344–47; E. H. Bunbury, *op. cit.*, Vol. II, pp. 95, 96, 539.

46. Strabo, *op. cit.*, Vol. I, p. 365.

47. T. L. Heath, *op. cit.*, pp. 345–46.

48. For a summary of the extant specimens of ancient cartography, see the article "Map" by E. G. Ravenstein in *Encyclopaedia Britannica*, 11th edition; also A. E. Nordenskiöld's *Periplus*, Stockholm, 1897, pp. 1–4. It is very probable that a few additional specimens of early maps have been uncovered by archaeologists since these texts were written.

49. This dialogue is quoted from A. E. Nordenskiöld, *op. cit.*, pp. 1–2.

50. *Ibid.*, p. 2.

CHAPTER II

1. His name is also spelled Dicaerchus. A Peripatetic philosopher, a geographer and historian, Dicaercus was said to be the first to devise a method of measuring the height of mountains. His principal work is a *Periegesis*. See T. L. Heath,

op. cit., pp. 306, 337, 339, 347; also E. H. Bunbury, *op. cit.*, Vol. I, pp. 616, 617, 628.

2. See R. Chambers, *The Book of days*, London, v.d., under December 24.

3. See Lancelot Hogben, *Mathematics for the million*, New York, 1937, pp. 37–68; also Ch. VIII "The world encompassed or spherical triangles."

4. See the *Oxford English Dictionary* under "Cancer."

5. Strabo, *op. cit.*, Vol. VIII, p. 129.

6. See the *Oxford English Dictionary* under "Capricorn."

7. Used as a noun, ecliptic is defined as "that great circle of the celestial sphere which is the apparent path of the sun among the stars, or that of the earth as seen from the sun; the plane of the earth's orbit extended to meet the celestial sphere." In 1940 the inclination was 23° 26′ 49.5″, and in 1950 it will be 23° 26′ 44.8″. On the terrestrial globe, the ecliptic is a great circle drawn so as to make an angle of about 23° 27′ with the equator.

8. For the mathematical determination of the ecliptic, see T. L. Heath, *op. cit.*, p. 131 *n*.

9. *Ibid.*, pp. 131 *n*, 132; Oenopedes of Chios, geometer and astronomer, is credited with the discovery of the obliquity of the ecliptic and the length of the Great Year (59 years) and the length of a year, which he said was 365 22/59 days.

10. Strabo, *op. cit.*, Vol. I, pp. 45, 364 *n*, 365, 371, 472, 507, 509, 515, 519.

11. *Ibid.*, Vol. I, p. 441 and note.

12. *Ibid.*, Vol. I, p. 507.

13. T. L. Heath, *op. cit.*, pp. 21, 65–66 and notes; see also Strabo, *op. cit.*, Vol. I, pp. 113, 361, 367, 425, 427, 431.

14. Strabo, *op. cit.*, Vol. I, p. 367.

15. *Ibid.*, Vol. II, pp. 135–43.

16. For a full discussion of the Atlantis story with valuable bibliographical notes, see Justin Winsor's *Narrative and Critical History of America*, Boston, 1889, Vol. I, pp. 15–46, 52, 382.

17. Strabo, *op cit.*, Vol. I, pp. 119, 255, 257, 439; Meroê described in Vol. VIII, p. 143.

18. E. H. Bunbury, *op. cit.*, Vol. I, p. 397.

19. On the location of Thule, see Strabo, *op. cit.*, Vol. I, pp. 233 ff.; Vol. II, p. 261; E. H. Bunbury, *op. cit.*, Vol. I, pp. 597, 612.

20. Strabo, *op. cit.*, Vol. I. p. 23.

21. *Ibid.*, Vol. I, p. 331.

22. *Ibid.*, Vol. I, pp. 332–33.

23. See Chaucer's *Treatise on the astrolabe*, edited by Walter W. Skeat, London, for the Chaucer Society, 1872; Robert Grant's *History of physical astronomy*, London, 1852; *M. Blundeville His Exercises*, London, 1594 (and later editions); Franciscus Ritter, *Astrolabium das ist: gründliche beschreibung und unterricht eines newen quadranten . . .* Nürnberg, *c.* 1650.

24. The longest day of the year was used on many of the maps in the *printed* editions of Ptolemy's *Geographia*. See Strabo, *op. cit.*, Vol. I, p. 283.

25. *Ibid.*, Vol. I, p. 3.

26. See the article "Eratosthenes" by T. L. Heath in *Encyclopaedia Britannica*, 11th edition.

27. E. H. Bunbury, *op. cit.*, Vol. I, pp. 615 ff. and folding map.

28. Strabo, *op. cit.*, Vol. I, p. 241.

29. *Ibid.*, Vol. I, p. 243.

30. *Ibid.*, Vol. I, p. 243.

31. E. H. Bunbury, *op. cit.*, Vol. I, pp. 304–05.

32. Strabo, *op. cit.*, Vol. I, p. 249.

33. E. H. Bunbury, *op. cit.*, Vol. I, pp. 627 ff.; Strabo, *op. cit.*, Vol. I, pp. 253, 317.

34. Strabo, *op. cit.*, Vol. I, p. 239.
35. E. H. Bunbury, *op. cit.*, Vol. I, pp. 631 ff.; Strabo, *op. cit.*, Vol. I, pp. 234–35.
36. E. H. Bunbury, *op. cit.*, Vol. I, p. 631.
37. Strabo, *op. cit.*, Vol. I, p. 265.
38. *Ibid.*, Vol. I, p. 331.
39. *Ibid.*, Vol. I, p. 359. Eratosthenes refers to things "in a line more or less straight." In the same vein Strabo mentions the need of a "metron" or standard of linear measure, p. 341.
40. *Ibid.*, Vol. I, p. 359.
41. Hipparchus of Micaea in Bithynia (fl. about 150 B.C.). Strabo refers to him as an authority on many subjects; references to him are scattered through Volume I of Strabo's *Geography, q.v.* See also J. B. J. Delambre, *op. cit.*, Vol. I, p. 173; G. C. Lewis, *op. cit.*, p. 207; Robert Grant, *op. cit.*, pp. 318, 437, *passim.*
42. Strabo, *op. cit.*, Vol. I, p. 23.
43. G. C. Lewis, *op. cit.*, pp. 205–57.
44. E. H. Bunbury, *op. cit.*, Vol. II, pp. 1–15.
45. For these and other pronouncements made by Hipparchus, see Strabo, *op. cit.*, Vol. I, p. 505 ff.
46. T. L. Heath, *op. cit.*, pp. 101, 172, 173, 200.
47. J. B. J. Delambre, *op. cit.*, Vol. I, p. 185.
48. Strabo, *op. cit.*, Vol. I, p. 509.
49. *Ibid.*, Vol. I, p. 515.
50. *Ibid.*, Vol. I, pp. 459–61 ff.
51. *Ibid.*, Vol. I, pp. 433 ff.
52. *Ibid.*, Vol. I, p. 449.
53. *Ibid.*, Vol. I, pp. 449, 451.
54. *Ibid.*, Vol. I, pp. 453, 455.

CHAPTER III

1. For a discussion of Ptolemy's background and dates see E. H. Bunbury, *op. cit.*, Vol. II, pp. 546 ff.; A. E. Nordenskiöld, *Facsimile-atlas to the early history of cartography*, Stockholm, 1889, pp. 1, 2.
2. For a summary of Ptolemy's various works, see the article by George Johnston Allman under "Ptolemy" in *Encyclopaedia Britannica*, 11th edition, pp. 622d, 623a. The publication of a complete edition of Ptolemy's works was first undertaken in Leipzig. The first volume, in two parts (1898, 1903), was the Greek text of the *Almagest*, edited by J. L. Heiberg. See also J. B. J. Delambre's *Connaissance des temps*, Paris, 1816.
3. The Heiberg edition of the Greek text of the *Almagest* (*cf.* note above), was the basis of an English translation by Robert Catesby Taliaferro (mimeographed), one of "The Classics of St. John's Program" 1938. For a summary of the contents of the *Almagest* see G. J. Allman, *op. cit.*, pp. 619–23.
4. G. J. Allman, *op. cit.*, p. 619.
5. *Ibid.*, p. 621b.
6. The text cited in the following pages is entitled *Geographia of Claudius Ptolemy . . .* translated into English and edited by Edward Luther Stevenson, New York Public Library, 1932. This is the publication of the Ebner manuscript (*c.* 1460) in the New York Public Library, edited with the aid of numerous early manuscript and printed versions of the work.
7. The quotation is from a paper read before the Association of American Geographers, 1942, by the Right Hon. Sir Halford J. Mackinder.

8. *Geographia,* Book I, Ch. I, pp. 25–26.
9. *Ibid.,* p. 25.
10. *Ibid.,* p. 26.
11. *Ibid.,* Book I, Ch. IV, p. 28.
12. *Ibid.,* Book I, Ch. II, p. 26c.
13. Ptolemy's own words, according to Taliaferro's translation of the *Almagest,* Book I, p. 36.
14. *Ibid.,* p. 36, "On the Arc between the Tropics."
15. *Ibid.,* pp. 66, 67.
16. *Ibid.,* pp. 67, 68.
17. Ptolemy's *Geographia,* Book I, Ch. II, pp. 26, 27 ff.
18. E. H. Bunbury, *op. cit.,* Vol. II, p. 519.
19. Ptolemy's *Geographia,* Book I, Ch. VI, p. 29.
20. For a general discussion of the map of Marinus taken largely from Ptolemy's *Geographia,* see E. H. Bunbury, *op. cit.,* Vol. II, pp. 519–45. See also Ptolemy's *Geographia,* Book I, Ch. VI through XXI (pp. 29–40).
21. Ptolemy's *Geographia,* Book I, Ch. IX, p. 31.
22. *Ibid.,* Book I, Ch. VIII, p. 31.
23. *Ibid.,* Book I, Ch. IX, pp. 31–32.
24. *Ibid.,* Book I, Ch. II, pp. 32 ff.
25. *Ibid.,* Book I, Ch. XVIII, pp. 38, 39.
26. *Ibid.,* Book I, Ch. XIX, p. 39.
27. *Ibid.,* Book I, Ch. XXII, pp. 40, 41.
28. *Ibid.,* Book I, Ch. XXI, p. 40.
29. *Ibid.,* Book I, Ch. XXIII, p. 41.
30. *Ibid.,* Book I, Ch. XXIV, pp. 42–45.
31. *Ibid.,* Book II, pp. 47 ff.
32. *Ibid.,* pp. 165–66.
33. For a discussion of this point, see the "Introduction" to Ptolemy's *Geographia, op. cit.,* by Joseph Fischer, S. J., especially p. 13. See also E. H. Bunbury, *op. cit.,* Vol. II, pp. 578–79; Nordenskiöld's *Facsimile-atlas,* p. 8.
34. This is true in both the extant manuscript copies and the more important printed editions.
35. The most satisfactory way of studying Ptolemy's errors is to make a side-by-side comparison of his map and a good modern map of the same area. If one chooses to read a fairly painless analysis of these errors, he may consult E. H. Bunbury, *op. cit.,* Vol. II, pp. 546–644. Not so painless is the monograph by Thomas G. Rylands, *The geography of Ptolemy elucidated,* Dublin, 1893. Contrary to the title, Rylands did not elucidate his subject so that the uninitiated can follow it readily.
36. See *The periplus of the Erythraean Sea* . . . translated from the Greek and annotated by Wilfred H. Schoff . . . New York, 1912; see also the annotated edition translated by William Vincent, in Vol. II of his *The commerce and navigation of the ancients in the Indian Ocean.* London, 1800–1807.
37. Ptolemy made many astronomical calculations from the parallel of Rhodes; these are found in Book II of the *Almagest.* Theon of Alexandria gave three possible reasons for Ptolemy's partiality to this parallel. (1) The height of the pole there was 36°, a whole number, while at Alexandria the height was supposed to be 30° 58'; (2) Hipparchus had made many observations at Rhodes which Ptolemy could check for accuracy; (3) Rhodes represented the mean climate of the seven climatic belts subsequently described.

CHAPTER IV

1. For background material on this subject, see C. Raymond Beazley, *The Dawn of Modern Geography*, London, 1897, Vol. I, pp. 1–20; *The Cambridge Medieval History*, edited by H. M. Gwatkin and J. P. Whitney, Cambridge, 1911, Vol. I, Chs. I–IV; *Encyclopedia of World History*, 1940 edition, pp. 113–55, for a brief sketch of the highlights of the period.
2. For other early pilgrims see C. R. Beazley, *op. cit.*, Vol. I, pp. 53–56.
3. See *Itinerary from Bordeaux to Jerusalem*, "The Bordeaux Pilgrim" (333 A.D.). Translated by Aubrey Stewart and annotated by Sir C. W. Wilson, London, Palestine Pilgrims' Text Society, 1887. See also C. R. Beazley, *op. cit.*, Vol. I, pp. 53–68. Beazley gives as the principal authority on medieval pilgrims Titus Tobler and Augustus Molinier's *Itinera hierosolymitana et descriptiones Terrae Sanctae . . .* 2 Vols., Geneva, 1879–1885. ("Publications de la Societé de l'Orient latin. Série géographique," I–II, IV.)
4. C. R. Beazley, *op. cit.*, Vol. I, pp. 241–44.
5. James Westfall Thompson, *The Middle Ages*, New York, 1931, Vol. II, p. 778, notes that the writings of Isidore of Seville (d. 636), of the "Venerable" Bede (d. 735) and the *Glossae Salamonis*, an encyclopedic dictionary, are representative of the scientific profundity of the seventh, eighth and ninth centuries; and that the *Natural History* of Pliny was the principal source of information for the three. Solinus, therefore, makes a fourth writer who leaned heavily on Pliny.
6. C. R. Beazley, *op. cit.*, Vol. I, pp. 243–73, gives a summary of geographical facts gleaned from the *Collecteana* or *Polyhistor* of Solinus.
7. Quoted from C. R. Beazley, *op. cit.*, Vol. I, p. 285, who used the Montfaucon edition of 1706–1707 in "Nova Collectio Patrum," Tome II.
8. See *The Christian Topography of Cosmas, an Egyptian monk*. Translated from the Greek and edited with notes and introduction by J. W. McCrindle, London, 1897, Publications of the Hakluyt Society, Series I, Vol. 98. See also the same text, edited with geographical notes by E. O. Winstedt, Cambridge, England, 1909. Citations are taken from the Hakluyt Society edition. For a list of the other writings of Cosmas, *cf.* pp. xxi–xxii; for a summary of his geographic credo, see C. R. Beazley, *op. cit.*, Vol. I, pp. 273–303. For sources used by Cosmas, see Beazley, Vol. I, p. 280.
9. Hebrews IX:1–2. According to Beazley (*op. cit.*, Vol. I, p. 287), it was Pamphilus who suggested the analogy, first used by Theodore of Mopsuestia.
10. Exodus XXXVII:10.
11. Job XXXVIII:38.
12. Cosmas, *op. cit.*, pp. 145 ff.
13. *Ibid.*, Book II, pp. 23 ff.
14. *Ibid.*, pp. 5, 14, 17, 86, 136–37.
15. For a summary of the Ravennese geographical principles, see C. R. Beazley, *op. cit.*, Vol. I, pp. 303–16; see also p. 529 for the various editions of the text. Citations are from Beazley.
16. C. R. Beazley, *op. cit.*, Vol. I, pp. 309 ff.
17. Isaiah XL:22 (King James).
18. Isaiah XI:12 (King James).
19. C. R. Beazley, *op. cit.*, Vol. I, p. 379 *n* (2):

> The ten references in question are: (1) In Varro, "De Re Rustica," i. 2. (2, 3) Propertius, "Elegies," iv. 11; v. 3. (4) Vitruvius, Architect. viii. 2, 6, etc. (5) Eumenius of Autun, "Oratio pro instaurandis scholis," chs. 20, 21. (6) Sue-

tonius, "Domitian," ch. 10. (7, 8) Pliny, "Natural History," iii. 3, 17; vi. 139. (9) Ovid, "Pontic Epistles," II, i. 37, etc. (10) Lampridius, "Life of Alexander Severus," ch. 45. All these are non-Christian and pre-Constantinian; the similar references of Vegetius, in his "Epitoma Rei Militaris" (iii. 6), addressed to Valentinian II. about A.D. 380; and of Cassiodorus in his "Letter to the Monks" (De Inst. Div. Script.), fall within the Christian period.

20. Beazley describes the maps of Cosmas and others in Vol. I, pp. 384 ff.; for some of the lost maps of this period, see pp. 388–89.
21. For a summary of medieval cartography of this period see W. L. Bevan and H. W. Phillott, *Mediaeval Geography. An essay in illustration of the Hereford Mappa Mundi*, London, 1873; see also *The study and classification of Medieval Mappae Mundi* by Michael C. Andrews, in *Archaeologia*, Vol. 75, London, 1926, pp. 61–76.
22. J. W. Thompson, *op. cit.*, Vol. I, p. xxi.
23. *Ibid.*, Vol. I, pp. xxii–xxiii.
24. C. R. Beazley, *op. cit.*, Vol. II, pp. 563–64 ff.
25. Genesis I:9 (King James).
26. In his *Admiral of the Ocean Sea*, S. E. Morison brands as "pure moonshine" (Vol. I, pp. 117–18) the meeting at Salamanca, where a council of divines was supposed to have turned thumbs down on Columbus and his scheme, as per Washington Irving's account.
27. Genesis II:8; III:24. For further information on the location of Paradise see C. R. Beazley, *op. cit.*, Vol. II, pp. 554 ff.; see also S. Baring-Gould, *Curious Myths of the Middle Ages*, London, 1884 [New Edition], pp. 250–65; on Columbus and the Terrestrial Paradise, see S. E. Morison, *op. cit.*, Vol. I, pp. 121, 124, 430; Vol. II, pp. 282–85.
28. C. R. Beazley, *op. cit.*, Vol. I, pp. 227 ff.; Bevan and Phillott, *op. cit.*, p. xvii.
29. Acts XVII:26.
30. C. R. Beazley, *op. cit.*, Vol. II, pp. 570–71, quoting from the Paris copy of the Lambert map.
31. T – O maps were written about Leonardo Dati in his poem *Della Sphera*, 1422:

> Un T dentro a un O mostra il disegno
> Como in *tre parte* fu diviso il mondo.

A diagram map of this kind will be found in most of the early editions of the *Origines* by Isidorus of Seville. See C. R. Beazley, *op. cit.*, Vol. II, pp. 576 ff.
32. Ezekiel V:5 (King James).
33. Bevan and Phillott, *op. cit.*, pp. xiii, xiv; C. R. Beazley, *op. cit.*, Vol. II, p. 575.
34. C. R. Beazley, *op. cit.*, Vol. II, pp. 573–75.
35. Numerous books deal with the Saint Brendan legend. See *Les voyages merveilleux de St. Brendan . . .* by F. Michel, Paris, 1878; also *Acta Sancti Brendani . . . Original documents connected with the life of St. Brendan*, by P. F. Moran, Dublin, 1872; also Bevan and Phillott, *op. cit.*, pp. xxv–xxvi.
36. The Prester John myth permeates the literature and maps of the period. He was probably the most real and influential of all mythical characters of the Middle Ages. For an account of him, see S. Baring-Gould, *op. cit.*, pp. 32 ff.; see also S. E. Morison, *op. cit.*, Vol. I, p. 43; Vol. II, pp. 21, 137–38, for his influence on Columbus.
37. The Ortelius map of the kingdom of Prester John appears in various editions of the *Theatrum*. The copy cited is in the French edition of 1574, *Theatre de l'univers . . .* and is the 52nd map.
38. For reference to Gog and Magog see Ezekiel XXXVIII:2; XXXIX:1; Revelations

XX:8; Bevan and Phillott, *op. cit.*, p. xxiii; C. R. Beazley, *op. cit.*, Vol. I, p. 357; S. Baring-Gould, *op. cit.*, pp. 36–40 ff.

39. Of the shorter accounts of the Crusades, by far the most readable is that written by Ernest Barker in the *Encyclopaedia Britannica*, 11th edition. He says, "the history of the Crusades must be viewed rather as a chapter in the history of civilization in the West itself . . . It is a chapter very difficult to write, for . . . a cautious writer who seeks to find documentary evidence for every assertion may be rather inclined to attribute to that influence little or nothing." In addition to the *Cambridge History of the Middle Ages* and J. W. Thompson (*op. cit.*) see Barker's article (*supra*), pp. 550–52, for a detailed analysis of the literature on the subject.

40. Ernest Barker, *op. cit.*, p. 524d.

41. *Ibid.*, p. 526c.

42. J. W. Thompson, *op. cit.*, Vol. I, p. 575.

43. See C. R. Beazley, *op. cit.*, Vol. II, pp. 279–320 ff., for a running outline of Carpini's journey. The first genuine and complete version of the text was edited by M. A. P. d'Avezac de Castera-Macaya, and appeared in 1839 in the fourth volume of the *Recueil de voyages et de mémoires* of the Geographical Society of Paris. See also the Hakluyt Society edition: *The texts and versions of John de Plano Carpini and William de Rubruquis*, edited by C. Raymond Beazley, London, 1903 (Extra Series, Vol. 13).

44. *The Journey of William of Rubruck* [Ruybrock, Willem van] *to the Eastern parts of the world 1253–55, as narrated by himself*. Translated from Latin MSS. and edited by William W. Rockhill. London, The Hakluyt Society, 1900 (Series II, Vol. IV). See also *The texts and versions of . . . William de Rubruquis* edited by C. R. Beazley. London, The Hakluyt Society, 1903 (Extra Series, Vol. 13). This version was edited from the account published by Richard Hakluyt, who used the manuscript of Lord Lumley.

45. C. R. Beazley, *op. cit.*, Vol. II, pp. 7, *passim*, Vol. III, pp. 15–160; see also the article by Beazley and Sir Henry Yule under *Polo* in the *Encyclopaedia Britannica*, 11th edition, for an exhaustive bibliography and summary of the travels of the Polos. An interesting and readable translation of Marco Polo's *Book* was published by the Argonaut Press, London, 1929: *The most noble and famous travels of Marco Polo together with the travels of Nicolò de' Conti*, edited from the Elizabethan translation of John Frampton, with introduction, notes . . . by N. M. Penzer. This edition also contains eleven valuable maps.

46. Henry Yule and C. R. Beazley, *op. cit.*, p. 8b.

47. After the Polos, all this territory remained *terra incognita* until 1860 or thereabouts, when it was again explored by Cooper, Garnier, Richthofen, Gill, Baber, and others. See Henry Yule and C. R. Beazley, *op. cit.*, p. 8c.

48. Henry Yule and C. R. Beazley, *op. cit.*, p. 10b.

49. For other medieval sources on China, see *Cathay and the way thither. Being a collection of medieval notices of China*, 4 vols. Translated and edited by Sir Henry Yule. London, The Hakluyt Society, 1913–1916 (Series II, Vols. 33, 37, 38, 41). These voyages include the travels of Friar Odoric, Ibn Batuta and Benedict Goës.

50. For a summary of the geographical sources available to the traveler and missionary of the late Middle Ages, see C. R. Beazley, *op. cit.*, Vol. III, pp. 4 ff.

51. For a good summary of the important explorations, discoveries and rediscoveries in this period, see C. R. Beazley, *op. cit.*, Vol. III, pp. 410–60.

52. *Ibid.*, Vol. III, pp. 423–28.

53. *Ibid.*, Vol. III, p. 431, discredits this traditional chapter in history, pointing out that the alleged sources, in the Admiralty Registers at Dieppe, were destroyed in 1694.

54. Of the more important references concerning Henry the Navigator, the following should be consulted: *Alguns documentos do archivo nacional da Torre do Tombo acerca das navegações . . . Portuguezas,* Lisbon, 1892; *Archivo dos Açores,* Ponta Delgada, 1878–1894; Gomes Eannes de Azurara, *Chronica do descobrimento e conquista de Guiné,* edited by Carreira and Santarem, Paris, 1841; C. R. Beazley, *Prince Henry the Navigator,* London, 1895; R. H. Major, *The Life of Henry of Portugal, surnamed the Navigator,* London, 1868.

55. For a translation of this charter, see Edward Gaylord Bourne; *Essays in historical criticism,* New York, 1901, pp. 174–75. In a note (p. 175), Bourne says the reading of the charter may be taken as a statement of Prince Henry's, because Affonso was only twelve years old at the time, and his two guardians were the Regent Dom Pedro and Prince Henry.

56. *The chronicle of the discovery and conquest of Guinea. Written by Gomes Eannes de Azurara.* Now first done into English by Charles Raymond Beazley and Edgar Prestage, 2 vols., London, The Hakluyt Society, 1896–99 (Series I, Vols. 95, 100), Vol. I, Ch. VII, pp. 27–29. Citations to Azurara are taken from this edition. See also Bourne, *op. cit.,* pp. 175–76. The long introduction to this first English translation of Azurara's Chronicle is an excellent study of Henry of Portugal, Azurara, and their times.

57. Azurara, *op. cit.,* Vol. I, Ch. VIII, p. 31.

58. Justin Winsor says that from 1469 King Affonso farmed out the African commerce, at the same time demanding that 500 miles a year be added to the southern limit of discovery along the coast. See Justin Winsor, *op. cit.,* Vol. II, p. 41.

59. For details of this voyage, see *A journal of the first voyage of Vasco da Gama, 1497–99.* Translated and edited by E. G. Ravenstein. London, The Hakluyt Society, 1898, Series I, no. 99, pp. 9–14. See also João de Barros, *Asia,* Dec. I, Book iii, Chapter IV; Duarte Pacheco Pereira, *Esmeraldo de situ orbis,* London, the Hakluyt Society, 1937. Series II, Vol. 79, pp. 15, 90, 92, 94. According to C. R. Beazley, Pacheco met Diaz returning from his great voyage at the Ihla do Principe. See also Galvano; *Descobrimentos (Discoveries of the World),* London, The Hakluyt Society, 1862, Series I, no. 30, p. 77; E. G. Ravenstein, "Voyages of Diogo Cão and Bartholomeu Diaz" In *Geographical Journal,* London, Dec., 1900, Vol. 16, pp. 625–55.

CHAPTER V

1. *M. Blundeville his exercises . . .* By Thomas Blundeville, Sixth edition, London, 1622, pp. 649–50. This edition is a compilation of several treatises by various authors besides Blundeville. The quotations cited appear in the introductory pages of "A new and necessarie treatise of navigation, containing all the chiefest principles of that arte." pp. 649 ff.

2. Graduated plotting charts with parallels and meridians laid down on a Mercator projection and corrected according to the best tables of "Meridional Parts" are issued by the U. S. Hydrographic Office.

3. Much of the cultural history of the Phoenicians has been uncovered by archeologists working in various parts of the Mediterranean, and it is fragmentary. For various classical references, see George C. Lewis, *op. cit.,* pp. 446–515. For a long bibliography on the subject, see George Rawlinson's *History of Phoenicia,* London, 1889.

4. Strabo, *op. cit.,* Vol 7, pp. 267–69. For a vivid word picture of the wealth of Tyre, see Ezekiel XXVII:12–27.

5. This passage is quoted by George Rawlinson, *op. cit.,* pp. 279–80; and by John Kenrick in his *Phoenicia,* London, 1855, pp. 234–35; both authors used the Schneider

edition of Xenophon, but came up with variant readings of the text; neither of which hurts the story or its point.

6. See Ronald M. Burrows, *The discoveries in Crete.* London, 1907.

7. For an excellent graphic presentation of the territory held by the Phoenicians at various periods, see William Smith's *An atlas of Ancient Geography*, edited by Smith and George Grove, London, 1874, Pl. 9.

8. Strabo, *op. cit.*, Vol. VII, p. 267; VIII, pp. 185–87.

9. Strabo, *op. cit.*, Vol. VII, p. 267.

10. Ezekiel XXVII:12.

11. Strabo, *op. cit.*, Vol. II, pp. 157, 159.

12. The power of amber to become charged with electricity by friction was first recorded by Thales of Miletus; his word "electrum" suggested the modern word electricity. See G. C. Lewis, *op. cit.*, pp. 458–61 and notes, regarding the classical sources of amber.

13. See Strabo, *op. cit.*, Vol. VIII, p. 77 on the construction of the Red Sea canal; and on the circumnavigation of Libya, see Vol. I, pp. 377–85; for other classical references to the subject, see G. C. Lewis, *op. cit.*, p. 497 and notes, 498 ff.

14. This passage is quoted from G. C. Lewis, *op. cit.*, p. 498. The circumnavigation of Africa by the Phoenicians is credited by Von Humbolt, Rennell, Heeren, Grote, Rawlinson and other authorities (see Lewis, p. 448, notes).

15. G. C. Lewis, *op. cit.*, p. 509.

16. For a translation of the Periplus of Scylax, see A. E. Nordenskiöld's *Periplus*, pp. 6–8, with important tables of distances on p. 8. Contrary to Rennell, Scylax reckoned that with a fair wind, a vessel could make 500 stadia a day and as much at night.

17. See A. E. Nordenskiöld's *Periplus*, pp. 11–14 for notes and a translation of the *Stadiasmus*.

18. *Ibid.*, p. 16, for notes on the possibility of still earlier charts.

19. In order to construct a mariner's chart, wrote Martin Cortès, "it shal be requisite to knowe two thynges. Whereof the one is the right *position* of places, or placing of countries and coastes. The other is the *distances* that is from one place to another." (*The arte of nauigation*, London, 1596.)

20. For these references to directions, see Strabo, *op. cit.*, Vol. I, pp. 11 *n*, 101, 105.

21. T. Blundeville, *op. cit.*, pp. 424–25.

22. See Silvanus P. Thompson, *The rose of the winds: the origin and development of the compass-card*, London, n. d., p. 4 *n*. (Read at the International Historical Congress, April, 1913. From the proceedings of the British Academy, Vol. VI.)

23. *Ibid.*, pp. 6–8.

24. *Ibid.*, pp. 8–10. See also Willebrordus Snellius, *Typhis Batavus*, Leyden, 1624, for full names of the winds in Dutch: *Noort; Noort-ten-oosten; Noort-noort-oost; Noort-oost-ten-noorden; Noort-oost*, and so on.

25. T. Blundeville, *op. cit.*, p. 682.

26. The invention of the compass is a highly controversial subject. A provocative article, if not the last word on the subject, was contributed by Heinrich Winter: "Who invented the compass?" (In the *Mariner's Mirror*, Cambridge, 1937, pp. 95–102.)

27. T. Blundeville, *op. cit.*, p. 682.

28. A. E. Nordenskiöld: *Periplus*, p. 49.

29. *Ibid.*, p. 49; see also S. P. Thompson, *op. cit.*, p. 3 for other writers who attested the powers of the magnetized needle. Thompson gives an interesting but brief summary of the history of the compass, pp. 1–4. See also *The letter of Petrus Peregrinus on the magnet, A. D. 1269*, translated by Brother Arnold, New York, 1904, pp. 37–41, for "Early references to the mariner's compass."

30. Petrus Peregrinus, *op. cit.*, p. 28. The translation by Brother Arnold was made from the printed edition of the *Epistola* prepared by Achilles Gasser, a physician of Lindau, and printed at Augsburg, 1558. Taisnier's pirated extracts of the text of the *Epistola* were translated by Richard Eden and were first printed in 1579. The only previous edition of the complete English translation was made by Silvanus P. Thompson, in an edition of 250 copies.

31. Petrus Peregrinus, *op. cit.*, p. 19.

32. See *William Gilbert of Colchester . . . on the loadstone and magnetic bodies and on the great magnet the earth, 1600*, translated by P. Fleury Mottelay, 1892, reprint by Edwards Brothers, Ann Arbor, 1938, pp. 2, 3. See also Silvanus P. Thompson: *William Gilbert, and terrestrial magnetism in the time of Queen Elizabeth: a discourse* [London, 1903] Royal Geographical Society Publications.

33. For a comparative study of two different renderings, see the translation issued by the Gilbert Club, London, 1900, with notes by S. P. Thompson.

34. Silvanus P. Thompson: *Notes on the De Magnete of Dr. William Gilbert*, London, 1901, pp. 4–5.

35. S. P. Thompson, *The rose of the winds*, pp. 20, 22; see also his *William Gilbert, and terrestrial magnetism . . .* pp. 2, 3.

36. See S. P. Thompson: *The rose of the winds*, pp. 6, 8, 21–24. An ingenious though fantastic theory as to the evolution of the fleur-de-lis, advanced by A. Schück in *Der Compass*, is outlined by Thompson on p. 31.

37. S. P. Thompson, *The rose of the winds*, p. 16 *n*; also his *William Gilbert, and terrestrial magnetism . . .*, p. 4; see also S. E. Morison, *op. cit.*, Vol. I, pp. 28–29, 246–47, 270–71, 279–81, Vol. II, pp. 64, 185–88; G. Hellman, *Meteorologische Zeitschrift*, Berlin, 1906, pp. 23, 145.

38. *Ibid.*, p. 4, 16 *n*. Mottelay, in his translation of Gilbert's *On the loadstone*, p. 252, has a note from A. M. Mayer's "The earth a great magnet," 1872, p. 253, as follows: "The fact that the needle does not point at all places to the true north was early known, but the discovery that it changed its direction with a change of place is generally attributed to Columbus. This is incorrect, for the needle's departure from the geographic meridian (called its *variation* or *declination*) is marked down for different points of the sea, on the atlas of Andrea Bianco, which was made in the year 1436; but what Columbus really did discover was a line of no variation 2½° east of the island of Corvo on the 13th of September 1492." In the same work (Mottelay, p. 8 *n*) the translator says, "At page 150 of the 1869 London edition of Mr. J. F. Nicholls' Life of Seb. Cabot, it is said the latter represented to the King of England that the variation of the compass was different in many places, and was not absolutely regulated by distance from any particular meridian; also, that he could point to a spot of no variation, and that those whom he trained as seamen, as Chancellor and Stephen Burrough were particularly attentive to this problem, noting it at one time thrice within a short space ('Biddle,' Memoir of Sebastian Cabot, 1831; Humboldt, in both his 'Examen Critique' and his 'Cosmos,' treating of 'Oceanic Discoveries')." See also S. P. Thompson, *William Gilbert, and terrestrial magnetism . . .*, pp. 1–9.

39. For a historical summary of terrestrial magnetism and its variations, see E. Walker's *Terrestrial and cosmical magnetism*, Cambridge and London, 1866; see also L. A. Bauer, *United States magnetic declination tables and isogonic charts, and principal facts relating to the earth's magnetism*, Washington, 1902.

40. S. P. Thompson: *William Gilbert, and terrestrial magnetism . . .* p. 4.

41. Halley made two voyages. For a bibliography on the subject, see *Correspondence and papers of Edmond Halley*, arranged and edited by Eugene F. MacPike, Oxford, 1932, p. 282. See also "Dr. Halley's first voyage: a journal of a voyage made for the discovery of the rule of the variation of the compass . . . 1699 and 1700,"

in Alexander Dalrymple's *A collection of voyages* . . . London, 1775; *Philosophical Transactions of the Royal Society*, Numbers 148, 195, 341.

42. See Michel Coignet: *Instrvction novvelle des poincts plus excellents et necessaires, touchant l'art de nauiguer* . . . Antwerp, 1581. The New York Public Library has a photostatic copy of this rare work from an original whose location is unknown.

43. The most readable account of Gerard Mercator, his career and the projection of his chart, was written by Elial F. Hall, "Gerard Mercator: his life and works . . ." (in the *Journal of the American Geographical Society of New York*, 1878, Vol. X, pp. 163–96). For a more comprehensive study, see J. Van Raemdonck: *Gérard Mercator: sa vie et ses oeuvres*, St Nicholas, 1869.

44. See Elial Hall, *op. cit.*, p. 181–82 for a translation of Mercator's explanation of his chart and projection.

45. Elial Hall quoting (p. 195) from William Barlowe's *The Navigator's Supply, &c.*, London, 1597.

46. L. C. Wroth, *The Way of a Ship, An essay on the literature of navigation science*, Portland (Me.), 1937, p. 62, quotes this passage from Wright's *Certaine errors in navigation*, London, 1599.

47. C. H. Deetz and O. S. Adams: *Elements of Map Projection with applications to map and chart construction*, Washington, 1938, p. 101. (U. S. Dept. of Commerce. Coast and Geodetic Survey. Special publication No. 68.)

48. Elial Hall, *op. cit.*, p. 183, 195. For a facsimile reproduction of Mercator's chart, Duisbourg, 1569, see E. F. Jomard, *Monuments de la géographie*, Paris, 1842–62, Pl. 1–8.

49. Elial Hall, *op. cit.*, p. 182.

50. See L. C. Wroth, *op. cit.*, p. 66. See also L. A. Brown, *Jean Domenique Cassini and his world map of 1696*, Ann Arbor, 1941, p. 16.

51. C. H. Deetz and O. S. Adams, *op. cit.*, pp. 101–36, 146, 147.

52. Elial Hall, *op. cit.*, p. 184.

53. A. E. Nordenskiöld's *Periplus*, pp. 1, 3, 16; see also p. 46 for a discussion of the probable date of this cartographic prototypes; also Pl. IV, which shows the similarity between the prototype and Mercator's chart.

54. *Ibid.*, p. 17a, 47d.

55. *Ibid.*, p. 21b, 18.

56. *Ibid.*, p. 48b. See also Note 38 above.

57. *Ibid.*, 51a–53d; see p. 53b–53c for a translation and definition of these terms. Bianco probably produced the first modern traverse table (1436) according to Nordenskiöld, p. 53d.

58. See Nordenskiöld's *Periplus*, p. 65, for a short account of Agnese. See also Henry R. Wagner, "The manuscript atlases of Battista Agnese" (in *The Papers of the Bibliographical Society of America*, Vol. XXV, 1931, pp. 1–110, including plates). This is an exhaustive study. Wagner appends a list of the known copies of Agnese atlases (pp. 55–103) and locates each one (pp. 108–09). Also appended is an excellent bibliography (pp. 104–08).

59. H. R. Wagner, *op. cit.*, pp. 1, 8–9.

60. For a list of these survivors, see Nordenskiöld's *Periplus*, pp. 59–63. Nordenskiöld (p. 69) is quoting from an English edition of the Waghenaer, London, 1612.

61. Henri Harrisse: *The discovery of North America*, London and Paris, 1892, p. 255.

62. See Edward Luther Stevenson: "The Geographical activities of the Casa de la Contratacion," in *The Annals of the Association of American Geographers*, Albany, 1927, Vol. 17, pp. 39–59. See also José de Veitia Linaje, *Norte de la contratacion de las Indias Occidentales*, Seville, 1672; also M. de la Puente y Olea, *Estudios Españoles los trabojos geographicos de la casa de contratación*, Seville, 1900.

63. H. Harrisse, *op. cit.*, pp. 258–67.

64. E. L. Stevenson, *op. cit.*, pp. 43, 44.

65. H. Harrisse, *op. cit.*, p. 265.

66. See Philip Lee Phillips: *A list of geographical atlases in the Library of Congress*, 4 vols. Washington, 1909–1920, Vol. IV, No. 5165. See also D. Gernez: "Lucas Janszoon Wagenaer. A chapter in the history of guide-books for sea-men," in the *Mariner's Mirror*, London, 1937, Vol. 23, pp. 190–97; 332–50.

67. For this and other editions of Wagenaer's sea-atlas, see P. L. Phillips, *op. cit.*, No. 3980, 3981, 5165. See also the note under No. 3981 by M. Rooses (Vol. III, p. 610b), taken from his *Christophe Plantin*, Anvers, 1882, p. 355; see also P. A. Tiele's *Nederlandsche bibliographie van land-en volkenkunde*, Amsterdam, 1884.

68. P. L. Phillips, *op. cit.*, Vol. III, No. 3981, p. 609.

69. A. E. Nordenskiöld: *Periplus*, pp. 107b, 110b.

70. D. Gernez, *op. cit.*, pp. 347–49.

71. P. L. Phillips, *op. cit.*, No. 1155 *n*, says 1689 was the date of the first edition of the *English Pilot*. For other editions, see Nos. 1157, 1158, 1160, 1162, 1163, 1164, 1168, 1171.

72. The great work on the history of the Dutch East India Company is François Valentijn's *Beschryving van oud en niew oost Indien*, 5 vols., Dordrecht, 1724–26. See also J. K. J. de Jonge: *De Opkomst van het Nederlandsch Gesag in Oost-Indien*, 13 vols., The Hague and Amsterdam, 1862–1888.

73. Frederick C. Wieder (ed.): *Monumenta cartographica; reproductions of unique and rare maps, plans and views in the actual size*, 5 vols., The Hague, Martinus Nijhoff, 1925–33. The text of Volume I bears the title "The Secret Atlas of the Dutch East India Company."

74. *Ibid.*, Vol. I, p. 145c.

75. For biographical material on Alexander Dalrymple, see "Memoirs of Alexander Dalrymple, Esq." in the *European Magazine*, London, Nov. and Dec., 1802, pp. 323–27, 421–24. This article also contains an extensive bibliography of his many writings. See also Great Britain, Hydrographic Office: *General instructions for the hydrographic surveyors of the Admiralty*. London, 1877.

CHAPTER VI

1. George P. Winship: *Printing in the 15th century*. Phila., 1940, pp. 1–12. (This work embraces the Rosenbach Lectures in Bibliography given in 1939.) For an interesting allusion to the probable significance of the "indulgence," see p. 12.

2. See John Johnson, *Typographia or the Printers' instructor* . . . 2 vols., London, 1824, Vol. 2, p. 217; see also Margaret Stillwell, *Incunabula and Americana*, New York, 1931, p. 8.

3. *Catalogue of Books mostly from the presses of the first printers* . . . collected by Rush C. Hawkins and catalogued by A. W. Pollard, Oxford, 1910, pp. xxv–xxxi.

4. Fust and Schoeffer used it in their Psalter of 1457 (M. Stillwell, *op. cit.*, p. 8). She says (p. 11) that the first humanistic type was used in Ulrich Boner's *Edelstein*, 1461.

5. The French "*taille douce*" or "*gravure au burin*."

6. Sidney Colvin: *Early engraving and engravers in England (1545–1695)* . . . London, 1905, p. 4.

7. For a detailed accounting of the various editions of Ptolemy's *Geographia* or *Cosmographia*, as it was later called, see Joseph Sabin, *A dictionary of books relating to America, from its discovery to the present time*, 29 vols., New York, 1868–1936. The annotations were written by Wilberforce Eames. A second list of

the editions of the *Geographia*, copiously annotated, will be found in A. E. Nordenskiöld's *Facsimile-atlas*, pp. 9–34, including the pseudo versions of the text.

8. On the perpetuation of the *Geographia* throughout the Middle Ages, see A. E. Nordenskiöld's *Facsimile-atlas*, p. 8.

9. See Edward Lynam's *The first engraved atlas of the world, the Cosmographia of Claudius Ptolemeus, Bologna, 1477*, Jenkintown, The George H. Beans library, 1941. See also Nordenskiöld's *Facsimile-atlas*, p. 32.

10. A. E. Nordenskiöld: *Facsimile-atlas*, pp. 9–10.

11. *Ibid.*, p. 13.

12. The map of Greenland appeared in the Ulm, 1482, edition of Ptolemy's *Cosmographia*, Sabin, *op. cit.*, Vol. XVI, p. 47–48. On the subject of map sources used by Columbus, see S. E. Morison, *op. cit.*, Vol. I, pp. 101–04. Morison's discussion of the Juan de la Cosa map will be found in Vol. II, p. 75. See also Justin Winsor, *op. cit.*, Vol. II, pp. 106, 206. The date of the Juan de la Cosa map has long been a controversial subject.

13. Among the more noteworthy maps produced in the early years of the sixteenth century were those by (1) Alberto Cantino, 1502; (2) Gregor Reisch, 1503; (3) Giovanni Matteo Contarini, 1506; (4) Martin Waldseemüller, 1507; Johann Ruysch, 1508; Bernardus Sylvanus, 1511; Joannes de Stobnicza, 1512.

14. Jan Hendrik Hessels: *Ecclesiae Londino-Batavae archivvm* . . . [correspondence between Abraham Ortelius and his friends] 3 vols., Cambridge, 1887–97. See a review of this work in the Proceedings of the Royal Geographical Society, Vol. X, London, 1888, p. 256, for the note cited here.

15. See *The cosmographiae introductio of Martin Waldseemüller in facsimile* . . . With an introduction by Joseph Fischer, S. J. and Franz von Wieser, New York, 1907.

16. *Ibid.*, pp. 7, 8; this suggestion was made three times; see pp. 18–30 of the facsimile edition above.

17. *Ibid.*, pp. 15–17 of facsimile edition above for the author's intentions regarding the map. For a facsimile of the large map see *Die älteste karte mit dem namen Amerika* . . . Edited . . . by Professor Joseph Fischer, S. J. and Professor Franz R. von Wieser. Innsbruck, 1903.

18. *The cosmographiae introductio*, p. 3. There are two variants of the text, one giving Waldseemüller as editor and one the Gymnasium.

19. *Ibid.*, pp. 29, 30. For a reproduction of this map, see A. E. Nordenskiöld's *Facsimile-atlas*, Pl. XLIII. A copy of the original map is in the collection of the American Geographical Society; a second is in the New York Public Library.

20. Sidney Colvin, *op. cit.*, pp. 4–6.

21. Elial Hall, *op. cit.*, p. 186 *n*, says that in 47 vols. of the *Journal* and 22 vols. of the *Proceedings* of the Royal Geographical Society there was no mention of Gerard Mercator.

22. I. J. Curnow, *The world mapped*, London, 1930, p. 72, locates a copy in Italy.

23. The article on "Mercator" in the *Encyclopaedia Britannica*, 11th edition, p. 149d, locates a copy of this map in the Plantin-Moretus Museum in Antwerp.

24. Elial Hall, *op. cit.*, p. 167. Beazley's article in the *Britannica*, 11th edition, says the globe was dedicated to Nicolas Perrenot, father of the Cardinal.

25. See Emerson Fite and Archibald Freeman, *A book of old maps*, Cambridge, Harvard University Press, 1926, p. 55 and notes; also A. E. Nordenskiöld's *Facsimile-atlas*, Pl. XLIII.

26. See John L. Motley: *The rise of the Dutch republic. A history*, New York, 1856, p. 150. See also Elial Hall, *op. cit.*, pp. 168 ff.

27. The map of Europe, as well as his maps of the world and the British Islands were

reproduced in Berlin by W. H. Kühl, 1891, from originals in the Stadtbibliothek of Breslau. See P. L. Phillips, *op. cit.*, No. 253.

28. Elial Hall, *op. cit.*, p. 171, says the map was really published, contrary to the opinion of previous scholars.
29. *Ibid.*, pp. 171–72.
30. J. H. Hessels, *op. cit.*, p. xxiii. See also Radermacher's letter to Jacob Cool, Middelburg, 25 July, 1603.
31. See Dard Hunter: *Paper making through eighteen centuries*, New York, 1930.
32. Radermacher to Cool. See J. H. Hessels, *op. cit.*, p. 772, Letter No. 330, Middelburg, Friday, 25 July, 1603.
33. *Ibid.*, p. 22, No. 10 — Joannes Terenumus to Ortelius, 15 June, 1561.
34. See *Catalogue of the John Carter Brown Library in Brown University* Providence, 1919, Vol. I, Part II, for a comparison of two variant copies of the first edition in that collection. See also P. L. Phillips, *op. cit.*, No. 386, 388 and a bibliographical account under No. 374. The biographical sketches of contributors to the *Theatrum* were extended in recent years and annotated by Leo Bagrow: "A Ortelii catalogus cartographorum" in *Petermanns Mitteilungen Ergänzungsheft*, Gotha, 1928, Teil [A–L], No. 199; 1930, Teil [M–Z], No. 210.
35. See P. L. Phillips, *op. cit.*, Vol. II Index, Vol. IV "Author List" for details concerning the various editions of the *Theatrum*; also P. A. Tiele's *Nederlandsche bibliographie*, Amsterdam, 1884. See also J. B. Thacher: *The continent of America*, New York, 1896, p. 254.
36. For other comments on the atlas see J. H. Hessels, *op. cit.*, letters No. 29, 30, 32, 33, 39 ff.
37. *Ibid.*, p. xxv ff.
38. *Ibid.*, letter No. 238.
39. Elial Hall, *op. cit.*, pp. 173, 174; *cf.* Duisburg, 1594 edition. See also P. L. Phillips, *op. cit.*, No. 3400 for the Duisburg 1595 edition.
40. See P. L. Phillips, *op. cit.*, No. 422; Sidney Colvin, *op. cit.*, p. 43.
41. P. L. Phillips, *op. cit.*, Nos. 422, 423.
42. *Ibid.*, Nos. 398, 399.
43. J. H. Hessels, *op. cit.*, Letter No. 32 — Mercator to Ortelius, 1570.
44. P. L. Phillips, *op. cit.*, No. 3392.
45. *Ibid.*, Nos. 162–65; see also Joseph Sabin, *op. cit.*, under "Bordone" for bibliographical notes.
46. P. L. Phillips, *op. cit.*, Nos. 1140, 3644.
47. *Ibid.*, No. 60 (Du Pinet); No. 65 (Romanus); No. 2815 (Camocio); Nos. 2948, 3145 (Tassin).
48. Thomas Chubb: *Printed maps in the atlases of Great Britain and Ireland* . . . London, 1927, p. 449.
49. See Sir Herbert George Fordham: "Note on a series of early French atlases, 1594–1637 . . ." in *Transactions of the Bibliographical Society*, fourth series, Vol. I, No. 3, December, 1920, p. 145. A copy of the atlas was offered for sale several years ago by Orion Booksellers of London (Catalogue No. 5) with a fairly detailed description of the volume. See also Ludovic Drapeyron's "communication" on the first national atlas of France, read at the 4th International Geographical Congress (Paris, 1890, Vol. I, pp. 406–08).
50. Bruzen de la Martiniere, Geographer to His Catholic Majesty, to Louis XV. This letter appeared as an introduction to the *Atlas de Poche, à l'usage des voyageurs et des officiers*, published by H. Du Sauzet, Amsterdam, 1734–38. (See P. L. Phillips, *op. cit.*, No. 584a.)
51. P. L. Phillips, *op. cit.*, Nos. 402–23.
52. Edward L. Stevenson, *Willem Janszoon Blaeu. 1571–1638* . . . , N. Y., 1914,

Hispanic Society Pub. No. 85, pp. 11–13; see also P. H. J. Baudet, *Leven en werken van Willem Jansz. Blaeu*, Utrecht, 1871.

53. E. L. Stevenson, *op. cit.*, p. 15.
54. *Ibid.*, pp. 26–28. The similarity between the Hondius world map of 1611 and Blaeu's world map of 1605 is striking.
55. J. H. Hessels, *op. cit.*, p. xxvi; Elial Hall, *op. cit.*, p. 170.
56. Sidney Colvin, *op. cit.*, p. 35.
57. E. L. Stevenson, *op. cit.*, pp. 30–35.
58. *Ibid.*, pp. 37–39.
59. *Ibid.*, pp. 22, 172–74.
60. *Ibid.*, pp. 16–17, quoting from Filips von Zesen: *Beschreibung der Stadt*, Amsterdam, 1664, pp. 215–16.
61. For further information on Blaeu's improved flat-bed press, see E. L. Stevenson, *op. cit.*, p. 17; see also J. Johnson, *op. cit.*, Vol. II, pp. 497 ff.; P. L. Phillips, *op. cit.*, No. 3430, and all titles listed under "Blaeu."
62. E. L. Stevenson, *op. cit.*, p. 17.
63. *Ibid.*, pp. 40–43; see also P. L. Phillips, *op. cit.*, Nos. 3420, 3421, 3430.
64. Sidney Colvin, *op. cit.*, pp. 6–7, 10. This strap-work was called *Compertimentum* in Italy.
65. See A. Lichtwark: *Der Ornamentstich der Deutschen Frü-Rennaissance*. Berlin, 1888, pp. 15–29.
66. Published in facsimile by Edward Bros., Ann Arbor, 1932, from the unique copy in the British Museum.
67. R. Tottill, *op. cit.*, fol. iiii.
68. *Ibid.*, fol. ii.
69. *Ibid.*, fol. vii.
70. *Ibid.*, fol. ix.
71. W. Salmon: *Polygraphice, or the arts of drawing, engraving . . . washing . . .* London, 1675, pp. 73 ff. The Library of Congress lists an edition of 1671. There were several later editions.
72. *Ibid.*, p. 172.
73. *Ibid.*, p. 217.
74. *Ibid.*, p. 320.
75. John G. M. Smith: *The art of painting in oyl, to which is added the whole art and mystery of colouring maps*, London, 1769, p. 95. There were various editions of this useful book. A. L. Humphreys, in his *Old Decorative Maps and Charts*, lists the ninth edition, London, 1788 — "the only treatise in which there is a special chapter on map colouring."
76. *Ibid.*, p. 96.
77. *Ibid.*, pp. 98, 99.
78. *Ibid.*, pp. 100, 102.
79. *Ibid.*, pp. 103–05.
80. *Ibid.*, pp. 106–10.
81. Sidney Colvin, *op. cit.*, p. 135.

CHAPTER VII

1. E. G. Ravenstein: *Martin Behaim, his life and his globe . . .* London, 1908, pp. 12–15.
2. T. Blundeville, *op. cit.*, p. 595.
3. *Ibid.*, pp. 599 ff., describes Blagrave's "Mathematicall Iewell"; for descriptions of other astrolabes see pp. 664 ff.
4. See L. C. Wroth, *op. cit.*, p. 88.

5. Edmund Gunter, *The workes of Edmund Gunter, containing the description of the sector, cross-staff, and other instruments* . . . London, third edition, 1653; for a bibliographical note on the subject, see L. C. Wroth, *op. cit.*, pp. 24–29.
6. Edmund Gunter, *op. cit.*, sign. Aa.
7. E. G. Ravenstein, *op. cit.*, p. 17; Blundeville, *op. cit.*, sig. Xx 3.
8. John Davis, *The Seamans Secrets*, London, 1607, reprinted in *The voyages and works of John Davis the navigator*, edited with an introduction and notes by Albert Hastings Markham, London, The Hakluyt Society, 1880, pp. 330 ff. For a bibliography on the subject see Appendix A, this volume. John Werner of Nuremberg, one of the earliest writers on navigation (who edited the 1514 edition of Ptolemy's *Geographia*), says that the cross-staff was a very ancient instrument, but that it was only then (1514) beginning to come into general use at sea. (See L. C. Wroth, *op. cit.*, p. 44.)
9. John Davis, *op. cit.*, pp. 330–33.
10. For a description and diagram of the English quadrant, see Nathaniel Colson's *Mariner's New Calendar*, London, 1762; Pierre Bouguer's "De la methode d'observer exactement sur mer la hauteur des astres." (In *Recueil des pieces qui ont remporté les prix de l'Académie Royale des Sciences*. Tome II. 1727–1733. Paris, 1752.)
11. Pierre Bouguer, *op. cit.*, pp. 1–15.
12. *Ibid.*, p. 29.
13. See *Correspondence and papers of Edmund Halley*, pp. 161–62.
14. *Ibid.*, pp. 3, 57, 60, 65. Halley's description of his collapsible reflecting quadrant, with diagram attached, ran as follows (pp. 161–62):

Let AB be a square brass hollow tube so strong as to bear its own length without bending. At A place the Eyeglass, and at B the objectglass of a Telescope of the length required. On this tube let the paralellogram CDEF of equall sides be affixed, which must be moveable on the four Centers C, D, E, F, each of the sides EC, CD, DF, being equall to the distance EF taken at convenience. On

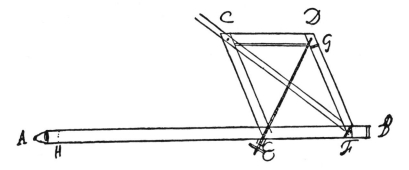

the side DF place an object glass of a Telescope as at G, and let it be as much a sphere as to have its focus at the distance of GF plus FH. And over all put a small brass ruler CF, having on the Center F a curious polisht mettall plate, or elce a fine thin plate of glass well foild, and cut so as to reach no lower than the center F, leaving the one half of the object glass at B open; then shall the Horizon be seen directly by the Telescope AB, and the Sun reflected from the plate F in the same point, and the altitude of the Sun be measurd by the Angle AFD., which may be opened or closed as occasion requires by a screw from the opposite angles DE: the which by its fineness and by dividing the number of parts in each revolution of an Index, may make the divisions as senble as can be required, and these divisions again are easily explicable by a small Table of Chords which at sight will give the degree and minute observed.

15. See an extensive biographical sketch of Newton, written by Henry Martyn Taylor in the *Encyclopaedia Britannica*, 11th edition. See also George J. Gray's *A bibliography of the works of Sir Isaac Newton . . .* 2nd edition, Cambridge, 1907. Newton's collected works were published by Dr. Samuel Horsley: *Isaaci Newtoni Opera quae exstant Omnia*, 5 vols., London, 1779–1785.

16. A description of Newton's quadrant was read before the Royal Society 28 October, 1742; it was published, with a plate, in the *Transactions*, Vol. XLII (1742–43), London, 1744, p. 155.

17. This description, with two plates, was published in the *Philosophical Transactions* for August and September, 1731 (No. 420), Vol. 37, London, 1733. In the same volume (No. 423) see "The description of a new quadrant for taking altitudes without an horizon, either at sea or land. Invented by Mr. John Elton." This paper, also, is accompanied by a plate.

18. See Harold E. Gillingham: "Early Philadelphia Instrument Makers," in *Pennsylvania Magazine*, Vol. 51, No. 3, Philadelphia, 1927. See also the article "Sextant" in the *Encyclopaedia Britannica*, 11th edition.

19. For a more detailed description, see text and plate cited in note No. 17 above, pp. 147–56. Hadley's improved instrument, with plate, is described on pp. 156–57.

20. See "An account of observations made on board the Chatham-yacht, August 30th and 31st, and September 1st, 1732 . . . for the trial of an instrument for taking angles . . . By John Hadley . . ." in *Philosophical Transactions* of the Royal Society for September and October, 1732. No. 425. Vol. 37, London, 1733, pp. 341–56.

21. See "A spirit level to be fixed to a quadrant for taking a meridional altitude at sea, when the horizon is not visible. By John Hadley." (In the *Philosophical Transactions* of the Royal Society for November and December, 1733, No. 430, Vol. 38, London, 1735, pp. 167–72.) Another ancient and honorable instrument for measuring angles was the mariner's bow. See "An account of Mr. Thomas Godfrey's improvement of Davis's quadrant, transferred to the mariner's-bow, communicated to the Royal Society, by Mr. J. Logan," in *Philosophical Transactions* of the Royal Society for December, 1734, No. 435, Vol. 38, London, 1735, pp. 441–50.

22. For a summary of the early astronomical tables produced in Europe and Asia, see the article "Astronomy" by Agnes Mary Clerke in the *Encyclopaedia Britannica*, 11th edition, pp. 810–11.

23. See L. C. Wroth, *op. cit.*, pp. 29–30, 44 ff.

24. For further information on Regiomontanus, see Pierre Gassendi, *Tychonis Brahei vita . . . Accessit N. Copernici, G. Peurbachii, et Joannis Regiomontani vita*, Paris, 1654; J. G. Doppelmayr, *Historische nachricht von den Nurnbergischen mathematicis*, Nürnberg, 1730; G. H. Schubert, *Peurbach und Regiomontan*, Erlangen, 1828.

25. *Regimento do estrolabio e do quadrante, tractado da spera do mundo*. Reproduction fac-similé du seul examplaire connu appartenant à la Bibliothèque Royale de Munich, Munich, Carl Kuhn, 1914. This volume, containing a long, informative introduction (pp. 1–31), is Vol. I of a series projected by Joaquim Bensaude under the general title: *Histoire de la science nautique Portugaise. . . .*

26. L. C. Wroth, *op. cit.*, pp. 50–52 ff.

27. See William Robert Martin's article "Navigation" in the *Encyclopaedia Britannica*, 11th edition, p. 288b; see also James II, King of Great Britain, *The royal charter of confirmation granted by His . . . Majesty to the Trinity House of Deptford-*

Strond for the government and increase of the navigation of England, London, 1825.

28. *Ibid.*, p. 293b, for the translated quotation, and for an account of other early printed Tables. See also *La Grande Encyclopédie* under "Annuaire du Bureau des Longitudes."

29. William Wales, scientist and explorer, made several important contributions to astronomy and navigation. His tables of equations of equal altitudes were included in his treatise on *The method of finding the longitude at sea, by time-keepers*, London, 1794.

30. W. R. Martin, *op. cit.*, p. 293b; the American version of the Nautical Almanac appeared under the title *The American ephemeris and nautical almanac*.

31. T. L. Heath, *op. cit.*, p. 23, refers to a handbook on nautical astronomy attributed to Thales; see also G. C. Lewis, *op. cit.*, p. 58.

32. T. L. Heath, *op. cit.*, p. 8 *n*.

33. *Ibid.*, pp. 101, 172–73, 200.

34. Martin Cortés: *The arte of nauigation* . . . London, 1589. See also T. S. Lecky: *Wrinkles in practical navigation*, revised and enlarged by William Allingham, London, 1910; pp. 383 ff.

35. S. E. Morison: "Columbus and Polaris," in *The American Neptune*, Vol. I, 1941, pp. 6–25, 123–37. This passage is quoted with the permission of the American Neptune, Incorporated.

36. T. Blundeville, *op. cit.*, pp. 713–27.

CHAPTER VIII

1. W. R. Martin, *op. cit.*, p. 284c.

2. See Richard Eden's "Epistle Dedicatory" in his translation of John Taisnier's *A very necessarie and profitable book concerning nauigation* . . . London, 1579 (?). (Quoted from *Bibliotheca Americana. A catalogue of books . . . in the library of the late John Carter Brown*. Providence, 1875, Part I, No. 310.)

3. J. J. Fahie, *Galileo. His life and work*, New York, 1903, pp. 172, 372 ff.; Rupert T. Gould, *The marine chronometer: Its history and development*, London, 1923, pp. 11, 12.

4. J. J. Fahie, *op. cit.*, pp. 372 ff.; E. L. Stevenson, *op. cit.*, p. 25. Galileo named the satellites of Jupiter the "Cosmian Stars" after Cosmo Medici (Cosmo II, grand-duke of Tuscany). See Galileo's *Opere* edited by Eugenio Alberi, 16 vols., Firenze, 1842–56. Tome III contains his "Sydereus Nuncius," pp. 59–99, describing his observations of Jupiter's satellites, and his suggestion that they be used in the determination of longitude.

5. J. J. Fahie, *op. cit.*, pp. 373–75.

6. R. T. Gould, *op. cit.*, pp. 4 and 4 *n*.

7. See Galileo's *Dialogues concerning two new sciences, by Galileo Galilei*, translated by Henry Crew and Alfonso de Salvio, introduction by Antonio Favaro, New York, 1914, pp. 84, 95, 170, 254.

8. See John L. E. Dreyer's article "Time, Measurement of" (in the *Encyclopaedia Britannica*, 11th edition, pp. 983d, 984a).

9. Thomas Burnet: *The theory of the earth* . . . London, 1684, p. 144.

10. See Charles J. E. Wolf, *Histoire de l'observatoire de Paris de sa fondation à 1793*, Paris, 1902; also *L'Institut de France* by Gaston Darboux, Henry Roujon and George Picot, Paris, 1907 ("Les Grandes Institutions de France").

11. C. J. E. Wolf, *op. cit.*, pp. 5 ff.

12. *Mémoires de l'Académie Royale des Sciences*, Vol. VIII, Paris, 1730.

13. C. J. E. Wolf, *op. cit.*, p. 4.

14. *Histoire de l'Académie Royale des Sciences*, Vol. I, pp. 45–46.
15. Justin Winsor, *op. cit.*, Vol. II, pp. 98–99 has an interesting note on the "log." In Pigafetta's journal (January, 1521), he mentions the use of a chain dragged astern on Magellan's ships to measure their speed. The "log" as we know it was described in Bourne's *Regiment of the Sea*, 1573, and Humphrey Cole is said to have invented it. In Eden's translation of Taisnier he speaks of an artifice "not yet divulgate, which, placed in the pompe of a shyp, whyther the water hath recourse, and moved by the motion of the shypp, with wheels and weyghts, doth exactly shewe what space the shyp hath gone." See the article "Navigation" in the *Encyclopaedia Britannica*, 9th edition. For further comments on the history of the log, see L. C. Wroth, *op. cit.*, pp. 72–74.
16. *Oeuvres de Fontenelle. Eloges.* Paris, 1825, Vol. I, p. 254.
17. Joseph François Michaud: *Biographie Universelle*, Paris, 1854–65. Cassini gave Jupiter's rotation as 9^h 56^m. The *correct* time is not yet known with certainty. Slightly different results are obtained by using different markings. The value 9^h 55^m is frequently used in modern texts.
18. The first edition of Cassini's work was published under the title *Ephemerides Bononiensés Mediceorvm sydervm ex hypothesibvs, et tabvlis Io: Dominici Cassini* . . . Bononiae [Bologne], 1668.
19. C. J. E. Wolf, *op. cit.*, p. 6.
20. For a detailed inventory of the equipment built and purchased by the Académie Royale, see C. J. E. Wolf, *op. cit.*, Chs. X and XII.
21. For a complete account of Picard's measurement of the earth, including tables of data and a historical summary, see the *Mémoires de l'Académie Royale des Sciences*, Vol. VII, Pt. I, Paris, 1729. See also the article "Earth, Figure of the" by Alexander Ross Clarke and Frederick Robert Helmert in the *Encyclopaedia Britannica*, 11th edition, p. 801.
22. *Mémoires de l'Académie Royale des Sciences*, Vol. VII, Pt. I. Pagination varies widely in different editions of this series.
23. *Ibid.*, pp. 306–07, gives a table of the linear measures used by Picard in making his computations. Measurements were made between the zenith and a star in the kneecap of Cassiopeia, probably δ (Al Rukbah). See the *Mémoires de l'Académie Royale des Sciences*, Vol. VII, Pt. II, Paris, 1730, p. 305.
24. For Cassini's status in the Académie Royale, see C. J. E. Wolf, *op. cit.*, Ch. XIII.
25. *Ibid.*, pp. 62–65. For an account of the great planisphere, see the *Histoire de l'Académie Royale des Sciences*, Vol. I, pp. 225–26; C. J. E. Wolf, *op. cit.*, pp. 116–30. A facsimile of one of the printed versions of the map, reduced, was issued with Christian Sandler's *Die Reformation der Kartographie um 1700*, Munich, 1905; a second one, colored, was published in 1941 by the University of Michigan from the original in the William L. Clements Library. For bibliographical notes regarding the publication of the map, see L. A. Brown, *Jean Domenique Cassini* . . . pp. 62–73.
26. The island of Ferro, the most southwest of the Canary Islands, was a common prime meridian among cartographers as late as 1880. It was considered the dividing line between the Eastern and Western hemispheres! (See Lippincott's *A complete pronouncing gazetteer or geographical dictionary of the world*. Philadelphia, 1883.)
27. L. A. Brown: *Jean Domenique Cassini* . . . pp. 42–44.
28. Cassini suggested two methods of adjusting a clock to *mean* time. The first was to make a series of observations of the sun (equal altitudes) and afterwards correct them with tables of the equation of time, and second, to regulate one clock to keep sidereal time by observing two successive transits of a star and correct the second clock from it.

29. Cassini's "Instructions" were printed in full in the *Mémoires de l'Académie Royale des Sciences*, Vol. VIII, Paris, 1730. For a translation into English see L. A. Brown, *Jean Domenique Cassini . . .* pp. 48–60.
30. L. A. Brown: *Jean Domenique Cassini . . .* p. 57.
31. Christian Huygens: *Horologivm oscillatorivm; sive de motu pendulorvm ad horologia aptato demonstrationes geometricae*, Paris, 1673.
32. Isaac Newton: *Philosophiae Naturalis Principia Mathematica*, 3 vols., London, 1687.
33. R. T. Gould, *op. cit.*, p. 9; also Henry S. Richardson's *Greenwich: its history, antiquities, improvements and public buildings*, London, 1834.
34. See Francis Baily's *Account of the Rev. John Flamsteed*, London, 1835.
35. R. T. Gould, *op. cit.*, p. 2.
36. See *Curious Enquiries*, London, 1687; R. T. Gould, *op. cit.*, p. 11. The title of Sir Kenelm Digby's famous work, which appeared in French as well as English, was *A late discourse . . . touching the cure of wounds by the powder of sympathy; with instructions how to make the said powder . . .* Second edition, augmented, London, 1658.
37. See Whiston and Ditton's *A new method for discovering the longitude*. London, 1714. The petition appeared in various periodicals: *The Guardian*, July 14; *The Englishman*, Dec. 19, 1713 (R. T. Gould, *op. cit.*, p. 13).
38. R. T. Gould, *op. cit.*, p. 13.
39. Gemma Frisius: *De principiis astronomiae et cosmographiae*, Antwerp, 1530.
40. Thomas Blundeville, *op. cit.*, p. 390.
41. 12 Anne, Cap. 15; R. T. Gould, *op. cit.*, p. 13.
42. R. T. Gould, *op. cit.*, p. 16. According to the Act of 1712 the Board was comprised of: "The Lord High Admiral or the First Lord of the Admiralty; The Speaker of the House of Commons; The First Commissioner of the Navy; The First Commissioner of Trade; The Admirals of the Red, White and Blue Squadrons; The Master of the Trinity House; The President of the Royal Society; The Astronomer-Royal; The Savilian, Lucasian, and Plumian Professors of Mathematics."
43. *Ibid.*, p. 20; this translation is from a paraphrase by Duro in his *Disquisiciones Nauticas*.
44. *Ibid.*, p. 25. The anagram was a device commonly used in the best scientific circles of the time to establish priority of invention or discovery without actually disclosing anything that might be seized upon by a zealous colleague.
45. *Ibid.*, pp. 27–30; Huygens described his pendulum clock in his *Horologium Oscillatorium*, Paris, 1673.
46. *Ibid.*, pp. 32, 33; Jeremy Thacker wrote a clever piece entitled: *The Longitudes Examined, beginning with a short epistle to the Longitudinarians and ending with the description of a smart, pretty Machine of my Own which I am (almost) sure will do for the Longitude, and procure me The Twenty Thousand Pounds. By Jeremy Thacker, of Beverly in Yorkshire. ". . . quid non mortalia pectora cogis Auri sacra Fames . . ."* London. Printed for J. Roberts at the Oxford Arms in Warwick Lane, 1714. Price Sixpence.
47. The invention of a "maintaining power" is erroneously attributed to Harrison. See R. T. Gould, *op. cit.*, p. 34, who says that Thacker antedates Harrison by twenty years on the invention of an auxiliary spring to keep a machine going while it was being wound. In spite of the magnitude of John Harrison's achievement, the inventive genius of Pierre Le Roy of Paris produced the prototype of the modern chronometer. As Rupert Gould points out, Harrison's Number Four was a remarkable piece of mechanism, "a satisfactory marine timekeeper, one, too, which was of permanent usefullness, and which could be duplicated as often

as necessary. But No. 4, in spite of its fine performance and beautiful mechanism, cannot be compared, for efficiency and design, with Le Roy's wonderful machine. The Frenchman, who was but little indebted to his predecessors, and not at all to his contemporaries, evolved, by sheer force of genius, a timekeeper which contains all the essential mechanism of the modern chronometer." (See Gould, *op. cit.*, p. 65.)

48. For a biographical sketch of Harrison see R. T. Gould, *op. cit.*, pp. 40 ff. Saunderson (1682–1739) was Lucasian professor of mathematics at Cambridge. Harrison's first "regulator" is now in the museum of the Clockmakers' Co. of London. "The term 'regulator' is used to denote any high-class pendulum clock designed for use solely as an accurate time-measurer, without any additions such as striking mechanism, calendar work, &c." (Gould, p. 42 *n.*)

49. *Ibid.*, pp. 40–41. Graham had experimented with a gridiron pendulum and in 1725 had produced a pendulum with a small jar of mercury attached to the bob which was supposed to counteract the expansion of the rod caused by a rise in temperature.

50. *Ibid.*, pp. 42, 43; Graham and Tompion are the only two horologists buried in Westminster Abbey.

51. *Ibid.*, pp. 45–46.

52. *Ibid.*, p. 47.

53. *Ibid.*, pp. 47–49, for details of the technical improvements made in No. 2 and No. 3.

54. *Ibid.*, p. 49. Some years later he was offered the honor of Fellow of the Royal Society, but he declined it in favor of his son William.

55. *Ibid.*, pp. 50, 53; for a full description of No. 4 see H. M. Frodsham in the *Horological Journal* for May, 1878 — with drawings of the escapement, train and remontoire taken from the duplicate of No. 4 made by Larcum Kendall.

56. *Ibid.*, p. 63.

57. *Ibid.*, pp. 55–56 and 56 *n.*

58. *Ibid.*, pp. 57 ff. On August 17, 1762, the Board refused to give Harrison a certificate stating that he had complied with the terms set forth in the Act of Queen Anne.

59. *Ibid.*, p. 59; see also *A narrative of the proceedings relative to the discovery of the longitude at sea; by Mr. John Harrison's time-keeper* . . . [By James Short] London: printed for the author, 1765, pp. 7, 8.

60. R. T. Gould, *op. cit.*, pp. 59, 60.

61. *Ibid.*, pp. 60 ff.; Act of Parliament 5 George III, Cap. 20; see also James Snort, *op. cit.*, p. 15.

62. R. T. Gould, *op. cit.*, pp. 61–62; 62 *n;* the unauthorized publication of Harrison's drawings with a preface by the Reverend Maskelyne, appeared under the title: *The principles of Mr. Harrison's time-keeper, with plates of the same*, London, 1767.

63. R. T. Gould, *op. cit.*, p. 63; see also Nevil Maskelyne's *An account of the going of Mr. John Harrison's watch* . . . London, 1767.

64. R. T. Gould, *op. cit.*, pp. 64–65.

65. *Ibid.*, p. 66; see also the *Journal of the House of Commons*, 6. 5. 1772.

CHAPTER IX

1. Michaud, *op. cit.*, under "Sanson."

2. *Ibid.*, under "Delisle"; see also *Nouvelle Biographie Universelle* under "Delisle"; Albert Isnard's "Joseph-Nicolas Delisle, sa biographie et sa collection de cartes géographiques à la Bibliothèque Nationale." (In France. Comité des travaux historiques et scientifiques. *Bulletin de la section de géographie*. Paris, 1915. Vol. 30, pp. 34–168.)

3. Michaud, *op. cit.*, under "Delisle, Guillaume."

4. *Ibid.*, under "Delisle, Joseph Nicolas."

5. See Pierre Clement, *Vie de Colbert*, Paris, 1846; *Lettres, instructions, et mémoires de Colbert, publiés d'après les ordres de l'Empereur* . . . Third edition, 9 vols., Paris, 1893.

6. *Lettres, instructions et memoires de Colbert* . . . Vol. IV, p. 28.

7. See Lucien Gallois: "L'Académie des sciences et les origines de la carte de Cassini," in *Annales de géographie.* Vol. 18, No. 99. Paris, 1909, pp. 193–204; No. 100, pp. 289–300.

8. L. Gallois, *op. cit.*, p. 196.

9. *Ibid.*, pp. 197–205. In his article "Map" in *Encyclopaedia Britannica*, 11th edition, p. 648d, Ravenstein says Vivier was the first cartographer to use hachures. See P. L. Phillips, *op. cit.*, No. 4254, for the Amsterdam edition of the Vivier map of Paris, which appeared in Vol. II (no. 2) of Frederik de Wit's *Atlas minor.*

10. See J. D. Cassini's "Observations astronomiques faites en divers endroits du royaume," in *Mémoires de l'Académie Royale des Sciences*, Vol. VII, Pt. I, Paris, 1729, pp. 349–75; in the same volume, see "Observations faites à Brest et à Nantes pendant l'année 1679," pp. 379–90.

11. For details concerning the extension of the meridian of Paris, see *Suite des mémoires de l'Académie Royale des Sciences*, 1718, Paris, 1720; see also the *Mémoires de l'Académie Royale des Sciences*, Vol. VII, Pt. I, Paris, 1729, especially the map, p. 430.

12. *Registres de l'Académie Royale des Sciences*, Vol. IX, p. 96.

13. L. Gallois, *op. cit.*, pp. 294–96; see also C. J. E. Wolf, *op. cit.*, pp. 120–22.

14. L. Gallois, *op. cit.*, pp. 296–97.

15. *Ibid.*, pp. 297 ff. See also *Histoire de l'Académie Royale des Sciences*, 1718, Paris, 1729, p. 245, "De la grandeur de la terre et de sa figure," Par M. [Jacques] Cassini. See all articles in the *Suite des Mémoires*, 1718, Paris, 1729, nearly all of which are concerned with the size of the earth and the length of a degree.

16. L. Gallois, *op. cit.*, pp. 299, 300.

17. *Ibid.*, p. 300; see also *Histoire de l'Académie Royale des Sciences*, 1733, Paris, 1735, pp. 389 ff.; *Suite des mémoires*, 1740, Paris, 1744.

18. See Charles Marie de la Condamine, *Journal du voyage fait . . . à l'équateur, servant d'introduction historique à la mésure des trois premiers degrès du méridien*, Paris, 1751 (to accompany the *Histoire de l'Académie Royale des Sciences* for 1751); also *La figure de la terre, determinée par les observations de MM. Bouguer et de la Condamine* . . . Paris, 1749. A Spanish expedition under Don Antonio Ulloa and Jorge Juan y Santacilia made an independent survey at the same time. See *Observaciones astronomicas y phisicas hechas de orden de S. M. en los reynos del Peru . . . Corregidas y emmendadas por el Autor*, Madrid, 1773. An account of the survey near the Arctic Circle was published by Moreau de Maupertuis under the title *La figure de la terre déterminée par les observations de Messieurs De Maupertuis, Clairaut, Camus, Le Monnier . . . et Outhier . . . accompagnés de M. Celsius . . . faites par ordre du Roy au Cercle Polaire*, Paris, 1738.

19. L. Gallois, *op. cit.*, pp. 301–03; see also *Histoire de l'Académie Royale des Sciences*, 1739, Paris, 1741, pp. 119–34; *Suite des Mémoires de l'Académie Royale des Sciences, 1740, passim.*

20. L. Gallois, *op. cit.*, pp. 304–05. The outline map bore the title *Nouvelle carte qui comprend les principaux triangles qui servent de fondement à la description géometrique de la France. Levée par ordre du Roy. Par Messrs Maraldi et Cassini de Thury, de l'Académie Royale des Sciences. Année 1744.* The textual explanation: "*Sur la description géometrique de la France*," by M. Cassini de Thury, appeared in the *Histoire de l'Académie Royale des Sciences*, 1745, Paris, 1749,

pp. 553–60. The 18-sheet map bore the title *Carte qui comprend touts les lieux de la France qui ont étés déterminés par les operations géométriques par Mr Cassimi de Thury de l'Académie Royale des Sciences. Tracé d'après les mesures et gravé par Dheulland. Aubin et Bourgoin le jeune scripsit. A Paris sur le quay de l'Horloge, en la maison de feu Mr Delisle . . .* [n.d.]

21. See Cassini de Thury: *Description des conquêtes de Louis XV . . . (A la suite de: Relation d'un voyage en Allemagne, qui comprend les opérations relatives à la figure de la terre . . .* Paris, 1775, pp. 123–94).

22. Michaud, *op. cit.*, under "Cassini, Jacques Dominique," says that two supplementary sheets were added, making 182 in all.

23. This General Staff map on the scale of 1:80,000 was issued by the Dépôt de la Guerre (now the Service Géographique de l'Armée). See Henri M. A. Berthaut, *La carte de France, 1750–1898,* 2 vols., Paris, 1898–99; see also his *Les ingénieurs géographes militaires, 1624–1831; étude historique,* 2 vols., Paris, Service géographique de l'armée, 1902.

24. See Nevil Maskelyne: "Concerning the latitude and longitude of the Royal Observatory . . . with remarks on a memorial of the late M. Cassini de Thury," in *Philosophical Transactions of the Royal Society,* Vol. 77, Pt. I, London, 1787, pp. 151–87. See also C. F. Cassini de Thury: "*La meridienne de l'Observatoire Royal de Paris, verifiée dans toute l'étendue du Royaume . . . pour lever une carte générale de la France,*" in *Suite des mémoires de l'Académie Royale des sciences,* 1740. Paris, 1744.

25. See Maskelyne's paper cited above, note 24. See also William Roy: "An account of the measurement of a base on Hounslow-Heath. Read from April 21 to June 16, 1785," in *Philosophical Transactions of the Royal Society.* Vol. 75, Pt. II, for 1785. London, 1785, pp. 385 ff.

26. *Ibid.,* pp. 385–87.

27. *Ibid.,* pp. 390–92.

28. *Ibid.,* pp. 397–401.

29. *Ibid.,* pp. 416–25; pp. 430, 432, 437.

30. *Ibid.,* pp. 431, 455, 456, 461, 478; see also William Mudge and Isaac Dalby, *An account of the operations carried on for accomplishing a trigonometrical survey of England . . .* 3 vols., London, 1799–1811, Vol. I, pp. 85, 86.

31. William Roy: "An account of the mode proposed to be followed in determining the relative situation of the Royal Observatories of Greenwich and Paris," in *Philosophical Transactions of the Royal Society,* Vol. 77, Pt. I, for 1787, London, 1787, pp. 188–226.

32. William Roy: "An account of the trigonometrical operation, whereby the distance between the meridians of the Royal Observatories of Greenwich and Paris has been determined. Read February 25, 1790," in *Philosophical Transactions of the Royal Society,* Vol. 80, Pt. I, for the year 1790, London, 1790, pp. 111–270.

33. *Ibid.,* pp. 112–14, 262.

34. *Ibid.,* pp. 121, 247.

35. Nevil Maskelyne: "Concerning the latitude and longitude . . . at Greenwich . . ." p. 183.

36. William Roy: "An account of the trigonometrical operation . . ." p. 205.

37. *Ibid.,* pp. 228–30.

38. *Ibid.,* p. 170.

39. *Ibid.,* pp. 249–59, 261–67.

40. W. Mudge and I. Dalby, *op. cit.,* Vol. I, p. 204.

41. Beginning in 1791 all expenses of the Survey were paid for by the Treasury, which committed itself to cover the work up to the amount of £3,000 per year. From 1790 to 1810 the amount was sufficient, according to Mudge. (*Westminster Re-*

view, Jan. to April, 1882, New Series, Vol. 61, London, 1882, pp. 492–521.) The French scientists had their own troubles. In 1793, Cassini de Thury was jailed by the revolutionary government. (*Quarterly Review*, Vol. 180, Jan. and April, 1895, London, 1895, p. 38.)

42. Josiah Pierce, Jr., "The Ordnance Survey of Great Britain — its history and object," *National Geographic Magazine*, Vol. II, 1890, Washington, 1891, pp. 243–60; "The Ordnance Survey" *Quarterly Review*, Vol. 180, Jan. and April, 1895, London, 1895, pp. 36–60; "The Romance of State-Mapping" (*Blackwood's Edinburgh Magazine*, Vol. 144, July-December, 1888. Edinburgh, 1888, pp. 384–98).
43. Jos. Pierce, *op. cit.*, p. 249; *Quarterly Review*, *op. cit.*, p. 43.
44. Jos. Pierce, *op. cit.*, p. 249–50; for a good biographical sketch of Colby see *Blackwood's Edinburgh Magazine*, *op. cit.*, pp. 387 ff.
45. *Westminster Review*, *op. cit.*, p. 497; Jos. Pierce, *op. cit.*, p. 257.
46. See John F. McLennan: *Memoir of Thomas Drummond*, London, 1867. Sir John Herschel described the first demonstration of Drummond's light in the Tower as follows:

> The common Argand burner and parabolic reflector of a British lighthouse were first exhibited, the room being darkened, and with considerable effect. Fresnel's superb lamp was next disclosed, at whose superior effect the other seemed to dwindle, and showed in a manner quite subordinate. But when the gas began to play, the lime being brought now to its full ignition and the screen suddenly removed, a glare shone forth, overpowering, and as it were annihilating, both its predecessors, which appeared by its side, the one as a feeble gleam which it required attention to see, the other like a mere plate of heated metal. A shout of triumph and of admiration burst from all present.

47. *Quarterly Review*, *op. cit.*, p. 43; Jos. Pierce, *op. cit.*, p. 251; Charles Close, *The early years of the Ordnance Survey*, Chatham, 1926; C. Close, *The map of England*, London, 1932.
48. *Quarterly Review*, *op. cit.*, p. 40; Jos. Pierce, *op. cit.*, pp. 252–53.
49. *Blackwood's Edinburgh Magazine*, *op. cit.*, pp. 387–90.
50. G. M. Wheeler, *op. cit.*, pp. 402–04.
51. *Ibid.*, pp. 90, 98, 99, 103, 109, 404–11.
52. *Ibid.*, p. 406; Arthur R. Hinks, *Maps and survey* . . . Cambridge [Eng.] 1944, p. 93.
53. G. M. Wheeler, *op. cit.*, pp. 89, 97, 102, 108, 345–47.
54. *Ibid.*, pp. 349, 352–57.
55. *Ibid.*, pp. 413–19.
56. *Ibid.*, pp. 89, 98, 102, 108, 353–60; A. R. Hinks, *op. cit.*, pp. 102, 103.
57. Wheeler, *op. cit.*, pp. 89, 90, 98.
58. *Ibid.*, pp. 103, 108, 109.
59. *Ibid.*, pp. 363 ff.
60. *Ibid.*, pp. 353, 360 ff.; A. R. Hinks, *op. cit.*, pp. 104, 105.
61. *Quarterly Review*, *op. cit.*, p. 39; G. M. Wheeler, *op. cit.*, pp. 263–66.
62. G. M. Wheeler, *op. cit.*, pp. 89, 94, 95, 102, 105, 265–66.
63. *Ibid.*, pp. 266 ff.; A. R. Hinks, *op. cit.*, pp. 89–91.
64. G. M. Wheeler, *op. cit.*, pp. 89, 96, 102, 106, 269, 270; [Imhof, Eduard] *Hans Konrad Gygers Karte des kantons Zürich von 1667* . . . Zürich, 1944. This publication includes a colored facsimile of the map.
65. G. M. Wheeler, *op. cit.*, pp. 307–08; see also P. L. Phillips, *op. cit.*, No. 3156; A. R. Hinks, *op. cit.*, pp. 106–08.
66. G. M. Wheeler, *op. cit.*, pp. 304 ff.
67. *Ibid.*, pp. 246–50.

68. *Ibid.*, pp. 230–31.
69. *Ibid.*, pp. 88, 94, 102, 104, 232 ff.
70. *Ibid.*, pp. 235–45.
71. *Ibid.*, pp. 464 ff.
72. *Ibid.*, pp. 90, 99, 464–96; *The writings of Thomas Jefferson*, Memorial edition, 20 vols., Washington, 1903–04, Vol. XIX, p. viii. For a list of the military explorations and surveys west of the Mississippi, with dates, see G. M. Wheeler, *op. cit.*, pp. 465, 466; also G. K. Warren, "Memoir to accompany the map of the territory of the United States from the Mississippi River to the Pacific Ocean." (In U. S. War Department. *Reports of explorations and surveys to ascertain the most practicable and economical route for a railroad from the Mississippi to the Pacific Ocean,* 12 vols., Washington, 1855–60, Vol. XI.) See also *Documents relating to the purchase & exploration of Louisiana.* I. The limits and bounds of Louisiana. By Thomas Jefferson . . . Printed from the original manuscripts . . . Boston and New York, 1904.
73. G. M. Wheeler, *op. cit.*, pp. 153, 464.
74. *Ibid.*, p. 81.
75. See Florian Cajori, *The chequered career of Ferdinand Rudolph Hassler . . . a chapter in the history of science in America*, Boston, 1929; G. A. Webber, *The United States Coast and Geodetic survey, its work, methods and organization*, Washington, 1929 (U. S. C. & G. Special Publication No. 23); U. S. C. & G. Survey, *The transcontinental triangulation and the American arc of the parallel*, by C. A. Schott, Washington, 1900.
76. See W. Thiele, *op. cit.*, pp. 127 ff.
77. G. M. Wheeler, *op. cit.*, pp. 100–03; see also pp. 467, 468, 490–94; *The United States Geological Survey: its origin, development, organization and operation*, U. S. Geological Survey Bulletin No. 227, Washington, 1904; *The United States Geological survey, its history, activities and organization*, Service Monograph of the United States Government No. I, New York, 1918.
78. W. Thiele, *op. cit.*, pp. 122 ff.; see also the letterpress on the verso of any U. S. Geological Survey "Top" sheet.
79. See Wolfgang L. G. Joerg: "Summary of Recent Reports on Natural Resources," in *Second Report of the Science Advisory Board*. Washington, 1935, pp. 397–422. See also Dr. Joerg's enlightening contributions to the state of maps and surveys within the various agencies of the United States government in the *American Yearbook*, New York, v.d.

CHAPTER X

1. G. M. Wheeler, *op. cit.*, p. 145.
2. *Ibid.*, pp. 101, 102, 147.
3. *Ibid.*, pp. 85, 101, 145.
4. *Ibid.*, pp. 82, 83, 148, 149.
5. *Ibid.*, pp. 149, 497, 498.
6. *Ibid.*, pp. 498–500; see also *Encyclopaedia Britannica* under "Chart" and "Surveying; nautical."
7. G. M. Wheeler, *op. cit.*, pp. 30, 31.
8. *Ibid.*, pp. 29–30.
9. Samuel Dunn's *A new atlas of the mundane system . . .* London, 1810, Pl. 24.
10. G. M. Wheeler, *op. cit.*, pp. 85, 144.
11. *Ibid.*, pp. 82, 147, 242; Charles H. Deetz, *Cartography*, U. S. Coast and Geodetic Survey, Special Publication No. 205, Washington, 1936, pp. 7 ff.; E. G. Ravenstein,

"Map" *Encyclopaedia Britannica*, 11th edition, p. 648d; see Michaud, *op. cit.*, for information on Marc du Carla Bonifas (1738–1816).

12. *La Grande Encyclopédie*, under "Système."

13. Pierre F. A. Méchain: *Base du système métrique décimal, ou, mesure de l'arc du méridien . . . exécutée en 1792 . . .* par MM. Méchain et Delambre . . . 3 vols., Paris, 1806–10.

14. *La Grande Encyclopédie*, under "Système."

15. See Hermann Wagner: *Der kartenmaszstab. Historisch-kritische betrachtungen*, in *Zeitschrift der gesellschaft für erdkunde zu Berlin.* 1914, pp. 1–34.

16. For a convenient table of scales showing the equivalents of (1) Common Representative Fractions, (2) Inches per Mile, (3) Centimeters per Kilometer, see E. C. Olson and A. Whitmarsh, *Foreign Maps*, New York and London, 1944, p. 166.

17. A. R. Clarke and F. R. Helmert, *op. cit.*, p. 810; see also Clarke's *Comparisons of standards of length of England, France, Belgium, Prussia, Russia, India and Australia, made at the Ordnance Survey Office*, Southampton, 1866.

18. See *La Grande Encyclopédie*, under "Système"; see also A. R. Clarke and F. R. Helmert, *op. cit.*, pp. 810–13.

19. "If the earth were represented by a spheroid with an equatorial diameter of 25 feet, the polar diameter would be approximately 24 feet 11 inches." (Charles H. Deetz and Oscar S. Adams: *Elements of map projection*, Washington, 1938, p. 9.)

20. For a historical summary of the more important geodetic operations in Europe, see G. M. Wheeler, *op. cit.*, p. 225 ff. See also A. R. Hinks, *op. cit.*, pp. 228–30.

21. For a bibliography of the important published works relating to this subject see G. M. Wheeler, *op. cit.*, pp. 539–46.

22. A. R. Clarke and F. R. Helmert, *op. cit.*, p. 803d; see also F. G. W. Struve's *Arc du méridien de 25° 20′ entre le Danube et la mer Glaciale, mesuré depuis 1816 jusqu'en 1855 . . .* St. Petersbourg, 1860.

23. G. M. Wheeler, *op. cit.*, pp. 226–27.

24. *Ibid.*, pp. 154, 227.

25. *Ibid.*, pp. 227–29; the members of the association were Austria, Belgium, Denmark, England, France, Germany, Greece, Holland, Hungary, Italy, Japan, Mexico, Norway, Portugal, Rumania, Russia, Servia, Spain, Sweden, Switzerland and the United States of America; see A. R. Clarke and F. R. Helmert, *op. cit.*, p. 810d.

26. P. F. A. Méchain, *op. cit.*, Vol. III, p. 104; see also Georges Perrier, "La figure de la terre," *Revue de géographie annuelle*, Tome II, Paris, 1908, pp. 201–409; A. R. Hinks, *op. cit.*, pp. 228 ff.

27. See John Fillmore Hayford: "Geodesy and Geophysics at Madrid," *Geographical Journal*, Vol. 64, London, 1924, pp. 477–81.

28. See *Compte-Rendu du congrès des sciences géographiques, cosmographiques et commerciales tenu à Anvers du 14 au 22 Août, 1871*, Tome I, Antwerp, 1872.

29. *Ibid.*, pp. xlvi–xlix.

30. For a list of the governments represented, and the delegates from each, see G. M. Wheeler, *op. cit.*, pp. 42–44.

31. *Ibid.*, pp. 23 ff.; for a bibliography on time reform and prime meridia, see pp. 32, 33.

32. *Ibid.*, pp. 26–29.

33. *Ibid.*, p. 31; see also M. J. de Rey-Pailhade, "Projet d'application du système metrique à la mesure des angles et du temps," in *Association Française pour l'avancement des sciences. Compte rendu de la 23me session, Caen, 1894*, Paris, 1895, pp. 941–46.

34. G. M. Wheeler, *op. cit.*, pp. 33 ff.

35. *Ibid.*, pp. 35–38, for a general history of time reform.

36. See the article "Time" in the *Encyclopaedia Britannica*, 14th edition. The Inter-

national Time Zones are well illustrated on the "Time Zone Chart of the World" published by the Hydrographic Office under the authority of the Secretary of the Navy. (No. 5192. 13th edition, October, 1946.)

37. See U. S. H. O. Chart No. 5192. This scheme of dividing the world into convenient time zones was used by the U. S. Navy and the other allied powers during World War II. It does not coincide in every detail with some of the hastily compiled Time Zone Charts issued by commercial publishers.

38. Albrecht Penck: "Die herstellung einer einheitlichen erdkarte im masstabe von 1/1,000,000," *International Geographical Congress. 5th. Berne, 1891. Compte Rendu.* Berne, 1892.

39. See Bailey Willis, "The international millionth map of the world," *National Geographic magazine*, Vol. XXI, Washington, 1910, pp. 125–32; also Eduard Brückner, *Rapport du président de la commission pour l'etablissement d'une carte de la terre . . . Report of the sixth international geographical congress, 1895.* London, 1896.

40. Thirty-two countries were represented at the meeting. See *Report of the eighth international geographical congress held in the United States.* (House of Representatives. 58th Congress, 3rd Session, Doc. No. 460. Washington, 1905.) For Prof. Penck's paper, "Plan of a map of the world — recent progress in the execution of a map of the world on the uniform scale of 1:1,000,000 (16 miles to the inch)" see pp. 553–57.

41. A. Penck, "Plan of a map of the world . . ." p. 556; see also B. Willis, *op. cit.,* pp. 127 ff.

42. See International 1/M map, Central Bureau, Southampton, England: *Carte du monde au millionième. Rapport pour 1921,* Southampton, Bureau Central, Ordnance Survey Office, 1921.

43. International 1/M map; *Rapport pour 1921,* pp. 19, 20.

44. *Ibid.,* p. 22.

45. For a good illustration of this problem, see "Notes on the transliteration of Arabic names for the 1/M map," in the *Geographical Journal,* Vol. 49, January to June, 1917, London, 1917, pp. 141–48.

46. See "The carte du monde au millionieme" by Col. Sir Charles Close in *Geographical Journal,* Vol. 83, January to June, 1934. London, 1934, pp. 323–24.

47. William Roy: "An account of the measurement of a base on Hounslow-Heath," p. 385.

48. A. R. Hinks: "The map on the scale of 1/1,000,000 compiled at the Royal Geographical Society under the direction of the general staff, 1914–1915," in *Geographical Journal,* Vol. 46, July to December, 1915. London, 1915, pp. 24–50.

49. Sir Charles Close, *op. cit.,* p. 323.

50. International 1/M map: *Rapport pour 1921 . . .* p. 9.

51. A. R. Hinks: *Maps and Survey,* p. 86.

52. *Ibid.,* pp. 86 ff.; see also "The present state of the *carte du monde au millionième,*" in *International Geographical Congress, 15th. Comptes Rendus . . .* Amsterdam, 1938, Tome 2, Travaux de la Section I, Cartographie, Leiden, 1938, pp. 150–55.

53. *Ibid.,* pp. 151–52.

54. "Arms and the Map. Military mapping by the Army Map Service," in *Print, a quarterly journal of the graphic arts,* Vol. IV, No. 2. Spring, 1946, pp. 3–16.

55. *Ibid.,* p. 6.

56. William Roy: "An account of the measurement of a base on Hounslow-Heath," p. 385.

Bibliography

This is a selective bibliography representative of the literature on cartography. Many of these volumes themselves contain long bibliographies should the reader care to pursue the subject further. To facilitate the use of the material and to help the reader in his selection of additional reading matter, the works listed are arranged according to subject.

General References

ALINGHAM, WILLIAM. *A short account of the nature and use of maps.* London, 1698.

Annales de géographie. . . . 30 vols. Paris, 1891–1921.

ARGENTINE REPUBLIC. *Catálogo de la biblioteca, mapoteca y archivo.* Buenos Aires, 1910.

ARMBRUESTER, RUDOLPH. Maps, their care and cataloguing. (In the *Library Journal.* New York, 1922, vol. 47, p. 830.)

BADDELEY, JOHN F. Father Matteo Ricci's Chinese world maps. (In the *Geographical Journal.* London, 1917, vol. 50, p. 254.)

BAKER, JOHN N. L. *A history of geographical discovery and exploration.* London [1931].

BALL, SARAH B. Maps and atlases — their selection and care. (In *Public Libraries.* Chicago, Jan. 1910, vol. 15, no. 1, pp. 11–15.)

BANCROFT, HUBERT H. *Central America.* 3 vols. San Francisco, 1882–1887.

BARBIERI, UBALDO. Cartografia. (In *Enciclopedia Italiana.* Milan, 1931, vol. 9, pp. 230–50.)

BARKER, WILLIAM H. The history of cartography. (In *Journal* of the Manchester Geographical Society. Manchester, 1923–1924, vol. 39–40, pp. 1–17.)

BARTHOLOMEW, JOHN G. The mapping of the world. Part 1. Topographical maps of Europe. [With a map.] (In the *Scottish Geographical Magazine.* Edinburgh, 1890, vol. 6, pp. 293–305.)

—— The mapping of the world. Part 2. Maps of Africa. [With a map.] (In the *Scottish Geographical Magazine.* Edinburgh, 1890, vol. 6, pp. 575–97.)

—— The mapping of the world. Part 3. Map of Asia. [With a map.] (In the *Scottish Geographical Magazine.* Edinburgh, 1891, vol. 7, pp. 124–52.)

BEANS, GEORGE H. *Maps ex Duke of Gotha collection* . . . Jenkintown, 1935. Contains maps printed in Italy prior to 1600.

BIBLIOGRAPHIE GÉOGRAPHIQUE INTERNATIONALE. *Bibliographie géographique* . . . *bibliographie annuelle* . . . Paris, 1896–1933.

BLAKIE, W. B. How maps are made. From the *Annual Report* of the Smithsonian Institution for 1893. Washington, 1894. Published originally in the *Scottish Geographical Magazine,* 1891, vol. 7, pp. 419–34.

BLISS, RICHARD. Classified index to the maps in Petermann's *Geographische Mittheilungen,* 1855–1881. Cambridge, Mass., 1884. Republished from *Library Bibliographical Contributions No. 16* of Harvard University.

—— Classified index to the maps in the publications of the Geological Society of London, 1811–1885. Boston, 1887.

—— Classified index to the maps in the Royal Geographical Society's publications, 1830–1883. Cambridge, Mass., 1886. Harvard University Library. Bibliographical contributions. no. 17.

BOGGS, SAMUEL W., and LEWIS, DOROTHY C. *The classification and cataloging of maps and atlases* . . . New York, 1945.

BRENT, GEORGE S. General index to the second ten volumes of the *Journal* of the Royal Geographical Society . . . London, 1853.

BRITISH MUSEUM. Dept. of Printed Books. King's Library. *Catalogue of maps, prints, drawings, etc. forming the geographical and topographical collection attached to the library of His late Majesty King George the Third* . . . London, 1829.

BROWN, LLOYD A. *Notes on the care and cataloguing of old maps.* Windham, 1941.

—— Special reference problems in map collections. (In *The Reference Function of the Library.* Edited by Pierce Butler. Chicago, 1943, pp. 144–62.)

BURNET, THOMAS. *The theory of the earth: containing an account of the original of the earth* . . . London, 1684.

CANADA. Archives. *Catalogue of maps, plans and charts in the map room of the Dominion archives* . . . Ottawa, 1912.

CHAVANNE, JOSEF. *The literature on the polar regions of the earth* . . . Vienna, 1878.

CLAUSSEN, MARTIN P., and FRIIS, HERMAN R. *Descriptive catalog of maps published by Congress 1817–1843* . . . Washington, 1941.

COLOMBIA. Biblioteca Nacional de Bogota. Catalogo de las cartas, planos . . . que existen en la biblioteca nacional de Bogota. (In *Boletin* de la Sociedad Geográfica de Colombia. Bogota, 1938, vol. 5, pp. 102–04, 218–24; 1939, vol. 6, pp. 38–46.)

COX, EDWARD G. Maps and atlases — a selected cartography. (In his *Reference Guide to the Literature of Travel Including Voyages* . . . Seattle, 1938, vol. 2, pp. 396–416.)

CURNOW, IRENE J. *The world mapped; being a short history of attempts to map the world* . . . London, 1930.

DALY, CHARLES P. Annual address: On the early history of cartography . . . (In *Bulletin* of the American Geographical Society. New York, 1879, no. 1, pp. 1–40.)

DAMPIER, WILLIAM. *A cruising voyage round the world.* London, 1697.

DEANE, CHARLES. Remarks on the death of Dr. J. G. Kohl. (In *Proceedings* of the Massachusetts Historical Society. Boston, 1879, vol. 16, pp. 381–85.) This paper contains an account of his life and writings.

DEETZ, CHARLES H. *Cartography.* Washington, 1936. U. S. Coast and Geodetic Survey. Special Publication No. 205.

DELAMBRE, JEAN B. J. *Histoire de l'astronomie ancienne.* 2 vols. Paris, 1817.

DICKINSON, ROBERT E., and HOWARTH, O. J. R. *The making of geography.* Oxford, 1933.

DU BUS, CHARLES. Edmé François Jomard et les origines du cabinet des cartes (1777–1862). (In France. Comité des travaux historiques. *Bulletin de la section de géographie.* Paris, 1931, vol. 46, pp. 1–128.)

DUNN, SAMUEL. *The description and use of the universal planispheres* . . . London, 1759.

DU VAL, PIERRE. *La connoissance et l'vsage des globes et des cartes de géographie.* Paris, 1654.

—— *Traité de géographie qui donne la connoissance et l'usage du globe et de la carte* . . . Paris, 1672.

ECKERT, MAX. *Die kartenwissenschaft; forschungen und grundlagen zu einer kartographie als wissenschaft* . . . Berlin and Leipzig, 1921.

—— *Kartographie; ihre aufgaben und bedeutung für die kultur der gegenwart* . . . Berlin, 1939.

—— On the nature of maps and map logic. (In *Bulletin* of the American Geographical Society. New York, June 1908, vol. 40, pp. 344–51.)

ENGELMANN, WILHELM. *Bibliotheca géographica* . . . Leipzig, 1858.

FAGE, ROBERT. *A geographical directory: or, a plain guide to the understanding of globes and maps* . . . London, 1677.

FITE, EMERSON, and FREEMAN, ARCHIBALD. *A book of old maps.* Cambridge, Mass., 1926.

FORDHAM, HERBERT G. *Maps: their history, characteristics and uses* . . . Cambridge, England, 1927.

Bibliography 343

GILBERT, EDMUND W. What is historical geography? (In the *Scottish Geographical Magazine*. Edinburgh, 1932, vol. 48, pp. 129–35.)

GREGORY, JOHN W. The evolution of the map of the world. (In the *Scottish Geographical Magazine*. Edinburgh, Feb. 1917, vol. 33, pp. 49–65.)

HAKLUYT, RICHARD. *The principal navigations, voyages, traffiques & discoveries of the English nation*. 12 vols. Reprinted Glasgow, 1903–1905. Works issued by the Hakluyt Society, Extra Series.

HAMY, JULES T. E. Les origines de la cartographie de l'Europe Septentrionale. (In France. Comité des travaux historiques et scientifiques. *Bulletin de géographie historique et descriptive*. 1888, pp. 333–432.)

HANTZSCH, VIKTOR, and SCHMIDT, LUDWIG. *Kartographische Denkmäler zur Entdeckungsgeschichte von Amerika, Asien, Australien und Africa* . . . Leipzig, 1903.

HARRINGTON, THOMAS. *A new introduction to the knowledge and use of maps* . . . London, 1773.

HARRISSE, HENRI. *The discovery of North America*. London, 1892.

HEAWOOD, EDWARD. The use of watermarks in dating old maps and documents. (In the *Geographical Journal*. London, 1924, vol. 63, pp. 391–412; see also vol. 64, pp. 237–40.)

HINKS, ARTHUR R. *Maps and survey* . . . Cambridge, England, 1944.

HOBBS, WILLIAM H. The discoveries of Antarctica within the American sector . . . Philadelphia, 1939. *Transactions* of the American Philosophical Society . . . New Series, vol. 31, Pt. I.

HOCKEN, THOMAS M. Some accounts of the earliest literature and maps relating to New Zealand. (In *Transactions and Proceedings* of the New Zealand Institute. Wellington, 1894, vol. 27, pp. 616–34.)

HUTTMANN, WILLIAM. On Chinese and European maps of China. (In *Journal* of the Royal Geographical Society. London, 1844, vol. 14, pp. 117–27.)

INSTITUTO HISTORICO, GEOGRAPHICO BRASILEIRO. *Catalogo das cartas geographicas hidrographicas, atlas, planos* . . . Rio de Janeiro, 1885.

JACOBS, JOSEPH. *The story of geographical discovery; how the world became known* . . . New York, 1902.

JERVIS, WALTER W. *The world in maps* . . . New York, 1938. A list, in chronological order, of ancient, mediaeval and modern maps: pp. 185–99.

JOMARD, EDME F. *Catalogue de cartes, plans et atlas de géographie provenant de la bibliothèque de M. Jomard* . . . Paris, 1864.

—— *La collection géographique de la bibliothèque royale en 1845*. Paris, 1845.

—— *Considération sur l'objet et les avantages d'une collection spéciale consacrée aux cartes géographiques* . . . Paris, 1831.

—— *Les monuments de la géographie* . . . Pub. en fac-similé de la grandeur des originaux. Paris, 1854–1862.

KEANE, JOHN. *The evolution of geography* . . . London, 1899.

KELTIE, JOHN S., and HOWARTH, O. J. R. *History of geography* . . . New York, 1913.

KOHL, JOHANN G. Substance of a lecture delivered at the Smithsonian Institution on a collection of the charts and maps of America. (In Smithsonian Institution. *Annual Report*, 1856. Washington, 1857.)

KRETSCHMER, KONRAD. *Geschichte der geographie* . . . Berlin, 1912.

LATHROP, JOHN. *A compendious treatise on the use of the globes, and of maps* . . . Boston, 1812.

LAUSSEDAT, AIMÉ. *Histoire de la cartographie* . . . Paris, 1892.

LENGLET DUFRESNOY, NICOLAS. *Méthode pour étudier la géographie* . . . 10 vols. Paris, 1768.

LETTS, THOMAS. Maps: handling, classifying, cataloguing. (In International Geographic

Congress. United States. *Report of the Eighth International Geographical Congress,* 1904. Washington, 1905, pp. 803–08.)

LÓPEZ DE VARGAS MACHUCA, TOMÁS. *Principios geograficos, aplicados al uso de los mapas* . . . Madrid, 1775.

MILLER, KONRAD. *Mappaemundi, die aeltesten Weltkarten.* 6 vols. Stuttgart, 1895–1898.

MORRISON, GABRIEL J. *Maps, their uses and construction.* London, 1901.

MULLER, FREDERICK. *Remarkable maps of the XV, XVI, & XVIIth centuries reproduced in their original size* . . . 6 Pts. Amsterdam, 1894–1897.

NEW YORK. Public Library. General atlases of geography (ancient and modern) in the New York Public Library. (In *Bulletin* of the New York Public Library, 1900, vol. 4, no. 2, pp. 63–69.)

—— *List of maps of the world, illustrating the progress of geographical knowledge from the earliest time* . . . New York, 1904.

NEWBIGIN, MARION I. The training of the geographer: actual and ideal. (In the *Scottish Geographical Magazine.* Edinburgh, 1925, vol. 41, pp. 27–36.)

NOLAN, JAMES B. Old maps; adventures of a map hunter. (In *Travel.* New York, 1926, vol. 46, pp. 30–32, 48.)

PHILIP, GEORGE. The enlargement of the geographical horizon . . . (In *Proceedings* of the Literary and Philosophical Society of Liverpool. London, 1896, vol. 50, pp. 313–39.)

PHILLIPS, PHILIP L. *A list of geographical atlases in the Library of Congress.* 4 vols. Washington, 1909–1920.

—— *A list of maps of America in the Library of Congress preceded by a list of works relating to cartography.* Washington, 1901.

RAISZ, ERWIN J. *General cartography* . . . New York, 1938.

REDLICH, OSWALD. *Historisch-geographische probleme.* Innsbruck, 1906.

REEVES, EDWARD A. The mapping of the earth — past, present and future. (In the *Scottish Geographical Magazine.* Edinburgh, Oct. 1916, vol. 32, no. 10, pp. 449–66.)

ROYAL GEOGRAPHICAL SOCIETY, London. *Catalogue of map room of the Royal Geographical Society.* London, 1882.

SAINT-YVES, G. *Les manuscrits géographiques de la bibliothèque de Marseilles* . . . Paris, 1896.

SANDLER, CHRISTIAN. *Die reformation der kartographie um 1700.* Munich and Berlin, 1905.

SANTAREM, MANUEL. *Essai sur l'histoire de la cosmographie et de la cartographie* . . . 3 vols., Paris, 1849–1852.

TAYLOR, EVA G. R. The earliest account of triangulation. (In the *Scottish Geographical Magazine.* Edinburgh, 1927, vol. 43, pp. 341–45.)

TIELE, PIETER A. *Nederlandsche bibliographie van land-en volkenkunde.* Amsterdam, 1884.

VIVIEN DE SAINT-MARTIN, LOUIS. *Histoire de la géographie* . . . Paris, 1873. Accompanied by his *Atlas dressé pour l'histoire de la géographie.*

WAGNER, HENRY R. Biblio-cartography. (In *Pacific Historical Review.* Glendale, Cal., 1932, vol. 1, pp. 103–10.

WERTHEIM, ALEXANDER. *Old maps and charts, a short guide for collectors.* Berlin, 1931.

WIEDER, FREDERIK C. (ed.). *Monumenta cartographica; reproductions of unique and rare maps, plans and views* . . . 5 vols. The Hague, 1925–1933.

WINSOR, JUSTIN. *The Kohl collection (now in the Library of Congress) of maps relating to America.* Washington, 1904. A reprint of Bibliographical Contribution No. 19 of the Library of Harvard University.

—— *Narrative and critical history of America.* 8 vols. Boston and New York, 1884–1889.

WINTLE, W. J. The romance of map-making. (In the *London Magazine*. London, Oct. 1902, No. 51, pp. 269–75.)

WRIGHT, JOHN K. *Aids to geographical research; bibliographies and periodicals.* New York, 1923. American Geographical Society. Research Series No. 10.

WROTH, LAWRENCE C. The early cartography of the Pacific. (In the *Papers of the Bibliographical Society of America*. New York, 1944, vol. 38, No. 2.)

Boundaries

ANDREWS, MICHAEL C. The boundary between Scotland and England in the Portolan charts. (In *Proceedings* of the Society of Antiquaries of Scotland. Edinburgh, 1927, vol. 60, pp. 36–66.) Contains, pp. 56–66, a list of fifteenth- and sixteenth-century charts.

BOGGS, SAMUEL W. *International boundaries; a study of boundary functions and problems* . . . New York, 1940.

—— The map of Latin America by treaty. (In *Proceedings* of the American Philosophical Society. Philadelphia, 1938, vol. 79, pp. 399–410.)

—— Problems of water-boundary definition. (In the *Geographical Review*. New York, 1937, vol. 27, pp. 445–56.)

The breviate in the boundary dispute between Pennsylvania and Maryland. Harrisburg, 1891. *Pennsylvania Archives*, Second Series, vol. XVI.

CLARK, FRANK E. *A treatise on the law of surveying and boundaries* . . . Indianapolis [1922].

DAWSON, SAMUEL E. The line of demarcation of Pope Alexander VI in A.D. 1493 . . . (In *Transactions* of the Royal Society of Canada. Ottawa, 1899, Ser. 2, vol. 5, pp. 467–546.)

DRAYSON, ALFRED W. *Practical military surveying and sketching, with the use of the compass and sextant* . . . London, 1869.

HINKS, ARTHUR R. Notes on the technique of boundary delimitation. (In *Journal* of the Royal Geographical Society. London, Dec. 1921, vol. 58, pp. 417–43.)

HOLDICH, SIR THOMAS H. Geographical problems in boundary making. (In *Journal* of the Royal Geographical Society. London, June 1916, vol. 47, pp. 421–40.)

HYDE, CHARLES C. Maps as evidence in international boundary disputes. (In *American Journal of International Law*. Concord, New Hampshire, 1933, vol. 27, pp. 311–16.)

JONES, STEPHEN B. *Boundary-making. A handbook for statesmen, treaty editors, and boundary commissioners.* Foreword by S. Whittemore Boggs. Washington, 1945.

LYONS, SIR HENRY G. Ancient and modern land measurement. (In the *Geographical Teacher*. London, 1926, vol. 13, pp. 425–32.)

PIERCE, J. W. The Ontario-Manitoba boundary. (In the *Canadian Surveyor*. Ottawa, 1938. Special ed. *Proceedings* of the 31st annual meeting of the Canadian Institute of Surveying, pp. 46–59.)

PHILLIPS, PHILIP L. The value of maps in boundary disputes. (In American Historical Association. *Annual Report* for 1896. Washington, 1897, vol. 1, pp. 455–62.)

STRICKLAND, JOSEPH S. J. *Documents and maps on the boundary question between Venezuela and British Guayana from the Capuchin archives in Rome.* Rome, 1896.

TAYLOR, EVA G. R. The plane-table in the sixteenth century. (In the *Scottish Geographical Magazine*. Edinburgh, 1929, vol. 45, pp. 205–11.)

VISHER, STEPHEN S. Influences locating international boundaries. (In *Journal of Geography*. Chicago, 1938, vol. 37, pp. 301–08.)

WHITE, JAMES. *Boundary disputes and treaties* . . . Toronto, 1914.

Compass and Magnetism

BAUER, LOUIS A. Halley's earliest equal variation chart. (In *Terrestrial Magnetism* . . . Chicago, 1896, vol. 1, pp. 28–31.)

—— Some bibliographical discoveries in terrestrial magnetism. (In *Nature*. London, 1895, vol. 52, pp. 79–80, 106, 343.) Contains a number of references to Halley's chart containing the lines of equal magnetism in the Atlantic Ocean.

—— *United States magnetic declination tables and isogonic charts . . . and principal facts relating to the earth's magnetism.* Washington, U. S. Coast and Geodetic Survey, 1902.

BERNARDIÈRES, OCTAVE M. G. J. DE. Physique du globe — sur la construction de nouvelles cartes magnétiques du globe . . . (In L'Académie des Sciences. *Comptes rendus*. Paris, 1895, vol. 121, pp. 679–84.)

BERTELLI, TIMOTEO. *La declinazione magnetica e la sua variazione nello spazio scoperte de Cristoforo Colombo* . . . Rome, 1892.

Catalogue of the Wheeler gift . . . in the library of the American institute of electrical engineers . . . 2 vols. New York, 1909. A classified bibliography of 5966 books and pamphlets relating to magnetism.

CHURCHMAN, JOHN. *An explanation of the magnetic atlas or variation chart hereunto annexed.* Philadelphia, 1790.

—— The magnetic atlas . . . (In *Monthly Magazine and American Review*. New York, Nov. 1880, vol. 3, pp. 342–49.)

DODSON, JAMES, and MOUNTAINE, WILLIAM. *An account of the method used to describe lines on Dr. Halley's chart of the terraqueous globe* . . . London, 1746.

FONTOURA DA COSTA, ABEL. *A marinharia dos descobrimentos* . . . Lisbon, 1933. Contains colored facsimiles of twenty-four compass roses from famous Portuguese charts.

GELLIBRAND, HENRY. *A discourse mathematical on the variation of the magneticall needle.* London, 1635. Facsimiledruck mit einer einleitung. Berlin, 1897. Half-title: Neudrucke von schriften und karten über meteorologie und erdmagnetismus [hrsg. von G. Hellmann] no. 9.

GILBERT, WILLIAM (of Colchester). Gilbert of Colchester, father of electrical science. A reprint of the chapter on electrics from *De Magnete*, Lib. 2, with notes by Silvanus P. Thompson. London, 1903. Gilbert Tercentenary Commemoration, Dec. 10, 1903.

—— *On the loadstone and magnetic bodies, and on the great magnet the earth.* Translated by P. Fleury Mottelay. New York, 1893. See also reprint for "The Classics of the St. John's Program." Ann Arbor, 1938.

HALLEY, EDMUND. *Correspondence and papers of Edmund Halley.* Arranged and edited by Eugene F. MacPike. Oxford, 1932.

—— Dr. Halley's first voyage: a journal of a voyage made for the discovery of the rule of the variation of the compass . . . 1699 and 1700. (In Alexander Dalrymple's *A Collection of Voyages* . . . London, 1775.)

—— Halley's earliest equal variation chart. Reproduced in facsimile . . . Text by L. A. Bauer. (In *Terrestrial Magnetism* . . . Chicago, 1896. Vol. I.)

HECK, NICHOLAS H. The magnetic survey of the United States. (In *Military Engineer*. Washington, 1938, vol. 30, pp. 13–17.)

HELLMANN, GUSTAV. Die anfänge der magnetischen beobachtungen. (In *Zeitschrift der Gesellschaft für erdkunde zu Berlin*. Berlin, 1897, vol. 32, pp. 112–36.)

—— Contributions to the bibliography of meteorology and terrestrial magnetism in the 15th, 16th, and 17th centuries. Chicago, 1893. Extract from Pt. 2 of the report of the Chicago meteorological congress. August, 1893.

—— Edmund Halley, W. Whiston, J. C. Wilcke, A. von Humboldt, C. Hansteen. Die ältesten karten der isogonen, isoklinen, isodynamen, 1701, 1721, 1768, 1804, 1825, 1826. Sieben karten. Berlin, 1895. Neudrucke von schriften und karten über meteorologie und erdmagnetismus.

LAMBERT, WALTER D. *Effect of variations in the assumed figure of the earth on the mapping of a large area.* Washington, 1924. U. S. Coast and Geodetic Survey. Special Publication No. 100.

On the cause of the change in the variation of the magnetic needle; with an hypothesis of the structure of the internal parts of the earth. (In *Philosophical Transactions* of the Royal Society of London. London, 1692, vol. 17, p. 563; 1809, Abridgement vol. 3, p. 470.)

PEREGRINUS, PETRUS. *Epistle of Peter Peregrinus of Maricourt to Sygerus of Foncaucourt Soldier concerning the Magnet.* Translated into English by Silvanus P. Thompson from the printed versions of Gasser, 1448, Bertelli, 1868, and Hellmann, 1898. . . . Amended from the Phillipps MS dated 1391. London, 1902.

—— *Epistle of Petrus Peregrinus on the magnet.* Reproduced from a MS written by an English hand about A.D. 1390. London, 1900.

—— *The letter of Petrus Peregrinus on the magnet,* A.D. 1269. Translated by Brother Arnold. New York, 1904.

PHAFF, J. M. Notes relative to a compass rose designed by C. de Bie of Vossemeer 1689, and early cartography. (In *Hydrographic Review.* Monaco, 1924, vol. 1, no. 2, pp. 129–39.)

REEVES, EDWARD A. Halley's magnetic variation charts. (In *Geographical Journal.* London, April, 1918, vol. 51, pp. 237–40.)

RUGE, SOPHUS. *Ueber compass und compasskarten.* Dresden, 1868.

SCHÜCK, ALBERT (Karl Wilhelm Albert). Das blatt der kompassrose. (In *Jahresbericht der Geographische Gesellschaft in München.* Munich, 1890, vol. 13, pp. 20–39.)

—— *Der kompass.* 3 vols. Hamburg, 1911–1918.

Some remarks on the variations of the magnetical compass, published in the Memoirs of the Royal Academy of Sciences, with regard to the general chart of those variations made by E. Halley; as also concerning the true longitude of the Magellan Streights. (In *Philosophical Transactions* of the Royal Society of London. London, 1714, vol. 29, p. 165; 1809, Abridgement vol. 6, p. 112.)

A theory of the variation of the magnetical compass. (In *Philosophical Transactions* of the Royal Society of London, London, 1683, p. 624; 1809, Abridgement vol. 2, p. 624.)

THOMPSON, SILVANUS P. *Hand list of the magnetic and electrical books in the library of Silvanus P. Thompson.* London, 1914.

—— *Notes on the De Magnete of Dr. William Gilbert.* London, 1901.

—— Petrus Peregrinus . . . (In *Proceedings* of the British Academy . . . London, 1905–1906, vol. 5, pp. 377–408.) This paper, read Nov. 28, contains a bibliography of the *De Magnete,* including the known manuscripts.

—— The rose of the winds: the origin and development of the compass card. London [1914]. Read at the International Historical Congress. April, 1913. From *Proceedings* of the British Academy, vol. VI.

—— *William Gilbert, and terrestrial magnetism in the time of Queen Elizabeth: a discourse.* London, 1903. Royal Geographical Society publications.

TODHUNTER, ISAAC. *History of the Mechanical theories of attraction and the figure of the earth* . . . 2 vols. London, 1873.

U. S. COAST AND GEODETIC SURVEY. *Principal facts of the earth's magnetism, and methods of determining the true meridian and the magnetic declination.* Washington, 1914.

WAGNER, HERMANN. Der kartenmaszstab. Historisch-kritische betrachtungen. (In *Zeitschrift der Gesellschaft für Erdkunde zu Berlin*. 1914, pp. 1–34, 81–117.) Mentions the probable first use of natural scale or Representative Fraction.

WAKELY, ANDREW. *The mariner's compass rectified* . . . London, 1726.

WALKER, EDWARD. *Terrestrial and cosmical magnetism*. Cambridge, 1866.

WINTER, HEINRICH. Who invented the compass? (In the *Mariner's Mirror*. Cambridge, 1937, vol. 23, pp. 95–102.)

Globes

ADAMS, GEORGE. *A treatise describing and explaining the construction and use of new celestial and terrestrial globes* . . . London, 1766. No less than thirty editions of this work were published between 1766 and 1810.

BIGOURDAN, GUILLAUME. Les anciens globes, tant célestes que terrestres. (In *La Science Moderne*. Paris, 1926, vol. 3, pp. 393–402.)

DE MORGAN, AUGUSTUS. *The globes, celestial and terrestrial*. London, 1845. This work is especially intended to accompany Malby's globes, published under the superintendence of the Society for the Diffusion of Useful Knowledge.

DELAMARCHE, CHARLES F. *Les usages de la sphère, et des globes céleste et terrestre* . . . Paris, 1791.

EWING, THOMAS of Edinburgh. *A system of geography* . . . *and a variety of problems to be solved by the terrestrial and celestial globes*. Edinburgh, 1816. Accompanied by his *New General Atlas*, 25th edition, published in 1878.

FENNING, DANIEL. *A new and easy guide to the use of the globes, and the rudiments of geography* . . . London, 1754.

HARDCASTLE, WILLIAM. *Eleven hundred questions on the use of the globes*. London, 1856. Various editions published; also a "Key" in 1856.

HARRIS, JOHN. *The description and use of globes and the orrery*. London, 1751.

HUES, ROBERT. *A learned treatise of globes* . . . London, 1639.

JUMP, JOHN. *Application des globes à la trigonométrie sphérique et à divers calculs d'astronomie et de géographie* . . . Paris, 1829.

LAHIRE, PHILIP DE. Description et explication des globes qui sont placéz dans les pavillions du château de Marly. Paris, 1704. (In *Journal des Sçavans*. Amsterdam, 1704, vol. 32, pt. 2, pp. 1040–47.)

MAINDRON, ERNEST. Le globe géographique de l'observatoire de Paris. (In *Revue Scientifique*. Paris, May 1887, vol. 13, no. 19, pp. 592–96.) An interesting account of the globe commenced in 1784 and finished in 1794.

MOLINEAUX, THOMAS. *A short introduction to the use of the globes* . . . London, 1792. The Molyneux globes. (In *Geographical Journal*. London, 1941, vol. 98, p. 215.)

MOXON, JOSEPH. *A tutor to astronomie and geographie. Or an easie and speedy way to know the use of both the globes, coelestial and terrestrial. In six books* . . . London, 1670.

RAEMDONCK, J. VAN. *Les Spheres terrestre et céleste de Gérard Mercator (1541 et 1551)*. Saint Nicolas, 1875.

RECLUS, JEAN J. E. *Projet de construction d'un globe terrestre à l'échelle du cent-millième*. Paris, 1895.

SCHEDLER, JOSEPH. *An illustrated manual for the use of the terrestrial and celestial globes*. New York, 1875. Appended: "Catalogue of J. Schedler's globes and maps."

STACKHOUSE, THOMAS. *The rationale of the globes, or a development of the principles on which the operations of these useful instruments are founded* . . . London, 1805.

STEVENSON, EDWARD L. *Terrestrial and celestial globes, their history and construction* . . . 2 vols. New Haven, 1921. Publications of the Hispanic Society of America, No. 86.

Terrestrial and celestial globes by Willem Blaeu. (In *Geographical Journal*. London 1938, vol. 91, pp. 295–96.)

VAREN, BERNHARD. Of the mutual situation of places and of the making of globes and maps. (In his *A Compleat System of General Geography*. London, 1733, vol. 2, pp. 686–729.)

Latitude

BASSETT, J. ANTHONY. *Latitude and longitude, and longitude and time* . . . Syracuse, 1883.

BASSLER, R. E. Early nautical instruments. (In the *Military Engineer*. Washington, 1937, vol. 29, pp. 200–02.)

BENSAUDE, JOAQUIM. *Histoire de la science nautique Portugaise*. Résumé. Geneva, 1917.

BESSEL, FRIEDRICH W. *Tabulae Regionmontanae reductionum observationum astronomicarum ab anno 1750 usque ad annum 1850 computatae*. Regiomonti Prussorum, 1830.

BLAGRAVE, JOHN. *The mathematical Iewel, shewing the making, and most excellent vse of a singular instrument so called* . . . London, 1585.

BLUNDEVILLE, THOMAS. *M. Blvndevile* [sic] *his exercises, contayning eight treatises, the titles whereof are set downe* . . . London, 1622.

—— A verie briefe and most plaine description of Mr. Blagrave, his astrolabe, which he calleth the mathematicall jewell. London, 1622. (In his *Exercises*. London, 1622, pp. 593–643.)

BOUGUER, PIERRE. De la methode d'observer exactement sur mer la hauteur des astres. (In *Recueil des pieces qui ont remporté les prix de l'Académie Royale des Sciences*. Tome II. 1727–1733. Paris, 1752.)

BROWN, BASIL J. W. *Astronomical atlases, maps and charts*. London, 1932.

CHABERT DE COGOLIN, JOSEPH B. Détermination de la latitude et de la longitude du Fort Saint-Philippe . . . (In *Histoire* de l'Académie Royale des Sciences. 1756. Paris, 1762, pp. 438–42.)

COLSON, NATHANIEL. *The mariner's new calendar*. London, 1677.

CUMMING, A. S. Gordon of Straloch's astrolabe. (In the *Scottish Geographical Magazine*. Edinburgh, 1926, vol. 42, pp. 79–82.)

CUNNINGHAM, DR. WILLIAM, OF NORWICH. *The cosmographical glasse* . . . London, 1559.

DANFRIE, PHILIPPE. *Déclaration de l'usage du graphomètre, par la pratique duquel l'on peut mesurer toutes distances des choses* . . . Paris, 1597.

DAVIS, JOHN. The seamans secrets. London, 1607. (With *The Voyages and Works of John Davis the Navigator*.) See next title.

—— *The voyages and works of John Davis the navigator*. Edited, with an introduction and notes by Albert Hastings Markham. London, 1880. Publication of the Hakluyt Society, No. 59.

DOPPELMAYR, JOHANN G. *Historische nachricht von den Nürnbergischen mathematicis*. Nürnberg, 1730.

ELTON, JOHN. The description of a new quadrant for taking altitudes without an horizon, either at sea or land. Invented by Mr. John Elton. (In *Philosophical Transactions* of the Royal Society. London, April, May and June 1732, vol. 37, No. 423.)

FRISIUS, GEMMA REINERUS. *Les principes d'astronomie et cosmographie* . . . Paris, 1556.

—— *De principiis astronomicae et cosmographiae*. Antwerp, 1530.

GASSENDI, PIERRE. *Tychonis Brahei vita* . . . *Accessit N. Copernici, G. Peurbachii, et Joannis Regiomontani vita*, Paris, 1654.

GELCICH, EUGEN. *Die astronomische bestimmung der geographischen koordinaten.* Leipzig, 1904.

GILLINGHAM, HAROLD E. Early Philadelphia instrument makers. (In *Pennsylvania Magazine*. Philadelphia, 1927, vol. 51, No. 3, pp. 289–308.)

GRAY, GEORGE J. *A bibliography of the works of Sir Isaac Newton* . . . 2nd edition, Cambridge, 1907.

GUNTER, EDMUND. *The workes of Edmund Gunter, containing the description of the sector, cross-staff, and other instruments.* London, 1653.

GUNTHER, ROBERT W. T. *The astrolabes of the world* . . . 2 vols., Oxford, 1932.

HADLEY, JOHN. An account of observations made on board the Chatham-yacht, August 30th and 31st, and September 1st, 1732 . . . for the trial of an instrument for taking angles . . . by John Hadley . . . (In *Philosophical Transactions* of the Royal Society. Sept. and Oct. 1732. London, 1733, vol. 37, No. 425, pp. 341–56.)

—— The description of a new instrument for taking angles. (In *Philosophical Transactions* of the Royal Society. Aug. and Sept. 1731. London, 1733. Vol. 37, No. 420, pp. 147–57.

—— A spirit level to be fixed to a quadrant for taking a meridional altitude at sea, when the horizon is not visible. (In *Philosophical Transactions* of the Royal Society. Nov. and Dec. 1733. London, 1735, vol. 38, No. 430, pp. 167–72.)

HALLEY, EDMUND. *Correspondence and papers of Edmund Halley.* Arranged and edited by Eugene F. MacPike. Oxford, 1932.

HORSLEY, DR. SAMUEL (ed.). *Isaaci Newtoni opera quae exstant omnia.* 5 vols. London, 1779–1785.

HUMBERT, PIERRE. La détermination des latitudes à la fin du XVIIe siècle. (In *Ciel et Terre*. Brussels, 1939, vol. 55, pp. 81–86.)

LA CONDAMINE, CHARLES MARIE DE. Description d'un instrument qui peut servir à déterminer, sur la surface de la terre, tous les points d'un cercle parallèle a l'équateur. (In *Histoire* de l'Académie Royale des Sciences, 1733. Paris, 1735, pp. 294–301.)

LAUSSEDAT, AIMÉ. *Recherches sur les instruments, les méthodes, et le dessin topographiques.* 2 vols. Paris, 1898–1903.

LECKY, THORNTON S. *Wrinkles in practical navigation.* Revised and enlarged by William Allingham. London, 1910. Later editions were published in 1912, 1918, 1925, and 1937.

LEYBOURN, WILLIAM. *An introduction to astronomy and geography* . . . London, 1675.

LOGAN, JAMES J. An account of Mr. Thomas Godfrey's improvement of Davis's quadrant, transferred to the mariner's-bow, communicated to the Royal Society, by Mr. J. Logan. (In *Philosophical Transactions* of the Royal Society, Dec. 1734. London, 1735, vol. 38, No. 435.)

LYONS, SIR HENRY. Ancient surveying instruments. (In *Geographical Journal*. London, 1927, vol. 69, pp. 132–43.)

MIDDLETON, GEORGE A. T. *Surveying and surveying instruments.* London, 1912.

MORISON, SAMUEL E. Columbus and Polaris. (In the *American Neptune*, Salem, 1941, vol. 1, pp. 6–25, 123–37.)

MORRIS, JOHN G. *Martin Behaim, the German astronomer and cosmographer of the times of Columbus* . . . Baltimore, 1855. Publications of the Maryland Historical Society. Vol. 3, no. 10.

RAVENSTEIN, ERNEST G. *Martin Behaim, his life and his globe* . . . with a facsimile of his globe . . . London, 1908.

REES, JOHN K. Variation of latitude. Washington, 1896. (In the *Report* of the Smithsonian Institution for 1894, pp. 271–79.)

REGIMENTO *do estrolabio e do quadrante; tractado da spera do mundo; introduction à la reproduction fac-similé de seul exemplaire connu appartenant à la Bibliothèque*

Royale de Munich. Munich, 1914. Vol. I of Joaquim Bensaude's projected *Histoire de la science nautique Portugaise.*

SCHUBERT, GOTTHILF H. VON. *Peurbach und Regiomontan* . . . Erlangen, 1828.

SCHÜCK, ALBERT (Karl Wilhelm Albert). Der Jakobsstab. (In *Jahresbericht* der Geographischen gesellschaft in München. 1894–1895. Munich, 1896, vol. 16, pp. 93–174.)

SLAFTER, EDMUND F. History and causes of the incorrect latitudes as recorded in the journals of the early writers . . . Boston, 1882. Reprinted from the *New England Historical and Genealogical Register.* April, 1882.

ZIEGLER, ALEXANDER. *Regiomontanus (Joh. Müller aus Königsberg in Franken), ein geistiger vorläufer des Columbus.* Dresden, 1874.

Longitude

ANVILLE, Jean B. B. D'. Mesure conjecturale de la terre sur l'équateur... Paris, 1736. (In *Journal des Sçavans.* Amsterdam, 1737, vol. 112, pp. 3–14.)

BAILY, FRANCIS. *Account of the Rev. John Flamsteed* . . . London, 1835.

BAUDET, PIERRE J. H. *Notice sur la part prise par Willem Jansz. Blaeu . . . dans le détermination des longitudes terrestre.* Utrecht, 1875.

BERTHOUD, FERDINAND. *De la mesure du temps, ou supplément au traité des horloges marines* . . . Paris, 1787.

BRITTEN, FREDERICK J. *Old clocks and watches and their makers* . . . London, 1932.

CARLOS, EDWARD S. *The sidereal messenger of Galileo Galilei.* London, 1880.

CASPARI, CHRÉTIEN ÉDOUARD. Les chronomètres de marine. Paris, 1894. *Encyclopédie scientifique des aide-mémoire.*

CASSINI, JACQUES. Reflexions sur la mesure de la terre, rapportée par Snellius dans son livre intitulé: Eratosthenes Batavus. (In *Histoire* de l'Académie Royale des Sciences. 1702. Second edition. Paris, 1720, Pt. II, pp. 60–66.)

CASSINI, JACQUES DOMINIQUE (compte de). *Mémoires pour servir à l'histoire des sciences et à celle de l'Observatoire Royal de Paris* . . . Paris, 1810.

—— *A voyage to California to observe the transit of Venus . . . to make experiments on Mr. Le Roy's timekeepers.* London, 1778.

CASSINI, JEAN DOMINIQUE. *Ephemerides Bononiensis mediceorvm sydervm ex hypothesibvs, et tabvlis lo: Dominici Cassini* . . . Bononiae [Bologne], 1668.

—— *La meridiana del tempio di S. Petronio tirata* . . . Bologna, 1655.

—— Oeuvres diverses de M. J. D. Cassini. (In *Mémoires* de l'Académie Royale des Sciences. Paris, 1730. Vol. VIII.)

CHABERT DE COGOLIN, JOSEPH B. *Voyage fait par ordre du roi en 1750 et 1751, dans l'Amérique septentrionale pour rectifier les cartes des côtes de l'Acadie* . . . Paris, 1753.

DARBOUX, GASTON. *L'Institut de France.* Paris, 1907. One of a series: "Les Grandes Institutions de France."

DELAMBRE, JEAN B. J. *Astronomie théorique et pratique.* 3 vols. Paris, 1814.

DIGBY, SIR KENELM. *A late discourse . . . touching the cure of wounds by the powder of sympathy; with instructions how to make the said powder* . . . London, 1658.

FAHIE, JOHN J. *Galileo. His life and work.* New York, 1903.

FERNÁNDEZ DURO, CESÁREO. *Disquisiciones nauticas* . . . Madrid, 1876–1881.

FOLKES, MARTIN. *Some account of Mr. Harrison's invention for determining the longitude* . . . London, 1742.

FONTENELLE, BERNARD LE BOVIER DE. Éloge de M. Cassini. (In *Histoire* de l'Académie Royale des Sciences. 1712. Paris, 1731, pp. 83–104.)

FUSS, PAUL H. VON. *Correspondance mathématique et physique de quelques célèbres géomètres du XVIIIᵉᵐᵉ siècle* . . . St. Petersburg, 1843.

GALILEI, GALILEO. *Le opere di Galileo Galilei*. Prima edizione completa. Edited by Eugenio Alberi. 16 vols. Florence, 1842–1856.

—— *Dialogues concerning two new sciences* . . . Translated . . . by Henry Crew and Alfonso de Salvio. Introduction by Antonio Favaro. New York, 1914.

GERMAIN, ADRIEN. Le premier méridien et la connaissance des temps. (In *Bulletin* de la Société de Géographie. 6th Series. Paris, 1875, vol. 9, pp. 504–21.)

GOULD, RUPERT T. *The marine chronometer: its history and development*. London, 1923.

GROS, CHARLES. *Échappements d'horloges et de montres* . . . *descriptif et historique* . . . Paris, 1913.

HARRISON, EDWARD. Idea longitudinis: Being a brief definition of the best known axioms for finding the longitude. (In the *London Gazette*. London, 1696. No. 3174.)

HILGARD, JULIUS E. Determination of transatlantic longitudes. Salem, 1874. (In the *Proceedings* of the American Association for the Advancement of Science. Aug. 1873. Salem, 1874, vol. 22, pp. 144–59.)

HUYGENS, CHRISTIAN. *Horologivm oscillatorivm; sive de motu pendvlorvm ad horologia aptato demonstrationes geometricae*. Paris, 1673.

JUAN Y SANTACILIA JORGE. *Observaciones astronomicas y phisicas* . . . *en los reynos del Peru* . . . *de las quales se deduce la figura y magnitud de la tierra, y se aplica á la navegacion*. Madrid, 1773.

LA CONDAMINE, CHARLES MARIE DE. *Journal du voyage fait par ordre du roi, à l'équateur, servant d'introduction historique à la mesure des trois premiers degrés du méridien*. Paris, 1751.

MASKELYNE, NEVIL. *An account of the going of Mr. John Harrison's watch* . . . London, 1767.

——*The British mariner's guide, containing complete and easy instructions for the discovery of the longitude at sea*. London, 1763.

MORI, ATTILIO. Le origini della carta del Cassini. (In *Rivista Geografica Italiana*. Florence, 1910, vol. 17, pp. 95–98.)

NEWTON, ISAAC. *Philosophiae naturalis principia mathematica*. 3 vols. London, 1687.

OLMSTED, JOHN W. The scientific expedition of Jean Richer to Cayenne (1672–1673). (In *Isis*. Bern, 1942, vol. 34, Pt. 2, No. 94, pp. 117–28.)

PICARD, JEAN. Mesure de la terre. (In *Mémoires de l'Académie Royale des Sciences de Paris depuis 1666 jusqu'à 1699*. Paris, 1729, Tome VII, Pt. I, pp. 133–90.)

—— Voyage d'Uranibourg, ou observations astronomiques faites en Dannemarck. (In *Mémoires de l'Académie Royale des Sciences de Paris depuis 1666 jusqu'à 1699*. Paris, 1729, Tome VII, Pt. I, pp. 193–230.)

PINGRÉ, ALEXANDRE G. *Voyage fait par order du roi en 1771 et 1772, en diverses parties de l'Europe, de l'Afrique et de l'Amérique* . . . Paris, 1778. This expedition was conducted by Verdun de la Crenne, and the Chevalier de Borda as well as Pingré.

POGO, ALEXANDER. Gemma Frisius, his method of determining differences of longitude by transporting timepieces (1530), and his treatise on triangulation (1533). (In *Isis*. Bruges, 1934–1935, vol. 22, No. 64, pp. 469–505.)

The Principles of Mr. Harrison's time-keeper, with plates of the same. Published by order of the Commissioners of longitude. London, 1767. This volume contains a preface by Nevil Maskelyne.

A proposal of a method for finding the longitude at sea within a degree, or 20 leagues. (In *Philosophical Transactions* of the Royal Society of London. London, 1731, vol. 37, pp. 185–95; 1809, Abridgement vol. 7, p. 501.)

PUISSANT, LOUIS. *Mémoire sur la projection de Cassini* . . . Paris, 1812.

RICHARDSON, HENRY S. *Greenwich: its history, antiquities, improvements, and public buildings*. London, 1834.

RICHER, JEAN. Observations astronomiques et physiques faites en l'isle de Caïenne. (In

Mémoires de l'Académie Royale des Sciences de Paris depuis 1666 jusqu'à 1699. Paris, 1729, Tome VII, Pt. I, pp. 233–326.)

SANDLER, CHRISTIAN. *Die reformation der kartographie um 1700.* Munich, 1905.

SCHÜCK, ALBERT (Karl Wilhelm Albert). Das horometer . . . (In *Geographischen Gesellschaft in München.* Munich, 1905, vol. 1, No. 2, pp. 269–83.)

SHORT, JAMES. *A narrative of the proceedings relative to the discovery of the longitude at sea; by Mr. John Harrison's time-keeper* . . . London, 1765.

Some remarks upon the method of observing the differences of right ascension and declination by cross hairs in a telescope. (In *Philosophical Transactions* of the Royal Society of London. London, 1720, vol. 31, pp. 113–19; 1809, Abridgement vol. 6, p. 494.)

TAISNIER, JOANNES. *A very necessarie and profitable booke concerning nauigation* . . . Translated . . . by Richarde Eden. [London, 1579?]

TAYLOR, EVA G. R. The geographical ideas of Robert Hooke. (In the *Geographical Journal.* London, 1937, vol. 89, pp. 525–38.)

—— Robert Hooke and the cartographical projects of the late seventeenth century (1666–1696). (In the *Geographical Journal.* London, 1937, vol. 90, pp. 529–40.)

THACKER, JEREMY. *The longitudes examined, beginning with a short epistle to the longitudinarians and ending with the description of a smart, pretty machine of my own which I am (almost) sure will do for the longitude and procure me the twenty thousand pounds.* . . . London, 1714.

WALES, WILLIAM. *The method of finding the longitude at sea, by timekeepers* . . . London, 1794.

WHISTON, WILLIAM, and DITTON, HUMPHRY. *A new method for discovering the longitude both at sea and land, humbly proposed to the consideration of the publick.* London, 1714.

WOLF, CHARLES J. E. *Histoire de l'observatoire de Paris de sa fondation à 1793.* Paris, 1902.

Projection

AVEZAC DE CASTERA-MACAYA, MARIE D'. Coup d'oeil historique sur la projection des cartes de géographie. (In *Bulletin* de la Société de Géographie. 5ᵉ serie. Paris, 1863, pp. 257–361.) Contains some interesting notes relating to early maps and map makers. This was also published in separate form in Paris, 1863.

BAILY, WALTER. A map of the world on Flamsteed's projection. (In *London, Edinburgh, and Dublin Philosophical Magazine.* 5th Series. London, May, 1888, vol. 21, pp. 415–16.)

CLOSE, SIR CHARLES. Map projections and sun compasses. (In the *Geographical Journal.* London, 1941, vol. 97, pp. 349–63.)

DE MORGAN, AUGUSTUS. *An explanation of the gnomonic projection of the sphere* . . . London, 1836.

DEETZ, CHARLES H., and ADAMS, OSCAR S. *Elements of map projection with applications to map and chart construction.* Washington, 1938. U. S. Dept. of Commerce. Coast and Geodetic Survey. Special publication No. 68.

DELAMBRE, JEAN B. J. De la projection stéréographique. (In *Mémoires* de l'Institut National des Sciences et Arts. Paris [1804], vol. 5, pp. 393–416.)

DONNE, BENJAMIN. *The use of the ge-organon and improved analemma* . . . Bristol, 1787.

DUCHESNE, CHARLES. L'enseignement des projections cartographiques. (In *Bulletin* de la Société Royale de Géographie d'Anvers. Anvers, 1907, vol. 31, pp. 65–94.)

GALL, REVEREND JAMES. Use of cylindrical projections for geographical, astronomical, and scientific purposes. (In the *Scottish Geographical Magazine*. Edinburgh, 1885, vol. 1, pp. 119–23.)

GARNETT, WILLIAM. *A little book on map projection* . . . London, 1921.

GERMAIN, ADRIEN. *Traité des projections des cartes géographiques*. Paris, 1866.

HALL, ELIAL F. Gerard Mercator: his life and works. (In *Journal* of the American Geographical Society of New York. New York, 1878, vol. X, No. 4, pp. 163–96.)

HINKS, ARTHUR R. *Map projections*. 2nd edition, revised. Cambridge, England, 1921.

HUNT, EDWARD B. Notes on map projections. (In the *American Journal of Science and Art*. New Haven, Nov., 1854, 2nd ser., vol. 18, pp. 326–40.)

JURISCH, CARL L. H. M. *A treatise on map-projection* . . . Cape Town, 1890.

KAMMERER, ALBERT. L'hemisphère australe en projection polaire équidistante du portulan Portugais anonyme du vieux séraï d'Istanboul . . . (In *Boletin* de la Sociedade de Geografia de Lisboa. Lisbon, 1940, vol. 58, pp. 373–78.)

REDWAY, JACQUES W. The reproduction of geographical forms . . . Boston, 1897.

REED, J. HOWARD. The elements of map projection. (In *Journal* of the Manchester Geographical Society. Manchester, 1895, vol. 11, pp. 232–47.) Gives illustrations of the various projections from Homer to modern times.

Map Trade

Die älteste karte mit dem namen Amerika . . . edited . . . by Professor Jos. Fischer, S. J. and Professor Franz R. von Wieser. Innsbruck, 1903.

Albert Dürer revived; or a book of drawing, limning, washing or colouring of maps or prints . . . London, 1666. According to Lowndes, an earlier edition was published. British Museum catalogues give an edition of 1660.

AUSSERER, CARL. Der atlas Blaeu der Wiener Nationalbibliothek. (In *Geographischen Gesellschaft in Wien*. Vienna, 1932, vol. 75, pp. 172–74.)

AVERDUNK, HEINRICH. *Gerhard Mercator und die geographen unter seinen nachkommen* . . . Gotha, 1914.

BAGROW, LEO A. Ortelii catalogus cartographorum. (In *Dr. A. Petermanns Mitteilungen Ergänzungsheft*, Gotha, 1928, Teil [A–L], No. 199; 1930, Teil [M–Z], No. 210.)

BAUDET, PIERRE J. H. *Leven en werken van Willem Jansz. Blaeu* . . . Utrecht, 1871.

BEAZLEY, CHARLES R. Sebastian Münster. (In the *Geographical Journal*. London, April, 1901, vol. 17, No. 4, pp. 423–25.)

BENEDICT, GEORGE H. Map engraving. (In the *Printing Art*. Cambridge, May, 1912, vol. 19, pp. 205–08.)

BERTOLINI, GIAN. Su l'edizione italiana dell'Ortelio. (In *Scritti de Geografia* . . . Florence, 1908, pp. 293–305.)

BOWLES, CARINGTON. *Carington Bowles's new and enlarged catalogues of useful and accurate maps, charts, and plans* . . . [London, 1786].

BOWLES, JOHN & SON. *A catalogue of maps, prints, copy-books, etc, from off copper-plates* . . . London [1753].

CARACI, GUISEPPE. *Tabulae geographicae vetustiores in Italia adservatae*. 3 vols. Florence, 1926–1932.

CARY, JOHN. Works published by John Cary, engraver and mapseller. (In his *Cary's Traveller's Companion*. London, 1810.)

Catalogue de livres, de cartes géographique . . . *Catalogue des plus nouvelles & des plus exacte carte* . . . *dressés sur les nouvelles obs. de* . . . *l'Académie Royale* . . . Leyden [1715].

Catalogue of books mostly from the presses of the first printers . . . collected by Rush C. Hawkins and catalogued by A. W. Pollard. Oxford, 1910.

CHUBB, THOMAS. *The printed maps in the atlases of Great Britain and Ireland; a bibliography, 1579–1870* . . . London, 1927.

CLEMENT, DAVID. Joannes Blaeu. A bibliography of the Blaeu atlases. (In *Bibliothèque Curieuse*. Göttingen, 1753, vol. IV, pp. 267–76.)

COLVIN, SIDNEY. *Early engraving & engravers in England (1545–1695)* . . . London, 1905.

CURNOW, IRENE J. *The world mapped; being a short history of attempts to map the world from antiquity to the twentieth century.* London, 1930.

DACIER, BON J. Notice historique sur la vie et les ouvrages de m. Barbié du Bocage. (In *Histoire et Mémoires* de l'Institut Royal de France. Académie des inscriptions et belles-lettres. Paris, 1831, vol. 9, pp. 132–45.)

DANIEL, JOHN. The seventeenth-century map-maker . . . (In the *Geographical Journal*. London, 1925, vol. 65, p. 85.)

DE VINNE, THEODORE L. *Notable printers of Italy during the fifteenth century* . . . New York, 1910. See pp. 37–52 for information on Sweinheim and Pannartz, printer and editor of Ptolemy, respectively.

DELAMARRE, CASIMIR. Pierre Antoine Tardieu, graveur de cartes. (In *Bulletin* de la Société de Géographie. 6e ser., Paris, 1871, vol. 1, pp. 73–76.)

DENUCÉ, JAN. Oud-Nederlandsche Kaartmakers. (In *Maatschappi der Anwerpsche Bibliophilen uitgave* nr. Antwerp, 1912–1913, vol. 44, No. 27 and 28.)

DU SAUZET, HENRI. *Atlas de Poche, à l'usage des voyageurs et des officiers.* Amsterdam, 1734–1738.

FADEN, WILLIAM, and JEFFERYS, THOMAS. Catalogue des cartes, plans, et cartes-marines . . . A Londres, 1774. Bound with their *A Catalogue of Modern and Correct Maps* . . . 1774.

—— *A catalogue of modern and correct maps, plans, and charts, chiefly engraved by the late T. Jefferys.* London, 1774.

FER, NICOLAS DE. Catalogue des ouvrages de géographie que l'auteur à mis au jour jusques en l'année 1716. (In his *Introduction à la Géographie*. Paris, 1717.)

FORDHAM, SIR HERBERT G. Christopher Saxton, of Dunningley. (In *Miscellanea* of the Thoresby Society. Leeds, 1927, vol. 28, pp. 357–84.)

—— *Exposition d'exemplaires choisis de cartes géographiques pour illustrer le developpement et le progrès de la cartographie anglaise* . . . [Cambridge, England, 1928]. Contains brief titles of 80 maps, chronologically arranged.

—— *Hand-list of catalogues and works of reference relating to carto-bibliography and kindred subjects for Great Britain and Ireland, 1720 to 1927* . . . Cambridge, England, 1928.

—— *John Cary, engraver, map, chart and print-seller and globe-maker 1754 to 1835* . . . Cambridge, England, 1925.

—— Liste alphabétique des plans et vues de villes, citadelles et forteresses qui se trouvent dans le grande atlas de Mortier, édition d'Amsterdam de 1696. (In France. Comité des travaux historiques et scientifiques, 1910. *Bulletin de Géographie Historique et Descriptive*. Paris, 1911.)

—— Note on a series of early French atlases, 1594–1637. Presented to the British Museum, 1920. (In *Transactions* of the Bibliographical Society. Second series. London, 1920, vol. I, p. 145.) "The Library. Fourth Series. London, etc., 1920–1921. Vol. I."

—— Some surveys and maps of the Elizabethan period remaining in manuscript . . . (In the *Geographical Journal*. London, 1928, vol. 71, pp. 50–60.)

GALLOIS, LUCIEN. *Les géographes Allemands de la renaissance.* Paris, 1890.

GENARD, MARIE N. J. P. La généalogie du géographe Abraham Ortelius. (In *Bulletin* de la Société Royale de Géographie d'Anvers. Anvers, 1881, vol. 5, pp. 312–49.)

GIUSEPPI, MONTAGNE S. The work of Theodore de Bry and his sons, engravers. (In *Proceedings* of the Huguenot Society of London. London, 1915–1917, vol. 11, pp. 204–26.)

GÜNTHER, SIEGMUND. *Peter und Philipp Apian, zwei deutsche mathematiker u. kartographen.* Prague, 1882.

HALL, ELIAL F. Gerard Mercator: his life and works. (In *Journal* of the American Geographical Society. New York, 1878, vol. 10, no. 4, pp. 163–96.)

HEAWOOD, EDWARD. Henricus Glareanus (sixteenth-century geographer) and his recently discovered maps. (In *Report* of the 73rd meeting of the British Association for the Advancement of Science. London, 1904, pp. 719–20.)

—— An unrecorded Blaeu world map of *c.* 1618. (In the *Geographical Journal.* London, 1943, vol. 102, pp. 170–75.)

HESSELS, JAN HENDRIK. *Ecclesiae londino-batavae archivvm . . .* [correspondence] between Abraham Ortelius and his friends]. 3 vols., Cambridge, 1887–1897.

HUCK, THOMAS W. The earliest printed maps. (In the *Antiquary.* London, 1910, vol. 46, pp. 253–57.) Describes the printing processes used on the maps in Ptolemy's *Geographia* and in Sebastian Münster's *Cosmography.*

HULST, FÉLIX A. J. VAN. *Ab. Ortelius,* Liège, 1846.

HUMPHREYS, ARTHUR L. *Old decorative maps and charts.* London and New York, 1926.

HUNTER, DARD. *Paper making through eighteen centuries.* New York, 1930.

IMRAY, LAURIE, NORIE and WILSON. *Three centuries of chart publishing.* 1670–1931. [London, 1931.]

Italian map collections of the sixteenth century. (In the *Geographical Journal.* London, 1927, vol. 69, pp. 598–99.) Contains a brief description of a "collection of Italian maps brought together by Antonio Lafreri. . . ."

JOHNSON, JOHN. *Typographia, or the printers' instructor: including an account of the origin of printing . . .* 2 vols. London, 1824.

JOMARD, EDMÉ F. Application du procédé Daguerre à la topographie. (In *Bulletin* de la Société de Géographie. 2d ser. Paris, 1839, vol. 11, pp. 108–11.)

JULIEN, ROCH. *Nouveau catalogue des cartes géographiques et topographiques . . .* Paris, 1763.

KAYSER, WERNER. Willem Janszoon Blaeu, globusmaecker, caertemaecker, boeckvercooper, 1571–1628. (In *Imprimatur ein Jahrbuch für Bücherfreunde.* Weimar, 1939, vol. 8, pp. 165–69.)

LAMPE, T. PETER. Improved map and chart pantograver. (In the *Military Engineer.* Washington, 1927, vol. 19, pp. 6–64.)

LARABEE, JOHN H. Modern methods of chart engraving. (In the *Military Engineer.* Washington, 1925, vol. 17, pp. 37–44.)

LENGLET DUFRESNOY, NICOLAS. Cartes de Charles Allard. (In his *Méthode Pour Étudier la Géographie.* 3rd edition, Paris, 1742, vol. I, Pt. 2, p. 288.)

—— Catalogue des cartes géographiques . . . du sieur Frederic deWit et Pierre Vander Aa, à Leyde. (In his *Méthode Pour Etudier la Géographie.* 3rd edition, Paris, 1742. Vol. I, Pt. 2, pp. 175–87.)

LETRONNE, ANTOINE J. Essai sur les idées cosmographiques qui se rattachent au nom d'atlas . . . (Extrait du *Bulletin Universel des Sciences.* Paris, 1831, section VII.)

LICHTWARK, ALFRED. *Der ornamentstich der Deutschen früh-renaissance.* Berlin, 1888.

LYNAM, EDWARD. *The first engraved atlas of the world, the Cosmographia of Claudius Ptolemaeus. Bologna, 1477.* Jenkintown, 1941.

—— Floris Balthasar, Dutch map-maker, and his sons. (In the *Geographical Journal.* London, 1926, vol. 67, pp. 158–61.)

McMURTRIE, DOUGLAS C. *Printing geographic maps with movable types.* New York, 1925.

MANNE, LOUIS C. J. DE. *Notice des ouvrages de M. D'Anville, premier géographe du roi . . .* Paris, An X, 1802. This work contains a catalogue of the maps engraved from D'Anville's surveys (pp. 45–102) compiled by B. J. Dacier, and a list of the works actually printed by him (pp. 103–120).

MARKHAM, CLEMENTS R. Lost geographical documents. (In the *Geographical Journal*, London, 1913, vol. 42, pp. 28–34.)

MOTLEY, JOHN L. *The rise of the Dutch republic. A history.* New York, 1856.

NISCHER VON FALKENHOF, ERNST. *Osterreichische kartographen* . . . Vienna, 1925.

NUNN, GEORGE E. *The mappemonde of Juan de la Cosa. A critical investigation of its date.* Jenkintown, 1934.

ORTROY, FERNAND G. VAN. *Bibliographie de l'oeuvre de Pierre Apian* . . . Besançon, 1902.

—— *Bibliographie sommaire de l'oeuvre mercatorienne* . . . Paris, 1918–1920.

—— *L'oeuvre cartographique de Gérard et de Corneille de Jode.* Gand, 1914.

—— *L'oeuvre géographique de Mercator* . . . Brussels, 1893.

PARTSCH, JOSEF F. M. *Philipp Clüver der begründer der historischen länderkunde.* Vienna, 1891.

RAEMDONCK, J. VAN. La grande carte de Flandre de 1540 faite par Gérard Mercator . . . (In *Bulletin* de la Société Géographie d'Anvers. Anvers, 1879–80, vol. 4, pp. 87–116.)

—— Relations commerciales entre Gérard Mercator et Christophe Plantin à Anvers. (In *Bulletin* de la Société de Géographie d'Anvers. Anvers, 1879, vol. 4, pp. 327–66.)

RATZEL, FRIEDRICH. *Abraham Ortelius* . . . [Altenburg, 1887].

RICHTER, HERMAN. Willem Jansz. Blaeu—en Tycho Brahes lärjunge. (In *Svensk Geografisk Arsbok.* Lund, 1925, pp. 49–66.)

ROLAND, FRANÇOIS. *Alexis-Hubert Jaillot, géographe du roi Louis XIV (1632–1712).* Besançon, 1919.

SALMON, WILLIAM. *Polygraphice; or, the arts of drawing, engraving* . . . London, 1675. See the 5th edition, London, 1685, pp. 204–11 for a chapter "of colours simple for washing of maps—of colours compounded for washing maps."

SMITH, JOHN G. M. *The art of painting in oyl, to which is added the whole art and mystery of colouring maps* . . . London, 1769.
There are various editions of this work, "the only treatise in which there is a special chapter on map colouring." The 9th edition was published in London, 1788.

STEVENS, HENRY N. *Ptolemy's Geography, a brief account of all the printed editions down to 1730.* London, 1908.

STEVENSON, EDWARD L. *Map of the world by Jodocus Hondius, 1611* . . . New York, 1907.

—— *Willem Janszoon Blaeu, 1571–1638; a sketch of his life and work, with an especial reference to his large world map of 1605* . . . New York, 1914. Hispanic Society Publication No. 85.

STILLWELL, MARGARET. *Incunabula and Americana 1450–1800.* New York, 1931.

TAYLOR, EVA G. R. *Late Tudor and early Stuart geography, 1583–1650.* London, 1934.

—— *Tudor geography, 1485–1583.* London, 1930.

THACHER, JOHN B. *The continent of America.* New York, 1896.

THOMPSON, DANIEL V. Medieval color-making . . . (In *Isis.* Bruges, 1935. vol. 22, p. 456.)

TIELE, PIETER A. *Nederlandsche bibliographie van land-en volkenkunde.* Amsterdam, 1884.

TOTTILL, RICHARD. *A very proper treatise, wherein is briefly sett forthe the art of limming* . . . London, 1573. Facsimile of the unique copy in the British Museum published by Edwards Bros., Ann Arbor, 1932.

VERTUE, GEORGE. *A description of the works of the ingenious delineator and engraver Wencelaus Hollar* . . . London, 1759.

WALDSEEMÜLLER, MARTIN. *The cosmographiae introductio of Martin Waldseemüller in facsimilie* . . . with an introduction by Joseph Fischer, S. J. and Franz von Wieser. Edited by C. G. Herbermann, New York, 1907. U. S. Catholic Historical Society Monograph No. 4.

WAUERMANS, H. E. *Histoire de l'école cartographique belge et anversoise du XVIᵉ siècle.* Brussels, 1895.

WINSHIP, GEORGE P. *Printing in the 15th century.* Philadelphia, 1940.

WINSOR, JUSTIN. The bibliography of Pomponius Mela, Solinus, Vadianus [i.e., Joachim Watt] and Apianus. (In his *Narrative and Critical History* . . . Boston, 1886, vol. 2, pp. 180–86.)

—— The general atlases and charts of the sixteenth and seventeenth centuries. (In his *Narrative and Critical History* . . . Boston, 1886, vol. 4, pp. 369–77.)

Middle Ages

Alguns documentos do archivo nacional da Torre do Tombo acerca das navegações . . . portuguezas. Lisbon, 1892.

ANDREWS, MICHAEL C. The study and classification of Medieval Mappae Mundi. (In *Archaeologia.* London, 1926, vol. 75, pp. 61–76.)

ANVILLE, JEAN B. B. D'. Dissertation on the extent of ancient Jerusalem. (In F. A. de Chateaubriand's *Travels to Jerusalem.* London, 1835, vol. 2, pp. 272–320.)

Archivo dos Açores. Ponta Delgada, 1878–1894.

AVEZAC DE CASTERA-MACAYA, MARIE D'. Note sur la mappemonde historiée de la cathédrale de Héréford . . . (In *Bulletin* de la Société de Géographie. 5ᵉ serie. Paris, 1861, vol. 2, pp. 321–34.)

BABCOCK, WILLIAM H. The problem of Mayda, an island appearing on medieval maps. (In the *Geographical Review.* New York, Jan.–June 1920, vol. 9, pp. 335–46.)

BARING-GOULD, SABINE. *Curious myths of the Middle Ages.* New edition. London, 1894.

BEAZLEY, C. RAYMOND. *The dawn of modern geography. A history of exploration and geographical science* . . . 3 vols. London, 1897–1906.

—— *Prince Henry the navigator.* London, 1895.

—— ed. *The texts and versions of John de Plano Carpini and William de Rubruquis.* London, 1903. Hakluyt Society, extra series, vol. 13.

BEVAN, W. L., and PHILLOTT, H. W. *Medieval geography. An essay in illustration of the Hereford Mappa Mundi.* London, 1873. This volume contains a good summary of medieval map making.

BORDEAUX PILGRIM, THE. *Itinerary from Bordeaux to Jerusalem.* "The Bordeaux Pilgrim" (333 A.D.). Translated by Aubrey Stewart and annotated by Sir C. W. Wilson. London, 1887. Publication of the Palestine Pilgrims' Text Society.

BOURNE, EDWARD G. *Essays in historical criticism.* New York, 1901. See especially chapter 6: "Prince Henry the Navigator," pp. 173–89.

The Cambridge medieval history. Edited by H. M. Gwatkin, and J. P. Whitney. 8 vols. Cambridge, 1911–1936. Excellent bibliography and comprehensive text.

Cathay and the way thither, being a collection of medieval notices of China. Translated and edited by Col. Sir Henry Yule. 4 vols. London, 1913–16. Hakluyt Society, Series II, vols. 33, 37, 38, 41.

CHARLESWORTH, MARTIN P. *Trade routes and commerce of the Roman Empire.* Cambridge, 1924.

CORTAMBERT, EUGÈNE. Quelques-uns des plus anciens monuments géographiques du moyen age conservés à la Bibliothèque Nationale. (In *Bulletin* de la Société de Géographie. 6ᵉ ser. Paris, 1877, vol. 14, pp. 337–63.)

CORTESÃO, ARMANDO. *Cartografia e cartógrafos portugueses dos séculos XV e XVI.* 2 vols. Lisbon, 1935.

Cosmas (Indicopleustes). *The Christian topography of Cosmas Indicopleustes;* edited with geographical notes by Eric O. Winstedt. Cambridge, England, 1909.

—— *The Christian topography of Cosmas, an Egyptian monk.* Translated and edited by J. W. McCrindle. London, 1897. Hakluyt Society, Series I, vol. 98.

Coulton, George G. *Life in the Middle Ages.* Selected, translated and annotated by G. G. Coulton. New York, 1930.

Eannes de Azurara, Gomes. *Chronica do descobrimento e conquista de Guiné.* Edited by Carreira and Santarem. Paris, 1841.

—— *The chronicle of the discovery and conquest of Guinea.* Written by Gomes Eannes de Azurara . . . done into English by Charles Raymond Beazley and Edgar Prestage. 2 vols. London, 1896–1899. Hakluyt Society, Series I, vols. 95 and 100.

Farrar, C. P., and Evans, A. P. *Bibliography of English translations from medieval sources.* New York, 1946.

Galvano, Antonio. *The discoveries of the world. From their first original unto the year of our Lord 1555.* Reprinted . . . and edited by Vice-Admiral Charles R. G. Bethune. London, 1862. Hakluyt Society, Series I, no. 30.

Heyd, Wilhelm von. *Histoire du commerce du Levant au moyen âge.* 2 vols. Leipzig, 1885–1886.

Kimble, George H. T. *Geography in the Middle Ages.* London [1938].

—— Portuguese policy and its influence on 15th century cartography. (In the *Geographical Review.* New York, 1933, vol. 23, pp. 653–59.)

—— Some notes on mediaeval cartography with special reference to M. Behaim's globe. (In the *Scottish Geographical Magazine.* Edinburgh, 1933, vol. 49, pp. 91–98.)

Koepen, Adolphus L. *The world in the Middle Ages, an historical geography* . . . New York, 1854.

Le Long, Jacques. Géographie ecclésiastique de la France. (In his *Bibliothèque Historique de la France.* Paris, 1768, vol. 1, pp. 71–84.)

Lelewel, Joachim. *Géographie du moyen âge* . . . 3 vols. Brussels, 1850–1852.

Major, Richard H. *The life of Henry of Portugal, surnamed the navigator.* London, 1868.

Michel, Francisque X. *Les voyages merveilleux de St. Brendan* . . . Paris, 1878.

Miller, Konrad. *Die ebstorfkarte, eine weltkarte aus dem 3 jahrhundert.* Stuttgart, 1900.

—— *Mappaemundi; die ältesten weltkarten.* 6 vols. Stuttgart, 1895–1898.

Moran, Patrick F. *Acta sancti Brendani* . . . *Original documents connected with the life of St. Brendan.* Dublin, 1872.

Morison, Samuel E. *Admiral of the ocean sea.* 2 vols. Boston, 1942.

Oberhummer, Eugen. Leonardo da Vinci and the art of the renaissance . . . (In *Geographical Journal.* London, May, 1909, vol. 33, pp. 540–69.)

Oman, Charles. *The Dark Ages, 476–918.* Period I. London, 1908.

Palestine Pilgrims' Text Society. *The library of the Palestine Pilgrims' Text Society.* 13 vols. London, 1885–1897. See all publications of this society for translations of important medieval texts relating to pilgrimages.

Polo, Marco. *The most noble and famous travels of Marco Polo together with the travels of Nicolò de' Conti.* Edited from the Elizabethan translation of John Frampton, with introduction, notes . . . by N. M. Penzer. London, 1929.

Portolan chart of Angelino Dalorto, 1325 . . . with a note on the surviving charts and atlases of the 14th century by Arthur R. Hinks. London, 1929. "Reproductions of Early Manuscript Maps." Royal Geographical Society.

Ravenstein, Ernest G., ed. *A journal of the first voyage of Vasco da Gama, 1497–1499.* London, 1898. Hakluyt Society, Series I, no. 99.

Ruybrock, Willem van. *The journey of William of Rubruck to the Eastern parts of* the world 1253–55, as narrated by himself. Translated from Latin manuscripts and edited by William W. Rockhill. London, 1900. Hakluyt Society, Series II, vol. 4.

SHEPHERD, WILLIAM R. *Historical atlas.* Seventh edition revised. New York, 1929.

THOMPSON, JAMES W. *The Middle Ages, 300–1500.* 2 vols. New York, 1931.

TOBLER, TITUS, and MOLINIER, AUGUSTUS. *Itinera hierosolymitana et descriptiones Terrae Sanctae* . . . 2 vols. Geneva, 1879–1885. Publications de la Société de l'Orient Latin. Série géographique, vols. 1–2, 4.

UHDEN, RICHARD. Die weltkarte des Isidorus von Sevilla. (In *Mnemosyne; Bibliotheca Classica Batavia.* 3ᵉ ser. Leiden, 1935, vol. 3, pp. 1–28.)

WRIGHT, JOHN K. *The geographic lore of the time of the crusades* . . . New York, 1925.

ZURLA, PLACEDO. *Di Marco Polo e degli altri viaggiatori Veneziani.* Venice, 1818.

National Surveys

ARNOUX, EDOUARD. *Notes sur le cadastre en France et sur l'impôt foncier et le cadastre à l'étranger.* Paris, 1891. (Extrait du "Dictionnaire des Finances.")

BAILY, FRANCIS. *An account of the revᵈ. John Flamsteed, the first astronomer royal* . . . London, 1835.

BARTHOLOMEW, JOHN G. The philosophy of map-making and the evolution of a great German atlas. (In the *Scottish Geographical Magazine.* Edinburgh, 1902, vol. 18, pp. 34–39.)

BERNHARD, HENRI. Les étapes de la cartographie scientifique pour la Chine. (In *Monumenta Serica.* Peiping, 1935, vol. 1, pp. 428–77.)

BERTHAUT, HENRI M. A. *La carte de France, 1750–1898.* 2 vols. Paris, 1898–1899.

—— *Les ingénieurs géographes militaires, 1624–1831. Étude historique.* 2 vols. Service géographique de l'armée. Paris, 1902.

BOUGUER, PIERRE. *La figure de la terre, déterminée par les observations de Messieurs Bouguer et de La Condamine* . . . Paris, 1749.

CAJORI, FLORIAN. *The chequered career of Ferdinand Rudolph Hassler* . . . *a chapter in the history of science in America.* Boston, 1929.

CARUSSO, C. D. *Importance de la cartographie officielle.* Geneva, 1886.

CASSINI, JACQUES. De la carte de la France et de la perpendiculaire a la méridienne de Paris. (In *Histoire* de l'Académie Royale des Sciences, 1733. Paris, 1735, pp. 389–405.)

—— De la grandeur de la terre et de sa figure. (In *Histoire* de l'Académie Royale des Sciences, 1718. Paris, 1719, pp. 245–256.)

—— De la grandeur et de la figure de la terre. (*Suite des Mémoires* de l'Académie Royale des Sciences, 1718. Paris, 1720.)

CASSINI, JACQUES, and CASSINI DE THURY, CÉSAR F. De la perpendiculaire à la méridienne . . . prolongée vers l'Orient. (In *Histoire* de l'Académie Royale des Sciences, 1734. Paris, 1736, pp. 434–52.)

CASSINI, JEAN D. Les hypothèses et les tables des satellites de Jupiter . . . (In *Mémoires* de l'Académie Royale des Sciences. Paris, 1730, vol. VIII, pp. 315–505.)

—— Observations astronomiques faites en divers endroits du royaume. (In *Mémoires* de l'Académie Royale des Sciences. Paris, 1729, vol. VII, Pt. I, pp. 349–75.)

CASSINI DE THURY, CÉSAR F. Description des conquêtes de Louis XV . . . (In *Relation d'un Voyage en Allemagne, qui Comprend les Opérations Relatives à la Figure de la Terre* . . . Paris, 1775, pp. 123–94.)

—— *Description géométrique de la France.* Paris, 1783.

—— La méridienne de l'Observatoire Royal de Paris, verifiée dans toute l'éntendue du Royaume . . . pour lever une carte générale de la France. (In *Suite des Mémoires* de l'Académie Royale des Sciences, 1740. Paris, 1744.)

—— Sur la description géometrique de la France. (In *Histoire* de l'Académie Royale des Sciences, 1745. Paris, 1749, pp. 553–60.)

—— Sur la jonction de la méridienne de Paris à celle que Snellius a tracée dans la Hollande . . . (In *Histoire* de l'Académie Royale des Sciences, 1748. Paris, 1752, pp. 123–32.)

—— Sur la perpendiculaire à la méridienne de l'observatoire . . . (In *Histoire* de l'Académie Royale des Sciences, 1736. Paris, 1739, pp. 329–41.)

CASTRO, MANUEL F. DE. *Notas para un estudio bibliográfico sobre los orígenes y estado actual del mapa geológico de Espana.* Madrid, 1874.

CHAPMAN, EDWARD F. The mapping of Africa. (In *Journal* of the Manchester Geographical Society. Manchester, 1895, vol. 11, pp. 192–202.)

CLEMENT, PIERRE. *Vie de Colbert.* Paris, 1846.

CLOSE, CHARLES. *The early years of the Ordnance Survey.* Chatham, 1926.

—— *The map of England.* London, 1932.

COLBERT, JEAN B. *Lettres, instructions, et mémoires de Colbert, publiés d'après les ordres de l'Empereur* . . . 9 vols. Paris, 1893.

D'AGAPEYEFF, ALEXANDER, and HADFIELD, E. C. R. *Maps.* Oxford, 1942.

DAHLGREN, ERIK W. *Les débuts de la cartographie du Japon.* Upsal, 1911. At head of title: Archives d'études orientales; publiées par J. A. Lundell. Vol. 4.

DRAPEYRON, LUDOVIC. L'évolution de notre premier atlas national sous Louis XIII et en particulier durant le ministère du Cardinal de Richelieu. (In France. Comité des Travaux Historiques et Scientifiques. *Bulletin de Géographie Historique et Descriptive.* Paris, 1890, pp. 260–84.)

DURAND, DANA B. The earliest modern maps of Germany and central Europe. (In *Isis.* Bruges, 1933, vol. 19, pp. 486–502.)

ENGELBRECHT, W. A. Outline of the history of Netherlands cartography and of its significance also for other countries. (In *International Geographical Congress. 15th. Comptes Rendus.* Amsterdam, 1938, vol. 1, pp. 85–98.)

EVELYN, JOHN. Of a method of making more lively representations of nature in wax than are extant in painting, and of a new kind of maps in bas relief; both practiced in France. (In *Philosophical Transactions* of the Royal Society. London, 1665.)

FEAD, MARGARET I. Notes on the development of the cartographic representation of cities. (In the *Geographical Review.* New York, 1933, vol. 23, pp. 441–56.)

FERNANDEZ DE CASTRO. (See CASTRO, MANUEL F.)

FLETT, SIR JOHN S. *The first hundred years of the Geological Survey of Great Britain.* London, 1937.

FORDHAM, SIR HERBERT G. *La cartographie des provinces de France, 1594–1757.* Cambridge [1912].

GALLOIS, LUCIEN. L'Académie des sciences et les origines de la carte de Cassini. (In *Annales de Géographie.* Paris, 1909, vol. 18, no. 99, pp. 193–204; no. 100, pp. 289–300.) Contains a transcript of the decree of Louis XIII, dated 1634, making Ferro the prime meridian of longitude for all French maps.

GENTHE, MARTHA K. German geographers and German geography. (In the *National Geographic Magazine.* Washington, Sept. 1901, vol. 12, pp. 324–37.)

GOUGH, RICHARD. *A catalogue of the books relating to British topography.* Oxford, 1814.

GREAT BRITAIN. ORDNANCE SURVEY. *Catalogue of the maps and plans and other publications of the ordnance survey of England and Wales, and the Isle of Man* . . . London, 1888.

—— *Comparisons of the standards of length of England, France, Belgium, Prussia* . . . London, 1866.

—— *Ordnance Survey alphabets.* [Southampton, 1934.]

—— *Report of the progress of the Ordnance Survey to the 31st December, 1893.*

HAXO, FRANCOIS N. B. *Mémoire sur le figuré du terrain dans les cartes topographiques.*

Paris, 1822. Contains much good material on topography, including use of hachures.

HINKS, ARTHUR R. *Maps and survey* . . . Cambridge, England, 1944.

HOTINE, MARTIN. The lay-out of the East-African arc. (In *Empire Survey Review*. London, 1934, vol. 2, pp. 357–67, 472–84; vol. 3, pp. 72–80, 203–18.)

HUMBERT, ABRAHAM. Lettre de Mr. Humbert . . . à M. de Camas . . . sur les principales cartes de géographie progres à composer un atlas de l'Allemagne. (In *Bibliothèque Germanique*. Amsterdam, 1734, vol. 30, pp. 175–203.)

[IMHOF, EDUARD] *Hans Konrad Gygers Karte des kantons Zürich von 1667* . . . Zürich, 1944. This publication is accompanied by a colored facsimile of the map itself.

INDIA. SURVEYOR GENERAL'S OFFICE. *A catalogue of maps, plans, and charts of the survey of India*. Calcutta, 1878.

INGLIS, HARRY G. R. *The early maps of Scotland, with an account of the Ordnance Survey*. Edinburgh, 1934.

INSTITUT ROYAL DES INGÉNIEURS NÉERLANDAIS. *Répertoire des cartes*. 5 vols. La Haye, 1854–67.

ISNARD, ALBERT. Joseph-Nicolas Delisle, sa biographie et sa collection de cartes géographiques à la Bibliothèque Nationale. (In France. Comité des travaux historiques et scientifiques. *Bulletin* de la Section de Géographie. Paris, 1915, vol. 30, pp. 34–168.)

JAMES, SIR HENRY. *Account of the methods and processes adopted for the production of the maps of the Ordnance Survey of the United Kingdom* . . . London, 1902.

JAPAN. GEOLOGICAL SURVEY. *The imperial geological survey of Japan* . . . Tokyo, 1923.

JOERG, WOLFGANG L. G. Summary of recent reports on natural resources. (In *Second Report of the Science Advisory Board*. Washington, 1935, pp. 397–422.)

JUAN, D. JORGE. *Observaciones astronomicas y phisicas, hechas de orden de S. M. en los reynos del Peru* . . . Corregidas y emmendadas por el autor. Madrid, 1773.

LA CONDAMINE, CHARLES M. DE. *Journal du voyage fait* . . . *à l'équateur, servant d'introduction historique à la mesure des trois premiers degrès du méridien*. Paris, 1751. To accompany *Histoire* de l'Académie Royale des Sciences for 1751.

LORIDAN, ABBÉ J. *Voyages des astronomes Français à la recherche de la figure de la terre et ses dimensions*. Lille, 1890.

McLENNAN, JOHN F. *Memoir of Thomas Drummond*. London, 1867.

MARCEL, GABRIEL A. *Les origines de la carte d'Espagne* . . . Mâcon, 1899.

MASKELYNE, NEVIL. Concerning the latitude and longitude of the Royal Observatory . . . with remarks on a memorial of the late M. Cassini de Thury. (In *Philosophical Transactions* of the Royal Society. London, 1787, vol. 77, pt. 1, pp. 151–87.)

MAUPERTUIS, MOREAU DE. *La figure de la terre déterminée par les observations de Messieurs de Maupertuis, Clairaut, Camus, Le Monnier* . . . *et Outhier* . . . *accompágnés de M. Celsius* . . . *faites par order du Roy au Cercle Polaire*. Paris, 1738.

MORI, ATTILIO. La cartografia dell'Italia dal secolo XIV al XVIII. (In *Bollettino* della R. Società Geografica Italiana. Serie 6. Roma, 1930, vol. 7, pp. 205–18.)

MUDGE, WILLIAM, and COLBY, ISAAC. *An account of the operations carried on for accomplishing a trigonometrical survey of England* . . . 3 vols. London, 1799–1811.

NEUMANN, KARL F. Catalogue des latitudes et des longitudes de plusieurs places de l'empire Chinois. (In *Journal Asiatique*. Paris, 1834, vol. 13, pp. 87–94.)

NISCHER-FALKENHOF, ERNST VON. The survey by the Austrian General Staff under the Empress Maria Theresa . . . and the subsequent initial surveys of neighbouring territories during the years 1749–1854. (In *Imago Mundi*. London, 1937, vol. 2, pp. 83–88.)

OLDHAM, HENRY Y. The early cartography of Japan. (In *Geographical Journal*. London, Sept., 1894, vol. 4, pp. 276–79.)

OLSON, E. C., and WHITMARSH, A. *Foreign maps*. New York and London, 1944.

The Ordnance Survey. (In the *Quarterly Review*. London, Jan. and April, 1895, vol. 180, pp. 36–60.)

PALMER, HENRY S. *The ordnance survey of the kingdom* . . . London, 1873.

PELLATI, N. Contribuzione alla storia della cartografia geologica in Italia. (In *International Congress of Historical Sciences.* Rome, 1903. vol. 10, pp. 131–63.)

PICARD, JEAN. Observations faites à Brest et à Nantes pendant l'année 1679. (In *Mémoires de l'Académie Royale des Sciences.* Paris, 1729, vol. VII, pt. I, pp. 379–90.)

PIERCE, JOSIAH, Jr. The ordnance Survey of Great Britain — its history and object. (In the *National Geographic Magazine.* Washington, 1891, vol. 2, pp. 243–60.)

PORTLOCK, LT. COL. JOSEPH E. *Memoir of the life of Major-General Colby, R. E.* 1869. (In Great Britain and Ireland. Army. Corps of Royal Engineers. Papers. New Series, vol. 1, 1851, etc.)

RICHTER, PAUL E. *Bibliotheca geographica Germaniae.* Leipzig, 1896.

ROSÉN, PER G. *The astronomic and geodetic work of the topographical division of the General Staff of Sweden.* Stockholm, 1882.

ROSNY, LÉON L. L. P. DE. La littérature géographique et la cartographie des Japonais. (In his *Feuilles de Momidzi.* Paris, 1902, pp. 55–76.)

ROY, WILLIAM. An account of the measurement of a base on Hounslow-Heath. Read from April 21 to June 16, 1785. (In *Philosophical Transactions* of the Royal Society. London, 1785, vol. 75, pt. II, pp. 385 ff.)

—— An account of the mode proposed to be followed in determining the relative situation of the Royal Observatories of Greenwich and Paris. (In *Philosophical Transactions* of the Royal Society. London, 1787, vol. 77, pt. I, pp. 188–226.)

—— An account of the trigonometrical operation, whereby the distance between the meridians of the Royal Observatories of Greenwich and Paris has been determined. Read February 25, 1790. (In *Philosophical Transactions* of the Royal Society. London, 1790, vol. 80, pt. I, pp. 111–270.)

SCHOTT, C. A. *The transcontinental triangulation and the American arc of the parallel.* Washington, 1900. U. S. Coast and Geodetic Survey publication.

SORIA, GASPAR. Biblioteca y mapoteca histórico-geográfica de la República Argentina. (In Argentine Republic. Instituto Geografico Militar. *Anuario.* Buenos Aires, 1913, vol. 2, pp. 85–116.)

THIELE, WALTER. *Official map publications. A historical sketch, and a bibliographical handbook.* Chicago, 1938.

TOWNSEND, MALCOLM. Glossary of geographical terms. (In his *An Index to the United States of America.* Boston, 1890.)

U. S. GEOLOGICAL SURVEY. *Topographic instructions of the United States Geological Survey* . . . Washington, 1928.

The United States Geological Survey: its origin, development, organization and operations. Washington, 1904. U. S. Geological Survey Bulletin No. 227.

U. S. WAR DEPT. GENERAL STAFF. *List of conventional signs and abbreviations in use on French and German maps* . . . Washington, 1918.

VANDERMAELEN, JOSEPH J. H. Les géographes des souverains qui régnèrent en Belgique 1550 à 1790. (In *Bulletin* de la Société de Géographie d'Anvers. Anvers, 1882, vol. 7, pp. 459–66.)

VIGNOLS, LÉON. Historique, entièrement inédit, de la carte topographique de France par Cassini . . . (In Congrès National des Sociétés Françaises de Géographie. 17° Sess., 1896. Lorient, 1897, pp. 359–67.)

VIVIEN DE SAINT-MARTIN, LOUIS. Esquisse historique de la cartographie de la France . . . (In *Bulletin* de la Société de Géographie. 4ᵉ ser. Paris, 1856, vol. 12, pp. 49–64.)

WARREN, GOUVERNEUR K. Memoir to accompany the map of the territory of the United States from the Mississippi River to the Pacific Ocean. (In U. S. War Dept. *Reports of Explorations and Surveys to Ascertain the Most Practicable and Economical Route for a Railroad from the Mississippi to the Pacific Ocean.* 12 vols. Washington, 1855–60, vol. XI.)

WAUGH, B. W. Completing the world's longest surveyed straight line. (In *Canadian Geographical Journal.* Ottawa, 1940, vol. 21, pp. 75–87.)

WEBBER, GUSTAVUS A. *The United States Coast and Geodetic survey, its work, methods and organization.* Washington, 1929. U. S. Coast and Geodetic Survey. Special Publication No. 23.

WHEELER, GEORGE M. *Facts concerning the origin, organization, administration, functions . . . of the principal government land and marine surveys of the world . . .* Washington, 1885. U. S. War Dept. Corps of Engineers.

—— *Report upon the third international geographical congress and exhibition at Venice, Italy, 1881, accompanied by data concerning the principal government land and marine surveys of the world.* Washington, 1885. U. S. War Dept. Corps of Engineers. For an invaluable bibliography of published works on national surveys, both topographic and geologic, in English, French, German, Italian, Danish, Spanish and Portuguese, see pp. 539–46.

WHITE, T. PILKINGTON. The romance of state-mapping. (In *Blackwood's Edinburgh Magazine.* Edinburgh, July-Dec., 1888, vol. 144, pp. 384–98.)

—— *The Ordnance Survey of the United Kingdom . . .* Edinburgh and London, 1886.

WINSLOW, ARTHUR. The art and development of topographic mapping. (In *Engineering Magazine.* October, 1893. New York, 1894, vol. 6, pp. 24–31.)

Ptolemy

BAGROW, LEO. The origin of Ptolemy's Geographia. (In *Geografiska Annaler.* Utgivna av Svenska Sällskapet för Antropologi Och Geografi. Stockholm, 1945, vol. 27, pp. 319–87.)

BUACHE, JEAN N. Mémoire sur la géographie de Ptolémée . . . (In *Histoire* de l'Académie Royale des Sciences. 1787. Paris, 1789, pp. 119–27.)

COOLEY, WILLIAM D. *Claudius Ptolemy and the Nile . . .* London, 1854.

MORALIA, THOMAS. Communique un catalogue de toutes les éditions des oeuvres de Claude Ptolémée . . . (In Franz X. Zach's *Correspondance Astronomique, Géographique . . .* Gênes, 1824. Vol. 10, pp. 46–53.)

NORDENSKIÖLD, ADOLF E. *Facsimile-atlas to the early history of cartography.* Translated from the Swedish original by Johan Adolf Ekelöf and Clements R. Markham. Stockholm, 1889.

Periplus of the Erythraean Sea . . . translated from the Greek and annotated by W. H. Schoff . . . New York, 1912.

PTOLEMY, CLAUDIUS. *Almagest: Ptolemy mathematical composition.* Translated into English from the Greek text of Heiberg by Robert Catesby Taliaferro. n. p., 1938. "The Classics of St. John's Program."

—— *Claudii Ptolemaei opera quae exstant omnia . . .* Leipsig, 1898. Vol. I, Parts I and II (1898–1903), consists of the Syntaxis mathematica (Almagest) edited by Johan Ludvig Heiberg.

—— *Geography of Claudius Ptolemy . . .* Translated into English and edited by Edward Luther Stevenson. New York, 1932.

RYLANDS, THOMAS G. *The geography of Ptolemy elucidated . . .* Dublin, 1893.

SMITH, WILLIAM. *An atlas of ancient geography.* (Dr. William Smith's Ancient Atlas.) Drawn by Dr. Charles Müller and edited by William Smith and George Grove. London, 1874.

TUDEER, LAURI O. On the origin of the maps attached to Ptolemy's Geography. (In *Journal* of Hellenic Studies. London, 1917, vol. 37, pp. 62–76.)

VIDAL DE LA BLACHE, PAUL M. J. Les voies de commerce dans la géographie de Ptolémée. Paris, 1896. Extract des Comptes Rendus de l'Académie des Inscriptions et Belles-lettres. Nov. 1896.

The Wilton codex of Ptolemy maps. (In the *Geographical Journal.* London, 1924, vol. 64, no. 3, pp. 237–40.)

Road Maps and Guidebooks

ANVILLE, JEAN B. B. D'. *Traité des mesures itineraires anciennes et modernes.* Paris, 1769.

BERGIER, NICOLAS S. *Histoire des grands chemins de l'empire Romain.* 2 vols. Brussels, 1736.

BUACHE, JEAN N. Observations sur la carte itinéraire des Romains appelée communement carte de Peutinger . . . (In *Mémoires* de l'Académie des Sciénces Morales et Politiques. Paris, 1804, vol. 5, pp. 53–62.)

CAVAILLÈS, HENRI. *La route Française, son histoire, sa fonction.* Paris, 1946.

CLOSE, CHARLES. The old English mile. (In the *Geographical Journal.* London, 1930, vol. 76, no. 4, pp. 338–42.)

COUSIN, LOUIS. *Observations sur le projet de carte itinéraire de la Gaule au commencement du Ve siècle.* Caen, 1868.

DEPT, GERARD GASTON. Notes sur la tabula Peutingeriana. (In *Revue Belge de Philologie et d'Histoire.* Brussels, 1931, vol. 10, pp. 997–1011.)

DESJARDINS, ERNEST. Communication de m. Ernest Desjardins au sujet de la table de Peutinger. (In *Bulletin* de la Société de Géographie. 5e ser. Paris, 1870, vol. 19, pp. 390–93.)

ESTIENNE, CHARLES. *La guide des chemins de France de 1553, par Charles Estienne.* Editée par Jean Bonnerot. 2 vols. Paris, 1936. Fascicule 265 de la Bibliothèque de l'École des Hautes Études. Vol. 2 contains a facsimile of the first edition of Estienne's *Guide.*

FORDHAM, SIR HERBERT G. *The earliest French itineraries, 1552 and 1591.* London, 1921.

—— The earliest tables of the highways of England and Wales, 1541–1561. (In *Transactions* of the Bibliographical Society. London, 1927, 2nd Ser., vol. 8, pp. 349–54.)

—— *An Itinerary of the 16th century. La guide des chemins d'Angleterre. Jean Bernard, Paris, 1579.* Cambridge, 1910.

—— *John Ogilby (1600–1676), his Britannia and the British itineraries of the eighteenth century* . . . London, 1925.

—— *Notes on British and Irish itineraries and road-books.* Hertford, 1912.

—— *The road-books and itineraries of Great Britain, 1570 to 1850.* Cambridge, England, 1924.

—— *Roads on English and French maps at the end of the seventeenth century* . . . Southampton, 1926.

—— *Studies in carto-bibliography, British and French, and in the bibliography of itineraries and road-books.* Oxford, 1914.

MILLER, KONRAD. *Itineraria Romana, Römische reisewege an der hand der tabula Peutingeriana.* Stuttgart, 1916.

PAWLOWSKI, GUSTAVE S. A. *Pierre Garcie dit Ferrande et son "Grand Routier"; notice additionnelle par M. Auguste Pawlowski* . . . Paris, 1902.

Sea Charts

ANTHIAUME, ALBERT. Les cartes géographiques et principalement les cartes marines dans l'antiquité et au moyen âge. (In France Comité des travaux historiques et scientifiques. *Bulletin de Géographie Historique et Descriptive.* Paris, 1912, pp. 355–443.)

—— *Cartes marines, constructions navales, voyages de découverte chez les Normands, 1500–1650.* Paris, 1916.

—— *Pierre Desceliers, père de l'hydrographie et de la cartographie françaises.* Paris, 1926.

BABCOCK, WILLIAM H. *Legendary islands of the Atlantic.* New York, 1922. American Geographical Society. Research series, no. 8.

BAKER, JOHN N. L. Some original maps of the East India Company. (In *K. Nederlandsch aardrijkskundig genootschap, Amsterdam.* Leiden, 1936, vol. 53, pp. 665–67.)

BARLOWE, WILLIAM. *The navigator's supply, &c.* London, 1597.

BEAUTEMPS-BEAUPRÉ, CHARLES F. *An introduction to the practice of nautical surveying and the construction of sea-charts.* London, 1823.

—— *Méthodes pour la levée et la construction des cartes et plans hydrographiques* . . . Paris, 1811.

BEGAT, PIERRE. *Exposé des opérations géodésiques relatives aux travaux hydrographiques exécutés sur les côtes septentrionales de France.* Paris, 1839.

—— *Traité de géodésie à l'usage des marins* . . . Paris, 1839.

BELLIN, JACQUES N. *Observations sur la construction de la carte des mers.* Paris, 1741.

—— *Observations sur la construction de la carte de l'océan méridional (entre l'Afrique et l'Amérique).* Paris, 1739.

BLACKROW, PETER. Navigation rectified: or, the common chart proved to be the only true chart. (In the *London Gazette.* London, 1689, no. 2467.)

BLUNDEVILLE, THOMAS. *M. Blvndevile his exercises* . . . Sixth edition. London, 1622.

BROWN, RALPH. Wind and current charts [and] miscellaneous maps and charts [by Matthew Fontaine Maury.] (In Brown's *Bibliography of Commander Matthew Fontaine Maury* . . . *Bulletin* of the Virginia Polytechnic Institute. Blacksburg, 1930, vol. 24, no. 2, pp. 60–61.) A list of Maury's wind and current charts is given on pp. 55–60.

BUCHON, JEAN A. C. *Notice d'un atlas en langue Catalane, manuscrit de l'an 1375, conservé parmi les manuscrits de la Bibliothèque royale.* Paris, 1839.

CAHILL, R. J. S. The world's air and ocean routes. Misleading maps . . . (In *Pacific Marine Review.* San Francisco, 1919, vol. 16, pp. 90–91.)

CHAPIN, HOWARD M. The French neptune and its various editions. (In *American Book Collector.* Metuchen, New Jersey, 1932, vol. 2, No. 1, pp. 16–19.)

CLARKE, JAMES S. *The progress of maritime discovery, from the earliest period to the close of the eighteenth century, forming an extensive system of hydrography.* London, 1803.

COIGNET, MICHIEL. *Instruction nouvelle des points plus excellens et necessaires, touchant l'art de nauiguer, ensemble vn moyen facile et tres sur pour nauiguer Est et Oest.* Anvers, 1581.

CORTÉS, MARTIN. *The arte of navigation. Contayning a briefe description of the sphaere* . . . London, 1596. The first edition of the translation was published in London, 1561.

COX, EDWARD G. Charts and sailing directions. (In his *Reference Guide to the Literature of Travel* . . . Seattle, 1938. Vol. 2.)

DAWSON, LLEWELLYN S. *Memoirs of hydrography, including brief biographies of the principal officers who have served in H. M. naval surveying service between the years 1750 and 1885.* 2 vols. Eastbourne, England [1883–1885].

DUNN, SAMUEL. *A new epitome of practical navigation; or, guide to the Indian seas.* London, 1777.

—— Remarks on the censure of Mercator's chart . . . (In *Philosophical Transactions* of the Royal Society, 1763. London, 1764, vol. 53, pp. 66–68.)

FOURNIER, GEORGES. *Hydrographie, contenant le théorie et la pratiqve de tovtes les parties de la navigation* . . . Paris, 1667.

FRANCE. Dépôt des Cartes et Plans de la Marine. *Analyse de la carte générale de l'océan Atlantique ou occidental* . . . Paris, 1786.

FRANCE. Service Hydrographique. *Catalogue des cartes, plans et ouvrages* . . . Paris, 1935.

—— Catalogue par ordre géographique des cartes, plans, vues de côtes, instructions nautiques. Paris, 1901. Marine et colonies. Service hydrographique. No. 739.

GARNETT, JOHN. Description and use of a new and simple nautical chart . . . (In *Transactions* of the American Philosophical Society. Philadelphia, 1804, vol. 6, pp. 303–18.)

GERNEZ, D. L'influence Portugaise sur la cartographie nautique Néerlandaise du XVIe siècle. (In *Annales de Géographie.* Paris, 1937, vol. 46, pp. 1–9.)

—— Lucas Janszoon Wagenaer. A chapter in the history of guide-books for sea-men. (In the *Mariner's Mirror.* London, 1937, vol. 23, pp. 190–97; 332–50.)

—— Les marins de l'antiquité se sont-ils servis de cartes nautiques? (In *Bulletin* de la Société Royale Belge de Géographie. Brussels, 1939, vol. 63, pp. 81–91.)

—— La première carte et les premières instructions nautiques modernes de la côte de Flandre. (In *Bulletin* de la Société Royale Belge de Géographie. Brussels, 1937, vol. 61, pp. 270–82.)

GREAT BRITAIN. Hydrographic Office. *General instructions for the hydrographic surveyors of the admiralty.* London, 1877.

HALL, ELIAL F. Gerard Mercator: his life and works . . . (In the *Journal* of the American Geographical Society of New York. New York, 1878, vol. 10, pp. 163–96.)

HANNO. *The periplus of Hanno; a voyage of discovery down the west African coast, by a Carthaginian admiral of the fifth century B. C.* Translated from the Greek, by Wilfred H. Schoff . . . Philadelphia, 1912.

HARRISSE, HENRI. *The discovery of North America.* London and Paris, 1892.

HEAWOOD, EDWARD. The world map before and after Magellan's voyage. (In *Geographical Journal.* London, June, 1921, vol. 57, pp. 431–46.)

JAMES II, KING of GREAT BRITAIN. *The royal charter of confirmation granted by his . . . majesty King James II to the Trinity-House of Deptford-Strond; for the government and encrease of the navigation of England . . .* London, 1685.

JOMARD, EDMÉ F. *Les monuments de la géographie ou recueil d'anciennes cartes.* Paris, 1842–62. Contains large-scale facsimiles of 21 rare and important maps and charts.

JONES, ERNEST L. *The evolution of the nautical chart . . .* [Washington, 1923].

JONGE, JOHAN K. J. DE. *De opkomst van het nederlandsch gesag in Oost Indien.* 13 vols. The Hague and Amsterdam, 1862–1888.

KENRICK, JOHN. *Phoenicia.* London, 1855.

KRETSCHMER, KONRAD. *Die Italienischen portolane des mittelalters . . .* Berlin, 1909.

LA RONCIÈRE, CHARLES G. M. DE. *Histoire de la Marine Française . . .* Paris, 1934.

LAURIE, RICHARD H., and WHITTLE, JAMES. Catalogue of pilots, charts, and other nautical works . . . London, 1821. With John Purdy's *Memoir, Descriptive and Explanatory . . .* London, 1822.

LEADER, JOHN T. *Life of Sir Robert Dudley, Earl of Warwick and Duke of Northumberland.* Florence, 1895.

LEWIS, CHARLES L. *Matthew Fontaine Maury, the pathfinder of the seas . . .* Annapolis, 1927.

LYONS, SIR HENRY. The sailing charts of the Marshall Islanders. (In the *Geographical Journal.* London, 1928, vol. 72, pp. 325–28.) An account of charts made from sticks by the natives of the Marshall Islands.

MEAD, HILARY P. *Trinity House.* London, 1947.

Memoirs of Alexander Dalrymple, Esq. (In the *European Magazine.* London, Nov. and Dec., 1802, vol. 42, pp. 323–27, 421–24.)

NANSEN, FRIDTJOF. Compass charts. (In his *In Northern Mists.* London, 1911. Vol. 2, pp. 215–36.)

NORDENSKIÖLD, ADOLF E. *Periplus, an essay on the early history of charts and sailing directions.* Stockholm, 1897.

ORR, MARY A. *Dante and the early astronomers . . .* London, [1914].

The periplus of the Erythrean Sea. Translated and edited by William Vincent. 2 vols.

London, 1800–07. (With his "Commerce and navigation of the ancients in the Indian Ocean.")

PILLSBURY, JOHN E. Charts and chart making. Annapolis, 1884. (In *Proceedings* of the United States Naval Institute. Annapolis, 1884, vol. 10, pt. 2, pp. 187–202.)

PUENTE Y OLEA, MANUEL DE LA. *Estudios españoles. Los trabajos geográficos de la Casa de contratación.* Seville, 1900.

RAEMDONCK, JEAN VAN. *Gérard de Cremer ou Mercator* . . . Saint Nicolas, 1870.

RAWLINSON, GEORGE. *History of Phoenicia.* London, 1889.

ROOSES, MAX. *Christophe Plantin; imprimeur anversois.* 2nd edition. Anvers, 1896.

Secret atlas of the Dutch East India Company. (See WIEDER, FREDERICK C.)

SELLER, JOHN. *Practical navigation: or, an introduction to the whole art.* London, 1672.

SNELLIUS, WILLEBRORDUS. Willebrordi Snellii à Royen. R. f. Tiphys batavvs . . . de navium cursibus, et re navali. Leyden, 1624.

SOMERVILLE, BOYLE T. The chartmakers. (In *Blackwood's Edinburgh Magazine*. Edinburgh, 1926, vol. 220, pp. 814–51.)

STEVENSON, EDWARD L. The geographical activities of the Casa de la contratación. (In the *Annals* of the Association of American Geographers. Albany, 1927, vol. 17, pp. 39–59.)

—— *Portolan charts, their origin and characteristics* . . . New York, 1911. Publications of the Hispanic Society of America, no. 82.

THOMAS, VAUGHAN. *The Italian biography of Sir Robert Dudley* . . . Oxford, 1858.

VALENTŸN, FRANÇOIS. *Beschryving van oud en niew oost Indien.* 5 vols. Dordrecht, 1724–1726.

VEITIA LINAJE, JOSÉ DE. *Norte de la contratación de las Indias Occidentales* . . . Seville, 1672.

WAGNER, HENRY R. The manuscript atlases of Battista Agnese. (In the *Papers* of the Bibliographical Society of America. New York, 1931, vol. 25, pp. 1–110, incl. plates.)

WAGNER, HERMANN. The origin of the mediaeval Italian nautical charts. In the *Report* of the International Geographical Congress. Sixth. London, 1895, pp. 695–702.)

WIEDER, FREDERICK C., ed. *Monumenta cartographica; reproductions of unique and rare maps, plans and views in the actual size.* 5 vols. The Hague, 1925–1933. The text of vol. 1 has title "The Secret Atlas of the Dutch East India Company."

WRIGHT, EDWARD. *Certaine errors in navigation, arising either of the ordinarie erroneous making or vsing of the sea chart, compasse, crosse staffe, and tables of declination of the sunne, and fixed starres detected and corrected.* London, 1599. In later editions the title was changed to read "Certaine errors in navigation, *detected and corrected* . . ."

—— A cruizing voyage to the Azores in 1589, by the Earl of Cumberland. (In Robert Kerr's *A General History and Collection of Voyages and Travels* . . . Edinburgh, 1824, vol. VII, pp. 375–96.)

—— *The description and use of the sphaere* . . . London, 1613.

—— The voyage of the Right Honourable George, earl of Cumberland to the Azores, etc. Written by the excellent mathematician and engineer, Master Edward Wright. (In John Pinkerton's *A General Collection of the Best and Most Interesting Voyages and Travels* . . . London, 1808–1814, vol. 1, pp. 804–19.)

WROTH, LAWRENCE C. *The way of a ship. An essay on the literature of navigation science.* Portland, Maine, 1937.

Strabo and the Ancients

BENN, ALFRED W. *The Greek philosophers.* New York, 1914.

BÉRARD, VICTOR. *Did Homer live?* Translated by Brian Rhys. London and Toronto, 1931.

Berger, Ernst Hugo. *Geschichte der wissenschaftlichen erdkunde der griechen*. Leipzig, 1903.

Bernhardy, Gottfried. *Eratosthenica, composuit Godofredus Bernhardy*. Berlin, 1822.

Blakesley, Joseph W. *A life of Aristotle* . . . Cambridge, 1839.

Bouché-Leclercq, Auguste. *L'astrologie Greque*. Paris, 1899.

—— *Histoire de la divination dans l'antiquité*. Paris, 1879.

Breasted, James H. *A history of the ancient Egyptians*. London, 1920.

—— *A teacher's manual accompanying the Breasted-Huth ancient history maps*. Chicago, [1918].

Budge, Ernest A. T. W. *Guide to Babylonian and Assyrian antiquities*. London, 1922.

Bunbury, Sir Edward H. *A history of ancient geography among the Greeks and Romans from the earliest ages till the fall of the Roman empire*. 2 vols. London, 1879.

Burnet, John. *Early Greek philosophy*. London, 1908.

Chambers, Robert. *The book of days*. 2 vols. London, v.d. Several editions were published between 1863 and 1914.

Chaucer, Geoffrey. *A Treatise on the astrolabe* . . . Edited by Walter W. Skeat. London, 1872.

Delepierre, Joseph Octave. *Le canard de la bibliothèque d'Alexandria*. (In *Miscellanies* of the Philobiblon Society, London, 1860–61, vol. VI.)

—— *Historical difficulties and contested events*. London, 1868.

Fairbanks, Arthur. *The first philosophers of Greece* . . . London, 1898.

Farrington, Benjamin. *Science and politics in the ancient world*. London, 1939.

—— *Science in antiquity*. London, 1936.

Gomperz, Theodor. *Greek thinkers*. London, 1901.

Gosselin, Pascal F. J. *Géographie des Grecs analysée* . . . Paris, 1790.

—— *Recherches sur la géographie systématique et positive des anciens* . . . Paris, 1798–1813.

—— Recherches sur les connoissances géographiques des anciens . . . (In *Mémoires de Littérature* . . . de l'Académie des Inscriptions et Belles-lettres. Paris, 1808, vol. 49, pp. 750–88.)

Gow, James. *A short history of Greek mathematics*. Cambridge, 1884.

Grant, Robert. *History of physical astronomy*. London, 1852.

Heath, Sir Thomas. *Aristarchus of Samos the ancient Copernicus. A history of Greek astronomy to Aristarchus*. Oxford, 1913.

Heidel, William A. Anaximander's book, the earliest known geographical treatise. (In *Proceedings* of the American Academy of Arts and Sciences. Philadelphia, April, 1921, vol. 56, no. 7, pp. 239–88.)

—— *The frame of the ancient Greek maps. With a discussion of the discovery of the sphericity of the earth*. New York, 1937. American Geographical Society Research, Series no. 20.

Herodotus. *Herodotus*, with an English translation by A. D. Godley . . . 4 vols. London and New York, 1921–1924. The Loeb Classical Library edition.

Hogben, Lancelot T. *Mathematics for the million*. New York, 1937.

Hutorowicz, H. de. Maps of primitive peoples. (In *Bulletin* of the American Geographical Society. New York, 1911, vol. 43, pp. 669–79.)

Kiepert, Heinrich. *A manual of ancient geography*. London, 1881.

Le Long, Jacques. Géographie ancienne des Gaules-cartes géographiques. (In his *Bibliothèque Historique de la France*. Paris, 1768, vol. 1, pp. 5–34.)

Lelewel, Joachim. *Pythéas de Marseille et la géographie de son temps* . . . Paris, 1836.

Letronne, Antoine J. *Sur les écrits et les travaux d'Eudoxe de Cnide* . . . Paris, 1841.

Lewis, Sir George C. *An historical survey of the astronomy of the ancients*. London, 1862.

Mahaffy, John P. *A history of Egypt under the Ptolemaic dynasty*. London, 1914.

MEYER, EDUARD. Aegyptische chronologie. (In *Abhandl. der Berlin Akad.* Berlin, 1904, p. 38.)

MÜLLER, KONRAD, and THEODORE. *Fragmenta historicorum Graecorum.* 4 vols. Paris, 1848–1853.

MÜLLER-FRAUENSTEIN, GEORG. Primitive map-making. (In the *Popular Science Monthly*. New York, Sept., 1883, vol. 23, no. 5, pp. 682–87.)

MYRES, JOHN L. An attempt to reconstruct the maps used by Herodotus. (In *Journal of the Royal Geographical Society*. London, Dec. 1896, vol. 8, pp. 605–31.)

NORDENSKIÖLD, ADOLF E. *Facsimile-atlas to the early history of cartography* . . . Stockholm, 1889.

PLATO. *Phaedo.* Translated by H. N. Fowler. London, 1914. The Loeb Classical Library edition.

RENNELL, JAMES. On the rate of travelling, as performed by camels; and its application, as a scale, to the purposes of geography. (In *Philosophical Transactions* of the Royal Society. London, 1791, vol. 81, pt. 2, pp. 129–45.)

RITTER, FRANCISCUS. *Astrolabium das ist: gründliche beschreibung uund unterricht eines newen quadranten* . . . Nürnberg, *c.* 1650.

SCHIAPARELLI, GIOVANNI V. *I precursori di Copernico.* Milan, 1873. Pubbl. del R. Osservatorio di Brera in Milano. No. iii.

SCOTT-ELLIOT, W. *The story of Atlantis* . . . London, 1896.

STRABO. *The geography of Strabo*, with an English translation by Horace Leonard Jones. 8 vols. London, 1917–1933. The Loeb Classical Library edition.

TERMIER, PIERRE. Atlantis. (In *Annual report* of the Smithsonian Institution, 1915. Washington, 1916, pp. 219–34.)

THIERSCH, HERMANN. *Pharos, antike, Islam und Occident; ein beitrag zur architekturgeschichte* . . . Leipzig and Berlin, 1909.

THOMAS, IVOR (trans.) *Selections illustrating the history of Greek mathematics*, with an English translation by Ivor Thomas. 2 vols. London and Cambridge, Massachusetts, 1941. The Loeb Classical Library edition.

THOMPSON, REGINALD C. *The reports of the magicians and astrologers of Nineveh and Babylon* . . . 2 vols. London, 1900.

THUILE, HENRI. *Commentaires sur l'atlas historique d'Alexandrie* . . . Le Caire, 1922. Publications spéciales de la Societé Sultanieh de Géographie du Caire.

TOZER, HENRY F. *A history of ancient geography.* Cambridge, England, 1935.

UKERT, FRIEDRICH A. Geographie der griechen und römer von den frühesten zeiten bis auf Ptolemäus. 6 vols. Weimar, 1816–1846.

ULRICHS, HEINRICH N. *An excursus on the topography of the Homeric Ilium.* London, 1847.

UNGER, ECKHARD A. O. Ancient Babylonian maps and plans. (In *Antiquity*. Gloucester, England, 1935, vol. 9, pp. 311–22.)

VINCENT, WILLIAM. *The voyage of Nearchus, from the Indus to the Euphrates* . . . London, 1797.

VIVIEN DE SAINT-MARTIN, LOUIS. *Etudes de géographie ancienne et d'enthnographie Asiatique* . . . 2 vols. Paris, 1852.

WALCKENAER, CHARLES A. *Recherches sur la géographie ancienne et sur celle du moyen âge* . . . Paris, 1823. Extrait des tomes V, VI et VII des *Mémoires* de l'Académie des Inscriptions et Belles-lettres.

WEIR, THOMAS. Astronomy in relation to geography. (In *Journal* of the Manchester Geographical Society. Manchester, 1892, vol. 8, pp. 211–25.)

ZELLER, EDUARD. *Outlines of the history of Greek philosophy.* Translated from the German by Sarah F. Alleyne and Evelyn Abbot. New York, 1890.

—— *Die philosophie der Griechen in ihre geschichtlichen entwicklung dargestellt.* 3 vols. Leipzig, 1920–1923.

World Cartography

Arms and the map. Military mapping by the Army Map Service. (In *Print, a Quarterly Journal of the Graphic Arts.* Woodstock, Vermont, 1946, vol. 4, no. 2, pp. 3–16.)

BARBIER, JOSEPH V. De la situation faite au projet de la carte du monde par les résolutions de la commission officielle de la décimalisation du temps et des angles. (In Congrès National des Sociétés Françaises de Géographie. St. Nazaire, 1898, pp. 281–83.)

—— Le projet de carte de la terre à l'échelle du 1:1.000.000. (In Association Française pour l'Avancement des Sciences. *Compte Rendu de la 23ᵐᵉ session.* Caen, 1894. Paris, 1895, pp. 915–41.)

—— Le projet de carte de la terre à l'échelle du 1/1.000.000ᵉ devant la commission technique de la Société de Géographie de l'Est. (In *Bulletin* de la Société de Géographie de l'Est. Nancy, 1894, vol. 16, pp. 263–308.)

BERGET, ALPHONSE. Les "cartes du monde" et la carte internationale au millionième. (In *Revue de Géographie Annuelle.* Paris, 1915, vol. 8, No. 2, pp. 1–31.)

BERTHAUT, HENRI M. A. Notice sur les cartes à l'échelle du 1.000.000ᵉ actuellement en cours au service géographique de l'armée. (In International Geographic Congress. *Report of the Eighth International Geographic Congress.* Washington, 1905, pp. 558–68.) House of Representatives. 58th Congress, 3rd Session, Doc. No. 460.

BIHOT, CHARLES. La carte internationale du monde à l'échelle du millionième. (In *Bulletin* de la Société Royale de Géographie d'Anvers, 1913. Anvers, 1914, vol. 37, pp. 267–82.)

BOGGS, SAMUEL W. The international millionth map of the world. (In the *Hydrographic Review.* Monaco, 1929, vol. 6, No. 2, pp. 181–85.)

BOWIE, WILLIAM. The function of geodesy in surveying. (In *Military Engineer.* Washington, 1924, vol. 16, pp. 140–43.)

—— No maps in a mapping age. (In *Civil Engineering.* Easton, Penna., 1936, vol. 6, pp. 88–90.)

BRÜCKNER, EDUARD. Rapport du president de la commission pour l'établissement d'une carte de la terre. *Report of the Sixth International Geographical Congress, 1895.* London, 1896.

BRUSSELS. Bibliothèque Royale de Belgique. *Exposition de cartes et plans organisée à l'occasion du congrès international de géographie historique . . .* Brussels, 1930.

CAYLEY, HENRY. On the colouring of maps. (In *Proceedings* of the Royal Geographical Society. London, 1879, vol. 1, pp. 259–61.) New monthly series. 1879.

CLARKE, ALEXANDER R. *Comparisons of the standards of length of England, France, Belgium, Prussia, Russia, India and Australia, made at the Ordnance Survey Office . . .* London, 1866.

—— Results of the comparisons of the standards of length of England, Austria, Spain, United States, Cape of Good Hope, and of a second Russian standard . . . with . . . notes on the Greek and Egyptian measures of length by Sir Henry James. (In *Philosophical Transactions* of the Royal Society. London, 1874, vol. 163, pp. 445–69.

FIELD, RICHARD M. Cartography and the war effort. (In *Bulletin* of the American Congress on Surveying and Mapping. Washington, 1943, vol. 3, no. 2, pp. 4–7.)

GREAT BRITAIN. War Office. *Rules for the transliteration of place-names occurring on foreign maps.* London, 1919.

HAYFORD, JOHN F. Geodesy and geophysics at Madrid. (In *Geographical Journal.* London, 1924, vol. 64, pp. 477–81.)

HEAWOOD, PERCY J. Map-colour theorem. (In the *Quarterly Journal of Pure and Applied Mathematics.* London, 1890, vol. 24, pp. 332–38.)

HILL, BRUCE C. Aerial photographic mapping. (In the *Military Engineer*. Washington, 1930, vol. 22, pp. 533–43.)

HINKS, ARTHUR R. The map on the scale of 1/1,000,000 compiled at the Royal Geographical Society under the direction of the general staff, 1914–1915. (In the *Geographical Journal*. London, July-Dec. 1915, vol. 46, pp. 24–50.)

INTERNATIONAL GEOGRAPHICAL CONGRESS. 15th. *Catalogue de l'exposition internationale de la cartographie officielle*. Leiden, 1938.

—— *Compte-rendu du congrès des sciences géographiques, cosmographiques et commerciales tenu à Anvers du 14 au 22 Aout, 1871*. 2 vols. Antwerp, 1872.

—— *Congrès international pour le progrès des sciences géographique, cosmographiques et commerciales. Catalogue de l'exposition ouverte du 14 au 27 Aout, 1871*. Anvers, 1871.

—— *Exposition catalogue général des produit exposés . . .* Par M. Felix Fournier. Paris, 1875.

INTERNATIONAL MAP COMMITTEE. *Carte du monde au millionième; comptes rendus des séances de la deuxième conférence internationale, Paris, Decembre, 1913*. Paris, 1914. Publication of the Service géographique de l'armée.

—— *Resolutions and proceedings of the International Map Committee assembled in London, 1909*. London, 1910.

INTERNATIONAL 1/M MAP. (Central Bureau, Southampton, England.) *Carte du monde au millionième. Rapport pour 1921*. Southampton, 1921. A bibliography of the International Map covering the years 1891–1920 is included in this publication (pp. 32–36).

—— *Rapport pour 1938*. Southampton, 1938.

MÉCHAIN, PIERRE F. A., and DELAMBRE, J. B. J. *Base du système métrique décimal, ou, mesure de l'arc du méridien . . . exécutée en 1792 . . . par MM. Méchain et Delambre . . .* 3 vols. Paris, 1806–1810.

Notes on the transliteration of Arabic names for the 1/M map. (In the *Geographical Journal*. London, Jan.–June 1917, vol. 49, pp. 141–48.)

OLSON, EVERETT C., and WHITMARSH, AGNES. *Foreign maps*. New York and London, 1944.

PENCK, ALBRECHT. Die herstellung einer einheitlichen erdkarte im masstabe von 1/1,000,000. (In International Geographical Congress. 5th. Berne, 1891. Compte Rendu. Berne, 1892, pp. 191–98.)

—— Plan of a map of the world . . . (In the *National Geographic Magazine*. Washington, Oct., 1904, vol. 15, pp. 405–08.)

PERRIER, GEORGES. La figure de la terre. (In *Revue de Géographie Annuelle*. Paris, 1908, Tome II, pp. 201–490.)

PICTET, MARC A. Considerations on the convenience of measuring an arch of the meridian, and of the parallel of longitude . . . (In *Philosophical Transactions* of the Royal Society. London, 1791, vol. 81, pp. 106–27.)

RANDALL, ROBERT H. Standards for map accuracy. (In *Bulletin* of the American Congress for Surveying and Mapping. Washington, 1943, vol. 3, no. 2, pp. 11–12.)

Report of the eighth international geographical congress held in the United States 1904. Washington, 1905. House of Representatives, 58th Congress, 3rd Session, Doc. No. 460.

REY-PAILHADE, M. J. DE. Projet d'application du système métrique à la mesure des angles et du temps. (In Association Française pour l'Avancement des Sciences. *Compte Rendu de la 23ᵐᵉ Session, Caen, 1894*. Paris, 1895, pp. 941–46.)

SANCEAU, CAPTAIN V. E. H. The present state of the carte internationale du monde au millionième. (In International Geographical Congress. 15th. Amsterdam, 1938. *Comptes Rendus*. Tome 2. Travaux de la Section I. Cartographie. Leiden, 1938, pp. 150–55.)

STRUVE, WILHELM FRIEDRICK G. W. *Arc du méridien de 25° 20′ entre le Danube et la mer Glaciale, mésuré depuis 1816 jusqu'en 1855* . . . St. Petersburg, 1860.

WHEELER, GEORGE M. *Report upon the third international geographical congress and exhibition at Venice, Italy, 1881, accompanied by data concerning the principal government land and marine surveys of the world.* Washington, 1885. U. S. War Dept. Corps of Engineers.

WILLIS, BAILEY. The international millionth map of the world. (In the *National Geographic Magazine.* Washington, 1910, vol. 21, pp. 125–32.)

Index